Anthony Burgess and America

Manchester University Press

Anthony Burgess and America

The untold story behind the American influences on Burgess's life, work, and legacy

by

Christopher W. Thurley

Manchester University Press

Published by Manchester University Press
Oxford Road, Manchester, M13 9PL

www.manchesteruniversitypress.co.uk

British Library Cataloguing-in-Publication Data
A catalogue record for this book is available from the British Library

ISBN 978 1 5261 7414 7 hardback

First published 2025

EU authorised representative for GPSR:
Easy Access System Europe, Mustamäe tee 50, 10621
Tallinn, Estonia
gpsr.requests@easproject.com

Typeset by Newgen Publishing UK

Contents

A timeline and bibliography can be found at the following links or by scanning the QR codes:

Timeline – https://www.manchesterhive.com/display/9781526174154/9781526174154.00015.xml

Bibliography – https://www.manchesterhive.com/display/9781526174154/9781526174154.00016.xml

List of illustrations

Acknowledgements

This project was only possible with the help of a community of scholars, colleagues, friends, and mentors who all helped me, in varying capacities, complete my work and get it to the quality and standard needed. First and foremost, thank you to Dr Alan Roughley (1952–2014) who gave me a chance to meet all these wonderful Burgess scholars all the way back in 2009, Dr Ben Forkner who gave me the initial idea for my doctoral work, Dr Jim Clarke who gave me the advice to pursue a PhD with my work before a book, and Dr Andrew Biswell for tirelessly working with me since 2014 to make this dream a reality and for vastly improving the quality of my work – this monograph owes its success to your guidance: thank you. Perhaps more importantly, depending on who you ask, thank you to my wife Julia Thurley, my daughter Sasha Rue Thurley, my son Leo Alexander Thurley, and my mother Terry Thurley for being the foundation that holds me up and supports me day in and day out – I LOVE YOU! Additionally, thank you to the Board of Trustees at the International Anthony Burgess Foundation (IABF) for trusting and supporting me through this journey, as well as the IABF staff who have assisted me with my research. Thanks to Gaston College for supporting me as a teacher and researcher. Special thanks to the early readers and commentators on my work who helped me as I started and continued researching and writing over the last decade: Rachel Brown, Yves Buelens, Dr Rob Spence, Dr Christine Gengaro, Aolani Gouge, Michele Domenech, Matthew Frost, and Dr Alan Shockley (1970–2020).

I'd like to use the rest of this space to just list as many people and organizations as I can to express my appreciation for all of them: Tamás Bényei, Dr Nuria Belastegui, Stephen Magdzinski, Dr Thomas Stumpf, Dr John Stinson, Dr Kent Mullikin, Dr Peter Valenti, Dr Rexford Brown, Dr Samuel Coale, Dr Thomas Staley, Dr Weldon Thornton (1934–2021), Dr William Pritchard, Rev. Patrick Samway, SJ, Dr Ronald Sharp, James Lieber, Edward Field, Greg Lazinsky, Herbert Gold, Dr Leah Schweitzer,

Dr Paul Phillips, Dick Cavett and Lisa Troland, Geoff Bartholomew, James Bevarly, Will Carr, Dr Martin Kratz, Dr Graham Foster, Dr Joel Minor, Dr Christopher Armitage, Dr Graham Woodroffe, Dr Anna Edwards, William Manley, Dr Anthony Levings, Dr Kenyon Wagner, Dr Barbara Lekatsas, Dr Allan Havis, Dr Joe Argent, Dr Ákos Farkas, Dr Jascha Kessler, Ryan Petty, Lara Hebald Embry, Allyson Heafner, Libby Stone, Samantha Little, Faith Barnes, Nicole Kaufman, John Withers, Morgan DePue, Barbara Wright, Michael Maciejewski, Rebecca Kouider, Michael Powell, Taylor Ewing, Dr William Blazek, Dr Paul Evans, Dr Paul Wake, Ian Carrington, Dr Jennifer Munroe, Marcella Patterson, Mirit Jakab, Daniel Schaarenberg, Kate Hawkins, Michelle Houston, Paul Clarke, the Manchester University Press editors and designers, Newgen, Sally Evans-Darby, and The Anthony Burgess Estate.

Archives and libraries at these institutions of higher learning: Amherst University, Baldwin Wallace University, Bloomsburg State University, Boston College, Bowling Green State University, Bucknell University, Centenary College of Louisiana, Central Michigan University, Choate School, City College of New York, City College of San Francisco, Clark University, College of St. Scholastica – Heidi Johnson, Colorado College, Columbia University, Community College of Allegheny County, Contra Costa College, Duke University, Earlham College, Eastern Washington University, East Los Angeles College, East Texas State University, Elmira College, Florida State University, Fordham University, George Washington University, Grand Valley State College, Hamline University, Harvard University, Indiana University of Pennsylvania, Kenyon College, Kingsborough Community College, Lafayette College, Long Island University, Massachusetts Institute of Technology, McMaster University, Mercer County Community College, Michigan State University, Mohawk Community College, Muhlenberg College, Notre Dame College of Maryland, Oberlin University, Ohio State University, Ohio Wesleyan University, Pennsylvania State University, Princeton University, Ramapo College, Rockhurst University, Sacramento State College, Sarah Lawrence College, Simon Fraser University, Stanford University, Stetson University, Texas Christian University – Special Collections, Mary Couts Burnett Library, The New School for Social Research, Tufts University, University of Buffalo – The Poetry Collection, Dr James Maynard and Dr Stephen McCaffery and the David Gray Library Chair Fellowship, University of California at Berkeley, University of California at Los Angeles, University of Delaware, University of Iowa, University of Kansas, University of Louisville, University of Massachusetts at Dartmouth, Claire T. Carney Library Archives, University of Michigan, University of Minnesota, University of Montana, University of New Hampshire, University of North Carolina at Chapel Hill, University of

Notre Dame, University of Oklahoma, University of Richmond, University of Rochester, University of Tennessee, University of Texas at Austin, The Harry Ransom Center, University of Victoria, University of Wisconsin, Stevens Point, Vanderbilt University, Washington College, Washington State University – Mark O'English, Washington University in St. Louis, Wester Chester County, NY, West Virginia State College, and Muskingum University – Nainsi Houston.

Organizations and businesses: Christian Science Monitor, The International Anthony Burgess Foundation, Library Association of the City University of New York, National Public Radio (NPR), The Adelaide Arts Festival, The American Library Association, The Hennepin County Library, The Modern Language Association, The Woodrow Wilson Center, Yaddo, Gaston College Library, Resources for American Literary Studies, Wrath-Bearing Tree, The Whitney Museum of American Art, 311, and the Anthony Burgess Centre.

To any person or entity I have forgotten, I am sorry. Such a solecism was not deliberate, but a *mea maxima culpa* on my end. Please use this space to write your name if you are one such being in absentia: ________________
____.

Introduction

> But ultimately a literature is not a matter for nationalistic or racial pride, since it is made out of a language, and a language becomes the property of anyone who decides to write in it. (Anthony Burgess, 'The Literature of the British from 1900 to 1982')[1]

There has been little scholarly work on the influence that the United States had on British author Anthony Burgess's writing and career. From 1966 until 1993, Burgess lived in America, taught in America, and visited and travelled extensively across the nation, ultimately visiting at least thirty-eight different American states, leaving only twelve states unvisited.[2] By the end of his life, he had visited over ninety colleges, high schools, or universities while living and working in the United States, all of which resulted in him speaking in front of tens of thousands of Americans, primarily college students, faculty, and other writers and artists. These visits consisted of lecture tours, teaching positions, hired writing and orchestral work, publicity tours, and writing residencies. Although largely ignored or glossed over by scholars, Burgess's constant interaction with Americans, American ideas and ways of living, and American culture had a significant impact on the author's writing, thinking, and lifestyle. Beginning with his first travel to the United States in March 1966, America afforded Burgess the economic security he was unable to find elsewhere as well as the popularity he desired. Having already published over a dozen of books by 1966, it was in America that his work was popular and being taken seriously, and eventually where it found its way into the higher education curriculum.[3]

The United States had a profound impact on Anthony Burgess's life, fiction, non-fiction, and career trajectory, helping him solidify his legacy. The impact that his time in America had on his fiction will be analysed herein by specifically looking at the American elements of five of his novels: *M/F* (1971), *The Clockwork Testament, Or Enderby's End* (1974), *Earthly Powers* (1980), *The End of the World News* (1982), and *Enderby's Dark Lady, or No End to Enderby* (1984). Additionally, thousands of pieces from

Burgess's canon (over fifty books, hundreds of articles, dozens of lectures, interviews, and archived personal correspondence) are used to evidence the interconnections between different forms of communication that Burgess presents, which should stand as proof of the complex canonical authorial dialogue taking place throughout his life's work – what could be called epitexts, as defined by the French literary theorist Gérard Genette.[4] Essentially, the culture of America and Burgess's American experiences are fused into the language of the particular novels selected here, and this ideologically infused language is a 'fundamental authorial intention' which is 'orchestrated' and 'refracted' at 'different angles through the heteroglot' – or different tongues – of cultural expression emanating from the United States during the time period Burgess was most engaged with the country.[5]

The idea of America, the culture and politics of America, and the country's literature and media influenced Burgess's thoughts on various issues and his authorial approaches to literature and non-fiction. *Influence*, as conceived of through my interpretation of the Russian cultural historian, philosophic anthropologist, and literary language theorist Mikhail Bakhtin's (1895–1975) corpus – particularly his collection of four essays in *The Dialogic Imagination* (1975) – and in the sense that it should be understood in this monograph, is exhibited when historical, biographical, literary, cultural, narrative, and aesthetic evidence reveals similarities between the author/author-figure/public personage and their fiction through literary borrowing, allusion, coincidence, parallelism, double-voiced discourse (*language in a fictional text that also resonates with the author*), monologism (*authorial perspectives and opinions infused into a literary narrative*), hidden polemics (*monologism used to express an author's opinion through a veil of supposed fictionality*), and heteroglossic dialogism (*assorted speech from a cultural/social milieu presented in a piece of fiction in an attempt to achieve verisimilitude, but which also reflects the author's influences*); more simply stated, this complex explanation could be equated with Genette's stance that the 'effect of the paratext [relevant contextual information outside the narrative of a literary text – as well as outside the physical object] lies very often in the realm of influence – indeed, manipulation – experienced subconsciously', where, despite this, any good reader or scholar is more certainly 'better off perceiving it fully and clearly' in order to better grasp the full function, and we may say *meaning*, of a text.[6] More simply, and due to these more esoteric terms being used infrequently in what follows, Burgess's novels are examined through a lens of juxtaposing Burgess's novels that discuss America with the more wide-ranging primary source evidence of how he wrote, spoke, thought, conversed, and discussed the United States and American culture/society in a myriad of different sources that include, but are not limited to, letters, articles, non-fiction, lectures, and interviews.

More specifically, these broad functions will be analysed in the following novels in these varying capacities: *M/F* (1971) in regards to Burgess's fascination with the subjects of pornography, sex, obscenity, incest, social myths, youth culture, and protest movements, as these all relate to and exist within American culture; *The Clockwork Testament, Or Enderby's End* (1974) as it pertains to Burgess's time in American higher education in New York City and elsewhere; *Earthly Powers* (1980) for its commentary on authorial narrative, fictionalized historical American personages, the long American novel, and American themes of race and politics; *The End of the World News* (1982) because of its American settings and Hollywood inspiration; and *Enderby's Dark Lady, or No End to Enderby* (1984) in order to assess Burgess's commentary on race and his literary disengagement with the United States as a subject for his fiction.[7] What becomes apparent after recognizing that 'every language in the novel is a point of view, a socio-ideological conceptual system of real social groups and their embodied representatives', and once the historical and biographical evidence has been collected, is that the United States triggered an experimental turn in Burgess's fiction, and the novels chosen here resemble tableaus from his lived life encountering American culture.[8] Recognizing this is important, but it is also crucial to remember that Burgess's American experiences afforded him a career in public speaking and teaching, which resulted in national fame and documentation on the many issues and topics of concern he engaged with publicly. The most important of these subjects to be covered in this monograph concern art (purpose, social impact, and production), literature (the future and state of the novel), obscenity (pornography, didacticism, and censorship), pop culture (music, television, film, and fame), education (curriculum, students, and the canon), authorship (authorial voice and the career of an author), politics (American conservatism and liberalism, counter cultures, social issues, and the Nixon and Ford eras), race (African Americans, American Jews, and the American racial melting pot), gender and sex (sexual permissiveness, homosexuality, and the roles of women), language (dialects, pronunciation, and meaning), and aesthetics (high and low art, pseudo-literature, and the literary continuum). Because of such a diverse and extensive relationship with the United States, it will become quite clear that Burgess's American experiences had a profound impact on the second half of his professional career, a point in great need of critical exploration.

Despite Ákos Farkas's many beneficial insights in his monograph, *Will's Son and Jake's Peer: Anthony Burgess's Joycean Negotiations* (2002), his claim that 'Burgess's distinguished professorship at various American universities had of course more to do with his reputation as the writer of *A Clockwork Orange* than anything he had produced as a scholar' is inaccurate for several reasons.[9] First, the *A Clockwork Orange* novel was only mildly popular after its release in 1962 – though Americans appear to have responded more conciliatorily to it than in the United Kingdom, with American scholars recognizing it early on as a serious contribution to literature – and only found the international fame it retains today after Stanley Kubrick's 1971/2 film of the same name.[10] Second, Burgess first visited the United States five years before Kubrick's *A Clockwork Orange* was initially released in the United States on 19 December 1971, when, in March 1966, he visited for a short lecture tour that began with a stop at Long Island University for a conference on 'literary translation', while going on to hold several visiting and permanent positions at colleges in the United States all before or during 1971.[11] Finally, Burgess was somewhat well known in America for his other novels, especially *Nothing Like the Sun* (1964), and non-fiction books, of which there were eight by 1971, including a biography of William Shakespeare and a book-length analysis of James Joyce's work.[12] Beginning in the mid-1960s, Burgess had also been in contact with American scholars and writing programmes. In the autumn of 1966, Burgess had met with Frederick Morgan of *Hudson Review* at the Café Royal in London, and in the spring of 1967, Burgess met with Leslie Fiedler, critic and writer who taught at the University of Buffalo, in the United Kingdom sometime shortly before autumn 1967, with the two staying in contact for over a decade.[13] Other visits and contact with Americans included a trip to Amherst University and Vanderbilt University in the spring of 1967, in addition to visits to Warner Brothers in 1967 and 1968.[14] Shortly after these visits, Burgess was requested for extended visits to the University of Buffalo, Columbia University, and the University of North Carolina at Chapel Hill, and in the spring of 1969 he even completed a small lecture tour of America before going on to spend over a month in Chapel Hill, North Carolina from 15 November through 20 December 1969 as a writer-in-residence. From this point on, and years before the *A Clockwork Orange* film brought on a cultural explosion, Burgess's new life consisted of being a speaker/teacher for hire in American higher education, as well as a hired writer for American stage and film projects.

As the 1970s began, Burgess accepted positions at Princeton University as a visiting lecturer (14 September 1970 to 30 June 1971), as an adjunct professor of writing at Columbia University (1 September 1970 to 15 May 1971), and then as a distinguished professor at the City College of New York (1 September 1972 to 31 August 1973).[15] In July 1971 and January 1972 Burgess also visited Minneapolis, Minnesota, in order to work on his translation of the stage-play *Cyrano de Bergerac* by Edmund Rostand, in addition to a myriad of lecture stops at places like Bowling Green State University, the University of Michigan, Michigan State University, the University of

Richmond, Virginia Commonwealth University, and a handful of other locations.[16] In Geoffrey Aggeler's *The Artist as Novelist* (1979), he characterized Burgess's frenetic work schedule as bouncing between 'some campus in Texas or Missouri, or conferring with theatre associates in Minneapolis or New York, or being interviewed by some professor with a tape recorder'.[17] Aggeler goes on to sound like the peripatetic author's publicist, saying that 'Mr Burgess never takes a holiday; whether he is in Malta, Rome, Sussex, or New York City, he works seven days a week.'[18] And the side effect of such prolonged and hectic travel around the United States was an increase in the amount of opinions Burgess had about the country he now worked in.

Despite Burgess's many protestations about American culture and life – 'In my old-fashioned way, I go on regarding George III as a bloody fool but the Declaration of Independence as a disaster. Come home, America. The British Commonwealth needs you' – he found the career he aspired to achieve resting in the vast expanse of a country that he had for almost half a century (1917–66) known only through books, music, and television.[19] His subsequent twenty-seven-year career (1966–93) travelling throughout America had a profound impact on him, a reality that is not hard to see for any reader aware of Burgess's work after 1968, which is made even clearer when the items stored in archives across America are introduced into the conversation.

A large portion of the research done for this monograph involves, and is informed by, primary sources from archives at American colleges and universities, and the two main archives accessed for this research include the Burgess collections at the University of Texas at Austin's Harry Ransom Center and the International Anthony Burgess Foundation. Moving beyond these well-known collections, I have gathered archived materials from over 100 American and Canadian institutions of higher learning and artistic organizations. Additionally, I have personally been in contact with more than thirty individuals who met or knew Burgess during the period covered in this monograph.

Burgess's *American* novels

In taking so many different aspects of Burgess's life and work into consideration, a unifying goal of this monograph is to attend to the problems of voice and persona as they are presented in a variety of texts and contexts. The separation between voice and text contributes circumstantially to Bakhtin's tenets of understanding context around language use and the *play* that different voices intrinsically embody, therefore distorting meaning while simultaneously constructing a contextualized lexical landscape. Such an approach essentially works to 'overcome the divorce between an abstract "formal" approach and an equally abstract "ideological" approach', which acknowledges both the 'private craftsmanship' and 'the social life of discourse outside the artist's study'.[20] Doing so means that all forms of utterance issued by Burgess can and are used to evaluate the individual orchestral elements of language inside and outside of the novels analysed here, since what occurred outside did have an effect on the text and does have an impact on how the texts are now understood, effects which can be assessed through Bakhtin's philosophy of language and in Genette's sense of how the epitext shapes how to see a text.

One important aspect to address are Burgess's autobiographies – used sporadically throughout this argument – since these lend insight into the author's life and experiences surrounding the production of his work, while also distorting a historical and biographical understanding of Burgess and his work. Even so, it may be that Burgess's autobiographies should be taken more seriously than some scholars and commentators have argued they should be. When Philippe LeJeune stated that Burgess was a slave to 'biography' because he wrote his autobiography only 'to cut the ground from beneath his biographers' feet', in the sense that he was racing to write a counternarrative to a biographer, or when Graham Woodroffe noted that Burgess's authorial mischievousness between his fiction and supposed non-fiction suggested that the 'only thing Burgess was really serious about was his music', and when William Boyd, who, in *The Burgess Variations* documentary, said that his confessions, or autobiographies, were 'some of his best *fiction*', what they are all really commenting on is Burgess's literary embellishment, not on the fact that the instances portrayed in these books are directly, though not always accurately, retold from how Burgess mis/remembered or refashioned/invented them from his actual life.[21] At the very least, they are a *truth*, though they may not be the *Truth*, because, of course, such a retelling is always flawed and relative, but biographical and historical research has uncovered and can uncover many shreds of truth behind Burgess's claims, especially those concerning locations and activities. Taking into consideration scholars' and philosophers' views on historicity, especially the idea that 'as a system of signs, the historical narrative points in two directions simultaneously: *toward* the events described in the narrative and *toward* the story type of mythos which the historian has chosen to serve as the icon of the structure of the events', what emerges after scrupulous attention to Burgess's published texts and archived materials is that the line between his life and his work was permeable, with both being absorbed into the other so that each reflected one another: the work has glimmers of the life and the life shows glimmers of the work.[22]

To begin, briefly, it's clear in many instances that in Burgess's articles for the *New York Times*, the *Times Literary Supplement*, *American Scholar*, and/or *Playboy* or *Penthouse*, where he expressed opinions about modern youth and the state of American education in the 1970s, these same opinions find different modes of expression and dialogic interrogation in *M/F*, *The Clockwork Testament*, *Earthly Powers*, *The End of the World News*, and *Enderby's Dark Lady*. Additionally, what is revealed are similarities in experience that directly translate into thematic components that shape the works. I argue here that in these texts, thematic inspiration has been derived largely from topics of American concern that ultimately drive the fiction through themes such as sex in the media, higher education, race, culture, literature, and language.

The evidence that helps emphasize this influence and the changes that occur in Burgess's texts before and after he visited America are analysed through a close examination of Burgess's pre-1966 novels to assess the vision of America that emerges. What is found is that Burgess essentially harbours pretty stock and repetitive views of American before he visits, and then his criticisms sharpen, increase, and grow more diverse (and often contradictory). Eventually, as is argued towards the end of this monograph, Burgess even became a kind of *American* author, or at the very least a prominent persona subsumed in the public intellectual and author role in the American media in the 1960s, 1970s, 1980s, and 1990s. Finally, the status of all the newly uncovered or forgotten lectures, interviews, and journalism is appraised based on the content written and the avenue of communication.

Partly because of Burgess's enthusiastic immersion into the mass media of radio and television, and the 1960s–1970s college lecture circuit, this approach draws on the detailed surviving record of Burgess's public persona (itself a form of multiple self-narration) that Burgess cultivated: the author, the journalist, the scholar, the teacher, the musician, the popular chat-show entertainer. Personal letters add another layer, revealing further acts of self-narration which are considered alongside Burgess's literary and broadcasting work. Bakhtin's theories of dialogic play and heteroglossia become important at this stage to help unravel the cacophony of Burgess's voices that occur in various media. At times, these voices are harmonious, and Bakhtin's assertion that the novelist's writings act as an 'orchestration of his themes and for the refracted (indirect) expression of his intentions and values' becomes apt.[23] At other times, a discordant nature emerges through contradiction, irony, or paradox between various levels of utterance.

Methodology

Although this monograph is tasked with looking at almost three decades of Burgess's life, while remaining predominantly focused on five books of his from 1971 through 1984, this approach attempts to deploy historical and contextual evidence alongside the whole of Burgess's canon beginning in the mid 1950s up until his death in 1993. The critical discourse on Burgess is likewise evaluated and utilized so as to situate Burgess's voice, and this monograph's voice, within a larger socio-historical and critical background. Seeing the Burgess-figure as a person, author, and character 'fraught with background' that exists nebulously across varying patterns of speech and platforms of tangibility opens new pathways of interpretation and explication regarding Burgess and his life, as well as his work.[24] The types of evidence used throughout this monograph therefore vary widely, but published materials will be, as a kind of theory of *work*, handled as being a more legitimate example of the public persona than the extemporaneous lecture comment or short letter, simply because to publish a document, a voice, or a line of thought is to present a refined, revised, and ruminated-upon use of language meant for a wide audience. Other forms of authorial communication, the *utterance* in Bakhtinian terms – taken outside the realm of fiction – are often, by the very nature of the setting in which they were produced, not necessarily meticulously thought out, revised, and meant for mass distribution or as a metonymic element indicative of the Burgess-gestalt. Even so, these kinds of communication have the potential, as will be argued here, to reveal more about the person behind the public façade. This does not strip these uses of language of significance, since, as Bakhtin notes and as will be evident in Burgess's overall polyphonic authorial multi-voicedness, almost every utterance is an 'intense interaction and struggle between one's own and another's word' where the end effect of this process is that 'they oppose or dialogically interanimate each other'.[25]

With the best attempt put forward, this exploration also does its best to ignore the mythic topoi Burgess propped up for himself – evidenced in dozens of examples where he provided exegeses of his own work (*The Artist as Novelist*, *Anthony Burgess*, *You've Had Your Time*, and in his journalism and non-fiction), fashioned his persona into characters in his two autobiographies, inserted his name/s into his fictions (*ABBA ABBA*, *The End of the World News*, *1985*, *The Wanting Seed*, etc.), or casted doubts on authorship (*A Clockwork Orange*, John Wilson, Joseph Kell's books, *The End of the World News*, Enderby's poems, etc.) – as well as the *grands récits* displayed in some of the secondary sources on his life and work.

Although an argument regarding Burgess's peculiar monoglossia in his fiction exists in the pages to come, that claim focuses particularly on his fiction, whereas Burgess the public figure occupied a more polyglottal space which was more cacophonous, diverse, and multitudinous. Burgess activated a monoglottal discourse in his fiction that tended to prescribe his fictional characters with voices too resonant of his public chorus (polyglot) of voices, including his personal convictions – a Burgessian monoglot language, lexicon, and ideology wrapped up in a *Burgessian 'we'* that includes his personal life experiences.[26] In the chosen novels for this monograph, the close parallelism between Burgess's fictional characters and the life he led contributes to his authorial monologism, a style that was moulded 'in the living heteroglossia of language, and in the multi-languagedness surrounding and nourishing his own consciousness', but which did not manifest in his literature in the way that Fyodor Dostoevsky, in Bakhtin's opinion an author who mastered the dialogic, would have.[27] The 'pure voice' of a dialogized and polyphonic character does not often, if at all, appear in these novels, since Burgess, in Bakhtin's estimation, does not provide the space, or else is not interested in attempting to achieve such a standard, where the author 'must to an extraordinary extent broaden, deepen and rearrange this consciousness (to be sure, in a specific direction) in order to accommodate the autonomous consciousness of others'.[28] Again, in Bakhtinian terms, Burgess created the illusion of heteroglossia in the novel by inventing 'superficial' dialogues which are, as will be explored, on many occasions 'isolated rhetorical polemics with another person'.[29]

All it takes is a general understanding of Burgess's life to begin recognizing the many overlaps and similarities between his life and work, but a more sustained investigation exposes more significant inspirations and influences, some, like with his time in the United States, that are immersive, enveloping, and emphatically self-allusive. Particularly in the five pieces of fiction chosen for this monograph, Burgess's double-voicedness exists as a monoglottal pastiche representation of heteroglottal American social discourse experienced by Burgess himself. Although his source content is heteroglossic – meaning that many different opinions, viewpoints, languages, cultural cues, and voices appear throughout these texts – his work is monoglottal in the sense that Burgess rarely attempts, with the subjects analysed throughout this monograph, to empathetically understand opposing opinions. A perfect example of this rests in Burgess's autobiographies, to be discussed throughout as examples of both fiction and non-fiction, which are distinctly exaggerated Burgessian visions of the author and public figure's life, and not necessarily that of the man, John Wilson. Where distortions arise between autobiography and historical evidence, there exist fissures that show Burgess's 'professional trickery', as Kenneth Toomey describes the production of fiction in *Earthly Powers* – or, as Burgess called it, 'formal trickery' – that clutters and traps a vision of the real, 'offering an unreal reality, lies'.[30] As mentioned earlier, although a large portion of Burgess's autobiographies can be credibly confirmed as being accurate, especially concerning general travel patterns and encounters, it is his shaping of these events, or *fidelity* as defined by Philippe LeJeune as being the point at which *information* is reshaped to emphasize *meaning*, that warrants further scepticism, because although *fidelity* exists outside of the realm of accuracy, such an approach – and acknowledgement of such a status – creates meaning from the text and paths of interpretation for the reader and scholar; this is all to say that through such interpolations of life into literature and literature into life, there exist layers of *information* and *meaning* to be derived from inconsistencies between these realms.[31] Burgess rationalized this mix of truth and fiction as he opened *Little Wilson and Big God* (1986), arguing that, philosophically, the 'autobiographer can see himself as the only true historian in the sense that he is presenting the life of perennial humanity', while also providing 'the raw material for the social historian, demonstrating what it was like to be imprisoned in a particular segment of time'.[32] He also blatantly admits that 'a good deal of real life has gone into my fiction, I forbear to unscramble it all into what has been fabled by the daughters of memory, though I have unscrambled some'.[33] Still, many details Burgess provides in his two autobiographies cannot be found anywhere else because they are the details of John Wilson's life, but in the act of laying out those half-truths, Anthony Burgess, the author and John Wilson's *nom de plume*, becomes the 'autophagous' literary author-personage of autobiography who feeds off the life and experiences of the multivariate identity.[34]

Indeed, although the novels analysed here cannot be strictly defined as *roman à clefs*, there exist many examples where Burgess directly fed off his life and the people who inhabited that realm in order to craft his fictions – the easiest example perhaps being Enderby's landlady in New York City, the 'rabid ideological man-hater' who is undoubtedly a suggestion of the poet, Adrienne Rich, whom Burgess rented an apartment from in New York City and describes in *You've Had Your Time* as 'a famous feminist and man-hater'.[35] The significance of this is that in making these connections, many of which are less explicit, the texts reveal new areas of understanding that beg for further investigation into the boundaries of Burgess's autobiografictional narratives in his novels, since, as Max Saunders notes in *Self Impression: Life-Writing, Autobiografiction, and the Forms of Modern Literature* (2010), a 'novel might be auto/biographical in its characters, but not in its plot or dialogue. Or, vice-versa: it might tell a real story, but reinvent the characters involved. Or it might use some real people, events, or language, but combine any of these with invented material. It might be true to autobiographical feelings about real events, but not to the events themselves'.[36] In identifying these overlaps, what is exposed are *patterns of influence*. It is for this reason that the many voices of Anthony Burgess, as they relate to his association with the United States, must be carefully and meticulously unravelled, delineated, circumscribed, assessed on matters of reliability and historical substantiation, and taken into consideration when discussing the life, fiction, and work of the author named Anthony Burgess, or else the rich extra-literary life of these texts cannot be adequately understood. Saunders's portmanteau neologism, autobiografiction, helps capture the sentiment that 'auto/biography can be read as fiction, and that fiction can be read as auto/biographical', therefore autobiografiction 'connotes more clearly the literary relationship ... between fiction and a self's autobiography', meaning the overlap between a public authorial projection and the work of such an author.[37] Assigning Burgess's literary work to be analysed in this monograph as working within the parameters set forth, this approach can then constructively and critically differentiate between varying levels of auto/biographical and historical information in order to lay out interpretative contexts that alter how readers of these Burgess texts can *see* and *understand* his life and work, especially in an American context.

Because Burgess experienced the United States as a public figure, Burgess's *work*, especially during this period of his life, must be defined as including the epitexts of correspondence, lectures, interviews, journalism, and non-fiction since these sources are artefacts of his public voice and persona that communicated his particular disposition as a public author-figure, and not to do so would be intellectually dishonest and historically misrepresentative because, as Bakhtin and Medvedev write in *The Formal Method* (1978), literature is a 'social phenomenon' where the 'very presence of the utterance is historically and socially significant' since it 'passes from natural reality to the category of historical reality'.[38] As David Lodge notes in *After Bakhtin: Essays on Fiction and Criticism* (1990), mid to late twentieth-century fiction writing 'has in fact probably never been more obsessively author-centred' because of the 'supplementary forms of exposure through the media-interviews and profiles in the press and on TV, prizes, public readings and book launches and so on' that have established a preoccupation with 'the author as a unique creative self, mysterious, glamourous origin of the text; and the questions one is asked on these occasions invariably emphasize the mimetic connection between fiction and reality'.[39] Burgess is a representative example of such a confluence of the historical record penetrating the literary shield due to his expressed public personal opinions revealing a tangled web of culturally heteroglossic and canonically allusive language.

This kind of crossover is important for understanding Burgess's fiction because he arguably could not even keep track of whether he was or was not one of his fully fictional characters, Enderby, stating in *Little Wilson and Big God* (1987), the first of his two autobiographies, that the 'dyspeptic poet who is, despite what the critics say, not myself, though he is the author of some of my poems as well as his own'.[40] In a single sentence Burgess contradicts himself, implying either dual authorship with a character of his own creation or else just teasing at the veil of authorial power. Even more revealing on this matter is that in a letter to Geoffrey Aggeler in 1969, Burgess remarked privately that the only poetry of his he valued had been preserved by and in Enderby.[41] His words elsewhere contradict the first notion that Enderby is not a kind of distortion of his own attitudes more completely, assuring that he was likely aware that Enderby was indeed, on many levels, a reflection of himself, explaining in an interview in 1985 that Enderby worked at a New York City college in *The Clockwork Testament* with a *disguised* name, not a fabrication, so as to present a kind of 'disguised autobiography', in Genette's terms in *Narrative Discourse* (1983).[42] Divulging even more, and substantiating this qualification, Burgess admits that, 'Yes, he [Enderby] went through my experiences', making at least the final two Enderby novels, narrated in third-person limited omniscient point of view, appear to be texts controlled by a puppet-master engaging in catharsis as Burgess fashions Enderby's life out of an often mock parallel life of his own.[43] Inarguably, *Burgess* appears both textually and paratextually across all of his work, in many different forms, with varying patterns, at different fronts, with different consistencies and emphases.

Taking the sometimes indecipherable line between Burgess and Enderby into account, the purpose of this monograph will not be to delve into the 'biographical origins of one's fiction, seeking to establish a perfect fit between the novelist's personal identity and his *oeuvre*', because no such 'perfect fit' exists, but what does exist is a preponderance of evidence that leads to the mimetic qualities of Burgess's work and biographical inspirations behind these literary products.[44] Not only do Bakhtin's theories on dialogical imagination become important when juxtaposing Burgess's views with his characters, but they are also important in the contextual and culturally rooted nature of language, how language cannot be fully understood without a historical matrix and frame of reference, described as the 'already uttered' timeline of language's evolution.[45] The heteroglot, which Bakhtin defines as being the model that authors utilize to construct their fantasies, intrinsically brings with it socio-historical significance, a point that challenges Burgess's arguments that literary language should exist in a temporal and political vacuum, that honest and true literature should not have a social purpose, 'since literature is, if it is true art, totally removed from the field of action, or rather (since literature is only words) from persuasion to action'.[46] Even though Burgess acknowledges that his opinion about the 'static aloofness of literature, may be regarded by some – including American Negroes and Central European Jews – as one of the privileges thrown up by Anglo-Saxon civilization on both sides of the Atlantic', which is shared by an author like Vladimir Nabokov, it is also argued in this monograph that Burgess adopts this view so that he may, as author-figure, evade culpability for uses of personal opinions and derogatory language within his texts and align himself with literary greats.[47] Indeed, Burgess contradicted himself routinely in his fiction and non-fiction when commenting on political matters, social problems, and the edifying role literature plays in culture, essentially and paradoxically confirming the cultural weight his use of language innately carried with it, confirming Bakhtin's supposition regarding the presence of 'double-voiced discourse' in the novel form that reveals dialogic fracturing.[48] For these reasons, Bakhtin's work provides a critical lens through which to legitimately analyse and deconstruct many of the biographical elements of Burgess's fiction during the period 1971–84, while also exposing fault lines between Burgess's authorial, public, and personal language.

A distinctive shift in tone and purpose found in Burgess's literary output at the beginning of the 1970s has been noted by Auberon Waugh, Paul Phillips, Jim Clarke, Geoffrey Aggeler, and John Stinson, among others, but all such analyses have avoided or ignored what is perhaps the biggest cause of such a change: his time in the United States.[49] It is not a coincidence that Burgess decidedly broke away from his former literary patterns once he began visiting the United States in the late 1960s. In fact, what took place in the United States not only influenced Burgess's work dramatically in content and purpose but also affected his general views of the ontology of literature itself. In his experiences throughout the United States, Burgess was introduced to many new ways of thinking about literature, the artistic process, and what it meant to be an artist, a scholar, an intellectual, and a public personality, so much so that he started embodying the American trait of experimentation that he saw as being integral to the American experience, be it literary or otherwise: 'America is increasingly expansive while England tends to contract. Thus linguistic experiment in art must, in America, seem an integral part of the social process.'[50] This is why a novel such as *M/F*, to be considered in Chapter 4, has a 'strong general correspondence with many of the most serious, "experimental" works of American fiction of the last twenty-five years or so [and] *M/F* can thus be read as either a structuralist or poststructuralist novel; modernist or postmodernist'.[51] Stinson's observation here is astute, and extends the argument made in his 1973 article, 'Anthony Burgess: Novelist on the Margin', that Burgess's work tends to straddle eras – he could have also added colonial and post-colonial.[52] In many ways, Stinson's comment is accurate because with novels such as *A Vision of Battlements* (1965), which is a mock-heroic inspired by Virgil's *Aeneid* in the same Joycean sense of *Ulysses*, he positions himself as a late modernist, but with novels such as *A Clockwork Orange* (1962), *M/F* (1971), *Napoleon Symphony* (1974), *1985* (1978), and *The End of the World News* (1982), his work shifts into the realm of the post-modern, while novels like

Byrne (1995), a mock-epic poem published posthumously, altogether upend any attempt to neatly chart the progression of Burgess's artistic development since he jumped back and forth between genres, eras, aesthetics, mediums, and styles throughout his entire career.[53] As Jim Clarke has noted about *M/F*, the text marks an experimental aesthetic turn in Burgess's fiction, which is argued in the later chapters to be particularly American and fits in with the experimental, crude, sardonic/comic, satirical, and inventive contemporary American novels of the period, such as Vladimir Nabokov's *Lolita* (1955), *Pale Fire* (1962), and *Ada or Ardor* (1969), William Burroughs's *Naked Lunch* (1959) and *Wild Boys* (1969), John Barth's *Sot-Weed Factor* (1960) and *Giles Goat-Boy* (1966), Philip Roth's *Portnoy's Complaint* (1969), Saul Bellow's *Herzog* (1964) and *Mr Sammler's Planet* (1970), Norman Mailer's *Why Are We in Vietnam?* (1967) and *Armies of the Night* (1968), Thomas Pynchon's *V.* (1963), *The Crying of Lot 49* (1966), and *Gravity's Rainbow* (1973), Gore Vidal's *Myra Breckinridge* (1968), Terry Southern's *Candy* (1958) and *Blue Movie* (1970), and even works like Henry Miller's *Tropic of Cancer* (1934), William Faulkner's *Absalom, Absalom!* (1936), and Ralph Ellison's *Invisible Man* (1952), all having themes redolent of those used by Burgess in *M/F* like incest, race politics, youth culture, myth, familial trauma, authorial and narratological play, and sexuality – Burgess having been, at the very least, aware of these works.[54] Becoming a part of the American literary scene in the mid-twentieth century provided Burgess with economic support, artistic courage, and a suitable environment to explore his literary faculties, which led to an evolution in his thinking about where and how literature fit into contemporary culture.

Although some scholars often dismiss these kinds of claims as being too close to the historic–allegoric method in Bakhtin's terms, or the intentional fallacy that seeks to pinpoint authorial intent to adjudge aesthetic quality, and the biographical fallacy that has the goal of connecting an author's life to their fiction for the mere sake of revealing glimmers of *truth* behind the texts, the claims made throughout this monograph draw attention to instances where the overlaps between author and work so egregiously invade each other's space that they reveal important and pertinent historical and biographical information that adds substantial context to Burgess's life and fiction.[55] These points are most beneficial and revealing when a topic Burgess – though this could be applied to any number of authors – discussed during a lecture turns up in an interview or a newspaper article, and then as a point in a novel. Examples abound, but the most significant case, to be discussed alongside an analysis of *M/F*, are Burgess's varied comments on pornography, specifically in an American context, which appear similarly in every medium Burgess communicated in, so that if we accept his various paths of communication as personas (journalist, teacher, author, television personality, etc.), then what occurs are trails of double-, triple-, and quadruple-voiced discourse across various modes of authorial 'literary performance', where the *private person* echoes the *television personality*, who then repeats the same comment as *the teacher* and *the author* during an interview, and so on, therefore exposing the authorial resemblances in the fiction and thus revealing layers of biographical and historical critical significance.[56] Using John Rodden's cogent definitional claim that literary interviews be accepted by the academic community, or at the very least literary historians, as examples of the 'rhetorical craft of artistic self-fashioning' and 'self-invention' which ultimately reveal glimmers of the 'psychology of authorship' and an explanation of how the production of autobiography can be accepted as a 'mode of literary performance' which contributes to an author's 'linguistic pattern', this monograph adopts this idea and applies it alongside Bakhtin's dialogism, Genette's paratexts, LeJeune's auto/biographical theories, and Saunders's autobiografiction, not just to formal literary interviews but, in Burgess's case, to any public performance as an author.[57]

As this monograph contests, the connections between Burgess and his characters, or even Burgess the author and Burgess the person in his autobiographies, are not separate and impenetrable spheres because a historical record exists, and therefore it is possible to pin down verifiable actual realities and track how these details have or have not been projected into fiction, non-fiction, and auto/biography. In *Self Impression*, Saunders suggests it is at the point where a reader may enter Burgess's texts with or without knowledge of his personal life that 'the paradox' begins: 'while every text is autobiography, no reader can know for sure in what way it is, because every reading is itself a species of involuntary and unconscious autobiography, and distorts the features of the writerly autobiographer into those of the readerly one'.[58] This monograph aims to delineate exactly where the American autobiographical elements exist in several of Burgess's novels to expose the boundaries and possibilities of the texts as conscious and unconscious autobiography, thus exposing a new facet of interpretation not only for the novels chosen here but also as a possible critical apparatus to one day be applied to Burgess's entire canon.

For over four decades, Burgess occupied an intersectional space where biography, autobiography, author, public persona, private individual, scholar, and journalist crossed paths and trod over each other's terrain, allowing him to assemble multiple identities for different purposes to be deployed depending on the time, setting, and audience. Effectively – what other Burgess scholars have also noted – Burgess fashioned for himself different personae in order to craft a more general 'autobiography of character' who wore many different masks.[59] Complex though this might be, it is not impossible to untangle his meandering web of identities, and, as expected in this complex web of narrative and discourse, it becomes unavoidable that research into Burgess's life and work reveals patterns of thought and recurring points of interest both within and outside his writings that are indispensable for an adequate approach to Burgess's work on and in America. Pinpointing, assessing, and analysing the many pieces of evidence that help support this layered historical, biographical, and narratological approach is not an attempt therefore to gauge the 'success of a work of literary art', but rather to contribute knowledge to the literary history of Burgess and, more particularly, to better understand the autobiographical allusiveness of his *American* novels.[60]

Notes

1 From *One Man's Chorus: The Uncollected Writings of Anthony Burgess*, ed. by Ben Forkner (New York: Carroll & Graf, 1998), p. 199.

2 Burgess visited every state except Alaska, Arizona, Arkansas, Maine, Mississippi, Nebraska, Nevada, New Mexico, North and South Dakota, Oregon, and Wyoming.

3 An example: teaching 'English 94: British and American Fiction since World War II' and English 293, a graduate course on twentieth-century fiction in the autumn of 1969, Dr Howard Harper at the University of North Carolina at Chapel Hill had included the following Burgess works in his syllabus: *A Vision of Battlements*, *The Right to an Answer*, *Tremor of Intent*, *ReJoyce*, *A Clockwork Orange*, *Honey for the Bears*, and *Nothing Like the Sun* (Howard Harper, Letter to Anthony Burgess, Fall 1969, University of North Carolina at Chapel Hill, Harry Ransom Center, The University of Texas at Austin).

4 Gérard Genette, *Paratexts: Thresholds of Interpretation*, trans. by Jane E. Lewin (Cambridge: Cambridge University Press, 1987; 1997), p. 5.

5 Mikhail Bakhtin, 'Discourse in the Novel', *The Dialogic Imagination: Four Essays*, ed. by Michael Holquist, trans. by Caryl Emerson and Michael Holquist (Austin, TX: University of Texas Press, 1981), p. 410.

6 Genette, *Paratexts*, p. 409.

7 Anthony Burgess, *M/F* (London: Penguin Books, 1971); Anthony Burgess, *The Clockwork Testament; or, Enderby's End* (New York: McGraw-Hill, 1974); Anthony Burgess, *Earthly Powers* (New York: Europa Editions, 1980; 2012); Anthony Burgess, *The End of the World News* (London: Penguin Books, 1982; 1984); Anthony Burgess, *Enderby's Dark Lady; or No End to Enderby* (New York: McGraw-Hill, 1984).

8 Bakhtin, *The Dialogic Imagination*, p. 411.

9 Ákos Farkas, *Will's Son and Jake's Peer: Anthony Burgess's Joycean Negotiations* (Budapest: Akadémiai Kiadó, 2002), p. 86.

10 Robert Spence, *The Reputation of Anthony Burgess* (Manchester: University of Manchester dissertation, unpublished, 2002), pp. 131–132; Andrew Biswell, *The Real Life of Anthony Burgess* (London: Picador, 2005), p. 258.

11 The film was released nationally on 2 February 1972.

12 Anthony Burgess, *English Literature* (Hong Kong: Longman Group, 1958; 1974; 1979); Anthony Burgess, *The Novel To-day* (London: The British Council and the National Book League – Longmans, Green & Co., 1963); Anthony Burgess, *Language Made Plain* (New York: Thomas Y. Crowell Company, 1964; 1965); Anthony Burgess, *Rejoyce* (New York: W.W. Norton, 1965); Anthony Burgess and Francis Haskell, *The Grand Tour* (New York: Crown Publishers, 1967); Anthony Burgess, *The Novel Now* (London: Faber & Faber, 1967; 1971); Anthony Burgess, *Urgent Copy: Literary Studies* (New York: W.W. Norton, 1968); Anthony Burgess, *Shakespeare* (New York: Carroll & Graf, 1970; 2002).

13 This meeting led to Burgess's 'Letter from England' to *The Hudson Review*. Burgess says to Morgan that the idea to do so was brilliant since Burgess had wanted to do this for some time: 'namely, tell a responsible and literate American organ what's going on in England (totally unbiased politically, naturally) at nicely spaced regular intervals. Please don't change your mind about that suggestion. … As you'll know, *The Hudson Review* is not merely known to exist in United Kingdom but is actually read. And so it should be. Again my thanks' (Anthony Burgess, Letter to Frederick Morgan, 18 March 1966, TS from London, Princeton University Library); Burgess visited the University of Buffalo in 1969 and 1976.

14 Farkas, *Will's Son and Jake's Peer*, p. 86; Biswell, *The Real Life of Anthony Burgess*, pp. 279, 293; Paul Phillips, *A Clockwork Counterpoint: The Music and Literature of Anthony Burgess* (Manchester: Manchester University Press, 2010), p. 110; Anthony Burgess, *You've Had Your Time: Being the Second Part of the Confessions of Anthony Burgess* (London: Penguin Books, 1990), p. 143; Burgess was invited by Dr William Pritchard, who wrote two of the first American academic criticisms of Burgess's work in his 1966 article 'The Early Novels of Anthony Burgess' in *The Massachusetts Review* and his 1967 article 'The Burgess Memorandum' in the *Partisan Review*.

15 Many of the professors who invited Burgess to visit their schools found his journalism and non-fiction works such as *Shakespeare* (1970) and *Re Joyce* (1965) to be highly entertaining as well as informative, and *Nothing Like the Sun* (1964) was also a favourite of many of these academics; the first known request to have Burgess work at the City College of New York came on 27 January 1972, when the *A Clockwork Orange* film had still not been released nationally in the United States.

16 Burgess's adaptation of Edmund Rostand's *Cyrano de Bergerac*, *Cyrano*, first opened at the Guthrie Theater in Minneapolis on 22 July 1971; Edmund Rostand, *Cyrano de Bergerac*, trans. and adapt. by Anthony Burgess (New York: Knopf, 1971).

17 Geoffrey Aggeler, *Anthony Burgess: The Artist as Novelist* (Tuscaloosa, AL: University of Alabama Press, 1979), p. 2.

18 Aggeler, *Anthony Burgess*, p. 2. He continues: 'No, Harold, he doesn't drink like Hemingway or Mr Fitzgerald. Sometimes he does leave that machine humming to itself while he brews himself a strong cup of tea, but his rest breaks are

few. Strong tea and cigar smoke are about all he will consume during a working day' (Aggeler, *Anthony Burgess*, p. 2).

19 Anthony Burgess, 'Letter from Europe', *American Scholar*, 40.1 (Winter 1970–71), 122.

20 Bakhtin, *The Dialogic Imagination*, p. 269.

21 Philippe LeJeune, 'Little Wilson and Big Rousseau? A Reading of the Preambles to Anthony Burgess's Confessions', *Anthony Burgess: Autobiographer*, ed. by Graham Woodroffe (Angers: Presses de l'Université d'Angers, 2006), p. 50; Graham Woodroffe, 'Introduction', *Anthony Burgess, Autobiographer*, p. 16; William Boyd, *The Burgess Variations*, BBC, 26–27 December 1999.

22 Hayden White, 'The Historical Text as Literary Artifact', *The Critical Tradition: Classic Texts and Contemporary Trends*, ed. by David Richter (Boston, MA: Bedford/St. Martin's, 2007), p. 1390.

23 Bakhtin, 'Discourse in the Novel', p. 292.

24 Erich Auerbach, *Mimesis: The Representation of Reality in Western Literature* (Princeton, NJ: Princeton University Press, 1953; 2003), p. 12.

25 Bakhtin, *The Dialogic Imagination*, p. 354.

26 Wayne C. Booth, 'Introduction', *Problems of Dostoyevsky's Poetics*, ed. by Caryl Emerson (Minneapolis, MN: University of Minnesota Press, 1984; 1999), p. xxi.

27 Bakhtin, *The Dialogic Imagination*, pp. 326–327.

28 Mikhail Bakhtin, *Problems of Dostoyevsky's Poetics*, ed. by Caryl Emerson, volume 8 (Minneapolis, MN: University of Minnesota, 1984), pp. 53, 68.

29 Bakhtin, *The Dialogic Imagination*, pp. 326–327.

30 Burgess, *You've Had Your Time*, p. 278; Burgess, *Earthly Powers*, p. 250; Anthony Burgess, 'Plain Man's Fancy', *Observer*, 5 November 1978, p. 30.

31 Philippe LeJeune, *On Autobiography*, ed. by Paul John Eakin, trans. by Katherine Leary (Minneapolis, MN: University of Minnesota Press, 1989), p. 23.

32 Anthony Burgess, *Little Wilson and Big God: Being the First Part of the Autobiography* (New York: Weidenfeld & Nicolson, 1986), p. 5.

33 Burgess, *Little Wilson and Big God*, p. viii.

34 Burgess, *Little Wilson and Big God*, p. 5.

35 Burgess, *The Clockwork Testament; or, Enderby's End*, p. 20; Burgess, *You've Had Your Time*, p. 269.

36 Max Saunders, *Self Impression: Life-Writing, Autobiografiction, and the Forms of Modern Literature* (Oxford: Oxford University Press, 2010), p. 8.

37 Saunders, *Self Impression*, p. 7.

38 Mikhail Bakhtin and P.N. Medvedev, *The Formal Method in Literary Scholarship* (Cambridge, MA: Harvard University Press, 1978; 1985), pp. 37, 120.

39 David Lodge, *After Bakhtin: Essays on Fiction and Criticism* (London: Routledge, 1990), pp. 15–16.

40 Burgess, *Little Wilson and Big God*, p. 185.

41 Anthony Burgess, Letter to Geoffrey Aggeler, 10 October 1969. TS. Lija, Malta. International Anthony Burgess Foundation.

42 Anthony Burgess, *Conversations with Anthony Burgess*, ed. by Earl Ingersoll and Mary Ingersoll (Jackson, MS: University Press of Mississippi, 2008), p. 147; Gérard Genette, *Narrative Discourse: An Essay in Method*, trans. by Jane E. Lewin (Ithaca, NY: Cornell University Press, 1983), p. 246.
43 Burgess, *Conversations with Anthony Burgess*, p. 143.
44 Lodge, *After Bakhtin*, p. 16.
45 Bakhtin, *The Dialogic Imagination*, p. 278.
46 Bakhtin, *The Dialogic Imagination*, p. 291; Anthony Burgess, 'Speaking of Books: The Writer's Purpose', *The New York Times*, 1 May 1966.
47 Burgess, 'Speaking of Books'.
48 Bakhtin, *The Dialogic Imagination*, p. 324.
49 Auberon Waugh, 'Auberon Waugh on New Novels', *The Spectator*, 19 June 1971; Paul Phillips, *A Clockwork Counterpoint: The Music and Literature of Anthony Burgess* (Manchester: Manchester University Press, 2010); Jim Clarke, 'Anthony Burgess's Structuralist Turn: Lévi-Strauss and Burgess's Aesthetics', *Anthony Burgess and France*, ed. by Marc Jeannin (Cambridge: Cambridge Scholars Publishing, 2017), pp. 107–125; Aggeler, *Anthony Burgess*; Geoffrey Aggeler, 'Introduction', *Critical Essays on Anthony Burgess*, ed. by Geoffrey Aggeler (Boston, MA: G.K. Hall, 1986); John J. Stinson, *Anthony Burgess: Revisited* (Boston, MA: Twayne, 1991).
50 Anthony Burgess, 'The Postwar American Novel: A View from the Periphery', *Urgent Copy*, p. 130. In *The Novel Now*, Burgess explains this stance a little further, saying that 'America is too big, and too little troped to a single centre of life and culture, to produce anything that can be called a provincial novel. ... It is the whole structure and ethos of a materialistic society that they revolt against. The most spectacular of the rebels are the Beats, though their literary record is meagre and their works amateurish. ... Their rebellion is really a withdrawal' (Burgess, *The Novel Now*, p. 152).
51 Stinson, *Anthony Burgess*, p. 109.
52 John J. Stinson, 'Anthony Burgess: Novelist on the Margin', *Journal of Popular Culture* (Summer 1973), 136–151.
53 Anthony Burgess, *A Clockwork Orange* (New York: W. W. Norton, 1962; 1986); Anthony Burgess, *A Vision of Battlements* (New York: W. W. Norton, 1965); Anthony Burgess, *Napoleon Symphony* (New York: Knopf, 1974); Anthony Burgess, *1985* (London: Beautiful Books, 1978; 2010); Anthony Burgess, *The End of the World News* (London: Penguin Books, 1982; 1984); Anthony Burgess, *Byrne* (London: Vintage, 1995).
54 Clarke, 'Anthony Burgess's Structuralist Turn', p. 108.
55 Mikhail Bakhtin, *Rabelais and His World*, ed. by Helene Iswolsky (Bloomington, IN: Indiana University Press, 1984).
56 Christopher W. Thurley, 'Anthony Burgess, Obscenity, and America', *Resources for American Literary Study*, 43 (2022), 130–160; John Rodden, *Performing the Literary Interview: How Writers Craft Their Public Selves* (Lincoln, NE: University of Nebraska Press, 2001), p. 1.
57 Rodden, *Performing the Literary Interview*, p. 1.

58 Saunders, *Self Impression*, p. 3.

59 Phillips, *A Clockwork Counterpoint*; Leonard R.N. Ashley, '"Unhappy all the time": Religion in Anthony Burgess's *Earthly Powers*', *Christianity and Literature*, 52.1 (Autumn 2002), 42.

60 W.K. Wimsatt Jr and M.C. Beardsley, 'The Intentional Fallacy', *The Sewanee Review*, 54.3 (July–September 1946), p. 468.

1

On his mind (1956–66)

> Americans, who contest the rule of the world with the Soviet Union, assume that they are in charge of Time. American Time is the only time. But there are at least three American Times, and the two great temporal contenders within the United States are the time of the East Coast and that of the Western seaboard. (Anthony Burgess, 'Thoughts on Time')[1]

The goal of this chapter is to provide an overview of how the topic of the United States was represented in fiction and non-fiction by Anthony Burgess *before* he first visited America in 1966. Doing so will also help solidify the two claims that Burgess was intertwined with American culture for almost his entire life, and that his later career was essentially and significantly shaped by the American marketplace. Burgess held many preconceptions about the United States, so it's crucial to chart the evolution of his opinions as multi-voiced through fiction and non-fiction. Although a good amount of critical work has been done on Burgess's life before 1966, with the first volume of his two autobiographies, *Little Wilson and Big God* (1986), acting as an important, though highly stylized and historically flawed, document, previous scholars have underestimated the thematic significance of America on the first decade of Burgess's authorial career (1956–66).

The ten years before Burgess visited America was a period filled with literary productivity, which produced some of his best-known work, making these works intrinsically significant to Burgess's life as a writer, as well as examples of how his work progressed. Before 1966, Burgess had over twenty books published – six non-fiction books and sixteen works of fiction – and over half of them contain material referring to the United States in some meaningful and/or insightful way. Still, the United States is usually discussed in these texts as a *concept* or *idea* of metonymic significance. Burgess essentially used and saw the United States as existing, as is delineated in Henry Miller's *Tropic of Cancer* (1961), 'always in the background', as if it did not actually exist, since America is, or was, just 'a name you give to an abstract idea'.[2]

The works assessed in this chapter are not limited to just the following publications, nor does the discussion of them here mean that some of these sources will not appear elsewhere throughout this monograph. Instead, the chosen pieces act as key examples of Burgess's early views of America during the first half of his writing career. Specifically, this chapter will assess the presence of the United States in the following seven novels: *Time for a Tiger* (1956), *The Enemy in the Blanket* (1958), *Beds in the East* (1959), *The Right to an Answer* (1960), *One Hand Clapping* (1961), *Honey for the Bears* (1963), and *A Vision of Battlements* (1965). The brief discussions of these works will provide background on Burgess's preconceptions of the United States in order to aid in the analyses in later chapters which look at Burgess's work in the United States after 1966.

Throughout his life, Burgess perceived the United States as being an alluring but altogether nascent, superficial, and irrational culture, as evidenced in his novels, journalism, public lectures, and interviews from the 1950s onwards, which will be the overarching focus of this monograph.[3] His opinions of American culture, coupled with his concern over the spread of Americanism, supported his stance that American culture and its form of materialism was corrosive and internationally invasive, a fear shared by characters in *Honey for the Bears* (1963) who remark that the United States would 'make plastic of the world' and displayed as a subtopic in several of Burgess's early novels.[4]

In one of the earliest dissertations on Burgess's work, Rexford Brown comments that the *Malayan Trilogy* (1964), or *The Long Day Wanes* in the United States, shows 'that the American "cultural advisors" ' sent to Malaya were portrayed in the trilogy as 'a new, more ruthless force that [was] more than willing to fill the vacuum left by the no longer tenable colonial idea' – an idea likely borrowed from Graham Greene's *The Quiet American* (1955).[5] It was not in Malaya, though, that Burgess first witnessed the destructive powers of the United States. Having left Southeast Asia in the late 1950s, Burgess's first memorable close contact with Americans actually came in April 1944 while living in Gibraltar, when he heard that Lynne, his first wife, had been attacked in London by 'a small gang of American men, presumably deserters, who had robbed her in the street and kicked her as she lay screaming', making Burgess reflect later that he had felt a 'rage' towards the American soldiers but not necessarily the United States as a whole.[6] In *Little Wilson and Big God*, Burgess explains that the attack 'had to be accepted as an evil enactment which had to have enactors of some nationality or other. It could have been Poles or French Canadians. The American aspect of the matter was accidental and unimportant'.[7] Being able to separate the two – countrymen and a group of violent vagabonds – exhibits Burgess's early ability to avoid being susceptible to acts of monolithic and generalized prejudice, as well as his growing intrigue with and distaste for the United States. Despite his calm and rational response to this act of violence, the United States was not shielded from his criticisms; before 1966, Burgess instead flung admonishments towards the United States that focused on his engagement with American mass media and the 'cheap, vulgar, silly, brutish, and nasty' American imports that flooded England, reflecting poorly, Burgess believed, on the British.[8]

Whatever immediate hostilities he claims to have had towards the United States – telling the *Oshkosh Advance-Titan* in 1975 that 'before his respect could return for America' he had to '"get this [*A Clockwork Orange*] out of his system"' – they soon evolved into fascination, and the boredom Burgess experienced in 1960s England enticed the writer to seek out the United States because it was a place rife with both progress and problems.[9] As Burgess stated many times throughout his career, his enduring interest in the United States stemmed from the country's – he casually stereotypes and generalizes without any examples – infirmities and entropic qualities:

> The state of American society is so warbley [sic] so uncertain, it's so emergent. Whereas in England you have … a sort of achieved society which is not always a good thing. … You need a very dynamic sort of society to produce fiction at all and America is a place for very good fiction or very good poetry.[10]

Unrest meant invigoration, something art needed, since good art, to Burgess at least, was not created from 'fixed, settled, tranquil' societies but rather from societies engaged with conflict and discordance, what Burgess called the 'dynamo', 'which produces the artistic impulse'.[11] In many ways, the chaos and flamboyance of the United States had been affronting Burgess since his childhood through films and music, only to escalate and move closer to Burgess during World War Two in the shape of American soldiers in Gibraltar, American soldiers in London, and, though it occurred three years before he occupied the same space, in Bamber Bridge, Lancashire, where a mutiny by African American servicemen occurred as a response to racism – a story Burgess repeated several times throughout his career.[12] There even exists a lifelong series of interactions with American artistic products as displayed in *Little Wilson and Big God*, making the pre-1966 context of Burgess's interactions with the United States, American goods, and American people crucial to this monograph's overall purpose.

The first glimpses of the United States in Burgess's fiction

A Vision of Battlements (1965), with the earliest evidence of the novel's composition going back to 1940 but which was drafted between 1951 and

1952, was Burgess's first novel and was based 'closely upon Burgess's experiences in Gibraltar'.[13] *A Vision of Battlements* is also Burgess's first novel to have an American character and to discuss American culture. Captain Mendoza, a Spanish American, describes the United States to Richard Ennis, the novel's protagonist, as being an abstract and factitious nation, echoing the earlier quote from Miller's *Tropic of Cancer*: 'One has produced Americanism, which is only a mental climate. America's not real, it's an idea, a way of looking at things.'[14] It's not surprising that Burgess, who had read Miller and not visited the United States but had also met war-fatigued and disillusioned Americans, would present a character who discusses the United States as a naïve, nebulous, and indeterminate far-off space where Pelagianism, or the rejection of sin (long before Allan Bloom suggested this in *The Closing of the American Mind* (1987) when he said that Americans had problems with their 'sense of *self*, not with any original sin or devils' in the 'peculiarly American way of digesting Continental despair', which was 'nihilism with a happy ending'), was not only admired but ingrained in the capitalist culture where *sin* was a cheap perfume, 'My Sin', and history was commoditized and 'artificial, like something on the movies'.[15] The presence of Mendoza and this description of the United States are important for two reasons: this is the first mention of the United States and American culture in Burgess's canon, with commentary on the country coming from his first American character who discusses cheap commodities, consumerism, the concept of the United States, popular mass media, and American literature, and this instance acts not only as the introduction to Burgess's frequent use of Augustinianism and Pelagianism in his fiction (see especially *The Wanting Seed*) but it is also simultaneously the first time that the United States is drawn into this dichotomy and defined by the terms of these two theological and eschatological philosophies, effectively resulting in the shared origin of two significant Burgess tropic motifs: the conceptualization of the United States and the parallelism existent between Americans and Pelagianism, as well as his fascination with this theological Manichaean dichotomy. This also means that the analyses that follow concerning the United States are as important to understand for Burgess studies as Burgess's relationship with theology, if not more so – a topic rigorously explored by Burgess scholars for decades whereas his interaction with the United States has largely been ignored – due to the coexistence of these two foundational themes.

With this accepted, it's then important to understand why the United States exists in Burgess's canon in the 1950s as a symbolic stereotype. Importantly, his encounters and memories of Americans during this time were not flattering, as is outlined in *Little Wilson and Big God*, where he detailed the friction between the Americans and the British in the 1940s: 'The Americans did not behave well. ... They expressed contempt for the limey cocksuckers. … They disclosed, as the more ignorant British did, a total misunderstanding of a colonial situation. They despised the colonisers and the colonised. The susceptibilities of foreigners were a joke.'[16] Burgess recounts that only 'the blacks showed any dignity', and because of such poor general behaviour many of the British soldiers 'went through a bad phase of Americanophobia', which Burgess also experienced until an American 'of Hispanic origin … named Baroja', the inspiration for his Mendoza, 'put me right'.[17] Paul Phillips in *A Clockwork Counterpoint: The Music and Literature of Anthony Burgess* (2010) states that it was in fact Captain Baroja who helped Burgess 'overcome his rage by explaining how the war demonstrated the existence of theological evil', while Andrew Biswell, Burgess's biographer, states in *The Real Life of Anthony Burgess* (2005) that this discussion 'crystallized his thinking about religion and politics'.[18]

The character of Richard Ennis in *A Vision of Battlements* exists as a reference point to how Burgess's view of the United States changed as time went on. Much like his first protagonist, author and character alike felt that the United States consisted of a great deal to be admired, especially in literature, with Burgess's novel remarking similarly that the United States had 'Whitman, for instance. There's nothing more stirring than that democratic vista'.[19] Burgess's non-fiction books before 1970 support this stance, with the following monographs dedicating large portions of space to American authors and novels, to be discussed elsewhere throughout this book: *English Literature: A Survey for Students* (1958), *The Novel To-Day* (1963), *The Novel Now: A Student's Guide to Contemporary Fiction* (1967), and *Urgent Copy* (1968). But the fact that there are similarities between Burgess and his early characters isn't necessarily a new observation, since other scholars have remarked that in his early novels characters such as Ennis, Crabbe, and Edwin Spindrift 'bear a striking resemblance to Burgess', primarily in the sense that the relation between author and characters rests in 'their contexts, experiences and associates', since 'Burgess's early protagonists live or visit places he lived and visited, work in jobs he worked at, often have unfaithful wives, and are commonly writers'. However, it's crucial to remember that these similarities do not in and of themselves prove anything about Burgess's texts; only precise archival and canon examinations can reveal the epitextual historical, cultural, and biographical elements that help to contextualize his novels and explicate them through Bakhtin's philosophic anthropology that designates language as double-voiced when it, 'within the boundaries of a single utterance', effectively produces 'two potential utterances [that] are fused, two responses are, as it were, harnessed in a potential dialogue'.[20] The similarities do not stop there, though, as will be much of the focus of this monograph. The lines of authorship, persona, and real person often parallel each other and frequently intersect, in effect providing a roadmap for the evolution and dialogic quality of some of Burgess's main themes – and, more specifically, his views of the United States. And though the plots, characters, and experiences in his novels may make 'for a charming story', often they are 'probably', Burgess's bibliographer notes, 'the literal truth – like most of Burgess's disclosures'.[21] If so, this makes cataloguing and analysing these many non-fiction/fiction overlaps immensely significant, if not crucial, to understanding Burgess's life and works, especially when investigating Burgess's elaborate commentary on all things Americana.

The image of the United States presented in *The Malayan Trilogy* (1956–59) is of a country which threatens to infiltrate the East through Americanization.[22] This is achieved largely through the movie industry, technological innovation, violence, pop music, and divorce – common areas of interest to Burgess and therefore also to his characters. The first occurrence of the word 'America' comes just twenty-five pages into *Time for a Tiger* when the literal intermixing of American culture with Malaya has reached the fictional state of Kuala Hantu, where 'smug American cars, radios blaring sentimental pentatonic Chinese tunes' mix with the sounds of trishaw bells ringing outside of the royal town that is 'dominated by an Istana designed by a Los Angeles architect, blessed by a mosque'.[23] Throughout the three novels, Americanism is intangibly omnipresent, with its influence occasionally sweeping down to interact with the characters. In one instance, looming Americanism is felt when a teacher is stolen away by 'a rather disreputable minor university in ... Louisiana, or certainly one of the southern states of America', as the unseen Gilkes was in *The Enemy in the Blanket*, or else by infiltrating young Malayan ruffians' ears as they flash switchblades and walk down the streets 'singing in authentic American' English lines from The Platters' 1955 single 'Only You', as occurs in *Beds in the East*.[24] Other characters are more suspicious of the invasive ubiquitousness of Americanization. For instance, Nabby Adams believes that a 'liking for iced beer was effeminate, decadent and American', what with all the refrigerators that the United States had, effectively flipping the generalized belief Burgess witnessed from Americans that 'all Brits are "fags"' in order to emphasize Nabby's machismo and the United States's outsider status.[25] So commonplace are Americans with refrigerators that Burgess frequently discussed the topic in interviews and lectures, and Adams even tells a story of having met an American from Texas who 'had some sort of refrigerating apparatus in the boot of his car'.[26] It was not just the seemingly opulent lifestyles Americans were accustomed to that Burgess took aim at, though, as several characters point out. Perhaps the more significant criticism Burgess applied throughout the texts was that for Malayans to adopt Western culture, as many of the Malayan 'bureaucrats from the traditional ruling class' did, was to, in effect, relinquish the country's, and the hemisphere's, grasp on the rich heritages and traditions of the many cultures present in Malayan society.[27] Indeed, one of the greatest fears present in Burgess's early novels was that of the homogenizing effect the United States had on both Malaya and England.

This is also evidenced with the school curriculum being described as far too focused on Western culture and the English language in *Time for a Tiger*, a factor that carried with it 'occidental bias' that had resulted in many of the alumni of the school despising 'their own rich cultures, leading them, deracinated, to a yearning for the furthest west of all', a sentiment that was brought on by an inculcation of 'the myths of cinema and syndicated cartoon [that] have served to unite the diverse races far more than the clump of the cricket-ball and the clipped rebukes and laudations of their masters'.[28] At one point, the narrator of *Time for a Tiger* reveals that an American had even been considered for a position at Victor Crabbe's first school in the trilogy. Ultimately not chosen, this immaterial and metonymic individual would have, if chosen, it is reasoned, been 'a complete betrayal of the ideals on which the Mansor School was based', and would have been seen as a 'surrender to a culture which, however inevitable its global spread, must for as long as possible meet a show of resistance'.[29] This resistance to Americanization, however futile, largely manifests in the British and European characters in the trilogy, with the Malayan characters often appearing either oblivious to, unconcerned about, or else apathetic to this impending takeover. The only exceptions exist in the final book of the trilogy, *Beds in the East*, when Indian and Malay characters rail against the omnipresent and commodifying forces of American influence that other, particularly younger, characters have adopted blindly. Parameswaran berates Syed Omar's Malayan family by lashing out at the young Malay youths who sing American pop and jazz songs with their 'long hair and ... American clothes, slouching round the town with companions'.[30] In the same chapter, Omar himself, upon hearing American music on a juke-box, castigates the same youth by arguing that they are 'not the men your fathers were, nor never will be. All this Coca-Cola and jazzing about. Where are the principles your fathers fought for? ... It's all these films from America. Soft living and soft thinking'.[31] Indeed, although Burgess himself played piano in a jazz band, jazz to Burgess symbolized youthful rebellion and was closely associated in his mind with the Beat Movement, where 'negro jazz finds an exact analogue in the prose of Jack Kerouac, with its free syntax, its sense of improvisation, its elimination of all punctuation except that corresponding to the wind-player's taking breath'.[32] This 'so-called beatnik idiom' he identified as being 'close to jazz in another way – the cultivating of "off-beat" accents, the avoidance of the unqualified statement', which the narrator in *Honey for the Bears* argues is 'the only dialectic these youngsters wanted ... the dialectic of jazz'.[33] A case of monoglottal heteroglossia yet again – *id est*, language infused with cultural elements which are appropriated and contorted by Burgess to fit into and adorn his personal and authorial value-system – the softening of the American mind was a trope that Burgess used on at least one other occasion when reflecting on a visit to the United States almost three decades later when he described having to speak to an 'audience softened by showbiz, about the threat to the liberty of expression which is arising in certain states of the Union'.[34] American living, Burgess would continue to believe, resulted in a malignant lethargy of mind which was ever more reason for the world to fear the international spread of American culture. The peculiar predicament with Malaya that Crabbe, and Burgess, realized was that this disparate and immiscible society was doomed to accept outside influences because of England's imperial approach that only provided an inconsiderate, lacklustre, and 'purely legal unification' onto a culture already too willing to accept the invasive nature of American popular culture that helped erect a 'superficial culture represented by American films, jazz, chocolate-bars, and refrigerators'.[35] Such a quandary, with Burgess's opinions likely influenced by Richard Hoggart's *The Uses of Literacy* (1957) which examined 'mass culture in Britain' and having much to do with Burgess's despising of pop music in general (a theme his contemporary Kingsley Amis also takes on in *Girl, 20* (1971) as a side effect of youth culture), essentially makes the preservation of cultures one of the paramount overarching themes of Burgess's Malay novels.[36]

Crabbe's comments about wanting to try to 'cultivate better inter-racial understanding, for one thing', by having 'meetings, say, once a week, to try and mix up the races a bit more', are absurd and comical considering Burgess's own opinions about the nature and duties of literary authors.[37] In *Beds in the East* (1959), Crabbe presents an impassioned plea to the diverse groupings of people in Malaya, only to be mocked and branded a communist for what is perceived as his unrealistic utopian idealism. Crabbe argues to a diverse Malayan audience, consisting of Tamils, Chinese, Indians, and so on, that there 'never seemed any necessity to mix. But now the time has come ... "there must not merely be mixing, there must be fusion" ', before being immediately mocked by Vythilingam as he retorts, 'Confusion'.[38] Predominantly, Burgess erred on the side of criticizing politics in general by calling out the faults and hypocrisies of any politician in order to establish an objective reality beyond and behind the rhetoric, but looking back at his life and work, the views and beliefs of a liberal individualist emerge.[39] His cosmopolitan nature, intellectualism, and endorsement of anti-war, anti-violence, and anti-gun political stances, as well as support for social benefit programmes coupled with a desire for fewer taxes, made him, albeit contradictory, a social liberal who leaned towards fiscal individualism, but who still had lingering, though latent, conservative matrimonial and religious views and values.[40] As will be discussed, many of these views were inspired by American issues and his opinions on such matters were expressed in relation to American political debates.

One of the most striking examples of Burgess discussing his work in relation to politics is his peculiar introduction to the Vintage edition of the *Malayan Trilogy* that includes a didactic plea about his work and how he wishes that 'this novel, which has its own elements of diversion, may, through tears and laughter, educate', effectively contradicting his many claims that the purpose of literature was not to teach its readers or attempt to change the world in any way, because they could not in effect do such things.[41] Burgess then reminds his readers that if American audiences had read the books, the content 'might have had some small effect on the attitude towards Orientals which, during the Vietnam adventure, vitiated any hope of American success' because of the Americans lacking the wherewithal to know who their friends and enemies were.[42] Burgess appears to be recounting an opinion held by at least two reviewers of *The Long Day Wanes* in the *Times Literary Supplement* and *New York Times Book Review* in 1965, who both came to the conclusion that individuals employed by the State Department, in either England or the United States, as well as Peace Corps volunteers, should read Burgess's collection of three novels.[43] The irony in all of this is not just that Burgess contradicts one of his most oft-repeated opinions about the historical and political significance of literature, but also that the *Malayan Trilogy*, though a group of novels about the end of colonialism, are equally prescient novels about the inevitable Americanization of the world. A staple of both colonial and post-colonial literature, these texts should also be included in the study of cultural documents that prognosticate the destructive and powerful military industrial complex that President Dwight D. Eisenhower warned Americans about in his farewell address in January 1961 and, ultimately, the calamitous American military involvement in both Korea and Vietnam throughout the 1950s, 1960s, and 1970s.

Nowhere else is the ominous presence of the United States more evident than at the end of the trilogy as Crabbe drowns in a remote river, either by accident or suicide, but not before witnessing the precursor of a now-independent Malaya being newly invaded not by the British imperial powers but rather an American superpower focused on taking stock of the territory, a power that believed there was much 'work to do in South-East Asia', a rather foreboding historical foresight and foreshadow of the United States's involvement in the Vietnam War between 1964 and 1975.[44] At the end of the trilogy, the United States is embodied in the character Temple Haynes, the linguist and technocrat, who knows little of Malaya's history and is detached from the realities of colonialism, making him only concerned with 'the linguistic angle', which brings with it 'the angle of inter-racial relations [and the] method of teacher training, time-and-motion study in industry, behavior-patterns, statistics, sociological surveys and, of course, demographic studies'.[45] Haynes refuses to see the larger context outside of his Western ideological blinders, arguing with American gusto that there was a 'great deal to do' with Malaya, and that it would 'cost a lot of money, of course, but it's the best possible investment', because the Americans could not 'afford to let the Communists get away' with influencing Southeast Asians.[46] Haynes, a character from 'some university or other. Under the auspices of some organisation or other', who resembles Graham Greene's quiet American, Alden Pyle, is a clandestine operative in the early days of American involvement with Southeast Asia.[47] Haynes is a somewhat benign and nebulous character who is described as being used to 'gracious living' and only interested with cataloguing languages, not conversing with people who speak those languages – making him also similar to Edwin Spindrift, the philologist protagonist of *The Doctor Is Sick*, since they spoke frequently of 'phonemes and semantemes and bilabial fricatives'.[48] Described as appearing 'pure Mayflower' with 'unempathetic features', the supposed benignity of Haynes melts away into a kind of hostile indifference as Haynes inspects Crabbe and the indigenous groups as specimens rather than humans, just as Greene's character Pyle is overly idealistic and naïve as he inconsiderately evangelizes York Harding's political theories to locals, which ultimately leads to his death as retaliation for his political games.[49] Similarly, Haynes, the indifferent technocrat, with his solemn and scientific modern sensibilities, unsympathetically views his time in Asia as a mundane but necessary intellectual and liberalizing task that would likely result in, as Pyle's British acquaintance Thomas Fowler notes, leaving the locals with 'a little equipment and a toy industry'.[50] Bringing news of the outside world, the world Haynes inhabits and will return to soon, he explains to Crabbe the news of how the European and transatlantic world has been changing over the years, especially with Europe being 'full of Coca-Cola signs', a world that Crabbe has been detached and insulated from by the jungles of Malaya.[51] Learning of this, Crabbe grows despondent, 'lost and boorish and crude', as he envisions the British consisting of 'merely gifted amateurs' when now was 'time for the professionals' like the United States technocrats and the inaugural and austere Singaporean government led by Lee Kuan Yew, who took power in June 1959.[52] Appearing ruthlessly logical, fastidious, and perspicacious, these attributes are otherwise presented ironically as detriments, as a sign of inhumaneness as the American people back in the West continue to be harshly criticized and portrayed as 'a race with as little sense of guilt as history', which resulted in the United States government being incapable of making sound international military and political decisions.[53]

The Americans that visit towards the end of *Beds in the East* are also not interested in cultivating or learning from Malayan culture during their travels. More specifically, two music professors from Columbia University are characters who are only concerned with documenting the ancestral sounds of the East, a practice that results in the scholar quickly dismissing Robert Loo's new Malayan compositions as examples of what Homi Bhabha called the 'ambivalence of colonial discourse' or cultural mimicry: 'We've heard it all before. We can do it far better ourselves. In fact, we didn't come out these thousands of miles to see a distorted image of ourselves in a mirror.'[54] Robert Loo, the young composer that Crabbe tries to mentor in *Beds in the East*, is not aware of this, nor does he see himself as producing music for a *nation*, since he is generally indifferent to his culture and Malayans' fascination with American music, remarking that the people 'of Malaya only want American jazz and ronggeng music. I am not composing for Malaya. I am composing because I want to compose. Have to compose'.[55] Unconcerned with the West's imposition, the American music scholars' quick dismissal still holds as a prime example of the Western world's 'desire for a reformed, recognizable Other, *as a subject of a difference that is almost the same, but not quite*'; this is why the portrayal of Americans is even worse than the colonizing British, at least through Burgess's texts, because the Americans are rejecting outright the realities of the culture by engaging in acts of confirmation bias to bolster the idealized image they seek.[56] The significance of what occurs in the *Malayan Trilogy* for this monograph is that many of the ideas and comments made about culture, the United States, and race turn up later in Burgess's career and, as a point of authorial inception, these early novels provide a kind of skeleton key to the development of such ideas.

In the first of his decidedly English novels, *The Right to an Answer* (1960), transatlantic activity manifests itself with J.W. Denham's partner Michiko San being attacked in Japan's American borough of Washington Heights – '(O Heights, O Washington, O Liberty)' – by American teenagers 'and, as far as I could find out, near-raped'.[57] Denham remarks that 'American teenagers, in their strange way, can hardly be blamed for anything either: chocolate malts (Jumbo ones) and juke-box trumpets shut ears and eyes to morality. (They were only kids, in a strange country, their father doing their duty for democracy etc.)'.[58] The problem, the book suggests (and indeed its author, despite Burgess's many comments on original sin), is that *youth* is not necessarily the cause of violence but a culture breeds certain inclinations; it is American culture that is producing this certain brand of nastiness. The adult Americans in the novel are presented as mere caricatures, symbols of excess and vanity, and as being mercurial when left to their own devices, all while having seemingly little control of their progeny.

Homogenously, the men are characterized as being 'super-fatted' and their wives as 'alluring for the most part but too aware of it', while their young children exhibit 'viciously bad bad behavior' that results in the tearing up of 'the school buses', smoking 'in public chimneyly', and throwing peach pits at people.[59] The derision is dense as Denham goes on to describe the older teenagers' destructive dispositions brought on by inflated and false senses of superiority that the American teens had acquired from being 'of the race of the makers of the not-sufficiently-punitive A-bomb'.[60] It's interesting that Burgess – and really Denham – see these teens' impediments as being associated with a delusionary deficiency of mind that was forged out of a social setting and cultural mindset – that being the United States and Americanism. A close inspection of this throughout his early novels cannot help but further support Burgess's tendency to display American culture, especially in the early 1960s, as being corrosive and infectious to the minds of its people, leading to an illusory sense of self-importance, a state of mind that he recognized as having contributed to atrocities and mass killings across multiple wars, specifically at this time the atomic bombs on Japan in 1945, the ineffectual blunder that was the Korean War (1950–53), and the early disinformation campaigns in Vietnam that further entrenched the American war effort in Southeast Asia.

Similarly to Burgess, Denham also questions what America even is – yes, a country, but having no real contact with the country, does it in fact exist at all if either author or character have never visited it? The United States exists here as a *ding an sich*, a noumenon, outside of experiential tangibility, that Denham envisions as a place he cannot see 'as anything other than a fine clever country that has been a little naughty but can have any time, as far as I am concerned, full dominion status', even though he, like Burgess, has conflicted feelings about the inception of the country to begin with: 'I don't accept the Declaration of Independence. I have never told any Americans this, naturally, but in my business and social dealings with these fine super-fatted people I have always assumed that they and I are much the same, and I have got on well with them accordingly.'[61] Burgess's *1985* (1978) novel in fact envisions a future when 'Who knows? – soon the Declaration of Independence may be repealed, and the English-speaking peoples of the world – or should I say the speakers of Workers' English? – reunited through a common purpose', and elsewhere, as will be discussed, Burgess ponders the effectiveness and legitimacy of both the Declaration of Independence and the United States Constitution.[62] Many of Burgess's own views on matters of statehood, American dispositions, cultural malaise and calamity, and consumerist attitudes remained unchanged throughout his entire life, but there does appear a more nuanced and placatory view of the United States and Americans when Burgess begins frequenting the country from 1966 onwards.

What both Denham and Burgess are criticizing is the sheer arrogance, entitlement, lack of humility, and historical detachment they believed Americans evinced as a people. Americans in Burgess's novels during this period often have as their defining trait economic power and little else. They are the individuals capable of having nice things, travelling, studying, and investing, but they lack humanistic compassion or any other redeeming qualities. In *The Right to an Answer* there exists an example of this economic power actually corrupting characters, in this case Burgess's protagonist. Denham protests that he has 'nothing against America, Americans' after the attack on Michiko San, sounding yet again like Burgess's response to Lynne's attack, but Denham's forgiveness appears to have been spurred on by a business deal since he was 'on the point of achieving a most diplomatic live-and-let-live arrangement about colour television with an American firm'.[63] This means that because of the likelihood that Denham had a business deal he could profit from, despite feeling 'anger, compassion and pity' for what had occurred, and 'demanding some kind of justice, in letting off hot air on social occasions with Americans', he instead rationalizes what has occurred by disassociating himself from the situation: 'for what, officially, was Michiko San to me?'.[64] The American influence here exploits the selfishness of humanity by turning Denham into the ruthless capitalist, only concerned with the profit motive, corrupted by the affluence of the United States, and therefore just as hollow and unkind as the other American characters he had once criticized. But Denham is not the only Burgess character to fall victim to the United States and American idealism, as his next novel the following year exhibits.

In 1961, Burgess published a novel under the second *nom de plume* Joseph Kell, entitled *One Hand Clapping*, which includes a Burgess-imagined United States for his characters Howard and Janet Shirley to travel around – indeed, they visit New York City, Cleveland, Detroit, Chicago, Salt Lake City, Los Angeles, San Francisco, and Miami – despite Burgess and his characters literally only knowing the United States through what they had seen 'on the films and on television'.[65] Howard and Janet are drawn to the United States, and popular consumerism, because of the cheap salvation and possible opportunities at wealth:

> If you just appeal to sex and easy sort of music and lyrics that'd make you want to puke and these kids clicking their fingers in a sort of stupid ecstasy, well then – What I mean is that you get so low it stands to reason you'll be appealing to the majority, the majority being stupid for the most part and just like animals.[66]

Aggeler notes that 'much of what she [Janet] finds attractive about life in her native land is imported from America', which was essentially flashy and attractive trinkets that are ultimately valueless, hollow ephemera of no cultural, historical, or intellectual significance.[67] Not only do Burgess's characters grow obsessed with the United States's exports, including the game-show format that Howard participates in which sparks the greed that leads to Janet killing him, but Burgess also manifests the idea of the United States as a concept directly into the photographic brain of Howard, who, having never visited the country, was still able to draw a map of the United States perfectly from memory. If what Mendoza said is right, that *Americanism* 'is only a mental climate' and *America* is 'not real, it's an idea, a way of looking at things', then Howard's possession of the United States in his mind as a simulacrum is indeed a lucid metaphor for a common Burgess trope: how the pernicious nature of the idea of the United States can take residence in an individual's cognitive space as an enticing two-dimensional abstraction.[68] When the two take off for the United States, although Burgess had no first-hand experience of the country in 1961, the conceptualizations are made tangible, and the narration reveals equally as much about the characters' experiences and perceptions as it does the author's understanding of the United States at the time the novel was written. The immensity, newness, and diversity of the United States intrigued Burgess in the early 1960s, and therefore he imagined, or has his characters experience, New York City as a place rid of the 'ghosts' floating around the provincial towns of England that made them 'seem a bit depressing and heavy somehow, but here in New York you didn't have that same feeling'.[69] What Burgess didn't capture in his sanguine estimation from across the Atlantic, but what he would slowly learn during his time in the United States, was that all that growth and activity in the United States also came with indefatigable societal hostility and unrest, realities that, he says in his unpublished essay on the Fourth of July celebrations in New York in 1986, could only be ignored or forgotten as 'long as the symbol of American freedom', the Statue of Liberty, still 'stands in New York Harbour'.[70]

In 1961, a contentious year, tempers flared in the American South and elsewhere as Freedom Riders systematically worked to get African Americans into voting booths, all while the Great Migration slowly continued and John F. Kennedy was inaugurated as the thirty-fifth President of the United States, going on to narrowly escape war with Cuba and the Soviet Union, only to be assassinated by an American veteran two years later. By 1966, as Hugh Brogan notes in his *Penguin History of the USA* (1999), though the image of the United States abroad may have remained somewhat steady, the country was undergoing ongoing turmoil as protests and riots broke out all over the nation: 'There had been nothing like these outbreaks since the American Revolution; even the labour troubles of the late nineteenth century had not posed such a fundamental challenge; but it was a challenge without hope.'[71]

Still, three years before Burgess first visited the United States, in *Honey for the Bears* (1963) the country exists in the novel as a thematic backdrop, an idea to be thrown into discussion by the novel's protagonist, Paul Hussey, or his American wife, Belinda, as they travel to the Soviet Union. Belinda, it is learned, spent her girlhood in Amherst, Massachusetts, and Paul, a Brit, sarcastically describes her as being a 'wicked plutocratic American'.[72] Elsewhere, the novel describes Americans as being grouped together 'listening to jazz' as they waited 'for the bomb to drop', depicting an image of a citizenry and nation essentially gripped by ir/rational fears all while the general population ignored the rest of the world and replaced any critical erudition or thought with the fear of one single word, *commie*, 'which was like Jew or n-----' due to the machinations of monomaniacs like 'Senator McCarthy'.[73] The United States and the Soviet Union appeared to Burgess as slightly distorted reflections of one another – 'America's different, of course, but America's really only a kind of Russia' – so much so that the Russian Alex character rhetorically asks a question Burgess pondered throughout his own life: what was the difference between the United States and the Soviet Union, two countries with diametrically opposed goals but who both utilized a state apparatus whose strength was maintained through fear, power, and irrationalism?[74] Russian Alex inquires, '"Russia or American," said Alexei Prutkov, "what's the difference? It's all the State. There's only one State"', and Paul himself soliloquizes that 'As for America, that's just the same as Russia. You're no different. America and Russia would make a very nice marriage.'[75] Writing in *Anthony Burgess: Revisited* (1991), John Stinson sums up the *Honey for the Bears* philosophy of the United States, stating that if 'Russia is strongly Manichaean, then so too is its fairly exact counterpart, America, with its sharp us/them attitude of the cold war era; America is afraid to reach out to make vital sustaining human contact with other peoples', an accurate assessment of how Burgess saw these two countries as two sides of the same coin, and a conceptual framework that would be fully fleshed out when Burgess explored myth, Americanism, incest, and miscegenation as a product of such insular and inbred patterns of cultural existence in *M/F* (1971).[76]

Beyond these types of mythic, dichotomous, and Manichaean issues, though, Burgess showed disinterest in the many other problems that plagued the United States throughout the 1960s, 1970s, and 1980s. If current events – such as the Civil Rights Movement, the Nuclear Non-Proliferation Treaty, or the bombing of the United States Embassy in Beirut, to name a few – did not coincide with Burgess's ongoing philosophical and literary interests, he rarely made an effort to engage honestly with those societal and political issues, the exception being when he forced contemporary issues into the confines of his own worldview, to be worked into his personal philosophical *grand récit*.

Despite all of the problems he was aware of, and despite Burgess's criticisms, once he arrived in the United States and began incorporating American themes into his literature, lectures, interviews, and journalism, opinions that largely voiced his disapproval 'of the Americanization of British culture as well as the socialized, secular, communization of much of the rest of the world', he still saw the United States as a place that took art seriously and a place that took the novel 'seriously because criticism is taken seriously'.[77] And once Burgess realized that he was to be taken seriously too, both monetarily and intellectually, as a composer and writer, the loathsome feelings he held during the Lynne-period of his life were assuaged and metamorphosed under pragmatic and endearing terms.[78] This is without even mentioning that 'the temptations of television appearances, which were easier than writing, were among the factors that were to drive me from Britain'.[79] What's clear, because it's repeated many times, often with a languid tone, was that 'it was gratifying [for Burgess] to be understood in America [and] humiliating to be misread in [his] own country. American critics forced [him] to take [his] own work seriously and to ponder whether the implied moral of the novel was sound'.[80] The subject of a dissertation by Rob Spence, *The Reputation of Anthony Burgess* (2002), found sustained support behind this claim by Burgess, with Spence noting that it was American scholars who 'quickly elevated Burgess's work to the status of literature worthy of study in higher education, and therefore appropriate as the subject of articles in learned journals', while in Britain, 'Burgess's work was not, and has still not been, admitted to the canon of modern literature, unlike the work of some of Burgess's contemporaries and near-contemporaries'.[81]

Regardless of whatever protestations Burgess had towards the United States, he could not deny the fact that it was in the United States that he would find a career as an intellectual and an author because beginning in the mid 1960s, Burgess's books were being taught by American professors and at both the undergraduate and graduate level as examples of valuable British contemporary art. It could perhaps be argued, then, that the author remembered as Anthony Burgess and who is revered today was *made* by the United States in the sense that without the mechanisms of media saturation and chaotic inspiration, Burgess's career and writings could have possibly slipped into obscurity apart from Americans' willingness to partake in and fund his life and work. And as his writing was taught and advertised in American universities, this meant essentially that Burgess's work had been accepted into the literary echelon of some American scholars, worthy of that sanctified space in the lecture hall, which provided Burgess with lucrative career possibilities – a benefit which was not given to him in the country of his birth, at least at the level he desired.[82] The reason for Burgess's popularity in the United States was broached by Paul Boytinck in his 1985 bibliography of Burgess's work, as he guessed that it, however ironically considering Burgess's sometimes incredibly merciless attacks on American culture and Americans, 'may well be that Americans are more receptive to his work than the English' because the 'typical Burgess openness endears itself to them; the standard English coolness would estrange and alienate them, and lead them to consult their God'.[83] Generally, in the 1950s, 1960s, and early 1970s in the United States, reviews and criticism of Burgess's work were frequently positive, although this would somewhat dissipate as time went on, but the reviews were not always, as was a common grievance to Burgess, best understood or appreciated at the level he desired. Several times, though, and this was what Burgess desired more than anything, his works were in fact understood *too* well, which was a realization that often terrified Burgess but also garnered his respect – the most popular instance to be discussed elsewhere is Thomas Stumpf's analysis of *A Vision of Battlements* at the University of North Carolina at Chapel Hill, who noticed that R. Ennis spelled backwards was, unbeknownst to Burgess, *sinner*:

> This fellow who was lecturing was a brilliant young man and had analyzed my work quite thoroughly. He emphasized that my characters always vomit, and that I always send them to the toilet. But he said something that shocked me then, and still does. He wrote the name of one of my first characters on the board – R. Ennis. 'You will notice,' he said, 'that that spells sinner backwards.' One cannot get away from oneself.[84]

Although reviewers of Burgess's books in England may have been a little more favourable to his work, what is certain is that the British academy rejected Burgess, a sore point for the author for nearly his entire life. Not only did his inability to be accepted into the literary elite circles of England push him away from the country of his birth, though; his push towards the United States also had little to do with taxes but much to do with money and culture. The unrest that was going on in the United States provided Burgess with ample writing material, a key interest in his desire to visit, saying on *The Dick Cavett Show* in March 1971 that there 'is plenty going on and there's plenty to write about. A bit too much if anything. ... I'm sorry about that'.[85]

To investigate Burgess's relationship with the United States, one must first begin before Burgess ever set foot in the country because his first experiences with the United States were with its exports, not its people, schools, or cities. Film, music, and literature were the first contacts Burgess had with American artistic products, with film being, he held, 'what America is truly about'.[86] While in the United States, Burgess was an avid viewer of older films on television, noting on multiple occasions that 'American television is essentially a movie museum', where he could watch 'at unearthly times'

Marx Brothers films such as *The Cocoanuts* (1929) and *Monkey Business* (1931), which he then attributed to the reason Americans did 'not get much reading done'.[87] These films are examples of some of the first media from the United States that he encountered as a youth, and was drawn to, even remarking that he loved the Marx Brothers since they were, to him, the 'most flamboyant expression of dissidence that the West has ever known'.[88] During the same formative years, Burgess also notes in *Little Wilson and Big God* (1986) that he viewed silent American films such as *The Sheik* (1921), *The Shriek of Araby* (1923), and *The Four Horsemen of the Apocalypse* (1921), while Madge, his stepsister, worked for the American film corporation, Famous Lasky.[89] Outside of films in these early years, it was the illustrations for the American author F. Scott Fitzgerald's short stories in the *Saturday Evening Post* that drew young John Wilson's attention.[90]

Bridging the gap

Reflecting on Burgess's time at the University of North Carolina at Chapel Hill in 1969, Ben Forkner, who met Burgess then and stayed in contact with him until his death in 1993, reflected that by the late 1960s Burgess had expressed that he couldn't 'read English writers anymore – that he can only read American writers'.[91] When visiting the Southern campus, Forkner recalls that Burgess 'did read widely in American literature but there were some gaps – the South, but he knew Thomas Wolfe when he came to Chapel Hill and he quotes Thomas a couple of times, but he didn't know much about Flannery O'Connor or Faulkner or Eudora Welty – he knew their names, but I don't think he read deeply in that sort of literature', which was not the case with 'someone like Ford Madox Ford, who Burgess idolized' and who, Forkner believes, was an author that 'sort of stirred Burgess's interest in American literature' because Ford had been 'so open to American literature, especially to Southern writers, and wrote so well about it that Burgess admired Ford above almost any other writer in the twentieth century, almost more so than Joyce, not more so, but alongside Joyce'.[92] Forkner isn't incorrect in this assessment since Burgess claimed in *You've Had Your Time* that Ford 'had prophesied that America's great literature would be a Southern product; and so it was, except for the North-Eastern Jews', also calling Ford, on multiple occasions, conceivably 'the greatest British novelist of the twentieth century'.[93] Still, though, this is not nearly the only early connection or perhaps the most significant that started to twine Burgess to the United States and the United States to Burgess.

During an interview in 1981, Burgess admitted that it was, as it had been since the 1960s, 'the contemporary American novelists that do interest me, not the British. And I feel very guilty about this. I cannot read people like Margaret Drabble and Iris Murdoch or any others. But I always read the Americans. I mean, you know, if it's new Philip Roth or William Styron I rush to get it. These I regard as great masters; Mailer in the same way'.[94] It is from the mid 1960s until the end of his life that Burgess's reading habits consisted largely of American authors who experimented with the ontology of the novelistic form, purpose, and product. His reading, as is evidenced by his remaining library and plethora of book reviews, was extremely broad. This wide scope of reading included a significant amount of work within the American literary sphere, as is evidenced both in non-fiction books like *Flame into Being* (1985) that reveal, as a reviewer notes on the back of the book, that writing of this nature often 'tells us as much about Burgess as about Lawrence', and with reviews of American academic books, novels, poetry, and anything else he was sent by publishers.[95] As for his own literary productions, he admits in the preface to his collection of journalism in *But Do Blondes Prefer Gentlemen? Homage to Qwert Yuiop* (1986) that 'I do not feel that American readers are likely to dismiss me as an unintelligible foreigner' because he was so well versed in the American literary tradition.[96] Aligning his work and his persona with this tradition in the early 1970s as the cosmopolitan European visitor to the United States, he did not do so naïvely or without years of consideration. This kind of respect for and interest in American literature began sometime in the 1950s when he was teaching literature in various capacities, as is noted in his 1963 publication, *The Novel To-Day*, where he addresses the failures of British literature of the time and argues that American literature had to break with the ubiquitous 'English literature' so as to be more specific, since regional literatures were gaining in popularity in the early 1960s: 'I say "novelists of the United Kingdom" advisedly. As we now accept that American Literature constitutes a separate and massive branch of Literature in English, so we are beginning to recognize the existence of several kinds of British Literature.'[97]

American literature had obviously already taken strides towards distinguishing itself long before the 1950s and 1960s, although the exact date is arguable, but the American Renaissance in the 1850s, which saw Nathaniel Hawthorne's 1850 publication of *The Scarlet Letter*, Herman Melville's 1851 publication of *Moby-Dick*, and Walt Whitman's 1855 publication of *Leaves of Grass*, tends to be an accepted marker of the unique emergence of a fervently American literary voice.[98] This is not to say that all that came before Whitman was not *American*, but that American literature up until roughly this point had struggled to produce non-European derivative literature. Burgess recognized this fact by claiming that it was James Fenimore Cooper, an author who came just before the American Renaissance, who ultimately 'spewed all the Englishry out of American imaginative writing in one quiet but devastating act. After it, real American fiction-writing could begin'.[99] At another time Burgess had altered his opinion and had yet still argued against the Whitman marker by claiming that this distinctive shift from British-influenced American literature came earlier then *Leaves of Grass* – establishing 'the thirty-six-year-old poet [Whitman] as that singer of democracy which expansive America needed' – through the works of Nathaniel Hawthorne, a stance likely influenced by Burgess's reverence for D. H. Lawrence, who did the same, in Burgess's own words, by pushing 'Walt out of the way' in order to tell 'America what the great grey poet really meant'.[100] Outside of discussing Lawrence, Burgess argued in his mid 1960s article on post-war American literature that 'We in England have wanted too long to regard the American Novel as a regional aspect of the English (national, not linguistic) Novel ... but the American Novel has (if we will be honest with ourselves) always been a distinct genre from Hawthorne onward.'[101] Part of Burgess's interest in the American process of literary production did not simply have to do with aesthetics but also with the societal acceptance of literature and the writers who produced it. By the mid 1960s, Burgess claimed that it was common for writers of the day to think of 'the future of the Novel in English as belonging wholly to America, with our Waughs and Greenes and Powells as provincial satellites, their art charming but calligraphic', which was partially due to the fact that 'with the exception of Kingsley Amis, no reputable novelist seems really to like it [in England]'.[102] Well recorded, commented on, and catalogued are Burgess's inspirations from Evelyn Waugh, his jealousy of Anthony Powell, and his love–hate relationship with Graham Greene, but one reason Burgess may have set Kingsley Amis outside of this generalization is that he saw in Amis's work a particularly American tone that, although desirous to stay in England, allowed Amis to draw 'his metaphors from the best sort of SF [science fiction] and jazz (Thelonius Monk) as well as linguistics (he knows all about phonemes) and depth psychology', which may have appeared to Burgess more experimental, less provincial, and therefore more appealing.[103] In fact, this was the characteristic that Burgess believed set American literature apart from the former imperial power, because American literary works opened outward to the rest of the world as expansive products that did not collapse inward, as he believed the British writers did parochially. Summarizing this feature in American literature in his 1979 non-fiction book *They Wrote in English: A Survey of British and American Literature*, Burgess stated that from 'about 1850 on', there existed a 'difference of tone' which attested to the large difference between American literary inventiveness and that of England.[104] The difference, he goes on to explain, did not rest simply in the variance of American speech, but more importantly in the 'matter of a continental approach to life as opposed to an insular one. Read one sentence of Henry James and you know you are back in the Old'.[105]

Other interesting stances that Burgess takes in *They Wrote in English*, though some may appear contradictory, are the superlative opinions he expresses about American authors even into the late 1980s, such as declaring that Benjamin Franklin was the 'author of the first masterpiece of United States literature – his *Autobiography*, published in 1817' due to a style that was 'plain and vigorous, eschew[ing] all shows of Augustan erudition, and possess[ing] a flavour that can only be termed American', positioning Edgar Allan Poe as the writer who produced America's 'first international literature', and calling Herman Melville 'perhaps the greatest of all American novelists'.[106] Peculiarly, Burgess does not accord similar admiration to African American writers, nor does he include many Black writers in the shaping of an American literary identity – a point to be discussed further on.[107] Other declamations regarding forming a national identity are held in more negative terms, like claiming that Henry David Thoreau's *Walden, or Life in the Woods* acts as 'a kind of small bible of anarchic individualism' that he believed was ubiquitous throughout American history; additionally, he remarks that Hawthorne's *The Scarlet Letter* represents a 'remarkable evocation of the repressive time when all sins were mortal, and adultery – now a tolerated American pastime' in what he proclaimed in the 1970s was the 'age of permissiveness'; most singularly backhanded, Burgess praises Mark Twain for his humour, satirical savagery, and mythopoeic ability in his writing that helped shape 'America's mythological view of itself' with Huck and Tom from *The Adventures of Huckleberry Finn* that simultaneously changed the way Americans were to write from that point on, since it 'became very hard to write in the old puddingy, earnest, sesquipedalian manner once Mark Twain had shown the possibilities of American English'.[108] Outside of Burgess's explicit comments about American literature, there exist fragments of circulated comments littered throughout his earlier works that provide more insight into how Burgess thought not only about American authors but also about Americans and American culture and society. At times, these specks of reference provide glimmers of Burgess's own perceptions and the perceptions of his characters, but elsewhere they provide significant clues about the evolution of Burgess's own views of the United States and his preoccupation with matters of American culture.

Notes

1 From *One Man's Chorus: The Uncollected Writings of Anthony Burgess*, ed. by Ben Forkner (New York: Carroll & Graf, 1998), p. 118.

2 Henry Miller, *Tropic of Cancer* (New York: Grove Press, 1934; 1961), p. 208.
3 Anthony Burgess, 'London Letter', *The Hudson Review*, 20.1 (Spring 1967); Anthony Lewis and Anthony Burgess, '"I Love England, But I Will No Longer Live There"', *New York Times*, 3 November 1968, pp. 285–310; Anthony Burgess, 'Letter from Europe', *American Scholar*, 32.1 (Winter 1972–73), 136.
4 Anthony Burgess, *Honey for the Bears* (New York: Norton, 1963), p. 256.
5 Rexford Brown, *Conflict and Confluence: The Art of Anthony Burgess* (published doctoral thesis, Graduate College of the University of Iowa, August 1971), p. 123; Graham Greene, *The Quiet American* (London: Penguin Books, 1955; 2004).
6 Andrew Biswell, *The Real Life of Anthony Burgess* (London: Picador, 2005), p. 107; Geoffrey Aggeler, *Anthony Burgess: The Artist as Novelist* (Tuscaloosa, AL: University of Alabama Press, 1979), p. 8.
7 Anthony Burgess, *Little Wilson and Big God: Being the First Part of the Autobiography* (New York: Weidenfeld & Nicolson, 1986), p. 302.
8 Aggeler, *Anthony Burgess*, p. 125.
9 Mike Bever, 'Burgess Displays the Artist and the Man', *Oshkosh Advance-Titan*, 20 March 1975, p. 18.
10 Anthony Burgess, 'Anthony Burgess Lecture', Sarah Lawrence College (1971), p. 26.
11 Anthony Burgess, 'Letter to Jacques S. Gansler', 29 November 1971, International Anthony Burgess Foundation Archives.
12 Anthony Burgess, 'Hot Pot and Tay', 1972, International Anthony Burgess Foundation Archive; Burgess, *Little Wilson and Big God*, p. 348.
13 Anthony Burgess, *A Vision of Battlements*, ed. by Andrew Biswell (Manchester: Manchester University Press, 1965; 2017); Paul Phillips, *A Clockwork Counterpoint: The Music and Literature of Anthony Burgess* (Manchester: Manchester University Press, 2010), p. 43. This was not the first to be published: 'The earliest surviving fragments of the novel which became *A Vision of Battlements* are to be found in Anthony Burgess's notebook from 1940' (Andrew Biswell, 'Introduction to *A Vision of Battlements*', p. 1).
14 Biswell, *The Real Life of Anthony Burgess*, p. 104; Burgess, *A Vision of Battlements*, p. 155.
15 Anthony Burgess, 'My Life and Times by Henry Miller', *New York Times*, 2 January 1972; Allan Bloom, *The Closing of the American Mind* (New York: Simon and Schuster, 1987), p. 147; Burgess, *A Vision of Battlements*, pp. 154, 156.
16 Burgess, *Little Wilson and Big God*, p. 302.
17 Burgess, *Little Wilson and Big God*, p. 302.
18 Phillips, *A Clockwork Counterpoint*, p. 42; Biswell, *The Real Life of Anthony Burgess*, p. 104.
19 Burgess, *A Vision of Battlements*, p. 155.
20 Jim Clarke, *The Aesthetics of Anthony Burgess: Fire of Words* (Cham: Palgrave Macmillan, 2017), p. 259; Mikhail Bakhtin, 'Discourse in the Novel', *The Dialogic Imagination: Four Essays*, ed. by Michael Holquist, trans. by Caryl

Emerson and Michael Holquist (Austin, TX: University of Texas Press, 1981), p. 361.

21 Paul Boytinck, *Anthony Burgess: An Annotated Bibliography and Reference Guide* (New York: Garland Publishing, 1985), p. xxi.

22 Anthony Burgess, *The Malayan Trilogy* (London: Vintage, 2000).

23 Burgess, *The Malayan Trilogy*, p. 25.

24 Burgess, *The Malayan Trilogy*, pp. 350, 412.

25 Burgess, *The Malayan Trilogy*, p. 61; Anthony Burgess, 'A Conversation with Anthony Burgess', *CBS News*, December 1980.

26 Anthony Burgess, ed. by George Malko, 'Penthouse Interview: Anthony Burgess', *Penthouse*, June 1972; Burgess, *The Malayan Trilogy*, p. 61.

27 Zawiah Yahya, *Resisting Colonialist Discourse* (Kebangsaan: Penerbit Universiti Kebangsaan, 1994; 2003), p. 65.

28 Burgess, *The Malayan Trilogy*, p. 29.

29 Burgess, *The Malayan Trilogy*, p. 30.

30 Burgess, *The Malayan Trilogy*, p. 408.

31 Burgess, *The Malayan Trilogy*, p. 440.

32 Phillips, *A Clockwork Counterpoint*; Anthony Burgess, 'Where Is English?', *New Society*, 21 July 1966, p. 100; Anthony Burgess, 'The Big Daddy of the Beats', *The Ink Trade: Selected Journalism 1961–1993*, ed. by Will Carr (Manchester: Carcanet Press, 2018), pp. 25–26.

33 Burgess, 'Where Is English?', p. 100; Burgess, *Honey for the Bears*, p. 149.

34 Anthony Burgess, 'Ah, Liberty', International Anthony Burgess Foundation Archive, unpublished, 1986, p. 4.

35 Burgess, *The Malayan Trilogy*, p. 452.

36 Rob Spence, 'Hogg, Hoggart and the Uses of Illiteracy: Anthony Burgess and Pop Music', *Anthony Burgess: Music in Literature and Literature in Music*, ed. by Marc Jeannin (Cambridge: Cambridge Scholars Press, 2009), p. 38; Kingsley Amis, *Girl, 20* (New York: Summit Books, 1971), p. 43.

37 Burgess, *The Malayan Trilogy*, p. 426.

38 Burgess, *The Malayan Trilogy*, p. 452.

39 Anthony Burgess, 'The Meaning of A Clockwork Orange' [Audio], Pennsylvania State University, 25 March 1975).

40 Brigid Brophy, 'American Policies in Vietnam', *The Times*, 2 February 1967.

41 Burgess, 'Introduction', *Malayan Trilogy*, p. x.

42 Burgess, 'Introduction', *Malayan Trilogy*, p. x.

43 Quoted in Boytinck, *Anthony Burgess*, pp. 77, 79.

44 Burgess, *The Malayan Trilogy*, p. 509.

45 Burgess, *The Malayan Trilogy*, p. 509.

46 Burgess, *The Malayan Trilogy*, p. 509.

47 Greene, *The Quiet American*; Burgess, *The Malayan Trilogy*, p. 509.

48 Anthony Burgess, *The Doctor Is Sick* (New York: W.W. Norton, 1960; 1997); Burgess, *The Malayan Trilogy*, p. 506–507.

49 Burgess, *The Malayan Trilogy*, p. 508.

50 Greene, *The Quiet American*, p. 88.

51 Burgess, *The Malayan Trilogy*, p. 510.
52 Burgess, *The Malayan Trilogy*, p. 510.
53 Burgess, *The Malayan Trilogy*, p. 511.
54 Homi Bhabha, *The Location of Culture* (London: Routledge, 1994); Burgess, *The Malayan Trilogy*, p. 572.
55 Burgess, *The Malayan Trilogy*, p. 404.
56 Bhabha, *The Location of Culture*, p. 86.
57 Anthony Burgess, *The Right to an Answer* (London: Hutchinson, 1960; 1980), p. 182.
58 Burgess, *The Right to an Answer*, p. 182.
59 Burgess, *The Right to an Answer*, p. 181.
60 Burgess, *The Right to an Answer*, p. 181.
61 Burgess, *The Right to an Answer*, p. 181.
62 Anthony Burgess, *1985* (London: Beautiful Books, 1978; 2010), p. 158.
63 Burgess, *The Right to an Answer*, p. 181.
64 Burgess, *The Right to an Answer*, p. 182.
65 Anthony Burgess, *One Hand Clapping* (New York: Carroll & Graf, 1961; 1999), pp. 146–150, 140.
66 Burgess, *One Hand Clapping*, p. 81.
67 Aggeler, *Anthony Burgess*, p. 148.
68 Burgess, *A Vision of Battlements*, p. 155; Burgess, *One Hand Clapping*, p. 100.
69 Burgess, *One Hand Clapping*, p. 140.
70 Lewis and Burgess, '"I Love England, But I Will No Longer Live There"'; Burgess, 'Letter from Europe', pp. 684–686; 'Interview with Anthony Burgess', *The Dick Cavett Show*, ABC Television Network: Daphne Productions and Rollins & Joffe Productions, 25 March 1971; Burgess, 'Ah, Liberty', p. 4.
71 Hugh Brogan, *The Penguin History of the USA* (London: Penguin Group, 1999), p. 639.
72 Burgess, *Honey for the Bears*, p. 12.
73 Burgess, *Honey for the Bears*, p. 92.
74 Burgess, *Honey for the Bears*, p. 172.
75 Burgess, *Honey for the Bears*, p. 93.
76 John J. Stinson, *Anthony Burgess: Revisited* (Boston, MA: Twayne, 1991), p. 39.
77 Samuel Coale, *Anthony Burgess* (New York: Ungar, 1981), p. 14; Anthony Burgess, 'The Postwar American Novel: A View from the Periphery', *Urgent Copy: Literary Studies* (New York: W.W. Norton, 1968), p. 131.
78 Anthony Burgess, *You've Had Your Time: Being the Second Part of the Confessions of Anthony Burgess* (London: Penguin Books, 1990), p. 326.
79 Burgess, *You've Had Your Time*, p. 106.
80 Burgess, *You've Had Your Time*, p. 61.
81 Robert Spence, 'The Reputation of Anthony Burgess' (Manchester: University of Manchester dissertation, unpublished, 2002), p. 19.
82 A course on contemporary fiction being taught at the University of North Carolina at Chapel Hill by Dr Howard Harper when Burgess was on campus listed his course readings as such: 'Dr. Howard Harper's English 94

undergraduate class on contemporary fiction taught Burgess's novels on these days: 12/2 – *A Vision of Battlements*, 12/9 – *The Right to an Answer*, 12/11 – *Tremor of Intent*; in English 293, a graduate course on 20th century fiction, he taught Burgess's books on these days: 12/3 – *Re Joyce*, 12/8 – *A Clockwork Orange*, 12/10 – *Honey for the Bears*, 12/15 – *Nothing Like the Sun*. "I'm going to take you at your word and invite you to come to my classes as often as you would like, and to do whatever you want to" ' (Howard Harper, 'Letter to Anthony Burgess', n.d., University of North Carolina at Chapel Hill: Harry Ransom Center).

83 Boytinck, *Anthony Burgess*, p. vi.

84 Starla Smith, 'Novelist Anthony Burgess – A Three-Time Failure?', *Iowa City Press-Citizen*, 20 October 1975, correspondence: University of Texas at Austin: Harry Ransom Center, Anthony Burgess Papers, Box 82; Anthony Burgess, 'First Novel', *One Man's Chorus: The Uncollected Writings of Anthony Burgess*, ed. by Ben Forkner (New York: Carroll & Graf, 1998), pp. 271–272.

85 'Interview with Anthony Burgess', 25 March 1971.

86 Anthony Burgess, 'Tercenart', n.d., International Anthony Burgess Foundation Archive, p. 2.

87 Anthony Burgess, 'One of the Minor Joys …', 1972, International Anthony Burgess Foundation Archive, pp. 116–117.

88 'Object of the Week: The Marx Brothers', The International Anthony Burgess Foundation, 19 June 2017, www.anthonyburgess.org/object-of-the-week/object-week-marx-brothers

89 Burgess, *Little Wilson and Big God*, pp. 31, 53.

90 Burgess, *Little Wilson and Big God*, p. 53.

91 Benjamin Forkner, phone interview with Christopher Thurley, 28 July 2016.

92 Benjamin Forkner, phone interview with Christopher Thurley, 28 July 2016.

93 Burgess, *You've Had Your Time*, p. 130; Anthony Earnshaw and Dr Marco Adria, 'Interview with Anthony Burgess', *Aurora*, 7 June 1988, Winter 1988.

94 Dana Gioia, 'Talking with Anthony Burgess', *Inquiry*, 2 February 1981, p. 24.

95 Anthony Burgess, *Flame into Being* (London: Abacus, 1985); 'I remember him as a kind of a dormant literary volcano – projecting a distinct air of danger, wreathed in cigar smoke, liable at any minute to erupt with a flow of molten judgments. For 30 years, from 1962, he wrote more than 400 reviews for the Observer. Among his "discoveries" were Sylvia Plath and the late Umberto Eco. Burgess on a Sunday would range from airport fiction (one of his great loves), to a new biography of Wagner, to a book on linguistics (another passion). He was the ideal weekend reviewer: generous, entertaining, witty, informative and wise. As a critic, he was what Thomas Carlyle called a "professor of things in general". In 1979, he was duly named critic of the year at the National Press Awards. In a moment worthy of *A Clockwork Orange*, his trophy was presented by Margaret Thatcher' (Robert McCrum, 'The "Lost" Novels That Anthony Burgess Hoped Would Make Him Rich', *The Guardian*, 18 March 2017, para. 3–4).

96 Anthony Burgess, 'Preface', *But Do Blondes Prefer Gentlemen? Homage to Qwert Yuiop and Other Writings* (New York: McGraw-Hill Book Company, 1986), p. xiv.
97 Anthony Burgess, *The Novel To-Day* (London: Longmans, Green & Co., 1963), p. 9.
98 Susan Belasco and Linck Johnson, *The Bedford Anthology of American Literature: Second Edition – Volume One: Beginnings to 1865* (Boston, MA: Bedford/St. Martin's, 2014), pp. 709–710.
99 Burgess also believed that Cooper was the 'first true American novelist with "The Spy"' ('Said Mr Cooper', para. 7), as he claims in 1972: Anthony Burgess, 'Said Mr Cooper to His Wife: "You Know, I Could Write Something Better Than That"', *The New York Times*, 7 May 1972, para. 3.
100 Anthony Burgess, *They Wrote in English* (proof copy, International Anthony Burgess Foundation Archive, 1989), p. 150; Burgess, *Flame into Being*, p. 86.
101 Burgess, 'The Postwar American Novel', p. 126.
102 Burgess, 'The Postwar American Novel', p. 126; Burgess, *The Novel To-Day*, p. 10.
103 Burgess, *The Novel To-Day*, p. 36.
104 Burgess, *They Wrote in English*, p. 154.
105 Burgess, *They Wrote in English*, p. 154.
106 Burgess, *They Wrote in English*, pp. 208, 147, 152.
107 Burgess, *They Wrote in English*, p. 33.
108 Burgess, *They Wrote in English*, pp. 149, 151, 153–154.

2

Burgess on the United States

America is full of foreigners, Whatever frightens America frightens the world.[1]

Introduction

What follows is a summary and analysis of Burgess's views on American youth movements, Burgess's status as an outsider in the United States, and the United States's cultural and social myths which allured and troubled Burgess. Assessing these three Burgess motifs is important due to the predominance of these themes in Burgess's literary work. Important to note is that this chapter argues that Burgess's public commentary on American culture and politics was substantial, stretched out over two decades, and was valued by American publishers and media, meaning that he had become far more than just an impartial visitor or infrequent commentator, but rather a persistent voice in American cultural and political discourse during the 1960s and 1970s. Additionally, this argument helps substantiate and necessitate the use of the Bakhtinian notions of heteroglossia, double-voiced discourse, dialogism, and the chronotope in order to exhibit the 'public nature of the human figure' that is Burgess and his canon.[2] Doing so contextualizes this monograph's approach and provides an essential and adequate exploration into Burgess's life, fiction, and author-status as it relates to the influence of the United States on his writing, career, and life.

Much of Burgess's commentary on the United States was in response to the varying aspects of the zeitgeist of the 1960s, 1970s, and 1980s, as evidenced in a wide array of books, television shows, movies, and art, so the focus will be placed on historical and ethnographic reporting with an emphasis on contemporary historical and literary commentary in order to most accurately display the kind of marketplace of ideas that Burgess himself was orbiting in. What comes out of this kind of approach, indeed what comes out of this chapter, is a more layered understanding of the relationship Burgess had with the United States, and in what types of topics he engaged with as matters of discussion, debate, concern, and interest.

Youthful American novelizing

By the mid 1960s, Burgess's intrigue with the United States was soon to be granted full experimental rights, as he and Liana Burgess, his second wife whom he married in 1968 after the death of Lynne, waded through the increasing requests for his presence – now, finally, being able to respond to requests he had received before Lynne died. The options for travel were at last open and the United States lived up to its motto of being the land of opportunity, especially, as Burgess observed, for writers, since he believed that the United States had the best writers of the time period – the 'best of the best is Nabokov' followed by 'Thomas Pynchon, who is perhaps America's best living novelist'.[3] On many occasions Burgess expressed his admiration for American literary achievements, holding the country's writers in higher regard than their British counterparts.[4] Into the 1980s, Burgess's opinion of American authors and the American literary scene waned somewhat, or perhaps he just grew exasperated with the United States's ability to churn out, in his opinion, the best writers and the best writing of the era in a place so complex and, at times, overwhelming and contradictory:

> I do feel, increasingly – and France must feel this also – that America is the country where the novel is finding its most typical twentieth-century expression, rightly or wrongly. I mean, the novel is a European creation, but I think America has taken it over, partly because the financial circumstances of the American novelist are so much more favorable than they are in Europe.[5]

Contradicting earlier comments, or having changed his mind, Burgess then says that he does not 'think that American novelists are any better than French writers or British writers, but they do have opportunities which we lack. … I don't like this. I'm patriotic enough to want it to have been made in Europe. … It is not a question of American energy; it is a question of American opportunity', going on to warn Americans that this supposed compliment was rather an advisory, stating that 'I don't think this is very good for Americans. We hear too many stories of American authors achieving great success and then committing suicide or dying of drink and despair. There is something perhaps wrong with this cult of fame and wealth in America'.[6] In this respect, that of fame, the United States would go on to become too exhausting for Burgess, and this was one reason he began to fall back to his earlier disdain for the country the longer he spent there, prompting reviews of his work such as this, addressing his 1974 novella

The Clockwork Testament, or Enderby's End: 'In what looks like his own testamentary farewell to New York and the American scene, Burgess is not only angry – his satirist prerogative – but apparently tired. His story seemed scratched together, his characters are clay pigeons to be shot at rather than people.'[7]

In Burgess's student guide to contemporary fiction, *The Novel Now*, published in January 1967, providing a slightly evolved (from the decade before) perception of the United States by expanding upon his previous acknowledgement that the country existed in a dualistic realm in the non-American mind, he makes the more nuanced claim that

> America is two things – a potential and an actuality, and the actuality can never live up to the potential. The vast resources of the country, its scenic beauty, the racial wealth of its population promises so much and, indeed, fulfils something of the promise, but never enough. A small country like England can be forgiven smallness of soul, but not a big country like America. That is why the persistent American theme is one of protest.[8]

Regardless of when Burgess first visited the United States, it is clear that he was observing the country via news, television, and movies, but to what exact extent remains a mystery. The various tableaus of the United States from outside the country likely included the assassination of President John F. Kennedy, the Watts Riots that broke out in Los Angeles, California, the Civil Rights Movement clashes, and student protests for free speech and against the Vietnam War, as well as the passing of Medicaid, the Voting Rights Act, and the Higher Education Act. So much was going on in the United States, especially compared to the far less tumultuous 1960s of England – although legalizing homosexuality and abortion, winning the World Cup, abolishing the death penalty, and the rise of The Beatles were no small achievements, they pale in comparison to the chaos erupting across the pond.

As Burgess's time spent in the United States increased throughout the 1970s and 1980s, with his trips becoming more frequent, consistent, and elongated, his views on matters of American novelizing evolved slightly; he remarked in 1972 that his personal tastes in novels began to grow discordant to the works being produced in the United States: 'I don't like earnestness in fiction, and there's no earnestness in Greene. There's a lot of earnestness in the American novel, however.'[9] Additionally, Burgess grew more and more dissatisfied with what he viewed as a general philistinism on the part of the American public, which he decried as being corruptive and obsessed with the myth of superiority and individualism; he remarked on this in a 1986 talk with an American journalist, saying the United States was an individualistic and materialistic country that too often commoditized sex.[10] It's clear that the sanguine view that Burgess temporarily had for the American literary experience in the 1960s and early 1970s, which included its treatment of writers, its pursuit of literary experimentation, and a vast and diverse culture that helped produce the previous two entities, had rotted away in his mind as he all too often apparently saw Americans commoditizing literature instead of understanding it and valuing it, to the point that he retorted on *The Dick Cavett Show* that 'Americans buy big books as a kind of furniture'.[11] The ideal society, to Burgess, was not to be found in the United States and in general always existed in some fictive imagined past which he sought to find anywhere he could throughout his life, only to be soured by the all-too-real modern world that he felt was trampling on the sanctities of yesteryear.

Throughout the 1960s and 1970s in the United States, Anthony Burgess watched as the college-age generation was heatedly involved in debates and protests that advertised their distrust towards the acting United States government and any hierarchical structure that possessed any modicum of societal power, including the universities they attended – a good sense of the atmosphere of the United States he witnessed is explored in Norman Mailer's new journalism take on anti-war protests in *Armies of the Night* (1968), and, more scholarly, as is recounted and dissected in critical history books such as *An American Ordeal: The Antiwar Movement of the Vietnam Era* (1990), *The War Within* (1994), and *Telltale Hearts: The Origins and Impact of the Vietnam Antiwar Movement* (1995), which closely assess the public opinions of Americans alongside Vietnam policy and the anti-war movement in order to reach the conclusions that the anti-war protest movements of the 1960s and 1970s, although amplifying concerns about the war, actually pushed American public opinion away from Vietnam withdrawal and an end to the war.[12] According to Burgess, and confirmed through historical accounts of the time period, there were professors who aligned themselves with the students who were engaged in youthful revolts against American society, which Burgess believed was a mistake because the young, despite whether they were right or wrong about the issues they were protesting, were essentially far too emotional and sensational to be given too much attention.[13] In his *A People's History of the United States of America* (1980), Howard Zinn articulated that these college students were 'heavily involved in the early protests against' the Vietnam War, amounting to '232 of the nation's two thousand institutions of higher education' having '215,000 students [who] participated in campus protests ... 3,652 had been arrested ... 956 had been suspended or expelled'.[14] Notoriously, at the climax of the country-wide protests, Zinn also reports that President Richard Nixon ordered the invasion of Cambodia on 30 April 1970, which resulted in students at Kent State University in Ohio gathering on 4 May

1970 'to demonstrate against the war', when 'National Guardsmen fired into the crowd', killing four students.[15] Uncharacteristically unconcerned with state-led murder in a democratic county, the research done for this monograph did not turn up a single significant mention of the Kent State Massacre by Burgess – aside from stating that the police on the University of North Carolina at Chapel Hill campus 'were there to patrol' and 'pre-empt student riots of the Kent State University kind'.[16] One of eight such articles Burgess wrote for *The American Scholar*, though having possibly written his summer 1970 'Letter from Europe' article before the event, it is peculiar that no mention of the Kent State incident appears here or in any later writings, with Burgess instead frequently directing his American-centric journalistic commentaries and perturbation during this period at student protests and counter-culture social turmoil, including hippies, a group he had called a 'bad influence' on college campuses.[17] This kind of description of American students was commonplace for Burgess, going so far as to recount in his autumn 1969 'Letter from Europe' that during his spring 1969 tour through the United States that took him 'to universities and colleges in the state of Washington, at Vancouver, in California, Colorado and New England ... as far north as Simon Fraser University, and as far south as Los Angeles', he witnessed student conformity in protest with 'little variation in the language and dress of rebellion' – a characteristic likely furthered and assisted by films and documentaries such as *The Strawberry Statement* (1970) and *Street Scenes* (1970).[18] Having grown increasingly irritated with counter-culture movements, and having been unwillingly absorbed into the dialogue of counter cultures after the release of Stanley Kubrick's *A Clockwork Orange* in December 1971, Burgess continued to condemn protestors, counter cultures, and youth movements not just throughout the 1970s but for the rest of his life. In fact, his 'Letter from Europe' series and his second autobiography, *You've Had Your Time* (1990), include perhaps the most insightful articulations of his opinions on the protest generation, despite being outright polemical in his 'Letter[s] from Europe' and sarcastically and humorously reflectional in *You've Had Your Time*: the 'forms asked for an evaluation of their lecturer's professional skill and (this being America) personality. Who were these children to presume to judge? I tore up the forms but kept the pencils. As I say, I had nothing to lose'.[19] In his autumn 1969 'Letter from Europe', the homogenization of protestation made him doubt the 'sincerity of student protest'.[20] Their insincerity, he goes on to explain and argue, likely stemmed from the coddling of their minds by the 'press and the commodity-sellers' who sold them the idea 'that youth is an achievement in itself', therefore making them less 'anxious to justify their existence existentially', since by protest alone they felt 'at least they are doing *something*', which must therefore be *right* – a uniquely American logic by Burgess's estimations.[21] What he meant by this was further explained publicly while speaking over a decade later in Washington, DC on 10 February 1981, when Burgess gave a lecture entitled 'Thoughts on Excellence' for the LTV Corporation to a crowd of American business and community leaders, which discussed many of his thoughts about the American ethos and mythos. Addressing the issue of American excellence, exceptionalism, ignorance, and arrogance, Burgess insisted that the American mentality, if it could be summarized, existed on a scale between two extremes. On one side of that scale was the zeitgeist of the American youth conjured up in the 1960s youth movements. Burgess summarizes this group, yet again, as possessing a philosophy that leaned towards 'being and not doing' – possibly gleaned from Jean-Paul Sartre's *Being and Nothingness* (1943), but to what extent is not known, though such a comparison should take place elsewhere since to examine this here would be digressive – with adherents to this philosophy believing that this disposition was god-like, an influence adopted from Eastern philosophy, likely influenced by reading Hermann Hesse.[22] The second extreme that some adhered to, oppositely and paradoxically, he contested, always using wide sweeping generalizations, were tenets set forth by the French philosophers Jean-Paul Sartre and Albert Camus, whose philosophies outlined that humans must *do* simply because they exist, despite the fact that everything humans do is essentially meaningless.[23] Burgess claimed that somewhere in between these poles was the predominant general American equilibrium: that the best course of action was *action* itself – doing for the sake of doing – especially when *doing* benefitted American civilization and not *doing* meant the opposite of excellence, therefore *to do action* must be the answer.[24] This approach to life and civilization appeared, by Burgess's calculations, to be innocent enough until it was revealed that Americans did not know their own limitations and therefore had the propensity to *do* too much. Such was the case with Americanism and Americanization of the world, and why Burgess applauded the United States's ingenuity and audaciousness while simultaneously speaking out against its incongruities, carelessness, and invasive nature.

Action, in and of itself, as a form of 'positive definition' which was 'dedicated to the maintenance and furtherance of civilization' by attempting to improve the body politic, was problematic, though, and Burgess was quick to point this out.[25] Applying this line of thought in an analogy, Burgess argued, rather insensitively and hyperbolically, that a 'European rapist will blame original sin' for his crime, while an 'American rapist will say it was all for the good of the victim' because all *American action* was rationalized as being *good* through sheer self-determination and cognitive dissonance – what Norman Mailer called the American schizophrenia.[26] This supposed dismissing of original sin and determinism so as to emphasize autonomy, free will, and individualism in order to achieve salvation led Burgess to not only equate Pelagianism with Americanism but also to see American culture as having the only popular culture capable of producing either fictional or real *Übermenschs* who could ignore the repressive philosophies of original sin and dismiss any sense of inferiority in the face of the universe.[27] As Burgess's argument goes, rather persuasively and chronotopically – in the sense that in existing within his various chronotopes, Burgess is therefore immersed in a 'social configuration of ideas about time and space that shapes and limits what it is possible to say or even to think about' – this philosophy of personage manifested itself in the particularly American creation of comics, superheroes, and pulp-fiction-like stories.[28]

Burgess's adversarial stance towards the baby boomer generation (born between 1946 and 1964), and the American culture they were creating, should come as no great surprise since he was in his fifties by the late 1960s and therefore had a drastically different worldview concerning the role of youth and the value and sanctity of higher education in a civilized society. Although there is no shortage of evidence to support this generational animosity, Burgess's more conservative alignment – 'a very very mild Conservative' – with the 'Black Papers' manifestos in England between the 1960s and mid 1970s (whose arguments have been largely accepted across political spectrums now) that denounced progressive education and student protests – the most notable being written and edited by A.E. Dyson and Brian Cox and which 'were not opposed in principle to progressive education, only to its excesses, fashionable in British schools in the 1960s and 1970s' by criticizing the 'selection for grammar schools at the age of 11, and advocated that it should be delayed until children were at least 13' – stands as one of the most significant examples.[29] In summary, Burgess appears to have largely stayed with the convictions and beliefs he outlined in his 1967 *Spectator* article 'The Purpose of Education', in which he laid out his theory of societal pedagogical epistemology:

> Schools should be small and dominated by intensely human teachers. This, I recognise, is the old way, and we cannot return to it so long as we are committed to giving everybody an education. But we should not be giving everybody an education. Some children – perhaps the majority – are ineducable beyond the stage of elementary skills, and they should not be allowed to hinder the progress of the educable. The important thing is that the vision of reality should continue to be transmitted. It must be transmitted to as many as possible, but it cannot be transmitted to everyone.[30]

In the same 'Letter from Europe' series mentioned previously, Burgess remarks that like 'many others of my class, I believed that to go to a university was an honor and that one must pay for the honor with hard work', going on to explain that even being admitted to a university was an achievement and not a 'right, even with the possession of high scholastic qualifications', despite being a period, 1937–40, he believed to have been filled with 'bad lecturing' and 'poor pedagogic practices'.[31] The poor conditions, Burgess satirizes, were reason enough to protest, and yet, 'we didn't – not many of us anyway'.[32] Presenting an example of legitimate conditions that warranted protest, Burgess argued that protestors in the United States lacked the justifiable, genuine, and immoral social conditions needed to react in such a way, stating that such agitators were not the weeds of a legitimate and strong 'democracy but of a society that is devoted to consumption', since this kind of reaction to societal conditions was a side effect of, he surmised, 'antithought, which is nurtured by the push-button demons of instant luxury'.[33] The types of protest he witnessed in the United States at this time were, to him, evidence of a 'type of vacancy, a time passing soap opera, something you do instead of work, instant uplift', not a meaningful reaction to unethical political ideologies and governments but rather an attempt to find 'something spectacular to make out of your excessive leisure', a leisure spent taking drugs and protesting, since outside 'of consumer goods production, life need only be drugs'.[34] Despite pointing out the many flaws and problems occurring in the United States during this time, chief among them being the Vietnam War (1955–75), Burgess never explicitly explained what he thought was an acceptable response to the actions of supposedly immoral or corrupt governments since all he focused on was where literature fit into this societal equation.

In the 1967 collection of writers' views on Vietnam, *Authors Take Sides on Vietnam*, many of Burgess's contemporary writers and popular thinkers provided their opinions about American involvement in Vietnam, predominantly expressing their opinion that the United States should indeed not be there. Most notably, James Baldwin stated that he was against the war because it was 'morally wrong and politically presumptuous', whereas Brigid Brophy, whom Burgess aligned with in a letter to the editor of *The Times* published on 2 February 1967, condemning the United States's involvement in Vietnam, argued she was against the war because she was naturally opposed to 'any power which marches into a foreign country, occupies half of it and, using that half as a base, bombs the other'.[35] Leslie Fiedler, who Burgess got to know in Buffalo, New York, concluded that, after explaining what he saw as the capitalistic ridiculousness of the whole situation, the United States must simply, '*Get out*', and Allen Ginsberg argued that the entire 'US intervention in Vietnam was always a mistake because the motives were wrong from the very beginning' due to the general parochial and ignorant nature of the United States.[36]

Although he was not included in that collection, Burgess took other avenues to voice his opinions. In his 1968 interview, 'I Love England, but I Will No Longer Live There' in the *New York Times*, despite being a detractor of United States involvement in Vietnam, Burgess railed against forms of protest always lacking substance and critical appeal because he perceived these responses to societal pressures as being 'so vague' and indeterminate: 'it can be Czechoslovakia one day, it can be Vietnam, it can be Biafra. Nobody gives a damn, it's a kind of lavatory, a kind of protest as a catharsis which probably the state looks kindly on' – perhaps it's no coincidence, then, that Enderby is the lavatorial poetry and social outcast/rebel who defies norms.[37] What he perceived as the overall disingenuousness of such protesting, from young people who were apt to protest just about anything and everything, was counteracted by the anathema he felt towards the actual war in Vietnam. Perhaps doing so to stand out, instead of throwing his negative opinion of the war behind the multitudes of authors who disapproved, Burgess focused his attention on the youth movements who were disrupting campuses in the wake of their protests. Always one to clearly articulate his distance from American culture in general, Burgess would frequently remind his audiences of his outside status: 'I'm an Englishman; I'm a foreigner: I'm an outsider'.[38] For instance, in the same interview in the *New York Times* above, Burgess blames his ideological stance on his Englishness and age which prevented him from finding protest movements, activism, and rebellious behaviour attractive or even beneficial in any way since only 'the young do daring things', adding that the much tamer British idea of rebellion was showing an 'American production [of] "Hair" ', subtitled *The American Tribal Love-Rock Musical*, the hippie-inspired Broadway musical infamous for its portrayal of drug use and its fully nude scene.[39] Another difference between, say, the 'Angry Young Men' of 1950s England and the United States, Burgess claimed, was that American youth were taken seriously after what Burgess saw as exhibiting juvenile and capricious behaviour, a reaction by the American public that Burgess abhorred since in England, if the youth had acted out – which he argued was rare – nothing changed since the 'young are a mere ornament, a mere decoration, a mere show. You get your bit of protest out of the way, and then on Monday things go back to gray normality'.[40]

By 1969, Burgess condescendingly and patronizingly teased that it was the 'continuation of the war in Vietnam [that] makes the students throw their cookies'; exhibiting this petulant behaviour was, he gathered, a by-product of the 'materialistic illiberalism of the American bourgeoisies' who routinely, and thoughtlessly, utilized 'weary icons – Che and Mao' as figureheads and symbols of their faux-rebelliousness.[41] What Burgess believed were unimaginative protests – much like Mailer does in *Armies of the Night*, though he still involved himself in the movement – he saw as being inspired by materialism, media, and clichéd icons which resulted in a banal and conformist activity he loathed, but it was the tendency of these protesting youth to also adopt an anti-intellectual and anti-establishment stance that incensed him.[42] Claiming to have seen in a 'California college' books being thrown 'through a window', among them 'Webster's Dictionary, Frazer's *The Golden Bough*, and the *Complete Poems of Percy Bysshe Shelley*', Burgess resented that the students were oblivious to the fact that these were 'the works of three revolutionaries'.[43] If to be believed, due to Burgess's tendency towards embellishment, though it is not out of the realm of possibility, this display of ignorance and disregard for knowledge deeply concerned Burgess since 'any violent rejection of traditional learning', he felt, should be cautioned and not condoned by 'various faculty people', who Burgess claimed had begun to side with the students and expressed to him during his visits at American universities that the 'time had come ... to consider the whole question of book learning from the very roots', and to potentially side with the youth's desire to 'begin with a kind of tabula rasa' where they attempt to 'ignore totally what's been done in the past, ignore lessons of the past, ignore the cyclical passion of human history, and think it's possible to start again'.[44] To those individuals, Burgess warned, on a 1972 episode of William F. Buckley's *The Firing Line*, that if the revolution of the young ever came, these intellectual traitors would likely only 'get some sort of special preference' just before being 'the first to be put up against the wall and have to face the firing squad'.[45] By 1973, Burgess continued being dismissive of youth movements and America's perceived submissiveness to the youth in an interview with the American teen magazine, *Seventeen*. The desire from American youth to quit or attempt to dismantle academia infuriated him, so the youth's willingness to, as the interviewer noted, 'reject what is going on in the educational system' and try to drop out because they didn't want to study, Burgess chalked up as being a character flaw of young people, since students 'should not be annoyed because learning is difficult. One should not regard things as being necessarily easy. Overcoming obstacles is one of the greatest pleasures in the world'.[46]

Preserving his conception of educational standards, with a stubborn disregard for initiatives attempting to give any willing citizen access to higher education, mattered far more to Burgess than any form of political activism or the social issues that brought on these responses. In the same *Seventeen* interview, Burgess argued that despite there being 'an image of youth taking over', it was all just a 'mere fantasy', because youth, by its very nature, was not 'ready to rule'.[47] An example of such an impoverishment of legitimacy and wisdom was exhibited in, Burgess goes on, the shoddy and sloppy conditions of the 'communes in California' that he states were 'pathetic', despite being founded upon admirable, though ignorant, ideals.[48] Consistently, what was ultimately at the core of his annoyance was that along with this apathy and disdain for learning came a failure to present refined modes of argumentation, thus it lacked an appreciation for nuance and subtlety. Recognizing and becoming infatuated with the conflicts, divisions, and consternations of everyday life was a trait of the young, Burgess believed, explaining eight months before his *Seventeen* interview, in his public *New York Times* letter to his students at the City College of New York, that 'youth is more aware of division than of continuity', which is why Burgess argued that young people grew frustrated by education because it trained the mind to find connections, whereas protesting and revolting were far more alluring because of the friction and discordance.[49] The letter was not received well by his students, as Barbara Lekatsas, a former student, has noted, but he also received negative responses from other college students around the country.[50] Responding to his letter on Christmas Eve 1972, Horace Porter, an African American recent college graduate, took Burgess to task by educating him on the perspective of a Black college graduate, stating that he deplored Burgess's 'sense of who and what is an American student' despite agreeing with the 'outrage at the general depravity of language sometimes found on campuses, but I am disappointed with what appears to be your feeling that "relevance" means Kesey, Vonnegut, and Burgess for the whites and soul food and bongo drums for the blacks'.[51] Porter provides context where Burgess had been working in generalizations and stereotypes in order to dismantle the clownish and dilapidated picture Burgess often portrayed when reporting on the topic of American higher education and its students and professors, a point to be discussed further in Chapter 4.

Although Burgess's rhetoric about student protests lessened, weakened, and altered as the mid 1970s rolled around, he still believed that the distinct rift between America's youth and the older generation that Burgess belonged to was the fault of America's general *modis operandi* and national philosophy. After announcing in 1973 that he had 'no stake in the establishment', he criticized his City College of New York students for not making the effort to reconcile their views with his perspectives: 'I read widely. I am curious as to what people write, and I am prepared to be sympathetic to students whose velleities I understand for the most part, but they don't make any effort to meet me. They won't read the books that I've read, although I read the books that they've read. They will not bring to a course I give the requisite background. ... They look for the wrong things in a book. They look for content rather than form, and they honestly believe the world can be changed' through literature.[52] Real, honest, and genuine literature was, to Burgess, eternally relevant to human nature and not ephemeral and definitely not something that existed as a provocation or call to activism, or a political statement – a belief that set him at odds with literature produced from the American Black Arts Movement and counter culture of the 1960s and 1970s – rather, good literature was supposed to present the truths of the world more plainly, and to a greater depth, than everyday reality is able to do. As far back as 1965, evidence of Burgess's opprobrium towards 'young intellectuals' exists, describing them as being a 'very austere people' who preferred 'a straight draught of didacticism to a tract disguised as entertainment', which made his incongruence with young intellectuals largely a disagreement about aesthetics, as was the case with many of his arguments concerning social matters.[53] Canonized high literature by its nature, and by the standards Burgess embraced, was different than what the youth tended to be drawn to, meaning authors and work like Hermann Hesse, whose 'studies of struggling youth' became 'part of an American campus cult indicating the desire of the serious young to find literary symbols for their own growing problems' and not for humanity and history as a whole.[54] To Burgess, literature was an atavistic activity – similarly to Bakhtin's dictum that 'of all words uttered in everyday life, no less than half belong to someone else' – that helped humanity engage with the past through linguistic and aesthetic means, to learn from, enjoy, and marvel at, in order to go forth with this knowledge as a means of avoiding and abolishing ignorance.[55] This is why Burgess felt that the 'great tendency of American youth … to treat novels not as a literary but as a philosophical experience' was absurd because legitimate and aesthete literary writers had 'no such message'.[56] Perhaps an act of self-protection which was coupled with his pedagogical approach to literature as both an author and teacher, Burgess held on to these beliefs. Whatever it was, Burgess's personal opinions on matters of literary purpose and pedagogy often conflicted with his American students and their ideas about literature, as can be gathered from his non-fiction, which then finds a home in his novels.

The ultimate irony of such castigations of the United States's youth culture regarding protest is that Burgess would eventually, in 1974's *The Clockwork Testament*, produce his own form of protest in the shape of a novella that used his recurring character, F.X. Enderby, to mock and ridicule all that Burgess despised during his New York years. As a reviewer stated in the *Times Literary Supplement* in June 1974, Burgess appeared to use this book as an assault 'against objects of his [Enderby's] creator's [Burgess's] scorn and dislike: most things in American civilization, and especially its protest culture'.[57] Burgess appears to have just not approved of younger people's modes of subversion, political activism not being an activity Burgess would ever partake in, but writing a novel was apparently acceptable.

The United States of America to Anthony Burgess

In many ways, despite some of its alluring qualities, Burgess saw the United States in the 1970s as a misguided and misinformed country. For Burgess, the United States purported many things but its slogan of democracy, peace, and individuality that emerged from the founding of the country and was solidified by the American Renaissance were not promises it ever meant to keep: 'America says one thing and means another. It doesn't want the free, individualistic person it pretends to value.'[58] In an interview at Rockhurst University in November 1975, Burgess expounded on this idea of American idealism being a farce:

> I hate to say this, because I try to be a good guest, but America is totally dishonest. Even Russia is more honest than America. Going through America, one is aware that its citizens are free; yet they behave as it is assumed people behave in Soviet Russia. Russian people assume they are not in a free country, but they behave as if they have a great deal of freedom. In the United States, it's the opposite way around.[59]

Here Burgess the author echoes what his character, Mendoza, had argued when talking to Ennis in *A Vision of Battlements* through what Bakhtin called the 'two speech centers and two speech unities: the unity of the author's utterance and the unity of the character's utterance' where 'the second unity is not self-sufficient' since it is 'subordinated to the first'.[60] Mendoza states that regardless of being diametrically opposed governmentally with Russia, who resembled 'the end-product of the Socialist process', the two countries, the United States and Russia, still acted in similar ways despite vastly different governing bodies: 'We're both the same, in a way. We both offer supra-regional goods – the icebox and the Chevrolet or the worker, standardised into an overcalled abstraction at a standardised production belt.'[61] Fourteen years before the Rockhurst interview, in *The Worm and the Ring* (1961) and through the same kind of subordinated speech, Howarth, the novel's protagonist, while in Paris, talks to an American wine salesman who explains why he had left the country, saying that Americans seemed not to even know there had been a large war raging across the ocean during World War Two:

> America's an abstraction, the way I see it. It's lost blood so fast it's only an idea now. I got so I couldn't taste anything any more. It was all two dimensions and everything deep-frozen. Russia and China and a bit of clear thought scaring the pants off everybody else. … America's too darn clean.[62]

Having feared the United States's volatility, been allured by its economic prowess, and finally having lived in and travelled throughout the country, Burgess's opinions of the United States towards the end of his life, having all been refracted through his cultural awareness, essentially came full circle by seeing the United States just as he had before visiting as an unstoppable, barrelling cultural, economic, and political monster, 'caught up in an exhilarating mindlessness as good as a course of adrenalin injections' that could not help itself but for working constantly, and futilely, to achieve the mythic image it had spent so long crafting of itself.[63] Since every 'social trend in every epoch has its own special sense of discourse and its own range of discursive possibilities ... then every thought, feeling, experience must be refracted through the medium of someone else's discourse, someone else's style, someone else's manner, with which it cannot immediately be merged without reservation, without distance, without refraction', Burgess, in his fiction, non-fiction, and journalism, echoes the themes of the zeitgeist.[64] The cultural theme of full and destructive subsumption of the individual within myth was picked up not only from his experiences but also, if not more so, from his reading of contemporary American literature, with such examples coming from Saul Bellow's Eugene Henderson who greedily yearns, '*I want*' in *Henderson the Rain King* (1959), to Gore Vidal's *Myra Breckinridge* (1968) whose titular character lusts to capture and consume all forms of sexuality, to Philip Roth's Peter Tarnopol in *My Life as a Man* (1974) who cannot help himself from spreading his semen around other people's homes. Indeed, literary American fiction that Burgess had read was alone enough to communicate to him, and the world, that the United States and Americans were insatiable, corrosive, eccentric, and diverse.[65] And although he found this peculiar cultural concoction to be both fascinating and provocative, the inevitable deterioration of Burgess's once-maligned embrace of the United States began in the late 1970s and early 1980s, which is evident through his marked decrease in visits, more sombre tone about the United States and Americans, and an increased general lack of concern with the country as was apparent across all of his modes of communication. Continuing to visit the United States all the way into January 1993, although much less regularly, these trips were also brief due to his failing health, but simultaneous with his decreased presence was the near-complete absence of the subject of the United States from Burgess's fiction after his metaphorical *au revoir* to the country in his final Enderby novel, *Enderby's Dark Lady, or No End to Enderby* (1984), to be discussed at length in Chapter 7.

The signs of Burgess's eventual retirement from cultural fame in the United States were existent in his earliest vituperations against the country, but as his commentary amassed over the years, a more grand narrative immersed in and evocative of an American heteroglossia, or socio-ideological language, reveals itself across his entire canon.[66] Appearing on *The Dick Cavett Show* in 1980, Burgess expressed his belief that shows like *Dallas* (1978–91) had contributed to Americans' self-conceptions being distorted, claiming that what American television had done, a medium consumed by Americans far more and in vaster quantities than literature, was reduce humans to bare elements, devoid of completeness and humanity – echoing the Federal Communication Commission's chairman Newton Minow's 1961 comment that television was a 'vast wasteland' of material.[67] In his 1982 article 'Cardboard Character' for *TV Guide*, he argued that the result of this was that American audiences were forced not to learn anything about 'real America', or anything for that matter concerning the 'real mentality of human beings', but instead were force-fed stories that leaned on 'the common denominators: sex, hatred':

> This JR character is unbelievable. ... I fear that television may so simplify people's view of their own mentalities that we will become sub-human. ... I am a writer because I believe in humanity. I believe in people. I believe people are immensely complicated things, immensely interesting, immensely complex. They're not simple; they're not cartoon characters. ... This helps in breeding a generation that has a very simplistic view of what human nature is.[68]

Continuing, Burgess widened this argument to include the European receptions to these types of television characters, stating that the United States had also force-fed Europe with shows where 'nobody reads, nobody thinks, nobody generates an idea other than a money-making or murderous one. In fact, we are very rarely presented with a whole human being'.[69] These types of characters in American television, Burgess gathered, only fed back into the United States's deterministic 'psychological tradition, which began with J.B. Watson and has culminated in B.F. Skinner ... where all men and women are free and self-determined', all coinciding with materialism to result in a country that 'likes to think of human beings as simple moving matter, not complex mind'.[70] Taking on a similar subject in his 1974 *Playboy* interview – an interview he claimed was not reported accurately – Burgess stated that Nietzsche's *superman* would have to be an American or else the comic book character, Superman, was indeed a manifestation of Nietzsche's ideas baked into pop culture, or, at the very least, the idea had to have been 'incarnated in America', a place with the 'superastronaut, the superpolitician – from Hamilton to Nixon – the supertechnician, the superscientist, even the super writer like [Norman] Mailer, this is a very American thing'.[71] Burgess explained that these entities were deemed 'super' because they soared 'above the purely human', which was yet again both good and bad: 'This probably explains why they make such a mess of the purely human, why such small considerations as concerning oneself with the rights of ordinary people go by the boards. Cartoons like *Superman*, *Batman* and *Captain Marvel* had to originate in America.'[72] What had occurred, Burgess contended, because these types of narrative frameworks were introduced and embraced by the

American populace, was that citizens of the United States were conditioned with myths and science fiction, so that this romanticized lens distorted their realities by forcing their perceptions into neatly drawn, quantified, qualified, and defined American mythical matrices, so that when the unthinkable occurred, like a manned successful mission landing on the moon on 20 July 1969, it would instantly be perceived as commonplace and expected – an event on which Burgess was commissioned by the *New York Times* to comment on.[73] This was done through no conscious act of their own, but rather this reaction was the fault of the paradigm they themselves had spun, consequently creating American culture, a culture with a predilection to be relentlessly unimpressed with life, disenchanted with the more common artful imaginative representations of the world, and therefore always in need and desirous of *more* and *better*.[74]

Although he adored the United States in many respects, it was a general detachment from reality that encouraged Burgess's opinion that the United States was a place capable and guilty of wholly forgetting the transgressions and achievements of the past, resulting in a kind of blind and bullish temperament that touted the idea of a sort of colonial democracy with the only goal of 'teaching the world the merits of consumption'.[75] The exception was with art and American literary experimentation, which was good as long as it was inspired by erudition and coupled with genius. As a writer, the United States and American authors inspired Burgess to experiment and provided him with plenty to talk and think about as he wrote throughout the 1970s and 1980s, which is why the United States appears in the foreground of five of his ten novels published between 1971 and 1984.

Equally important to Burgess was the United States's obsession with myths and innovation that resulted in deeply embedded cultural convictions which Burgess found endlessly provocative and inspiring aesthetically, although not necessarily socially inviting or beneficial. This myth-building, carried out in all facets of American daily life, Burgess partially attributed to the United States's obsession with and productivity in the art of cinema and the entertainment industry, which he felt ended up, over time, turning 'most institutions ... into myth', resulting in the myth trying to 'self-consciously ... maintain itself', therefore inevitably leading to disaster due to the unattainable and unrealistic goals and pursuits Americans strived for.[76] In fact, one of the United States's most celebrated forms of business was the Hollywood film industry, whose sole purpose was to explore the realm and possibilities of visual storytelling, and these visual representations had soon became more vivid and realistic than anything that had ever come before them, so that by the 1960s and 1970s 'film culture [had] permeated American life in a way that it never had before and never has since'.[77] The verisimilitude of Hollywood films had paradoxically altered reality, with films such as

Easy Rider (1969) being a reflection of this specifically for the hippie demographic, thus furthering the gap between reality and make-believe – the counter culture had produced a film evocative and emblematic of its own intentions and philosophies, while also compounding this image by influencing the very same counter culture that had provoked such a creation.[78] The two worlds, myth/visual storytelling versus reality, relied upon each through the use and understanding of symbols, iconography, characters, and tales, which soon supplanted the more mundane materiality of everyday American life – more broadly, the white picket fences, the combat hero, the cowboy, the businessman, the hippie, the Black radical, and the subservient housewife, all symbols and tropes perpetuated by and mirrored back onto the society that created the medium to begin with.

Although Burgess understood that the United States had economically, artistically, and politically advanced by living according to various social and cultural doctrines and myths, he felt that many of these aspects of American life also acted as a detriment to the psyche of the American soul, or at the very least threw the country's understanding of itself into disarray, a point of discussion still being heatedly debated, discussed, and analysed into the twenty-first century with books such as Heather Cox Richardson's *How the South Won the Civil War: Oligarchy, Democracy, and the Continuing Fight for the Soul of America* (2020) and Jon Meacham's *The Soul of America: The Battle for Our Better Angels* (2018) attempting to put into perspective what *progress* looks like in American history by dispelling and contextualizing certain rosy retrospective American lore.[79] Even though the United States had proved itself, by Burgess's standards, in the 1960s to be far from perfect and not quite 'excellent' due to its many misgivings and blunders both militarily and socially – since to say that something is excellent 'you must at first at least be harmless' – the country still clung to projections of excellence, leading him to evaluate that Americans and American culture refused to honestly and sincerely grapple with its issues, instead choosing to take the paths of least resistance in order to feed upon delusional, illogical, and romantic visions of nationalistic perfection.[80] Burgess attributed this national myopia to, first, Americans forgetting about the rest of the world and, second, the country forgetting about the facts of history, arguing that Americans needed to remember that, despite the individualistic 'pull yourself up by the bootstraps' mentality, there were uses 'for everything, even the loathsome bureaucratic machine. America needs a measure of socialization, as Britain needed it. Things – especially those we need most – don't always pay their way, and it is here that the state must enter, dismissing the profit element'.[81] Disheartened with its ubiquitous, and often ruthless, capitalist and market mentality – ironically, because he enriched himself in such a system, complaining that it was 'not easy for the artist to live in a capitalist society' – Burgess saw the United States, though it treated its writers better than in England, as missing out on many of the intensely humanistic elements needed in modern societies, which is a similar assessment to historian Hugh Brogan's comment that the United States had a cultish subservience towards a 'consumer society with a taste for cheap salvation'.[82] The Burgessian persona, rife with heteroglossic dialogism, displays Burgess's authorial monologism in his 1974 novel *The Clockwork Testament*, where he more accurately echoes Brogan's critique of American culture when the narrator describes Americans as adhering to and seeking out the 'synchronic sweet and savoury, a sign of their salvation, unlike the timid Latin races'.[83] Swirling in the American cultural milieu of the 1970s, the 'cheap salvation' of Americans, which could be summarized as an essentially ego-maniacal materialism, was also a point Burgess expressed about the United States in his journalism into the 1980s. Remarking in an unpublished piece about a recent trip he had taken to Washington, DC, Burgess says that the Americans he had encountered had 'bowed down for a time to impossible gods, and now they could return to Oklahoma City or Dallas to worship their more tangible God – the one who announces salvation through the three-car garage and the thousand acre ranch', as a way to express how Americans rationalized the guilt of being aware of corrupt state action but went on living as if nothing had happened.[84] Common for the period, Norman Mailer described this self-same disposition in *Armies of the Night* on numerous occasions, going so far as to explain how Americans could rationalize their way of life due to a kind of insanity brought on by a 'fiercely controlled' schizophrenia that employed various means of cognitive dissonance to both love and hate the state, the Vietnam War, and Christianity.[85]

The United States's struggles with truth (the propaganda of the 1940s, the presidential lies of the 1960s and 1970s, etc.), self-awareness (the materialism, the pleas for isolationism as well as an increase to the military industrial complex bent on eradicating communism, etc.), honesty (the Central Intelligence Agency's involvement in other country's elections, particularly Central and South American countries in the 1970s, and McCarthyism, etc.), and overall genuineness (the myths and realities of the American dream, Hollywood, institutionalized racism, Christian fundamentalism, etc.) are reflected upon in Burgess's *1985* (1978) by arguing, in a Socratic catechistic dialogue between two personages, that the United States had these problems because of excessive hubris, not to be, Burgess appears to suggest, equated with the type of superiority complexes found in dictatorships that had occurred in Europe, but rather as a national character flaw forged out of the United States's revolutionary beginnings.[86] This led, the text argues, to the United States government overcompensating for a perceived sense of superiority, therefore resulting in a litany of militaristic and social faux pas. This overconfidence was also a side effect of a naïve presumptuousness only existent in a nation that was new to such potent and vast power:

> There's nothing in the traditions of the United States which predisposes them to authoritarianism on the European model. The hysterical anti-communism of the fifties can be seen as a symptom, though an unpleasant and dangerous one, of an ingrained hatred of centralized authority. You can't deny that America did a great deal to promote democratic self-determination in western Europe. Truman, Acheson, Marshall Aid. There was a kind of arrogant assumption on America's part that she knew best, that God had endowed her with a moral superiority that was the reward of an enlightened democratic tradition, but that's very different from collectivist tyranny.[87]

This critique of the United States's collective psyche presented through a dialogue between what appears to be a contrived Burgess personas was likely influenced and informed by an American novel mentioned by Burgess frequently, in *1985* and elsewhere in letters and articles, *It Can't Happen Here* (1935) by Sinclair Lewis.[88]

Lewis's protagonist, Doremus Jessup, describes the Americans in the novel as learning 'in school that God had supplanted the Jews as chosen people by the Americans, and this time done the job much better, so that we were the richest, kindest, and cleverest nation living; that depressions were but passing headaches'.[89] Similarly again, Burgess's remarks on the United States's inability to listen to the rest of the world and take guidance from history are presented by Jessup as he summarizes the not-so-fictional American belief that governing was easy despite 'foreigners' making up a 'bogus mystery' of the struggles to maintain a nation, since 'politics were really so simple that any village attorney or any clerk in the office of a metropolitan sheriff was quite adequately trained for them'.[90] This naïve overconfidence, and refusal to acknowledge expertise, remains a criticism for the United States, as more than half of the electorate still struggle immensely with understanding national history and political facts, a trait Burgess was introduced to from American fiction and then experienced first-hand while living in and travelling around the United States.[91]

In *1985*, 'Epilogue: An Interview', Burgess juxtaposes Lewis's novel with what he perceived were the problems that still existed among Americans into the late 1970s, indeed what could be recognized as being easily exhibited in something like Hunter S. Thompson's *Rolling Stone* periodicals covering the 1972 presidential campaign and which were ultimately published in *Fear and Loathing on the Campaign Trail '72* (1973).[92] Burgess's text explains that Lewis's novel shows 'how a tyranny can come about through the American democratic process, with a president American as apple pie, as they say – a kind of cracker-barrel Will Rogers type appealing to the philistine anti-intellectual core of the American electorate', which is not entirely dissimilar to Thompson remarking that the palpable angst and hatred of the common American was virulent to the point that the so-called 'Silent Majority was so deep in a behavioral sink that their only feeling for politics was a powerful sense of revulsion', redolent of fascism, wherein they desired that in the 'White House was a man who would leave them alone and do anything necessary to bring calmness back into their lives even if it meant turning the whole state of Nevada into a concentration camp for hippies, n-----s, dope fiends, do-gooders, and anyone else who might threaten the status quo'.[93] Burgess used the American cowboy vaudeville actor Will Rogers as a kind of metonymy for the all-American White man in just the same way that James Baldwin used Gary Cooper – probably more accurately in that Rogers was a Cherokee Native American – in his 1965 debate with William F. Buckley to evoke the concept of the symbol of American personhood and identity, only in Baldwin's case to be deceived in thinking he belonged to the White, heterosexual male in-group. Burgess uses this same kind of figure as a symbol to raise just the same scepticism: that these metonymies of American*ness* can be deceptive, are fictive, and have the possibility of exuding particularly *un*-American qualities. Sharpening his criticism, Burgess, while carrying out a stream-of-consciousness interview between a Burgess persona and a fictional American interlocutor, goes further to argue that such seemingly un-American attitudes are actually deeply entrenched in the American political and cultural scheme, by using a kind of caricatured American stereotype, both ignorant and jingoistic, as well as provincially intolerant, that is ultimately rooted in some truth:

> Core? More than the core, the whole fruit except for the thin skin of liberalism. My old pappy used to say: Son, there ain't no good books except the Good Book. Time these long-haired interlettles got their comeuppance, and so on. And so book-burning, shooting of radical schoolmasters, censorship of progressive newspapers. Every repressive act justified out of the Old Testament and excused jokingly in good spittoon style.[94]

An intricately assembled narrative that is fashioned between a fictional American interviewer of twenty-seven years old and a Burgess persona, this fictional interview erects two layers of authorial distance between John Wilson and the Burgess persona (persona, Anthony Burgess; author, John Wilson) and three layers between the interviewer and the actual author (interview format→fictionalized American→Anthony Burgess as author→ John Wilson), which all takes place as a commentary on the matters of a story that precedes this invented dialogue, all in a single book of the same name. The dialogue presents a counterpoint to a piece of fiction, the *1985* novella that is the majority of the book, and must be taken as at least partially autobiographical because Anthony Burgess, the author listed on the book, is the creator of the entire scenario, is addressed as 'you', assuming this means the author of the book, and therefore both asks the questions and provides the answers, thereby directing the entire exchange towards common tropes and motifs utilized and discussed by the public figure of the same name, all with similar language and opinions expressed by the author extraliterarily. Since, as Michael Holquist explains in *Dialogism: Bakhtin and His World*, Bakhtin's theories focus on 'literary texts [as] utterances, words that cannot be divorced from particular subjects in specific situations', the knowledge of epitextual orbital 'activity of the author' and the 'place they hold in the social and historical forces at work when the text is produced and when it is consumed' therefore must be taken into consideration and be recognized as 'active elements in a dialogic exchange taking place on several different levels at the same time' as the 'words in literary texts'.[95] Although Burgess's epitextual dialogue often so closely overlaps with his literary texts, and textual *others* are clearly painted with the monologism of the author, Burgess does not achieve what Bakhtin argued Fyodor Dostoevsky achieved: the literary illusion as if the 'character were not an object of authorial discourse, but rather a fully valid, autonomous carrier of his own individual word', because the language of Burgess's characters is too clearly monologic in that it is too closely similar to Burgess's heteroglossic interactions with the contemporary American discourse.[96] It's possible that this text could be defined, using terms from Max Saunders's *Self Impression: Life-Writing, Autobiografiction, and the Forms of Modern Literature* (2010), as meta-auto/biografiction in the sense that the text is a piece of fiction interspersed with biographical commentary on fictional and non-fictional personas, ultimately revealing autobiographical details and opinions of and about the text's author while existing as a dialogue about authorial intent and authorial self- and cultural criticism – similar in some ways to the intricate narration split between the fictional author, John Shade, with fictional annotations by Charles Kinbote in Vladimir Nabokov's, *Pale Fire* (1962), one of Burgess's most admired *American* authors, for whom he published the poem 'To Vladimir Nabokov on His 70th Birthday' in a special issue of *TriQuarterly*.[97] Understanding and recognizing the layered and multifaceted realities of his texts and the language used within them then allows for the aforementioned responses to be taken as either 'a "real" referential system (in which the autobiographical agreement, even if it comes by way of the book and the writing, has the value of act), and a literary system (in which the writing no longer aspires to transparency but is able to mime perfectly, to mobilize the beliefs of the first system)', or both, as is substantiated and argued here.[98] Since an interview of a literary author often has 'an intrinsic duality' that both adds 'to an author's *oeuvre* as well as offering a commentary or critique of that *oeuvre*', this interview-narrative structure, created with unnamed personas, actually exists through a triple function that simultaneously evokes a literary and authorial identity coupled with self-referential commentary.[99] This must be the accepted way of understanding this text because Burgess's comments align with his own public persona, therefore contributing yet another utterance to his monologized dialogism which simultaneously helps craft a multilayered understanding of how he felt about the United States (in the answer responses), Americans (while asking and contextualizing questions as a fictional American), and American authors (while alluding to Lewis's fiction). Working from this assumption, it is important to understand that at the heart of Lewis's novel is the premise that 'the installation of a fascist government will not be a [grand] revolution or *coup d'état*; rather, the groundwork for fascism has already been constructed in the ideological worldviews of the majority of Americans', meaning that the 'riposte to the claim that "It can't happen here" is "It already has"', a notion Burgess either recognized himself or adopted from Lewis and repeated.[100] Identifying Burgess's experiences with and thoughts on Lewis's novel is important because doing so informs Burgess's readers, and indeed readers of this monograph, of how his perception of the United States was informed by Lewis's novel specifically, and American literature more generally.

Taking on what he perceived were the ingrained problems with American doctrines on 4 July 1971, a national American holiday, Independence Day, Burgess, or a persona of his, published an article in the *New York Times* that argued provocatively and somewhat satirically that the United States's ingrown contradictions and failures were, 'not altogether jocularly', due to the 'sacrosanct Constitution' which he deduced needed to 'be repealed, the Presidency be liquidated in favor of the British monarchical system (republics rarely work well), and that the South be made to secede from the Union. Add to this program the total disarming of the country, and then genuine reform in other areas might begin'.[101] Four months later in November 1971, Burgess was even more direct, stating that the American Constitution was 'out of date' and that 'republics tend to corruption', while providing the clarifying snippet that 'Canada and Australia have their own problems, but they are happier countries than America'.[102] More provocatively, on multiple occasions, Burgess even satirically suggests that instead of adopting a monarchical system – an opinion even suggested by Hunter S. Thompson in *Fear and Loathing on the Campaign Trail '72* – the United States should just return to the throne of England due to the faulty nature of a republic government.[103] Were they to be 'back under the British crown', he argued, Americans 'would be a lot happier', a point he continued repeating into the 1980s.[104] The most significant reason Burgess made these types of arguments had to do with his perception of the United States being a place striving to adhere to a doctrine that was unrealistic, which resulted in the country and its citizens never attaining the goals they purported to embrace, therefore causing more problems than these creeds helped to solve. Being overwhelmed with what he perceived as the impractical and romantic doctrines established by the American Constitution, Burgess argued they had to be changed in order to dismantle the mythic and futile dreams of full egalitarianism that were proclaimed in a document far too 'wide open to great state power as any constitution is' due to its having been written by the '18th century rational mind'.[105]

The difference between the rational and enlightened American minds of the eighteenth century is communicated and echoed, monologically for Burgess, through his time-travelling teacher in *The Clockwork Testament* who narrates to his students at the end of the book that the United States is 'a great free complex or federation of states that are welded together under a most un-British constitution – rational, frenchified, certainly republican' document.[106] In his non-fiction book on New York City, for the Time-Life Great Cities series, *New York* (1976), this description of the American political system exists in direct opposition to how Burgess describes the particularly European motivation behind assembling the British Constitution, by claiming that the British document is crafted using *a posteriori* logical appeals based on observation and then related to philosophies in order to inform ethics, politics, and governance, while the Americans tended to utilize *a priori* logical applications that forced philosophy upon observations, with his non-fiction text acting as a kind of dialogic response to his fiction:

> In Europe things come about and then have to be justified philosophically; in America things are grandly and innocently created out of a philosophy. England's Constitution grew, or accumulated, haphazardly, empirically, without even a scrap of paper to write it on; that of the United States emerged boldly and idealistically, influenced by a treatise on law, *De l'Esprit des lois*, written by the French philosopher Montesquieu.[107]

Such a kind of *a priori* application could, Burgess posited, lead to a discordance, an antibiosis forged out of incongruence that was destined to always be more inadequate than an informed and advised *a posteriori* and organic *ad hoc* approach – again, the United States's failings, he perceived, were baked into the founding of the country.

In his 1972 article, 'One of the Minor Joys', Burgess again lets on that his opinions on matters of American politics existed in very similar terms across all different kinds of writing and performances he conducted, this time prefacing his opinion with an apocryphal anecdote of travelling to Tennessee and happening upon 'a portrait of George III above somebody's sideboard' which acted as segue into a discussion about how he used to lecture to American audiences and would sometimes, yet again, 'not altogether jocularly', suggest that the 'United States should abandon the republican principle and come back to the fold'.[108] Bringing politics into the debate, Burgess begins arguing that with Nixon again winning the American presidency in November 1972, 'there might well be support for such a program, if insinuated with enough cunning' – anything was possible, Burgess postulated, after the rise of the 'Jesus Freaks and the Mansonian diabolists'.[109] Burgess supposedly expressed a similar sentiment in his September 1974 interview with *Playboy* when he explained some of his grievances towards both the United States and England:

> I feel that the prose of the Declaration of Independence is the most beautiful, the most inspiring, the very perfection of the English language. I admire those men of 1776, although I think they did the wrong thing in many ways. ... we never would have had this horrible nonsense with the Presidency, which has caused so much trouble in America. I don't think this mode of culture is really fitted for republicanism. The Americans are really a limited-monarchy people.[110]

Burgess often argued that the United States Constitution was an impractical and far too ideological document that acted as one of the singular most significant contributing factors in the United States's perpetuation of their myth of supremacy, of revolt, and of having created the perfect societal system. The document's Edenic appropriation, he felt, was a dangerous presupposition that led to all sorts of other problems.

The opinion he held about the presumptuous and faulty nature of the Constitution, although sharing an opinion with anti-federalists during the country's founding, was also shared by Frederick Douglass and some members of the Black Power Movement, who believed that the 'Constitutional tradition was always corrupt and was constructed as a defense of slavery'.[111] Fuelling his disdain for the idealistic document was largely Burgess's hatred for politicians, which is why he, however seriously or not, suggested the dissolving of the presidency and the Constitution altogether, two entities he felt professed too much and were built upon illusory foundations – saying in his 1973 *Paris Review* interview (done seemingly entirely through the mail, with Burgess having 'full control over [the] text') that the 'U.S. presidency is a Tudor monarchy plus telephones' – that were rarely dealt with critically and honestly. In a Norwegian television interview in 1981, Burgess was quite direct about his contempt for governments and the people who ran them:

> I am frightened of governments and we are governed too much – they don't like individualism ... I hate politics; I hate politicians. ... they're all the same tending toward all powerful governments, so many laws, frightened of the

police and tickets and taxes and I never feel free. It's a job of government to make people feel unfree.[112]

Regardless of the transgressions the United States committed while he lived and travelled throughout the country, Burgess never expressed allegiance to a political party – since in republican democracies, like the United States, presidents 'are at the mercy of party. The election of the head of state is part of a democratic process which entails the regular swing from one ideology to another. A president is committed to a one-sided philosophy, that of his party. Being a politician, he is corruptible' – but instead admonished whomever the leading politicians were at the time, which just so happened to predominantly be Republicans during Burgess's most active time in the United States: 1969–77.[113] His attacks on politicians were due to his belief that more evil than any founding document, myth, or police presence were politicians by their very nature, since Burgess had deduced that politicians had to always be diametrically opposed to the efforts of artists, especially literary authors, since 'the writer is concerned with the truth. The state is not', and therefore by ontological purpose alone, politicians had to 'think of truth as a commodity'.[114]

After President Gerald Ford's 'truth is the glue' comment during his inaugural remarks on 9 August 1974, Burgess used this concept as an example of partisan and personal views being expressed as objective fact, thereby distorting reality for political gain.[115] Accompanied by illustrations from Ralph Steadman, Burgess wrote a poem entitled 'O Lord, O Ford, God Help Us, Also You' for the *New York Times* in December 1974. The poem, written in heroic couplets, ruthlessly mocks President Ford: 'I gawped at New York television while / Your Ford, unflawed by an ironic smile, / Announced to the whole world: *Truth is a glue.* / O Lord, O Ford, God help us, also you'.[116] The rest of the poem, packed with slights against American leaders and statesmen by accusing 'Men we thought big [who] are now revealed as little' of being 'Conniving and contriving, mean and brittle, / Power-hungry merely, greedier than us, / Vindictive, ignorant, pusillanimous, / Liars, vulgarians, and ugly too', is a requiem for 1974, a year the poem describes as a 'Satanic mill. / Has any twelvemonth fed us more with fear? / Was ever a more salutary year? / At least we're learning and no more pretend / That history moves to a Hegelian end'.[117] After such an apparently awful year, with Nixon's resignation coming on 8 August 1974, Burgess's poem surmises that 'America as Eden's dead and gone, / The Devil rides, and so on and so on', largely because Americanism, being equated through a biblical metaphor here with lost innocence, superficiality, arrogance, proud ignorance, and blind adherence to myths and ahistoricity, has led to the prevalence and glorification of petulant youth culture contaminating logic, erudition, and common sense, 'As if the drughead's *Nothin', man, in books* / Infects the castles where our rulers sit / (History, that other Ford once said, is s--t)' – the reference to Henry Ford is to his infamous 1921 comment that 'History is bunk'.[118] The American culture of the 1970s created an atmosphere, the poem laments, where 'politics was metaphysics, art, / Eloquence, knowledge of the human heart, / That is now sunk into a disrepute / Shameful and shameless, all too absolute'.[119] Concluding, Burgess's poem pleads with its readers to 'Watch out for pederasts in Central Park, / Read Plato and not Playboy', even though Burgess's works of fiction during this period were filled with the expletives he chose to censor himself with here (assuming this was not an editor's decision), and just two months previous to the publication of this poem, he had completed an extensive interview in *Playboy*, which is all not to mention that even the poem itself, decrying the youth and anti-intellectualism, was illustrated by one of the co-creators of Hunter S. Thompson's Gonzo journalism which idolized drug culture; in being knowledgeable of these epitextual elements and exterior dialogues and heteroglossia, there occurs a muddling or tarnishing of Burgess's points, all while simultaneously representing not only the cultural contradictions of the 1970s but also what Bakhtin calls the 'socio-ideological contradictions' that existed at the time and are recognized in hindsight at the point of this examination.[120] This irony was apparently lost on him, or else ignored, since no comment exists on these peculiarities.

Echoing his proclamation that 'All governments are evil' in the *New York Times*, Burgess took his perturbations to the university lecture circuit stage to publicly address American audiences on these matters.[121] One such time occurred in his lecture entitled 'A Visit with Anthony Burgess' at Tufts University on 3 March 1975 where Burgess began by broadly stating that any state or governmental apparatus 'itself is possibly as good an example of evil as we will find in the world and it is all the more evil because it believes itself to be good' since the 'machine called the state, is not primarily concerned with anything except preserving itself with its own self-continuation'.[122] He goes on to explain to his American audience that he was not just simply 'digging at your president' because he 'would say the same about the Prime Minister of my own country and the President of my adopted country [Italy]', but rather his stance on this topic was directed by the belief 'that salvation does not belong in the divine vision, it does not belong in religion, it certainly does not belong with the state. It probably belongs with art because the artist does not promise, the artist delivers'.[123] What politicians were not drawn to, Burgess goes on to argue, was good honest, transcendent, and profound art because these types of works had subversive qualities to them. Conversely, politicians were drawn to 'bad art' since this quality served 'the purpose of over-simplification' for their 'over-simplified mind[s]', which is why, he gathered, it was rare to see politicians banning 'television soap operas' or 'the best sellers of Arthur Hailey or Harold Robbins', and instead tried to put 'out of circulation Vladimir Nabokov' since this writer's work always strove against 'a pure stasis of beauty', effectively complicating humans' perceptions of the world.[124] Finally, and perhaps most interesting about this polemic, is that Burgess goes on to briefly address his apolitical aesthetic motivations, admitting to feeling 'guilty sometimes because I'm not using my art for improving the world in the sense which politicians use it, but I feel that this residuum of pure beauty that ... may well be the one thing that will save us'.[125]

Writing in 'tercenart', an article employing a fictive future English language designed to show the degradation of the tongue over time, which was meant for the Arts and Leisure section of the *New York Times* but never published, Burgess imagines a narrator writing in 2076, the 300-year anniversary of the founding of the United States of America, celebrating and god blessing 'the triunited states of america, canada and mexico', with its 'final cracked fanfare to the republican principle' that has led to the 'forthcoming restoration of the monarchy and the reestablishment of the democratic actuality after decades of presidential abuse'.[126] The return to a monarchy is not a panacea, the imagined narrator warns, since the citizens of the United States will still need to 'anticipate new modes of jubilance and new concepts of treason', since corrupt leadership was unavoidable.[127] Thankfully, though, the text communicates, the restorative quality of art would 'continue in its unregenerable autonomy to celebrate only itself', because where art acts as an example of the 'ultimate freedom', and therefore 'the ultimate treason', it must also exist to challenge the current apparatuses of social control.[128] Articulating yet again the artist-versus-state/politician dichotomy, this piece provides another example of the kinds of unsolvable conflicts that drove so much of Burgess's fiction, because the ideas and philosophical underpinnings behind politics, ethics, and social issues mattered the most to him, not the ephemeral and protean political ideologies discussed by political parties. For this reason, throughout his entire life Burgess's fiction remained predominantly 'apolitical', while Burgess the public figure rarely ever discussed political parties and only publicly admonished politicians he felt were blatant unethical fools and/or miscreants. Socially and politically, what Burgess witnessed in the United States concerned him a great deal, and he had opinions on these matters, but this was never meant to be his admission to a particular brand of political thinking. To Burgess, what the United States needed was rationalism, rigidity, and a populace with minds open to the world. This was very unlikely to occur, he gathered, with the social conditions and thinking of the American populace he witnessed throughout his visits.

In a 1975 lecture at Clark University in Massachusetts, Burgess told his American audience that as they were approaching the 200-year anniversary of the country's founding in 1976, they should still keep their egos in check: 'As you gloat over your Bicentennial, remember that your country was founded by men who could not make it at home.'[129] This intentional oversimplification, and humorous reductionist perspective, is a reflection of Burgess's overarching view that the United States was a place unable to contend with worldly matters because it was a country populated by individuals given to flights of escapism and bent on insular thinking. Although likely expressed to get a laugh, Burgess could have more legitimately commented on the fact that, as Nancy Isenberg did masterfully in her 2016 book *White Trash: The 400-Year Untold History of Class in America*, Americans have always had a poor grasp on the history of the nation, especially its founding. This historical amnesia and inclination towards the romanticization of reality, she argues, is a reflection 'of the larger cultural impulse to forget – or at least gloss over – centuries of dodgy decisions, dubious measures, and outright failures'.[130] Although Americans' obliviousness to many of the world's realities was increasingly frustrating to Burgess, it was the country's higher education institutions, literary authors and scholars, and artistic communities – be that Broadway, Hollywood, or literary societies – that made it worth engaging with both financially and intellectually, despite its many shortcomings.

American language, reviews, and literature

In 1967, having visited the United States but before his close and continued relationship with the country had really begun, Burgess described himself as 'one of those sentimentalists who like to emphasize the unifying elements in British and American culture and turn a blind eye (this is known as the Nelson touch) [referring to the leadership style of the eighteenth-century British flag officer in the Royal Navy, Admiral Horatio Nelson (1758–1805)] to the divisive ones'.[131] Regardless of how much time Burgess spent in the United States, he frequently padded his persona as an outsider and a stateless expatriate bound to no place specific in order to emphasize that instead of being a man beholden to a country, he was a lover of ideas and aesthetics that were cosmopolitan in nature – this also provided him with distance and detachment which helped him avoid harsher criticisms. Regardless of his posturing as a non-committal wanderer, he was able, when travelling, to adopt a certain level of cultural identity to the point of acceptance, but it was never enough for him to be fully assimilated into any culture. This afforded Burgess the right to always plead his temporary status as a visitor who should not be taken too seriously in his observational convictions – especially when it came to the United States. Although examples abound of how he did this in multiple countries, in the United States this became a harder act to sell, since he found himself very much in the mainstream culture, and his hundreds of lectures in front of thousands of Americans for over a decade were far too much engagement for him to act as if he were only a temporary social commentator. In the same 1974 *Playboy* interview mentioned previously, after almost a decade of travelling around the United States and after having lived in New Jersey and New York for the better part of two years, Burgess presented this evasive technique by stating that he firmly held onto the cultural identity of an Englishman who had 'no place in America at all, except that I have an actual bond with America because we share a common culture', which he delineated as existing largely in the shape of the English language.[132] In what could be considered his seminal published article on the topic of American and British English, 'A Gift of Tongues: Ameringlish Isn't Britglish', published in the *New York Times* in September 1973, Burgess explores the differences between English usages from both sides of the Atlantic, a topic he also explored in his article 'Ameringlish Usage', a book review of John Simon's *Paradigms Lost: Reflections on Literacy in Decline* (1980) that tangles with the same content and is republished in *But Do Blondes Prefer Gentlemen?* (1986) as 'Ameringlish'. The genesis of Burgess's thoughts on these matters, though, comes earlier, at a lecture he gave at Duke University in spring 1973.[133]

On 17 April 1973, Burgess gave a lecture entitled 'British and Ameringlish' at Duke University in Durham, North Carolina, for the Blackburn Literary Festival, an experience memorialized in *You've Had Your Time* and *M/F*. An unpublished typescript entitled 'Neologism' at the International Anthony Burgess Foundation is actually a collection of about three separate articles which are believed to have been produced by Burgess for the Duke lecture and the subsequent *New York Times* article. The copy that exists is somewhat disorganized and possibly incomplete, having been broken up into several sections that do not necessarily form a cohesive whole. Existing in the document is a typescript of the article that appears in the *New York Times*, as well as a 'Postscript', possibly all meant to be completely separate but which have since been pushed together in the archive, that hands the literary English mantle over to Americans for the reason that the 'mother-country' had grown exhausted, whereas vitality was 'very much available in the rebellious daughter who has become the world's stepmother'.[134] More intriguing is the 9 September 1973 publication in the *New York Times*, 'A Gift of Tongues: Ameringlish Isn't Britglish' that analyses the American tongue, which repeats Burgess quips such as that because of their speech he always felt as if 'all Americans are well-educated, since none of them ever drops an aitch, even when mugging you – except in "herb" '.[135] Two main tenets of his approach to the American usage of English are that 'what is right for Ameringlish is not so for Britglish and vice versa', as well as what he claimed was the static and enduring quality of American English that had not 'hardly changed since 1620'.[136] Along with the Americanization of the world, and what he saw as the dissolving British international reputation, Burgess argued that the American use of English had become, without a doubt, 'the model of spoken English ... not despised and diminished Britain'.[137] But strange to Americans, he pondered, was that despite the ubiquitousness of American English, Americans still acted 'strangely provincal [sic], even colonial, in its lack of confidence in its own language', relenting, however seriously or not is unclear, that 'perhaps it would be wisest to take Alistair Cooke', the British-born American journalist, 'as the model speaker for Ameringlish, as opposed to Britglish'.[138] This supposed diffidence concerning the American tongue, Burgess laid out, brought along with it the singularly American 'difficulty in achieving a mode of converse which shall strike a mean between heavy formality and folksiness – there is a tendency for it to be either brutally and sentimentally colloquial or pentagonally grandiloquent'.[139] The paradoxical nature of Americans' use of their form of English led to further semantic disruptions due to the inharmonious and contradictory nature of the United States internationally popularizing the most predominant variation of English while also exhibiting the country's innate and insular parochial idiosyncrasies both in its language and its popular thought – a country fascinated with international popularity but whose other half despised the international community. Speaking to William F. Buckley Jr, the conservative public commentator and a man whose form of American English could be described as exceedingly ornate and eloquent, Burgess said that he had discerned among New Yorkers a use of language that was 'extremely vague' and 'extremely emotive'.[140] Assuming that, as is likely, this description of 'emotive' language is referring to African American English – which Burgess strongly admonished, calling it 'a tongue of deprivation' – and the vernacular of the young, Burgess is arguing that emotion and imprecision was polluting and altering what he believed were the admiring qualities of the vernacular.[141] His mocking depictions, glaringly monoglot in the sense that he is not attempting to achieve verisimilitude or empathetic portrayals, of these modes of speech are exhibited to some degree in all the books chosen for this monograph and will be discussed at length in the chapters that follow.

Mocking or not, outside of his novels Burgess publicly stated that he had not felt 'qualified to use the American language', believing that the

American use of English was distinctly separate lexically and orthoepically from the British English he utilized.[142] One such reason for this was that Burgess held the belief that beneath the colloquialisms of American English rested evidence of, symbolically, what it meant to be an American.[143] Burgess defined language or a vernacular as being 'a system of sounds made by the vocal organs of a particular group of people, possessing meaning for that group of people. And existing continuously for a given period of history', so to know about American usage was to see inside the American psyche.[144] The added emotion, the vagueness, and the diffidence swirling around on the American English tongue all fused together into a metaphorical semiotic hybrid that created a deeply insecure and fractious argot which provided its speakers not with a fear of language use but rather a fear of ideas. Whether it was the plebeian or the scholar, Burgess saw a lethargy of the mind being shaped out of a grammar that reflected this laxness. Taking into consideration the prescriptive desires of the American psyche, the laxness of tongue, and the insecurities towards engaging with complex ideas, Burgess upbraided Americans' fearfulness of words like '"communism" without giving themselves a chance to examine the referent of the term'.[145] A decade later, Burgess addressed this subject again in the epilogue of *1985* in which he interviewed himself, questioning the American understanding of the word and subsequently American English's equivocative semantics, prompting the more robust Burgessian-personae-interlocutor to rhetorically ask, 'Isn't the term communism a vague counter, all overtones and no fundamental note, in the minds of most Americans?' before patronizingly implying that Americans have nothing to worry about with communism since 'communism is what happens to Lower Slobovia, not the United States'.[146] Burgess was almost assuredly also conjuring up the popular Orwellian dictum from 'Politics and the English Language' (1946) that 'if thought corrupts language, language can also corrupt thought. A bad usage can spread by tradition and imitation even among people who should and do know better'.[147] Indeed, Burgess was and is still not incorrect in his criticisms, since many Americans even at the time of writing this monograph use the words 'communism' or 'socialism' as catch-all words for anything bad or distasteful without any knowledge of the etymologies or politico-economic concepts. It is this kind of irrational fear mixed with ignorance that embodied, and indeed enraptured, the American psyche as Burgess perceived it, as his *1985* persona summarizes these inclinations as being yet another side effect of a culture that tended towards 'pure verbalization, especially in public utterances' that lacked any actual substance, meaning, purpose, grounding, or awareness.[148]

Arrogance without erudition was once again exposed, this time intrinsically part of Ameringlish, a cognitive–lingual connection which simultaneously influenced the spread of Americanism that, evoking Orwell yet again in the meaninglessness of certain words such as 'democracy', Burgess repined was 'bad in that it is fundamentally hypocritical. Talk of the "free world" often means an obsession with American security, American trade, the augmentation of an American-led community dedicated to more and more feverish material consumption; it does not necessarily mean the spread of democratic rights'.[149] It was especially for this reason that Burgess lashed out at such types of dissemination because 'America, transmitting her power through the world, pretends that she is crusading; this is the unforgivable hypocrisy'.[150] Thankfully, though, Burgess admitted, certain American writers fought against the slippery slope of Americanization through the laxness of the American tongue which help proliferate the potentially harmful myths of the United States, making the claim in 1972 that writers such as Norman Mailer and Saul Bellow had 'slapped the American tongue back to life after a long period of sentimental or demagogic or journalistic devitalization', which was only slowed down by the 'beat whiners' who had rhapsodized 'loosely, making poetry a new kind of demagogic noise, while the older poets shaped, chiselled and saw there was still much to learn from the past'.[151] It was apparently up to these writers, and writers like Burgess who criticized these trends in the American tongue, to keep the language sharp, accurate, and meaningful because it risked being swept away by the incessant vagaries occurring in the American popular public realm of speech. It was, Burgess decried, also up to immigrants to assimilate to the American way of life, which very much included language, to fulfil the purpose of immigration and to live by the American code of conduct.[152]

In 1962, when *A Clockwork Orange* was published, Burgess also recalled that it was Americans, not the British, who best understood the book and upon publication found a larger audience, though still relatively small, reflecting in 1991 on *The Larry King Show* that 'in England they thought it was a kind of a feast of violence, but, the American critics I read seemed to think that it was a kind of, you know, a deeper moral meaning about free will'.[153] Later into 1977, though, Burgess had apparently thoroughly had enough of the severe criticism from both reviewers in England and the United States when he sharpened his counterattack in the May 1977 *Chicago Tribune* article 'A Writer Snarls Back at Critics'. In the article Burgess not only provides an enumerated list of questions that critics should be able to answer if they desire to be an effective critic, but he also focuses on his own experience as a critic in order to give advice, not without first picking out individual papers and articles to direct his rage. He goes after three American papers directly, citing 'the snarls of the Kalamazoo Courier, the condescension of the North Charleston Examiner [these first two apparently being fictional], [and] the qualified laudations of the Cleveland Plain Dealer', as well as pointing out two that provided positive or hyperbolic reviews of the novel which included the 'praise of Time, the enthusiasm of Newsweek, the hysteria of The Village Voice'.[154] The most damning comment cuts to the heart of Burgess's never-ending concern with the United States that until 1977 he had often diluted, and that was his utter disdain for much of the United States, the majority really, since it could not achieve the level of high culture, intelligence, reasonableness, and compassion he sought in a society, by moving to single out 'reviewers in Oregon, the Dakotas, Nevada, and other territories far from the heart of culture [viz. the vertical Europe which is Manhattan]', and it is mainly for this group, those outside of culture, that Burgess delves into his 'elementary tips' for being a constructive and helpful reviewer.[155] Due to the severity of such a retort, in many ways 1977 could be seen as the year in which Burgess's relationship with the United States began to sour irretrievably, just a decade after he first visited, so that his initial poor opinions of the country had in fact come full circle.

Despite having severely reduced his visits towards the last decade of his life and harbouring many disparaging views of American culture into the mid 1980s, Burgess never quite lost his interest in American authors. He even rationalized his interest in the United States by associating the country with authors and ideas he revered by situating British authors with American experiences, however ludicrously or inaccurately. Repeated on multiple occasions in books, journalism, and interviews, Burgess argued that the tongue of Shakespeare was indeed the tongue of American English; not wholly inaccurate but definitely an oversimplification.[156]

Attempting to predict changes in American English in 2067, Burgess argued that the American dialect of English would take over as the English lingua franca in large part due to his idea that although the United States was a 'progressive country', 'American speech is highly conservative. One cannot imagine its being very different a century – or even two centuries – from now', which existed as his support linking Shakespeare to the United States: 'English spoken four years after Shakespeare's death – by the Pilgrim Fathers of 1620 – that still provides the phonetic norm for these United States'.[157] Similarly, in 1970, Burgess went further with this supposed link between the playwright and country by deploying contemporary language usages as examples for the connection, explaining that 'Shakespeare died four years before the landing on Plymouth Rock', therefore making 'him a pillar of American culture', especially in the sense that Shakespeare's 'language, especially in its pronunciation (as I've tried to demonstrate all over the Union), is far closer to Nixonian or Black Panther English than to the dialect of Elizabeth II'.[158] In rooting Shakespeare with the United States, this provided Burgess a cultural bridge, a tactic he frequently employed with other writers in order to adjust and construct a mythical lineage between him and greatness – whether it was the Joyce, Ireland, and Irish/Scottish Burgess/Finnegan heritage he conflated, the Lawrence, Nottinghamshire, and Manchester parallel, Shakespeare and the United States, Burgess and the United States, or any other less blatant examples.[159] Doing so afforded Burgess the possibility not only of inserting himself into an overall literary mythos but also of infusing himself into his own literary topos with less friction, advantageously confirming on one instance in 1989 that literary characters 'are always fragments of the personality of the creator. Is Hamlet Shakespeare? Yes. So is Anthony'.[160]

To muddy the authorial waters even further, in attempting to produce layers of myth between author, characters, and author-figure, Burgess declared on various occasions that notwithstanding these connections in cultural lineage and universal characterizations, 'A novel is written by a persona, whatever that is. That's why I don't write poetry – it's much too naked. I'd rather hide behind somebody. That's the difference between a poet and a novelist: the novelist hides behind people, the poet comes out pretty directly.'[161] Erecting these facades that separate Burgess from his characters is a weak attempt to distance himself from some of the biographical similarities that lie just barely under the surface, and any reader even vaguely aware of Burgess's life can easily see the sources of illumination behind such projections. Even so, the barriers, and the slight distortions written into them, afford Burgess some degrees of separation that shielded, and shield, him from accusations of libel, catharsis, and straight biography. Ironically, and contradictorily, when analyzing other authors' works, he admitted that 'books stem out of some great personal agony – and the book itself was an attempt to exorcise, cathartise and so forth', all while claiming that his own work did not play by the same rules he set out for other authors.[162] This is essentially posturing, and part of the authorial image that Burgess plays with – playful or not, he was also all too cognizant of the real-world consequences that could stem from how he handled his biographical, historical, fictional, and literary projections and images. By producing a kind of transworld dialogue that exists between transworld identities, Burgess effectively crafts for himself a mythic status that aligned his own writing with literary icons and vast cultural history, and both admitted authorial inspiration and denounced autobiographical elements. This pattern of dialogic play, metanarratives, and transworld identities began to reach their apotheoses, although having always been present in Burgess's writings, during the years when he started spending a significant amount of time in the United States.

Notwithstanding Burgess's Shakespearean English approximation to American English, in his 1964 non-fiction book on language, *Language Made Plain*, Burgess expresses his fear and hostility towards Americans' use of English. Admitting that the 'world is shrinking' and 'supra-national communities are being painfully forged' due to the increasing travel of peoples between countries and continents, Burgess's argument for the book is that learning others' languages will become a necessity despite the ubiquitous spread of English, particularly American English.[163] Wasting little time to admonish contemporary American English, Burgess asserts that he has 'very powerful prejudices about what I call Americanisms' because he saw in American neologisms the 'essence of Americanism', which he believed was 'a threat to the British Way of Life'.[164] He goes on to admit that such a fear is 'obviously nonsense' because of the irrationality in fearing English usage, like the phrase, 'I guess', which Burgess estimated was likely 'at least as old as Chaucer, pure British English, something sent over in the *Mayflower*'.[165] Even so, he decides sardonically to reject 'reason' in preference for 'blind prejudice' by internalizing the use of such a phrase 'as a betrayal of the traditions of my national group'.[166] Again, much like Orwell's proclamations in 'Politics and the English Language', it's not necessarily that Burgess merely feared the use of silly phrases being incorporated into the British lexicon but rather that these turns of phrase stood as examples of poor quality of thought which consequently had the likelihood of deteriorating language's main role as being accurate and evocative, a fear intrinsically aligned with the United States's cultural power over the rest of the world. Further on in *Language Made Plain*, Burgess explains why he believes Americans do not adopt British terms but Brits adopt American terms, stating that this is an effect of the fact that 'the propaganda traffic is one-way: eastwards'.[167]

The United States therefore, to Burgess, did not simply corrupt language but also corrupted thought via a pathway of lexical subversiveness. But the danger did not stop here for Burgess; evoking patterns of similarities between his comments on language use and what occurs to the characters in *One Hand Clapping* (1961), American English, he asserts, is coupled with American capitalism and consumerism. Going hand in hand, he saw this corrosive infiltration as occurring almost subliminally through the most popular medium of the 1960s: television. He depicted England as a subservient and willing consumer of a degenerative culture that 'gladly buys American' despite the fact that 'Americans have to be persuaded to reciprocate'.[168] Brits, Burgess argues, sacrifice their culture in order to pander to the economic whims of the American superpower by creating television shows 'designed with an American audience in view' and with British actors who have 'to portray American characters, even when the locale is British; or else American actors are imported to fill traditionally British rôles'.[169]

Conspiratorially or presciently, Burgess saw this type of cultural exchange as being a way for the United States to pave 'the way for the ultimate victory of American phonemes and American usage. ... It is not really possible to resist such process, however hard the forces of conservatism or inertia dump their dead weight on the threshold'.[170] The United States was both a country and culture to be feared by Burgess's estimations, and yet Americanization was a force that was somewhat futile to resist, which was likely a reason he succumbed to spending so much time in the United States – he recognized that what the country offered him and his career far outweighed the more pernicious and global issues it presented. Indeed, much of the fault that lied in the allure of the United States was due to how Burgess perceived England and its many faults. The malaise of British culture, the lack of literary experimentation, taxes, and the treatment of its writers, specifically Burgess, were some of the main reasons that Burgess turned to the United States and why many of his characters also see the country as the shining example of opportunity.

Published in 1986, Burgess's novel *The Pianoplayers* envisions an early twentieth-century Blackpool, England, which closely resembles the city of Manchester in which Burgess was born, with characters that are clearly inspired by his childhood. The United States shows up yet again, distant but as a symbol of escape and possibility for Ellen Henshaw's father when he dreamily waxes upon the idea that the family could

> go to the States, that's what we'll do. We'll go to America, others have done it before us, as a matter of fact the States was made by people like you and me, not satisfied with the life back here. We'll go to the States and we'll make a fresh start.[171]

For Burgess, in the 1960s, this sentiment must have been felt too because that is exactly what he did. Not only this, but Burgess was also dissatisfied with British society and literary production, and in the United States there was the possibility to reinvent himself and be noticed both monetarily and aesthetically for the literary craftsman that he had become.

Burgess was not the only one interested in American literary pursuits; he makes the claim on a litany of occasions that Britain as a whole was 'jealous of the North American achievement in literature south of the Great Lakes and the 49th Parallel' and beyond.[172] Burgess was taking notice of the advances being made by American writers, and as an author he wanted to be a part of this change. That being said, Burgess still saw many faults in the American approach to, and glorification of, the literary arts. At one point, in 1973, he criticized two of the United States's predominant modernist authors, F. Scott Fitzgerald and Ernest Hemingway, by stating that he didn't 'think Fitzgerald's books [were] great – style too derivatively romantic, far less of that curious freshness of vision than you find in Hemingway', arguing that although Hemingway was 'a great novelist ... he never wrote a great novel (a great novella, yes)', going on to criticize the Americans' reception to literature, stating that the failure of these great writers to produce great work did not matter because 'America likes its artists to die young, in atonement for materialist America's sins'.[173] By the mid 1980s, Burgess felt that England had overcompensated in its desire to catch up with the American literary machine, arguing in an interview in 1985 that the British were too influenced by the United States, causing England to become 'regarded as an outpost of America'.[174] Regardless of this, Burgess was inspired by American productivity, applauded many of its advances in the arts, and took advantage of the monetary benefits that becoming popular in the United States bequeathed upon its contributors; he was tempted by the prospects of becoming an *American* author, but this was something that could never have been achieved for various philosophical, geographical, and personal reasons. In the same interview quoted above, Burgess admits that he had been enticed on many occasions to come back to the United States after he left several permanent residences in the early 1970s, saying that the United States is 'an extension of my own country. ... I've always been tempted to become an American author, but I probably left it to too late [sic]. I shall probably die by the Mediterranean, not by the Hudson'.[175] In a 1975 interview with Don Crinklaw in the *St. Louis Post-Dispatch*, Burgess admitted that he had always felt that he had never 'been part of a culture and must spend the rest of my life looking for one', though he, however honestly, guessed that if he had found a culture to assimilate with, it would have been either the United States or Canada, because like Crabbe, both the character and the author wanted 'to be wanted', and it was in North America where Burgess was reciprocated the most in this desire.[176] The problem, Burgess explains further, was that American culture specifically, or 'Anglo-American culture', was an imposing and materialistic culture, a characteristic that would eventually repel Burgess from the United States in the mid 1980s.[177]

Conclusion

Burgess's intrigue with the United States began with the ubiquitous and invasive nature of its culture, but what kept him returning throughout the 1960s and 1970s, and even 1980s and 1990s, was that 'American authors earn more' and 'are given sinecures in universities', and Burgess was happy to partake in such a system, believing that, after having worked in the United States 'off and on, for the last eight years', it was honestly 'the country where the English language will come to its finest flower, chiefly because the conditions for writing books are a little more propitious than they are in England'.[178] The constant unrest in American streets, cities, and campuses was an added bonus, since there was so much to think about, but eventually all these factors became oppressive instead of inspirational as Burgess aged.[179] What deterred him was not just his failing health into the mid to late 1980s but seemingly the United States's short attention span, franticness, ignorance, apathy, and provincialism, as well as its inability to learn from its mistakes and broaden its perspective regarding its place in the world. Reflecting on his time in the United States while writing *You've Had Your Time* (1990), he recalls that 'there had been a time when America knew me as a writer; it did not take long to be forgotten'.[180]

While living and working in the United States, Burgess believed the country provided writers with valuable ideas to write about, and it was all the better that this source material was harboured in a culture that he felt appreciated, supported, and cultivated its writers. The same, of course, could not be said of England. Although the United States was the country Burgess needed for his intellectual, pedagogical, and aesthetic interests to be fed, it was not the country he was to call home or where he would become fully assimilated, largely because the United States was just too foreign, too loud, too fast for him – good for inspiration but not for the act of writing.[181] Such a general distaste for the country is even felt across the extensive and multi-modal/voiced oeuvre of Burgess's American commentaries, where he is intrigued enough to respond and use the miseries of the United States for writing fodder, but not interested enough in the scholarly sense to fully understand and engage with the myriad of topics he glints upon in his various fiction and non-fiction and private and public texts and utterances. And in the late 1970s it is clear that Burgess had grown weary of the United States, as evidenced by his marked decrease in the time he spent there, firmly solidifying his identity and legacy as a predominantly European writer who was strongly influenced by the United States, so much so that the country popped up everywhere in his work as a fascination and *idée fixe* that kept on feeding his artistic mind, but only as a far-off muse that delivered writing fodder when needed.[182]

Notes

1 Anthony Burgess, Standard Diary 1964, Sunday 5 July, International Anthony Burgess Foundation Archives.

2 Mikhail Bakhtin, *Rabelais and His World*, ed. by Helene Iswolsky (Bloomington, IN: Indiana University Press, 1984), p. 160.

3 'Author Discusses Novel', *The Ohio State Lantern*, 2 February 1973, para. 7; Anthony Burgess, *Conversations with Anthony Burgess*, ed. by Earl Ingersoll and Mary Ingersoll (Jackson, MS: University Press of Mississippi, 2008), p. 78.
4 Burgess, *Conversations with Anthony Burgess*, p. 21.
5 Burgess, *Conversations with Anthony Burgess*, p. 140.
6 Burgess, *Conversations with Anthony Burgess*, p. 140.
7 Quoted in Paul Boytinck, *Anthony Burgess: An Annotated Bibliography and Reference Guide* (New York: Garland Publishing, 1985), p. 25.
8 Anthony Burgess, *The Novel Now* (London: Faber & Faber, 1971), p. 204.
9 Burgess, *Conversations with Anthony Burgess*, p. 93.
10 William Manley, interview with Christopher Thurley, 6 December 2017, telephone.
11 'Interview with Anthony Burgess', *The Dick Cavett Show*, ABC Television Network: Daphne Productions and Rollins & Joffe Productions, 3 December 1980.
12 Norman Mailer, *Armies of the Night: History as a Novel/The Novel as History* (New York: Plume, 1968; 1994); Charles DeBenedetti and Charles Chatfield, *An American Ordeal: The Antiwar Movement of the Vietnam Era* (Syracuse, NY: Syracuse University Press, 1990); Tom Wells, *The War Within* (Berkeley, CA: University of California Press, 1994); Adam Garfinkle, *Telltale Hearts: The Origins and Impact of the Vietnam Antiwar Movement* (New York: St. Martin's Press, 1995).
13 Anthony Burgess, 'The Young', *The Firing Line*, Southern Educational Communications Association, 21/31 December 1972, University of Buffalo Archives; Anthony Burgess, 'A Candid Interview with the Author of *A Clockwork Orange*', interview with Katherine Pritchard, *Seventeen*, 32.8, August 1973.
14 Howard Zinn, *A People's History of the United States* (New York: Harper Perennial – Modern Classics, 1980; 2003), p. 490. While reading commentary from Zinn about the United States, it is important to understand criticisms to his (in)famous narrative as well: 'Like traditional textbooks, *A People's History* relies almost entirely on secondary sources, with no archival research to thick its narrative. Like traditional textbooks, the book is naked of footnotes, thwarting inquisitive readers who seek to retrace the author's interpretative steps. And, like students' textbooks, when *A People's History* draws on primary sources, these documents serve to prop up the main text, but never provide an alternative view to open up a new field of vision' (Sam Wineburg, 'Undue Certainty: Where Howard Zinn's *A People's History* Falls Short', *American Educator* (Winter 2012–13), 28).
15 Zinn, *A People's History*, p. 490.
16 Anthony Burgess, *You've Had Your Time: Being the Second Part of the Confessions of Anthony Burgess* (London: Penguin Books, 1990), p. 204.
17 Anthony Burgess, 'Letter from Europe', *The American Scholar*, 39.3 (Summer 1970), 503.
18 Anthony Burgess, 'Letter from Europe', *American Scholar*, 38.4 (Autumn 1969), 684.

19 Burgess, *You've Had Your Time*, p. 275.
20 Burgess, 'Letter from Europe' (Autumn 1969), p. 685.
21 Burgess, *You've Had Your Time*, p. 278; Burgess, 'Letter from Europe' (Autumn 1969), p. 685.
22 Jean-Paul Sartre, *Being and Nothingness* (New York: Washington Square Press, 1943; 1993); Anthony Burgess, *On the Novel* (Manchester: International Anthony Burgess Foundation, 1975; 2019), p. 62.
23 Anthony Burgess, 'Thoughts on Excellence', *Excellence: The Pursuit, the Commitment, the Achievement* (Washington, DC: LTV Corporation, 1981), p. 103.
24 Burgess, 'Thoughts on Excellence', pp. 102–104.
25 Burgess, 'Thoughts on Excellence', p. 26.
26 Anthony Burgess, 'The People Are Decent Enough: The Trouble with Americans', *New York Times*, 4 July 1971, para. 2; Mailer, *Armies of the Night*, p. 188.
27 Anthony Burgess, 'Cynical about the Great Words', *Conversations with Anthony Burgess*, p. 29: 'This supercession of god, especially by an ego-driven rationality which itself threatens to become god-like (or *übermensch* in Nietzschean terms) is the Apollonian stance. From it stems the impulse to improve upon the world that manifests as Apollonian art, in which man is forced to assume the responsibilities of a divinity and recreate the world so as to improve upon nature' (Jim Clarke, *The Aesthetics of Anthony Burgess: Fire of Words* (Cham: Palgrave Macmillan, 2017), p. 72).
28 Kent Puckett, *Narrative Theory: A Critical Introduction* (Cambridge: Cambridge University Press, 2016), p. 15.
29 Anthony Lewis and Anthony Burgess, '"I Love England, But I Will No Longer Live There"', *New York Times*, 3 November 1968, p. 57; A.E. Dyson, 'Culture and Anarchy, 1869; 1969', *Critical Quarterly*, March 1969; Brian Cox, 'A. E. Dyson, 1928–2002', *Critical Quarterly*, 45.1–2 (16 September 2002), pp. v–vi.
30 Anthony Burgess, 'The Purpose of Education', *Spectator*, 3 March 1967, p. 11.
31 Burgess, 'Letter from Europe' (Autumn 1969), p. 685.
32 Burgess, 'Letter from Europe' (Autumn 1969), p. 685.
33 Burgess, 'Letter from Europe' (Autumn 1969), p. 686.
34 Burgess, 'Letter from Europe' (Autumn 1969), p. 686; Burgess, 'The Purpose of Education', p. 11.
35 Brigid Brophy, 'American Policies in Vietnam', *The Times*, 2 February 1967; *Authors Take Sides on Vietnam*, ed. by Cecil Woof and John Bagguley (New York: Simon and Schuster, 1967), pp. 19, 25.
36 *Authors Take Sides on Vietnam*, pp. 34, 36.
37 Lewis and Burgess, '"I Love England, But I Will No Longer Live There"', p. 53.
38 'Interview with Anthony Burgess', *The Dick Cavett Show*.
39 Lewis and Burgess, '"I Love England, But I Will No Longer Live There"', p. 53.
40 Lewis and Burgess, '"I Love England, But I Will No Longer Live There"', p. 53.
41 Andrew Biswell, *The Real Life of Anthony Burgess* (London: Picador, 2005), pp. 103–104; Anthony Burgess, 'Letter from Europe' (Autumn 1969), p. 684;

Anthony Burgess, 'Thoughts on the Thoughts', *Spectator*, 219 (15 September 1967), p. 298.
42 Mailer, *Armies of the Night*, p. 156.
43 Burgess, 'Letter from Europe' (Autumn 1969), p. 684.
44 Burgess, 'Letter from Europe' (Autumn 1969), p. 684.
45 Burgess, 'The Young', p. 1.
46 Burgess, 'A Candid Interview with the Author of *A Clockwork Orange*', p. 236.
47 Burgess, 'A Candid Interview with the Author of *A Clockwork Orange*', p. 236.
48 Burgess, 'A Candid Interview with the Author of *A Clockwork Orange*', p. 236.
49 Anthony Burgess, 'My Dear Students; a Letter', *New York Times*, 19 November 1972, p. 22.
50 Barbara Lekatsas, interview with Christopher Thurley, 9 March 2019, telephone.
51 Horace A. Porter, 'To Do One's Thinking, or Think One's Doing', *New York Times*, 24 December 1972.
52 Anthony Burgess, 'Dressing for Dinner in the Jungle', *Conversations with Anthony Burgess*, p. 88.
53 Anthony Burgess, 'The Two Shaws', *Spectator*, 14 May 1965, p. 67.
54 Burgess, *On the Novel*, p. 62.
55 Mikhail Bakhtin, *The Dialogic Imagination: Four Essays*, ed. by Michael Holquist, trans. by Caryl Emerson and Michael Holquist (Austin, TX: University of Texas Press, 1981), p. 339.
56 Peter Kunigk, 'Burgess on His Art: Writers in "Bad Way"', *The Lafayette*, 6 April 1973, p. 6.
57 Boytinck, *Anthony Burgess*, p. 24.
58 Burgess, 'Cynical about the Great Words', p. 24.
59 Quoted in M.R. Jr Knickerbocker, 'Anthony Burgess to Speak at Rockhurst', *News from Rockhurst College*, n.d., Kansas City, MO, p. 3.
60 Mikhail Bakhtin, *Problems of Dostoyevsky's Poetics*, ed. by Caryl Emerson, Theory and History of Literature, volume 8 (Minneapolis, MN: University of Minnesota, 1984), p. 187.
61 Anthony Burgess, *A Vision of Battlements* (New York: W.W. Norton, 1965), p. 155.
62 Anthony Burgess, *The Worm and the Ring* (Brighton: William Heinemann, 1961; 1970), p. 175.
63 Anthony Burgess, 'Ah, Liberty', International Anthony Burgess Foundation Archive, 1986, p. 5.
64 Bakhtin, *Problems of Dostoyevsky's Poetics*, p. 202.
65 Saul Bellow, *Henderson the Rain King* (London: Penguin, 1959); Gore Vidal, *Myra Breckinridge* and *Myron* (New York: Knopf, 1968; 1987); Philip Roth, *My Life as a Man* (New York: Rinehart, and Winston, 1974), p. 212.
66 Bakhtin, *Dialogic Imagination*, p. 287.
67 Rodney A. Smolla, 'The Life of the Mind and a Life of Meaning: Reflections on *Fahrenheit 451*', *Michigan Law Review*, 107.895 (April 2009), p. 907.
68 'Interview with Anthony Burgess', *The Dick Cavett Show*; 'We are all made of what we read, hear and see, and what we read, hear and see had better be

good; else we are in trouble. We may conceivably put to rule over us a President whose image we first encountered in a B film [Ronald Reagan] (not a production of *Hamlet*) and whose simplistic characterisations we identify with reality. Reality is not *Dallas*, but we are in danger of wanting reality to be *Dallas* because of our hankering after simplicity. Life, of course, is far from simple' (Anthony Burgess, 'Cardboard Character', *TV Guide*, 1982, unpublished; IABF Archive, p. 3).

69 Burgess, 'Cardboard Character', p. 1.

70 Burgess, 'Cardboard Character', p. 2.

71 While at Rockhurst University in Missouri on Sunday 2 November 1975, after taking a question concerning this *Playboy* interview, Burgess explained that the interviewer, C. Robert Jennings, had misrepresented him and 'was conducted by a very pleasant young man from Harvard, who was ill. He was suffering from nephritis and his wife had just left him, probably because he had nephritis, and he was worried to death about his situation at the time, and I knew it could not be a satisfactory interview, moreover, the mail service in Italy was not functioning, it was impossible for any American to write to me in Italy, as he could have done and sent to me what he had written, and said "Is this right?" So the thing went out unchecked and some ridiculous statements were made, which I did not. … I've never been reported totally accurately' ('Anthony Burgess to Discuss "The Use of Art" ', Rockhurst University – The Roy A. Roberts Visiting Scholar Lecture – 2 November 1975). Contradicting this to some extent, Liana noted in a letter that despite the 'rather revolting and sleek masturbatory pictures they publish rather good and important interviews. One of the most serious depth interviews with Anthony was published in *Playboy*' (Liana Burgess, Letter to Francisco (Paco) Porrua, 19 March 1978, series II, correspondence, 1956–97: University of Texas at Austin: Harry Ransom Center, Anthony Burgess Papers, 78.1–5); Anthony Burgess, 'Playboy Interview: Anthony Burgess; a Candid Conversation', *Playboy*, 21.9 (September 1974), p. 84.

72 Burgess, 'Playboy Interview', p. 84.

73 Burgess, 'Playboy Interview', p. 84; Anthony Burgess, Letter to Geoffrey Aggeler, 10 October 1969, International Anthony Burgess Foundation.

74 Clifford Geertz, *The Interpretation of Cultures* (New York: Basic Books, 1973), p. 5.

75 Anthony Burgess, *1985* (London: Beautiful Books, 1978; 2010), p. 64.

76 Anthony Burgess, *New York* (Amsterdam: Time-Life, 1976), p. 76.

77 Peter Biskind, *Easy Riders, Raging Bulls: How the Sex-Drugs-and-Rock 'N' Roll Generation Saved Hollywood* (New York: Simon and Schuster, 1998), p. 17.

78 Biskind, *Easy Riders, Raging Bulls*, p. 125.

79 Jon Meacham, *The Soul of America: The Battle for Our Better Angels* (New York: Penguin Random House, 2018).

80 Burgess, 'Thoughts on Excellence', p. 78.

81 Anthony Burgess, 'Is America Falling Apart?', *New York Times*, 7 November 1971, para. 8.

82 Anthony Burgess, 'Artist's Life', *One Man's Chorus: The Uncollected Writings of Anthony Burgess*, ed. by Ben Forkner (New York: Carroll & Graf, 1998),

p. 209; Hugh Brogan, *The Penguin History of the USA* (London: Penguin Group, 1999), p. 588.

83 Anthony Burgess, *The Clockwork Testament; or, Enderby's End* (London: Hart-Davis, MacGibbon, 1974, p. 18).

84 Anthony Burgess, 'A Trip to Washington', February 1981, Harry Ransom Center Archive, p. 4.

85 Mailer, *Armies of the Night*, p. 188.

86 Zinn, *A People's History of the United States.*

87 Burgess, *1985*, p. 64.

88 Anthony Burgess, Letter to Max Steele, 3 February 1970. TS. Lija, Malta (Letters to Anthony Burgess. Max Steele Papers. The Louis Round Wilson Special Collections Library. Southern Historical Collection. University of North Carolina at Chapel Hill).

89 Sinclair Lewis, *It Can't Happen Here* (New York: Signet Classics, 2014; 1935), p. 373.

90 Lewis, *It Can't Happen Here*, p. 373.

91 'National Survey Finds Just 1 in 3 Americans Would Pass Citizenship Test', Woodrow Wilson National Fellowship Foundation, 3 October 2018, https://woodrow.org/news/national-survey-finds-just-1-in-3–americans-would-pass-citizenship-test

92 Hunter S. Thompson, *Fear and Loathing on the Campaign Trail '72* (New York: Simon and Schuster, 1973; 2012).

93 Burgess, *1985*, p. 219; Thompson, *Fear and Loathing on the Campaign Trail '72*, p. 442.

94 Burgess, *1985*, p. 219.

95 Michael Holquist, *Dialogism: Bakhtin and His World* (London: Routledge, 1990), p. 68.

96 Bakhtin, *Problems of Dostoyevsky's Poetics*, p. 5.

97 Max Saunders, *Self Impression: Life-Writing, Autobiografiction, and the Forms of Modern Literature* (Oxford: Oxford University Press, 2010); Burgess, 'A Candid Interview with the Author of *A Clockwork Orange*'; Carol Rumens, 'Poem of the Week: To Vladimir Nabokov … by Anthony Burgess', *The Guardian*, 19 April 2021, www.theguardian.com/books/2021/apr/19/poem-of-the-week-to-vladimir-nabokov-by-anthony-burgess; Anthony Burgess, *Collected Poems*, ed. by Jonathan Mann (Manchester: Carcanet, 2020).

98 Philippe LeJeune, *On Autobiography*, ed. by Paul John Eakin, trans. by Katherine Leary (Minneapolis, MN: University of Minnesota Press, 1989), p. 126.

99 Jerome Boyd Maunsell, 'Literary Interview as Autobiography', *The European Journal of Life Writing*, 5 (2016), p. 3

100 Robert McLaughlin quoted in Gary Scharnhorst, 'Afterword', *It Can't Happen Here*, p. 386.

101 Burgess, 'The People Are Decent Enough', para. 5.

102 Burgess, 'Is America Falling Apart?', para. 21.

103 Thompson, *Fear and Loathing on the Campaign Trail '72*, pp. 468–469.

104 'The English author Anthony Burgess', *NRK TV* (16 October 1981), https://tv.nrk.no/program/FOLA02008681
105 Keith Runyon, 'Burgess on Burgess: "Clockwork Orange" Author Tells How He Ticks', *The Courier-Journal*, 24 April 1973, para. 29.
106 Burgess, *The Clockwork Testament; or, Enderby's End*, p. 124.
107 Anthony Burgess, *The Great Cities – New York* (Amsterdam: Time-Life Books, 1976), p. 161.
108 Anthony Burgess, 'One of the Minor Joys ...', 1972, International Anthony Burgess Foundation Archive, para. 5.
109 Burgess, 'One of the Minor Joys ...', para. 5.
110 Burgess, 'Playboy Interview', p. 84.
111 Allan Bloom, *The Closing of the American Mind* (New York: Simon and Schuster, 1987), p. 33.
112 Anthony Burgess, Letter to John Cullinan, St. Lawrence University, 16 June 1971, University of Texas at Austin: Harry Ransom Center Archives, box 82; John Cullinan, Letter to Anthony Burgess, 12 February 1971, St. Lawrence University Canton, New York, University of Texas at Austin: Harry Ransom Center Archives, box 82; Anthony Burgess, 'The Art of Fiction', *Paris Review*, ed. by John Cullinan, 1973 (2005), p. 157; 'The English author Anthony Burgess'.
113 Anthony Burgess, 'The Royals', *One Man's Chorus: The Uncollected Writings of Anthony Burgess*, ed. by Ben Forkner (New York: Carroll & Graf, 1998), p. 103.
114 Anthony Burgess quoted in Jeff Kindler, 'Burgess: The Artist Delivers', *Observer*, Tufts University, 7 March 1975, p. 4.
115 Anthony Burgess quoted in Kindler, 'Burgess', p. 4.
116 Anthony Burgess, 'O Lord, O Ford, God Help Us, Also You', *New York Times*, 29 December 1974, para. 2.
117 Burgess, 'O Lord, O Ford, God Help Us, Also You', para. 1.
118 Burgess, 'O Lord, O Ford, God Help Us, Also You', para. 2.
119 Burgess, 'O Lord, O Ford, God Help Us, Also You', para. 2.
120 Burgess, 'O Lord, O Ford, God Help Us, Also You', para. 5; Mikhail Bakhtin, 'Discourse in the Novel', *The Dialogic Imagination*, p. 291.
121 Burgess, 'O Lord, O Ford, God Help Us, Also You', para. 3.
122 Anthony Burgess, Lecture at Tufts University, Tufts University, 4 March 1975.
123 Burgess, Lecture at Tufts University.
124 Burgess, Lecture at Tufts University.
125 Burgess, Lecture at Tufts University.
126 Anthony Burgess, 'Tercenart', International Anthony Burgess Archive, pp. 1–2.
127 Burgess, 'Tercenart', pp. 2–3.
128 Burgess, 'Tercenart', pp. 2–3.
129 Anthony Burgess quoted in John White, 'Thus Spoke the Novelist', *The Scarlet*, Clark University, 18 April 1975, para. 4.
130 Nancy Isenberg, *White Trash: The 400-Year Untold History of Class in America* (New York: Penguin Books, 2016), p. 12.
131 Anthony Burgess, 'Don't Cook Mother Goose', *New York Times*, 5 November 1967, para. 1.

132 Burgess, 'Playboy Interview', p. 82.
133 Anthony Burgess, 'A Gift of Tongues: Ameringlish Isn't Britglish', *New York Times*, 9 September 1973; Anthony Burgess, 'Ameringlish', *But Do Blondes Prefer Gentlemen? Homage to Qwert Yuiop and Other Writings* (New York: McGraw-Hill Book Company, 1986), pp. 211–214; Anthony Burgess, 'Ameringlish Usage', *New York Times*, 20 July 1980; 'The Man Who Made "A Clockwork Orange" Tick: Anthony Burgess', *The Chronicle*, 16 April 1973, p. 9.
134 Anthony Burgess, 'Neologism' (unpublished, International Anthony Burgess Archive, 1973), p. 1.
135 Burgess, 'A Gift of Tongues', para. 2.
136 Burgess, 'Ameringlish Usage', para. 5; 'Interview with Anthony Burgess', *The Dick Cavett Show*, ABC Television Network: Daphne Productions and Rollins & Joffe Productions, 1 April 1971.
137 Burgess, 'A Gift of Tongues', para. 11.
138 Burgess, 'A Gift of Tongues', para. 11.
139 Burgess, 'A Gift of Tongues', para. 10.
140 Burgess, 'The Young', p. 6.
141 Burgess, 'Ameringlish Usage', para. 2.
142 Burgess, 'Dressing for Dinner in the Jungle', p. 99.
143 Burgess, 'Dressing for Dinner in the Jungle', p. 99.
144 Anthony Burgess, *English Literature* (Hong Kong: Longman Group, 1958; 1974; 1979), pp. 12–13.
145 Anthony Burgess, 'Politics in the Novels of Graham Greene', *Urgent Copy: Literary Studies* (New York: W.W. Norton, 1968), p. 17.
146 Burgess, *1985*, p. 226.
147 George Orwell, 'Politics and the English Language', *Horizon*, April 1946, p. 174.
148 Burgess, *1985*, p. 226.
149 Orwell, 'Politics and the English Language', p. 169; Burgess, 'Politics in the Novels of Graham Greene', p. 17.
150 Burgess, 'Politics in the Novels of Graham Greene', p. 17.
151 Anthony Burgess, 'Here's to Me and My Generation – Mr Burgess Makes a Christmas Toast', *New York Times*, 24 December 1972, para. 6.
152 Burgess, *New York*, pp. 45–46.
153 Anthony Burgess, 'Interview with Anthony Burgess on Mozart', *Larry King Show Live*, Mutual Broadcast System, 3 December 1991, George Washington University Archives.
154 Anthony Burgess, 'A Writer Snarls Back at Critics', *Chicago Tribune*, 2 May 1977, p. 24.
155 Burgess, 'A Writer Snarls Back at Critics', p. 24.
156 Christine Ro, 'How Americans Preserved British English', BBC, 8 February 2018.
157 Anthony Burgess, 'The Future of Anglo-American', *Harper's Magazine*, February 1968, pp. 55–56. Burgess repeated this idea on *The Dick Cavett Show* and in his 1992 linguistics book *A Mouthful of Air* in varying ways: 'That English had already been transported to Jamestown, Virginia, in 1607, but

the Massachusetts settlement, with Boston built in 1630, represents definitive colonization, stretching up to Maine and down to South Carolina. ... This was the language that Shakespeare had spoken. The new Americans had no poet of his stature, but they did have Mistress Anne Bradstreet' (Anthony Burgess, *A Mouthful of Air: Language, Languages ... Especially English* (New York: William Morrow and Company, 1992), p. 273).

158 Anthony Burgess, 'Is Shakespeare Relevant?', *New York Times*, 11 December 1970, para. 3.

159 'Being myopic myself, I suspect that Shakespeare was myopic' (Anthony Burgess, *Shakespeare* (New York: Carroll & Graf, 1970; 2002), p. 28).

160 Burgess, *Conversations with Anthony Burgess*, p. 183.

161 Lauren Weiner interview with Anthony Burgess, 'Shakespeare, Human Choice, and the Goddess-Muse', *Kenyon Collegian*, book 783, 16 October 1980, p. 4.

162 'What's It Going to Be Then, Eh? A Look At: Stanley Kubrick's "A Clockwork Orange"', Another 'Sound on Film' Broadcast Transcript: WKCR-FM/Columbia University Radio, April 1972, IABF Archives, p. 7.

163 Anthony Burgess, 'Preface', *Language Made Plain* (New York: Thomas Y. Crowell Company, 1964; 1965).

164 Burgess, *Language Made Plain*, pp. 3–4.

165 Burgess, *Language Made Plain*, pp. 3–4.

166 Burgess, *Language Made Plain*, pp. 3–4.

167 Burgess, *Language Made Plain*, p. 179.

168 Burgess, *Language Made Plain*, p. 179.

169 Burgess, *Language Made Plain*, p. 179.

170 Burgess, *Language Made Plain*, p. 180.

171 Anthony Burgess, *The Pianoplayers* (New York: Washington Square Press, 1986), p. 151.

172 Anthony Burgess, 'Taking Canada Seriously', *But Do Blondes Prefer Gentlemen?*, p. 404.

173 'Although he [Fitzgerald] could write a bad story, he could not write badly. It is the good writing here that is likely to infuriate the reader more than the slick pert plots. Fitzgerald should have been getting on with his novels, not wasting his talent on sub-literary prostitution. ... Moreover, he had a public of great size which didn't even know that he was a novelist. It required an integrity that ran counter to the American Way of Life to sustain the role of novelist at all' (Anthony Burgess, 'Dollars and Dolours', *The Observer*, 2 December 1979, p. 36); Anthony Burgess, 'The Art of Fiction', *Paris Review*, ed. by John Cullinan (1973; 2005), p. 28.

174 Anthony Burgess, 'Getting Your Day's Work Done', *Conversations with Anthony Burgess*, p. 153.

175 Burgess, 'Getting Your Day's Work Done', p. 152.

176 Don Crinklaw, 'Burgess's Eccentric Odyssey', *St. Louis Post-Dispatch*, 4 May 1975, p. 113; Anthony Burgess, *The Malayan Trilogy* (London: Vintage Books, 2000), p. 53.

177 Burgess, *The Malayan Trilogy*, p. 53.

178 Lewis and Burgess, '"I Love England, But I Will No Longer Live There"', p. 45; George Malko, 'Penthouse Interview: Anthony Burgess', *Penthouse*, June 1972, p. 118.
179 'Interview with Anthony Burgess', *The Dick Cavett Show*, ABC Television Network: Daphne Productions and Rollins & Joffe Productions, 25 March 1971.
180 Burgess, *You've Had Your Time*, pp. 350–351.
181 Burgess, 'A Candid Interview with the Author of *A Clockwork Orange*', p. 250.
182 Adam Roberts's novel *The Black Prince* is inspired by a one-page idea from Burgess that explicitly mentions the desire to use John Dos Passos's 'Camera Eye' technique as a mode of storytelling (Adam Roberts, 'Black Prince: Money Money Money', *Morphosis*, 7 June 2019, https://amechanicalart.blogspot.com/2019/06/black-prince-money-money-money.html).

3

M/F (1971)

> Politics is a simplification of human life, as is raw sex. Both provide the real international pseudo-literature. The didactic and the pornographic span the globe. Real literature has difficulty in getting a visa issued. (Anthony Burgess, 'A Babble of Voices')[1]

Introduction

Anthony Burgess's 1971 novel, *M/F*, was originally conceived of as a novel entitled 'The Riddle Solver – A Novel', or 'The Incest Play', or 'The Solver of Riddles', with a main character named Gerald Emmett, which changed to Miles Faber sometime in the mid 1960s. Such a change might have been an attempt at alluding to all or some of the following possibilities: the book publisher, the *Fahrenheit 451* character Max Frisch's (another M.F.) novel *Homo Faber* (1957) in which the main character Walter Faber appears to commit incest through an act of fate, Christopher Isherwood and W.H. Auden's play *Ascent of F6* (1936) published by Faber with an anti-hero named Michael Forsyth (MF) Ransom, and/or an approximation of 'fæder' for 'father' or Latin for 'craftsman' or 'soldier', making Miles Latin for 'soldier', the 'soldier maker', or riddle fighter, similar to Oedipus.[2] The title of the novel can also be written as *MF*; indeed, Burgess used this spelling in *You've Had Your Time*, opting to 'forget the other variants of the title', but throughout this monograph it will be written with the slash so as to remind readers of the supposed theme of structuralism, thus including a geometric line separating the letters, and also to call attention to the novel's similarity in title to Roland Barthes's structuralist monograph from the year before its publication, *S/Z* (1970).[3] This decision also emphasizes the advancement of literary experimentation exhibited in Burgess's aesthetic vision beginning in the 1970s, experimentation that was influenced by United States culture, as will be evidenced by addressing a slew of lectures, interviews, journalism, and books that comment on, include, or else use American society and culture as a source of inspiration via its 'realm of influence'; therefore these pieces act as epitextual commentaries on the novel and its themes to be discussed.[4]

In many ways the 1970s were Burgess's *American* years and *M/F* is decidedly Burgess's first *American* text. To say this novel is *American* means that this text should be recognized as Burgess's first clearly and predominantly American-inspired fiction, as opposed to the United States merely and briefly being alluded to in his earlier fiction, a fact that is supported by the novel's themes, content, setting, characters, and characterizations. The entire presupposition of the novel is based upon Burgess's ideas concerning race, 'miscegenation', youth culture, obscenity, sex, and American myth and mores as a way to craft an anthropologically structuralist novel which explores 'the co-relation between riddles and incest'.[5] Additionally, and what will be the focus of this chapter, a point not explored yet by Burgess scholars, is that *M/F* also exists as a utilization of Burgess's public discourse and dialogues on pornography, obscenity, and materialism as distinctively American traits, which can be witnessed by looking at Burgess's commentary on and dialogue with the American cultural heteroglot which is packed full of 'voices among which his own voice must also sound', therefore 'these voices create the background necessary for his own voice'.[6] Although academic discussion of *M/F* has largely focused on the text's structuralist in/aspirations, defined by Burgess as being 'about the structures that the human brain imposes on the world about it', the significance of the story's mythic American underpinnings (Algonquin legend, youth culture, American counter culture, incest, obscenity, and miscegeny in American society) is often overlooked by scholars so as to focus on the structuralist origins.[7] This is unfortunate due to how important the American aspects are to the central inspiration for the novel, beginning with the 'American Indians', whose 'legends', Burgess explains in the 'Oedipus Wrecks' chapter of *This Man and Music* (1982), 'presented the same collocation' of Oedipus and therefore left 'no question of cultural transmission from East to West, so it had to be assumed that the incest-riddle structure was built into certain cultures and was an emanation of human need', making incest, Burgess goes on to suggest, innate not just to human civilization but especially to North America.[8] Alongside this inspirational cue is the fact that Burgess had been thinking about writing 'a structuralist novel, based on a Lévi-Strauss thesis, with the framework of an Algonquin legend about incest', a point expressed publicly during an interview with the *New York Times* in 1968, and so *M/F* came to fruition through a marriage between European philosophy and American myth, whose intention was voiced through an American newspaper.[9]

One year before the aforementioned interview, appearing in the *Washington Post Book World* on 26 November 1967, Burgess reviewed Claude Lévi-Strauss's lecture, 'The Scope of Anthropology' (1966), by relating Lévi-Strauss's concept of anthropology that insisted 'on the universality of *structures* of social beliefs and taboos' to literature beyond Oedipus, landing on one of his own novels, *Tremor of Intent* (1966).[10] Believing that he had, in presenting the suggestion of incest between brother and sister, reproduced and essentially proven, subconsciously on some level, Lévi-Strauss's hypothesis that humanity communicates 'by means of symbols and signs', and that at its core, 'incest prohibition is thus the basis of human society, and in a sense it is the society', Burgess remarked that 'I've been manipulated by [Lévi-Strauss]' and in recognizing that, he now wanted to 'find' – though a better word may be *interpret* literature through a Lévi-Straussian lens – 'that other authors, as well as Joyce and myself, have been manipulated too'.[11] Published in *The Malahat Review* in January 1971, an interview with Burgess revealed his future novel-writing plans, where he explained that he intended to 'exploit the Algonquin legend', the same covered by Lévi-Strauss in his lecture, of 'the boy who was bound to commit incest because he could answer all the riddles correctly, which is a direct tie-up with Oedipus', going on to state that he had worked this idea out by creating a world which is the present but is 'subtly different [with] People you've never heard of – great writers, greater than Shakespeare, great politicians; so the reader is all the time trying to piece together a world which is a parallel world to our own but not another planet'.[12] Burgess foresaw this theoretical and experimental shift in literature at least back in 26 March 1965 when he published 'What Now in the Novel' in the *Spectator* and expressed the opinion that he felt English literature was 'already swinging to a new interest in form rather than content, and that that is where the significant pattern of the next ten years must lie'.[13] Published only a year after Roland Barthesx's *S/Z* (1970), a structuralist analysis of Honoré de Balzac's work, *M/F* is evocative of a period focused on structuralism and interested in literary *trompe l'oeil* and experimentation, as the first publication's cover art – peritextual evidence – reveals with an M.C. Escher-esque design.[14]

Still, even with these grand theoretical inspirations, with which Burgess publicly prefaced his work, there exists much contention over whether this text is actually *structuralist*, as defined specifically by Lévi-Strauss's theories, but to explore this imbroglio would demand far more attention and research down a different critical avenue, and therefore would be a digression to the approach laid out here. In Burgess studies alone, notwithstanding the internecine debates between different structuralist schools of thought, there exists debate about Burgess's structuralist self-directed classification, what Burgess called a 'law' in his *Oedipus the King* (1972) adaptation, and one such stance is laid out by Jim Clarke, who believes Burgess's structuralist application was well intentioned, though imprecise, with only the *content*, but not the *form*, driving the supposed Lévi-Strauss brand of structuralism: 'specifically his [Lévi-Strauss] method of structuralist social anthropology, became for Burgess the raw material of his novel, not so much the structure of the fiction as the principles driving its content'.[15] Remarking to Carol Dix in 1972 about the inspiration Lévi-Strauss had on his thinking, Burgess's comments are evidence of how he took a nuanced and elaborate anthropological theory, influenced and evolved from earlier structuralist poetics, and reduced it to an aesthetic inspiration which would focus on the 'co-relation between riddles and incest' where the 'characters had to make sense in structural terms' – what those terms are is unclear – so that when 'you would realise that the main character is a Negro. Then really you ought to go back and read it again'.[16] This appears to be, in essence, the extent of connectedness that Burgess surmised existed between his novel and the concepts of Lévi-Strauss, though a thorough and precise literary analysis is still needed. For the purposes of this monograph, though, this is enough to begin from, and however inaccurate the mythic and theoretical inspirations are, it is important to recall that Burgess's theme of incestual Americans had actually begun years before with Belinda Hussey, the Massachusetts native, from *Honey for the Bears* (1963), whose own father engaged in incest with his daughter, and, with the topic of incest alone, in *Tremor of Intent* (1966).[17] Seven years after *Honey for the Bears* was first published, and after having spent a sporadic four-year period in the United States teaching and lecturing, Burgess's intertextual motif appeared again in the United States where Miles would begin his incestuous/mythic journey, this time with supposed theoretical backing.

More in line with the Bakhtinian, biographical, and historical analyses to come, it is important to acknowledge that *M/F* is closely pre-dated and post-dated by other American-centric texts such as Burgess's 'Letter from Europe' series with the *American Scholar* magazine, his 'Viewpoint' series in the *Times Literary Supplement*, and several *New York Times* articles discussing New York City, literary relevance, the decline of American culture, university students' academic abilities, and what he called the 'permissive' age, or a 'period of inattentiveness', as Frank Kermode put it when discussing the same time period.[18] All of these documents are significant historical items for trying to understand Burgess's experiences in the United States in the early 1970s, and in some cases these pieces act as communicative continuations of the themes laid out in *M/F*, resulting in an elongated epitextual authorial discourse on such subjects.

Burgess and the United States in *M/F*

Teaching at both Princeton University as a visiting lecturer and Columbia University as an adjunct professor of writing, at the beginning of 1971, when *M/F* was first published, Burgess had spent the two years prior to the novel's publication engaging in a 1969 lecture tour throughout the United States, where he visited over a dozen university campuses from the West to East Coasts, including visits to Deià, Mallorca, for a lecture to American students in conjunction with Dowling College's satellite campus and a one-month residency at the University of North Carolina at Chapel Hill in November to December 1969. In the autumn of 1970, in addition to accepting two teaching positions, Burgess also accepted requests for one-night lectures as far west as East Lansing, Michigan and as far south as Richmond, Virginia, all while speaking at various colleges and organizations all over New York State. Due to this, the late 1960s and early 1970s can be considered the point at which Burgess was fully immersed into American society and culture. This influence can be seen throughout almost all of his work of the decade, with biographical and historical context directly related to his American travels appearing in his publications: *Puma* (1976) – initially conceived of as 'Cat's Day' – was Burgess's attempt at a Hollywood apocalypse film turned novel, which he began writing in Iowa – all while 'teaching 85 students and assorted class visitors in the School of Letters this month [and] working with the music department in conjunction with the presentation of his own symphony' – and uses New York City as its setting; *The Clockwork Testament* (1976) is a novella that exists as a castigation of American higher education and pop culture; *New York* (1976), a commissioned non-fiction picture book on his adopted home; *1985* (1978), a strange bifurcated novel/commentary/hypothetical dialogues where the epilogue is a mock hidden polemical interview with an American student in which the interlocutor, the unnamed author of the story who also monologically echoes Burgess, critiques Americans and American culture; *Ernest Hemingway and His World* (1978), a biography on the famous American author that he also uses as a commentary on modernist American authors and the fallibility of American fame; and then, finally, *Earthly Powers* (1980) comes at the beginning of the next decade but is really a book of the 1970s and resembles Burgess's attempt to achieve the *big* American novel that spans decades and takes American counter culture and hippiedom on as a central plot device.[19]

The authorial intent behind *M/F* and the text's own self-awareness is latent in the novel, since Miles, along his journey, encounters example upon example of characters alluding both to the text itself as a kind of hermeneutic palimpsest document and to the contemporary American culture of Burgess's world which has created the myth. The novel ends with the admission that Professor Keteki produced an academic thesis on 'Volitional Solecisms in Melville', or, oxymoronically, intentional mistakes, on the American author of the classic American Renaissance novel, *Moby-Dick* (1851) – one cannot ignore the demotic allusion to a phallus here as well. Additionally, Dr

Keteki also met Faber's grandfather at Columbia University, the college Burgess was in discussion with Frank MacShane to teach at in 1970 and which he had visited in December 1969, which is an example of literary and biographical overlap that emphasizes that the free will of the characters always rests in the hands of a creator, an artist or a god, so that even though the text and Miles's journey are problematized by misadventure, everything from Miles's narrative to Burgess's text is deliberate. In the sense of *M/F*, this means Miles's deviation from the family pattern is therefore not an act of breaking away from fate, but that his fate was to not follow familial tradition (at least in the narrative he supplies), just as by experimenting with the novel, Burgess is actually just mimicking other kinds of American-style experimental literature of the time. This isn't to say that *M/F* is a dull plagiarized text, or that we 'have to conclude that it is a decided failure, however artfully and cleverly contrived', as Samuel Coale does, but rather that there is a sense of ersatz originality existent throughout all layers of the artifice.[20] Burgess ends the novel with a description of the power and importance of miscegenation as a way to start over, to wipe the slate clean, and to void out the unthinking traditions that influence the future: 'a fine humane political ideal but its aesthetic results are often undesirable', says Miles to his wife, 'two totally opposed ethnic types. … I am black. A Chinese woman with a black man' who 'have no children of their own' with adopted Italian children so as to drive the 'melting pot' trope as an ongoing symbol 'of an American culture bordering on a return to pure nature'.[21] As a whole, and for these reasons, it could be argued that *M/F*'s sole purpose and main intent is to be a structuralist plea for the United States to forget about race consciousness, since 'Burgess sees race consciousness itself as fundamentally absurd', and for the United States to become a mixed-raced society as a path to shed historical guilt and myth.[22]

As much as a dismissal of race politics in the United States, *M/F* also takes on the lackadaisical American college student and hippie culture, the same group he encountered in mid September 1969 when he lectured in Deià, Mallorca, at the satellite Mediterranean Institute of Dowling College in New York, where he gathered useful observations of Americans abroad and was indeed writing *M/F* during his time there.[23] Burgess describes the experience in *You've Had Your Time* (1990), commenting that there were no Catalonians about, just 'expatriate Anglophones, the greatest of whom was Robert Graves', with the school running 'a course in European studies, which meant, on the basic level, learning how to subsist on fresh fish, coarse bread, and harsh red wine' by young Americans who 'were very ill and cried for hamburgers and Coca-Cola'.[24] In a description by Burgess in a separate article, he painted a similar picture of Deià, situating himself against the backdrop of hippie American students that he contended with:

> I even gave a lecture in a suit and collar and tie, a thing unheard of before in Deià. [A place] overlax place with no garbage collection, a credulity about lunar magic, hippies sick because they had to subsist on fish and red wine and could not get Coca-Cola and hamburgers.[25]

The American obsession with Coca-Cola is memorialized in *M/F* when Miles first orders 'a soft drink new to me – Coco-Coho', in bottles, 'owl-shaped' so as to immediately work American consumerism and poor nutrition into the Algonquin myth realm – the 'mistress of owls' who is the riddle maker, the Algonquin equivalent of the sphinx.[26] Later in the novel, Miles uses several empty cases of 'Coco-Coho (not so new then: the drink was already in the Caribbean) crates' to sit on.[27] Burgess's actual trip became a partial inspiration for the Americans Burgess presented in *M/F* as well as the fictional Caribbean island Castita, Grencijta (meaning 'big city') that, like Deià, is a place 'ennobled by the presence of a very civilized poet' but not 'itself highly civilized'.[28] Castita arose out of this image, providing Burgess with a snapshot of Americanization abroad and the counter culture, as Aggeler, whom Burgess had met for the first time only months before visiting Deià, put it, an influence 'that could breed Miles Faber and export so much of the vulgarity and cheapness', qualities that also gratified, as discussed previously, Janet Shirley in *One Hand Clapping* (1961), prompting Burgess to wonder 'whether the West could be saved from the various forms of "incest" mirrored in its racial attitudes and cultural values'.[29] Although Burgess, before visiting the United States, had some inclination to believe that the country's cultural contributions were largely ignoble rather than noble, these opinions were contradicted frequently and evolved over time, with *M/F* being his first outright novelistic castigation of the country, as well as direct inspiration from the country, with more novels to follow with the same goal. Even though he gained much in the United States, his success in the country never pushed him into a position of servile adoration.

M/F kicked off this decades-long theme by using Burgess's own definition of structuralism, however much that may deviate from Claude Lévi-Strauss's definition which was derived from Ferdinand de Saussure's emphasis on 'semiology' as it relates and is 'attributed to it as its object of study the life of signs at the heart of social life', then extrapolated by Lévi-Strauss to include 'mythic language, the oral and gestural signs of which ritual is composed, marriage rules, kinship systems, customary laws, and certain terms and conditions of economic exchange'.[30] Even though the novel is purported by its author to be designed around this theoretical matrix, *M/F* can also easily be seen as a novel in which the Black American protagonist's identity, influenced by his family, culture, education, and the ideals of American society, perceives mythic and social structures influencing and directing his actions. Ironically, and self-reflexively, Burgess's text of *M/*

F is also the by-product of Burgess's own experiences of and observations on the 1970s American society he encountered – the heteroglossia of the 'era's many and diverse languages' and 'extraliterary genres' – which, in effect, reflect the language of the text, making the novel then an externality of Burgess's own personification of the contemporary heteroglossia as 'incarnated in individual human figures, with disagreements and oppositions individualized', where such 'oppositions of individual wills and minds are submerged in *social* heteroglossia, [so that] they are reconceptualized through it'.[31] In Bakhtinian terms, the connections between authorial presence and text are wound up in the language, where the 'artistic image of a language must by its very nature be a linguistic hybrid (an intentional hybrid): it is obligatory for two linguistic consciousnesses to be present, the one being represented and the other doing the representing'.[32] In *Problems of Dostoyevsky's Poetics* (1984), Bakhtin explains the scholarly obligation of looking at the author, the chronotope, and the text as being necessary because 'an artistic image, of whatever sort, cannot be invented, since it has its own artistic logic, its own norm-generating order', and therefore 'the creator must subordinate himself to this order', an order and purpose still ordained by the author, whose ideas, like those 'of Dostoevsky the thinker, upon entering his polyphonic novel, change[s] the very form of their existence, they are transformed into artistic images of ideas: they are combined in an indissoluble unity with images of people'.[33] The difference between this example and Burgess's work and characters is that in Burgess's case, his narratives are often not nearly as dialogically balanced enough to produce a polyphonic novel, since the 'monologic isolation' of his authorial purposes is often easily discernible, a point of explication in this chapter.[34]

This concept is evident throughout *M/F*, most particularly with Burgess's decades-long epitextual commentaries on race, American culture, obscenity, pornography, offensive language, censorship, and, ultimately, aesthetics. These topics and themes are displayed just as prominently in *M/F* as when Burgess discussed these matters at public lectures around the United States and in American and international publications.[35] One aspect of the subject of censorship and offensive language that Burgess explored was the role race and gender played in the use of some epithets – again, race and sexuality being major themes in *M/F*, though the subjects rest in the background of the plot, unlike in *The Clockwork Testament*, *Earthly Powers*, and *Enderby's Dark Lady* . In fact, Burgess often conflated the discussions of racial and gender equality into a kind of catch-all topic as a target for his attacks that, when it came to race and gender, often meant that he entirely disregarded the roles racism and sexism have played in popularizing certain words, terms, and sentiments: 'racial squeamishness goes on – I remember an American Shylock who had to mess up the blank verse by omitting "Jewish" in "Jewish gabardine" – but literary sex can go as far as it likes, which is pretty far', and more to the point when he said that the 'word "chairperson" ... is a form of censorship; we can't change the past that is immutably enshrined in our language. This is no different from the movement to "de-n-----fy" Mark Twain'.[36] Indeed, history cannot be changed, but Burgess's facile argument here assumes that a culture cannot attempt to make amends for the fact that, as Jabari Asim notes in *The N Word* (2007), the 'language of racial insult ... runs like an electric current through' so much of White Western culture, literature, and language, a fact that should, for the sake of intellectual conversation, be understood before discussing the use of certain words.[37] Instead, Burgess oversimplifies the entire debate by expressing that there is either a fear of language (and anything language describes) or censorship. And to Burgess, a fear of certain words and/or the fear of sex or violence in art, he would go on thinking, was ridiculous because 'being disturbed is part of the human condition' and therefore art must deal in these matters.[38] Having summarized this point, it should be clearer now that *M/F* should be recognized as Burgess's formal introduction into the so-called American permissive age, where he embraced and used more abrasive and explicit language that more closely resembled the American popular and literary culture being produced in the 1960s and early 1970s.

Thus, *M/F* is the effect of the United States's impact on Burgess's artistic sensibilities during this time period, sensibilities that are displayed and played out in the novel but which also take other forms throughout all of his major *American* pieces to be discussed in this monograph. Because of this significance, such an analysis is also essential to the broader macrocosmic understanding of Burgess's *American* work as shining examples of Bakhtin's theories being played out on a twentieth-century multimedia scale, where more so than ever before, and with an author rife with examples of this being played out publicly, Burgess's literary 'language is not an abstract system of normative forms but rather a concrete heteroglot conception of the world', where his language exhibits 'the "taste" of a profession, a genre, a tendency, a party, a particular work, a particular person, a generation, an age group, the day and hour', so that each 'word tastes of the context and contexts in which it has lived its socially charged life; all words and forms are populated by intentions', since 'Contextual overtones (generic, tendentious, individualistic) are inevitable in the word'.[39]

To argue that *M/F* is Burgess's first *American* text because of its inspirations and content does two very important things: first, it delineates a timeline for which this monograph can proceed in order to analyse the overarching idea of Burgess's American inspirations that are evident in his fiction; and, two, in looking closely at Burgess's cultural dialogism concerning race, American culture and youth, pornography, obscenity, and censorship, such a discussion assists with attempting to understand his own conception of aesthetics, and therefore simultaneously provides a view of how his life experiences influenced his fiction.

Race, youth culture, and *M/F*

M/F opens with the twenty-year-old Miles Faber – the titular MF of the title, Miles being Latin for 'soldier' and faber meaning 'maker', as well as the potential *mezzo forte*, mother-fucker who has a mother-father/male-female problem – explaining his past act of 'public copulation' which took place under the 'chaste Massachusetts moonlight … outside of the F. Jannatu Memorial Library … as a mode of protest … against tyrannical democracies, wars in the name of peace, [and] students forced to study', all while claiming to have kept a gaze fixed on the 'assistant librarian, Miss F. Carica during his act of copulative protestation'.[40] In opening the novel with a satirical presentation of a stereotypically exhibitionist, highly sexualized, entitled, and inconsiderate American youth supposedly protesting, which is narrated and perhaps written by a middle-aged, possibly fifty-year-old, Miles who, within the first paragraph of the novel, casts doubt on his own narrative – 'I do not think, for instance, that I really replied' – the text of *M/F* instantly lays out a challenging and untrustworthy narrative environment.[41] Burgess's supposedly structuralist novel focusing on a young Black American student, since the '*Zeitgeist* has always been the emanation of a minority', is intentionally aimed at the protesting youth cultures of the 1960s and early 1970s whom Burgess had already criticized in articles – articles which should be accepted as parallel narratives, like his 'Letter from Europe' series in autumn 1969 and summer 1970, as well as his *New York Times* article, 'Is Shakespeare Relevant?', published in December 1970 in the same year as the release of *M/F*.[42] In particular, Burgess described these kinds of students, especially those studying literature, as moaning against structuralism as a literary theory, because, Burgess assumed, when students complained about something, it was likely due to their distaste for 'academic rigour, especially in a field like literature, where they expect to be permitted to burble about beauty and social significance and the effects of terminal tuberculosis on Keats's attitude to love'.[43] His general comments on matters of societal unrest are somewhat diverse in opinion, though, when at an 'Obscenity and the Novel' lecture at Contra Costa College in March 1969, Burgess told the crowd that campus unrest is 'primarily sociological' with 'vague goals' and therefore has a 'fictitious cause …. And when a cause is fictitious, I'll have no part of it at all', though he did make one important exception: 'Black students have every right to riot. But they should not be vague about what they're rioting about because "freedom" is not enough.'[44] Shortly after Miles's public sex act, his 'fellow-students' even present an 'agitation' on campus by protesting for his reinstatement after being kicked out of school for the transgression, leaving no doubt of parodic cultural elements.[45] Examples such as this abound throughout the novel as evidence of acts of double-voiced discourse that serve 'two speakers at the same time and [express] simultaneously two different intentions' between both Burgess and Miles.[46] Through Miles's narration and descriptions, Burgess attempts to describe a hive-minded student body whose outbursts are ultimately acts of conformity to their objectiveless outrage, which Burgess suggests is in itself incestuous due to the homogeny that moulded these students into having a 'collective existence' where *identity* is 'swallowed in purpose or ritual. Slogans at the point of orgasm'.[47] Only a dozen pages in, Burgess makes it quite clear that his American experiences up until 1971 would be at the forefront of this novel and that this is going to be a very different novel than any of his previous work.

The novel is, in summary, about 'a twenty-year-old college student who has just been dismissed from college for publicly fornicating with someone named Carlotta as a form of unspecified protest near the college library', where Miles, the novel's protagonist, appears as 'Burgess's evocation of a typical addlepated student of the late Sixties. His present desire is to get to the Caribbean island of Castitian poet and painter, Sib Legeru', whose name 'means incest'.[48] Originally named Gzeijitte in the country of Vilpeisi in Burgess's personal notebooks, the name is changed to Castita which is Italian for chastity, but it is also suggestive of castes, and possibly castration, since the act of incest is an act of abominable destruction in the novel, a novel, it should be remembered, where every proper noun acts as a double, or even triple, entendre of some sort, usually to do with animals, as Burgess himself informed his audiences: 'Nearly all people Miles will meet in the course of the narrative will either have animal names or resemble animals.'[49] Positioned in the Caribbean, this location may be symbolic in the sense that the Caribbean has been a more colonially exploited and terrorized geographical location than its close neighbour the United States, which, although once a colony and plagued with internal colonialism in the form of slavery and racial segregation, has had the luxury of repeatedly practising some form of geopolitical isolationism over the last 200 years and thus has escaped the historically pernicious and tyrannical subjugation caused by colonialism on many Caribbean islands. Between the fifteenth and twentieth centuries, the Caribbean islands were largely non-autonomous and unwillingly occupied and exploited by dozens of other world powers, resulting frequently in predominantly impoverished and heterogenous populations with diverse cultural identities. For these reasons, this particular location, as contrasted to Miles's United States citizenry, is then significant so as to present a dichotomy between, to use Bakhtinian terms, a centripetal (the United States) and a centrifugal (Castita) force. The United States, in *M/F*, is an incestuous and homogenous centralizing force that is the homeland of the incestuous actors, while the novel-form itself, Bakhtin argues, and the Caribbean setting both act as the decentralizing, centrifugal forces which destabilize, ironically, also through potential acts of incest.[50] The language of the characters, as well as their backgrounds, influences, and discourses, are soaked too in the extra-literary heteroglossia of Burgess, so that every utterance in the novel 'serves as a point where centrifugal as well as centripetal forces are brought to bear', both poly- and monoglottal, so that the 'process of centralization and decentralization, of unification and disunification, intersect in the utterance; the utterance not only answers the requirements of its own language as an individualized embodiment of speech act, but it answers the requirements of heteroglossia as well, it is in fact an active participant in such speech diversity'.[51] As narrated in *M/F*, 'communication has been the whatness of communication' in the novel, therefore the acts of dialogic stand alone and are balanced separately between the poles of cultural influence, of text to author, of character to riddle, of meaning to interpretation, of text to intertext.[52] An aspect of *M/F*'s mythic-Americanness also has to do with the fictional author, Sib Legeru, which Burgess created in order to resemble a Hermann Hesse and/or Kurt Vonnegut-type figure – writers he admonished on several occasions for pandering to the youth. Legeru is the enigmatic writer(s) that Miles hungers for because the author-figure exists for Miles as an icon of the 'only sanity in the world', whose work ironically and fatefully pulls Miles closer to committing incest since, as Joseph Darlington points out, Sib Legeru means ' "sibling-legging", or lying with one's sibling in Anglo-Saxon'.[53] Believing that the United States and the American mind were innately incestuous, Burgess infuses this and several other subjective Americana topoi into *M/F* as founding principles upon which the novel is structured. Burgess's active engagement with explaining the significance of the text in the several public analyses he provided, as well as the literary allusions and directed exegetical textual commentary that exist within the story, begs that the text be exposed and analysed beyond just the significance of the signs and symbols in the text, so as to also identify any and all social, historical, and authorial inspirations that the text and its author suggest.

An avid reader of all of Burgess's writing up until the publication of *M/F* may have been able to see the connections Burgess was making between his own life, as well as his opinions on youth culture, race identity movements, and American culture with incest, but as time went on and his work accrued, the evidence for such overlaps grew considerably. More obvious than Burgess's growing epitext in the 1970s, though, was the bridge which Claude Lévi-Strauss's ideas provided to Burgess in order to bring his ideas into an organized artistic vision. In Lévi-Strauss's *The Scope of Anthropology*, the theorist argues that in 'North America, puzzle situations are found whose origins are incontestably indigenous', which may have confirmed Burgess's predisposition to think of the United States as an incestuous nation, as Stinson noted in *Anthony Burgess: Revisited* (1991) when he argued that Belinda Hussey's incest story from *Honey for the Bears* may act as a metaphor for the United States being 'afraid to reach out to make vital sustaining human contact with other peoples', therefore making the country's choice 'not to "marry" outside its own family ... a kind of symbolic "incest"'.[54] This insight is supported in Geoffrey Aggeler's *Anthony Burgess: The Artist as Novelist* (1979), where Burgess remarked that the United States's intentional attempt at acquiring the world through culture, or Americanization, was despicable to Burgess since he essentially saw this act as an attempt for American culture to feed off itself and influence itself as a completely homogenous, self-sufficient, inward-looking nationality designed for betterment only through a type of jingoistic incestuous indulgence.[55] This provincial ethnocentrism, he argued, was embodied in the twentieth-century American persona, which effectively produced a revamped form of manifest destiny and therefore became a theme Burgess explored in *M/F* in order to criticize the American inclination to 'preserve "freedom" through incestuous avenues', meaning that in order to preserve the idea of *America*, all 'non-American cultures must either be resisted or Americanized'.[56] Similarly, Aggeler notes that Burgess saw Americans' tendency to focus on race consciousness, either willingly or unwillingly, especially as evidenced in the various racial identity movements (most likely the Black Power, Black Arts, and Black Is Beautiful Movements), as a prime example of such self-imposed racial insularity, or, more figuratively, incestuousness.[57] At the end of the novel, Miles, and Burgess through an act of double-voicedness with 'its presence felt by the novelist in the living heteroglossia of language, and in the multi-languagedness surrounding and nourishing his own consciousness', warns readers of the novel that if they are hungry for meaning, they can perhaps take this moral, 'that my race, or your race, must start thinking in terms of the human totality and cease weaving its own fancied achievements of miseries into a banner. Black is Beauty, yes, BUT ONLY WITH ANNA SEWELL PRODUCTS'; through the artifice of Burgess's monologic narrative, this is a direct attack simultaneously from a White Anglo-Celt author on a Black American movement and a Black American affronting his own in-group.[58] Either oblivious to the terror waged on Black communities in the United States over the last two centuries, ongoing during the publication of *M/F*, or else uncaring about the severity, Burgess ignored this reality and just saw racial identity collectives and Americanization as being incestuous, and therefore in need of resistance.

More directly inspirational, Stinson notes, by pulling details from Burgess's second autobiography, *You've Had Your Time* (1990), is that the genesis of *M/F* came to Burgess several years before he started working on the book in 1969, when the author had met the American actor William (Bill) Conrad, 'who played Cannon in the television series', and who also was initially listed as the producer for Burgess's 'musical comedy based on the life of Shakespeare, tentatively titled "The Bawdy Bard"', and had also 'expressed a half-serious desire to make an all-black film on Oedipus, calling it *Mother Fucker*'.[59] Playing off of the strangely incestual obscenity, motherfucker, used prominently in poetry of the Black Arts Movement by writers such as Sonia Sanchez in her poem 'TCB' published in *We a BaddDDD People* (1970) and Amiri Baraka, whose phrase in the poem 'Black People!' was adopted by the anarchist anti-war movement, 'Up Against the Wall, Motherfuckers' (as well as being a brief gang in England whose subset would create the King Mob gang of Sex Pistols lore), Aggeler notes in the 'Introduction' to *Critical Essays on Anthony Burgess* (1986) that the term had a 'wide range of usages in the North American black idiom', going on to claim that Burgess simply extrapolated the incest trope 'further to encompass all the maladies currently afflicting Western culture'.[60]

A better environment and culture for Burgess to act out the concept of 'the puzzle and the sexual taboo', the metaphorical 'knot that it is dangerous to untie since, untying it, you are magically untying the knot that holds the natural order together', could not be found than in the United States, a place that, he said in 1970, 'none of us can do without, our smart, clever, harassed step-mother, with so many gifts and so many anxieties, who best gets our love and devotion when she least seems to seek it'.[61] The characterization of Western civilization having the United States as a stepmother works immediately within the miscegenation and incest framework that Burgess manipulates in *M/F* and discusses publicly: that all humanity is the same race, and to think otherwise by sticking to one's racial tribe was to increase the likelihood of incestuous activities:

> Our cerebral structuring of the outside world is not something clever, or educated, or scientific, and the modern West is no better at doing it than was, or is (forget about was, which brings in time and history, and these are not important), tribal Africa. Man is everywhere and always man.[62]

The central and unifying theme of miscegenation that carries out this structuralist endeavour in the novel is presented through a memory of Miles's father's interest in the 'cause of miscegenation', which he held 'very much at heart'.[63] Miscegenation, or the act of mixing races for procreation – a term historically manufactured by anti-abolitionists to mock abolitionist views of desegregation, but which had already entered the American lexicon by the time this became known, and can have pejorative connotations, although it was a word that was adopted by Black authors like Charles Chesnutt as synonymous with race amalgamation; all details, seemingly, unbeknownst to Burgess – was, to Burgess, an issue that was not up for debate; it was just a fact of life. Indeed, Burgess believed that the 'whole pattern of Western culture [was] incestuous' because of hypocrisies like 'race consciousness,' which was 'symptomatic of an incestuous pull'; this, Burgess thought, was increasingly disturbing since he felt that the time had 'come for the big miscegenation [where] all of the races must overcome their morbid preoccupation with color identity and face the merger that is inevitable in any event'.[64] These types of ideas, through an act of dialogic interrelation, turn into the divine inspiration Miles's reaches after drinking 'Dutch courage' in a paradoxical Bakhtinian and Eliotian epiphany:

> *Dare to try to disturb the mystery of order.* For order has both to be and not to be challenged, this being the anomalous condition of the sustention of the cosmos. Rebel becomes hero; witch becomes saint. Exogamy means disruption and also stability; incest means stability and also disruption. You've got to have it both ways, man.[65]

Using a kind of Dennis Hopper, *Easy Rider* (1969) parlance to mimic the counter-culture generation of American hippiedom, anarchism, and free love vernacular, Burgess is able to envision profundity intertwined with frivolousness – perfect for the collegiate youth culture of America and for the Burgessian mix of high and low culture.[66]

It's because of this too that the tone, diction, lexicon, and content in *M/F* decidedly shift from much of Burgess's older work to be more raw and bawdy, with this story being now rid of the euphemisms like those found in the *Tremor of Intent* sex scenes, the linguistic obfuscation of Alex raping, masturbating, and killing in *A Clockwork Orange*, and the self-censorship through phonemic wordplay ('for cough' for *fuck off*) of certain four-letter words in *Inside Mr Enderby*; indeed, *M/F* is more sexually explicit than much of his previous fiction and more interested in explicit acts, descriptions, and discussions of sex.[67] Such a trait was common in film and literature in the sex-obsessed and self-conscious 1960s and 1970s, especially so in American fiction in the decade and a half leading up to 1971 with books like Terry Southern and Mason Hoffenberg's erotic and incestual *Candy* (1958), William Burroughs's orgiastic junkie nightmare of *Naked Lunch* (1959), Henry Miller's many descriptions of sex and 'cunts' in *Tropic of Cancer* (1934/61), Hubert Selby Jr's depressive and debauched exploration of drug addicts in *Last Exit to Brooklyn* (1964), Sanford Friedman's

Totempole (1965) exploring the geneses of homosexuality and pursuits of sexual fulfilment, Gore Vidal's trans woman *Myra Breckinridge* (1968) who commits sexual violence – a novel Burgess described as being one that 'cannot really be excerpted, since its chief merit lies in its being a compendium of film disguised as a novel; it has to be swallowed whole', John Updike's vivid sex scenes in *Couples* (1968), though Canadian, Mordecai Richler's *Cocksure* (1968), which satirized the sexual proclivities of Hollywood, Philip Roth's neurotic masturbator in *Portnoy's Complaint* (1969), and Saul Bellow's voyeuristic and exhibitionist penile presentation scene in *Mr Sammler's Planet* (1970), all books and authors Burgess was at the very least aware of.[68] With the American authors pushing the envelopes of how far literature could go with sex, it is in *M/F* that Burgess finally used his fiction to enter the dialogue and contribute a kind of commentary on the topics of sexual explicitness, pornography, and obscenity, subjects that Burgess addressed for years in public lectures and journalism, dating back to at least 1964 when Burgess defended *Naked Lunch* from the 'pornographic hounds', to 1966 when Burgess said that Selby's *Last Exit to Brooklyn* was the least obscene book because of its 'wholly compassionate' tone, which all led to the end of 1967 when Burgess published 'What Is Pornography?' in order to formally get down to the ontology of obscenity and pornography, going on to begin lecturing on these subjects beginning in March 1969 while on an American university lecture tour.[69] Although his fascination with discussing aesthetics and pornography, definitions of obscenity, and arguments concerning censorship publicly began before Burgess first visited the United States in 1966 – largely influenced by James Joyce's *A Portrait of the Artist as a Young Man* – his American experiences appear to have significantly heightened and increased this interest.[70]

One need not look further than Miles's *Americanness*, which is partial and inauthentic, but which brings with it a myriad of indirectly or implied stases, characteristics, cultural identities, and mythic qualities that reveal a cipher, which helps unlock Burgess's supposedly structuralist, and more accurately American, turn in fiction writing. Peppered with American slang that Joseph Darlington has catalogued, consisting of 'freak', 'bitch', 'bastard', 'man', and 'pal', *M/F* is Burgess's first attempt to produce a novel for, and on, the same American audiences who read the comic, though erudite, popular American novels of Bellow, Mailer, Roth, Vidal, and Burroughs, which is proved by the fact that the text is distinctly inspired by the United States since, as Aggeler states, it is quite 'clear that Burgess's American experiences, perhaps as much as his reading of Lévi-Strauss, have had a great deal to do with generating his vision of incest', and the many inspirations explained by Burgess in *This Man and Music* (1982) appear to confirm such an assertion, at least partially.[71]

Burgess defined incest as being 'the insoluble puzzle' only to be solved by the Oedipal character trope, a character who symbolically disrupted nature through incest, thus committing the 'ultimate perversion of nature' where 'nature is shocked to death'; Burgess even went on to translate and adapt Sophocles' play for the Guthrie Theater in Minneapolis, Minnesota – a place where Burgess imagines Val from *The End of the World News* playing Macbeth at the 'Old Guthrie' – which opened on 17 October 1972.[72] *M/F*, Burgess argued, could never, due to its mythic gravitational 'incest-puzzle correlation', take place in England because, Burgess states somewhat accurately, in 'England, certainly, incest only became a crime in 1908', since it was, he suggests, not that big a deal and therefore there existed 'no long history of the deep-seated horror that found expression in the myths of the Greeks and the Indians', a point Burgess feeds his character, Mr Pardaleos, after asking for his opinion on incest: 'Incest, incest. Keeping sex in the family. Most cultures have pretty rigid taboos on incest. My own ancestral one, for instance. Oedipus, Electra, all that. Some don't care much. England didn't. They didn't bring in their Incest Act till 1908.'[73] Notwithstanding that in the United States incest was against the law in some sense since at least 1793, this story, with its Black American protagonist, still had to manifest in twentieth-century America because of the fact that Burgess believed there existed the 'perception of an incestuous pattern in American racial consciousness that mirrors incestuous yearnings in art or "antiart"'.[74] Indeed, in the United States of *M/F*, incest and sex are just as ingrained in the culture and identity of the society as, if not more than, Burgess believed existed with the Algonquin Native Americans, so much so that these ideas and themes appear routinely, consciously, and subconsciously, as Burgess's epitextual 'rhetorical craft of artistic self-fashioning' and 'self-invention' divulges, with the menu in a New York cafeteria forming an acrostic that spells *incest with mother*: 'Indiana (or Illinois) nutbake. Chuffed eggs. Saffron toast. Whiting in tarragon, hot. Michigan (or Missouri) oyster-stew. Tenderloin. Hash, egg. Ribs.'[75] To even speak of such matters is through coded language, symbolizing the ubiquity of such shame, while also addressing the difficulty in untangling and confronting it. To Burgess, the United States lacked guilt because of its relatively young age, but if it were guilt the American writer wanted, he argued, then they would have 'to seek it in the Electra motif or in homosexuality'.[76] Therefore, the Oedipal, Black, capricious, young, and precocious American protagonist, Miles Faber, or Homo Faber, becomes a uniquely American framework that Burgess used to explore a pubescent nation, enraptured by myth, obsessed with sex, volatile and yet responsive, but also able to decode these sensibilities, all while being fated towards incestuous desires due to the country's insular preoccupation with racial consciousness – the topics, the experimentation, the setting, the characters, and Burgess's largely American life at this point in his career all point to a singularly American piece of fiction.

Perhaps most singularly American is the emphasis on race which is in the background of the entire novel. Although the topic of interracial incest had been an American literary plot device from at least William Faulkner's masterpiece, *Absalom, Absalom!* (1936), it was the American writers in the 1960s and 1970s who rejected established norms and experimented with crafting an American mythos, like Thomas Pynchon, author of such novels as *V.* (1961) and *The Crying of Lot 49* (1965), which were potential inspirations to Burgess's style when he conceived of *M/F*. Remarking on Pynchon's writing in 1981, Burgess said that American authors had done very well in getting beyond having intellectuals as protagonists, using Pynchon, an author whom his second wife Liana had translated into Italian, as an example of a writer who had 'gone outside of literature totally' and crafted 'a mythology of his own, a mythology of the television commercial or a cartoon strip' which he used as a content source because an author had to always 'have something to refer to, some set of cultural props'.[77] Seeing *M/F* as exhibiting this kind of literary framework helps make sense of the text through this American lens, though this framework could be applied to other pieces by Burgess since he frequently rotated sets of reusable themes (Manichaeanism, Augustinianism, Pelagianism, original sin, political power), topics (obscenity, higher education, inter-cultural exchanges, sexuality, race), and props in his fiction (pop music, college students, music, literary figures, myth, etc.), many of which are discussed in this monograph. Despite some reused subjects and topics, Burgess shifted towards a new type of fiction in *M/F*, a fiction that moves not only to an Americanized perspective but also 'from an Anglocentric perspective to an international viewpoint' that can be seen via 'the symbolism of *M/F* ... reframed as a set of signifiers in transition between mythologies', which allowed Burgess to rely on new material to present his bricolage.[78] More specifically, this novel marks a point of production when Burgess's fiction began moving away from Asia, England, Russia, and Europe in order to create a story out of cultures that had been largely unexplored in his fiction before 1970. In addition to his move into American and Caribbean cultural identifiers, this move also indicates that Burgess's writing, as Dominic Green notes in 'The Most of Anthony Burgess' in 2017, 'recoiled from Sixties England ... and became less English', leading to 'Joycean experiments' that became 'elaborate, [with] the display of foreign tongues more aggrandizing, the fascination with French theory more irritating', which resulted in Burgess 'now writing literature about literature', perhaps loosely and distantly inspired by

Americans like William Burroughs, whom he first met in 1963, though by writing far less chaotic gallimaufry, who were engaging in similar Joycean literary experiments in books like the so-called *Nova Trilogy* (1961–67) and *Naked Lunch* (1959).[79]

While reviewing *Incubus* by Giuseppe Berto in 1966, Burgess explains the American literary trope of pushing out into the expanse of the American landscape which would simultaneously revert to European introspection along the journey, an aesthetic technique which takes shape in *M/F* and is evidence of his changing style within the novel: 'The big American novels thrust out into the Atlantic or else into the West; when they're tempted to set their comfortable *mise en scène* in an inward-looking, self-satisfied township, then they become European and can admit the ghastly luxuries of incest and family guilt.'[80] Finally put into his fiction, *M/F* marks a significant turning point in Burgess's writing career, as many Burgess scholars agree. Unique in his categorizations, Jim Clarke, the author of *The Aesthetics of Anthony Burgess* (2017), has argued that *M/F* signalled Burgess's turn towards producing literature that explored Nietzsche's *The Birth of Tragedy* (1872) term, the 'Apollonian mode' of creation that, Clarke insists, allowed Burgess to 'clearly identify his own existing Dionysian mode of chthonic inspiration' by incorporating 'Lévi-Strauss's metonymic form of cultural expression' into his work.[81] Whether or not this is an accurate analysis is beside the point, since regardless of Clarke's exegetical efficacy, what this critical point makes clear is that there is a scholarly consensus that Burgess's work appears to decidedly shift in tone and form with the publication of *M/F*. This newly acquired vehicle of literary ingenuity, Joe Darlington argues, also simultaneously facilitated Burgess's 'vision of the destiny of world culture' that moved 'from the local to the global'.[82] In zooming in on the local vision of the American identity using a worldly American protagonist, Burgess explores an identity that he believed was Americanizing the world – stating that Italy, France, Australia, and others were all becoming 'a kind of small America'.[83] Doing so also allowed him to assess what he believed was, as he told Aggeler and expressed elsewhere, 'the absurd and incestuous black preoccupation with race', meaning the emphasis on closed-off self-sufficiency advocated by the American Black Power Movement – which was a response to racist White policies and political practices enacted over generations, and which Norman Mailer in *Armies of the Night* (1968) described as effectively succeeding in 'rendering the white man invisible at will for the black' – so as to emphasize the theme of incest, and what Burgess appears to designate as anti-social cultural practices.[84] Towards the end of *M/F*, the narrative pulls out of this myopic view to take in a panoramic vista of the world, distinctly non-American as Miles has settled in Bracciano, Italy, the location of Burgess's home during the time of writing the novel, so that 'in noisy Italian peace and far away from the increasing stresses of New York', the protagonist 'can write this chronicle of a few days in my early life', to be published by 'Stearns and Loomis in London', the middle names of two prominent American expat modernist authors, T.S. Eliot and Ezra Pound, thus making a full separation from the United States impossible.[85]

Wholly ignoring the 400 years of systematic oppression targeted at Black people in America, not to mention the very recent conclusion of the Civil Rights Movement less than three years before its publication, *M/F* also acts as a condemnation of African American identity movements, with Burgess publicly arguing that it was 'about time the blacks got over this business of incest, of saying they're beautiful and they're black, they're going to conquer, they're going to prevail'.[86] Despite having travelled to around a dozen states by 1971, during one of the United States's most tumultuous political and cultural periods that provided the author with an abundance of diverse and complex experiences and ideas, African Americans' struggles was apparently a topic Burgess learned little about or else was apathetic towards. Even so, as Thomas Stumpf notes in his article, 'The Dependent Mind: A Survey of the Novels by Anthony Burgess', the unrest in the United States in the late 1960s suited Burgess well since he had the tendency to place his characters in environments that had cultural dissonance or '*Kulturkämpfe*, pitting one culture and its representatives against others and noting the usually confused, frequently tragicomic outcomes'.[87]

In the early 1970s, the motives and dispositions of young Americans were changing drastically alongside and due to cultural and educational revolutions, with largely young college student populations rebelling against the established order of the United States government, which was often met with potent military and police force against protestors.[88] Off the streets, though a part of the protests, were also battles to change and broaden academic collegiate curriculums to include more accurate portrayals of American culture, especially in the humanities. These curriculum changes were what Richard Hofstadter, in *Anti-Intellectualism in American Life* (1963), called a 'de-intellectualized curricula', a term which would likely be recognized in the twenty-first century as veiled racism or else White bias since such commentary was, at its core, just an attempt to discredit new initiatives to include more contemporary topics and histories of peoples of colour in college curriculums so that, as James Baldwin remarked, in managing 'to change the curriculum in all the schools so that Negroes learned more about themselves and their real contributions to this culture, you would be liberating not only Negroes, you'd be liberating white people who know nothing about their own history'.[89] Over thirty years later, though this debate continues at the time of this writing, Stanley Fish debated against continued attacks on similar kinds of curriculum changes, arguing that after the 'Immigration Act of 1965, and the reawakening of interest in ethnic origins ... it would be surprising had there *not* been significant changes in the materials making their way into the curriculum and onto the reading lists of our colleges and universities'.[90] However, resistance to change was – and perhaps still is – a key characteristic of Americans, who, in several polls in 1966 when asked about the Vietnam War effort, largely supported increases of military strength, seeing the venture as a 'necessary evil', since 'American opinion was ambivalent, as it is on many issues' and the general public was 'not about to turn against their president of their country if either withdrawal or victory could not be quickly established'.[91]

On one occasion Burgess claims that – though there exists no proof of this except that large student protests were occurring in Washington State during March 1969 – a protesting student even went so far as to burn down an entire 'fascist fucking library' just because Hermann Hesse could not be the subject of a PhD.[92] At the University of North Carolina at Chapel Hill in 1969, Burgess recalls seeing armed policemen, Black protestors, and demonstrations occurring on campus; at Princeton and Columbia University, Vietnam War protests took place routinely, and on American television in May 1970 there was coverage of students being shot and killed by the Ohio National Guard at Kent State University. In *MAD* magazine's October and December 1969 editions there were sections entitled 'Brawls of Ivy Department; MAD's 1969 College Riot Preview' and 'Clash-Program Department; A MAD Look at Modern College Courses'.[93] In the October edition of this satirical comic magazine, read widely by young people at the time, the aforementioned section presents a list of the 'top ten' colleges with the best riots so far that year on campus. The number one school was where Burgess would begin teaching in September 1970: Columbia University, which was followed by three other schools Burgess would go on to visit over the next several years: New York University, the University of Chicago, and Duke University. In the December 1969 edition of *MAD*, released while Burgess was on the University of North Carolina at Chapel Hill's campus, there appeared a four-page grouping of photos with captions showing helmeted police with batons, handcuffs, and guns alongside screaming students, some bloodied, some wielding megaphones, burning flags or brandishing guns and picket signs. Taken at campuses across the United States – the University of Wisconsin, City College of New York, Harvard University, Columbia University, and Princeton University – these pictures are chaotic and indicative of the overall zeitgeist. None of these stories or encounters were displayed on the cover of the *New York Times*, a publication read largely by the older generation, during the month of December, since that space was reserved for articles discussing the Nixon administration, Black Panther shootings, and other such articles with headlines such as

'The Hippie Mystique', 'Foes of War Hold Modest Protests', and '63 Arrest, 8 Policemen Hurt as 3,000 Protest Nixon's Visit'. Although the many protests throughout the country, and world, were covered hundreds of times in smaller articles in later pages in November and December 1969, not one article was accompanied by similar images to those displayed in the satirical youth publication, *MAD* magazine.[94]

With nearly 50,000 American and closer to 100,000 Vietnamese deaths by the end of 1969, and with American opinions on the war becoming less supportive, to mock the anti-war protest college youth culture could definitely be categorized as a conservative stance, especially likely to come from someone of an older generation.[95] Although *M/F* certainly fits into the milieu of early 1970s bawdy though erudite American literary fiction, many of the hidden polemics Burgess embeds in the text certainly align themselves in opposition to the liberal, progressive, and Democratic political boundaries in American politics at the time. And in *M/F* it is unmistakable that Burgess opens the novel by parodying what he saw as the ridiculousness of the New Left and college student youth culture. While talking to the character Loew, Miles explains the chaos on campus at an American university while justifying his recent exhibitionism by describing the overall campus setting as a place filled with 'Firearms flashing on the campus. Books burned at sundown – reactionary Whitman, fascist Shakespeare, filthy bourgeois Marx, Webster with his too many words. A student has a right to fuck in public' – that is, the obscenity of everyday life in the United States and the proud know-nothingness of its student population.[96] The similarities to Burgess's actual encounters and commentaries are striking, and having the sexual exhibitionism incorporated into this description allows Burgess, and the text, to connect themes of the counter culture with pornography and obscenity, often the topic of the lectures Burgess himself was giving on American campuses across the country. After spending months on end in the United States during a time with such political and social unrest, it's no surprise that Burgess's interactions with students resulted in the creation of Miles Faber, a character who exists as the epitome of American excess, arrogance, intelligence, sexual vitality, and, because of Burgess's own views and the necessities of exploring Algonquin myth in a contemporary United States, incestual urges. Clearly influenced by contemporary American culture, it's important to recognize, though, that the world of Miles Faber is not an attempt at verisimilitude or realism, since his ludicrous and farcical journey is based more on a myth which is distorted through Burgess's heteroglossic monologism than reality. Structured upon and derived from this Native American Algonquin myth, this story is acted out in an American society that condemned 'incest because it's the negation of social communion. It's like writing a book in which every sentence is a tautology', where the young Black American, Miles, who thinks 'contracepted incest should be a human right', cannot help but pursue a path that leads to incest, which he learns is a genealogical trait passed down from his father – as with Oedipus, his destiny is written in the stars (and stripes?).[97]

Not only is the urge to commit an act of incest in Miles's genes, but he is also blindly and hereditarily drawn to insubordination since he simply extends his father's 'feeble gesture of a rebel of the last generation'.[98] Embedding Miles's actions even further in literary and social myth, Miles's father had fears that Miles would commit the same incestual blunder he had: 'He [Miles's father] was obsessed by a fear that if you met her [Miles's sister] you might conceive, against your will no doubt, undoubtedly against your will, an identical passion of unlawful degree. Hellenic, again. The curse on a house. As flies to wanton boys. Sport of the immortals.'[99] This dictum establishes the mythic trope of the novel which is activated by an Oedipal fate that is fuelled by a *deus ex machina* of mythic proportions, all entwined with modern American culture, while also alluding to the final line of Thomas Hardy's *Tess of the d'Urbervilles* (1891) and King Lear's own struggles to avoid the inevitable collapse of his family which is blamed upon the gods, so that the novel again explores another motif of Burgess's: free will. Although Miles breaks the pattern and shatters the myth, at first it appears as though the Faber family has no such autonomy due to the supplanting of their free will by and through the anthropological structuralist observations of Lévi-Strauss. After defying this fate, or structuralist theory, Dr Fonanta – '*zoon phonanta*, the talking animal, man' who also lectures at Columbia University, as Burgess was preparing to do – attempts to calm Miles by summarizing everything that had happened to him at the end of the novel: 'you have exorcised the curse. ... There'll be no more incest in the Faber family'.[100] Although this literary stratagem is intentionally contrived and meant to act as an example of myth having been infused into the American, and human, psyche, *M/F* as a literary text which was produced by Anthony Burgess also exhibits the heteroglossic qualities that Bakhtin notes in 'Epic and Novel', where he discusses the novel genre's ability to 'criticize itself', thus assisting with the understanding of the authorial process of producing such a text.[101] Conveniently, Bakhtin does well to analyse the kind of literary ingenuity Burgess attempts in *M/F* that uses anthropology, personal experience, and cultural awareness to create a novel which utilizes a literary 'language [that] renews itself by incorporating extraliterary heteroglossia and the "novelistic" layers of literary language'.[102] This layering of myth, riddle, allusion, self-reflexivity, and narrative unreliability produces a literary work which has 'become dialogized, permeated with laughter, irony, humor, elements of self-parody and finally – this is the most important thing – the novel inserts into these other genres an indeterminacy, a certain semantic openendedness, a living contact with unfinished, still-evolving contemporary reality (the openended present)', since Burgess's commentary on American society, and what New Historicists call the 'life-world' of both the text and the author, was only just beginning to be novelized and is only beginning to be explicated at the time of writing this monograph.[103] Miles's journey to break with familial tradition (or curse) is also the United States's struggle to break with what Burgess saw as harmful traditional behaviour, and the text itself is an attempt for Burgess to break away from his previously European paradigmatic perspective by using a mythic and theoretical matrix as the foundation for a mimetic reconceptualization of the genre of American literary experimentation during the 1960s and 1970s.

Although Miles may be the mythic production of American ideals, he is not the only indication that Burgess's text is an imaginative critique of the United States. In the realm of literature, the American preoccupation with goods and the harnessing of the consumer ethos, Burgess gathered in 1986, led the younger college generation to resist 'Milton or Samuel Johnson' – an example also used partially by Allan Bloom in *The Closing of the American Mind* (1987) when he criticized young people who wished to trash the classical curriculum canon because 'after all, what do Shakespeare and Milton have to do with solving our problems? Particularly when one looks into them and finds that they are the repositories of the elitist, sexist, nationalist prejudice we are trying to overcome' – because of their insistence on 'relevance and the virtue of understanding their own age through its writers', which meant 'Brautigan's *Trout Fishing in America* or Kesey's *One Flew Over the Cuckoo's Nest*', thus prompting faculty to grant permission for 'postgraduate students to write theses on Norman Mailer, J. D. Salinger and even Truman Capote'.[104] Burgess waffled in his opinion of some of Mailer's work – calling *Ancient Evenings* (1983) 'a big thing – you cannot ignore it' – but was adamant at this time that he and Saul Bellow were the best American authors who had both awakened the American tongue, but for Capote, Burgess's most telling comment was when he described him as a 'bloody fool' who 'has written' but is not a 'genuine writer'.[105] With this in mind, the tossing of Mailer's name into *M/F*, with a chalked 'SCREW MAILER' on a brick wall behind a recently mugged old man, must either be a sign of the 'induced consumer appetite of this civilization' responding to literature it did not understand or like, since Mailer was probably more right than left on the political spectrum, or an allusion to the author in order to show a society that was responding to the commercial materialism of Mailer's *non-fiction* of the late 1960s which had interrupted his novelizing – which option here is not quite clear.[106] What is clear, though, is that a false-idol author drew Miles to Castita through the feeling of hunger for Sib Legeru as the 'only sanity in the world', something Burgess felt that the Beat poets, and several other authors and personages like Hermann Hesse and Kurt Vonnegut, were cultivating with their pseudo-literary escapist fiction.[107] To Burgess, academic institutions' acceptance of such authors was a sign of the dumbing down of culture and the forced forgetfulness and disrespect of history. Not naïve to the more general Western world's push in the direction of modernization, Americanization, and commodification, Burgess conceded that he was aware this was occurring in Europe too, 'owing to American influence', a dispiriting piece of reality for him to digest as a self-proclaimed 'old-fashioned' British European who found this shift entirely too 'unEuropean'.[108]

What Burgess witnessed travelling to American universities throughout this period is what Hugh Brogan, historian, describes as being a time when 'young people, who from the gilded shelter of universities which their parents' money had bought for them and in many cases built for them (never had the colleges and universities of America raised funds more successfully than during the fifties and early sixties) looked out with absolute intolerance on the modern world, and condemned it as unclean', which was brought on by the 'sixties youth movement, which had originated in the Freedom Riders, when college America had not only discovered, to its horror, just how racialist and brutal parts of the country were, but also that there was effective action it could take to improve matters'.[109] American college students during the 1960s and 1970s had a desire for action that was necessitated by the very real dangers and pressures of the world around them, resulting from a newly realized autonomy, but this also had the unfortunate side effect of a sort of cultural–historical blinding where these newly enlightened students refused to see the benefits of understanding the past because the present appeared so worthy of attention. They essentially rationalized that if the present had so many problems, then the past that had given birth to the present was also part of the problem; this of course stood in stark opposition to Burgess's view of the world, where he represented the antipodal view that 'there is no present. The present is only the past. The present is becoming the past now'.[110] This was a point Burgess appears to have never ceased believing in, as he repeats this line of thought in a 1987 letter to a Russian newspaper editor, *Literaturnaya Gazeta*, stating that:

> Our Western young have nothing to believe in except the ability to prolong the present – which means ignoring the past and the future – chiefly through the use of drugs. They have no moral standards. Sex is freely available, though possibly AIDS is beginning to act as a deterrent (not a moral one, of course). It is probably true of all of us that we are substituting fear (super-Chernobyls, atomic war, the death of the planet) for morality. Christianity has failed, except in America, where fundamentalist Christianity is proving reactionary and dangerous.[111]

Driven almost solely by emotional obstinacy, Burgess was unable to empathize with these youth movements, providing a good explanation of his stance on the subject while on an episode of *The Firing Line* television show with William F. Buckley Jr in 1972 entitled 'The Young':

> I have a bias toward reason, inevitably, but I can see that when government is so degraded, so low as merely to act on emotional appeals, possible emotional appeals must be made. But one doesn't regard the emotional appeal, therefore, as of a higher order than the rational appeal. It is the device you have to use in a particular set of circumstances. ... Behind the protest against the Vietnam War, a protest in which I most thoroughly involve myself, there is a certain measure of reason. It is wrong for a war to be waged which is not likely to produce any end which tends towards the betterment of human society. It is wrong to kill people for no reason whatsoever. It is wrong to expend money. ... Well, the young who protest against the Vietnam War, of course, are thoroughly right to do so and I say again it is a measure of the ineptitude of government that government will only listen to loud voices and will not listen to reason. But this association of the anti-Vietnam war front or faction with the young is again something very strange and something very peculiar. It's as though the young themselves have preempted this attitude toward the Vietnam War.[112]

A more nuanced and accepting view of youth, this is an example of a very rare occasion where Burgess explicitly stated his support for a cultural or political movement. Remarking on his relationship to Burgess in the early 1970s at Princeton University, a former student of his, James Lieber, remembered that Burgess, at the height of the Vietnam protests and unrest, never commented on American social issues in the classroom, saying that he 'seemed to like it [the Vietnam protests] and he seemed quite comfortable with it', but he never expressed his take on it outright, which Lieber found strange because 'it came up everywhere else and that was what was on people's minds. ... He wasn't critical of President Nixon and Henry Kissinger, people like that. ... They didn't seem to be on his screen in any way'.[113] Some explanation of this may come from Burgess's 1972 *Penthouse* interview where he rationalized his idiosyncratic stance, stating that:

> America once felt no guilt; no sense of history, no sense of guilt. Probably in the last few years, Americans have learned to be guilty, but they've learned to be guilty on a kind of spectacular American scale instead of just living with guilt as we do in Europe. The My Lai business was a terrible shock; why should it have been such a terrible shock? This is what human beings are like. Why should Americans be any different? Yet Americans always assume that they are different; this is the place where you've escaped from guilt, and Sin is over there in the Old World.[114]

This perhaps played into Burgess's opinion that reason had to prevail in social movements like this, and all he saw was a lot of emotion being flung back and forth at the forefront of these debates, topics explored in Mailer's books, *Why Are We in Vietnam?* (1967) and *Armies of the Night* (1968), as well as a point of concern dissected in the histories of the anti-war Vietnam movements by DeBenedetti and Chatfield in *An American Ordeal* (1990) and Garfinkle in *Telltale Hearts* (1995), which attempt to deduce whether the actions and approaches of the anti-war movement actually were detrimental to their pursuits, with DeBenedetti and Chatfield coming to the conclusion that although the 'antiwar movement did not force the United States to quit the war', it was still important since its 'political significance was, instead, that it persistently identified that choice as the essential issue of American foreign policy and national identity'; Garfinkle's arguments are less subtle, concluding emphatically that 'the radicalization of the antiwar movement in the 1965–69 period seems to have strengthened the prevailing "middle" view that the United States should neither leave Vietnam nor escalate the war sharply, but should keep U.S. troops there and simultaneously try to end the war by negotiation'.[115] Clarifying his perspective even further with Buckley Jr, Burgess stated that 'emotion and reason should ride hand in hand together' because when 'we can explain our emotions in syllogistic terms, then we can push on ahead with our emotions and make them as emotional as we like', but when 'emotion merely springs out of prejudices, sectarian prejudices, such as much of the emotion in the South between the whites and the blacks, then of course we have to be much on our guard', and the same went for 'today's youth', who have 'a good deal of the emotionalism that is ... not backed by reason'.[116] This was why Burgess also cautioned against Americans aligning themselves with any youth movements, and consequently why he was also hesitant to voice his support, because he saw the 'American young' as being 'well-meaning but misguided', and therefore they 'must not themselves be taken as guides', feeling instead that the 'guides, as always, lie among the writers and artists' – what kind of writer, he does not explain, but we can assume not a Sib Legeru or a Kurt Vonnegut.[117] Miles appears as a condemnation to such 'youth' thinking, ultimately with his act of public copulation and literary journey ending in no significant beneficial societal or personal enlightenment; it's actually the failure of these things, and the failure of consummating incest, that enables him to ultimately realize that breaking these patterns and cycles of action may free him from such arbitrariness so that he may be able to engage in 'Higher Games', meaning loftier goals in life, like matchmaking his adopted son and daughter in an act of somewhat 'unincestuous' incest in order to sit back and 'enjoy the movement of life – kids falling in love, performing birds'; in other words, beauty.[118]

It's not until Miles is able to escape the United States, his family, and the Western hemisphere that he can do this, though, finally allowing him, at the end of the novel, to shed the skin of his former American self, able now to Faber, or create. As an American, to whatever degree, sex and protest mixed with societal violence and assaults on sexuality, art, and social decency, are a part of Miles and his environment as he walks around early in the novel in a 'jeweled codpiece' in 'hot tiffanied Manhattan', thinking of his outfit for the following day, 'a bare penis in blue underpants, ejaculating into Buttermilk Channel' or perhaps 'catheterized by Brooklyn Bridge', which Miles sees potentially as a 'living dildo, rather, if you saw Harlem River as the isolating order of Hudson and East, a slim knife cutting off your manhood, white boy'.[119] Anything goes in the environs of this United States, and perhaps the real one too, this 'free society' to the point of absurdity that was void of rational behaving youth, with Miles's American standing in as a caricature of the problems Burgess personally identified as plaguing American students, campuses, and the cultural landscape.[120]

Sex and *M/F*

Like Miles in *M/F*, Burgess saw himself, especially later in life, as being '*used* .... Being an exhibitionist ... I had been a dildo; I had been one of those complicated Japanese sex-robots that cost so much; I had been Chester's expendable emanation, sexed but nameless', with American audiences devouring and sucking him dry night after night in classrooms, lecture halls, and interviews and through television appearances.[121] He continued writing and lecturing about ideas concerning pornography, obscenity, censorship, didacticism, and literature throughout the United States, and elsewhere, between 1968 and 1982, with lecture titles such as 'Contemporary Authors', 'The New Morality', 'The Novel in Our Culture', 'Obscenity and Pornography', 'Obscenity and the Novel', 'Obscenity, Pornography and Their Limits', 'The Use of Art: And It's Relationship to Morality, Pornography, and Propaganda', 'What Is Pornography?', and 'Wild World of the Modern Novel', and he would go on mentioning such subjects in various forms all the way up until his death in 1993 – with even his posthumous novel in verse, *Byrne* (1995), also exhibiting some discussion of sex, obscenity, and pornography.[122] He was desperate for money in the 1960s and 1970s due to taxes in England, and as he and Liana grew more dispirited with Malta, he realized that lecturing would provide him with the means to pay for another move, correctly as it turns out, since Burgess earned hundreds of thousands of dollars doing such tours and visits.[123] *M/F* was written at the height of these thematic interests, though his commentary on such topics had been building in his mind for years before the novel was published.

In *Urgent Copy: Literary Studies* (1968), Burgess's article, 'What Is Pornography?', was republished from publication in *The Spectator* on 1 December 1967.[124] The article was inspired by Britain's successful prosecution and banning of Selby's novel, *Last Exit to Brooklyn* (1964), under the 1959 Obscene Publications Act (this verdict was overturned in the Court of Appeal in 1968), a book consisting of 'a series of interlinked fictions about perverse and violent sex in the squalider purlieus of New York' – 'The things that go on in New York. The Indies far safer' – which Burgess defended for right of publication in court, humbly claiming 'to offer myself' to help.[125] Along with Frank Kermode, who covered the trial in some detail in *Modern Essays* (1971), Burgess was an advocate for the publication of the book which was being decried as 'a piece of outrageous pornography', but Burgess didn't particularly like the novel, stating his difficulty in objecting to its ban because he had to 'pretend that a very mediocre book was good art whose literary qualities were its best defence'.[126] Although he thought the book failed 'as good art', he believed it had some value in that it revealed a dark reality of American poverty and could perhaps make people want to 'do something charitable to people whose tragic lives arouse Aristotelian pity and terror'.[127] Burgess attended the court appeal among eleven other defence witnesses at the 'Magistrates' Court, Marlborough Street, in mid-November 1966'.[128] Although Burgess seemed disheartened after getting involved with the debate surrounding the book, due to his dislike for the collection of short stories, his public experience dealing with this issue serves as one of his earliest public authorial engagements with the topics of censorship, pornography, obscenity, and aesthetics. After having written an introduction for the reissued second edition of *Last Exit to Brooklyn*, he lamented that for posterity it would look as though he commended the novel by 'its very presence at the head of the book', which he makes clear was not the case.[129] Still, Burgess did not squander the opportunity at the head of the novel, instead releasing a harsh diatribe aimed at the minds wishing to censor that which scared them, characterizing the magistrates and public figures as missing the point and being feeble-minded:

> It is the frivolous mind that responds with pious horror to distasteful subject-matter and ignores the genuinely moral purpose for which the subject-matter is deployed. Look into the repressive mind and you will see fear or obsession or both. The mature and well-balanced mind is, when shocked at revelations of human depravity or social sickness, concerned with making that shock fire a reforming zeal or, at least, stoke compassion. Repression does not come into it; rather, the need is felt to extend sympathy by publicizing the bad news, broadcasting the agony.[130]

The prefatory note continues by summarizing Selby's book and approach to fiction, concluding that the work is in fact a product of a literary fiction writer and not a piece of pornography by stating that 'true obscenity uses literary condiments to inflame the palate; Selby, committing himself from the very first page to an unedited recording, totally eschews the devices of titillation. Pornography is not made this way'.[131] Burgess does admit that 'American books like *Last Exit to Brooklyn* and the sodomistic *Totempole* go about as far as fiction may be expected to go', really a remarkable false comparison between genres since *Totempole* is simply a gay bildungsroman with only two semi-explicit sex scenes, though due to anti-gay prejudice at the time of its publication many reviews attacked the novel.[132] Selby's lucid, direct, and disturbing (and far more explicit and gritty than Friedman) style, Burgess argues, is reminiscent of the landscape which he intended to depict, and therefore he is being accurate, something not present in pornography because pornography deals not with reality 'but with fantasy'.[133] What Selby shows his readers, Burgess – and indeed Kermode, by what he called 'moral power' – contends, though apparently without confirmation from Selby himself, *should* be offensive, not because it is indecent but because it *exists* in real life; real people in the real world live in the squalor presented in the book and that is what should be offensive. Advocates of censorship instead tried to silence the very representation of the signified. Burgess blames these accusers for being vapid and selfish, themselves hoping rather not to 'wish to intervene' with the real-world inspiration for the novel, deciding instead to try to ban professed pornographic representations when what should really happen is a call to 'change the society in which this thing can happen'.[134] Finally, Burgess sums up the entire problem of censorship, pornography, and art, and the conflation that occurs among them, as being a misattribution of the 'nature of the kinesis'.[135]

This theme of non-intellectuals misunderstanding and misperceiving what is and what is not pornographic and didactic, compared and contrasted to what is and is not *art* or *literature*, is what drove Burgess's interest in this topic since he also argued, near the end of his life, that nothing is 'less pornographic than intellection'.[136] Intellect was also a quality lacking in the political arena, as Burgess, always sceptical of governments and their powers, warned his audience in a 1969 lecture at Colorado College, saying, 'When they start telling us what is obscene, telling us our morals, then we should tell them where to get off. … There are other fields where we are disgusted, but the government does nothing about them.'[137] In 1973, these kinds of arguments would take place in the *New York Times* with his article 'For Permissiveness with Misgivings', as he defended the Golden Age of Porn film *Deep Throat* (1972) against censorship from the Supreme Court, since porn, attempting to 'arouse sexual desire', could not be obscene because obscenity was, by definition, only 'the merely disgusting (like ordure in the streets or a useless and bloody war) and we ought to need no warning against the danger of throwing up'.[138]

Exacerbated by his time in the United States, where he lectured frequently on pornography, *M/F* is Burgess's first novel to incorporate the concepts of pornography, obscenity, and censorship together explicitly and exhaustingly in his storytelling – although there are fragments of these separate elements scattered across his entire canon. The physical product of pornography, descriptions of sexually charged situations, obscenity, expletives, and egregious sexual acts take place routinely in *M/F* because they must in order to be evocative of the proliferation of pornography and obscene language that began in the late 1960s and 1970s in popular American culture that was largely the effect of what Burgess deemed as social *permissiveness*, or decadence, therefore positioning *M/F* simultaneously as a novel in the same genre as the fashionable popular American literature of the time.[139] Assessing and analysing his work on the subjects of pornography, obscenity, didacticism, and censorship is important because Burgess's overall feelings towards these topics all coalesced and significantly impacted his personal philosophy of aesthetics that took shape in the literary aims, content, and purpose of his work from the mid-1960s onward. The motif of obscenity is weaved unabashedly into *M/F*, a novel Burgess was writing during his censorship battles in Malta that led to his eventual move to Rome, through various means as yet another way to capture the zeitgeist of American culture during his time in the United States.

While living in Malta in June 1970, Burgess gave a lecture entitled 'Obscenity and the Arts' for the Malta Library Association to 'an audience of three hundred' Maltese Jesuits, during a time when he had been publicly castigating the Maltese government for censorship.[140] For this occasion, Burgess changed the 1960s American anti-Vietnam War magazine *Horseshit* example to a euphemism: 'Equine Ordure', which has within its pages, Burgess explains, 'mostly...drawings of elderly people making love'.[141] Developing some of these ideas over almost two decades, Burgess would return to the topic, even borrowing the title of this lecture in a 1988 *Times Literary Supplement* piece entitled 'Obscenity and the Arts – A Symposium', where Burgess once again emphasized that 'all actions termed obscene exist, or are capable of existing, in the real world, and art merely affirms that they are there', and that all of his arguments are only concerned with 'true art', and pornography 'cannot be that, since it does not represent the real world, turning it into an impossible pornotopia where the only events are orgasms', where despite its lack of artistic ingenuity, the 'State would be showing blatant hypocrisy in banning it'.[142] Subtle are the changes in his arguments, where several exist, but for the most part his early lectures act as evidence of the genesis of his ideas on the subjects, ideas which would come into direct conflict with political apparatuses.

Nowhere else was the relationship between pornography and aesthetics made clearer than when Burgess spent time in the United States, where pornography intrinsically began wrapping itself up with his ontological aesthetic commentary about society and art due to his belief that best-selling fiction was a mixture of the didactic and the pornographic that abandoned the duties of a literary author for cheap popular salvation rather than earnest attempts to exploit language in order to produce an intellectually dense text that had the capability to 'change your life'.[143] Burgess was very much aware of and interested in the distinctly American brands of pornographic invention that began growing into the American psyche during the late 1960s and early 1970s that led up to the 1973 'Miller vs. California' Supreme Court decision that found that 'obscene materials did not enjoy First Amendment protection', with obscene materials being defined as depending on whether (a) 'the average person, applying contemporary community standards would find that the work, taken as a whole, appeals to the prurient interest', (b) 'the work depicts or describes, in a patently offensive way, sexual conduct specifically defined by the applicable state law', and (c) 'the work, taken as a whole, lacks serious literary, artistic, political, or scientific value'.[144] With pornography, and also incest, being popular cultural motifs in American literature and film, really with the entire Western world, during this period – with films like *Rebel without a Cause* (1955), *Lolita* (1962), *Candy* (1968), *Midnight Cowboy* (1969), *Beyond the Valley of the Dolls* (1970), *Tropic of Cancer* (1970), *The Devils* (1971), *Deep Throat* (1972), *Fritz the Cat* (1972), and *Deliverance* (1972), and books such as *Tropic of Cancer* and *Capricorn* (1934/61), *V.* (1963), *Myra Breckinridge* (1968), *Ada* (1969), *Wild Boys* (1969), *Portnoy's Complaint* (1969), and *The Breast* (1972), to only name a few that included obscenity, incestual themes, pornography, sexual violence, and explicit sexual acts – *M/F* should be recognized similarly as a cultural identifier of the zeitgeist of 1960s and 1970s popular culture in the United States, alongside other such authors as Saul Bellow, William Burroughs, Henry Miller, Vladimir Nabokov, Thomas Pynchon, Philip Roth, Terry Southern, and Gore Vidal.

During one of the most obscenity-filled portions of *M/F*, Miles stumbles upon his doppelganger – perhaps a little like the incestuous twin Uncle Jack in *Candy* – Llew's bedroom filled with pornographic items, among them a paperback book he had been reading 'called *Giant Cock*, no fairy tale but obviously a loose story of crude leering conquests dripping with gissum, a representation of women's agony as pleasure', therefore presenting Miles with an image of himself, a reflection, not as an exhibitionist but as a masturbator and potential rapist of his sister (as Llew tries), as well as perhaps also presenting the question to him of whether he was capable of committing incest with his sister.[145]

Upon further investigating the room, there also exists a 'cupboard full of tattered sex magazines published in, of all places, Adelaide, South Australia, the cover of one of which showed a girl screwing a complaisant kangaroo with a dildo' – not surprisingly, Adelaide is the city that Burgess travelled to in March 1970 for the Adelaide Arts Festival in order to present a lecture on censorship.[146] Other examples of sexualized material abound throughout the novel, with records from groups like the 'Punishings from the Rods', 'The Dea Dea Tease', and 'Nekro and the Philiacs', a paperback entitled 'Faggots for the Burning – a study of irregularities in high American places, significant exposure, very popular at that time' sitting on the knee of a fellow bus rider towards La Guardia airport in New York City, the 'dirty sex film called *The Day After*', the description of sexual relations with a family member as 'the whole works: *eiaculatio seminis inter vas natural mulieris*, and no pills or diaphragms or pessaries', and Miles's doppelganger reading yet another 'profane book'.[147] The exact Latin phrasing aforementioned actually comes from Joyce's *Ulysses* in the Wandering Rocks episode when questioning whether Sister Mary Patrick had committed adultery with her husband's brother; the Latin is translated as 'ejaculation of semen within the natural female organ'.[148] By alluding to what is considered one of the greatest novels of the twentieth century, *Ulysses*, a novel which also uses a myth, derived from Homer's *The Odyssey*, as a structural source, and which was initially banned in England for obscenity upon publication in 1922, Burgess is conjuring the spirit of a modernist text which pushed the boundaries of literary experimentation and the presentation of real life in literature, regardless of how sexually explicit it was. In an article commemorating Joyce's centenary in 1982, Burgess stated that just because 'sex and obscenity were aspects of the programme of realism', this did not make them pornographic, because Joyce's language obfuscated any such titillation and was therefore 'very remote from pornography'.[149] At a tribute festival at the University of Rochester in New York in 1972, Burgess explained how the 'virtue of obfuscation' is why *Ulysses* was not pornographic, and how, similar to his own *A Clockwork Orange*, the two novels use slang or 'obscure symbolism' to shield against 'violent pornography' or Joyce's character 'alone facing the universe'.[150] In 1975, Burgess even compared *Ulysses* with the novels of the era of *M/F*, stating in *On the Novel* that 'lesser novelists, working in a more permissive age, can record cognate agonies. Generally speaking, any novelist writing after the publication of Hubert Selby's *Last Exit to Brooklyn* or Gore Vidal's *Myra Breckinridge* can expect little objection, on the part of either publisher or police, to language or subject-matter totally unacceptable, under the obscenity laws then operating', making it even less unsurprising to see how Burgess was attempting, in *M/F*, to insert his work into the heteroglottal discourse of literary obscenity and of American permissiveness of the 1960s and 1970s.[151]

Ulysses and *Finnegans Wake* are also books about families – with Burgess even suggesting that the 'real problems of *Finnegans Wake* are not semantic but referential. Joyce loves to mystify, and the mysteries yield less to the language scholar than to the diligent enquirer into the facts of Joyce's life, or the lives of his friends' – especially families with fathers who masturbate in public and have incestuous dreams about their daughters, with the separation between these two characters being just that, *public* and *dream*, since, as Burgess commented on regularly, *Ulysses* is Joyce's daytime (public) novel, while *Finnegans Wake* is his nighttime (private/dream) novel.[152] In *M/F*, Miles too straddles the gap between these dichotomies, between public acts and fantasy, tangible true life and myth, free will (daytime) and predetermination (night). At one point in the novel, Miles bridges the daytime and nighttime, sexual explicitness and incest, while being directed to daydream by Pardaleos, whose guided questions ask about whether Miles could be blamed for 'thinking that the old were mad' before Miles begins, at the request of Pardaleos, to fantasize about voyeuristically watching as a son and mother engage in copulation:

> The mother had no face, but her body was clearly defined – big breasts, belly, buttocks shining sweatily in the morning light. The son was bony and over-eager. Their engagement was urgent and he came as quickly as a young rooster. Then he lay back, wet and panting, and his face was something like mine. … It was just sex. If it were a sort of morality cartoon you could stick a shocking label on – SONFUCKSMOTHER. Primal sense isn't revolted, except perhaps aesthetically. It's ideas, words irrational taboos, pseudo-ethical additives that that [sic].[153]

As much a book about generational differences, for all of its sexually dubious content, *M/F* fits neatly into an American pop culture from the 1950s on with films like *Rebel without a Cause* (1955) that has a teenage daughter desirous to kiss her father on the lips and active defiance from children to parents.[154] In the late 1950s and 1960s, the United States started to lose the aesthetic of 'such mushy fantasy', and *M/F* resembles such a shift in American influence as this quality looms over the novel even after Miles leaves the States; this tale perhaps even closely resembles Terry Southern and Mason Hoffenberg's licentiously surreal tale of an American college girl's exploration of the country and her body, which includes acts of masturbation, incest, and sadomasochism, as well as poet idolization and Eastern philosophy, in *Candy* (1958), which was made into a film in 1968 with the likes of Marlon Brando and Ringo Starr.[155] Like Miles, he and the titular character Candy cannot outrun *sex*, and so, in *M/F*, whether in the United

States or abroad Miles's landscape is riddled with phalluses: 'living dildo', 'I had been a dildo', 'great phallic spike', 'wooden phallic spike', 'plastic representation of a male sexual apparatus', and so on like a Freudian nightmare.[156] Thus, *M/F* acts as a vehicle to explore and utilize the mythic themes surrounding incest, Americanism, and human sexuality in order to show how 'transposing the liberation of the psyche to the social level, we have killed our neuroses and now live in a permissive world. But permissiveness turns out to be very naïve'.[157] The naïvety Burgess speaks of here is not only Miles's youth, but also the novel's circuitous and ultimately meaningless journey, filled with dead ends and let-downs.

One such let-down comes when, upon solving several riddles in a public square in Castita, solutions of which are not shared with readers of the book, *M/F*'s narrator, Miles, fears being 'arrested for uttering a public obscenity' in order to respond to the last riddle, the answer being *fuck*.[158] Just as Miles refuses to provide closure in the denouement of the novel by telling readers to produce their own meaning, Burgess's text and its characters often encounter riddles and provocations with no solid purpose or explicit answers, leaving Miles to question the entropic nature of his life at the end of chapter 14 with, 'What had I done to deserve these problems?'[159] Attempting to tackle the seeming meaninglessness and relativity of life, and indeed of art, several characters of *M/F* assert that there is not always meaning attached to life occurrences and/or literature, since good literature is not meant to provide that meaning – a direct attack on the Puritan American tradition 'that to read a book for pleasure alone is probably sinful; to read a book for information is probably holy'.[160] It is this aesthetic point too that is a key driver of the *M/F* structuralist plot that seeks to show 'myth *is* language: to be known, myth has to be told', therefore the difference between pornography and real literary art that *suggests* and provides a written structural approach to myths of American culture is that real literary art must innately and simultaneously exist, in Burgess's aesthetic terms, in a stasis between pornographic and didactic writing in order to be true to literature, and in the case of *M/F*, structuralism (through a Joycean lens, Burgess defines these terms first in *Joysprick* (1973) and then in *This Man and Music* (1982) with the same inspirations, but now applied to the continuum of pornography and didacticism):

> Improper art is either pornographic or didactic: proper art is static. One can diagrammatize this concept as a continuum, with the pornographic at one end, the didactic at the other, and the static attempting to maintain a middle position. The artist is always in danger of moving from his static posture and embracing either the pornographic or the didactic. If the two ends of the continuum are joined, making a cycloid, then the didactic and the pornographic meet. In a great deal of Class 1 fiction the didactic justifies the pornographic.

> Indeed, the best-selling formula for our time insists on the combination of frank sex and technical information. The reader enjoys sex, and, if he feels any shame in this, it can dissolve in a sense of virtue that he is learning how an airport is run, or a bank, or the White House, or a nuclear installation. In Class 2 fiction sexual or aggressive emotions may be aroused, but their arousal and purgation are subordinate to the total structure. In true pornography the pornograph – book or picture – is a mere device for procuring discharge. Very little Class 1 fiction is pornographic in this sense, but titillation is an avowed aim, as is the conveying of information.[161]

A *real* literary novel, of the 'Class 2' variety, although it can 'be temporarily adjudged pornographic', is meant to act as art of and within itself, not as an inspiring work meant to teach the reader.[162] Exceptional literature, Burgess expressed, should provide no moral lesson, no unifying accepted point – echoing the narrator in *Kingdom of the Wicked* (1985) when he says that 'literature ceases to be literature when it commits itself to moral uplift: it becomes moral philosophy or some such dull thing' – which is why *M/F* tampers with this idea in presenting, at its core, a meaningless plot, which is only meant to work into a pattern ordained by structuralism, to a character that has little more free will than Oedipus – ordered by nature, ordered by the author, ordered by fate.[163]

In the sense that *myth* is being used here, the word is meant to refer to traditional folk tales that are up for cultural interpretation; just as *M/F* is Burgess's attempt at digging down to anthropologically significant structural matters, the text should be analysed in a sense that contextually assesses what Bakhtin described as 'makeup of a given national language' that is 'surrounded by an ocean of heteroglossia, heteroglossia that is, moreover, primary and that fully reveals an intentionality, a mythological, religious, socio-political, literary system of its own, along with all the other cultural-ideological systems that belong to it'.[164] In this frame of reference, the text of *M/F* is perhaps more self-aware than any other Burgess novel, and may also include some of the most significant extra-literary authorial commentary to push the novel into realms of exegesis that Burgess desired more than many of his other novels – *A Clockwork Orange* being the large exception.

In a very post-modern move, Burgess uses the narration of the novel self-referentially in order to refer to the diegesis itself more blatantly than he had ever done up until the writing of *M/F*, when Miles dismisses any seriousness the book may be accumulating by making the reader aware of the indeterminate and fictive nature of what they read:

> I recognize the difficulty my reader is now going to experience in accepting what I wish to be accepted as a phenomenon of real life and not as a mere property of fiction. The trouble is that he, you, is, are only too willing to accept it in that latter capacity, and this inevitably impairs ability to accept it in the

> former. A camera trick, a split frame! The deployment of coincidence to the end of entertainment.[165]

'Amateur art', Miles narrates, is signalled by 'too much detail to compensate for too little life' to either criticize young people's philosophies of art, or ironically, because *M/F* is in fact a book filled with details and 'little life', none if not derived by myth and the character's mythic referents.[166] At its core, *M/F* is an experimental novel focused only on details, on invention, on social trends, on perspective and inspiration, which Burgess took great pride in and claimed was meant for 'the intelligent young' but was, he argued, though without proof and which is unlikely because the novel was out of print by 1980, not to be fully appreciated until 'ten years after publication'.[167] Depending on the sensibilities of the reader, *M/F* is either considered one of Burgess's best pieces of work or, and this is more widely accepted, as one of his worst: 'If we look at the novel as "straight-forward, traditional and realistic," then we have to conclude that it is a decided failure, however artfully and cleverly contrived.'[168] Rather than agree or disagree with this aesthetic and literary judgement, what this monograph is attempting to do is pinpoint the novel as unequivocally Burgess's American turn in literature, as evidenced by the genre, content, and influence the United States had on the text. What can be agreed upon is that *M/F*, regardless of its artistic value, is an incredibly important book to understand Burgess's aesthetic shift and his views on important subjects that he engaged with routinely outside of the book, because the novel's focus 'is broader than art'.[169]

In his shift to engage with and comment on American culture, while also criticizing the self-important novels of the 1950s and 1960s that young readers, by Burgess's estimations, looked to for guidance and meaning – *Siddhartha* (1951 United States release), *The Catcher in the Rye* (1951), *Fahrenheit 451* (1953), *The Lord of the Flies* (1954), *On the Road* (1957), *To Kill a Mockingbird* (1960), *The Electric Kool-Aid Acid Test* (1968), *Slaughterhouse-Five* (1969), and so on – Burgess stuffs Miles's world full of pornographic content and questions of virtue so as to ridicule the habits of permissive culture and low aesthetic value that makes the characters, and readers, question the art produced in such an environment. One such example comes when Miles expresses that he had once met the famous author of dirty writings, Yumyum Carlotta, who is then immediately insinuated to be the cause of society's ills by a Castitian inspector.[170] The ultimate irony of the novel and Miles's quest to find the elusive poet, Sib Legeru, is that the authors of Sib Legeru's *works* are revealed to be Miles's family and friends when they were young adults, whose writings Dr Fonanta, another co-author, describes as exhibiting 'the nastiest aspects of incest – and I use the term in its widest sense to signify the breakdown of order, the collapse of communication, the irresponsible cultivation of chaos'.[171] Through contrived and sanguine youthful minds who wrote 'pseudoworks' – defined as being disingenuous and bogus (Burgess used the term publicly to describe writing that lacked literary elements, while the terms 'pseudo-works' and 'pseudo-students' also appear in *The Clockwork Testament* to describe school*work* and *students* not worth Enderby's time) – although they desired meaning so badly, the texts of Sib Legeru are examples of a combination of an absence of meaning that could only come from 'sniggering boyscout codishness' that was essentially the perfect mix of the didactic and pornographic.[172] The author referred to as 'Sib Legeru' is summarized as being a façade for a group of adolescent and sophomoric writers pandering and engaging in a 'therapeutic experiment' that involved 'spurious joy in spurious creation, followed by the salutary horror of seeing how mad and bad and *filthy* the pseudoworks were', to invoke the image of a kind of quasi-utopian hippie cult that writes poor poetry.[173] Dr Fonanta continues Burgessianly, professing that the true artist's, and therefore the truly enlightened human's, job is, as Burgess similarly states in 'Epilogue: Conflict on Confluence' in *Urgent Copy*, 'to impose manifest order on the universe, not to yearn for Chapter Zero of the Book of Genesis', a mistake Burgess felt many of the popular writers of the time made.[174] Even more biographically, Burgess appears to describe himself through the personage of Fonanta: 'I wanted to specialize in the psychology of incest, but the scope is surprisingly limited. So I dabble still – music, literature, light philosophy. Art, I believe, will prove man's salvation, but not. This. Kind. Of. Pseudo. Art.'[175] This is particularly autobiografictional and double-voiced, since Burgess had used and would go on to use some of these ideas in non-fiction and fiction, saying in a 1975 interview that 'Man must be free. He must find his own salvation through art', and remarking many times that he thought of himself more as a composer than an author, even noting in the closing to *Mozart and the Wolf Gang* (1992) that he felt he owed 'more to the great composers than to the great writers'. Connecting such points opens the text of *M/F* up to the 'fluidity or permeability of genres and categories' beyond the structuralism that is commonly discussed; this cannot help but be the context in which the text should be understood due to the blatant acts of '*Doubly-oriented speech*, that is, speech which not only refers to something in the world but refers to another speech act by another addresser.'[176] Again, the closely biographical details are crucial to understanding all the Burgess texts discussed in this monograph, and *M/F* acts as a seminal jump in this kind of analysis that exposes his biographical fissures and disguised treatises that exist, in this case with pornography, aesthetics, and the United States.

American materialism and *M/F*

What Burgess perceived as – and this is clearly not a unique idea, especially at this time – the *Americanization* of the world, he felt was not 'necessarily a bad thing' but 'an excellent thing' if all that came from the United States was finding a restaurant with a 'refrigerator there' or finding that one could 'get ice in your gin and tonic'.[177] What worried Burgess about Americanization was not the technological advancements and amenities, not even to a certain extent the type of consumerism which improved human life; rather, it was the cultural heritage aspect that he feared. He felt the world was commodifying around an American idealism where people only saw the 'exotic' in countries that could not afford Americanization, meaning 'no home comforts, pepper, unleavened bread'.[178] This is what he referred to on one occasion, although not as the progenitor of the phrase which the *Oxford English Dictionary* notes as coming into use in 1950, as the 'cocacolonization' of the world, which he believed made its way into American collegiate curriculums by sheer cultural pressure from a 'highly competitive market' that stemmed from students' rights 'to assert the ethos of consumerism'.[179] The close association between Americans and economics and business is blatantly evident in at least nine of Burgess's novels (the others being *A Vision of Battlements* with Mendoza explaining the cheapness of 'standardised production belt' America, the *Beds in the East* with Temple Haynes and the opportunistic American capitalists, *The Right to an Answer* with Denham's colour television job opportunity, the Enderby novels with the American show-business market, *One Hand Clapping* where the United States is the exotic untouched and wealthy cinematic false utopia, *1985* with commentary on the corrosiveness of American thinking and ingenuity, *Earthly Powers* as a land of seemingly endless sinecures and paid speaking and writing opportunities, and *The End of the World News* with class struggles in the Trotsky narrative and the space exploration and the higher education system in the Puma narrative).[180] In *M/F* this topic surfaces alongside a critique of materialist culture, which, to Burgess, was not culture at all, as is evidenced when Miles's family assumes he is studying business management, but the major did not work out for him so he was 'advised to transfer to something useless', meaning Elizabethan English literature, which he claims still had a good amount to contribute to business philosophy, what with the 'intrigues, stabs in the dark, fraternal treachery, poisoned banquets'.[181] Burgess often characterized the United States as being a country that found the humanities, largely, to be nonsense – despite 'the spirit of exact knowledge that put American men on the moon [which] is to be found here also in these conscientious but exciting combings through the thinning hair of Joyce scholarship' – because the disposition of the country recognized and advocated for the profit margin far more than it did for the advancing of philosophical wisdom.[182] Remarking on this peculiar trait of Americans in 1981, Burgess said that colleges acted as a kind of 'final stage of necessary education: it is not very often the threshold of a life of scholarship. Universities themselves, not being owned by the state, are run like businesses and, like businesses, they have to compete for trade'.[183]

If *M/F* is indeed a text of criticism aimed towards Burgess's American experiences and American culture, as this chapter attests, then the language of the novel must be recognized as exhibiting what Burgess felt was American English's 'puritanical evasiveness', where euphemism and suggestion are used routinely and every scrap of language has meaning and significance, even down to the use of pink substances in the book.[184] Burgess associated the colour *pink* with being evocative of 'American innocence' which turns to brain matter that is consumed in *M/F*, a metaphorical disintegration of intellect in the mouth of an American exhibited when Mr Pardaleos scoops 'up pink brain-stuff'.[185] Miles feels – echoing Strauss's work in *The Raw and the Cooked* (1964) wherein Strauss explores the semiotics of food across cultures – as if he had just consumed an ancestor or a piece of the past after his meal: 'I felt as though I'd eaten my father, a cast coffined ham with poached eggs for eyes, his brain a soufflé, his fingernails alive and prickling'.[186] Summarizing in 'The Use of Codes', published in *The Art of Telling* (1983), Frank Kermode describes Strauss's work, sounding eerily similar to what Burgess is trying to encapsulate here, as citing 'a myth, found, he says, all over America, that links eclipses, rotting meat, disease, and incest. Without the tabu on incest (of which Miles's genetic arguments are merely a minor reinforcement) there could be no order, no human system-making'.[187] Since Burgess claims that eating American food during the winter holiday season made him want 'to be an American', after a Princeton-American dentist fit four lower fake teeth into his mouth with 'a prosthesis of solid pink American workmanship' just 'in time for the roast turkey' at both Christmas and 'its Thanksgiving rehearsal', a mouth filled with American innocence and evasiveness during the most consumerist holiday of the year fits nicely into the *M/F* world.[188] This *fit* is further supported as either an act of self-mythologization or inspiration, since Miles himself is born on 'Christmas Eve. Two minutes to midnight' (this is also the time of year Janet and Howard Shirley visit the United States), effectively moulding Miles into a mythic personage who symbolizes overt and unabashed American materialism and excess that has washed over a supposedly sacred Christian holiday (as Miles takes on Llew's name as a form of Noel or Nowell).[189] The ironic and antithetical nature of the mythic – in the sense that it is not based on any factual knowledge of Jesus's birthdate – Christmas holiday has popularly warped the Christian significance into the epitome of American exceptionalism and hypocrisy distorted through America's reductionist views that lead to an altered reality, a 'simplification; a reflection of the "melting pot" of popular American imagery' that often boils down to an American obsession with money in Burgess's fiction.[190]

Behind many of Burgess's criticisms or protestations about American greed, hubris, and power, Burgess knew that at the core of his travels to the United States was that he too visited American shores because of the money, therefore admitting to the fact that the almighty currency rules and runs everything – the artist and the businessman – a 'depressing reality' that Burgess never got over; Miles concurs when he states that 'the facts of economic life are desperately cruel'.[191] For these reasons, somewhat cathartically for Burgess, Miles is an American metaphor, a symbol, existing as the synecdoche of all America – an image of the depressing reality at the core of human nature and modern society that we are all stuck in systems of cultural, social, and familial webbing.

Conclusion: the significance of *M/F*

During an interview in 1973 for *Studies in the Novel* out of North Texas State University, Burgess expressed concern with the scholarly tendency to ignore the 'folk history' and 'folk mythology' contextually surrounding authors and their works because of the valuable nature of what such information could lend to critical inquiry.[192] He argued that in England, folksiness is 'very much a part of English life. You can't avoid it. It's not contrived. It's natural. Things don't change very rapidly there. So you're always aware of the past in England and probably far more than in America, although in parts of America you're aware of the past: New England and so on', which makes sense in the context of *M/F*, considering Miles attended college in Massachusetts and is plagued by his familial history.[193] Both inside and outside of his fiction, Burgess expressed that he had witnessed the (particularly American) youth of the day's desire to overthrow 'the past – all the past, indiscriminately', with populations from two particular countries actively seeking to destroy the past completely:

> We are living in an age in which two great nations are committed to the destruction of the past. Both the United States and the Soviet Union dream of a radiant future into which the past can uncoil no qualifying tentacles. The past may be permitted to subsist as the material for museums and cinematic entertainments, but only to be wondered at, derided, mocked, accepted as the garishly coloured matter, ignorant, unscientific, unhygienic, which the radiant future is to supersede.

Shockingly omitted here is the 'Cultural Revolution' taking place in China.[194] At the time of writing *M/F*, Burgess declared the United States to be a country whose 'character is still emerging', a character too that had been up until 1970 long diluted by a kind of naïve relativism that sought relevance, an idea informed by such authors in the Burgess orbit as B.F. Skinner, particularly in his 1948 utopian novel *Walden Two*.[195] Sounding like something out of Aldous Huxley's *Brave New World* (1932) or the history-destroying precepts of Mao Zedong's 'Cultural Revolution' (1966–76) – which was often lauded by American counter-culture youth groups, specifically the May Second Movement, though general student populations were seen pinning 'Mao badges onto their lapels' and quoting 'from his "Little Red Book" on the walls of their lecture halls', even with 'Black Panther leader Eldridge Cleaver once' calling Mao the ' "baddest [expletive] on planet earth" ' – the characters in *Walden Two* express that in their new scientifically progressive and positivist society, which acts as a precursor for Skinner's own science of behaviourism to emerge decades later, there was no room for history since 'History tells us nothing. … Nothing confuses our evaluation of the present more than a sense of history.'[196] American culture and the education system that Burgess engaged with during his four years travelling and living in the United States between 1966 and 1970 gave him the opinion that 'American education doesn't pay enough attention to history or to language', so in his first literary response emanating from his increasingly close relationship with the United States, Burgess constructs *M/F* around a prefigured cultural and mythic stratagem which includes the pornographic, the incestuous, and the obscene, intertwined with youth culture, in-breeding, and racial identity movements to produce an experimental novel that takes on a theoretical structure to show the post-modern collapse of culture occurring in the United States.[197] Burgess pursues this, it is suggested here, all while inserting himself into the American literary discourse of the 1960s and 1970s, so that when Miss Emmett remarks that the 'Americans are clever people' regarding either-or-both spying and/or meteorology, it becomes clear that the United States's scientific and observational influences are far-reaching, but ultimately Miles, and, due to the mythic and sexual circumstances, humanity, finds salvation outside of the United States, with a multi-ethnic marriage and adopted children, thus rejecting commodification, Americanization, and incestual habits for a more worldly, historical, and heterogenous existence.[198] As Fonanta states, incest signifies, as noted before, 'the breakdown of order, the collapse of communication, the irresponsible cultivation of chaos'; Burgess is therefore identifying 'incest with the narcissistic attributes of contemporary culture', that is to say American culture, which 'Faber himself is a product of'.[199] The American abdication of historical, cultural, and humane social and political practices, matched up against Lévi-Strauss's mythic but more importantly anthropological dictum that humanity must never lose 'sight of the fact that existing societies are the result of great transformations occurring in mankind at certain moments in prehistory and at certain places on the earth, and that an uninterrupted chain of real events relates these facts to those which we can observe', affords Burgess not only a grand structure to infuse into the diegesis but also an approach to the story that acts as a vehicle for his own interests and ideas through the use of contemporary, experimental, and topical issues and themes.[200]

It should be recalled that the text of *M/F* exists on two parallel planes simultaneously, where

> behind the narrator's story we read a second story, the author's story; he is the one who tells us how the narrator tells stories, and also tells us about the narrator himself. We acutely sense two levels at each moment in the story; one, the level of the narrator, a belief system filled with his objects, meanings and emotional expressions, and the other, the level of the author, who speaks (albeit in a refracted way) by means of this story and through this story.[201]

Applying this Bakhtinian theoretical, philosophically anthropological, and historical lens reveals these many embedded details and layers of meaning in and surrounding Burgess's novels (the paratexts), thus producing an incredibly rich and beneficial commentary on Burgess's life and work; in fact, with *M/F* specifically, the application of this apparatus may even be crucial to fully understanding and evaluating the text as well as acting as an example of the complexities to appear in Burgess's later fiction. Indeed, the United States was both the catalyst and paradoxically the anticatalyst to Burgess's experimental and dialogic turn in the 1970s, as he expressed in 1973: '"If I were writing what I wanted to," he said, "I would be writing highly experimental fiction which no one would buy"'.[202]

One review in the *New York Times* described Burgess as a 'puzzling writer' who has 'read almost too much' because he too often 'seems merely to be manipulating the received literary past', where 'puzzles are not always art', which makes *M/F*, to this critic at least, 'too contrived .... It is a mechanical bird, technically marvelous but secretly dead'.[203] Another review argued that Burgess was no longer interested in telling stories but rather had fallen into his own character, 'Dr. Spindrift's predicament – becoming so absorbed by the fascinating life there is in words that he forgets they are "part of the warm current" of a larger life', while Auberon Waugh deduced that Burgess had only written the novel to 'demonstrate his intellectual superiority over the reviewers. Well, he has succeeded. I can't make head or tale [sic] of it'.[204] Aesthetic judgements aside, for any serious Burgess scholar *M/F* is the turning point for Burgess both aesthetically and in terms of his writing career – despite the poor sales of *M/F*, small advance, limited translation history, and generally indifferent reception – as his popularity, due to Kubrick's *A Clockwork Orange*, was soon to blossom across the world, but mostly in the United States, and his work from this point on takes a decidedly American turn.[205]

In that vein, *M/F* is also a message *to* or *about*, not necessarily *for*, the younger generation of American students he was teaching at the time. The text even explicitly warns its (especially younger) readers against trying to distil a moral or purpose from the narrative, 'not even an espresso cupful of meaningful epitome or a Sambuca glass of abridgement', thus Miles, and Burgess, ask the reader to accept the story as is and appreciate it for its 'literary value' and nothing else.[206] In describing all writing as only *communication* that 'has been the whatness of the communication', the *M/F* text asks that the message from the writing alone, like Lévi-Strauss notes about language and myth, be the answer; but even Miles-Burgess cannot help themselves as they sarcastically call on academics to find meaning beyond the signifiers and the signifieds, to establish 'separable meaning' because it is the professors' jobs 'to make a meaning out of anything'.[207] Of course, the irony is that the book, which is littered with symbols, riddles, clues, and layers of meaning all crafted upon a theoretical concept, actually has a more simple, selfish, and biographical contextual objective below the superficial surface of the plot. Miles, and by extension Burgess, are teasing the reading audience, asking them both to simply accept the novel as is and also to solve the riddle, therefore directing the narrative communication with the reader into a type of paradoxical call and response, a Gordian knot that has no fixed answer. Just as incest is the falling in upon one's own genetics, the text collapses back onto itself as well, producing a contradiction of narrative invention that mimics that of the characters and plot, and since the 'collapse of cultures in incestuous and unproductive coupling results in a loss of meaning', the novel ends without a literary denouement and the characters themselves disappear into a sea of 'internationalism embodied in a diversity of nationalisms'.[208]

Ending in 1999 on Lake Bracciano, Italy, the fifty-year-old, Black American, Miles Faber and his Chinese wife, Ethel, have several adopted children 'of varying colours and nationalities', again a metaphor for the melting pot of the United States, none of whom share their parents' genes because Ethel believes that the 'true genetic blending of her race and my own' usually produces 'undesirable' offspring.[209] Despite Miles begging 'her to consider being impregnated by some other man', Ethel would not because she 'never allowed her ancestral moral principles to be impaired either by the Western permissive ethos or by my own what she considers extravagant desire for her ivory beauty to be transmitted to the future by any means other than the celebration of my verses'.[210] So, it appears that 'out of "creative miscegenation" and incest [there emerges] a new order of love and responsibility', in the case of *M/F*, for an American, Miles, who had once overheard in a diner at the beginning of the novel that in the United States there was 'instant soup' that symbolized 'the New World's rejection of history, but in France there are still kitchens where soup has simmered for all of four centuries', thus guiding and informing him about where a more genuine and sophisticated existence can be achieved.[211] In recognizing this, and that he can break the pattern of incest, Miles has then made history by being individualistic and iconoclastic in rejecting the mythic social patterns and urges which have ensnared his family and his countrymen.

Miles, at fifty years of age, the same number of states in the American Union, has his story brought to a close with a family that acts as a microcosm of the diverse American experiment. Burgess had not wound his riddles as tight, or with such nuance, as Joyce's *Finnegans Wake*, so his warning that 'Riddles are there for a good purpose – not to be answered' cannot be heeded since the riddles, as prepositioned by the author, itch to be unravelled.[212] Assuredly his first American novel, *M/F* also acutely resonates with Bakhtinian theory, leaving it as a prime example of Burgess's literary cultural dialogism that often utilizes an authorial hidden polemic behind his work, perhaps most notably and explicitly in the *American* novels explored throughout this monograph. *The Clockwork Testament* (1974) elongates the monologic expression of *M/F*, in many ways sounding like an extension of some of the narrative hostilities expressed, by exploring and commenting on such Burgess motifs as the 'so-called democracy' of the United States where the 'kids had to have what they wanted', where the fictional University of Manhattan has 'halfhearted student demonstrations against or for the dismissal of somebody' with 'a brave girl stripping in protest', where inside Enderby tells one of his students that the 'autobiographical element' in his poem is incestuous since the poem expresses a childhood desire of greed for his mother's breasts.[213] When encountering parodic and caricatured Americans, they note that 'sex and violence' are 'always the answer' for entertainment, and yet a portion of the population sees art and entertainment (be that Shakespeare or films of sexual violence against nuns) as the culprit of society's ills, so that 'for the sake of society there must be control' because there are 'too many dirty books and movies and also violent ones'.[214] Both texts exhibit cultural heteroglossia as presented through a 'dialogical relationship between the text and its contexts' because to 'understand means to be able to relate a text to other texts', but there is no character-to-character dialogic balance, just as Miles's path is preordained and monologic in Burgess's authorial and narrative mission, though in *The Clockwork Testament* Burgess seems to have dropped the pretence and become more explicit and severe, largely abandoning any elaborate mythic or structural base in order to carry out a cathartic, double-voiced, acerbic, though barely concealed, hidden polemic which lashes out at his newfound American popularity, this time with far fewer riddles and coded language that disguise the text's, and the author's, intentions.[215]

Notes

1 From *Index on Censorship*, PEN International, International Anthony Burgess Foundation Archives, 1978; 1981, p. 39.
2 Anthony Burgess, Standard Diary 1964, Saturday and Sunday 22 and 23 February, International Anthony Burgess Foundation Archive; Anthony Burgess, Standard Diary 1964, Wednesday, Thursday, Friday 26–28 February, International Anthony Burgess Foundation Archive.
3 Anthony Burgess, *You've Had Your Time: Being the Second Part of the Confessions of Anthony Burgess* (London: Penguin Books, 1990), pp. 208–210, 221, 231–232.
4 Gérard Genette, *Paratexts: Thresholds of Interpretation*, trans. by Jane E. Lewin (Cambridge: Cambridge University Press, 1987; 1997), p. 409.
5 Anthony Burgess, 'Anthony Burgess: Interviewed by Carol Dix', *The Transatlantic Review*, 42/43 (Spring/Summer 1972), p. 187.
6 Mikhail Bakhtin, *The Dialogic Imagination: Four Essays*, ed. by Michael Holquist, trans. by Caryl Emerson and Michael Holquist (Austin, TX: University of Texas Press, 1981), p. 278.
7 Anthony Burgess, 'Culture as a Hot Meal', *Spectator*, 11 July 1970.
8 Anthony Burgess, 'If Oedipus Had Read His Lévi-Strauss', *Urgent Copy: Literary Studies* (New York: W.W. Norton, 1968), p. 259; Anthony Burgess, *This Man and Music* (New York: McGraw-Hill Book Company, 1982), p. 163.
9 Anthony Burgess and Anthony Lewis, '"I Love England, But I Will No Longer Live There"', *New York Times*, 3 November 1968.
10 Burgess, 'If Oedipus Had Read His Lévi-Strauss', pp. 258, 260.
11 Claude Lévi-Strauss, 'The Scope of Anthropology', *Current Anthropology*, 7.2 (April 1966), 115, 118; Burgess, 'If Oedipus Had Read His Lévi-Strauss', p. 261.
12 Anthony Burgess, 'Going on Writing till Ninety or One Hundred', *Conversations with Anthony Burgess*, ed. by Earl Ingersoll and Mary Ingersoll (Jackson, MS: University Press of Mississippi, 2008), pp. 21–22.
13 Anthony Burgess, 'What Now in the Novel', *Urgent Copy* (New York: W.W. Norton, 1968), p. 155.
14 Raman Delden, ed., *The Cambridge History of Literary Criticism: From Formalism to Postructuralism*, volume 8 (Cambridge: Cambridge University Press, 2008); Anthony Burgess, *M/F* (London: Jonathan Cape, 1971).
15 Jim Clarke, 'Anthony Burgess's Structuralist Turn: Lévi-Strauss and Burgess's Aesthetics', *Anthony Burgess and France*, ed. by Marc Jeannin (Cambridge: Cambridge Scholars Publishing, 2017), pp. 111–112.
16 Burgess, 'Anthony Burgess: Interviewed by Carol Dix', p. 187.

17 Anthony Burgess, *Honey for the Bears* (New York: W.W. Norton, 1963; 1996), p. 113; Anthony Burgess, *Tremor of Intent* (New York: W.W. Norton, 1966), p. 222.

18 Anthony Burgess, 'Letter from England', *American Scholar*, 36.2 (Spring 1967), 261–265; Anthony Burgess, 'London Letter', *American Scholar*, 37.4 (Autumn 1968), 647–649; Anthony Burgess, 'Letter from Europe', *American Scholar*, 38.4 (Autumn 1969), 684–686; Anthony Burgess, 'Letter from Europe', *American Scholar*, 38.2 (Spring 1969), 297–299; Anthony Burgess, 'Letter from Europe', *American Scholar*, 39.3 (Summer 1970), 502–504; Anthony Burgess, 'Letter from Europe', *American Scholar*, 40.3 (Summer 1971), 514, 516, 518, 520; Anthony Burgess, 'Letter from Europe', *American Scholar*, 41.3 (Summer 1972), 425–428; Anthony Burgess, 'Letter from Europe', *American Scholar*, 40.1 (Winter 1970–71), 119–122; Anthony Burgess, 'Letter from Europe', *American Scholar*, 41.1 (Winter 1971–72), 139–142; Anthony Burgess, 'Letter from Europe', *American Scholar*, 32.1 (Winter 1972–73), 135–138; Anthony Burgess, 'Viewpoint', *Times Literary Supplement*, 11 May 1973; Anthony Burgess, 'Viewpoint', *Times Literary Supplement*, 22 June 1973; Anthony Burgess, 'Viewpoint', *Times Literary Supplement*, 23 March 1973; Anthony Burgess, 'Cucarachas and Exiles, Potential Death and Life Enhancement', *New York Times*, 29 October 1972; Anthony Burgess, 'Is America Falling Apart?', *New York Times*, 7 November 1971; Anthony Burgess, 'Pornography: "The Moral Question Is Nonsense"; For Permissiveness, with Misgivings', *New York Times*, 1 July 1973, pp. 18–19; Anthony Burgess, 'My Dear Students; a Letter', *New York Times*, 19 November 1972; Frank Kermode, 'Obscenity', *Modern Essays* (Glasgow: Fontana Press, 1971; 1990), p. 84.

19 Anthony Burgess, 'The Art of Fiction', *The Paris Review*, ed. by John Cullinan, 1973, p. 123; Anthony Burgess, 'Penthouse Interview: Anthony Burgess', ed. by George Malko, *Penthouse*, June 1972, p. 115; Gladys Carr, Letter to Liana and Anthony Burgess, 7 March 1977, Series III. Contracts and Royalty Statements, 1956–97: University of Texas at Austin: Harry Ransom Center, Anthony Burgess Papers, 85.1; Paul Wake, 'Introduction', *PUMA* (Manchester: Manchester University Press, 2018), pp. 5, 11; Starla Smith, 'Novelist Anthony Burgess – A Three-Time Failure?', *Iowa City Press-Citizen*, 20 October 1975, Correspondence: University of Texas at Austin: Harry Ransom Center Anthony Burgess Papers, Box 82.

20 Samuel Coale, *Anthony Burgess* (New York: Frederick Unger Publishing, 1981), p. 117.

21 Burgess, *M/F*, p. 204; Joseph Darlington, 'Tea, Coca-Cola and Wine: Culinary Triangles in Anthony Burgess's *M/F*', *Anthony Burgess and France*, ed. by Marc Jeannin (Newcastle-upon-Tyne: Cambridge Scholars Publishing, 2017), p. 143.

22 Geoffrey Aggeler, *Anthony Burgess: The Artist as Novelist* (Tuscaloosa, AL: University of Alabama Press, 1979), p. 204.

23 Deborah Rogers, Letter to John Burgess Wilson, 20 September 1969, University of Texas at Austin: Harry Ransom Center, 78.5.

24 Burgess, *You've Had Your Time*, p. 199.

25 Anthony Burgess, 'The Magus of Mallorca', *But Do Blondes Prefer Gentlemen? Homage to Qwert Yuiop and Other Writings* (New York: McGraw-Hill Book Company, 1986), p. 370; Burgess repeats almost verbatim this same comment in an article published in *But Do Blondes Prefer Gentlemen*: 'There used to be young Americans who saved up money just to fly to Liverpool, not because the Beatles were there but because the Beatles had long left here. I taught a group of American students in Deyá, home of Roberto the Heavies or Robert Graves, who could not stomach a diet of wine and fish and rice but seriously suffered because of a lack of Coke and burgers' ('Thoughts on Travel', *But Do Blondes Prefer Gentlemen?*, p. 47).
26 Burgess, *M/F*, p. 21; Lévi-Strauss, 'The Scope of Anthropology', pp. 118–119.
27 Burgess, *M/F*, p. 68.
28 Burgess, *You've Had Your Time*, p. 199.
29 Aggeler, *Anthony Burgess*, p. 144.
30 Lévi-Strauss, 'The Scope of Anthropology', p. 114.
31 Bakhtin, *The Dialogic Imagination*, pp. 411, 326.
32 Bakhtin, *The Dialogic Imagination*, p. 359.
33 Mikhail Bakhtin, *Problems of Dostoyevsky's Poetics*, ed. by Caryl Emerson, Theory and History of Literature, volume 8 (Minneapolis, MN: University of Minnesota, 1984), p. 65.
34 Bakhtin, *Problems of Dostoyevsky's Poetics*, p. 92.
35 Christopher W. Thurley, 'Anthony Burgess, Obscenity, and America', *Resources for American Literary Study*, 43 (2022), 130–160.
36 Anthony Burgess, 'Swing of the Censor', *The Spectator*, 21 June 1969, p. 16; Mary Ann Grossman, 'Banned Books Testify to Fear of Ideas', *St. Paul Pioneer Press*, 28 September 1985, the University of Texas at Austin: Harry Ransom Center Archives, para. 28.
37 Jabari Asim, *The N Word* (Boston, MA: Houghton Mifflin Company, 2007), p. 3.
38 Anthony Burgess, 'Obscenity and the Arts – A Symposium', *Times Literary Supplement*, 12–18 February 1988, p. 159.
39 Bakhtin, *The Dialogic Imagination*, p. 293.
40 Burgess, *M/F*, p. 9.
41 Burgess, *M/F*, pp. 9, 217–218.
42 Anthony Burgess, *On the Novel* (Manchester: International Anthony Burgess Foundation, 1975; 2019, p. 37; Burgess, 'Letter from Europe' (Autumn 1969), 684–686; Burgess, 'Letter from Europe' (Summer 1970), pp. 502–504; Anthony Burgess, 'Is Shakespeare Relevant?', *New York Times*, 11 December 1970.
43 Anthony Burgess, 'Signals', *But Do Blondes Prefer Gentlemen?*, p. 199.
44 Jerry Belcher, 'An Author Speaks: Goals of Campus Riots Too Vague', *San Francisco Examiner*, 14 March 1969, p. 36.
45 Burgess, *M/F*, p. 10.
46 Bakhtin, *The Dialogic Imagination*, p. 324.
47 Burgess, *M/F*, p. 14.
48 Coale, *Anthony Burgess*, pp. 108, 117.

49 Burgess, Standard Diary 1964, Wednesday, Thursday, Friday 26–28 February, International Anthony Burgess Foundation Archive; Burgess, *This Man and Music*, p. 166.
50 Mikhail Bakhtin, 'Discourse in the Novel', *The Dialogic Imagination: Four Essays*, pp. 271–273.
51 Bakhtin, 'Discourse in the Novel', p. 272.
52 Burgess, *M/F*, p. 218.
53 Burgess, *M/F*, p. 50; Darlington, 'Tea, Coca-Cola and Wine', p. 138.
54 John J. Stinson, *Anthony Burgess: Revisited* (Boston, MA: Twayne, 1991), p. 39.
55 Anthony Burgess quoted in Aggeler, *Anthony Burgess*, pp. 205–206.
56 Anthony Burgess quoted in Aggeler, *Anthony Burgess*, pp. 205–206.
57 Lévi-Strauss, 'The Scope of Anthropology', pp. 118–119; Burgess, *Honey for the Bears*, p. 117.
58 Bakhtin, *The Dialogic Imagination*, p. 326; Burgess, *M/F*, p. 219.
59 Stinson, *Anthony Burgess*, p. 105; Charles Champlin, 'Anthony Burgess Bounces Back in Blighty', *Los Angeles Times*, 9 June 1968.
60 Burgess, *You've Had Your Time*, p. 208; Geoffrey Aggeler, 'Introduction', *Critical Essays on Anthony Burgess*, ed. by Geoffrey Aggeler (Boston, MA: G.K. Hall, 1986), p. 14; Sonia Sanchez, 'TCB', *You Better Believe It*, ed. by Paul Breman (New York: Penguin, 1973), p. 367; Adam Garfinkle, *Telltale Hearts: The Origins and Impact of the Vietnam Antiwar Movement* (New York: St. Martin's Press, 1995), p. 163; Jon Savage, *England's Dreaming: Anarchy, Sex Pistols, Punk Rock, and Beyond* (New York: St. Martin's Press, 1992).
61 Burgess, 'If Oedipus Had Read His Lévi-Strauss', pp. 259–260; Burgess, 'Letter from Europe' (Summer 1970), 504.
62 Burgess, 'Culture as a Hot Meal', p. 13.
63 Burgess, *M/F*, p. 13.
64 Mark Sussman, 'The "Miscegenation" Troll', *JSTOR: Daily*, 20 February 2019, https://daily.jstor.org/the-miscegenation-troll; Charles Chesnutt, *The Future American*, *The Norton Anthology of American Literature: 1865–1914*, ed. by Robert S. Levine (New York: W.W. Norton, 2017), pp. 1175–1179; Aggeler, *Anthony Burgess*, p. 204.
65 Bakhtin, *The Dialogic Imagination*, p. 324; Burgess, *M/F*, p. 195.
66 Dennis Hopper, *Easy Rider* (Columbia Pictures, 1969); Anthony Burgess, *1985* (London: Beautiful Books, 1978; 2010), p. 75.
67 Burgess, *Tremor of Intent*, p. 98; Anthony Burgess, *A Clockwork Orange* (W.W. Norton, 1962; 1986), pp. 25, 33; Anthony Burgess, *Enderby* (New York: Ballantine Books, 1973), p. 89.
68 Terry Southern and Mason Hoffenberg, *Candy* (New York: Grove Press, 1958; 1996); William S. Burroughs, *Naked Lunch* (New York: Grove Press, 1959; 2001); Henry Miller, *Tropic of Cancer* (New York: Grove Press, 1934; 1961); Hubert Selby Jr, *Last Exit to Brooklyn* (London: Calder & Boylars, September 1968); Sanford Friedman, *Totempole* (San Francisco, CA: North Point Press, 1965); Gore Vidal, *Myra Breckinridge* and *Myron* (New York: Knopf, 1968; 1987); Anthony Burgess, Untitled draft, *Times Literary Supplement*, 20 April

1977, University of Texas at Austin: Harry Ransom Center, box 62, fol. 2; Mordecai Richler, *Cocksure* (McClelland &Stewart, 1968); Philip Roth, *Portnoy's Complaint* (Vintage International, 1969; 1994); Saul Bellow, *Mr Sammler's Planet* (Fawcett Publications, 1969).

69 Anthony Burgess, 'On the End of Every Fork', *The Guardian*, 20 November 1964, p. 9; Anthony Burgess, 'New Fiction', *Listener*, 20 January 1966, p. 109; Anthony Burgess, 'What Is Pornography?', *Urgent Copy*, pp. 254–257.

70 James Joyce, *A Portrait of the Artist as a Young Man* and *Dubliners* (New York: Barnes & Noble Classics, 1914; 2004), pp. 182–183.

71 Darlington, 'Tea, Coca-Cola and Wine', p. 153; Aggeler, *Anthony Burgess*, p. 203; Burgess, *This Man and Music*.

72 Burgess, 'If Oedipus Had Read His Lévi-Strauss', p. 259; Sophocles, *Oedipus the King*, translated and adapted by Anthony Burgess, 'To the Reader' and 'An Exchange of Letters' (Minneapolis, MN: University of Minnesota Press, 1972), pp. 1–6, 81–94; Anthony Burgess, *The End of the World News* (London: Penguin Books, 1982; 1984), p. 213.

73 Philip Johnston, 'How Incest Slipped from Statute Book; Changes Aim to Reflect Altered Make-Up of Households', *Daily Telegraph*, 21 November 2002; Burgess, 'If Oedipus Had Read His Lévi-Strauss', pp. 259–260; Burgess, *M/F*, p. 47.

74 Leigh B. Bienen, 'Defining Incest', *Northwestern University Law Review*, 92.4 (1997–98), 1504; Aggeler, *Anthony Burgess*, p. 94.

75 John Rodden, *Performing the Literary Interview: How Writers Craft Their Public Selves* (Lincoln, NE: University of Nebraska Press, 2001), p. 1; Ben Masters, *Novel Style: Ethics and Excess in English Fiction since the 1960s* (Oxford: Oxford University Press, 2017), pp. 48–49; Burgess, *M/F*, pp. 21–23; Burgess, *This Man and Music*, p. 168.

76 Anthony Burgess, 'Dark Disease: A European Tradition', *Urgent Copy: Literary Studies*, p. 31.

77 Dana Gioia, 'Talking with Anthony Burgess', *Inquiry*, 2 February 1981, p. 25.

78 Darlington, 'Tea, Coca Cola and Wine', p. 147.

79 Dominic Green, 'The Most of Anthony Burgess', *The New Criterion*, 36.2 (October 2017), 30; Barry Miles, *Call Me Burroughs: A Life* (New York: Hachette Book Group, 2013), p. 409.

80 Burgess, 'Dark Disease', p. 30.

81 Clarke, 'Anthony Burgess's Structuralist Turn', p. 115.

82 Darlington, 'Tea, Coca-Cola and Wine', p. 157.

83 Anthony Burgess, 'Morbus Gallicus', *But Do Blondes Prefer Gentlemen?*, p. 97.

84 Aggeler, *Anthony Burgess*, p. 204; Burgess, 'Morbus Gallicus'; Burgess, 'Letter from Europe' (Winter 1970–71), 119–122; Anthony Burgess, 'Isn't It Time for Britain to Become a GI Bride?', *The Los Angeles Times*, 16 May 1979; Anthony Burgess, 'Anthony Burgess Lecture: "The Writer's Daily Damnation"', Sarah Lawrence College: Sarah Lawrence College Archives, 19 January 1971; Norman Mailer, *Armies of the Night: History as a Novel/The Novel as History* (New York: Plume, 1968; 1994), p. 101.

85 Burgess, *M/F*, p. 216; Robert Spence, 'The Reputation of Anthony Burgess' (Manchester: University of Manchester dissertation, unpublished, 2002), p. 140.
86 Aggeler, *Anthony Burgess*, p. 204.
87 Thomas Stumpf, 'The Dependent Mind: A Survey of the Novels by Anthony Burgess', *Anthony Burgess Newsletter* (Anthony Burgess Center, University of Angers, 2000), p. 6.
88 Charles DeBenedetti and Charles Chatfield, *An American Ordeal: The Antiwar Movement of the Vietnam Era* (Syracuse, NY: Syracuse University Press, 1990); Garfinkle, *Telltale Hearts*.
89 Richard Hofstadter, *Anti-Intellectualism in American Life* (New York: Vintage Books, 1963), p. 301; James Baldwin, 'A Talk to Teachers', *James Baldwin: Collected Essays*, ed. by Toni Morrison (New York: The Library of America, 1998), pp. 678–686.
90 Stanley Fish, *There's No Such Thing as Free Speech: And It's a Good Thing Too* (New York: Oxford University Press, 1994), p. 51.
91 Garfinkle, *Telltale Hearts*, p. 15.
92 'Vietnam War: Student Activism', Civil Rights and Labor History Consortium at the University of Washington, 2008, https://depts.washington.edu/antiwar/vietnam_student.shtml; Burgess, *You've Had Your Time*, p. 196.
93 Frank Jacobs, 'Mad's 1969 College Riot Preview', *MAD Magazine*, October 1969; 'A Mad Look at Modern College Courses', *MAD Magazine*, December 1969.
94 Steven V. Roberts, 'The Hippie Mystique', *New York Times*, 15 December 1969; Paul L. Montgomery, 'Foes of War Hold Modest Protests', *New York Times*, 14 December 1969; Homer Bigart, '63 Arrested, 8 Policemen Hurt as 3,000 Protest Nixon's Visit', *New York Times*, 10 December 1969.
95 'Vietnam War U.S. Military Fatal Casualty Statistics: Electronic Records Reference Report', National Archives; 'Mass Atrocity Endings', Tufts University; DeBenedetti and Chatfield, *An American Ordeal*.
96 Burgess, *M/F*, p. 11.
97 Burgess, *M/F*, pp. 49–50. It may be that because of this supposed mythical structuralism, what Burgess is actually doing here, more accurately and in more familiar territory, is simply what he had done several times before, and would go on to do, which is using an outside source as a structure and inspiration for one of his novels – a Joycean tactic in *Ulysses* that Burgess used with Wagner's *Der Ring des Nibelungen* for *The Worm and the Ring* (1961), Virgil's *Aeneid* for *A Vision of Battlements* (1965), Beethoven's *Eroica* and the Prometheus myth with *Napoleon Symphony* (1974), the Bible for *Moses* (1976), *Man of Nazareth* (1980), and *Kingdom of the Wicked* (1985), the Orpheus myth for *Beard's Roman Women* (1976), Keats and Belli for *ABBA ABBA* (1977), and Byron's *Don Juan* for *Byrne* (1995). The noticeable difference here is that for *M/F*, the source material is North American and not European, making it an aberration among the rest of his oeuvre.
98 Burgess, *M/F*, p. 50.

99 Burgess, *M/F*, p. 51.
100 Burgess, *M/F*, pp. 179, 211.
101 Bakhtin, *The Dialogic Imagination*, p. 6.
102 Bakhtin, *The Dialogic Imagination*, p. 7.
103 Bakhtin, *The Dialogic Imagination*, p. 7; Christine Gallagher and Stephen Greenblatt, *Practicing New Historicism* (Chicago, IL: The University of Chicago Press, 2000), p. 13.
104 Anthony Burgess, 'The Academic Critic and the Living Writer', *Times Literary Supplement*, issue 4363, 14 November 1986, para. 5; Allan Bloom, *The Closing of the American Mind* (New York: Simon and Schuster, 1987), p. 353.
105 'Ten O'Clock News; Anthony Burgess'. 1983-04-12. WGBH, American Archive of Public Broadcasting (GBH and the Library of Congress), Boston, MA and Washington, DC, http://americanarchive.org/catalog/cpb-aacip-15-mg7fq9qg1t; Anthony Burgess, 'Here's to Me and My Generation – Mr Burgess Makes a Christmas Toast', *New York Times*, 24 December 1972; Anthony Burgess, 'Interview with Anthony Burgess on Mozart', *Larry King Show Live*, Mutual Broadcast System, 3 December 1991. George Washington University Archives; Lynn Darling, 'The Haunted Exile of Novelist Anthony Burgess', *Washington Post*, 26 December 1980; Anthony Burgess, 'Viewpoint', *Times Literary Supplement*, 23 March 1973, p. 322.
106 Burgess, *M/F*, p. 25.
107 Burgess, *M/F*, p. 54.
108 Burgess, 'The Academic Critic and the Living Writer', para. 5; 'As the youth of Europe became more and more Americanized [in the 1950s], in dress, speech, music, literature, outlook and even in eating habits, it turned away, or thought it did, from American leadership in politics and ideology' (Hugh Brogan, *The Penguin History of the USA*, 2nd edition (London: Penguin Group, 1999), p. 600.
109 Brogan, *The Penguin History of the USA*, p. 657.
110 Anthony Burgess, 'The Young', *The Firing Line*, Southern Educational Communications Association, 21 and 31 December 1972, University of Buffalo Archives, p. 12.
111 Anthony Burgess, Letter to Vladimir Abarinov, 20 June 1987, University of Texas at Austin: Harry Ransom Center Archives, Gabriele Pantucci Collection, container 7.
112 Burgess, 'The Young', pp. 10–11.
113 James Lieber, interview with Christopher Thurley, 28 March 2017.
114 Burgess, 'Penthouse Interview', p. 116.
115 Norman Mailer, *Why Are We in Vietnam?* (New York: Picador, 1967); Mailer, *Armies of the Night: History as a Novel*; DeBenedetti and Chatfield, *An American Ordeal*, p. 408; Garfinkle, *Telltale Hearts*, p. 14.
116 Burgess, 'The Young', p. 12.
117 Burgess, 'Is America Falling Apart?', pp. 16–17.
118 Burgess, *M/F*, p. 219.
119 Burgess, *M/F*, p. 24.
120 Burgess, *M/F*, p. 24.

121 Burgess, *M/F*, pp. 36–37.
122 Anthony Burgess, *Byrne* (London: Vintage, 1995); Thurley, 'Anthony Burgess, Obscenity, and America', pp. 130–160.
123 Lecture tour contracts evidence at the Harry Ransom Center and International Anthony Burgess Foundation.
124 Anthony Burgess, 'What Is Pornography?', *Urgent Copy*, p. 254.
125 Frank Kermode, 'Obscenity', *Modern Essays* (London: Fontana Press, 1971; 1990), pp. 71–89; Burgess, *M/F*, p. 76; Burgess, *You've Had Your Time*, pp. 134–135.
126 Kermode, 'Obscenity', pp. 71–89; Burgess, *You've Had Your Time*, p. 135.
127 Burgess, 'What Is Pornography?', p. 255.
128 John Sutherland, *Offensive Literature: Decenshorship in Britain, 1960–1982* (London: Barnes and Noble Books, 1982), p. 67.
129 Anthony Burgess, 'Introduction', *Last Exit to Brooklyn* (London: Calder & Boylars, September 1968); Burgess, *You've Had Your Time*, p. 135.
130 Burgess, 'Introduction', *Last Exit to Brooklyn*, p. xiv.
131 Burgess, 'Introduction', *Last Exit to Brooklyn*, p. xv.
132 Anthony Burgess, '*Ulysses*: How Well Has It Worn?', *Urgent Copy*, p. 83; Sanford Friedman, *Totempole* (Berkeley, CA: North Point Press, 1965).
133 Burgess, 'Introduction', *Last Exit to Brooklyn*, p. xvi.
134 Kermode, 'Obscenity', p. 76; Burgess, 'Introduction', *Last Exit to Brooklyn*, p. xvi.
135 Burgess, 'Introduction', *Last Exit to Brooklyn*, p. xvii.
136 Anthony Burgess, 'On Wednesday He Does His Ears', *New York Times*, 14 October 1990, para. 5.
137 Paul Reville, 'Novelist Anthony Burgess Explores Obscenity, Libel', *The Tiger*, Colorado College, 21 March 1969.
138 Anthony Burgess, 'Pornography: "The Moral Question Is Nonsense"; For Permissiveness, with Misgivings', *New York Times*, 1 July 1973, p. 19.
139 'Review', *Publishers Weekly*, 8 February 1971; Anthony Burgess, 'Sex Permissiveness "Hardly Affects the Serious Artist"', *The Palm Beach Post*, 1 July 1973, p. 72.
140 Anthony Burgess, 'Obscenity and the Arts' (Valletta, Malta: Malta Library Association, 1973), p. 4; Andrew Biswell, 'Anthony Burgess's Censorship Scandal in Malta: A Timeline', The International Anthony Burgess Foundation, 10 June 2020, www.anthonyburgess.org/blog-posts/anthony-burgesss-censorship-scandal-in-malta-a-timeline.
141 Burgess, 'Obscenity and the Arts', p. 4.
142 Anthony Burgess, 'Obscenity and the Arts – A Symposium', *Times Literary Supplement*, 12–18 February 1988, p. 159.
143 Anthony Burgess, 'Introduction: A Celebration of Translation', *Return Trip Tango and Other Stories from Abroad*, ed. by Frank MacShane and Lori Carlson (New York: Columbia University Press, 1992), p. xviii; Anthony Burgess, *They Wrote in English* (proof copy, International Anthony Burgess Foundation Archive, 1989), p. 6.

144 'Miller v. California', *Oyez*, www.oyez.org/cases/1971/70–73.

145 Southern and Hoffenberg, *Candy*; Burgess, *M/F*, pp. 97–98. A handkerchief of Llew's is found later, providing evidence of what Llew used these mediums for: 'Llew's handkerchief – gissum-stiff – that I wiped the blood away' (Burgess, *M/F*, p. 110).

146 Burgess, *M/F*, p. 101; Burgess, *You've Had Your Time*, p. 214. Burgess is listed in the writers' section of the programme for the Adelaide Festival of the Arts (6 to 28 March 1970) accompanied by authors Edna O'Brien, Stefan Heym, and Edward Franklin Albee. The biographical description reads: 'English writer ANTHONY BURGESS was born in 1917 and was educated in Manchester. ... His use of words is exciting: one critic has called him "a swarm of words looking for a structure to settle on"' ('The Adelaide Festival of Arts, 6–28 March 1970: Souvenir Program', The Australian Council for the Arts, 'Writers' Week', International Anthony Burgess Foundation Archive, p. 60).

147 Burgess, *M/F*, pp. 144, 142, 147, 148, 101.

148 James Joyce, *Ulysses* (New York: Dover Publications, 1922; 2009), p. 214.

149 Anthony Burgess, 'Joyce as Centenarian', *But Do Blondes Prefer Gentlemen?*, p. 432.

150 'University of Rochester Pays Tribute to Benefactor', *New York Times*, 11 November 1972, para. 16.

151 Burgess, *On the Novel*, pp. 115–116.

152 Anthony Burgess, *Joysprick: An Introduction to the Language of James Joyce* (New York: Harcourt, Brace, Jovanovich, 1973), p. 138; Anthony Burgess, *Rejoyce* (New York: W.W. Norton, 1965), p. 25.

153 Burgess, *M/F*, pp. 48–49.

154 Nicholas Ray, *Rebel without a Cause* (Warner Brothers, 1955).

155 Burgess, *M/F*, p. 23; Southern and Hoffenberg, *Candy*, directed by Christopher Marquand (ABC Pictures, 1968).

156 Burgess, *M/F*, pp. 24, 37, 66, 68, 107.

157 Anthony Burgess, 'Thought on the Present Discontents', *But Do Blondes Prefer Gentlemen?*, p. 19.

158 Burgess, *M/F*, p. 75.

159 Burgess, *M/F*, p. 161.

160 Anthony Burgess, 'Contemporary Authors: The Works of Anthony Burgess', Pennsylvania State University, 1982. Of the puritanism of the United States, Burgess also says, 'The situation is even worse in America, where the Puritanism of the Pilgrim Fathers made adultery a capital offence and, in consequence, inaugurated the modern age of easy divorces or serial polygamy' (Anthony Burgess, 'France and Myself', *One Man's Chorus: The Uncollected Writings of Anthony Burgess*, ed. by Ben Forkner (New York: Carroll & Graf, 1998), p. 71).

161 Claude Lévi-Strauss, 'The Structural Study of Myth', *The Critical Tradition: Classic Texts and Contemporary Trends*, ed. by David Richter (Boston, MA: Bedford/St. Martin's, 2007), p. 861; Burgess, *This Man and Music*, p. 158; Burgess, *Joysprick*, p. 15.

162 Burgess, *This Man and Music*, p. 157. These distinctions turn into Class 1 and 2 in Anthony Burgess, 'Craft and Crucifixion – The Writing of Fiction', *One Man's Chorus: The Uncollected Writings of Anthony Burgess*, p. 259.
163 Anthony Burgess, *Kingdom of the Wicked* (New York: Arbor House, 1985), p. 7.
164 Bakhtin, *The Dialogic Imagination*, p. 368.
165 Burgess, *M/F*, p. 95.
166 Burgess, *M/F*, p. 66.
167 'Author Anthony Burgess Talks about His New Novel Any Old Iron', *BBC Sounds*, 18 August 1989, www.bbc.co.uk/sounds/play/p03m0s7y?fbclid=IwAR2jBl8pDkrBXBziQ9VQ73QIi-v_4KCqQYgXDHUhPF5JnhWDvZ6jNT8P4ss; Burgess, *You've Had Your Time*, p. 232.
168 Coale, *Anthony Burgess*, p. 117.
169 Aggeler, *Anthony Burgess*, p. 204.
170 Burgess, *M/F*, p. 89.
171 Burgess, *M/F*, p. 214.
172 Burgess, *M/F*, p. 214; Anthony Burgess, lecture at Tufts University, 4 March 1975; Anthony Burgess, *The Clockwork Testament; or, Enderby's End* (London: Hart-Davis, MacGibbon, 1974), p. 20.
173 Burgess, *M/F*, p. 214.
174 Burgess, *M/F*, p. 214; Anthony Burgess, 'Epilogue: Conflict and Confluence', *Urgent Copy*, p. 265.
175 Burgess, *M/F*, p. 212.
176 Martin Covert, 'Burgess on Art, God, Good, Evil', *The University of Tennessee Daily Beacon*, 17 April 1975, p. 105; Anthony Burgess, *Mozart and the Wolf Gang* (London: Vintage, 1992), p. 145; Max Saunders, *Self Impression: Life-Writing, Autobiografiction, and the Forms of Modern Literature* (Oxford: Oxford University Press, 2010), p. 191; David Lodge, *After Bakhtin: Essays on Fiction and Criticism* (London: Routledge, 1990), p. 33.
177 Anthony Burgess, 'Playboy Interview: Anthony Burgess; a Candid Conversation', *Playboy*, September 1974, p. 84.
178 Anthony Burgess, 'Thoughts on Travel', pp. 48–49.
179 Burgess, 'The Academic Critic and the Living Writer', para. 5.
180 Anthony Burgess, *A Vision of Battlements* (New York: W.W. Norton, 1965), p. 155; Anthony Burgess, *The Malayan Trilogy* (London: Vintage Books, 2000); Anthony Burgess, *The Right to an Answer* (London: Hutchinson, 1960; 1980); Anthony Burgess, *One Hand Clapping* (New York: Carroll & Graf, 1961; 1999); Burgess, *1985*; Anthony Burgess, *Earthly Powers* (New York: Penguin, 1980); Burgess, *The End of the World News*.
181 Burgess, *M/F*, p. 11.
182 Anthony Burgess, 'One of the Minor Joys …', 1972, International Anthony Burgess Foundation Archive, para. 8.
183 Anthony Burgess, 'A Trip to Washington', February 1981, Harry Ransom Center Archive, p. 3.
184 Anthony Burgess, 'The Mystery of Evil', *But Do Blondes Prefer Gentlemen?*, p. 506.

185 Burgess, *M/F*, p. 49.
186 Burgess, *M/F*, p. 49.
187 Frank Kermode, 'The Use of Codes', *The Art of Telling: Essays on Fiction* (Cambridge, MA: Harvard University Press, 1983), p. 80.
188 Burgess, *You've Had Your Time*, p. 229.
189 Burgess, *M/F*, pp. 13, 202.
190 History.com Editors, 'Christ Is Born?', 20 December 2019, www.history.com/this-day-in-history/christ-is-born; Darlington, 'Tea, Coca-Cola and Wine', p. 142.
191 William Manley, interview with Christopher Thurley, 6 December 2017; Burgess, *M/F*, p. 36.
192 Anthony Burgess, 'Dressing for Dinner in the Jungle', *Conversations with Anthony Burgess*, p. 80.
193 Burgess, 'Dressing for Dinner in the Jungle', p. 80.
194 Anthony Burgess, *Any Old Iron* (New York: Washington Square Press – Pocket Books, 1989), p. 333.
195 Burgess, 'Letter from Europe' (Summer 1970), 504; B.F. Skinner, *Walden Two* (Indianapolis, IN: Hackett Publishing Company, 1948; 1976; 2005).
196 DeBenedetti and Chatfield, *An American Ordeal*, p. 118; Julia Lovell, 'Mao's Global Legacy of Revolution and Bloodshed', *The Wall Street Journal*, 5–6 October 2019, p. C4; Skinner, *Walden Two*, pp. 181, 224.
197 Burgess, 'Playboy Interview', p. 236.
198 Burgess, *M/F*, p. 127.
199 Coale, *Anthony Burgess*, p. 122.
200 Lévi-Strauss, 'The Scope of Anthropology', p. 116.
201 Bakhtin, *The Dialogic Imagination*, p. 314.
202 Gretchen Robinson, 'British Author Discusses His Controversial Novel', *The Greenville News*, 11 January 1973, p. 29.
203 Christopher Lehmann-Haupt, 'Incest in the Widest Sense …', *New York Times*, 29 March 1971, p. 31.
204 Paul Boytinck, *Anthony Burgess: An Annotated Bibliography and Reference Guide* (New York: Garland Publishing, 1985), p. 86; Auberon Waugh, 'Auberon Waugh on New Novels', *The Spectator*, 19 June 1971, p. 850.
205 Andrew Biswell, International Anthony Burgess Foundation, email sent to Christopher Thurley, 21 May 2021.
206 Burgess, *M/F*, p. 218.
207 Burgess, *M/F*, p. 218.
208 Darlington, 'Tea, Coca-Cola and Wine', p. 156.
209 Burgess, *M/F*, p. 217.
210 Burgess, *M/F*, p. 217.
211 Coale, *Anthony Burgess*, p. 120; Burgess, *M/F*, p. 22.
212 Burgess, *M/F*, p. 194.
213 Burgess, *The Clockwork Testament; or, Enderby's End*, pp. 44, 54, 62.
214 Burgess, *The Clockwork Testament; or, Enderby's End*, pp. 70, 81.
215 Erkki Peuranen, 'Bakhtin: Soft and Hard', *Dialogues on Bakhtin: Interdisciplinary Readings*, ed. by Mika Lähteenmäki and Hannele Dufva (University of Jyväskylä: Centre for Applied Language Studies, 1998), p. 30.

Burgess Explains 'Orange':

FRIDAY, S

Self-evil Better Than Imposed Good

By Pat Conrad
Staff Writer

A Clockwork Orange. Perhaps you read the book, or saw Stanley Kubrick's film version, or perhaps both. Chances are the title itself, let alone the movie, left you very bewildered as to its meaning.

Author Anthony Burgess cleared up whatever confusion existed in the minds of the "attentive" audience, as he called it, with an exceptionally well-presented lecture on Wednesday evening. However, he began by expressing his disagreement with the subject matter. "The author lays the egg; it is the job of the critics to eat it." He added, with a little humor intended, "I don't like the book anyway."

He mentioned that he began the novel title-first, the title coming from an old East London dialectic expression meaning "queer, bizarre." About that time he had the idea that "the Anglo-American state robs fruitful human beings of their juiciness, making them dried up 'clockwork oranges.'" The juiciness is man's free will to choose a moral good and a moral evil. "We have to be free to choose whoever we are," he stated. "It is better to choose evil than to have good imposed upon you."

He was alarmed by the idea that the state might be able to cure criminals of their violent bent. He saw such an idea as a sin by the state, because it would take away the criminals' freedom of choice. From his own experience he looks at criminals with a forgiving eye, realizing that they are human beings with a free will. From all this he developed **A Clockwork Orange**.

photo by Tom Sherry
Author Anthony Burgess

Mr. Burgess explained that violence was not the point of the book, but it had to be incorporated to show man's freedom to choose evil. He wanted to take the reader into ultraviolence, meaning "beyond violence" (not "extreme violence," as it has been misinterpreted).

He also mentioned that, when the book was first chosen around 1965 to be made into a movie, he wanted the Rolling Stones with Mick Jagger as the lead to be the "droogs." The chance to produce the movie was turned down, however, until Kubrick took it a few years later.

In answer to some questions afterwards, Mr. Burgess explained some of the finer aspects of his book and expressed some of his views on politics and social problems.

The slang spoken by the main characters throughout the novel was invented by Mr. Burgess himslf because actual slang, he felt, quickly becomes outdated. His slang is a mixture of Russian and English, the languages of the two superstates.

A point of special interest in Mr. Burgess' lecture was that **A Clockwork Orange** was one of the last of five novels to be written within a year, the amount of time doctors once gave the author to live. Hence, it was written very speedily.

In speaking about Kubrick's movie version, he stated that "no author is ever pleased with the movie version of his own book because literary experience lets the reader's imagination draw the intended images whereas cinematic experience robs the viewer of his imagination. He went on to point out several areas of disagreement between his novel and Kubrick's movie.

Figure 3.1 Anthony Burgess lecture covered in the campus newspaper, *The Indiana Penn* (29 September 1972). Indiana University of Pennsylvania Libraries Special Collections and University Archives.

Popular novelist Anthony Burgess, the author of Clockwork Orange, visited LC and lectured to a full house in Dillard Fine Arts Center Monday night. Mr. Burgess also spoke to several classes.

Figure 3.2 Anthony Burgess at Lynchburg College (26 March 1975). Courtesy of the University of Lynchburg.

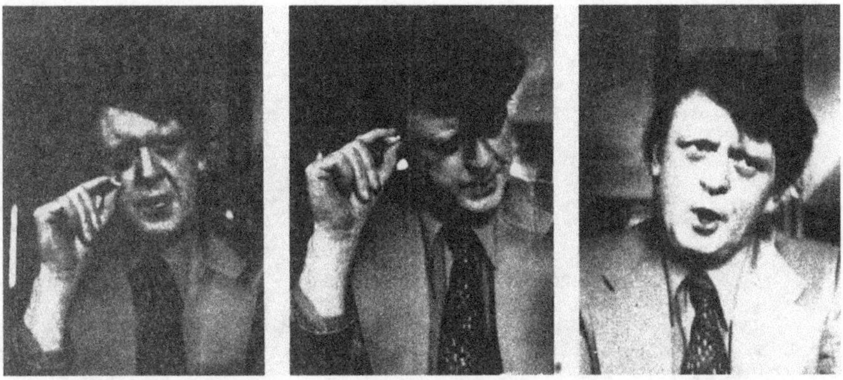

Figure 3.3 Anthony Burgess at Ohio State University, published in *The Ohio State Lantern* (2 February 1973). Courtesy of The Ohio State University Libraries.

PAGE 6 FRIDAY MARCH 7, 1975

Burgess cont.pg.1

When asked his opinion on Solzhenitsyn's exile and flight for 1 literary freedom, Mr. Burgess was adamant in his opinion: "I think Solzhenitsyn is the most over-rated writer of the 20th century. His work is wordy and verbose. I admire him for his morals and convictions, but he is terribly over-praised. I think that he and Pope John are exaggerated heros."

Particularily fond of apple pie, the author inhaled his, grabbed his briefcase, and in excusing himself, proceeded downstairs. (Don't want to keep everyone waiting.") On stage, he looked a little embarrassed with Dean Howard's praising introduction, them refusing to use the sound system, took control of the packed audience.

"I'm from Lancashire," he stated, "different from the England of Robert Morley and London. We're more friendly, more open, more aquaintaince-minded. Therefore I am different as an Englishman and a novelist."

The son of show business parents, he had originally used the piano a a creative outlet and as a source to scratch out a living.

The scare of a terminal illness inspired him to write five and a half novels in twelve months. It was during this time that "A Clockworl Orange" was written. Mr. Burgess seemed to approach "A Clockwork Orange" simply because he had to. The publicity of the movie seems to have left him bitter about his own creation. "Clockwork" was written because of my own fear of what was happening in Britian at the time (late 50's early60's). Juvenile delinquency was rampant. The government proposed to take drastic action through the process of "conditioning"therefore turning teenagers into 'useful citizens'.

"Man should not be manipulated by the state, turned into a good creature that will be incapable of doing evil. Man should be free on a moral sphere. He should be free to choose between good and evil. I believe it is better to choose evil then not to choose at all."

Violence upsets the author, but he felt the need to write about it. "Man has a right to choose violence or not to choose it. The writer has a great responsibility in areas such as these. What a writer will create in fiction, some people will take as real left People claim that "A Clockwork Orange" caused people to go off the handle and be violent. I wrote the book ten years before movie was made and only after the movies was shown did these acts of violence occur. Now I am getting the blame for it. The novelist's duty is to be honest and open at all costs. The novelist must never preach, only show the world in specific detail

Mr. Burgess finished his lecture by reading an excerpt from "Cyrano" dealing with the problem of compromising. "We must be free of a filthy world" he read. At the end, he said "Ladies and Gentlemen, may your noses also be big."

It was a great pleasure to have such an open, witty, intelligent man as our guest on campus. "What good is, I'm not sure." he said. "All that is recognized as desirable; is good I suppose." Yes, he is right, for he has lived both good and evil and is not afraid to share the experience. The Modern Renaissance Man.

TM in the AM and PM

By Bill Freitas

If you happen to be walking through the library or passing one of the lounges and see me sitting with my eyes closed, please don't disturb me! I may be meditating. I won't be wearing a white robe, beads or sandles and I won't be sitting in a lotus position on the floor because I couldn't get into one if I tried. No, I will just be sitting there comfortably in a chair with my eyes closed, just as over 100 fellow SMU students do twice a day when they practice Transcendental Meditation.

The popular name for Transcendental Meditation is its abbreviation: TM. The TM club of SMU was formed 2½ years ago as a chapter of the Student's International Meditation Society (SIMS). Its purpose is to unite the students who already practice TM and encourage the student body to discover the benefits of TM.

Transcendental Meditation is neither concentration nor contemplation: it requires neither mood making nor positive thinking. TM is not a religion and does not in any way conflict with any religion of today. TM has absolutely nothing to do with drugs. TM is not a philosophy and when a person starts TM he does not have to change his ways of thinking or acting.

Rather, TM is a very simple, natural process of the mind, easily learned by anyone, which allows a person to experience a very deep state of restfulness. This state of rest has been shown to be twice as deep as even the deepest point of sleep. Although we become very rested when we meditate, we don't loose awareness as we do when we sleep. In TM we become more alert, in fact, our awareness increases. We need sleep at night to get rid of the fatigue that we have accumulated from the experience of a day's activity. But the rest we gain in sleep is not deep enough to get down to the deeper stresses caused by tension. In a very natural way TM provides the deep rest necessary to dissolve these deep stresses and tensions. Once they are gone, they are gone for good.

Psychologists say that we are using only a small portion of our mental potential, maybe 15 or 20 percent. Stress in our nervous system interferes with the expression of intelligence and creativity. Removing this tension results in increased energy and developed intelligence and creativity.

After meditating, students find that they naturally engage in activity more effectively without accumulating stress and strain. Without this tension students can pay better attention in classes, study more effectively, learn more easily and the whole educational experience becomes more meaningful and enjoyable, the way it should be.

The benefits continue into all areas of life. A person naturally acts in a more loving and creatively intelligent manner by unfolding the full potential of his heart and mind, making life a joy both for himself and others.

A more thorough discussion will be held on Transcendental Meditation at two different times next week. They will be on Tuesday, March 11, and on Wednesday, March 12, at 3:30 pm in Group I, Room 103.

For anything concerning TM on-campus, contact me, Bill Freitas or Jackie Lemlin at the Yearbook office, ext. 692. ▫

SMU Women's Center presents film

The women's health movement is making waves in the medical industry. Doctors are becoming aware that more and more women will no longer treat them as high priests in charge of all knowlede concerning the female body. There is a growing desire among women to unravel the mystery of their bodies and thereby to regain control over them. This desire is manifested in many ways. "Taking Our Bodies Back: The Women's Health Movement" is a film which deals with 10 critical areas of the movement, from the simple but revolutionary concept of self-help to the vital issue of informed surgical consent. March 10, the Women's Center will present this film, followed by a self-help demonstration by the New Bedford Women's Health Center.

Highlights of the film will include an actual home childbirth. In a hospital, birth is often treated like a disease, to be dealt with routinely using drugs and surgery. At home, supported by family and friends, the woman was much more in control of her own delivery. The viewer will also witness the procedure of the new early uterine evacuation technique of abortion. Other subjects include the following: a gynecological examination, hysterectomy, minority women, drug company attitudes, breast cancer, "knowing our bodies" in high school, and self-help.

The New Bedford Women's Health Center will demonstrate, using a plastic speculum, how to give oneself a cervical examination. They will also explain the proper technique of self breast examination.

The program should be practical and enlightening for any woman interested in becoming more aware of her physical and emotional self. It will be presented Monday, March 10, 7:30, Orange dormitory, 2nd floor, the multipurpose room. ▫

What does female situation entail?

Women across the nation are forming support groups for the dual purpose of self-discovery and a better understanding of what the female situation entails. How does our culture shape our nature? What are our roles in this male-oriented, capitalist system and why are they this way? These and many more questions call for discussion and analysis by women themselves. If we share our opinions and struggles, we will learn what we need to heal in ourselves and also what needs to be healed in our society. By studying and discarding traditional definitions of womanhood, we will be better prepared for a pursuit of humanness and self-actualization. We can begin to view life in a more fluid way, a way that welcomes change and encourages personal development.

If you're interested in participating in an awareness group, please visit the Women's Center at one o'clock on Monday, March 10. We will be meeting once per week to learn more about each other - past and present - and set out toward becoming stronger human beings in the future. New films, speakers, and contemporary publications will be employed as means for stimulating and improving communication. If you cannot be with us at this time, leave your name, schedule, and telephone number at the Center and perhaps a more suitable time can be arranged.

For centuries, female energy has been negated. Let us balance this by positively asserting and developing it in today's world! ▫

Figure 3.4 Anthony Burgess lecture and campus newspaper, *The Torch*, coverage while speaking at the University of Massachusetts at Dartmouth (7 March 1975). Special Collections and University Archives Research Center, UMass Amherst Libraries.

Figure 3.5 Anthony Burgess lecture covered in the campus newspaper, *University of Montana Student Newspaper* (4 April 1975). Courtesy of the University of Montana.

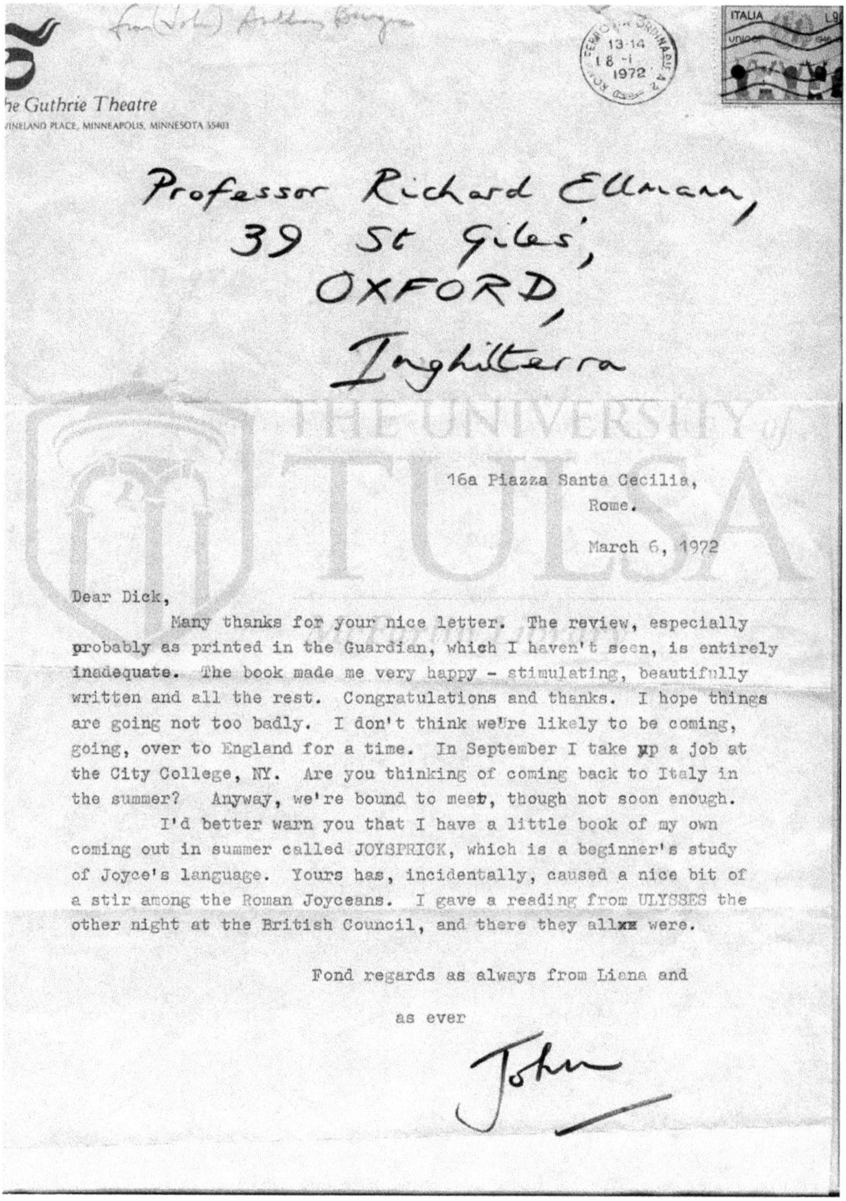

from (John) Anthony Burgess

he Guthrie Theatre
VINELAND PLACE, MINNEAPOLIS, MINNESOTA 55403

ITALIA

13-14
18 -I
1972

Professor Richard Ellmann,
39 St Giles',
OXFORD,
Inghilterra

16a Piazza Santa Cecilia,
Rome.

March 6, 1972

Dear Dick,

Many thanks for your nice letter. The review, especially probably as printed in the Guardian, which I haven't seen, is entirely inadequate. The book made me very happy - stimulating, beautifully written and all the rest. Congratulations and thanks. I hope things are going not too badly. I don't think we're likely to be coming, going, over to England for a time. In September I take up a job at the City College, NY. Are you thinking of coming back to Italy in the summer? Anyway, we're bound to meet, though not soon enough.

I'd better warn you that I have a little book of my own coming out in summer called JOYSPRICK, which is a beginner's study of Joyce's language. Yours has, incidentally, caused a nice bit of a stir among the Roman Joyceans. I gave a reading from ULYSSES the other night at the British Council, and there they all were.

Fond regards as always from Liana and

as ever

John

Figure 3.6 Anthony Burgess to Richard Ellman, the Joyce scholar, on Guthrie Theatre, Minneapolis, MN, letterhead paper (6 March 1972). The University of Tulsa Special Collections and University Archives, McFarlin Library.

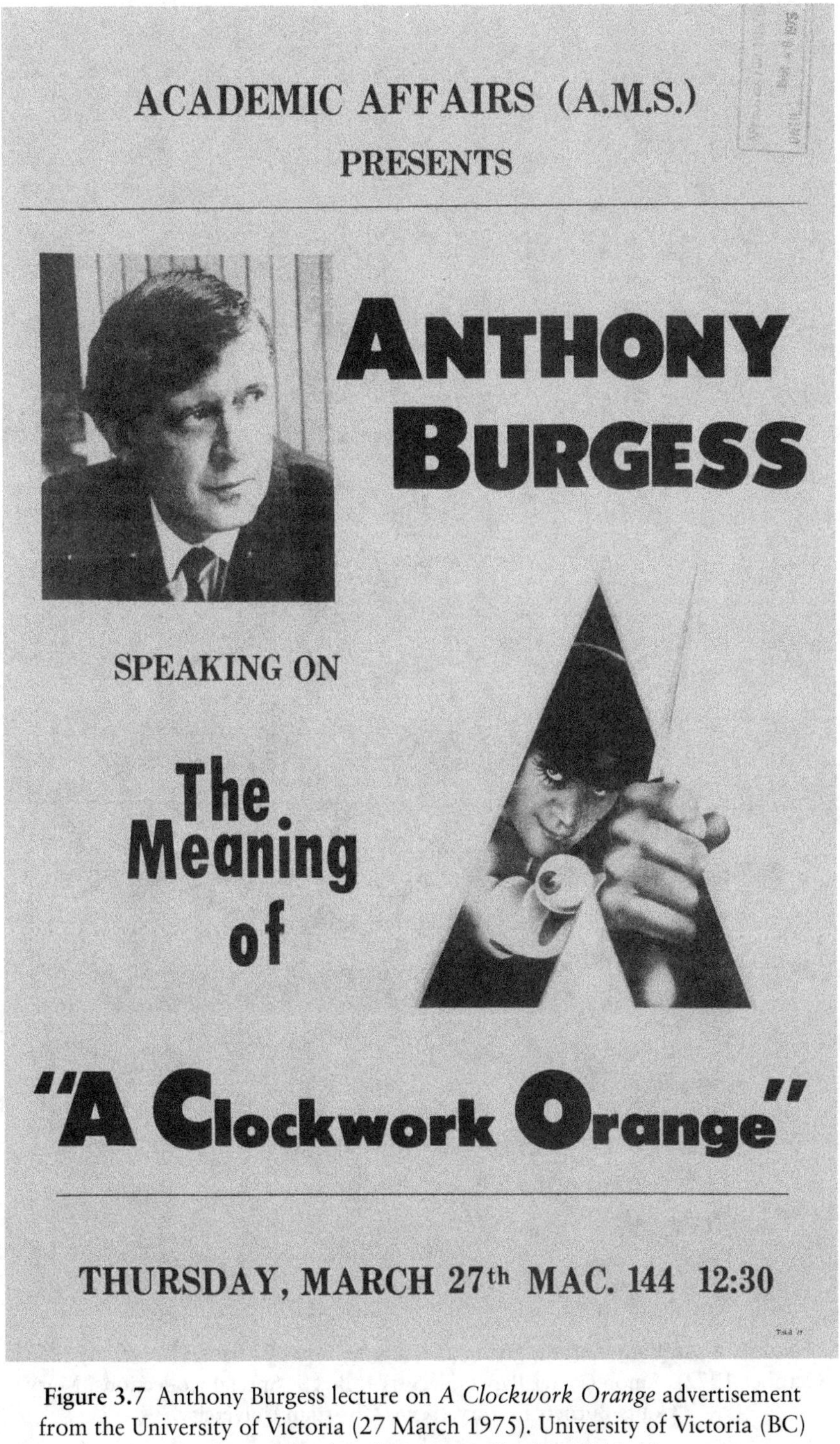
ACADEMIC AFFAIRS (A.M.S.)
PRESENTS
ANTHONY
BURGESS
SPEAKING ON
The
Meaning
of
"A Clockwork Orange"
THURSDAY, MARCH 27th MAC. 144 12:30

Figure 3.7 Anthony Burgess lecture on *A Clockwork Orange* advertisement from the University of Victoria (27 March 1975). University of Victoria (BC) Archives, Poster and Notice Collection 2016–13.

Figure 3.8 Anthony Burgess giving a lecture at Texas Christian University (25 October 1972). Amon Carter Papers, MS 014, Box 1, Special Collections, Mary Couts Burnett Library, Texas Christian University.

Figure 3.9 Drawing of Anthony Burgess in *Inquiry* for Dana Gioia's 'Talking with Anthony Burgess', 2 February 1981. Special Collections Department at Princeton University Library, Box 16, Folder 1 of the Hudson Review Archives (C1091).

4

The Clockwork Testament, or Enderby's End (1974) and *New York* (1976)

> Hogg frowned slightly. 'But,' he said, 'it can't be. It says here that this K had delusions about other people stealing his work and making horror films out of his poetry. That's not quite the same, is it? I mean, this bloody man Rawcliffe did pinch the plot of my *Pet Beast* and make a bloody awful Italian picture out of it. I even remember the name. *L'Animal Binato* it was called in Italy – that's from Dante, you see: *The Double-Natured Animal* or something like it – and in England it was called Son *of the Beast from Outer Space.*' He read more intently, frowning further. 'What's all this,' he said, 'about a sexual fixation on this bloke K's stepmother? That can't be me, this bloke can't. I hated her, you know how much for I told you. And,' he said blushing, 'about masturbating in the lavatory. And about this woman being very refined and trying to make a real married man out of him.' (Anthony Burgess, *Enderby*)[1]

> A tense city, and yet I thrive in it. For violence is only one side of the coin. Dante's Florence, too, was violent and so was Shakespeare's London. In a totally tranquil city you will find dusty ideas and no art; human energy can erupt in an offence against a person or his property, but it can also do so in a symphony. New York's destructive dynamism has its mirror-image: a dynamism that is creative, ever-moving, self-renewing. (Anthony Burgess, *The Great Cities – New York*)[2]

Introduction and overview

Initially conceptualized as a non-fiction philosophical reply to the onslaught of positive and, more significantly, negative attention Anthony Burgess received due to Stanley Kubrick's film version of *A Clockwork Orange* (1971), the single written chapter of 'The Clockwork Condition' (1973), first published in 2012, deals with many of the same subjects Burgess decided to satirize and present as parodic fiction in *The Clockwork Testament, or Enderby's End* (1974), another partially experimental short novel which is actually an assemblage of a transcript, film script, narrative, and science fiction twist ending that acts as a commentary on literary adaptation and the status of art in society, as well as an attack on Americans and American culture – elements redolent and therefore evocative of the time period in Canadian author Mordecai Richler's *Cocksure* (1968), a novel Burgess reviewed, saying, 'I wish I'd written it myself', which too has an emphasis on the Hollywood film business, a partial film script, television show dialogue, and surreal scenarios.[3] Wrapped up in this socio-authorial literary response are patterns which exhibit, strikingly, Burgess's heteroglossic (social multi-voicedness) and polyphonic (authorial, character, and narrative dialogue and epitexts) monoglossia as presented through a barely concealed hidden polemic. As Ákos Farkas notes in *Will's Son and Jake's Peer* (2002), *The Clockwork Testament, or Enderby's End* 'viciously satirize[s]' American culture as Burgess witnessed it in the early 1970s, resulting in this text being a prime example of a novelized authorial hidden polemic which castigates 'the cultural philistinism attributed to Americans' by the author-figure.[4] The short novel plays out Burgess's hidden polemic through his recurring character Francis Xavier (F.X.) Enderby in the Bakhtinian sense that the 'author's discourse is directed toward its own referential object, as is any other discourse, but at the same time every statement about the object is constructed in such a way that, apart from its referential meaning, a polemical blow is struck at the other's discourse on the same theme, at the other's statement about the same object', with 'the other' being American authors, intellectuals, students, and popular culture icons.[5] The characters and situations Enderby encounters closely resemble those of Burgess's own experiences, with many of the American characters Enderby meets acting as stereotypical conglomerative caricatures of the personages he interacted with during his American travels. The entire farcical and satirical novel has an air of sarcasm and unreality to it which is a side effect of the hidden polemic that treats 'other's words ... antagonistically, and this antagonism, no less than the very topic being discussed, is what determines the author's discourse'.[6] This fictional antagonism, when juxtaposed with Burgess's 'public epitexts' (lectures, interviews, autobiography, non-fiction, and journalism), reveals the (not so) furtive nature of his polemical discourse, which in turn makes *The Clockwork Testament* perhaps the most important text to analyse when looking at Burgess's relationship with the United States because it is one of the most autobiograficational novels he produced, since it brazenly 'incorporates lived fact', which then and also, because of the nature of the text, provides a detailed commentary on Burgess's thinking about American culture, American higher education, New York City, and the American zeitgeist of the mid 1970s.[7]

Background, context, allusions, and epitexts: *The Clockwork Testament*

Since the purpose of this chapter is to explore how *The Clockwork Testament* is highly auto/biographical and cathartically satirical in the sense that Burgess uses the novel and his character, Enderby, to carry out a hidden polemic focused on Burgess's own life in New York City in the early 1970s, it is also important to recognize that the novel is steeped in the cultural milieu of the time, thus making the text, as is the argument for this entire monograph, and indeed all of his *American* work, highly heteroglot in the sense that Burgess's language is 'borrowed' from the time and environment (the chronotope) in which he had his American experiences, resulting in 'stylization, parody, or some analogous phenomenon'.[8] This novel, by its very nature of fitting into this burlesque genre, as Bakhtin defines it, is 'itself stratified and heteroglot in its aspect as an expressive system ... in the forms that carry its meanings', in the sense that to parody or satirize, the inspiration must come from a cultural milieu, and all that is needed to reveal this 'life-world' of the text is the historical context, which in this case is the cultural, biographical, and historical background and voices consciously surrounding Burgess which are infused into his language and motivations, as well as those he chose to caricature: students, New Yorkers, television personalities, and academics.[9] Enderby's descent into the madness of American life (quarrels, sex, and violence) is mirrored by what Burgess witnessed in the cultural maelstrom that was New York City in the early 1970s as a public figure, conditions that he felt were paradoxically 'totally representative of the human condition' – a term used when describing Minos's labyrinth, 'beauty and knowledge built around a core of sin, the human condition', Enderby's *Pet Beast* epic poem in *Inside Mr Enderby* (1963) and also the title of André Malraux's 1933 novel, *La Condition Humaine*, better known to English readers as *Man's Fate*, which presents a rugged view of violence, sex, and drug habits occurring within the 1927 Shanghai Massacre through the eyes of, largely, four different individuals.[10] Using Enderby for the purpose of unrestrained critique accommodated various layers of criticism, which does not exclude Burgess's own purposes since he, as has been expressed by Jim Clarke in *The Aesthetics of Anthony Burgess*, 'actively embraced the fictionalizing function of writing his self and, in doing so, produced a transcendent resolution of the depressing poststructuralist conclusion that all such writing is a reduction of, or violence committed upon, the self', effectively producing *The Clockwork Testament* as a kind of ascetic cathartic by-product of this period of his life.[11]

This may be why violence, or the subject of violence, appears in every aspect of life in *The Clockwork Testament* – not entirely different from the hellish landscape occupied by Alex and his droogs in *A Clockwork Orange* and not overly surprising too since *The Clockwork Testament* first began, among several other inspirations, with the intent to contemporize Dante's *Inferno* narrative, something Burgess also claims to have tried in *Any Old Iron* – whether on college campuses, New York City trains and sidewalks, or television shows watched by Enderby, and/or while being a guest on a talk show where he is goaded into defending the violence used in his adapted screenplay of *The Wreck of the Deutschland* (similarly, Burgess stated that one day he envisaged himself producing a 'choral and orchestral setting of *The Wreck of the Deutschland*', a poem he thought 'not likely to be filmed'); Enderby defends the violence of the film by claiming that there is 'more juvenile violence in America than anywhere else in the world. Not that I object to violence (*Audience protest.*) You can't change things without [constructive] violence'.[12] This is not too great an exaggeration in the 1970s in New York City, with statistics later in the decade showing in stark terms a persistent problem that began in the early 1970s: '1,814 homicides in 1980 – three times what we have today', which was largely due to fiscal problems that forced the New York Police Department 'to lay off 50,000 employees in 1975', leading the police force to 'shrink by 34%, while serious crime increased by 40%'.[13] This was a symptom Burgess saw the beginnings of since much of 'New York City's crime happened on the subway in the late '70s', with the 'Lexington Avenue Express' being nicknamed 'the "Mugger's Express"'.[14] Keeping this in mind, essentially Enderby is shaped and cultivated by this violent environment, leading him to swordfights on the subway, with the film based on his work acting as a perfect supplement to the realities that were occurring in the streets.[15] Enderby broadens his castigations of the United States beyond his immediate horizons and argues that the country's current chaos is due to its former violent colonial history with England: 'hypocritical country where everybody had a gun. ... You baggers (?) were violence when you broke away from us in 1776. Not blaming you for that of course. You wanted to do it and were term into do it (??). You were wrong of course. Might still be a bit of law and order if you were still colonial territory. Not ready for self gov (*Audience protest and some A*)'.[16] Immediately put on the defensive, Enderby haphazardly debates with Sperr Lansing during his chaotic television appearance that is soon overrun by other guests, constantly interrupted by commercials, ultimately leading Enderby to be asked to leave, but not before going on several tangents that could have come straight out of one of Burgess's own lectures: 'Cant stand the bloody place [England]. Americanized. The past is the only place worth living in. Imaginary past. ... Curious thing about America is that it was founded by people who believed original sin and also priesty nation (???) but then you had to watch for signs of gods grace and this was in commercial success making your own way building heaven on earth and so on this led to American plagiarism (?)', which should be *Pelagianism*.[17] *The Clockwork Testament*-Enderby may, for these reasons, be the most audacious incarnation of Enderby and therefore, due to this, exposes the dark recesses of Burgess's own ego, since Enderby does without a doubt occasionally speak directly on Burgess's behalf by using the author's own ideas, terms, and words to communicate through his character, yet it would be an error to say that the two are interchangeable: 'America was an English colony, and now England is an American colony.'[18] Despite the nastiness of Enderby in *The Clockwork Testament* and Burgess's own record of occasionally being quite cold, distant, and rude, Burgess was more often than not, as Gore Vidal put it, 'amiable, generous and far less self-loving than most writers', which makes Enderby appear to be a Mr Hyde-like construction who acts upon the nasty id-like desires and opinions that Burgess, professional author, restrains.[19]

Even so, the striking autobiograficitional nature of *The Clockwork Testament* was recognized at the time it was published – McGraw-Hill declared the book out of print in October 1989 – with reviews explicating the novel to reveal evidence of the kind of Bakhtinian categorization presented here by explaining that the story is rife with 'straw dialogues, set pieces that Enderby wins outright or wins covertly because the ostensible winners reveal their boorishness by their conquest', since Burgess deliberately manufactured such parodic characters as quick victims of Enderby's loathing and Burgess's 'mastered distaste'.[20] Burgess's bibliographer, Paul Boytinck, also notes this overlapping of author and fiction in the text by explaining that in *The Clockwork Testament*, Enderby, 'afflicted with aphasia following a heart attack, invents a minor Elizabethan with the unlikely name of Gervase Whitelady', an act which Burgess claimed he, though perhaps this is fiction too – one can never be too sure with Burgess – committed when he 'delivered a similar lecture or mini-lecture on one fictitious Grasmere Tadsworth', which may have simply been Burgess characteristically mixing his fiction with his lived life, his lived life with fiction, and/or simply an error due to William Wordsworth having lived in the British village of Grasmere.[21]

In an unpublished article from 1972 that is archived at the International Anthony Burgess Foundation in Manchester, United Kingdom, Burgess writes about his time teaching creative writing in the United States and the feelings he was confronted with over such a position as a creative instructor of literature:

> I have just completed a semester in creative writing (fiction) and – accepting for the sake of argument, meaning the job, that creative writing can be

> taught – I feel that I've let my students down in various ways, the principal way being the collective approach, or group therapeutic, whereas what the young writer needs is individual tuition. This means, to make amends, I must spend every Monday of the new semester in 90-minute sessions with students in duos, solos not being practicable, starting at 8:30 in the morning and ending at dinner time. It is feared by my colleagues, and rightly, that this may suggest a new tutorial pattern for everyone, but, granted the same and still arguable premise about the teachability of the subject, what way out is there? Another way in which I seem to have failed my students is in not disclosing sufficiently my own professional 'secrets' – how to choose the names of characters, how to characterize through dialogue alone, how to set up a cocktail party scene, how to describe the sexual act without brash explicitness and so on. But my fear has always been – a fear I share with many professional fiction writers who teach for a living – that I may impose a style instead of teasing a number of different styles out. Nevertheless, the view is held here that style can be taught, and that there might even be a kind of style kit with which to equip students.[22]

Similar to Burgess's own satirical mocking, Enderby too jeers at scholarly literary inquiries along with the teaching of creative fiction, with Enderby pondering to himself that he could 'always say that he had been trying out a new subject called Creative Literary History. They might even write articles about it: *The Use of the Fictive Alternative World in the Teaching of Literature*'.[23] These kinds of ridiculous literary escapades – perhaps Burgess would mock this very monograph – is further still vaguely ridiculed in conjunction with a colleague of his in the same aforementioned article, where Burgess claims that the Modern Language Association (MLA) convention – founded in 1883 and one of the world's largest scholarly associations – just 'provides a platform for the wild-eyed prophecies of Leslie Fiedler, for whom literature has apparently come to an end, but it is chiefly a kind of flesh market in which teachers of languages (including English) try to get better jobs'.[24]

Being so similar to Burgess's actual or exaggerated life in the early 1970s, the short novel *The Clockwork Testament*, called a novella by Burgess in *You've Had Your Time* (1990), is an authorial interpretation and embellishment of the author's existence, which also voices Burgess's grievances through double-voiced hidden polemic, during a time period when, at the time of publishing, the popularity of Stanley Kubrick's *A Clockwork Orange* was beginning to subside, although it was still increasingly popular; in *A Clockwork Orange: Controversies* (2011), Peter Krämer explains that Kubrick's film was 'mentioned frequently' at the 'end-of-the-year critical overview for 1972 and 1973', having grossed '$12 million with another $1.5 million being added in 1973 and about half a million dollars in each of the next few years'.[25] Despite the success of the movie, and the increase in speaking engagements offered, Burgess frequently commented to his audiences that he was still very poor, telling the New England Library Association in New Hampshire in October 1972 that 'now that I'm even more famous, this has been my worst financial year'.[26] Although the film was widely popular, 'the critical reception of [Kubrick's] *A Clockwork Orange* was by no means unanimously positive', and, more often than not, queries about the film's violence and sex fell to Burgess, who was, as John Stinson notes in *Anthony Burgess: Revisited* (1991), frequently assaulted 'with questions about the glorification of violence and the social responsibility of the artist'.[27] *The Clockwork Testament* afforded Burgess an avenue of response to the whirlwind of popularity surrounding the movie based on his novel, in much the same way that Jean Cocteau was able to respond in his similarly named *Le testament d'Orphée* (1960) to his 1949 film *Orphée* – both *The Clockwork Testament* and Cocteau's film act as an homage to and explanation of previous work, and an attempt to distance the artist from his artistic voice.[28] The Cocteau inspiration seems plausible too since the novel – after the notion of 'The Clockwork Condition' was abandoned – was initially suggested to have the title *Enderby in New York*, which then changed to *Death in New York* on one of the surviving typescripts as an ode to Thomas Mann's *Death in Venice* (1912), and ended up using the word *testament* to denote a declaration or commentary on one's property, in this case Burgess and Cocteau's allusion to the artist's previous work through an artistic act that is distinctly different and yet provides a new perspective on past achievements.[29]

Clearly inspired to respond to the ordeals of his life and work, only one month after completing his stint as the distinguished visiting professor of English position at City College of New York on 31 August 1973 – Kurt Vonnegut took over the position after Burgess's departure – Burgess finished writing *The Clockwork Testament* in Rome, taking only three weeks to write the novel, after having explained in personal correspondence that he was in the process of writing a satire based on the public attacks focused on him and his ripostes, which alludes to two articles that covered these debates in *The Times*, London.[30] In 1972 Burgess had signed a contract with the American 'hustler and literary agent', Thomas P. Collins, to write a non-fiction book under the title 'The Clockwork Condition', but after being unable to complete this nebulous philosophical work, as well as an incomplete 'George' or 'American trilogy', he wrote *The Clockwork Testament* instead, the only book to appear under the contract with Collins.[31]

Tom Collins, as he is addressed in *You've Had Your Time*, is described by Burgess as a 'former Jesuit priest' who tracked Burgess down in his apartment in New York City and offered to 'make me rich' if Burgess would agree to write three novels: 'George Gershwin (*The Rhapsody Man*),

George Patton (*The True Patton Papers*) and George III (*The Man Who Lost America*)', promising that if Burgess could at least produce outlines for each, he, Collins, could 'guarantee advances totaling a million dollars'.[32] Although never fully written or published, what exists of *The American Trilogy*, as they would be referred to by Burgess, is a letter to Collins from September 1972 in the International Anthony Burgess Foundation's archive which summarizes the three books and includes Burgess's thoughts on how to approach this project, one that he grew to believe was 'intended to appeal to a wider audience than the author has previously sought – nothing hermetic about them, no torturous syntax or wanton wordplay, but, if possible, a certain connotative richness behind the comparative simplicities of the prose'.[33] Intertwined with *The Clockwork Testament*, Burgess explains, however untrustworthy it may be in his autobiography, though still revealing slivers of truth, that Collins 'required something small and thoughtful to be written immediately' while Burgess was still working on the trilogy, as a sign of dedication, which in effect produced the 'novella called *The Clockwork Testament*' which was 'written in ten days and made into a beautifully illustrated book by an artistic team brought together by Tom Collins. Knopf published this, and I received money for it, though not much', whereas Tom Collins was paid 'five thousand pounds advance' and 'kept it all', leading to Robert Lantz and Deborah Rogers, Burgess's New York and London agents, joining forces and 'deploring my unprofessionalism, innocence, and treachery' for having dealt with Collins without their guidance.[34]

Beginning to be greatly dissatisfied with American culture and life while teaching at City College of New York, Burgess turned down a visiting professorship at Columbia University for the 1974–75 academic year, at first accepting the offer and then changing his mind, purportedly due to health issues, deciding to instead get back to writing and largely avoid the United States until his spring 1975 lecture tour.[35] *The Clockwork Testament* appears to be a cathartic attempt at ridding himself of the many objections, which had reached a boiling point after Kubrick's film release, that Burgess had about the United States, many of which have been previously discussed, though these issues had grown and evolved between 1966 and 1973. Despite this, and/or perhaps because of it, with several critics commenting on Burgess using *The Clockwork Testament* as an 'answer to critics' which was 'based on Burgess's own experience', and an expression of 'his contempt for American culture', the novel attracted some positive American attention, especially concerning the biting satirical humour of the small book.[36] J.D. O'Hara, reviewing the novel in the *New York Times*, disregarded Burgess's castigations of American culture as a 'transmogrified' attempt to 'really and clearly' explain what he meant in his 'moral and religious novel "A Clockwork Orange"', all while displaying descriptions of New York City that were so entertaining that 'anyone considering a trip to the Big Apple should read it for its street scenes alone'.[37] Although the book was finished in July 1973, shortly after a United States lecture tour, and published in early 1974, in the United States with illustrations from the Quay Brothers, *The Clockwork Testament* could be seen as a 'vicious poke' at American culture, but this apparently did not in the least dissuade publishers and universities from desiring to pay Burgess to write and speak for their American audiences.[38] Between March and April 1975, Burgess carried out a four-months-long lecture tour across the country and went on to spend four weeks at the University of Iowa as a visiting lecturer (5–31 October 1975) – he would go on to turn down lectureship invitations for the 1976–77 academic year with the school, despite at once claiming that one 'of my aims in coming back to Iowa is to work on a biggish novel and to teach Joyce'.[39] More surprisingly perhaps is that despite the harsh treatment of New York City and the United States in the novel and press, Burgess was commissioned in 1976 to write an entire book on his adoptive home, New York City, for Time-Life, entitled plainly *New York*, which was reported as repeatedly slipping 'into the style of a smooth, fact-jammed, Time-Life-research article – although the publisher reports that Burgess did his own research and all of the writing except the captions for the many excellent photos ... Burgess may be separated from New York but it is still his mistress'.[40] Another reviewer even went so far as to argue that they could not think of a 'better moment for this book [*New York*] to appear than now when it is fashionable to snicker at New York's financial plight, shudder at its crime, condemn its huge welfare system', and that perhaps Burgess's 'honesty and warmth, and the camera artists who have complemented his text with splendid and remarkable photographs will convince those of little vision that New York is not dead'.[41]

Regardless of the strange allure Burgess had with American readers, which he had started really focusing on since 1971 with *M/F*, it's important to historically and authorially contextualize *The Clockwork Testament*, both before and after its publication, with a 'Januslike gaze in two directions at once' in order to recognize it as a novel reflective of Burgess's struggles to become acclimated with American culture, American higher education, and the United States's relentless fascination with fame, as a willing, though somewhat reluctant, temporary visitor.[42]

Burgess's outsider status – 'I was not of their world' – among American academic scholars at universities throughout the United States probably started, or else was clearly defined, in 1969 at the University of North Carolina at Chapel Hill when he made multiple requests to be awarded a PhD in English literature for his published work, or else to be admitted onto the doctoral programme, and possibly to join the faculty, though all such requests were ultimately denied and Burgess's obtuseness towards scholarly establishments continued to swell over the subsequent three years he spent fulfilling duties as a writer-in-residence, an adjunct faculty member, a visiting professor, and a distinguished professor at, respectively, University of North Carolina at Chapel Hill, Columbia University, Princeton University, and City College of New York.[43] All of these experiences at these institutions of higher learning ripple through Burgess's literature from 1971 onward. In looking at *The Clockwork Testament, or Enderby's End* and *Enderby's Dark Lady, or No End to Enderby* (1984), any reader even vaguely familiar with Burgess's teaching positions in the United States would be able to surmise that Burgess was using autobiographical material in order to facilitate, or else produce, auto/biographical fiction, but not necessarily to create strict *romans à clef*, as Burgess himself defined this genre by stating that a true *roman à clef* made it 'necessary for the reader to consult the real-life personages and events that inspired it', though, he remarked, it could be true, in the more 'general sense', that 'every work of literary art requires a key or clue to the artist's preoccupations', whereas a true and strict *roman à clef* was more 'particular in its disguised references'.[44]

Visiting the University of North Carolina at Chapel Hill in November to December 1969 was a halfway mark or the turning point in Burgess's career as a writer which appears to be subconsciously confirmed when he tells his readers about his time at the University of North Carolina close to the midpoint of the Penguin edition of *You've Had Your Time*. Burgess decided to end the first part of his biography by morphing into his new *nom de plume*: 'now Burgess', by shedding the letters of his earlier life's name: John Wilson.[45] The foreshadowing of his new life as a writer peeks through earlier instances in *Little Wilson and Big God* – 'I was touching the borders of the literary life' – as he begins to contemplate what to do next after ending his hopes of being a composer in his 'late thirties' and after his failure as an army grunt pushed him even closer to his love for teaching and learning while holding a position in the Army Education Corps during World War Two.[46] In all sincerity, Burgess was always a writer, but this proclivity did not astutely manifest until his Malay teaching tenure in the British Colonial Service came to an end and the honest creation of fictional characters for the selling of words began.[47] He completed his first autobiography by proclaiming to have taken a firm stance as a new writer who was to set off to work, 'and I did'.[48] It was at this point, somewhere roughly in the late 1950s and early 1960s, that Burgess picked up the story of his life in the second part of his autobiography and where his rise to fame as a cosmopolitan author started to take shape. Burgess laboured under forms – forms of music, forms of the novel, forms of the low, common, and demotic as well as the high, artful, erudite, and esoteric, and forms of all of these matters intersecting – so it's no surprise that he ended his pre-professional life of writing in *Little Wilson and Big God* and started a book to record his new authorial life in *You've Had Your Time*.[49]

Of course, the second book of confessions was written by this 'professional' author reflecting on the days of struggling to survive, even though, at the time when the story picks up, Burgess had already written seventeen novels. Still, Burgess's novels sold meagrely and he never found a solid popularity during this period, therefore he considered himself an *écrivain très peu connu* or 'little-known writer' who was on the precipice of 'giving up altogether the tapping out of ill paid words'.[50] Along with this financial struggle came the decline of Burgess's first wife's health, essentially barring Burgess from taking part in much travel overseas, especially not for tours or residencies. The letters abroad came in from universities, but Burgess had to turn them down as he slowly awaited the death of his first wife. With that death came depression at first, and then release, and then freedom. That freedom allowed for him to take advantage of a market he had known for some time would provide him with economic salvation. Since receiving a review by Naomi Bliven in *The New Yorker* after the 1960 publication of *The Right to an Answer*, where the reviewer found the novel to be ' "not a joke but a nicely controlled examination of some human predicaments that is cunningly disguised as entertainment" ', Burgess gathered that he had made his 'American début', at least to reviewers, since he surmised that 'the great American public was indifferent', claiming to have decided that it 'was important, from now on, to appeal to Americans' because 'they had the money'.[51]

The highly autobiographical content in *The Clockwork Testament* was something Burgess even openly admitted on several occasions, remarking in *The Times* on 6 August 1973 that his views about the reception of Kubrick's *A Clockwork Orange* would be published in his upcoming novel, and later on, while at Pennsylvania State University in 1982, he stated that *The Clockwork Testament* was in fact 'pretty much based on my own experience with *A Clockwork Orange* – being blamed for all the sins of the world', where 'based on' can be equated with autobiography in the same sense that all autobiography is also simply *based on* an author's life, through their biased perspective as seen through their distorted and selfish perception, since, as John Sturrock notes in *The Language of Autobiography* (1993), 'all autobiographical stories are in practice part portrait, just as all self-portraits are in part story – autobiography wills the unity of its subject'.[52] Furthermore, the research conducted for this monograph reveals that not only are there many biographical parallels between Burgess and Enderby – they are exactly the same age, share similar experiences, several opinions are double-voiced, their narrative voices intertwine, and their comments overlap – but Enderby also acts not as Burgess's biographer, Andrew Biswell has argued, a 'grotesque autonomous figure who shares little of the author's true personality', but as a kind of autobiografictional authorial conduit for Burgess's thinking and frustrations.[53] Although intrinsically separated from Burgess through the act of writing, the two are nonetheless inescapably connected, a point recognized by Burgess in the 'A Prefatory Note' which begins *Enderby's Dark Lady*, in which he states that 'Enderby demanded that he be killed off' and so Burgess 'duly murdered [Enderby] with a heart attack', though in reality, Burgess ponders, no character can ever fully die despite the advancement of a character's life being cut off the day their 'creator will die'.[54] On *The Larry King Show* in 1991, Burgess explained that his autobiographical exploits may not simply be mythmaking, as some noted Burgess scholars have conceded, but their inaccuracy could be attributed to the fallibility of Burgess's memory, mixed with his proclivity for embellishment:

> I think the real danger of writing about yourself especially if you are a professional novelist is that you may start telling lies. You may start wanting to entertain the reader than to tell the truth. I think on the whole I've been fairly truthful but it was not enjoyable.[55]

Such pontifications could be applied to any character and author, though, so what Burgess appears to be doing here is downplaying and overshadowing the similarities which exist between this particular creation of his in order to trivialize such connections, but the significance of revealing the links between author and character in the case of Burgess and Enderby cannot be overstated, since to unravel one is to expose the other. Recognizing this allows for readers of the novel to then organize and assess certain themes as being reflections and exaggerations of Burgess's own views on American culture, particularly regarding the American higher education system, the position of an author among scholars, and cultural aspects of the United States that involve race, celebrity, politics, and youth.

It could be argued that were it not for the fandom in the wake of the popularity of Stanley Kubrick's *A Clockwork Orange*, Burgess may not have grown so dispirited with the United States, but what is certain is that the film based on his novel had an intense impact on the frequency with which he communicated with American audiences and the tone he employed when engaging with American popular media. This effect was largely due to his view of Americans' propensity for melodrama, as he attempted to encapsulate when claiming to have given an interview about the inspiration behind writing *A Clockwork Orange* – regarding catharsis after Lynne had been attacked during World War Two – only to see a headline shortly afterwards that read 'CLOCKWORK ORANGE GANG KILLED MY

WIFE – AUTHOR', though there remains no actual proof of such a column. This therefore also signals that Burgess himself was a grand and casual inventor of half-fictions and embellishments about his own life, and so he is not to be *entirely* trusted when it comes to history and always must be fact-checked, though his many exaggerations are proof in and of themselves of his constant heteroglossic monologic double-voiced authorial discourse that weaves and spirals in and out of his fiction and non-fiction.[56] What remains true is that Burgess was a target for the blame of violence seen in the wake of Kubrick's film, especially after a series of copycat crimes and the attempted assassination of Governor George Wallace by Arthur Bremmer, who suggested that the film may have had a violent effect on his thinking.[57] Misunderstood, sensationalized, and blamed for provoking real violence due to the violence in *A Clockwork Orange*, a novel Burgess was never very proud of outside of the linguistic inventiveness in Nadsat – he ranked the novel as a 'Class 2' work of literary art among the ranks of *Ulysses* and *Lolita* – he claimed that he did 'not always like what I myself write about' and that he was 'nauseated by the content of my *A Clockwork Orange*', though he contradicted this in the 1986 Norton 'Introduction' to the novel where he stated that he 'enjoyed raping and ripping by proxy' due to his, and he argued, any author's 'cowardice that makes him depute to imaginary personalities the sins that he is too cautious to commit for himself'; cowardly in this sense, Burgess appears to have again used the novel-form, this time with Enderby, to, by proxy, carry out condemnation he personally held against certain individuals and a country as a whole.[58] In *The Clockwork Testament*, Burgess and Enderby assert that the United States was 'eccentric' and 'great on conformity', as has already been evidenced on Burgess's behalf in the previous chapters, so for this novel the author bestowed these opinions upon his protagonist, much more than he had in the two previous Enderby books, *Inside Mr Enderby* (1963) and *Enderby Outside* (1968), as a way to surreptitiously mock his experiences with fame, violence, and social scapegoating in the United States, all while going on the offensive against those who held this question to him: 'Don't you think there's enough juvenile crime in our streets without filth like yours abetting it?'[59]

In fact, the diatribe that is *The Clockwork Testament* was years in the making. Having unceremoniously left Princeton University in June 1971, after having been forced to teach creative writing courses for a programme Burgess publicly described as a 'kind of sideshow' to the *real* academic activities taking place on campus, and later as a topic that is 'mostly useless', while at Columbia University the programme had been more esteemed, with students who were 'published novelists or short story writers, and the discussion of a limp metaphor or contused phrase has relevance to a great tough audience, actual or potential, honking out there through the streets of Manhattan', Burgess had become significantly disgruntled with American higher education after being turned down for a PhD at both the University of North Carolina at Chapel Hill and Princeton.[60] Despite his salary being $15,000 for the year with a $1,000 travel grant (roughly over $110,000 in 2022), with his rent for Dr Bede Liu's house being around $275 a month at 32 Western Way, Princeton, NJ 08540, the year was difficult for Burgess as a teacher.[61] But with two appearances on *The Dick Cavett Show* on 25 March 1971 and 1 April 1971, articles in the *New York Times*, and creative work in Minneapolis, Minnesota for his translation of *Cyrano de Bergerac*, he was beginning to gather more and more American popularity – achievements that did not necessarily sit well with the elites at Princeton University, as Burgess discussed on Dick Cavett's show, saying that 'Princeton is more English than England' and that it was expressed to him the school did not 'want members of our staff belittling themselves by appearing on commercial programs of this nature'.[62] Burgess also grew aggravated by some of his students at the Ivy League school, summarizing one situation at Princeton nearly twenty years later in his second autobiography, *You've Had Your Time* (1990), by explaining that the 'Princeton Creative Writers were not serious' due to the 'relegation of Creative Writing to an extra-academic region' which, he claims, attracted a classful of newly accepted female students and one African American student – female education at Princeton began in 1969 – who exhibited militant feminist and anti-White ideas in their poetry which focused on 'cutting the balls off men', with the 'sole black male' focusing on 'white castration only, with the penis occasionally thrown in as a kind of *bonne bouche*'.[63] When telling this story in his autobiography, Burgess repeats almost verbatim the words of Enderby when he claims to have asked a student what poetry was made out of: 'Poetry, said the black man, hating me with hot eyes, was essentially emotion, but I said it was essentially words'; in *The Clockwork Testament* this appears as, ' "Poetry is made out of emotions," he pronounced. "Oh no," Enderby said. "Oh very much no. Oh very very very much no and no again. Poetry is made out of words" ', whose meanings, the Enderby of *Inside Mr Enderby* (1963) ponders, 'The meaning? Meaning was no concern of the poet' and Burgess, the author, agrees in a non-fiction book review, stating, 'Poetry, as Mallarmé said, is made out of words, not ideas.'[64] Similar in many ways, both Burgess and Enderby were struggling with entertaining new modes of youthful thought in the early 1970s, with both character and author expressing, again with an almost one-to-one similarity, that they were too old-fashioned for these young college students: Enderby remarks that between him and his students there 'was no communication; he was too old-fashioned; he has always been too old-fashioned', and in Burgess's summer 1971 'Letter from Europe', he remarks that he wonders, 'in my old-world old-fashioned way', how these young writers

> bring themselves to use such words, show such intimate knowledge of such remote sexual deviations? Rape and almost ecstatic obscenity are nowadays openly exploited in the very first paragraph, leaving nothing for the final one but some drug-induced vision of hell. Can Creative Writing, or creative writing, go on much longer in this way? When is the new puritanism coming?[65]

Apparently not accepted by the older scholars of the time either, and too old to fit in with the undergraduate youth, Burgess's prime audience appears to have been highly educated, young adult White men, but anything out of that demographic left him out of place and obtuse. Again, reflecting on that time in his life in *You've Had Your Time*, Burgess commented that he 'was doing no good at Princeton' and that the 'Burgess family was not wanted in Princeton [for] publicly displayed disloyalty', with personal accounts of his time there substantiating his apparent disgruntled depressiveness as he played the part of the eccentric author who was not to be bothered with the ramblings of these *too* young and too wealthy American college students.[66] Forty-six years later, Lieber distinctly remembers Burgess as a kind of affront to the establishment, an affront to the pomp and circumstance of such an elite school, so much so that he reflects that having Burgess as a teacher 'was a great opportunity' because Burgess did not

> indulge or placate people, and that certainly was a good thing for me, it was refreshing. ... I felt like that helped me mature. ... Princeton was kind of an incubator at that time, but Burgess was more about, 'let's get real, this is the real world, your writing is shit, don't bother.' ... So that was good and he was quite funny ... naturally funny, a funny person.[67]

Although this characterization fits quite neatly with some other less appealing characterizations of Burgess, his time at Princeton does appear to be quite singular in his distaste for his students, his teaching, and life in general – still, Burgess wrote while maintaining his teaching duties, having finished the overture of *Blooms of Dublin* while on campus, and even at one time proposed to write 'a Princeton novel, rather like DEATH IN VENICE, ready by end of autumn and, indeed, to bring it over to England'.[68] Lieber even commented on the fact that during this time he remembers Burgess looking very old and worn down, so it is possible that this was a period of depression or some other aspect of poor health that was contributing to his overall dissatisfaction. More support for this speculation comes from Rexford Brown, who, in 1971, finished his dissertation 'Conflict and Confluence: The Art of Anthony Burgess' at The University of Iowa, after having talked to Burgess during 'three long phone conversations' in order to help him with his dissertation approach.[69] During his interaction with Burgess, Brown got the sense that Burgess 'was subject to periodic depressions', who, although kind to Brown, 'called himself a hack', and yet still came off as 'so voluble. ... He was very un-self-conscious, and I had the feeling he was smoking all the time when I ... talked to him. Just very encouraging'.[70] His frustrations were clearly accumulating, though what was to come only made things worse; his despondency would reach a climax when Kubrick's *A Clockwork Orange* was released in New York City on 19 December 1971. By this time too, the letters about concerns regarding representation and payment from the film between Burgess and his literary agent at the time, Deborah Rogers, had reached tense heights, culminating in the decision to get a lawyer by January 1972.[71]

Still, at one point, in early 1972, Burgess agreed to 'join Malcolm McDowell for a one-week publicity tour of New York City to promote' Kubrick's film. According to Robert Hofler's interview with McDowell in *Sexplosion: From Andy Warhol to A Clockwork Orange* (2014), the meeting of the two men began with 'Burgess asking McDowell, "Have you shit today?"'[72] After confirming that he had, McDowell claimed that 'Burgess launched into a scatological dissertation until their first interview of the morning' on Monday, but on Wednesday of the same week 'McDowell noticed a distinct change in his publicity date's attitude toward Kubrick and his film. "Burgess realized he's been cheated because he wasn't paid anything"' for the film.[73] Despite the venom accruing in Burgess's feeling towards Kubrick, it seems likely that he acted as Kubrick's mouthpiece to perhaps, at first, remain in good standing with Kubrick due to a desire to have his Napoleon movie idea made into a reality, one that would ultimately never come to fruition. Still, the increased attention led to a flood of university offerings, chief among them being from the City College of New York for a one-year distinguished visiting professor of English position that paid $31,275 with a $5,000 supplement for the term.[74] Exhausted and bitter from not receiving credit and royalties from Kubrick's film, although Burgess stood to benefit from the book sales, by the summer of 1972 Burgess apparently welcomed a change to his jet-setting lifestyle to take the university position. Despite having purported in the summer of 1972 in his 'Letter from Europe' that the 'nomadic sort of existence that, at an age proper for settling down, I find suits me best', Burgess admits that he had 'a lost soul' and settled down to the next American challenge.[75]

Burgess's display of public disloyalty against Princeton occurred on *The Dick Cavett Show*, an intellectual late-night comedy talk show that aired on and off from 1968 up until 2007, which was hosted by a television personality who Burgess greatly respected as being a 'witty, erudite, eloquent alumnus of Yale', who had 'read Henry James, whereas Carson probably hasn't heard of Henry James'.[76] Vaguely alluded to in *The Clockwork Testament*,

Dick Cavett's show playfully morphs into the 'Cannon Dickson Show', though it is unlike Cavett in that it has 'mostly show-business personalities' and resembles more closely a Johnny Carson, *The-Tonight-Show*-like television programme, while the 'Sperr Lansing Show is, well, *different*' – perhaps a pun on 'shake spear', a surname that the second half of Enderby novels often played with – in the sense that scholars appear on the programme, which is closer to Cavett's show, therefore crafting a similar though different, backwards and exaggerated, American reality for Enderby as Burgess did for Miles in *M/F*.[77] Indeed, Enderby even describes talk shows – 'sort of a thin man with a fat jackal. Both leer a good deal, but one supposes they have to' – almost exactly as Burgess described other late-night shows other than Cavett's to the host in 1974, telling Cavett during a discussion about his newly released memoir, *Cavett* (1974), that his show was the 'only popular show ... built on language', explaining to him that in Burgess's opinion,

> you're the only person in this kind of business who is concerned about words. Most of the talk show pundits one sees – that thin man with the fat jackal, I forget their names. ... These other people. They're full of expletives. They're full of sounds like 'Yeah. Yeah,' and 'I guess so,' and 'Wow'.[78]

Doing a mock American accent on those last words, Burgess appears to be acting out a scene in his own work on television, all while also explaining that the novelist's job is to lie: 'writing novels is lying; it's telling lies'.[79] At the core of lies are truths, but Burgess is clearly tying a complex knot of narrative that exists both intra- and extra-textually, which is layered in the text of *The Clockwork Testament*.

So, what Midge Tauchnitz appears to suggest when they state that the Lansing show is *different* is that *this* show, despite the type of guest, is apparently less refined and more focused on sensationalism, which can be discerned from Tauchnitz's lack of knowledge in even knowing when Gerard Manley Hopkins (1844–89), a Victorian poet, died: '"did you try [contacting] Hopkins?" "No luck there either. Nobody knows where he is"'.[80] In a letter to Geoffrey Aggeler in 1975, Burgess explained that the other characters to appear on television with Enderby, Professor Balaglas, Ermine Elderly, and Lansing, are all nominatively 'really tied up with [Gerard Manley] Hopkins', with Balaglas's arguments on the television show being 'lifted verbatim from B. F. Skinner's *Beyond Freedom and Dignity*', or 'ULTRA LIBERTATEM DIGNITATEMQUE' ('beyond freedom and dignity'), as Burgess put it.[81]

Not entirely verbatim, though exact phrases do appear; what happens is that Balaglas's comments are essentially paraphrased remarks from Burrhus Frederic (B.F.) Skinner (1904–90), an American behavioural psychologist with such publications as *The Behavior of Organisms: An Experimental*

Analysis (1938), *Walden Two* (1948), and *Beyond Freedom and Dignity* (1971), which have been distorted through a very poor transcription of the fictional television show discussion, possibly with the very real-world use of protecting Burgess from accusations of plagiarism.[82] For instance, in Skinner's monograph, *Beyond Freedom and Dignity*, he explains that ' "Brainwashing" is proscribed by those who otherwise condone the changing of minds simply because the control is obvious. A common technique is to build up a strong aversive condition, such as hunger or lack of sleep and, by alleviating it, to reinforce any behaviour which "shows a positive attitude" towards a political or religious system. A favourable "opinion" is built up simply by reinforcing favourable statements. The procedure may not be obvious to those upon whom it is used, but it is too obvious to others to be accepted as an allowable way of changing minds'. In Enderby's world, where Burgess displays a poor transcription that also affords space to mock through semantical and malapropic irony, this turns into Balaglas's statement that 'Positive rain forcemeat (?). Instructive urge is not killed (kwelled)? By prison or punishment. Brainwashing that is to say negative through fear of pain already tried but is fundamentally inhuman (e?). We must so condition human mind that reward is expected for doing good not the other way about.'[83] Balaglas also sounds a bit similar to T.E. Frazier from *Walden Two* when Frazier is summarized as yearning for 'control of the physical and social environment', whereas Burgess's creation sermonizes that 'for the sake of society there must be control'.[84] Similarly too is that Balaglas mentions the use of prison volunteers, 'as well as in our universities', as does Skinner when discussing in *Beyond Freedom and Dignity* a Supreme Court decision to recognize the power of 'positive inducement'.[85] Going on, Balaglas continues, Frazier-like, to argue that 'we are committed to control of the violent-ment (?) and as works of art and movies', and though *control* is a fundamental precept in Skinner's theories, the psychologist makes no such emotional and dictatorial pleas about censorship in his monograph, though he does deconstruct the concept of a permissive society, a topic Burgess returned to frequently, saying that, 'Permissive practices have many advantages. ... Permissiveness is not, however, policy; it is the abandonment of policy, and its apparent advantages are illusory. To refuse to control is to leave control not to the person himself, but to other parts of the social and non-social environments.'[86] Dedicated to caricaturing Skinner, Burgess's Skinnerian clown, which is a simplistic reduction of the actual person and ignores any nuance in his actual opinions/arguments/findings, represents more what Burgess willed into Skinner's argument than Skinner's arguments themselves, so that when Burgess's parodic double-voiced monoglottal scenario plays out, it is in essence only a stage filled with fools for Enderby/Burgess to mock. Noting in 'The Functions of the Rogue, Clown and Fool in the Novel' section in the 'Forms of Time and of the Chronotope in the Novel' chapter in *Discourse in the Novel*, Bakhtin says that these types of characters in literature, rogues (Enderby) and fools/clowns (the rest of the cast), at their essence just wear masks, which for the rogue reveals that he still has 'some ties that bind him to real life' whereas 'the clown and the fool ... are "not of this world," and therefore possess their own special rights and privileges', in this instance because Burgess's monologic vision trims these characters down to shallow two-dimensionality so that they may be mocked and 'laughed at by others, and *themselves* as well' to the point that this 'laughter bears the stamp of the public square where the folk gather'.[87] By distorting Skinner's arguments, presenting a caricature of late-night television, sharing arguments with his characters, and presenting this all through a poorly edited transcription, Burgess has produced a singularly monologically double-voiced unbalanced polyphonic hidden polemic, with superficial comic characters who, by their very nature as clowns, 're-establish the public nature of the human figure: the entire being of characters' which are 'utterly on the surface' where 'their entire function consists in externalizing ... a human being, via parodic laughter', all so that Burgess can mock public figures, defend his aesthetics, and provide a satirical literary counternarrative to the actual life of the novel's author.[88] This entire complicated apparatus is assembled to direct its assault towards American culture and Burgess's current American experience during a time when Burgess referred, in 'The Clockwork Condition', to the peculiar disposition of the author as being one who was 'a mere entertainer, a sort of clown' who 'mimes' and 'makes grotesque gestures', and because of this, an author could be 'pathetic or comic and sometimes both'.[89]

Motivation for the entire television show scene seems to have emanated from Burgess's appearances on Dick Cavett's show, and more specifically his appearance on 25 March 1971, when Burgess claims in his second autobiography that Cavett encouraged him 'to say hard things about Princeton', which is what led him to receiving some sort of condemnation from the administration at Princeton. However, the reality is that Cavett simply asked Burgess about his time as a professor at Princeton, and Burgess, ever the talker who was easily goaded, launched into an orated comedic obloquy about teaching fiction writing, meeting with students and parents, and the quality of his office and job in general.[90] To perhaps his largest crowd yet, although he had presented this argument elsewhere, Burgess revealed that the very job he had been hired to do – that is, teach creative writing – was, he believed, ludicrous because *talent* was unteachable.[91] After being asked by Cavett if one could teach writing, Burgess replied, 'Well, if there are any Princetonians watching, I'd better say yes you can do it', but if they were not watching, he goes on to say, he would more accurately state that 'you can't do it. I'd say that you can teach people how to put a scene together, you can teach people how to write verse, but you can't teach them to have original ideas or to have a knowledge of life', a poor choice of words for marketing the university, though altogether not an unpopular opinion among professors during a time when authors were increasingly filling university English departments across the United States.[92]

A week later on 1 April 1971, Burgess returned to Cavett's show and his criticism of Princeton University continued, this time with Burgess stating that he was ashamed of asking his students to his office since there were 'no carpets on the floor and nowhere to hang coats. There is plenty of whiskey and that sort of thing, but nothing to drink it out of. I'm ashamed so I usually meet them in the pub. In the pub they say they're too young, so we end up meeting in the street and risk arrest'.[93] It was after this televised interview that the relationship between Burgess and Princeton appears to have fractured in some way; he claims such behaviour in class and in public were deemed unworthy of Princeton's standards to some degree, and he was rebuked for it, though no hard evidence exists to confirm this.[94] In an awkward *volte-face*, Burgess returned to *The Dick Cavett Show* almost nine months later on 19 January 1972, apparently ashamed of some of the effects his behaviour had had at the school. After being asked again about his time at Princeton, a much more sombre Burgess presented a final note about it to Cavett, afterwards asking for the conversation to move away from this topic once he had made his peace: 'Lovely town, Princeton, delightful town, delightful university, delightful people. But I wasn't happy there. It was probably my fault. Let's leave it at that. Probably my fault. Princeton is a fine university, one of the greatest universities in the world. I wasn't good enough for it.'[95] Adding a little more detail, Burgess stated that he was reprimanded, since the school did not want faculty members on television, especially an intrusive and 'possibly drunken British [writer] who may deflect them from the path of righteousness, make them drunk, and possibly make them lose their jobs. … Probably, I'm sick about it. But probably it's better for Princeton and myself not to meet again'.[96] After his time at Princeton University ended on 30 June 1971, it seems that whatever damage was done to the relationship between school and author was not irreparable since Burgess did in fact return for a reading of his work on 29 September 1972 – refusing to read from *A Clockwork Orange*, he chose to instead read from *M/F*, his translation of *Cyrano de Bergerac*, and the unfinished *Napoleon Symphony* – and was scheduled to come back in 1973, but he had to cancel at the last minute.[97]

Similarly, though to a lesser degree, cantankerous, loquacious, and bombastic as Enderby himself, Burgess's life in the United States was certainly drumming up content worthy of a novel, and this is of course what would happen. Although these accounts of the early 1970s are from informal interviews, private correspondence, and an autobiography known for its looseness of truth and objective details, nevertheless Burgess's auto/biographical reflection in *The Clockwork Testament* is, as Max Saunders explains about this brand of literature in *Self Impressions: Life-Writing, Autobiografiction, and the Forms of Modern Literature* (2018), a 'legacy to posterity' which acts out an authorial performance of 'anthropological necessities', making it too, then, innately distorted and biased but relative and relevant because it serves 'as an expression of belief, or of the desire to believe', in a sense, 'that there are truths that inhere in fictions' – or, as Kenneth Toomey says, 'the gist is true'.[98] In a sense, too, this tenet is at the core of Bakhtin's thought, that history, in this case authorial history, itself becomes 'the frame' which draws 'characters out of their isolation' by a novelist who uses the 'materials of everyday speech' as Burgess witnessed them to reframe reality, or autobiography, as novel, thus making it 'properly historical'.[99] In many ways, Burgess's autobiografiction is an attempt at relaying (his) truth and his reality, his perspective, just not under the auspices of autobiography, a practice and approach to literature which was representative not only of modernist fiction but also of influential literature of the late modernist and post-modernist periods by American authors Burgess was publishing alongside, such as Henry Miller with his trilogy, *The Rosy Crucifixion*, where *Sexus* (1949), *Plexus* (1953), and *Nexus* (1959) are thinly fictionalized novels of Miller's real life in the United States before he departed for Paris; Jack Kerouac's *roman à clef*, *On the Road* (1957), presents slightly fictionalized versions of his travels and encounters with Neal Cassady, Allen Ginsberg, and William Burroughs, among others, as being the misadventures of Sal Paradise and Dean Moriarty; Norman Mailer's *Armies of the Night* (1968), as the subtitle suggests, is 'History as Novel; The Novel as History', so that this non-fiction novel of the new journalism era actually recalls and describes the historical events of the October 1967 March on the Pentagon, but, in describing the scene as Mailer encountered it, it is embellished and presented through a subjective authorial perspective without an attempt at objectivity; Hunter S. Thompson's *Fear and Loathing in Las Vegas* (1971) goes even further with new journalism, effectively producing his own style, or Dr Raoul Duke's style, of gonzo journalism, where the trip and personal experience, infused with drugs, actually takes over the non-fiction element, therefore turning the autobiographical into the fantastic; Charles Bukowski's *Post-Office* (1971) is an autobiografictional novelization of Bukowski's time working for the United States Postal Service, as told through his literary alter ego, Henry (Hank) Chinaski, a practice he utilized for over two decades of novels; and, finally, though to only name a few with such similarities, is Saul Bellow's Pulitzer Prize-winning *Humboldt's Gift*

(1975), yet another *roman à clef* that is perhaps more fictionalized than the previous novels, though closely based on Bellow's life and his relationship with the poet Delmore Schwartz, wherein he uses the story for the more grand purposes of exploring the role of art in modern American culture – a novel Burgess described as a 'masterpiece of rich humor and pathos'.[100]

Fictions, non-fictions, and autobiographies: New York City in *The Clockwork Testament*

Leaving Princeton University in summer 1971, Burgess accepted the 'Distinguished Professor of Literature' position at City College of New York for $36,275 for the 1972–73 academic year to begin on 1 September 1972.[101] In *The Clockwork Testament*, Enderby is invited to an approximation of City College of New York, the fictional University of Manhattan, in order to 'pass on some of his Creative Writing skill to Creative Writing students' and apparently to weed out students with poor writing skills and those who succumbed to plagiarism, though perhaps this is an ironic and parodic contemporary nod towards the Oulipo experimental French literature collective and William Burroughs's experimental *Nova Express* trilogy (1961–67), both of which were exploring the practices and limits of reusing text and collaborative textual productions in the early 1970s, a style Enderby twists to comedically mock the standards of the courses: 'one postgraduate student had received a prize for a poem that turned out to be a passage from a vice-presidential speech copied out in reverse and then seasoned with mandatory obscenities'.[102] In some ways, Burgess was essentially doing this kind of pastiche work himself, borrowing ideas and inspirations across multiple pieces of his own writings in order to assemble a text drawn from his experiences. In *The Clockwork Testament*, more so than any other novel of his, Burgess's fiction, journalism, public utterances, and autobiography exist on a parallel plain, exhibiting the 'trope of fiction as true autobiography ... groups of works; or across the group of works constituting a writer's entire oeuvre, when true autobiography is located [in] multiple works rather than in a single book', due to Enderby engaging in embellishments and fictionalized events that deviate only slightly from Burgess's path as both the author and character were living and teaching in New York City.[103] Enderby's adventures and the plot and purpose of the novel exhibit autobiografictional traits, such as the 'autobiographical spiritual experiences adopting fictional forms' when Enderby encounters many similar experiences to Burgess while in New York City, or perhaps this is the other way around, where Burgess patterns his memories on his character in his autobiography, but either way, the text, and his texts, is/are highly evocative of an autobiograficational satire meant as a cathartic release for the author, while also, ironically, fulfilling a contractual obligation to Tom Collins.[104]

Burgess's enforced, possibly inaccurate, and retroactive chronology of his autobiography shows, when compared to records and his literature, the powers of his autobiographical imagination. This becomes even more evident in such instances as when Enderby describes several 'black girl students', 'evidently waiting for ... Assistant Professor Zeitgeist or some such name', in order to signify Enderby's association with being forced to cohabitate with the spirit of the times, the professor Enderby shared an office with, 'beguiling their wait with loud manic music on a transistor radio'.[105] This fictional anecdote, perhaps inspired by an incident Burgess actually experienced, is mirrored and repositioned in *You've Had Your Time*, in which Burgess, autobiographer, describes a time outside his lecture hall at City College of New York when several African American students 'waited with competing cassette recorders of the kind called ghetto blaster', provoking Burgess to rebuke them, only to receive 'coarse threats in return, as well as scatological abuse which was unseemly in any circumstances but monstrous when directed at even an undistinguished professor'.[106] The exchange that follows this in *The Clockwork Testament* between Enderby and these students exhibits either how Burgess remembered and fabricated this actual event in *You've Had Your Time* or else how Burgess used a fictional encounter created by him in one of his novels as a way to mythologize his own experiences in his autobiography, there being always a 'fictional element in all autobiography', or even, though less likely considering the considerable amount of accurate reporting that exists throughout Burgess's autobiography, a completely manufactured autobiographized literary event.[107] Nevertheless, what follows is an unfiltered expostulation and contemptuous inner dialogue by Enderby which acts out frustrations, through mockery and double-voicedness, that Burgess expressed publicly on multiple occasions when he 'dismissed Black English, as spoken in the impoverished American ghettoes', and, recounting in his 'Viewpoint' article in the *Literary Supplement* having given a lecture at a Poets, Essayists, and Novelists (PEN) symposium in 1973, Burgess claims to have expressed that he 'deplored Blackspeak, which is ghetto language coddled by linguistic experts, cherished by remedial English teachers (who should know better), presented as a potentially serious literary medium and, as I see it, innocently – whatever, again, that means – used as a device for encouraging inarticulacy' – topics discussed at length in the chapter on *Enderby's Dark Lady*.[108] Insulting and ignorant as this may be to twenty-first-century sentimentalities, this was a relatively popular opinion at the time, but Burgess then uses this opinion as his source for parody and mockery when Enderby remarks to the students that

> 'This is, after all, the English Department of a University.' And then: 'Shut that bloody thing off.' 'You goan fuck yoself, man.' 'You ain't nuttin but shiiit, man.' Abdication. What did one do now – slap the black bitches? Remember the long servitude of their people and bow humbly? ... Enderby slapped the black bitch on the puss. No, he did not. He durst not. It would be on the front pages tomorrow.[109]

Instead of reacting violently, Enderby replies, '"Abdication of authority. Is that expression in your primer of Black English?"', to which the students mockingly retort, '"Pip pip old boy"', before sounding a bit like *A Clockwork Orange* Nadsat mixed with vulgar American-*go-fuck-yourself*-isms: '"And all that sort of rot, man." "You go fuck yo own ass, man"' – a term used as a crucial plot point in Richler's *Cocksure* (1968), when the Star-Maker reveals that he has turned himself into a hermaphrodite who could have sex with himself .[110] The restraint shown by Enderby not to lash out violently at these paper-thin stereotyped background characters is the restraint shown by any rational, non-violent, and professional educator, but this does not excuse the nasty thoughts, publicized through narrative, that Enderby has towards the students, and suggests ultimately that, because the humour is directed at monologic and derisive metonymic caricatures – partially even resembling, as defined by Bakhtin, a poorly concocted Menippean satire that displays a 'carnivalized genre' that is 'extraordinarily flexible' in its 'bold and unrestrained use of the fantastic and adventure' – the text's purpose is to display an authorially and 'internally motivated' opinion, that of Burgess's.[111] In *You've Had Your Time*, Burgess concludes the very similar memory of confrontation with students by simply quixotically wondering, 'What would Bertrand Russell have done?', to apparently allude to, and empathize with, the renowned philosopher's dubious and shameful dismissal from City College of New York on the grounds of being too '"morally unfit" to teach at the institution' in 1940 by Bishop Manning of the Protestant Episcopal Church, who denounced his appointment because he believed Russell was 'a man who is a recognized propagandist against both religion and morality, and who specifically defends adultery' – though the school board supported the appointment, the case was brought to the New York Supreme Court and Russell's appointment was terminated by Justice McGeehan on 'dangerously broad' grounds.[112] A massive false equivalence, Burgess simply evokes the wrongs of the past to mockingly question the environment of his historical present.

Burgess did not save his personal criticisms for his fiction and autobiographies, though, as he was frequently publishing articles in national newspapers, including two comedically cynical polemical criticisms of New York City, college students, and the United States in the *New York Times* in October and November 1972. It is worth noting, too, that Burgess was not the only author in residence at this time who found the environment at City College of New York difficult, with his colleague, Joseph Heller, author of *Catch-22* (1961), also reflecting on his time at the college in his memoirs, *Now and Then* (1998), and also remembering that he

> admired the way Burgess could take even the most hostile of these students seriously. He knew and remembered their names. He gave serious thought to even their most absurd statements. He wanted to know their backgrounds .... In all my life, even at its most compassionate moments, I have not come close to reaching that enormous inner generosity that characterised Anthony Burgess.[113]

Despite the generosity that Heller witnessed, both of Burgess's articles, 'Cucarachas and Exiles, Potential Death and Life Enhancement' and 'My Dear Students', caused a stir and elicited 'To the Editor' responses from New Yorkers.[114] On 19 November 1972, Burgess wrote an open letter, 'My Dear Students', to address the frustrations that would end up being double-voiced and fictionalized in *The Clockwork Testament* and imaginatively recalled in *You've Had Your Time*. Calling himself a 'temporary professor' to feign genuineness in his public letter to his students, Burgess sounds Enderbian as he describes witnessing a 'near-illiterate black ... being allowed credits for soul-cooking and bongo-drum playing' which he understood as being a result of collegiate standards which purport that the 'youth must be served, the ills of the past must be expiated by a lowering of standards, [and] professors must be no better than their students'.[115] Going on to disparage and discount contemporary writers like Kurt Vonnegut – his soon-to-be successor – and even himself, by stating that students should not study contemporary authors, at least not yet, he attacks the insolence and laxness he saw in contemporary collegiate American education programmes, programmes that had courses 'in classics that asks for no Latin or Greek, Virgil in translation being good enough, or an in-depth survey of the prosody of Allen Ginsberg'.[116] This supposed laxness he saw even manifesting itself in 'undergraduate life-styles' by contributing to the many ills he saw in humanities programmes in the American higher education system, going so far as to say that he felt this lethargy of academic rigour seeping into his own instruction, 'permitting a relaxation of standards that I would never have tolerated while I was a professional teacher'.[117] On the Manhattan University campus, Enderby describes the setting as being once the 'centre of incorrupt learning' that had become 'a whorehouse of progressive intellectual abdication' where the students, or 'kids', had to be pleased, 'this being a so-called democracy: courses in soul cookery, whatever that was, and petromusicology, that being teen-age garbage now treated as an art, and the history of black slavery, and innumerable branches of a subject called sociology'.[118] This leads the narrator, and we can assume Enderby/ Burgess – though Burgess doesn't appear to have had such a hostile view of sociology, he did remark in 'The British Observed' that anthropology has congenial human-centric purposes whereas statisticians and sociologists abstract material gathered by scientists, therefore 'the people can never really win' – to believe that such an abdication of duty had resulted in the United States, and Americans, ignoring and disrespecting the history, tradition, and scaffolding of human knowledge: 'The past was spat upon and the future was ready to be spat upon too, since this would quickly enough turn itself into the past.'[119]

Oddly enough, it was these social aspects of the American experience that Burgess did not seem wholly concerned about; rather, it was the mythos and the opportunity that drew him in. Similar to Janet's emphasis in *One Hand Clapping* on the invigorating qualities of the New York lifestyle, after having lived in New York City, a common aphoristic anecdote Burgess would tell periodically involved his opinion that the city warded off suicidal thoughts because it was fervently and violently *alive*:

> I often feel suicidal in Rome, Paris and London, and there is no antidote there except drink or literature. In New York, when the desperate mood comes on, all I have to do it to descend to the subway after midnight and observe the omnipresent evidence of violence there, and then the urge to go on living rushes in with the speed of a suburban express.[120]

Burgess told this almost identical story on *The Dick Cavett Show* on 4 December 1980 to sardonically, and apocryphally, express the inspiring entropy of New York City that he described in his book *New York* (1978) as being 'restless, febrile, neurotic, brutal, endlessly creative, endlessly destructive, prizing the new for novelty's sake, bizarre in its cultural and racial variety ... perpetual decay and perpetual rebirth'.[121]

Burgess's November 1972 article, exploring similar themes, was not received well by his students, or other academics, especially the African American scholar Horace Porter who in his 'Letter to the Editor' on Christmas Eve 1972 professionally excoriated Burgess, urging him to remember the historical context behind his criticisms:

> It is important that you recall that the likes of me were barred, blocked and hosed from university doors well into the sixties and that I, like thousands of my colleagues, arrived on the very tail of a decade which may have been both the most dramatic and traumatic in American history. War. Assassinations. Hippies. Riots. Sex. Pot. Acid. Rock. The decade of bells, bombs and buttocks. And hair! So when I arrived at Amherst in the fall of 1968, I had to contend with the sins of the white fathers, the contemporary crisis of the American society, and the confusions of my own black, adolescent soul. Yes, I asked for

> 'relevant' courses and issued demands and protested for Black Studies because that seemed at the time, the most effective way of driving away the three-legged giant of a demon which was out to get me. Since I was coming of age, it seemed infinitely more important to me as a black to read DuBois and Baldwin instead of Chaucer. They provided light for that frightening journey through the wilderness of my past.[122]

The deserved criticism, and crucial piece of epitext that evidences the cultural dialogue Burgess was immersed in, never received a response from Burgess – at least not publicly or discovered yet – but it stands as a testament to how much Burgess, and Enderby, were out of touch with American history and new fields of critical thought concerning race, youth, counter culture, and minority movements, while also being overly willing to express condemnation and insult towards these movements, much as the older, Whiter, generation of Americans were also doing at the time. But it was not just his students and time on campus that he felt was contributing to a certain lowering of standards, but American society and culture in general, especially in New York City.

Enderby, and indeed Burgess, suggests that it is New York City itself which leads to such deprivations of tongue and decorum, describing Manhattan as a place 'otherwise dirty, rude, violent, and full of foreigners and mad people' that also had a 'wide variety of dyspeptic foods on sale in the supermarkets'.[123] The rudeness and violence Enderby refers to resembles, and in many cases mirrors, occasions, and reflections Burgess-the-journalist and public personality catalogued in 'Cucarachas and Exiles, Potential Death and Life Enhancement' published less than a month earlier than 'My Dear Students' on 29 October 1972. Despite feeling 'simpatico' in New York City since it was 'seething with exiles', Burgess claims to have, on multiple occasions after he had written several critical articles on the United States and New York City, received 'several abusive phone calls' from more parochial and philistine Americans, telling him to 'eff off back to effing Russia, you effing corksacking limey effer', because he had nonchalantly, and more specifically, 'suggested some time ago, in these columns, that America would be better off for a bit of socialized medicine'.[124] Such abusive and disproportionate responses to such banal common sense Burgess attributed in his November 1971 article, 'Is America Falling Apart?', to an agony that he claimed was 'not to be associated with breakdown so much as with the parturition of self-knowledge'.[125] The detached insularity of the United States, detached from Europe's history, it seems, is what Burgess most feared about the opinions being formed and shaped in the general American psyche, which were independent from the rest of the Western world's collective knowledge and also resistant to outsider perspectives that provided a foil to so many of these idiosyncratic American incongruences.

What other expatriate authors like Christopher Isherwood admired about the United States, or at least what his main character George in *A Single Man* (1964) admired about the country, was that Americans – eerily redolent of a post-modern American novel like *White Noise* (1985) by Don DeLillo which concludes on the note that 'everything we [Americans] need that is not food or love is here in the tabloid racks. The tales of the supernatural and the extraterrestrial. The miracle vitamins, the cures for cancer, the remedies for obesity. The cults of the famous and the dead' – had 'retired to live inside our advertisements, like hermits going into caves to contemplate', all while banishing the world of the historical and the tangible so as to 'sleep in symbolic bedrooms, eat symbolic meals', and be 'symbolically entertained', something George notes terrified Europeans, including the visiting European and occasional New Yorker Anthony Burgess.[126]

Whereas Isherwood went to the United States to escape from Europe's history and cultural weight, Burgess went to the United States to partake of its riches and to witness the culture as an observer and critic, all while trying to bring a little bit of Europe with him. For taking such *un-American* stances in the press, though, Burgess claims to have even received 'scarifying letters' from a Hibernico-Cherokee author, James Drought, who informed him that he was a 'penilambent parasite and that the British have achieved nothing in 2,000 years'.[127] In his 23 March 1973 'Viewpoint' article in the *Times Literary Supplement*, this story evolved to levels of hyperbole and extravagance worthy of Enderby, with Burgess claiming to be fearful of (we can infer the same individual mentioned previously) a 'seven-foot failed Cherokee writer who threatens to come to West End Avenue with a tomahawk'.[128] In similar grandiose terms, Burgess's article claims that, a point echoed in Enderby's New York tale, a 'Black voice', appearing to mean a Black person, then arose from the audience to ask, after his comments about 'blackspeak', whether he honestly thought ' "you're going to get away with that remark?" '.[129] These events, if they can be trusted at all, began as humorous and daring stories of his time in New York City, or mythologizing his bold personality against the backdrop of an even bolder city, all to end up conflated, morphed, and barely fictionalized in *The Clockwork Testament*, in which Enderby describes being thrust into debates about racial identity politics over an article *he* had written:

> He had written a very unwise article for a magazine, in which he said that he thought little of black literature because it tended to tendentiousness and that the Amerindians had shown no evidence of talent for anything except scalping and very inferior folkcraft. One of his callers, who had once termed him a toothless cocksucker (that toothlessness had been right, anyway, at that time anyway), was always threatening to bring a tomahawk to 91st Street and Columbus Avenue, which was where Enderby lodged.[130]

Burgess lived at 93rd and Broadway, only two blocks from his fictional character, just barely disguising the similarities with slight changes and shrinking the more chaotic and expansive events of his life down into a controlled autobiograficational burlesque with 'anti-stylization of someone else's style, often combining with a clear parodying of that style' that is at its core a reduction in seriousness from *A Clockwork Orange*, Jean Cocteau's *Le testament d'Orphée*, Dante's *Inferno*, and Thomas Mann's *Death in Venice*, in order to satirize and mock the United States and Americans.[131]

To those whom the flesh-and-blood Burgess claims to have 'bow[ed]' his head to and replied only with 'sullenness and silence' in his awkward interactions, he used his non-fiction and, more harshly, his fiction, especially Enderby and *The Clockwork Testament*'s narrator, to take them to task through condescension and ridicule through a distorted hidden polemic propped up upon real-life personages crafted into, barely or clearly, caricatures.[132] Noticed by Stinson in *Anthony Burgess: Revisited* (1990), in *The Clockwork Testament* 'the distance between Burgess and Enderby has greatly shrunk', therefore creating a text that is perhaps the most egregious example of Enderby communicating a double-voiced diatribe against those who frustrated his creator.[133] Another such crucial moment occurs when both the character and creator are scheduled to live in the apartment of a professor who is on sabbatical, which was the actual case while Burgess lived in the poet and teacher Adrienne Rich's apartment while she was on 'a year's research leave', which Burgess even suggests was also the apartment Enderby stayed in when he wrote that Enderby was 'blamed daily over the telephone, as I was for the film of *A Clockwork Orange*, in Adrienne Rich's flat, which Enderby inhabits alone, masturbating and gorging on the wealth of Manhattan'.[134] Twelve years younger than Burgess, the activist, feminist, and poet was likely viewed by Burgess as being the epitome of the radical protesting intellectual American that elicited so much ire from him, despite expressing some admiration for her poetry.[135] Through this juxtaposition, it's no wonder that Burgess, and Enderby, perceived himself as a symbol of the 'old-guard' moving into the territory of radical counterculture movements of the 1970s in New York City.[136] Increasingly political, Rich's activism stood in stark contrast to Burgess's supposed avoidance of political issues and focus on traditional literary genres, although both were likely seen as firebrands to the established hierarchies of the Ivy League universities they taught at, just for different reasons.

Upon moving into her apartment, though, it was not politics or activism that drew a dividing line between the two authors: it was cockroaches and rent. While spending her time 'in Cambridge, Massachusetts' for a sabbatical, and knowing about Burgess's upcoming appointment, Rich 'wrote to Burgess with a suggestion that he should rent her apartment at 670 West

End Avenue in New York' for '$500 per month in rent, but Burgess (who complained that he was not allowed to sublet his flat on Piazza Santa Cecelia in Rome, and would therefore have to pay double rent) managed to negotiate this figure down to $400 per month', though Burgess's archived chequebook shows a payment to Rich for $475 in January 1972, so his negotiating skills may not have been as satisfactory as first thought.[137] Once settled in the Manhattan apartment, having received no 'mention of cockroaches' when Rich was trying to persuade the Burgesses to move into the property, Burgess and Liana 'were disturbed to see a large poster in the street outside their apartment, which advertised (in Spanish) the services of a cockroach exterminator', only to find their fears confirmed 'when Rich wrote to them a few weeks later with the news that her regular exterminator normally visited on the second Tuesday of each month, and she urged Burgess to put his name down for a visit in order to enjoy a bug-free existence'.[138] This did not sit lightly with the Burgess family, resulting in the aforementioned 'Cucarachas and Exiles' *New York Times* article, and then, ultimately, Burgess weaved this idea into *The Clockwork Testament*. Enderby updates readers on his acclimatization to New York City by expressing that he had, beginning the second chapter, become, 'so far as use of the culinary resources of the kitchen (at night the cockroaches' playground) were concerned, one hundred per cent Americanised'.[139] New York City citizens responded to the *New York Times* article swiftly, with the author receiving, as Biswell explains, 'a deluge of letters ... mostly from his neighbours in the apartment building who resented him for having revealed their guilty secret'.[140] The 'enemies' in Enderby's building, on the same hall, and likely resembling Burgess's neighbours, are similarly incensed with Enderby over a film attributed to him, this time *The Deutschland*, for which Enderby wrote the screenplay that was based on of the nineteenth-century poem, 'The Wreck of the Deutschland' (1875) by Gerard Manley Hopkins – an allusion to Stanley Kubrick's film adaptation of Burgess's own *A Clockwork Orange*. Enderby describes the motley neighbour crew as consisting of 'a gap-toothed black writer and his wife; a single woman with dogs who had objected to his mentioning in his magazine article the abundance of cockroaches in this part of Manhattan, as though it were a shameful family secret; a couple of fattish electronic guitarists who had smelt his loathing as they had gone up together once in the elevator', all of which he guesses were likely 'affronted by the film just this moment referred to'.[141] In fact, an actual neighbour of Burgess's during this time, Anne McCormick, took to writing to the *New York Times*, appearing in a 'To the Editor' column where she remarked that 'contrary to [Burgess's] statement', the apartment he was in was 'not on Broadway and 93rd Street, but in an older cooperative middle-class building on West End Avenue and 93rd' which was 'not a "cotton mill" nor [did it have] a sidewalk littered with broken bottles. And there are many tenants who would be glad to help solve his cockroach problem'.[142] Burgess provided a reply to McCormick's 'needlessly grouchy and captious' message, retorting that 'I don't actually live on the corner of 93rd Street and Broadway, but that's where I ask cab drivers to take me to', the 'building opposite me looks even more like a broken down Lancashire cotton' building, and that he had just recently 'extracted a fragment of broken bottle from my broken shoe. The cockroach problem has, thank you very much, at last been solved', but, he summarizes, if that clarification was needed, 'perhaps my view of a "broken-down" district differs radically from that of Mrs. McCormick, but I do know that in London the bulldozer would already be at work', ending rhetorically that if 'this is urban renewal, what is New York dilapidation like?'[143]

The similarities between editorial, public statement, and fictional text are incontrovertible and possibly the reason that Burgess forged these elements together years later in the second part of his autobiography, where he described the situation in more detail and still with the same hyperbolic vitriol as decades earlier, saying that the Burgesses were to

> take over the tenth-floor apartment of the poetess Adrienne Rich on Riverside Drive. She, a famous feminist and man-hater, was to assume a year's residence in a Mid-West university. We were not permitted to enter her flat until we had been examined by the committee of the apartment block, and this did not propose to convene a meeting until after Labor Day. So, very expensively, we occupied a suite in the Algonquin Hotel.[144]

It is no secret that this debacle led Burgess to 'taking revenge on Adrienne Rich for having rented him an infested apartment in a seedy neighbourhood' by incorporating a 'cruel caricature of Rich' into *The Clockwork Testament* via the fictional landlady who is not named, but 'said to be [a] lesbian poetess', with 'another crazed feminist' breaking into Enderby's apartment and threatening 'him with a loaded pistol' to 'take off his clothes' and micturate upon a 'volume of his own poems'.[145] Burgess seems to have envisioned himself as a traditionalist figure moving into the apartment, and indeed city and country, of what he may have thought was a poet of the radical countercultural avant-garde who was perhaps just an ephemeral by-product of the popular zeitgeist. Such a characterization isn't very accurate, though, as Rich, who was once married to a man and had three children – not formally announcing that she was a lesbian until 1976 – was often described as being, as she is here by the American poet John Ashbery, 'a traditionalist poet, but not a conventional one. … Miss Rich is … a metaphysical poet', and in her obituary in 2012 she was described as being 'triply marginalized – as a woman, a lesbian and a Jew' and 'concerned in her poetry, and in her many essays, with identity politics long before the term was coined' where she investigated how 'the personal, the political and the poetical were indissolubly linked' and 'remained celebrated for the unflagging intensity of her vision, and for the constant formal reinvention that kept her verse'.[146] Although the relationship between the two writers started off well, with Rich reaching out to Burgess offering to sublet her apartment, the relationship began to sour almost immediately, with a proposed sublet fee and a questionnaire and interview for acceptance, not to mention Rich requiring Burgess take care of her fish and plants, while also having to get the apartment sprayed for cockroaches once a month; upon moving out, the fish and plants were dead and, as was usual with Paolo Andrea's sleep habits (Burgess's son with Liana), a mattress was ruined by urine (the same happened in Princeton), all of which was billed to Burgess after he vacated.[147]

As he was known to do, Burgess fits himself, and Enderby, into such grand literary, theological, philosophical, and atavistic narratives that are concerned with the life of the artist, the *legitimate* poet who was concerned with the ontology of poetry, which to Burgess, and largely to Enderby, appears to have excluded any poets who were overly focused on emotions or politics, as Burgess saw, however inaccurately, Rich and other such poets concerned with *identity*, since her and writers like her often produced work that got, as Burgess describes political literature in *They Wrote in English* (1989), 'in the way of the universal statement' since they do not 'generalize' wrongs 'into universal wrongs, speaking for mankind and not just a part of it', therefore leaving these individuals to not create 'genuine literature'.[148] Burgess's attacks on and categorization of Rich seem misplaced and undeserving, though, considering the poet was highly esteemed, and incredibly versatile, often even discussing topics in her poetry that were central themes for Burgess, such as censorship, art, and lived life in 'The Burning of Paper Instead of Children' (1968), myth and experimental film in 'I Dream I'm the Death of Orpheus' (1969), the androgynous qualities of writers in 'The Stranger' (1972), and bodily functions in 'The Phenomenology of Anger' (1972).[149] As for the other side of this story, Rich's opinions of Burgess and his literary games 'are likely to remain mysterious, at least for the time being', because when she 'sold her papers to Harvard University, she stipulated that certain parts of the collection, including her private papers and letters, should remain under lock and key until 2050'.[150] What exists, though, is her 1972 poem, 'The Ninth Symphony of Beethoven Understood at Last as a Sexual Message', which one can assume is directed at Burgess (and Alex of *A Clockwork Orange* by association) since it describes a

> man in terror of impotence
> or infertility, not knowing the difference

> a man trying to tell something
> howling from the climacteric
> music of the entirely
> isolated soul
> yelling at Joy from the tunnel of ego
> music without the ghost
> of another person in it, music
> trying to tell something the man
> does not want out, would keep if he could
> gagged and bound and flogged with chords of Joy
> where everything in silence and the
> beating of a bloody fist upon
> a splintered table.[151]

It's intriguing to think that Rich may actually be commenting on, though not explicitly, Burgess's authorial monoglottism with the lines, 'music without the ghost / of another person it', since there exists a very legitimate argument, as this monograph lays out, that a significant portion of Burgess's oeuvre, to varying degrees, is highly autobiographical while also exhibiting cultural heteroglossia and a 'philosophy of culture' which is dialogic in the extra- and inter-literary sense with so many epitextual aspects, though his authorial fictional presentations are often much less dialogic and are fashioned around a singularly, often biographical, authorial vision that takes over the narrative and the language of his characters.[152] This kind of authorial and philosophical monomania, where Burgess reuses and refocuses on a relatively short list of philosophical and theological precepts, and his life experiences, may have been recognized here by Rich as the poem notes, and is designated as a way to protect the author behind the *silent* artwork. Taking the chance to fictionalize, and simultaneously viciously parodying and satirizing his communication and interactions with a contemporary American author, Burgess took vengeance on Rich and others through an authorially savage double-voiced technique which also acts as a passive aggressive – since the fictionalizing is vague and thinly disguised – literary hidden polemic, and the epitexts surrounding this representation are crucial to exhuming the layers of authorial inspiration in the life-world of the text.

It wasn't just Rich who Burgess was taking aim at, though. Burgess lashes out at the status of American culture, more virulently and caustically than he himself was known to do, through situational satire and Enderby, who describes the absent landlady's apartment as being filled with books that 'sternly turned the backs, spines rather, of their contents towards him' threateningly at the sans-spectacles Enderby, appearing through his bad eyesight to communicate to him that it was not his business to know what worlds those books created or addressed, because the world of the activist, the protestor, was 'concerned with the *real* issues of life, meaning women downtrodden by men, the economic oppression of the blacks, counter-culture, coming revolt, Reich, Fanon, third world' – these are allusions to Charles A. Reich's monograph *The Greening of America* (1970) that, on the cover of the book no less, warned of 'a revolution coming' which would 'not be like revolutions of the past. It will originate with the individual and with culture', and Frantz Fanon, the French West Indian post-colonial author of *Black Skin, White Masks* (1952) and *The Wretched of the Earth* (1961), with the former including a preface by Jean-Paul Sartre and which would go on to become 'a key text for radical students and served as an inspiration for the Black Power movement in the United States'.[153] Enderby, the supposed Male Chauvinist Pig ('MCP') – foreseeing his own future: Burgess would go on to be called the Sexist Pig of the Year in 1980 by the Women in Publishing organization – naked at this point, blurrily stares at the books of the 'supposedly oppressed – blacks, homosexuals, women' and perhaps on these sneering covers resents the very language in the titles, just as Burgess mocked and attacked his neighbour, McCormick, who, Burgess gripes, used 'cant terms like *multi-ethnic* – a hybrid bit of gobbledygook which makes me feel like adding to the Saturday night street vomit'.[154]

Just as Enderby is trying to better make out the titles of the volumes on the bookshelf, a female student, Lydia Tietjens – signalling again that the text is soaked in authorial and literary allusiveness with this allusion to the promiscuous wife, Sylvia Tietjens, of the main character of Ford Madox Ford's tetralogy, *Parade's End* (1924–28) – walks into his apartment to beg for a better grade, prompting Enderby to cover 'his genitals with his poem', his manhood quite literally being defended by his traditionalist poetry.[155] Invasive, disruptive, and threatening, New York City, and indeed the United States, would assuredly lead to 'Enderby's End', perhaps even due to the lasciviousness of Ms Tietjens, and to the exasperation of Burgess, perhaps also like Thomas Mann's similarly edentulous Gustav von Aschenbach who succumbs to cholera, which the tale of Enderby appears to liken to the intellectual smothering of the Women's Liberation and/or Black Power Movements, making Enderby appear as Von Aschenbach feels as he attempts to reconcile his demise: 'public faith in [poets] is utterly ludicrous, and educating the populace, the younger generation, through art is a hazardous enterprise that should be outlawed. For how can a man be a fit educator if he had an inborn, natural, and incorrigible preference for the abyss?'.[156]

Thinking that *The Clockwork Testament* would be 'Enderby's End', or the last adventure, because Burgess appears to have grown tired and worn out on Enderby, Burgess disposes of him through the common – aside from the science fiction, space travel premise – literary convention of killing off the protagonist in the final chapter. Remarking on the killing of perhaps his most notable character, Burgess said that he had 'tried to kill this character off in a novel because I was fed up with him. I didn't want anything more to do with him'.[157] As audiences would find out in 1984, though, with *Enderby's Dark Lady, or No End to Enderby*, Enderby was to return since this 'character is living a kind of hypothesis [with] two possible paths open to him' because he 'had to go to America' in order to choose between New York where 'he would die' or Indianapolis where 'he would live', with either story being true, but 'Both stories, no. Either story is true but not both' – though, since the books are both published, they then both must *exist* and therefore in essence must in some sense be *true*.[158] Despite what Burgess said about accepting the realities or truths of either *Enderby's Dark Lady* or *The Clockwork Testament*, as a point of scholarly inquiry they must be accepted as parts of the whole Enderbian tetralogy that is encompassed within the entire Burgess canon. *The Clockwork Testament* is in fact the end of one manifestation of Enderby; the end of the Enderby who was produced out of catharsis and frustration regarding the life that Anthony Burgess had lived as an American educator and public figure between September 1970 and July 1973, largely in and around New York City.

Regardless of some of the negative attention he received for his comments on New York City and the United States, Burgess was still commissioned to write the 1976 Time-Life book *New York*, in which he still did not hide some of his criticisms of the city even though the book as a whole is a far less perturbed commentary that utilizes a more data- and research-driven contextual understanding of the city and its inhabitants. What is meant by this is that in this book, Burgess acknowledges the concept, as B.F. Skinner defined in *Beyond Freedom and Dignity* (1971), that 'unsuspected controlling relations between behavior and environment' exist everywhere, and that many of the poor in New York City have been victims of situational and environmental oppression.[159] In *New York*, Burgess presents an unusually optimistic and progressive, as well as Skinnerian, insight when he writes that his narrative displays a 'pattern in New York's demographic history' that shows the 'fresh influx of immigrants is despised and feared, and detestable qualities are attributed to its members', though 'we do not have to take them totally seriously' because these

> new settlers, like many of their predecessors, have to live in slums among small-time criminals, and that their consequent fights to survive often take an anti-social form. But what looks like congenital criminality now may one day be viewed in retrospect as justifiable aggression by people shouldering to find a place in the sun.[160]

What is shocking about this concession is that Burgess essentially breaks with his earlier opinions concerning 'autonomous man' and adopts a view more sympathetic to and parallel with Skinner, the behavioural psychologist who helped inspire *A Clockwork Orange* from his novel *Walden Two* (1948), who resembles Professor Man Balaglas in *The Clockwork Testament*, and was a target for Burgess, after the release of Kubrick's film adaptation of *A Clockwork Orange*, in 'The Clockwork Condition'. In 'A Fable for Social Scientists', Burgess said it was strange that Skinner's behaviourist conditioning techniques were 'the way both the USA and Russia seem to think things ought to be done. In that respect they are coeval. And they are both ripe for the pendulum theory'.[161] It was not only in fiction and non-fiction that Burgess mentioned Skinner; he was actually placed into a documentary as a kind of counterpoint to Skinner in July 1975. Pennsylvania State University produced the documentary *Behavioural Revolution* which included interviews with both Burgess and Skinner, filmed at separate times, with Burgess apparently responding to one of Skinner's claims about improving society by countering that he could

> quite clearly see that we could live in a very happy society if Skinner had the control of it, but of course Aldous Huxley said the same thing: the whole point about his *Brave New World*, is that people are happy. People are totally happy ... but his point, I think a true point, is that happiness is not enough.[162]

Before the publication of *New York*, Burgess appears to have wholeheartedly accepted the myth of complete and unadulterated autonomy, allowing him to perceive individuals as being completely free of influence from their environments, and it is not until *New York* that Burgess recognizes how race, socio-economic status, and access to social programmes create cyclical disparities and disenfranchisement. Even in admitting this, Burgess still perceived that the dilapidation of New York City was a symptom of overarching societal beliefs and perspectives, a moral and philosophical problem ultimately, as he was never unable to let go of his individualistic Manichaean outlook. Pointing out in this coffee-table book which was heavily edited to match the 'house style' at Time-Life – 'Because deadlines were so pressing we had already gone ahead with our own revise of the chapter. However, we were able to incorporate much of your additional material and I think you will agree when you see the page proofs that the final version does full justice to the rest of the book' – that the graffiti that littered New York City's streets 'could be interpreted as the strangled cry of men crushed by the megalopolis and seeking identity', Burgess also generously acknowledges the counter-cultural understanding of this new form of artistic street expression, being 'taken seriously by students of sociology', as a sign of rebellion 'against the circumambient ugliness created by city planners, property developers and powerful corporations'.[163] Burgess goes on to defend the city planners, though, who he says were not the cause of 'Manhattan's ugliness' because the 'ordinary citizens' tended 'to treat their city as a *thing*, not as a living organism – a thing for using, exploiting, maltreating, never cherishing'.[164] His line of logic partially blames both the common people and the economic powers of the system that developed the city. Predominantly, Burgess feared and spoke out against governments, superstructures, and institutions of power, but regarding New York City, he also preached social responsibility and grew so frustrated with the city's apparent lack of decorum that in *The Clockwork Testament*, Burgess's Enderby focuses more widely on the responsibility of individuals in a society, on autonomous man, and not on the power structure that created an environment that produced these types of individuals – a point he addressed in the obscenity trial against Hubert Selby Jr's *Last Exit to Brooklyn* years before, which was discussed previously. Between his non-fiction, journalism, and fiction lies Burgess's contradictory notion that American society at his time of writing was experiencing a period of chaotic moral and philosophical decay, despite the fact that he noted that 'art and the humane scholarship are flourishing here, as they are not, for instance, in England'. And yet, Burgess still expressed views about the important role of the individual in society in opposition to collectives, especially government, while also expressing opinions that, as noted before, Americans could benefit from 'socialized medicine', meaning government-paid – these political and social debates need not be mutually exclusive, though they are often debated in such a way, but Burgess appears to play whichever line of argument suits his needs best at a specific moment while ignoring the overarching contradictions in the subtleties and complexities of the problems associated with these varying political philosophies.[165] Looking to *New York*, a piece of non-fiction, provides readers with a backdrop with which to help interpret Burgess's fiction because the two modes of writing are, especially when discussing the topics of the United States, American culture, and New York City, coming from such similar and personal backgrounds – this non-fiction book is also important for understanding *Puma*, as evidenced in Paul Wake's new edition of the text and discussed here in Chapter 6.[166] In *New York*, as stated previously, Burgess appears to have finally recognized and admitted that humans, and human behaviour, are influenced by their surroundings, saying even that 'I do believe that decent living conditions can be fine solvents of anti-social behaviour', that free will is an extension of this, as a by-product of such a system, and that humans cannot exercise free will without a certain level of social stability.[167] Elaborating, Burgess alludes to the fact that authors in their works do not, perhaps cannot, show 'the whole panorama' of New York City because it is much easier to 'create a city of their own than to reproduce the reality', effectively positioning *The Clockwork Testament* into this reflective requital and qualifying the artistic purpose and inspiration behind Burgess's film script for the unproduced, epitextually important, *The Eyes of New York* (1976).[168] Burgess opens this more creative work, when compared to *New York*, meant as narration over scenes of New York City, grandly, allusively, literarily, and, of course, redundantly, by using some of his most common American and New York City tropes, motifs, and subjects in an attempt at encapsulating the full breadth of New York City's, and the United States's, different-and-many-voicedness, or social heteroglossia:

> Call me Ishmael. Call me Mario. Call me Ivan Ivanovich. Call me Yan Yansen. Call me Jack Matsuki. Call me Poh Soo Jing. Call me anything you like: the name doesn't matter. But before anything, call me a New Yorker. Being a New Yorker, I'm the child of immigrants. All New Yorkers are immigrants or the sons or daughters of immigrants. There are of course, the Red Indians who were here already – the so-called vanishing Americans. ... But the city the world knows was made by immigrants, and nearly nine million immigrants dwell in it. ... Call me a New Yorker, but also call me a man who uses his eyes. In fact, I'm a photographer. That's my trade .... Hoping someday to produce a book with a very few words and a great many pictures – all mine, and all of New York City .... We talk a lot in New York, but we don't listen much .... Look at their eyes, drinking in the new world.[169]

Echoing that it 'was an American face that exuded American optimism', New York City is presented in Burgess's fiction as an emblem of the United States as a whole, 'where for most of these immigrants from America the only serious religion is ambition', and due to the human crucible that it was, it encompassed to Burgess all of the characteristics and diverse problems that the entire country was grappling with.[170] Although the circumstantial epitextual biographical evidence around these texts helps substantiate that Burgess did evolve and mature in his thoughts about American culture, having less vitriolic and more nuanced views about the country – 'Here's to liberty. And what precisely do you mean by *liberty*? Ah, be quiet' – he still enjoyed using the tropes of his earlier writings and musings, so that these two images of New York, produced several years after *The Clockwork Testament*, present a picture of New York City that is similar to how Enderby encountered it – except Enderby only experienced a microcosm, less grand, captured only in a small section of Manhattan.[171]

Historical and contextual knowledge of such epitextual discourse and dialogue between authors and in the literary world makes *The Clockwork Testament* appear increasingly not so much just a hidden polemic but something closer to an obstreperous *roman à clef* burlesque, and any such attempt to argue that there is 'no claim to be made that Enderby and Anthony Burgess agree with one another on the subjects of poetry and criticism, whatever occasional similarities are to be found', is both naïve and contra-contextual, since such thinking could result in producing a significant gap in the understanding of this text that is a necessity to be explored to explain the literary and authorial history of Burgess's recorded life and work.[172]

American education and culture in *The Clockwork Testament*

Whether it was his experiences at City College of New York, the dangers in the streets, the cockroaches, the conflicts over living quarters, the students, and/or the increased attention brought on by Kubrick's *A Clockwork Orange*, Burgess was clearly disgruntled in the early 1970s and it was manifesting in Enderby's penultimate novel. Interviewed by Bill Meehan in the *Columbia Daily Spectator* for the May 1973 issue, Burgess decided to lash out Enderbianly, as can be noticed by the title of the interview alone: 'Burgess: Interview with an Erudite Elitist'.[173] Focusing on the topic of the democratization of education, higher education that was accessible to all, or open enrolment, a popular point of discussion at the time and something Burgess was witnessing first-hand at the City College of New York, Meehan asks Burgess about many of the topical issues going on in 1970s American higher education, especially in New York City. Ultimately, Burgess explained what he had communicated in multiple published items, that 'there are some institutions that cannot, except at grave peril, be democratized, and universities are among them', and allowing everyone the same access to the same education without exclusionary qualification processes set up to differentiate between the various capabilities of students, he thought, would result in a 'lowering of standards', which would therefore imply 'the right to a degree', therefore disallowing centres of higher education the luxury to impose 'the disciplines that prevailed at Oxford or Cambridge'.[174] It was in the American democratized classroom, Burgess contends from his experience, that idealism, which is taken to mean 'aspiration' by Burgess, was running rampant and was in need of being managed; he explains in this diatribe that in one class specifically, a course he taught on James Joyce, he was 'appalled by the lack of high school preparation for a group like that'.[175] The low quality of his students' abilities led Burgess to question his effectiveness as a teacher, confessing that he claims that he had to give several high grades simply to 'justify myself that I taught the course'.[176] Satirizing this event in *The Clockwork Testament*, Enderby has students demanding they receive A's, with one female student, the aforementioned Lydia Tietjens, visiting his apartment for an interview, and to offer her body as an enticement to receive a better grade: ' "I have to get A's. I just have to." ' And then: ' "It *is* hot" ' as she sheds some clothing.[177] This supposed lack of focus on actual academic duties and a sense of entitlement, or at least students' desire for grades rather than knowledge, was deeply disconcerting to Burgess and something he suggests was attributed to a society and culture that did not value actual academic learning or intellectual language use, nor did this country have an early education system which prepared students for such ventures – 'the IPA, or International Phonetic Alphabet, which ought to be the first thing taught in our schools, though it never is'.[178] Burgess felt that the failure of American pre-collegiate education was caused by the fact that 'few in America seem to regard the instruction of the young as a vocation ... moreover, the general lack of an educational philosophy puts teachers in the position of not knowing what they are doing or why'.[179] Consequently, the doubt he assumed in his abilities, created by this type of poor performance from his students, prompted him to reflect on how he understood the idea of higher education, reflecting that a bachelor's degree was something that used to be, in his day, 'a fairly high qualification' that, he states, indubitably resulted in a sense of elitism simply out of exclusionary practices demanding students struggle with a great amount of work to accomplish such a feat: 'This is what it was all about, the amassing of knowledge and the equipping of the brain for dealing with scholarship and learning in general.'[180] He even prophesies, rather accurately, a future where the 'Ph.D. standard will, in time, be *that* standard; therefore, we'll have to think of some new kind of degree, beyond the Ph.D. We'll have to think of some new kind of university and so it will go on forever if we are lowering our standard',[181] and if it came to this, Burgess continued prognosticating, dangers would lie ahead: 'If we *are* lowering our standards, then we have to think of a higher standard and a higher body of learning.'[182] Having witnessed what he believed was a lowering of standards directly when he taught in the United States, he decided to comment on the state of collegiate education in the country not only through his own autobiography, interviews, and articles but also through his fictional characters. Again, Enderby, in *The Clockwork Testament*, goes on a tangent to his class after a student rebukes him for using the N-word by remarking, 'you play your little games with yourself. All this shit about words. Closing your eyes to what's going on in the big big world' – this repetition sounds like an allusion to the 'big big big deng' or 'money' in *A Clockwork Orange* that Alex sneers at towards his droogs and their desires to be 'big bloated capitalist[s]', while also being redolent of one of John Dos Passos's *U.S.A. Trilogy* novels, *The Big Money* (1936), a series of novels he advised a student on at Princeton University and novels which use the techniques of 'The Camera Eye' and 'Newsreel' to tell the story, stylistic approaches that would go on to be utilized in the unfinished *Black Prince* historical film screenplay that was adapted and finished by Adam Roberts in 2018: allusion upon allusion, dialogue upon dialogue.[183] In fictionalizing a common language battle waged across campuses during this period, and still now, Burgess sets up a dialogic situation of idealism versus the emotionally detached inquiries of scholarship. Enderby, although with resemblances to his creator, pales in a formal and professional comparison – all evidence suggests – and tackles the situation melodramatically, unempathetically, and unprofessionally by retorting, ' "Don't call me *maaaaaan*. … All that's going to save your immortal soul, *maaaaaan*, if you have one, is words. Words words words, you bastard." '[184] Fictionally, Enderby vicariously carries out the battle that Burgess was struggling with – like when he told Dick Cavett, on the subject of having to teach creative writing, that to write literature, 'You've got to have a lot of words. … Good poems come not from the heart but from the brain' – by expressing some of the frustrations that were plaguing Burgess, as an avenue of release so that he could contemplate his role in an American university in order to, finally, magnify the topic and inflate its importance to biblical or dystopic levels of severity in Enderby's fictional world.[185] Another such moment occurs when Enderby yells at his students that they won't be able to fight what is coming in the future, perhaps also double-voicing Burgess's own frustrations at the time of composing this novel:

> You can't fight. You'll never prevail against the big bastards of computerized organisations that are kindly letting you enjoy the illusion of freedom. The people who write poems, even bad ones, are not the people who are going to rule. Sooner or later you're all going to go to jail. You have to learn to be alone – no sex, not even any books. All you'll have is language, the great conserver, and poetry, the great isolate shaper. Stock your minds with language, for Christ's sake. Learn how to write what's memorable. No, not write – compose in your head.[186]

The paranoia of Enderby feeds off of Burgess's own anxiety and frustrations that in turn helps bring the prophetic tantrum to a peak of comedic hyperbole. Wrapped up in the context of Burgess's epitextually evidenced thought processes while in New York in the early 1970s, it's easy to see what was having an influence on his writing and why. Burgess's teaching experiences at City College of New York, Princeton University, Columbia University, and the University of North Carolina at Chapel Hill, in addition to hundreds of lectures and class visits across the country, as well as his own hegemonic views of literature and education, are here deformed, distorted, and transmuted into the world of Enderby and left up to the anti-hero to deal with the subject in his own hyperbolic, though authorially directed, way, which results in Enderby's students yelling back at their arrogant professor with rage, extolling, 'You bastard. You misleading reactionary *evil* bastard', thus proving Burgess's point more than Enderby's that the young and supposedly liberal counter cultures of the period were often illiberal in their desires, meaning that they would rather denounce contrarians than allow for discourse, with Burgess again sounding similar to Enderby when he stated in a 1969 *Spectator* article, entitled 'Swing of the Censor', that a society 'shall never be free to have, under the tolerance of the law, all the verbal experiences we desire. ... Cunt and bugger can get on the literary bus only because kike and n----- have been ordered off. Society, it seems, can only function so long as there are verbal taboos, and the semantic area is immaterial'.[187] Andrew Biswell argues that this final standoff between Enderby and his students 'is entirely symmetrical in its prejudices', and therefore dialogic, largely because Utterage is 'given the final word in the argument', but this doesn't stand up to or help explain the unbalanced embedded 1970s racism of the text in its entirety. Just because one has a final statement does not mean one has won the argument, especially when this student, a thin caricature to begin with, is calling Enderby a 'reactionary *evil* bastard' for simply quoting from Elizabethan playwright Ben Jonson's 'Cynthia's Revels: Queen and huntress, chaste and fair' sonnet – in fact, this would prove the point that Utterage doesn't know what he is talking about.[188] And though *The Clockwork Testament* is not a *racist* text, meaning that it does not extol and support racist attitudes or ideologies, it still has historically racist elements among any of Burgess's attempts to, as Biswell notes, challenge 'a few of the standard clichés about race and violence' by having the 'noisy ethnic people' discussing poetry while the 'three nice WASP boys', White Anglo-Saxon Protestant, attempt sexual violence; still, the jokes and jibes are tired and contrived, drawing more attention to the ingrained racism of the early to mid-twentieth-century outlook than towards the attempt to cherish diversity or enlighten race consciousness in America – similar too to the dangling addition of Miles's race at the end of *M/F*, a point Thomas Nelson Winter made when reviewing the novel, saying that the 'only flaw is that a single, offhand sentence in the epilogue changes the complexion of the entire book'.[189]

Making Burgess's points even more unconvincing as a supposed piece of autonomous fiction is that, in the case of *The Clockwork Testament* especially, the author indeed claims to even have experienced similar reactions, likely not as hostile, when Burgess would teach creative writing courses and openly criticize the legitimacy of such teachings. Essentially, he claims, the position of a creative writing teacher could be boiled down to 'pouring over subtly unsatisfactory pieces of writing' to no clear goal, arguing that despite 'Mr Hiram Hayden's [editor at *The American Scholar*] achievements in this field of parapedagogy, I don't think Creative Writing really exists as a subject', resulting in Burgess's own students, he felt, getting the impression that he was simply 'an aged outsider, foreign moreover, who is incapable of appreciating' their craft and academic scope.[190] In 1978, the first part of Burgess's *1985* draws out this idea of ineffective education standards and practices further by investigating the ontology of epistemology: 'if men are born free, it is only in the Ingsoc sense that animals too are born free: freedom to choose between two courses of action presupposes knowledge of what the choice entails', therefore humans must, the narrator evaluates, 'gain knowledge through direct experience, like the burnt child fearing the fire, or else through the experience of others which is contained in books'.[191] The voices of the fictional students in Enderby's classroom, an exaggerated approximation of what Burgess experienced, are the voices of a generation who found their purpose in the 'neo-anarchists' like that of 'the film-maker Dennis Hopper: "There ain't nothing in books, man"', which Burgess objects to by explaining that what these celebrity-types did not understand was that learning is 'cow-like rather than lion-like' in the sense that it 'takes a long time to gain, by browsing over a field, the protein available in a quick meal of meat', and it was, by his estimations, the *old* like him who offered 'the meat of education' whereas the 'counter-culture goes back to grass' – a sloppy metaphor.[192] Not only was it the counter culture that Burgess saw as stifling the modes of efficacious humanistic learning, but, in *Language Made Plain* (1964), Burgess also laid this responsibility at the threshold of 'systems of education' that 'have done nothing to foster and everything to dull' the 'natural curiosity about the most fundamental of all social activities' that every human should have.[193]

What Burgess saw taking place on American campuses throughout the 1970s did not really provide him with much evidence to the contrary. Burgess was more than stimulated in his scholarly inclinations with the brilliance of many of the United States's brightest scholars, academics, and students, even though he still believed that what the United States was doing in higher education was self-defeating and somewhat futile to the overall vision and goal of supreme epistemological ends, saying in 1973 that there were far too many American universities and that 'the number of students in each of them is far too great', which resulted in students and institutions that fell into a dilapidation of standards: 'I've got to have an A. The sheer horrible innocence of it. Who the hell didn't feel he'd got to have an A?'.[194] Speaking at Bucknell University, Burgess goes further to explain that once again, the United States's obsession with grandiosity and excellence had turned universities into 'academic factories' with students who were not, he felt, 'sufficiently prepared for university life. Few of them know anything about the past, and they're not interested in foreign languages. This worries me a great deal'.[195] In *New York*, Burgess even suggests a plan for education in the United States, relying largely on what he saw as the travesty of Anglo-American English usage, suggesting that a 'central policy for New York education should be simply enough and should be concerned primarily with language', since, 'for good or ill, the common tongue of New York is English'; therefore, to live

> in New York is to commit oneself to such mastery of the language as will enable one to cope with communication outside one's own ethnic group: to use English as a *lingua franca*. To bring up a family in New York means committing one's children to attempted mastery of the language that Washington, Jefferson and Martin Luther King use.[196]

As noted previously, what immigrants and those fetched against their will had brought to the United States was inventiveness, diligence, and healthy diversity, but the problem with this was the constant ethnic battles for identity, discouraging even Enderby, when the oblivious character in exhaustion asks his students to 'imagine a period when this kind of race-hate stupidity is all over'.[197] The problem was that, in the United States, these many immigrants had had their names stripped away, their native tongues lost, to only experience a homogenizing effect of English on the population, the United States lacking a national language, so that, in Burgess's own words, 'English would never be a *real* language' in the United States but rather just 'the tongue an Italian and a Chinese would use to talk to each other, or else an Irishman and a Polish Jew. ... The Italians didn't want to become Shakespeare or Milton or Washington or Jefferson or Lincoln – masters of the tongue that the Pilgrim Fathers had brought over in 1620' – echoing arguments from the late nineteenth century, once spouted by prominent American leaders like Theodore Roosevelt in his *American Ideals* (1897) proclamations.[198] The protean nature of such a language in the American zone, to Burgess, led to a degradation of the power of English, where it began to lose its veracity which was epitomized in a city like New York City, where 'nobody listens to a man's voice in New York, no matter how loud. Words hugely written, images, huge-limbed, bright-coloured – these do the shouting. The eye again. Everything in New York is addressed to the eye'.[199] Communication, then, the act of sharing meaning, takes on a wholly new shape in the mind of a New Yorker, possibly in Americans as a whole. Mixed with forgetting the past, indeed shirking it entirely, Burgess was concerned – with other educators – that the ability to contextualize and think critically was being lost on the generation coming to age in the 1970s and 1980s. In *New York*, one of the few books of Burgess's where he actually quotes and cites research and researchers, he supports this claim with a comment from Professor William Riley Parker of Indiana University who in 1961 said that there 'is not a single assumption that I as a teacher of graduate students in English can make about either the knowledge or skill they have already supposedly acquired. I cannot assume knowledge of the simplest Bible story or myth or fairy tale or piece of children's literature'.[200] It was this type of inability to understand historical literary allusion and context that frightened Burgess and which makes its way into *The Clockwork Testament* with the arrogant and boisterous film actor. In New York City, where the novella takes place, Enderby recognizes this lack of refined communicative ability being sewn into the cloth of the culture, where it was humans' eyes that had to drink in information 'bewildered, overwhelmed, almost persuaded' by the sheer quantity of messages being delivered on an average bustling day in New York City.[201] Burgess wonders if this type of information gathering and presentation is even communication, rhetorically answering that graffiti is only 'one-way communication' used to voice that the 'city is ourselves. Ourselves remembering ourselves – no longer the wide-eyed strangers with bundles, fed like the inmates of a prison, screened and examined and teste[d] to see if we're worthy to enter the land. ... This is art. Poor art sometimes, often unprofessional. Art nonetheless', and art

> is communication of a different kind from the advertiser's images or the politician's rhetoric. It's not good saying: what's it about[,] what does it mean? Ultimately it means itself. But underneath it there [is] a philosophy hard to put into words. Pride, resentment, fear – they're all in it. You could sum it up by saying it's a device for confronting the city. For though the city is people, it's also a juggernaut that crushes people.[202]

New York City, therefore, is a place of unending ingenuity and creation, but with creation comes its opposite – death, dismay, and frustrative tension. By circumventing language altogether, the people of New York City evade the powers of language and resort to the image. This appears to be a compliment in this essay, but in *The Clockwork Testament* this takes on a different nature, where the students are focused on present ideas that disregard the past, the language use is faulty and fragmentary, and death follows life far too closely, as Enderby is met with a procreative act and is then immediately confronted with death that acts as the great corollary to bring in a balance of desires: ' "Oh, this is all too American," Enderby said. "Sex and violence. What angel of regeneration sent you here?" For there was no question of mumbling and begging now. *Endberbius trumphans, exultans*.'[203] For these reasons, when Burgess entered City College of New York in 1972, having several years of experience teaching in the United States at this point, he sought to attempt to counteract these deleterious American traits with his own brand of education, refusing to goad the education path of creative writing. His aims were to provide his students with real-life, honest, and blunt feedback, and therefore not to 'teach them anything beyond "the professional trickery" of his craft' and going against their expectations to 'join them in ejaculations of the "Wow-that's-great-Janice!" sort that even the most jejune lines of quasi-poetry invariably called forth'.[204] This did not mean, though, that Burgess was wholly devoid of providing constructive and empathetic feedback to students either. He was, as was commented on many times, an extremely giving and conscientious instructor who spent a great deal of time and care with his students' work. Bruce Parks, a former student of Burgess's at City College of New York, remembered his creative writing class time with Burgess, 'which was held in the evenings in his apartment on 93rd street. We sat in the living room around the coffee table, freshly provisioned for each class with large bottles of red and white wine', filled with Burgess encouraging his students and always finding 'something good in our work to point out'.[205] Regardless of the one African American student – likely fashioned into Lloyd Utterage in *The Clockwork Testament* – who was 'impeccably mannered', 'brilliant', and a 'perfect gentleman to all of the women in the class, to Mrs. Burgess, to Francesca (their housekeeper/governess), but [who] transformed into a Mr Hyde when it was his turn to read', having written 'the most alarming prose, full of racial hate and murder and gore. It went on and on, week to week', Burgess, Parks writes, still always 'seemed to have no cautions ... and always encouraged us' and would even sometimes 'read a student's work out loud himself, adding to it a new dimension brought by his dramatic voicing and diction, and it made everyone's writing sound pretty good', concluding that the path of the creative writer would likely not be a career for the majority, if not all of the students, but that his students 'would be better people for the pursuit, even if we didn't succeed, than we would be if he were to discourage us'.[206] As has been deduced throughout the research for this monograph, Burgess was not such a rigid curmudgeon as he, and others, sometimes painted him to be – that was definitely one part of his demeanor, but a minor part magnified to mythical proportions in his fiction and non-fiction writings.

On *The Firing Line* with William F. Buckley, Burgess explained how he perceived human intelligence, opinions that somewhat defied his classicist and austere proclamations in regards to education, by stating that he

> never paid a great deal of attention to this method of assessing one's intelligence. I think my own IQ is very low, very low indeed. ... No, I have never accepted the notion of an undifferentiated intelligence quotient. I believe in the Binet double system, whereby one can be very stupid at many things but rather clever in others.[207]

In fact, Burgess's feelings about creative writing, as a scholarly academic programme, were shared and are shared by many academics still. In 1975, Geoffrey Aggeler wrote to Burgess mocking such academic pursuits in agreeance with Burgess's perspective, saying that in Utah, where Aggeler taught, there was a newly instituted 'Creative Writing program' that offered 'a PHD in Creative Writing, and our Creative Writing products are about the only ones right who seem to be getting jobs as teachers of English', which he felt was bursting with irony since these students, the graduates of this track, were 'by and large, not merely illiterate but anti-literate' and refused 'to read and consider their own sanctified sensations the only critical touchstone worth heeding. One of them nearly wrecked my graduate seminar in Elizabethan Tragedy two years ago by an exercise of what can only be described as militant obtuseness'.[208] In fact, Burgess was merely the loudspeaker to one side of the argument that was raging in American higher education at the time. He was shunned frequently for being this voice simply because he was an outsider, but as will be explained further, Burgess was becoming, during his time in the United States, fully steeped in the ways and patterns of the country that made him into a kind of ersatz genuine American voice. Critics even took notice of this because since Burgess had been visiting the United States, his inventiveness in the literary arts continued to expand, no longer being pigeonholed by the label of British novelist but rather a cosmopolitan figure that transcended those boundaries, themes, and products of literary output. Through the American experience, be it via higher education, show business, or day-to-day life during the years he lived in the United States, Burgess began to embody, communicate, and reflect American values and modes of experimentation, especially concerning literature and education. Although many of the experiences Burgess revisits in his literature come from periods when he was living in the United States, his broad knowledge of how the country looked as a whole came from his extensive travels for lecture tours – a practice he said 'is an American institution' in the sense that the 'whole American educational system has been built up on the notion that it's a good thing to have lecturers, and if you can get some exotic person, it's all the better. This goes back a long way, to the 19th Century. I think what they really get is contact with an alien mind – a different accent to begin with, a different mode of using the language, a different way of thinking. It's what Brecht called the A-effect – the alien effect. ... Americans are quite willing to have their peace disturbed' – which gives stories such as *The Clockwork Testament* the ability to go beyond the limits of just New York City to mention many other states, towns, and groups of people he encountered elsewhere.[209]

His cynicism had been fed by so many encounters with what he saw as the inexperienced and vapid across the United States that he came to the (not completely inaccurate) conclusion that real literature is only for a certain group of people with exceptional cognitive capabilities and intentions. This idea clearly materialized out of his first-hand observation of an open-access higher education setting during his teaching stint at City College of New York, which only fuelled his beliefs as they were supported time and again, accumulating during his experiences at various other American universities. Burgess was struggling with a student population that didn't see the importance, significance, or relevance of literature, and it greatly bothered him. Students' pleas regarding relevance, he railed against in his November 1972 *New York Times* article, seemed to 'have a strong taint of reasonless rebelliousness about it – the quality of one's own thing. I doubt if one can run a scholarly course on one's own thing'.[210] In his own *The End of the World News* (1982), Val, a science fiction author, laments this same problem, stating that an author has

> certain obligations to his readers. Life put the riddles, the writer's job was to try and answer them, and so on. 'Science fiction, is let's be honest, ultimately triviality,'[211] Val said. 'It's brain-tickling, no more. The American mediocrity, which rejects Shakespeare, Milton, Harrison and Abramovitz, has led us to this nonsense – a university course in, let's face it, trash. Christ, we should be studying Blake and Gerard Manley Hopkins'.[212]

These trivialities Burgess saw in popular forms of writing that his students claimed were *relevant* and therefore important, which Burgess found increasingly annoying – 'relevance, whatever that means'.[213] In 'My Dear Students', Burgess diminishes his lashing out with a typical Burgessian sardonic undercut to supersede his own authority, qualifying that although he has these ideas, many of them accusatory, 'I am a novelist and not a scholar' and therefore, it can be inferred, he means to say that he should not be taken too seriously.[214] Regardless of his attempts to belittle his own opinions, likely in order to mitigate censure, these were still his students, so he makes the article prototypically blithe in order to alleviate some of the causticity of his thoughts by attempting to appeal to ethos so as not to offend, stating that 'I love you all dearly because you are decent, serious, concerned, worried to death. You are much as I was in 1937–40.'[215] The main difference that Burgess recognized between him and his students was his belief that the past was something he used 'to teach me; you tend to abominate the past as the source of all hypocrisy, humbug and evil'.[216] This is the quintessential point that Burgess sees as separating the students of the 1960s and 1970s from the student he was in the 1930s and 1940s. Being born into the end of World War One, often acknowledged as a largely meaningless war, and seeing the precipitous evil of World War Two – which Burgess admitted was a necessary war – Burgess viewed the past and history as something to be revered, protected, learned from, and used as a guide into the future. As a student of the classics who produced allusive literature that referred to these documents, and something of a traditionalist when it came to literary knowledge, Burgess was a man who lived in the past in his own head.[217] His main concerns, when it came to how he felt about the past, were concerns of literature and culture, since literature, as he defined it, had to be worthy of study, and therefore he believed that not much of this type of material existed in the present – *literature* was always a product of the past that had survived time in order to teach him about the present and how to create his own literary voice that could one day be inducted into that very same canon of *true* literature. Writers like Tom Wolfe,[218] Kurt Vonnegut,[219] and Hermann Hesse, he claims, appealed to younger readers on purpose, which reflected back on their abilities as writers because there was 'usually something wrong with writers that the young like'.[220] Because interest by the young meant there existed some sort of blemish, and because he believed wholeheartedly in the validity and sanctity of the past, Burgess stated that he 'wouldn't give a course that covered *any* author later than, say, Graham Greene or Evelyn Waugh'.[221]

The generation that he was teaching tended to see the world wars as being wasteful in both life and resources; furthermore, that same generation, especially the American group he witnessed in the 1970s, were now watching as new wars, like the Korean War (1950–53) and Vietnam War (1955–75), ended or unfolded with debatably Pyrrhic victories or military impasses and gridlocks that weren't worth the expenditures and therefore were essentially trivial. The generation that had started these wars was Burgess's generation that was born into war, possibly seeing it as a way of life in the modern world. But this assumption on the part of these students was largely incorrect and inaccurate, since there exists no solid example of Burgess finding common ground with the educated baby boomers who started these wars. Burgess, although furtively, sided with the younger generation in his dismissal and despising of the useless Pacific wars. Ostensibly a belief that Burgess could have supported publically with little negative impact, he appears to have ignored these issues almost completely, only mentioning the United States's foreign wars several times, quite likely just because it was too *relevant*, too contemporary, and therefore too much a cynosure of the times to avoid completely; Burgess likely did not engage directly and frequently with this subject-matter because, having not accumulated enough time for people to gestate with the idea of those wars and their impacts, he thought it too soon to comment. Hugh Brogan in his *The Penguin History of the USA* summarizes American student involvement with the 1960s and 1970s protest movement as being a time of constant rebellion which was 'borne like a virus by American students' who used college as a form 'of evasion ... so-called college deferment, by which youths could put off their military service until they had finished their education – which helps to explain the then-common phenomenon of the thirty-year-old American students, whose college days seemed to be endless'.[222] In fact, it was quite strange at the time for there to be any writers that actually supported the war in Vietnam, with the *New York Times* even reporting that John Updike was 'the only major American writer who was "unequivocally for" U.S. involvement in Vietnam'.[223]

Understanding his opinions about teaching in general and teaching in the United States specifically helps in codifying this perspective and helps present a clearer picture of how Burgess struggled both internally and externally in the world of authors and professors, ultimately coming to the conclusion that the world of artists fit him better, but that he could never escape that he was, however begrudgingly, that 'dreadful word, an intellectual'.[224]

American myth and violence in *The Clockwork Testament*

Understanding that *The Clockwork Testament* exists among and alongside other essential authorial and historical utterances – and should be contextualized as such to ascertain meaning – that help define its contours, it is easier to recognize the significance of the descriptions of the landscape which include embedded cultural iconography. Enderby describes wealthy Americans as being 'still humble provincials. Ichabod', from Washington Irving's 'The Legend of Sleepy Hollow' (1820), a story Burgess said in *They Wrote in English* (1989) 'had given a myth to the whole world', and whose protagonist is naïve, credulous, austere, and inglorious in his rustic oppositions to high culture as he 'tarried' out his days in the 'fixed', 'unobserved', and 'drowsy, dreamy' town of Sleepy Hollow, whose inhabitants are separated from the 'restless country' and world outside of their small town's borders, with Ichabod Crane and the 'Sleepy Hollow Boys' acting as ingrained symbols of what Burgess saw as a cultural characteristic that many Americans could not shake.[225] This mythic and ideological underbelly also exists televisually in *The Clockwork Testament* through a children's cartoon programme that Enderby has happened upon, which conceals matters of high significance in low art. The entertainment of children is mixed in with propagandistic political ideologies that bleed through into the 'talking animals in reds, blues, and yellows' that barely contain the 'chained wit and liberalism of the creators escaping from odd holes in the fabric: that legalistic pig there was surely the Nice-President?', making Enderby question his own assertions about matters of communication in artful representations, all while suggesting that the 'story of Augustine and Pelagius' could be presented 'in cartoon form' as an entrenched American social dichotomy.[226]

The ridiculousness of the subversive and iconoclastic practice of oversimplifying, so as to commoditize infantilization – like the Superman-Shakespeare T-shirt in *Enderby's Dark Lady* to be discussed in Chapter 7 – complex and intricate ideas to that of a children's show is exactly what Burgess despised about the Americanization, and democratization, of (high) culture, since when American culture swallowed and ingested such aspects of culture, Burgess appears to suggest that the product becomes transmogrified and cheapened to mere material, not as intellectual matter to be examined and better understood, but to be bought and consumed – Burgess was known to 'ramble on about materialism' and certainly many of his representations of and comments on the United States include this criticism.[227] The United States was the reducer of beauty to commodity to Burgess, and American television specifically was something to be loathed, despite his attraction to the medium as a 'movie museum': 'it is the quality of the TV output that turns me from a good guest of America into a snarling ingrate. ... I consider that America should be abysmally ashamed of its television programs [with] the NBC and RKO drivel shin[ing] in clear and idiotic as the moon'.[228] Here, Burgess wonders not when the individual will take responsibility for the televisual drivel but when the 'great federal corporation[s], financed out of license fees, [are] going to take over the task of adult communication in this important medium?', something he feared since 'television has become, for most Americans and Europeans too, their sole purveyor of drama', a problem since 'television programmes and the films ... are in the service of unreality, the hiding of the nature of the human duty and the doling out of anodynes as a substitute', which was ultimately 'evil' because it set 'a premium on ignorance'.[229] To Burgess, this faltering dissemination of poor-quality television was culturally degrading and also 'symptomatic of the disease of timocracy that is the root of most of America's troubles'.[230] Reversing course on the subject of censorship towards the end of his life, he remarked that he was 'for censorship in the medium' of film and television – even choosing self-censorship of *Man of Nazareth* in the Spanish editions in order to assist with publication:

> Anthony and I suggest for the Argentinian edition this fairly simple cuts [sic]: from page 69 of the manuscript to the end of the chapter. at the beginning of the next chapter (chapter three, page 78 of the original), delete this in the first line. page 97 of the original, in the middle, three lines are to be cut (He saw himself with his dead wife Sara, live again and lively in bed, etc. till 'flooded'.) ... I think it should work. If these cuts clear the way to publication in the Argentine, they are more than welcome. The main point is not there. To quote a poet whom you don't like *rosa no buscaba rosa, buscaba otra cosa.*

The 'danger of television, especially when its standards are virtually established by commercial interests, is that it is an agent of social degradation', making it ultimately 'far more frightening than the prospect of *A Clockwork Orange* getting to the screen'.[231]

As his views on the perniciousness of television were evolving, alongside his own increased presence on television, it's no wonder that Enderby is thrust into the American public limelight by appearing on a talk show, the fictional Sperr Lansing Show. All *The Clockwork Testament* provides its readers with is an error-filled '*PARTIAL TRANSCRIPT*' created by an apparently uncultured American, all for a recording of the show that was ultimately '*NOT USED*'.[232] It can be deduced that the transcriber is apparently quite ignorant, uneducated, somewhat illiterate, hard of hearing, and/or unused to a British accent, due to a significant amount of Enderby's dialogue being marked as 'unintelligible' or 'unintell', and although other characters are similarly mis-transcribed, an error which is either unrecognized by the transcriber or catalogued with the use of '(*?*)' or some such variation, this is not the same as Enderby's commentary being marked as being completely unintelligible, or '(*Unintell*)'.[233] Caricaturing the transcriber, who is the narrator for a large portion of chapter 7, using this tactic, it is in instances such as when Enderby tries to remark that 'A British monk called Morgan, in Greek, Pelagius, taught no natural propensity to evil. Heresy and Evil is in everybody', but where the transcriber hears and records, 'A British monkey called Morgan in Greek Plage us (*??????*) taught not national pensity (*?*) to evil. Errorsy (*?*)', that the transcriber's cognition is distorted so as to represent American intellectual simplicity; ironically, what the transcriber has no problem recording accurately is that 'Evils in everybody. Desire to kill rape destroy mindless violence.'[234] This may suggest that Americans are well aware of evil and violence and so are well accustomed to the language of such, while the unintelligible portion is too esoteric to grasp – the theme of Pelagianism and American culture being a subject discussed all the way back in Burgess's first published novel with his first American character, Mendoza, in *A Vision of Battlements*, a point discussed in Chapter 2 of this monograph.

Enderby's commentary on how the United States rationalized condemning artful violence as opposed to actual violence opens up yet another avenue in which, as Jim Clarke notes, 'Enderby, not unlike Ronald Beard [of *Beard's Roman Women*], inhabits possible worlds that reflect upon and deviate from Burgess's own experiences.'[235] More outlandish and stubbornly opinionated than Burgess himself, Enderby, although he has appeared to be outside and unaware of politics in the past, takes on Burgess's own arguments with a somewhat inconsistent characterization due to Enderby's newfound awareness of the American social zeitgeist of the 1970s by even commenting on the hypocrisy of American involvement in the Vietnam War. Enderby does so not by outrightly condemning it but rather by pointing out the fact that the United States provides polemics against violent films and art, and then does nothing about the violence caused by wars. This is worked into Enderby's and also Burgess's overarching argument concerning varying levels of evil and good, and how these terms are relative to the context in which they take place. While naked, talking to the student who had entered his apartment unbeknownst to him, testicles still in plain view, Enderby says that evil is

> the destructive urge. Not to be confused with mere wrong. Wrong is what the government doesn't like. Sometimes a thing can be wrong and evil at the same time – murder, for instance. But then it can be right to murder. Like you people going round killing the Vietnamese and so on. Evil called right.[236]

After his student remarks that she never said that the Vietnam War was right, Enderby counters that the United States 'government did. Get this straight. Right and wrong are fluid and interchangeable. What's right one day can be wrong the next. And vice versa. It's right to like the Chinese now. Before you started playing Ping-pong with them it was wrong' – in a reference to the so-called 'Ping-Pong Diplomacy' of the Nixon administration, a fitting metaphor to display the folksiness and unseriousness of American politics and culture.[237] Further on, Enderby takes to this line of reasoning again on television, arguing to his interlocutors, in a very Burgessian manner, that 'Human beings are defined by freedom of choice. Once you have them doing what theyre told is good just because theyre going to get a lump of sugar instead of a kick up the ahss (?!) then ethnics no longer exists' (here with the intended play on ethnics versus ethics in the transcription), ending his rant just as the host cuts off Enderby: 'The State could tell them it was good to go off and mug and rape and kill some other nation. That's what its been doing. Look at your bloody war in …', we can assume, Vietnam.[238] The television personalities find Enderby to be a manic character, rightly so, but they also refuse to take any of his points seriously by instead just pushing their agenda of sensationalism: 'SPERR: I thought you said you liked violence (*prol A*). ENDERBY: Never said that you silly bagger (*?*)', only to have his points curtailed by commercial breaks.[239] Additionally, Enderby is cut off just before explaining that to be revolted and offended by the violence in the film based on his screenplay, which was based on Hopkins's *The Wreck of the Deutschland*, where the film included acts of sexual violence committed by Nazis against nuns, is a ludicrous proposition while a futile war rages on the other side of the world and with its horrors being televised on the news. Dealing with very similar circumstances, in which Burgess was 'accused of concocting a piece of violent pornography' for having written *A Clockwork Orange* which was turned into a massively popular film by Stanley Kubrick, all while a large portion of America supported a war in which thousands of Americans and Vietnamese were killing each other every year between 1965 and 1972 in Vietnam, the furore over the film seemed ludicrous, especially considering that the threats targeted at Kubrick even provoked the director to withdraw the film from British theatres and block the video release – and the United States's involvement in the Vietnam War didn't end until spring 1975.[240]

The facts of the United States's ironies and contradictions are perfectly suited for satire and dark, morbid comedy that humorizes the ridiculous, and however clunky, that is what *The Clockwork Testament* is attempting to do, using lived experience by its own author. In his summer 1971 'Letter from Europe', Burgess tried to align his knowledge of eighteenth-century London to the stark and violent streets of New York by quipping that there existed an atmosphere of 'eighteenth century Grub Street swirling around Amsterdam Avenue and 110th' due to a 'fair number of my Columbia students [being] mugged by the new Mohawks, and I myself once had to brandish a heavy stick in counterthreat, (this, though, was down near 13th St)'.[241] Burgess explains that living in New York City periodically, then working at Princeton University but visiting Columbia weekly to teach as an adjunct instructor,[242] provided him with the ability to 'enter Modern American Urban Life with a vengeance', dispelling the notion of the 'ivory towers' in the 'Groves of Academe' after seeing him 'swelter on the I.R.T. train, which has been immobile between stations for forty-five minutes, or dodging axes or coshes, or vomiting after twenty-five cent pizza on uptown Broadway'.[243] It was this environment that Burgess saw as being 'at the center of most of the New York Creative Writing I read', which shocked him since the harsh language of these surroundings was often 'in the work of the girls than of the men', making him question his 'old-world old-fashioned way' where 'sweet young writing misses bring themselves to use such words, show such intimate knowledge of such remote sexual deviations?'.[244] As Enderby noted too, although New York was a wild place, filled with fear and excitement, there 'was this to be said for New York: it was not dull'.[245] Although expressed frequently in his non-fiction writing, *The Clockwork Testament* is the first Burgess novel to deal honestly and singularly with New York City to either the laudation or chagrin of resident New Yorkers. New York City appears consistently throughout a handful of Burgess's novels, but it is only in *The Clockwork Testament* where the setting of New York City is not just a backdrop, an idea meant to facilitate some other literary gains, but one of the sole purposes of writing the story. With it, meaning the story, comes everything that New York City is usually characterized as having: too many people, loud noises, crass language, plenty of food, provocative students and artists, and crazed inhabitants lurking behind every corner. *The Clockwork Testament* acts as a stereotype and honest vision of the city through the voice of an author who was seeing it as an outsider, through a literary character who was pushed into an environment in which he was never going to belong. Even more revealing about the times and the situations that were occurring on the street and in collegiate classrooms are Enderby and Burgess's comments about race and poverty that provide a much more nuanced view than the landscape crafted in *The Clockwork Testament*. To the twenty-first-century reader, this may not appear to be the case in several instances in *The Clockwork Testament*, but critics during the 1970s took notice of the honesty and forthrightness, an example coming from Bernard Bergonzi's 1972 *The Situation of the Novel* in which he claims that even before *The Clockwork Testament*, Burgess's fiction exhibited a 'unique sense of humour combined with a desolate philosophical despair that makes Burgess one of the few novelists to whose work the much-abused label "black comedy" can reasonably be applied', largely through a common theme of 'underlying subjects [of] racialism, which Burgess sees in more complex terms than the conventional Western liberal' does not evoke, that of the 'alienating structures of imperialism'.[246] *The Clockwork Testament* clearly works into this definition, but it may ultimately be the sloppiest and most inarticulate of Burgess's presentations of his racially themed literary pursuits.

Race, sex, and *The Clockwork Testament*

As discussed at length previously, despite being in line with some of Burgess's views on race and language, Enderby is especially, or uniquely in *The Clockwork Testament*, racist, sexist, impatient, and untrusting, even crudely describing an encounter with a student through objectification:

> He was close to her now and saw that she was a nice little thing he supposed she could be called, with nicely sculpted little tits under a black sweater stained with, as he supposed, Coke and Pepsi and hamburger fat (*good food* was what these poor kids needed), long American legs in patched worker's pants.

Another has 'a cheese-paring nose, a wide American mouth that was a false promise of generosity, the face of a girl who wanted an A'.[247] Employing certain thematic traits in his fiction, a common theme in Burgess's American novels, which is often double-voiced by the author publicly, such as the malnutrition of American young that appears in *M/F* as well as elsewhere in *The Clockwork Testament* – 'poor kids. Half-starved, seeing visions, poisoned with cokes and hamburgers' – is the representation of American students as being highly sexualized, malnourished, politically and emotionally charged, and focused on 'passing' college rather than learning.[248] The emphasis on the body and sexuality was, Enderby gathers, an American trait, as he thinks it strange 'how one never bothered to take in the face here in America, the face didn't matter except on films, one never remembered the face, and all the voices were the same'.[249] Similarly inauthentic and stereotyped, Enderby, and it wouldn't be entirely unreasonable to suggest, Burgess, in many ways – through double-voiced discourse and hidden polemic as an avenue to present a kind of veiled displaced satisfaction so as to maintain plausible deniability – perceived African American students as being incompetent, angry, and disrespectful. The two most significant examples are with the character Priscilla who is described as being a 'lazy black insolent bitch, thought Enderby, but evidently illiterate' – and not, it can be judged, in the Pam Grier, capital "B", *Black Bitch* of *Coffy* (1973) and *Foxy Brown* (1974) way that had an empowering sense of 'combined beauty, sexuality, and violence' – and Lloyd Utterage, whose name alone, as Biswell notes, evokes a person who 'exists in a state of utter rage' and who Enderby describes on one account as 'guffaw-sneer[ing] in a way that Enderby could only think of as *n-----ish*'.[250] When looking at these lines individually, it's not hard to see how Enderby's perspective and narrative, as well as the narrative of the text, could be described as being influenced by or reminiscent of the minstrel caricatures of African Americans in the late nineteenth and early twentieth centuries, but also by what Paul Gilroy described in *The Black Atlantic* (1993) as the 'updated minstrel antics' of a person like Jimi Hendrix (1942–70), the legendary psychedelic rock guitarist, whose onstage persona would be 'wild, sexual, hedonistic, and dangerous', resulting in the effect of producing a 'neo-minstrel buffoonery' which was 'received as a sign of his authentic blackness by the white rock audiences on which his burgeoning pop career was so solidly based'.[251] In this sense, being as ignorant and oblivious as he was of Black culture, Burgess's understanding and characterization of such characters borders on the racist and the minstrel-like, a genre and characterization that he, and the majority of White populations, had likely encountered in media far more than the images of compassion laid out by the Black authors he respected and admired like James Baldwin and Ralph Ellison, and so his characters are a reflection of that, though they do speak up for themselves (in an ironic sense) and therefore just barely miss being as stock and stereotypical as a Stepin Fetchit or as lowbrow as early Jim Crow comedies.[252] Such a characterization of his attitudes is supported by instances when, speaking at Sarah Lawrence College in January 1971, Burgess expressed the sentiment that the United States was a place doing well for art, which was not so for him in Europe because:

> There is very little that comes out of England or even out of France that interests me but a great deal that comes out of America is very interesting indeed. Not only people like R. Ellison who must write, must bring his other novel out soon. Not only black novelists but also the Jewish novelist people like Malamud and Bellow and Philip Roth but there is some tough traditional writing going on in America. There is some very heartening experimental writing.

He even described Bellow's plots in 1987 as being 'Christmas trees, if the goy metaphor is acceptable, hung with toys of intellectual speculation. Or, to borrow one of his own images, his novel is stuck like a pomander with the pungent cloves of ideas'.[253]

In 1974, Burgess still held rather strict conservative British prejudices which were altogether not dissimilar to the views espoused in Allan Bloom's *The Closing of the American Mind* (1987), regarding feminism as being an 'enemy of the vitality of classic texts', opinions that would have not felt out of place in the 1940s and 1950s in any Western country, but which were certainly beginning in the mid-1970s to become outdated for liberals, as well as more generally recognized as being inaccurate and cruel.[254] Largely progressive and having liberal tendencies towards ethnic diversity, Burgess still unapologetically utilized racial epithets because he appears to have been largely naïve of the history of African Americans in the United States.[255] By 1976, in *New York*, there appears to have been a significant shift in Burgess's thinking on the subject, since he acknowledges 'the conflict of black and white' and seems to have grown discouraged by the particularly American brand of racial hostility, though, as evidenced in his August 1976 article 'Dirty Words' published in the *New York Times*, he was still more concerned by what may be called *political correctness*.[256] 'The Nonsensical Use of "Neuter" Words', also known as 'Dirty Words', is an article in which Burgess argued in support of the use of racial epithets and inaccurate pronouns because, he contends, when these words are censored or changed we thrust language use into a realm guarded by magical thinking:

> We're supposed to be living in a scientific age, and yet never has man been more ready to ascribe magic to mere verbal counters. We all have to make the effort to love language rather than fear it and to refuse to attach partisan meanings to words. Layers of meaning are a different matter. All of us share responsibility for managing word-frontiers. Hunkies, n-----s, micks, kikes, everybody.[257]

Utilizing selective philosophizing, Burgess picks and chooses when and where society should be 'scientific', which appears to rest solely with the use of language. How Burgess could then turn around and claim on *The Dick Cavett Show* and *After Dark* that words like 'shit' and 'fuck' disturbed him – as well as Enderby in *Enderby's Dark Lady* constantly asking that the word 'shit' not be uttered – is not only illogical and inconsistent but also baffling as to how he could be so naïve as to ignore the fact that profanity takes shape in many different words with many different purposes.[258] For him to ignore the fact that a word like the N-word has a long, painful, and abusive history reinforces the argument that only certain histories interested Burgess. Being wholly, apparently, unaware that the N-word has served primarily 'even in its contemporary "friendlier" usage – as a linguistic extension of white supremacy', as a form of 'language of oppression' that still 'endures, helping to perpetuate and reinforce the durable, insidious taint of presumed African-American inferiority' is one of the startling gaps, if not the most startling, in Burgess's cosmopolitan nature and persona.[259] In the interest of historicizing his comments, though, it's important to remember that the derogative power of this epithet has increased significantly over time to the point that in the United States in 2025 this word has evolved into perhaps the most insulting and incendiary word in the English language; in the 1970s, that was not necessarily the case – of course, it was still highly offensive, but the word had not taken on as much vitriol as it has in the twenty-first century – with blaxploitation films like *The Legend of Nigger Charley* (1972) and *Boss Nigger* (1974) appearing in cinemas around the country.[260]

And so, by 1976, Burgess still held to the belief that language could not carry with it the power of racial hatred, since words were just signifiers for ideas, and if words were given too much power, then censorship would ultimately prevail. This is not an inaccurate *a priori* view, but it is naïve and intellectually dishonest and lazy since it ignores the cultural and humanistic power that language, a very Bakhtinian notion, does have in order to fuel racial hatred, to subordinate, and to repress certain groups, as Stanley Fish masterfully displayed in his lectures-turned-monograph *There's No Such Thing as Free Speech* (1994), in which he opens by explaining that any such attempt to rid words of historical context is also an attempt to 'deprive moral and legal problems of their histories so that merely formal calculations can then be performed on phenomena that have been flattened out and no longer have their real-world shape'.[261] Much like Edwin Spindrift in *The Doctor Is Sick* (1960), Burgess commits his character's same digression of treating people and words like things to be dissected, detached from the emotional and historical baggage they bring. In *New York*, though, now writing non-fiction as 'Anthony Burgess', and not a thinly disguised cathartic parody or partial Menippean satire, and therefore more likely to be confronted for his opinions, Burgess begins to grant the subject of race sincerer attention that takes into account the nuance, subtleties, and complexities of being a minority American – either that, or the editors and publishers filtered or altered his commentary.[262] Indeed, New York City is where Burgess gained his largest and most significant education in all things America, largely due to New York City being so diverse, so active, and so disparate from much of the rest of the country, therefore acting as an epitomic synecdoche for the nation, in a wider sense, as a whole. One such concession that Burgess makes in this non-fiction book is that despite other ethnicities and nationalities being victims of the United States's widespread ability to be bigoted and vindictive, the vast sum of vitriol always seemed to come down the hardest and most consistently on African Americans:

> It is perhaps not surprising that many of the newly arrived Irish immigrants, who were themselves despised and rejected by the haughty Teutprot Establishment, used the blacks as convenient scapegoats for their frustration and resentment. Barred from the professions and most of the trades, blacks also competed with the Irish for jobs.[263]

Although Burgess occasionally referenced Frantz Fanon mockingly, this aligns essentially with Fanon's point that the 'scapegoat for white society – which is based on myths of progress, civilization, liberalism, education, enlightenment, refinement – will be precisely the force that opposes the expansion and the triumph of these myths. This brutal opposing force is supplied by the Negro'.[264]

And one of the biggest problems that Burgess saw facing the country, and the city, was the disconcerting problem with accepting its African American populations as brethren, something that, even though he contributed, however unwillingly or unknowingly, to the anti-Black narratives of the 1970s, he found it deeply troubling, stating that the 'problems of diversity overwhelm any sense of glory' in New York City, perhaps in the United States as a whole, because the problem had grown to such drastic levels that the 'black-white confrontation in New York can find no parallel in the various racial and religious enmities of the 19th Century'.[265] In a distinctly different tone from other comments on these matters in the past, Burgess even admits to being largely ignorant of the struggles of African Americans and as knowing only a glimpse of their world through literature by viewing 'the black experience' through Ralph Ellison's *Invisible Man* (1952), which he claims opened his mind to the African American experience more so 'than a whole library of cold documents', calling it 'a towering masterpiece'.[266] This perceptive observation he claims to have encountered on his own as he walked through Harlem one day, the 'only white man around, and met neither hostility nor curiosity but a kind of willed indifference', becoming himself 'an invisible man', prompting him to escape quickly 'back to my white world'.[267] The level of empathy reached here by Burgess deviated from his otherwise elitist egotism that fueled much of his social commentary, as will be discussed at further length when looking at *Enderby's Dark Lady* in Chapter 7. But for Burgess to recognize that Ellison's unnamed character in his 'masterpiece', and in fact all African Americans, could not escape this same invisibility, and that they were condemned to working in a 'paint factory that has the slogan: "Keep America Pure with Liberty Paints"', is significant in that he appears to have finally realized the peculiar historic position of the Black body throughout American history that was 'essential for the making of pure whiteness: the black keeps America pure by becoming a scapegoat for its sins', in much the same way that James Baldwin argued, in 'A Talk to Teachers', that the White world manufactured Blackness as something opposed to White standards over the assumption that Black people are 'a kind of criminal [and] that's the only way he can live'.[268] In a startling epiphany that acts as a stark contrast to the content in *The Clockwork Testament*, which complicates, though doesn't upend, the hidden polemical grounds of the text, in a definitive differentiation between artist and artistic creation, and not lessening the hidden invective to diminish Enderby to the likes of Nabokov's Humbert Humbert, as Biswell compares, this just shows Burgess's evolution and the slight disparities between author and character, as well as how drastically Burgess could alter his voice for different audiences, like when he makes the political proposition to the world, to the United States, to New York City, that 'We need what New York potentially has: the glory of diversity.'[269] Where this again becomes double-voiced and an example of hidden polemic, though, since Enderby himself is a caricatured Burgess, a Hyde-like extension of the author and one who verbalizes his most dubious and shady opinions left largely under- or undeveloped in non-fiction, is just one sentence later when Burgess states, innocently enough, that 'When we can all see this, there will be no need for talk of toleration, or of revenge, conquest and destruction', which in essence came from the mouth of Enderby years earlier: 'I mean, imagine a period when this kind of race-hate stupidity is all over, and yet the poem – *perennius aere*, you know – still by some accident survives.'[270] All the way back to *Beds in the East* (1959), this line of thought is expressed between Vythilingam and Nik Hassan, when Hassan argues that in the new Malaya there 'must be inter-marriage, there must be a more liberal conception of religion, there must be art and literature and music capable of expressing the aspiration of a single unified people', again, innocent enough, but this time largely ignoring the injustices of colonialism.[271] This approach to race relations is nothing new to practitioners of Critical Race Theory, and really most intellectual discourse; what Burgess is doing here, through fiction and non-fiction, is handing the onerous onus of ceasing racism over to people of colour by arguing that it is their fault for recognizing race, when such a practice, known as colour-blindness – not to be confused with Burgess's physical monochromacy – is essentially a scapegoat for recognizing historical wrongs by allowing a society to only redress 'extremely egregious racial harms, ones that everyone would notice and condemn', whereas the baked-in institutionalized racism can continue to 'keep minorities in subordinate positions' by not being addressed.[272] Seeing the Black–White problem and division as 'the most disturbing feature of recent years', Burgess still sticks to one of his original points in *New York*, largely that any racially conscious artistic aims should still be avoided since, as he saw it, any type of '"ethnic" literature is divisive' since the 'glory of diversity must presuppose a unity' and therefore reduce aesthetic-literary productions and reveal socio-political shortcomings, in turn revealing that a completely diverse and fully realized view of New York City was still a long way off – on the subject of White-on-Black violence and discrimination, Burgess is on the whole profoundly silent, though this may be because the realities of the plight of African Americans in the United States over the last 300 years are only receiving the scholarly and investigative insight necessary in the last three decades since his death, in such popular and comprehensive publications as Philip Dray's *At the Hands of Persons Unknown: The Lynching of Black America* (2002), Ibram X. Kendi's *Stamped from the Beginning: The Definitive History of Racist Ideas in America* (2017), and Isabel Wilkerson's *The Warmth of Other Suns* (2011) and *Caste: The Origins of Our Discontents* (2020), to be incredibly brief.[273] By remarking through double-voiced discourse on these matters of race in *The Clockwork Testament*, ironically, this would actually make, by Burgess's own definition, this novel, and perhaps others, part of the sect of literary output that does not achieve a literary symbiosis because it unequivocally represented authorial political statements and displayed ingrained authorial bias and racism by having the Enderby-Burgess narrator describe the varied ethnicities both encountered on the 'mean streets' of New York City as being 'full of black and brown menace'.[274]

Enderby, picking up where Burgess left off in 'Dirty Words' where Burgess naïvely presented the false equivalency that 'hunkies, n-----s, micks, kikes, everybody' all equally share 'responsibility for managing word-frontiers', responds to Utterage's angry and vindictive poetry – 'It will be your balls next, whitey, / A loving snipping of the scrotum / With rather rusty nail scissors, / And they tumble out then to be / Crunched underfoot crunch crunch' – by returning to prosody and linguistics, wholly blind to the sensibilities that rest behind the words he uses (not necessarily as good poetry, but of the cultural frustrations) and that which is symbolically signified, or what Bakhtin explains about language being 'not a neutral medium'; rather, language 'is populated – overpopulated – with the intentions of others': 'I take it that this term *whitey* is racialist and fill of opprobrium and so on. Suppose now we substitute for it the word *n-----*'; 'I mean, if, as you said, the point is the hate, then the hate can best be expressed – and, indeed, in poetry must be expressed – as an emotion available to the generality of mankind. So instead of either *whitey* or *n-----* you could have, er, *bohunk* or, say *kike*. But *kike* probably wouldn't do'; 'Since the end words are disyllabic or er yes trisyllabic but never monosyllabic.'[275]

Utilizing Burgess's fascination with this issue, which the author did not adjust until close to his death when in *A Mouthful of Air* (1992) he called such terms the 'language of abuse', Utterage and Enderby play out the problem that Burgess laboured over and was especially concerned with while in the United States.[276] Where race and art overlapped, where politics intruded upon the liminal point of creative expression, this was the space Burgess abhorred, or was at least disinterested in, like when he gave only one small paragraph to 'black poets in America' in *They Wrote in English* (1989) because he did 'not think that black poetry is, as yet, very important poetry' since too much of it 'proclaims the black experience aggressively and this approaches propaganda rather than art'; where Burgess rationalizes and deliberates, Enderby sneers invectively.[277] Utterage responds to Enderby asking if the pseudo-professor thought – resembling an experience Burgess himself claims he had, as was mentioned previously – he would get away with such use of language; Enderby, feeling hurt and surprised at such a threatening retort, is silenced until another student remarks, 'he's British. He doesn't understand the ethnic agony', which Enderby appreciates as a prosodic term and nothing else: ' "That's rather a good phrase," Enderby said. "It doesn't mean anything, of course. Like saying *potato agony*" '.[278] Wholly incapable of recognizing or unwilling to recognize the divergent point of view, Enderby ponders the use of imaginative language and its variance with 'the defilers of language' that include 'Your President, for instance. The black leaders. Lesbian power, if such a thing exists', to once again stress Enderby's, and largely Burgess's, perspective of refusing to accept or entertain a world in which politics and art exist on the same field of discourse.[279] These were spaces that Enderby and Burgess could not reconcile; they could not be convinced that social issues/politics and art could exist within the same sphere. More startling, though, is that Burgess was an admirer of George Orwell, Aldous Huxley, and Sinclair Lewis, authors whose most famous novels (*1984*, *Brave New World*, and *It Can't Happen Here*) are drenched in political and social commentary, so it's shocking, or rather characteristically hypocritical, being the author of such books as *The Wanting Seed* and *1985* that are filled with political ideologies, that Burgess could not fathom a world in which socio-political disturbances become aesthetically and legitimately charged in fine literature – though perhaps Burgess's classical, early twentieth-century, Eurocentric, and Catholic education at Xaverian College and Manchester University is perhaps the source of such thinking, and/or perhaps he just did not care about issues concerning race.[280] Still further, and elsewhere, Burgess remarks that it's not the politics of theology behind literature, or within it, that he's concerned with, since he suggests that 'politics are an irrelevance in literature, just as theology is. I cannot tolerate John Milton's regicidal puritanism, but I worship his poetry' and that abhorrent politics may actually be a prerequisite to being a 'good' writer, as with Eliot and Pound.[281] Explaining further in the same article, 'Why Were the Revolutionaries Reactionary?', Burgess says this:

> For art, certainly literature, has to be judged in terms of human values: it promotes properties like love, tolerance, redemption. It is impossible to imagine a literature based on hate and damnation. When I taught in America, certain of my black students brought me poems about the desirable castration of white men. I was sincerely reviled for not approving of them. Literature does not work in that way. It cannot base itself on sectarian prejudices. A Nazi poetry is a contradiction in terms. Literature assumes that all mankind is one, occasionally rejoicing but mostly bewildered and suffering, certainly mortal. Literature thus puts politics in the right place: as a system for maintaining minimal order and looking after the drains. Politics is not important enough to be a theme for literature.[282]

Even so, it's not difficult to see where Burgess plays favourites with what is and what is not acceptable political fodder for literature.

In 1975, Burgess egregiously contradicts himself again during a lecture at Tufts University, during which he claimed that he 'could never be a socialist, a conservative, a fascist, or a communist; I could only be an activist. ... And this, I suppose, crystallizes itself, as far as I am concerned, with a particularly simple aesthetic philosophy'.[283] Calling himself an activist is striking because of Burgess's stance on American student protests, but here he aligns this activism with aesthetic pursuits – that his art is action and a commentary on societies, which always stood opposed to the 'state of ignorance' employed by state apparatuses that ignore the struggle between 'the individual and the thing which surrounds him, namely the state'.[284] Juxtaposed to *The Clockwork Testament*, this makes it seem like Burgess isn't quite sure what he believes. Taking liberties with the scene between Utterage and Enderby, Burgess presents, through a 'systematically monologic worldview' and voice, an utterance-Utterage that/who does not, and indeed cannot, honestly or empathetically 'recognize someone else's thought, someone else's idea, as an object of representation', and therefore this Black student simply sees the outsider British poet/teacher as having committed a transgression in absentia and therefore is due for a particularly weak riposte: 'His people started it. N-----whippers despite their haw-haw-haw old top.'[285] Everything, Burgess appears to communicate, always came back to the sins of the past, but it was not the history of racial abuses that Burgess was concerned with, it was always a more romantic vision of philosophy and art, the birth of the humanities, not necessarily the covert transgressions of governments, racist politics, and the status of the hoi polloi – an activist maybe, but very much focused on *high culture* and, most definitely, *of his time*.

Finally, Enderby – far more clueless than Burgess, with Burgess aiming to outrage the very same people he caricatures – ignores the attacks outright and focuses on the semantics and diction, not the personage utilizing them, to respond that Utterage has 'the makings of a word man. You'll be a poet someday when you've got over all this nonsense', before letting the letters and the sounds of the N-word drip off his tongue to experience the vocalization – something his audience clearly perceives as offensive – out loud in front of the whole class as an example of an act of 'prosodic analysis', repeating

> *n------whipper* swiftly and quietly like a tongue-twister. ... *N-----* and *whipper*, you see, have two vowels in common. Now note the opposition of the consonants – a rich nasal against a voiceless semivowel, a voiced stop against a voiceless. Suppose you tried *n------killer*. Not so effective. Why not? The *g* doesn't oppose well to the *l*.[286]

Reaching the tipping point of Utterage's patience, Enderby is finally threatened by the student, a bit of emotional language that Enderby finally recognizes as being *dangerous* to which he responds violently in kind: '"I understand that you want to cut a white man's genital apparatus off. Well, come and try. But you'll get this sword in your black guts first." He drew an inch or so of steel.'[287] Reeling from the class's insubordination, Enderby utilizes the Burgessian defence of inquiring whether Utterage, the class's *token Black male*, has a 'monopoly of abuse' in an attempt to invalidate the frustrations of *the* angry Black man, but also the stereotyped wholistic anger of the contemporary African American experience.[288] The answer, as any historically aware reader would easily understand, is, especially in the United States, yes, Black people do have and have had the monopoly on suffering in the American experience; though Henry Louis Gates Jr does warn against engaging in the 'rivalry over victim status: the sort of Oppression Sweepstakes that ran through so much harebrained attitudinizing of the seventies and eighties', this statement does not mean that Black people in America are not the only population to have suffered, but that to draw a comparison between any White counterpart would be a fallacy of false parallelism or false equivalency, with only Native Americans as a possible counterargument to this claim, a population that Enderby also lashes out at in equally offensive terms, by characterizing a Native American student as 'Running Deer', as a 'cunning know-all of the Kickapoo nation ... a very cunning young redskin sod, [who] ought to be kept on his reservation'.[289] This attempted humour at the expense of the monologic cardboard characters, devised from a biased and monologic observation of a foreign social heteroglossia, and all told through a monological parody that acts polyphonically, though the characters are cheap imitations of the real experiences encountered by Burgess, makes the scenarios of the text, especially in the scenes covered here, far more troubling than funny, more insulting than mock-heroic.

Burgess and Enderby alike struggle to remove their own prejudices in order to recognize the plight of others through acts of selfish introspection where they legitimize their assumptions by describing the world around them as supreme observers, a symptom of an antiquated British worldview, refusing to shatter their own national myths and histories of subjugation in order to more objectively rationalize the realities of the world around them; in effect, to dialogize the literary setting. Enderby is erratic, myopic, comedic, bigoted, vicious, patronizing, and ultimately ridiculously contrived, predetermined to play the lead role in a manufactured ploy to divest his, and his creator's, audience of Americans of any reasonable human intellect. The manufactured plot is of course Burgess's own making in order to exploit the characters' own partialities into a farcical display of incongruency and ignorance, effectively producing what Bakhtin called 'a *voiceless object of that deduction*', and nowhere else is this more evident than when the text addresses race.[290]

Conclusion: Endergess or Burgby

Enderby plays the fool, and perhaps the *vice* character, as much as his students, but it's important to keep in mind that despite Burgess's own warning to the reader, from the narration of Enderby, that art is not 'important because of the biographical truth of the content', this is simply an attempt to shield the authorial purpose.[291] This novella *is* inescapably a monoglottal product of Burgess's life and craft, which can easily be discerned by investigating the life of the public figure known as Anthony Burgess. This understanding cannot be taken as a dichotomist balancing act that anoints one perspective as 'correct' or 'accepted', but should instead be taken into consideration as one essential interpretation meant to be understood among a kaleidoscopic vision of the realities of both Enderby and Burgess. Burgess, and Biswell, are right, to a point, that this interpretation cannot be accepted as a straight biographical extension of the writer, since every genre is not made of 'pure entities', but this also affords room to recognize the similarities between Burgess and his literary work that cannot and should not be completely ignored as long as those connections be qualified as exhibiting symbolic distance that is rife with irony.[292]

Being an outsider to the social issues of the United States, Enderby is distinctly less sympathetic than his creator, and although Burgess and Enderby share many similarities in character, this is the defining dissonance between the Burgess–Enderby parallel characterization – Burgess learns, changes, adapts, admits to mistakes, and grows, while Enderby is largely a static character, not really a protagonist because of his stubbornness and refusal to change, traits which ultimately lead to his death. The irony, too, is that Burgess uses this text to cathartically release his anger with being discordant with the American experience, while largely ignoring or else blind to the fact that the very same groups he castigates were dealing with similar conflicts of identity. Enderby manifests Burgess's polarities of emotional dispositions, engendering his hatred, anxieties, and frustrations, as well as his feelings of inadequacy and love for language as art, but the large difference is Enderby's capriciousness, lack of self-awareness, and recklessness in the way he sees the world, while Burgess, although not always, was more conscious of his self *within* society, since he at least attempted to be empathic and caring during most public occasions, though he was only human and definitely had his share of gaffs and insults.[293] One such event occurred when he visited Fordham University on 2 June 1973 for a pre-graduation ceremony, afterwards rebuking the audience and faculty in the 22 June 1973 'Viewpoint' article in the *Times Literary Supplement*. George W. Shea, dean of the Liberal Arts College at Fordham University, publicly responded in a 'Letter to the Editor: Anthony Burgess at Fordham' in the *Times Literary Supplement*, where he explained that despite being treated cordially and with great respect, Burgess acted cantankerously, at one point demanding a glass of gin before the ceremony, which was granted by Shea, only to be rewarded with Burgess lamenting that the academic robe given to him 'was not trimmed with ermine, and a cap which, shaking his disheveled locks, he refused to put on', and then while 'downing the gin, he talked of his work, [and] was rude to a young Jesuit who dared to come in to admire him without putting on a Roman collar'.[294] Shea attributed Burgess's perturbations to having 'judged, for no reason I can find, that Fordham is part of an American scheme to destroy all that is valuable in the great university tradition of the West'.[295] Director of the creative writing programme at the City College of New York, one Leo Hamalian, and 'Burgess's "boss" during the year he spent' at the university, then responded to defend Burgess's character days later, and Burgess would go on to write a 'Viewpoint' article about the incident stating that the Fordham event had 'summed up' to him 'everything that was wrong with education and society and the church', before claiming that afterwards he had been 'accosted by a black man who reviled me for [his] espousal of an inegalitarian philosophy of higher education'.[296] Burgess did not return at length to the United States again until spring 1975, having returned to Rome to write *The Clockwork Testament*.

Enderby in *The Clockwork Testament* experiences the same uncomfortable realization that he too, like his creator before him, has been exploited, used, willingly and with permission, so that he could not be entirely ashamed of such an admission because it was the unfortunate role of the artist in the modern, especially Americanized, world. Enderby, though, exhausted and stressed by this inner conflict and frustration, is killed by it. Achieving detumescence after violence and sex in a single evening, 'He felt pretty good, as they said in American fiction, though distended. All he needed now, as again they would say in American fiction, and he laughed at the conceit, was a woman', as he slips off into death by fourth heart attack and is observed by the time-travelling students.[297] Enderby's death at the end of the novella keeps with the literary allusiveness – Cocteau dies and ascends at the end of the *Testament of Orpheus*, Dante is led into purgatory, and Aschenbach dies in the final pages of *Death in Venice* – while also acting as a symbol of the inhospitableness of the United States for the 'great' poet, Enderby, who is killed by the exhaustion of sexual intercourse as the television plays the 'morning news, which is all bad', of course – more sex and violence.[298]

Very much still alive, though, was Burgess, and his literary and professional life would look much different after *The Clockwork Testament*, especially as his involvement with the United States dwindled after 1976 and he solidified his presence in the world of literature and letters as a solidly European author. The next three chapters will look at the lingering American content present in *Earthly Powers* (1980), *The End of the World News* (1982), and then, finally, *Enderby's Dark Lady* (1984) as Burgess's farewell novel to the United States.

Notes

1 Anthony Burgess, *Enderby* (New York: Ballantine Books, 1973), p. 236.
2 Anthony Burgess, *New York* (Amsterdam: Time-Life, 1976), p. 156.
3 Andrew Biswell, International Anthony Burgess Foundation, email sent to Christopher Thurley, 21 May 2021; Anthony Burgess, 'The Clockwork Condition', *A Clockwork Orange: The Restored Edition*, ed. by Andrew Biswell (New York: W.W. Norton, 1962; 2012), p. 221; Anthony Burgess, 'Introduction: A Clockwork Orange Resucked', *A Clockwork Orange* (New York: W.W. Norton, 1962; 1986), p. v; Mordecai Richler, *Cocksure* (Toronto: McClelland & Stewart, 1968).
4 Ákos Farkas, *Will's Son and Jake's Peer: Anthony Burgess's Joycean Negotiations* (Budapest: Akadémiai Kiadó, 2002), p. 104.
5 Mikhail Bakhtin, *Problems of Dostoyevsky's Poetics*, ed. by Caryl Emerson, Theory and History of Literature, volume 8 (Minneapolis, MN: University of Minnesota, 1984), p. 195.
6 Bakhtin, *Problems of Dostoyevsky's Poetics*, p. 195.
7 Richard Macksey, 'Foreword', *Paratexts: Thresholds of Interpretation* (Cambridge: Cambridge University Press, 1987/97), pp. xviii–xix; Max Saunders, *Self Impression: Life-Writing, Autobiografiction, and the Forms of Modern Literature* (Oxford: Oxford University Press, 2010), p. 286.
8 Bakhtin, *Problems of Dostoyevsky's Poetics*, p. 186.

9 Mikhail Bakhtin, *The Dialogic Imagination: Four Essays*, ed. by Michael Holquist, trans. by Caryl Emerson and Michael Holquist (Austin, TX: University of Texas Press, 1981), p. 288; Christine Gallagher and Stephen Greenblatt, *Practicing New Historicism* (Chicago, IL: The University of Chicago Press, 2000), p. 13.

10 Anthony Burgess, *The Clockwork Testament; or, Enderby's End* (London: Hart-Davis, MacGibbon, 1974), p. 124; Burgess, *Enderby*, p. 13; André Malraux, *Man's Fate* (New York: The Modern Library, 1934; 1961).

11 Jim Clarke, *The Aesthetics of Anthony Burgess: Fire of Words* (Cham: Palgrave Macmillan, 2017), p. 264.

12 Anthony Burgess, 'Book Proposal for "The Clockwork Condition"', 7 June 1972, International Anthony Burgess Foundation Archives (uncatalogued); Anthony Burgess, 'Craft and Crucifixion – The Writing of Fiction', *One Man's Chorus: The Uncollected Writings of Anthony Burgess*, ed. by Ben Forkner (New York: Carroll & Graf, 1998), p. 260; Anthony Burgess, 'Gerard Manley Hopkins 1844–1889', *One Man's Chorus: The Uncollected Writings of Anthony Burgess*, p. 336; Burgess, *The Clockwork Testament*, p. 77; Anthony Burgess, 'Success', *One Man's Chorus: The Uncollected Writings of Anthony Burgess*, p. 171.

13 Christina Sterbenz, 'New York City Used to Be a Terrifying Place', *Business Insider*, 12 July 2013.

14 Sterbenz, 'New York City Used to Be a Terrifying Place'.

15 Burgess, *The Clockwork Testament*, pp. 92–93.

16 Burgess, *The Clockwork Testament*, pp. 43, 77.

17 Burgess, *The Clockwork Testament*, p. 77.

18 Anthony Burgess, 'England in Europe', *One Man's Chorus: The Uncollected Writings of Anthony Burgess*, p. 108.

19 Gore Vidal, 'Not So Poor Burgess', *The Observer*, 28 November 1993, p. 64.

20 Len Carr, Letter to Gabriele Pantucci, 10 October 1989, University of Texas at Austin: Harry Ransom Center Archives, Gabriele Pantucci Papers Series I and II; W.T. Lhamon, 'Recent Fiction', *New Republic*, 22 February 1975, p. 29.

21 Paul Boytinck, *Anthony Burgess: An Annotated Bibliography and Reference Guide* (New York: Garland Publishing, 1985), p. vi; Anthony Burgess, 'The Private Dialect of Husbands and Wives', *Vogue*, 1 June 1968, p. 118.

22 Anthony Burgess, 'One of the Minor Joys …', 1972, International Anthony Burgess Foundation Archive.

23 Burgess, *The Clockwork Testament*, p. 51.

24 Burgess, 'One of the Minor Joys …'.

25 Anthony Burgess, *You've Had Your Time: Being the Second Part of the Confessions of Anthony Burgess* (London: Penguin Books, 1990), p. 285; Peter Krämer, *A Clockwork Orange: Controversies* (London: Palgrave Macmillan, 2011), pp. 92–93.

26 Mike Power, 'Author Would Expunge "Clockwork" from Record', *The Portsmouth Herald*, 6 October 1972, p. 11.

27 Krämer, *A Clockwork Orange*, p. 87; John J. Stinson, *Anthony Burgess: Revisited* (Boston, MA: Twayne, 1991), p. 95.

28 *Testament of Orpheus*, dir. Jean Cocteau (Cinédis and Les Editions Cinégraphiques, 1960).

29 Robert Lantz, 'Letter to Burgess', 16 August 1973, International Anthony Burgess Foundation Archive; Thomas Mann, *Death in Venice*, trans. by Joachim Neugroschel (New York: Penguin Books, 1998); *Testament of Orpheus*, dir. Jean Cocteau.

30 Andrew Biswell, *The Real Life of Anthony Burgess* (London: Picador, 2005), p. 351; 'Kurt Vonnegut Named CCNY Professor', *The Bridgeport Telegram*, 25 May 1973, p. 16; William Mallet, Letter to Anthony Burgess, 7 October 1973, International Anthony Burgess Foundation Archive; Sheridan Morley, 'Anthony Burgess Answers Back', *Times*, 6 August 1873, p. 7c; Marcel Berlins, 'Lawyers Reject Author's Attack', *Times*, 7 August 1873, p. 2.

31 Robert McCrum, 'The "Lost" Novels That Anthony Burgess Hoped Would Make Him Rich', *The Guardian*, 18 March 2017; Alison Flood, 'The Clockwork Condition: Lost Sequel to *A Clockwork Orange* Discovered', *The Guardian*, 25 April 2019, www.theguardian.com/books/2019/apr/25/the-clockwork-condition-lost-sequel-to-a-clockwork-orange-discovered; George Armstrong, 'Pith of the Orange', *The Guardian*, 30 July 1973, p. 1; Anthony Burgess, Letter to Aggeler, 24 December 1974, International Anthony Burgess Foundation Archive.

32 Burgess, *You've Had Your Time*, p. 255.

33 Anthony Burgess, 'American Trilogy', 18 September 1972, Thomas P. Collins International Anthony Burgess Foundation Archive); McCrum, 'The "Lost" Novels That Anthony Burgess Hoped Would Make Him Rich'.

34 Burgess, *You've Had Your Time*, pp. 285–286.

35 Anthony Burges, Letter to Professor Martin Meisel, 2 February 1974, Harry Ransom Center Archives, 80.5.

36 'Review of The Clockwork Testament; Or, Enderby's End', *Saturday Review/World*, 25 January 1974, p. 44; Peter Prescott, 'Among the Yahoos', *Newsweek*, 7 April 1975, p. 89; Peter Prince, 'Intramural', *New Statesman*, 21 June 1974, p. 894; 'Review of *The Clockwork Testament; Or, Enderby's End*, *Booklist*, 1 March 1975, p. 669.

37 J.D. O'Hara, 'The Clockwork Testament or Enderby's End', 2 February 1975, p. 4.

38 Burgess, *The Clockwork Testament; or, Enderby's End*, p. 126; 'Review of *The Clockwork Testament; Or, Enderby's End*, p. 669.

39 John C. Gerber, Letter to Anthony Burgess, University of Iowa, 14 April 1975, University of Texas at Austin, Harry Ransom Center Archives, 81.2; John C. Gerber, Letter to Anthony Burgess, University of Iowa, 31 October 1975, University of Texas at Austin, Harry Ransom Center Archives, 81.2; Nicholas Gerogiannis, Letter to Anthony Burgess, *The Iowa Review*, 19 May 1976, University of Texas at Austin, Harry Ransom Center Archives, 81.2; Anthony Burgess, Letter to James Klein Fleming, 8 December 1976, Correspondence: University of Texas at Austin: Harry Ransom Center Anthony Burgess Papers, Box 82.

40 Clarence Olson, 'For the Love of a City', *St. Louis Dispatch*, 17 April 1977, p. 40.
41 Nicholas J. Loprete, 'Review of *New York*', *Best Sellers*, 37.4 (July 1977), 115.
42 Katerina Clark and Michael Holquist, *Mikhail Bakhtin* (Cambridge, MA: Harvard University Press, 1984), p. 202.
43 Thomas Stumpf, interview with Christopher Thurley, 1 July 2015; Anthony Burgess, Letter to Ben Forkner, 26 July 1971, Harry Ransom Center, The University of Texas at Austin; Anthony Burgess, Letter to Ben Forkner, 9 May 1979, Harry Ransom Center: The University of Texas at Austin; Anthony Burgess, *This Man and Music* (New York: McGraw-Hill Book Company, 1982), p. 33; Brian Swann, 'Burgess Memories: Brian Swann', International Anthony Burgess Foundation, 18 May 2018; Christopher Armitage, email to Christopher Thurley, 20 October 2017; Benjamin Forkner, phone interview with Christopher Thurley, 21 November 2015; Benjamin Forkner, phone interview with Christopher Thurley, 13 June 2016.
44 Anthony Burgess, *On the Novel* (Manchester: International Anthony Burgess Foundation, 1975; 2019), p. 63.
45 Anthony Burgess, *Little Wilson and Big God: Being the First Part of The Autobiography* (New York: Weidenfeld & Nicolson, 1986), p. 448.
46 Burgess, *Little Wilson and Big God*, pp. 285, 109.
47 Burgess, *Little Wilson and Big God*, p. 413.
48 Burgess, *Little Wilson and Big God*, p. 448.
49 Burgess, *You've Had Your Time*, p. xi.
50 Burgess, *You've Had Your Time*, pp. 198–199.
51 Burgess, *You've Had Your Time*, p. 36.
52 Morley, 'Anthony Burgess Answers Back', p. 7c; Saunders, *Self Impression*, p. 8; Anthony Burgess, 'Contemporary Authors: The Works of Anthony Burgess', Pennsylvania State University. 1982; John Sturrock, *The Language of Autobiography: Studies in the First Person Singular* (Cambridge: Cambridge University Press, 1993), p. 5.
53 Burgess, *The Clockwork Testament; or, Enderby's End*, pp. 27, 97; Biswell, *The Real Life of Anthony Burgess*, p. 221.
54 Anthony Burgess, 'A Prefatory Note', *Enderby's Dark Lady; or No End to Enderby* (New York: McGraw-Hill, 1984), pp. 7–8.
55 Anthony Burgess, 'Interview with Anthony Burgess on Mozart', *Larry King Show Live*, Mutual Broadcast System, 3 December 1991, George Washington University Archives.
56 Anthony Burgess, 'Letter from Europe', *American Scholar*, 41.3 (Summer 1972), 426.
57 Vincent LoBrutto, *Stanley Kubrick: A Biography* (New York: Da Capo Press, 1999), p. 368; Biswell, *The Real Life of Anthony Burgess*, p. 365.
58 Burgess, *This Man and Music*, p. 157; Anthony Burgess, 'Ugh – Letters to the Editor', *Times Literary Supplement*, 2 January 1964, p. 9; Anthony Burgess, *A Clockwork Orange* (New York: W.W. Norton, 1962; 1986), p. ix.
59 Burgess, *The Clockwork Testament; or, Enderby's End*, pp. 21, 10.

60 Brian Swann, 'Burgess Memories: Brian Swann', International Anthony Burgess Foundation, 18 May 2018, www.anthonyburgess.org/burgess-memories/burgess-memories-brian-swann; Burgess, 'Craft and Crucifixion – The Writing of Fiction', p. 264; Burgess, 'Letter from Europe' (Summer 1971), pp. 517–518.
61 Bede Liu, Letter to Anthony Burgess, 12 July 1971, The University of Texas at Austin: Harry Ransom Center Archives.
62 Christopher Armitage, email to Christopher Thurley, 20 October 2017; Rexford Brown, phone interview with Christopher Thurley, 5 January 2017; 'Interview with Anthony Burgess', *The Dick Cavett Show*, ABC Television Network: Daphne Productions and Rollins & Joffe Productions, 19 January 1972.
63 Burgess, *You've Had Your Time*, p. 225.
64 Burgess, *You've Had Your Time*, p. 225; Burgess, *The Clockwork Testament; or, Enderby's End*, p. 58; Burgess, *Enderby*, p. 24; Anthony Burgess, 'All Too Irish', *But Do Blondes Prefer Gentlemen? Homage to QWERT YUIOP and Other Writings* (New York: McGraw-Hill Book Company, 1986), p. 435.
65 Burgess, *The Clockwork Testament*, p. 63; Burgess, 'Letter from Europe' (Summer 1971), p. 518.
66 Burgess, *You've Had Your Time*, pp. 227, 230; James Lieber, phone interview with Christopher Thurley, 28 March 2017; Rexford Brown, phone interview with Christopher Thurley, 5 January 2017.
67 James Lieber, phone interview with Christopher Thurley, 28 March 2017.
68 Anthony Burgess, Letter to Deborah Rogers, 6 August 1971, Series II, Correspondence, 1956–97: University of Texas at Austin: Harry Ransom Center Archives, Anthony Burgess Papers, 78.1–5.
69 Rexford Brown, phone interview with Christopher Thurley, 5 January 2017.
70 Rexford Brown, phone interview with Christopher Thurley, 5 January 2017.
71 Deborah Rogers, Letter to John Burgess Wilson, 5 February 1972, University of Texas at Austin: Harry Ransom Center, 78.5; John Burgess Wilson, Letter to Deborah Rogers, 13 March 1972, University of Texas at Austin: Harry Ransom Center, 78.5.
72 Robert Hofler, *Sexplosion: From Andy Warhol to A Clockwork Orange – How a Generation of Pop Rebels Broke All the Taboos* (New York: itbooks, 2014), p. 249.
73 Hofler, *Sexplosion*, p. 249.
74 Theodore Gross, Letter to Anthony Burgess, City College of New York, 27 January 1972, University of Texas at Austin: Harry Ransom Center Archives, box 80, fol. 4.
75 Burgess, 'Letter from Europe' (Summer 1972), p. 425.
76 Burgess, *You've Had Your Time*, p. 230; 'Interview with Anthony Burgess', *The Dick Cavett Show*.
77 Burgess, *The Clockwork Testament; or, Enderby's End*, p. 24, 22 December 1972.
78 Burgess, *The Clockwork Testament; or, Enderby's End*, p. 24; 'Interview with Anthony Burgess', *The Dick Cavett Show*, 4 September 1974.
79 'Interview with Anthony Burgess', *The Dick Cavett Show*, 4 September 1974.
80 Burgess, *The Clockwork Testament*, p. 25.

81 Anthony Burgess, Letter to Geoffrey Aggeler, 25 May 1975, International Anthony Burgess Foundation Archive; Paul Phillips, *A Clockwork Counterpoint: The Music and Literature of Anthony Burgess* (Manchester: Manchester University Press, 2010), p. 148; Burgess, Letter to Geoffrey Aggeler, 25 May 1975, International Anthony Burgess Foundation Archive.

82 B.F. Skinner, *The Behavior of Organisms* (New York: Appleton-Century, 1938); B.F. Skinner, *Walden Two* (Indianapolis, IN: Hackett Publishing Company, 1948; 1976; 2005); B.F. Skinner, *Beyond Freedom and Dignity* (New York: Alfred A. Knopf, 1971).

83 Skinner, *Beyond Freedom and Dignity*, p. 96; Burgess, *The Clockwork Testament*, p. 78.

84 Skinner, *Walden Two*, p. 107; Burgess, *The Clockwork Testament*, p. 81.

85 Skinner, *Beyond Freedom and Dignity*, p. 39.

86 Burgess, *The Clockwork Testament*, pp. 79–81; Skinner, *Beyond Freedom and Dignity*, p. 84.

87 Mikhail Bakhtin, 'Forms of Time and of the Chronotope in the Novel', *The Dialogic Imagination*, pp. 159–160.

88 Bakhtin, 'Forms of Time and of the Chronotope in the Novel', pp. 159–160; Burgess, 'The Clockwork Condition', p. 222.

89 Burgess, 'The Clockwork Condition', p. 222.

90 Burgess, *You've Had Your Time*, p. 230.

91 Burgess, 'Letter from Europe' (Summer 1971), p. 518; Anthony Burgess, 'Thoughts on Excellence', *Excellence: The Pursuit, the Commitment, the Achievement* (Washington, DC: LTV Corporation, 1981), p. 24.

92 'Interview with Anthony Burgess', *The Dick Cavett Show*, 25 March 1971; Charles J. Shields, *The Man Who Wrote the Perfect Novel: John Williams, Stoner, and the Writing Life* (Austin, TX: University of Texas Press, 2018), pp. 205–207; Anthony Burgess, ed. by George Malko, 'Penthouse Interview: Anthony Burgess', *Penthouse*, June 1972, p. 118.

93 'Interview with Anthony Burgess', *The Dick Cavett Show*, 1 April 1971.

94 'Interview with Anthony Burgess', *The Dick Cavett Show*, 19 January 1972.

95 'Interview with Anthony Burgess', *The Dick Cavett Show*, 19 January 1972.

96 'Interview with Anthony Burgess', *The Dick Cavett Show*, 19 January 1972.

97 'Visiting Lecturer in Creative Arts (Writing): 1970–71 Schedule', Princeton University, The University of Texas at Austin, Harry Ransom Center Archive, 81.4; John Wilheim, 'Novelist Burgess Attracts 300 for Dramatic Reading', *The Daily Princetonian*, 2 October 1972, p. 3.

98 Saunders, *Self Impression*, p. 176; Anthony Burgess, *Earthly Powers* (New York: Europa Editions, 1980; 2012), p. 62.

99 Ken Hirschkop, 'Mikhail Bakhtin: Historical Becoming in Language, Literature and Culture', *The Cambridge History of Literary Criticism: Twentieth-Century Historical, Philosophical and Psychological Perspectives*, volume 9 (Cambridge: Cambridge University Press, 2008), p. 150.

100 Henry Miller, *Sexus: The Rosy Crucifixion 1* (New York: Grove Press, 1962; 1965); Henry Miller, *Plexus: The Rosy Crucifixion 2* (New York: Grove Press, 1963; 1965); Henry Miller, *Nexus: The Rosy Crucifixion 3* (New York: Grove

Press, 1960; 1965); Jack Kerouac, *On the Road* (New York: Penguin, 1957; 2016); Norman Mailer, *Armies of the Night: History as a Novel/The Novel as History* (New York: Plume, 1968; 1994); Charles Bukowski, *Post-Office* (New York: Ecco, 1971; 2002); Saul Bellow, *Humboldt's Gift* (New York: The Viking Press, 1973); Anthony Burgess, *They Wrote in English* (proof copy, International Anthony Burgess Foundation Archive, 1989), p. 18.

101 O.L. Chavarria-Aguilar, Letter to Anthony Burgess, 3 May 1972, Harry Ransom Center Archives, 80.4.

102 Burgess, *The Clockwork Testament*, p. 14.

103 Saunders, *Self Impression*, p. 255.

104 Saunders, *Self Impression*, p. 198; McCrum, 'The "Lost" Novels That Anthony Burgess Hoped Would Make Him Rich'.

105 Burgess, *The Clockwork Testament*, p. 61.

106 Burgess, *You've Had Your Time*, p. 275.

107 Brian McHale, *Postmodernist Fiction* (New York: Routledge, 2001), p. 203.

108 Dominic Green, 'The Most of Anthony Burgess', *The New Criterion*, 36.2 (October 2017), 28–32; Anthony Burgess, 'Viewpoint', *Times Literary Supplement*, 23 March 1973, p. 322.

109 Burgess, *The Clockwork Testament*, p. 61.

110 Burgess, *The Clockwork Testament*, pp. 54–55; Richler, *Cocksure*, p. 211.

111 Bakhtin, *Problems of Dostoyevsky's Poetics*, p. 113.

112 Burgess, *You've Had Your Time*, p. 275; Graham Foster, 'Object of the Week: Burgess Lecturing on Marlowe', The International Anthony Burgess Foundation, para. 3; Paul Edwards, 'How Bertrand Russell Was Prevented from Teaching at the College of the City of New York' (1956), www-cdf.lbl.gov/~mikesh/russell.pdf, p. 2.

113 Will Carr, 'A Class Act: Anthony Burgess at City College New York', The International Anthony Burgess Foundation, 24 July 2020, www.anthonyburgess.org/blog-posts/a-class-act-anthony-burgess-at-city-college-new-york.

114 Anthony Burgess, 'Cucarachas and Exiles, Potential Death and Life Enhancement', *New York Times*, 29 October 1972; Anthony Burgess, 'My Dear Students; a Letter', *New York Times*, 19 November 1972.

115 Burgess, 'My Dear Students; a Letter', para. 7.

116 'Kurt Vonnegut Named CCNY Professor', p. 16; Burgess, 'My Dear Students; a Letter', para. 11.

117 Burgess, 'My Dear Students; a Letter', para. 11–12.

118 Burgess, *The Clockwork Testament; or, Enderby's End*, p. 44.

119 Anthony Burgess, 'The British Observed', *But Do Blondes Prefer Gentlemen?*, p. 121; Burgess, *The Clockwork Testament*, p. 44.

120 Burgess, 'Cucarachas and Exiles, Potential Death and Life Enhancement', para. 14.

121 Burgess, *New York*, p. 6.

122 Barbara Lekatsas, phone interview with Christopher Thurley, 9 March 2019; Horace A. Porter, 'To Do One's Thinking, or Think One's Doing', *New York Times*, 24 December 1972, p. 32.

123 Burgess, *The Clockwork Testament*, p. 17.

124 Burgess, 'Cucarachas and Exiles, Potential Death and Life Enhancement', pp. 28, 37.
125 Anthony Burgess, 'Is America Falling Apart?', *New York Times*, 7 November 1971, para. 15.
126 Don DeLillo, *White Noise* (New York: Viking Penguin, 1985), p. 326; Christopher Isherwood, *A Single Man* (New York: Farrar, Straus and Giroux, 1964), p. 91.
127 Burgess, 'Cucarachas and Exiles Potential Death and Life Enhancement', p. 28.
128 Anthony Burgess, 'Viewpoint', *Times Literary Supplement*, 23 March 1973, p. 322.
129 Burgess, 'Viewpoint', p. 322.
130 Burgess, *The Clockwork Testament*, p. 9.
131 Bakhtin, *Problems of Dostoyevsky's Poetics*, p. 197.
132 Burgess, 'Cucarachas and Exiles, Potential Death and Life Enhancement', p. 28; Burgess, 'Viewpoint', p. 322.
133 Stinson, *Anthony Burgess*, p. 95.
134 Andrew Biswell, 'Adrienne Rich, Anthony Burgess and the Cockroaches', The International Anthony Burgess Foundation, 30 March 2012, www.anthonyburgess.org/blog-posts/adrienne-rich-anthony-burgess-and-the-cockroaches-by-andrew-biswell; Burgess, *You've Had Your Time*, p. 285.
135 Biswell, 'Adrienne Rich, Anthony Burgess and the Cockroaches'.
136 Biswell, 'Adrienne Rich, Anthony Burgess and the Cockroaches'.
137 Biswell, 'Adrienne Rich, Anthony Burgess and the Cockroaches'; Anthony Burgess, chequebook, 1972, International Anthony Burgess Foundation Archive.
138 Biswell, 'Adrienne Rich, Anthony Burgess and the Cockroaches', para. 6.
139 Burgess, *The Clockwork Testament*, p. 19.
140 Biswell, 'Adrienne Rich, Anthony Burgess and the Cockroaches', para. 7.
141 Burgess, *The Clockwork Testament*, p. 10.
142 Anne McCormick, 'Meeting New York Realistically', *New York Times*, 19 November 1972.
143 Anthony Burgess, 'Meeting New York Realistically', New York Times, 19 November 1972.
144 Burgess, *You've Had Your Time*, p. 269.
145 Biswell, 'Adrienne Rich, Anthony Burgess and the Cockroaches', para. 8; Ákos Farkas and Evgeniya Laverycheva, 'Lilies That Fester: *The Clockwork Testament* as a Campus Novel', *Burgess and Droogs: A Post-Centennial Collection of Essays*, 20 (2022), 94–95.
146 John Ashbery, 'Tradition and Talent', *Adrienne Rich's Poetry and Prose*, ed. by Barbara Charlesworth and Albert Gelpi (New York: Norton Critical Edition, 1993), p. 279; Margalit Fox, 'Adrienne Rich, Influential Feminist Poet, Dies at 82', *New York Times*, 28 March 2012, www.nytimes.com/2012/03/29/books/adrienne-rich-feminist-poet-and-author-dies-at-82.html.
147 Biswell, 'Adrienne Rich, Anthony Burgess and the Cockroaches'; Bede Liu, Letter to Anthony Burgess, 12 July 1971, The University of Texas at Austin: Harry Ransom Center Archives; Thomas Kuhn, Letter to Anthony Burgess, 8 June 1971,University of Texas at Austin: Harry Ransom Center Archives.

148 Burgess, *They Wrote in English*, p. 33.
149 Adrienne Rich, 'The Burning of Paper Instead of Children', 'I Dream I'm the Death of Orpheus', 'The Stranger', and 'The Phenomenology of Anger', in *Adrienne Rich's Poetry and Prose*, pp. 40–43, 52–53, 55–59.
150 Biswell, 'Adrienne Rich, Anthony Burgess and the Cockroaches', para. 9.
151 Adrienne Rich, 'The Ninth Symphony of Beethoven Understood at Last as a Sexual Message', Copyright 2002 by Adrienne Rich. Copyright 1973 by W.W. Norton, from *The Fact of a Doorframe: Selected Poems 1950–2001*.
152 Rich, 'The Ninth Symphony of Beethoven Understood at Last as a Sexual Message'; Hirschkop, 'Mikhail Bakhtin', p. 152.
153 Burgess, *The Clockwork Testament*, p. 28; Charles A. Reich, *The Greening of America* (New York: Random House, 1970); Ziauddin Sardar, 'Foreword to the 2008 Edition', *Black Skin, White Masks* (London: Grove Press, 1952; 2008), p. ix.
154 Burgess, *The Clockwork Testament*, p. 21; Edward Champion, 'Burgess's Powers Are Still Strong', *The Guardian*, 5 February 2008; Anthony Burgess, 'Grunts from a Sexist Pig', *But Do Blondes Prefer Gentlemen?*, p. 1; McCormick and Burgess, 'Meeting New York Realistically', p. 118.
155 Burgess, *The Clockwork Testament*, p. 28.
156 Mann, *Death in Venice*, p. 363.
157 Clarke, *The Aesthetics of Anthony Burgess*, p. 268.
158 Clarke, *The Aesthetics of Anthony Burgess*, p. 268.
159 Skinner, *Beyond Freedom and Dignity*, pp. 19–20.
160 Burgess, *The Great Cities – New York*, pp. 41, 44.
161 Skinner, *Walden Two*; Burgess, 'The Clockwork Condition', pp. 69–75; Anthony Burgess, 'A Fable for Social Scientists', International Anthony Burgess Foundation Archives, pp. 1–12; 'An Interview with Anthony Burgess: "The Challenge of Our Time"', *Jim Nelson Black* (The University of Texas at Arlington, 15 May 1973; 2016), p. 8.
162 Anthony Burgess, appears in *Behavioral Revolution*, Pennsylvania State University, July 1975, Program 5, University Libraries: Pennsylvania State University Archives.
163 Andrew Biswell, International Anthony Burgess Foundation, email sent to Christopher Thurley, 21 May 2021; Christopher Farman, Letter to Anthony Burgess, 17 May 1976, Series II, Correspondence, 1956–97: University of Texas at Austin: Harry Ransom Center, Anthony Burgess Papers, 78.1–5; 'New York, Time-Life Contract', 24 June 1975, International Anthony Burgess Foundation Archives (uncatalogued); Burgess, *The Great Cities – New York*, p. 50.
164 Burgess, *The Great Cities – New York*, p. 50.
165 Burgess, 'Is America Falling Apart?', para. 16–17; Burgess, 'Cucarachas and Exiles, Potential Death and Life Enhancement', para. 4.
166 Anthony Burgess, *Puma*, ed. by Paul Wake (Manchester: Manchester University Press, 2018).
167 Burgess, *The Great Cities – New York*, p. 46.
168 Burgess, *The Great Cities – New York*, p. 6.

169 Anthony Burgess, 'The Eyes of New York', 1976, University of Texas at Austin, Harry Ransom Center Archives, p. 1.
170 Anthony Burgess, 'Marilyn', *One Man's Chorus*, p. 380; Burgess, *The Great Cities – New York*, p. 43.
171 Anthony Burgess, 'Ah, Liberty', International Anthony Burgess Foundation Archive, unpublished, 1986, pp. 3–5.
172 Michael Rudick, 'Enderbyan Poetics: The Word in the Fallen World', *Critical Essays on Anthony Burgess*, ed. by Geoffrey Aggeler (Boston, MA: G.K. Hall, 1986), p. 111.
173 Anthony Burgess, 'Burgess: Interview with an Erudite Elitist', ed. by Bill Meehan, *Columbia Daily Spectator*, 6.3 (1 May 1973).
174 'Everyone should be able to enter college, Burgess said, but standards should be tougher in academics. There's too many useless courses being taught, he said, but he doesn't think young men are really qualified to choose their own education' (quoted in Mark Zimmerman, ' "People are dull; art is to shock" ', *The University of Tennessee Daily Beacon*, University of Tennessee Libraries, Knoxville, Special Collections, 17 April 1975, para. 8); Burgess, *You've Had Your Time*, p. 275; Burgess, 'Burgess: Interview with an Erudite Elitist', p. c4.
175 Burgess, 'Burgess: Interview with an Erudite Elitist', p. c5.
176 Burgess, 'Burgess: Interview with an Erudite Elitist', p. c5.
177 Burgess, *The Clockwork Testament; or, Enderby's End*, p. 36.
178 Phyllis Malamud and Anthony Burgess, 'For Love or Money', *Newsweek*, 4 June 1973, International Anthony Burgess Foundation Archive, para. 3; Anthony Burgess, 'Father of the OED', *One Man's Chorus*, p. 351.
179 Burgess, *The Great Cities – New York*, pp. 140–141.
180 Burgess, 'Burgess: Interview with an Erudite Elitist', p. c5.
181 'The real universities will, in time, sink to a secondary level, and real real universities will supervene. This will go on forever ... "parity of esteem." ... It is an aspect of the egalitarian heresy that informs all progressive politics. The real, and heroic, student protest takes place beyond the Iron Curtain, where the resuscitative light of a humane philosophy tries to advance against the totalitarian darkness, although it rarely prevails' (Anthony Burgess, 'Letter from Europe', *American Scholar*, 38.4 (Autumn 1969), 686.
182 Anthony Burgess, 'The Young', *The Firing Line*, Southern Educational Communications Association, 21 December 1972; 31 December 1972. University of Buffalo Archives, p. 2.
183 Burgess, *The Clockwork Testament; or, Enderby's End*, p. 60; Burgess, *A Clockwork Orange*, p. 52; John Dos Passos, *U.S.A.: The 42nd Parallel; 1919; The Big Money* (New York: The Library of America, 1938; 1996); James Lieber, phone interview with Christopher Thurley, 28 March 2017; Adam Roberts, *The Black Prince* (London: Unbound, 2018); Adam Roberts, 'The Black Prince: An Interview with Adam Roberts', International Anthony Burgess Foundation, 9 October 2018, www.anthonyburgess.org/publications/black-prince-interview-adam-roberts
184 Burgess, *The Clockwork Testament; or, Enderby's End*, p. 60.

185 'Interview with Anthony Burgess', *The Dick Cavett Show*, 25 March 1971.
186 Burgess, *The Clockwork Testament; or, Enderby's End*, p. 64.
187 Burgess, *The Clockwork Testament; or, Enderby's End*, p. 65; Anthony Burgess, 'Swing of the Censor', *The Spectator*, 21 June 1969, p. 16.
188 Biswell, *The Real Life of Anthony Burgess*, p. 352.
189 Biswell, *The Real Life of Anthony Burgess*, p. 352; Burgess, *The Clockwork Testament; or, Enderby's End*, pp. 91–92; Thomas Nelson Winter, 'A Protean Work: Review of Anthony Burgess, MF', Faculty Publication, Classics and Religious Studies Department, University of Nebraska at Lincoln, 21 March 1972, p. 83.
190 Burgess, 'Letter from Europe' (Summer 1971), p. 516.
191 Anthony Burgess, *1985* (London: Beautiful Books, 1978; 2010), p. 75.
192 Burgess repeated this point in a 1976 lecture for the International Shakespeare Association Congress in Washington, DC: 'For the young especially the inarticulate leaders of youthful revolt are great because of their in-articulateness. Only politicians are articulate, and they're all liars. Ergo, wordmen are liars, unless they can put their words to music. Mr Dennis Hopper, the filmmaker and hero of *Easy Rider* said: "There ain't nothin' in books man." A rock-group in my own country recently pronounced: "Education's a dead scene. Youth susses things out on its own"' (Anthony Burgess, 'Shakespeare as Culture Hero in an Anti-Heroic Age', Plenary Lecture: Shakespeare in America: The International Shakespeare Association Congress, 21 April 1976, Washington, DC, University of Texas at Austin: Harry Ransom Center Archives, box 81, fol. 2, para. 2); Burgess, *1985*, p. 75.
193 Anthony Burgess, *Language Made Plain* (New York: Thomas Y. Crowell Company, 1964; 1965), p. 9.
194 Milton Talbot, 'Burgess on "Orange": "Not One of My Best"', *Tuesday's Bucknellian*, 17 April 1973, p. 1; Burgess, *The Clockwork Testament; or, Enderby's End*, p. 39.
195 Talbot, 'Burgess on "Orange"', p. 1.
196 Burgess, *The Great Cities – New York*, pp. 140–141.
197 Burgess, *The Clockwork Testament; or, Enderby's End*, p. 59.
198 Burgess, 'The Eyes of New York', p. 2; Theodore Roosevelt, *American Ideals*, *The Norton Anthology of American Literature: 1865–1914*, ed. by Robert S. Levine (New York: W.W. Norton, 2017), pp. 1169–1172.
199 Burgess, 'The Eyes of New York', p. 2.
200 Burgess, *The Great Cities – New York*, pp. 140–141.
201 Burgess, 'The Eyes of New York', p. 3.
202 Burgess, 'The Eyes of New York', p. 3.
203 Burgess, *The Clockwork Testament; or, Enderby's End*, p. 110.
204 Farkas, *Will's Son and Jake's Peer*, pp. 39–40.
205 Bruce Parks, 'My Time with AB: Recollections of Professor Burgess at City College and a Visit to Bracciano', *End of the World Newsletter*, The International Anthony Burgess Foundation (July to August 2009): 03.11–5.
206 Parks, 'My Time with AB': 03.11–5.

207 Burgess, 'The Young', p. 7.
208 Anthony Burgess, Letter to Geoffrey Aggeler, 25 May 1975, International Anthony Burgess Foundation Archive.
209 Dennis Stack, 'Burgess Explores A-Effect', *Kansas City Star*, 9 November 1975, p. 14E.
210 Burgess, 'My Dear Students; a Letter', p. 22.
211 Toomey echoes this purpose: '"What, Mr Toomey, do you seek out of life?" A very straight question. "To enjoy it. To fix the phenomena of human society in words"' (Burgess, *Earthly Powers*, p. 242).
212 Anthony Burgess, *The End of the World News* (London: Penguin Books, 1982; 1984), p. 30. Further on in the novel, Burgess waxes on the subject even more: 'There is only the past, and the glory of the past is not order, for order is an abstraction imposed by that non-existent thing called the present. The glory of the past is riot, profusion, a chaos of flowers. ... Let us glory in having added more and more to the past, increased the roar of its music and the chaotic profusion of its flowers' (Burgess, *The End of the World News*, p. 216). Geoffrey Aggeler describes Burgess's sentiment thus: 'Burgess has also been disturbed that American students have "cut themselves off completely from the past, from the whole of the past"' (quoted in Geoffrey Aggeler, *Anthony Burgess: The Artist as Novelist* (Tuscaloosa, AL: University of Alabama Press, 1979), p. 99).
213 Burgess, *You've Had Your Time*, p. 276.
214 Burgess, 'My Dear Students; a Letter', p. 22.
215 Burgess, 'My Dear Students; a Letter', p. 22.
216 Burgess, 'My Dear Students; a Letter', p. 22.
217 'Because there's nothing else, because there is no present. The present is only the past. The present is becoming the past now. That's all I'm saying' (Burgess, *The Firing Line*, p. 12).
218 Burgess's ongoing disproval of Wolfe is listed at several points throughout this book, but it's telling that in Burgess's article 'Thoughts on Excellence', which was presented at the Washington Seminar in Washington, DC on 10 February 1981, with Tom Wolfe as a co-presenter, Wolfe wrote a glowing approbation of Burgess as a writer and intellectual. The piece acts as an admittance that Wolfe, possibly despite the criticisms, if he had known of them, was still 'a great, great admirer of Anthony Burgess', who, Wolfe claims, is among British writers only paralleled by Graham Greene who are 'often and steadily mentioned as candidates for the Nobel Prize' (Burgess, 'Thoughts on Excellence', p. 19). Wolfe goes on to sum up Burgess's career as one filled with 'single-mindedness' which helps exemplify the themes of the conference. Wolfe ends his introduction by telling a story of going to a party to celebrate Burgess's 1976 Time-Life book on New York City. The party, filled with 'two or three thousand other Anthony Burgess admirers' – hyperbole? Condescension? Satire? – went on as everyone in attendance found out that Burgess was not actually there but instead in Egypt 'involved in making a movie about Jesus' (Burgess, 'Thoughts on Excellence', p. 19). Wolfe also wrote the foreword to Burgess's article that

came from the lecture which was published in Burgess, *Excellence: The Pursuit, the Commitment, the Achievement*.

219 'I do remember one thing. His damning of Kurt Vonnegut's writing with the remark that if you need proof of his being a bad writer you need only note his extreme adoration by the young' (Dick Cavett, 7 October 2016).

220 Burgess, 'Playboy Interview', p. 74.

221 Burgess, 'Playboy Interview', p. 76.

222 Hugh Brogan, *The Penguin History of the USA*, 2nd edition (London: Penguin Group, 1999), p. 658.

223 Hofler, *Sexplosion*, p. 54.

224 Burgess, *Little Wilson and Big God*, p. 262; 'Although he enjoys university teaching, he does not see himself as any sort of intellectual ("If I am one, I'm fighting against it all the time")' (Aggeler, *Anthony Burgess*, p. 27).

225 Burgess, *The Clockwork Testament*, p. 69; Burgess, *They Wrote in English*, p. 145; Washington Irving, *The Legend of Sleepy Hollow* (London: Bloomsbury Books, 1820; 1994), pp. 7–12.

226 Burgess, *The Clockwork Testament*, p. 67.

227 Burgess, *Enderby's Dark Lady; or No End to Enderby*, p. 60; William Manley, phone interview with Christopher Thurley, 6 December 2017.

228 Burgess, 'One of the Minor Joys …'; Burgess, 'Letter from Europe' (Summer 1971), p. 518.

229 Burgess, 'Letter from Europe' (Summer 1971), p. 518; Anthony Burgess, 'Cardboard Character', *TV Guide*, 1982, International Anthony Burgess Archive; Anthony Burgess, 'The God I Want', *The God I Want* (Indianapolis, IN: The Bobbs-Merrill Company, 1967), p. 70; Joseph Darlington, 'Reviews: No End to Anthony' (Oxford: Oxford University Press, 2018).

230 Burgess, 'Letter from Europe' (Summer 1971), p. 518.

231 Liana Burgess, Letter to Paco, 18 February 1978, Series II, Correspondence, 1956–97: University of Texas at Austin: Harry Ransom Center, Anthony Burgess Papers, 78.1–5; Anthony Burgess, 'Stop the Clock on Violence', *The Ink Trade: Selected Journalism 1961–1993*, ed. by Will Carr (Manchester: Carcanet Press, 2018), p. 253.

232 Burgess, *The Clockwork Testament*, p. 75.

233 Burgess, *The Clockwork Testament*, pp. 76–78.

234 Burgess, *The Clockwork Testament*, p. 77.

235 Clarke, *The Aesthetics of Anthony Burgess*, p. 269.

236 Burgess, *The Clockwork Testament*, p. 33.

237 Burgess, *The Clockwork Testament*, p. 33; David Devoss, 'Ping-Pong Diplomacy', *Smithsonian Magazine*, April 2002, www.smithsonianmag.com/history/ping-pong-diplomacy-60307544

238 Burgess, *The Clockwork Testament*, p. 79.

239 Burgess, *The Clockwork Testament*, p. 77.

240 Anthony Burgess, 'Contemporary Authors: The Works of Anthony Burgess', Pennsylvania State University, 1982; Burgess, 'Stop the Clock on Violence', p. 251; Krämer, *A Clockwork Orange*, p. 118.

241 Burgess, 'Letter from Europe' (Summer 1971), pp. 517–518.

242 'I had expected, when I came to live a year in New Jersey, that my trips to New York would be very frequent. With all its faults, New York is the most visitable place, with a lot going on, and the people are warmer and more communicative than they are in New Jersey. But the journey in and out is tiring, and each evening tends to be spent at home, taking in America vicariously through the color television. Although color-blind, I like color' (Burgess, 'Letter from Europe' (Summer 1971), pp. 517–518).

243 Burgess, 'Letter from Europe' (Summer 1971), pp. 517–518.

244 Burgess, 'Letter from Europe' (Summer 1971), pp. 517–518.

245 Burgess, *The Clockwork Testament*, p. 111.

246 Bernard Bergonzi, *The Situation of the Novel* (London: Pelican Books, 1972), p. 210.

247 Burgess, *The Clockwork Testament*, pp. 29, 39.

248 Anthony Burgess, 'The Purpose of Education', *The Spectator*, 3 March 1967; Burgess, *The Clockwork Testament*, p. 30.

249 Burgess, *The Clockwork Testament*, p. 29.

250 Jack Hill, *Coffy* (American International Pictures, 1973); Jack Hill, *Foxy Brown* (American International Pictures, 1974); Patricia Hill Collins, *Black Sexual Politics: African Americans, Gender, and the New Racism* (London: Routledge, 2004), p. 124; Burgess, *The Clockwork Testament*, pp. 21, 63; Biswell, *The Real Life of Anthony Burgess*, p. 351.

251 Paul Gilroy, *The Black Atlantic* (Cambridge, MA: Harvard University Press, 1993), p. 93.

252 'Ten O'Clock News; Anthony Burgess'. 1983-04-12. WGBH, American Archive of Public Broadcasting (GBH and the Library of Congress), Boston, MA and Washington, DC, http://americanarchive.org/catalog/cpb-aacip-15-mg7fq9qg1t

253 Anthony Burgess, 'Anthony Burgess Lecture: "The Writer's Daily Damnation" ', Sarah Lawrence College: Sarah Lawrence College Archives (19 January 1971), p. 26; Anthony Burgess, '*More Die of Heartbreak* by Saul Bellow, Secker and Warburg Price?', University of Texas at Austin: Harry Ransom Center Archives, Gabriele Pantucci Collection, container 7.

254 Allan Bloom, *The Closing of the American Mind* (New York: Simon and Schuster, 1987), p. 65.

255 Andrew Biswell, 'Anthony Burgess and Politics', The International Anthony Burgess Foundation, 23 May 2022, www.anthonyburgess.org/blog-posts/anthony-burgess-and-politics/?fbclid=IwAR1Ua0hB-TvQUAV-MW4POGzwxetnIt7-swzCol7rmHtVYdb6-5Jgn7fsMJI

256 Burgess, *The Great Cities – New York*, p. 35; Burgess, 'Guest Observer: Dirty Words'.

257 Burgess, 'Guest Observer: Dirty Words', p. 5.

258 'Profanity, according to the FCC, includes language that "denotes certain of those personally reviling epithetic naturally tending to provoke resentment or denoting language so grossly offensive to members of the public who actually

hear it as to amount to a nuisance'" (quoted in Jabari Asim, *The N Word* (New York: Houghton Mifflin Company, 2007), p. 175).

259 Asim, *The N Word*, p. 4.

260 Martin Goldman, *The Legend of Nigger Charley* (Paramount Pictures, 1972); Jack Arnold, *Boss Nigger* (3P Productions, 1974).

261 Michael Holquist, *Dialogism: Bakhtin and His World* (London: Routledge, 1990), pp. 43–49; Stanley Fish, *There's No Such Thing as Free Speech: And It's a Good Thing Too* (New York: Oxford University Press, 1994), p. viii.

262 'New York, Time-Life Contract', 24 June 1975, International Anthony Burgess Foundation Archives (uncatalogued).

263 Burgess, *The Great Cities – New York*, p. 36.

264 Frantz Fanon, *Black Skin, White Masks* (London: Editions de Seuil; Pluto Press, 2008), p. 150.

265 Burgess, *The Great Cities – New York*, p. 44.

266 Burgess, *The Great Cities – New York*, p. 44; Burgess, *They Wrote in English*, p. 17.

267 Burgess, *The Great Cities – New York*, p. 44.

268 Burgess, *The Great Cities – New York*, p. 44; James Baldwin, 'A Talk to Teachers', *James Baldwin: Collected Essays*, ed. by Toni Morrison (New York: The Library of America, 1998), p. 684.

269 Biswell, *The Real Life of Anthony Burgess*, p. 221; Burgess, *The Great Cities – New York*, p. 44.

270 Burgess, *The Great Cities – New York*, p. 44; Burgess, *The Clockwork Testament*, p. 59.

271 Anthony Burgess, *The Malayan Trilogy* (London: Vintage Books, 2000), p. 452.

272 Richard Delgado and Jean Stefancic, *Critical Race Theory: An Introduction* (New York: New York University Press, 2001), p. 22.

273 Burgess, *The Great Cities – New York*, pp. 44, 49; Philip Dray, *At the Hands of Persons Unknown: The Lynching of Black America* (Ann Arbor, MI: University of Michigan Press, 2002); Ibram X. Kendi, *Stamped from the Beginning: The Definitive History of Racist Ideas in America* (New York: PublicAffairs, 2017); Isabel Wilkerson, *The Warmth of Other Suns* (New York: Random House, 2011); Isabel Wilkerson, *Caste: The Origins of Our Discontents* (New York: Random House, 2020).

274 Burgess, *The Clockwork Testament*, p. 20.

275 Burgess, 'Guest Observer: Dirty Words'; Bakhtin, *The Dialogic Imagination*, p. 294; Burgess, *The Clockwork Testament*, pp. 58–59.

276 Anthony Burgess, *A Mouthful of Air: Language, Languages ... Especially English* (New York: William Morrow and Company, 1992), p. 285.

277 Burgess, *They Wrote in English*, p. 33.

278 Burgess, *The Clockwork Testament*, p. 59.

279 Burgess, *The Clockwork Testament*, pp. 59–60.

280 Biswell, *The Real Life of Anthony Burgess*, p. 50.

281 Anthony Burgess, 'Why Were the Revolutionaries Reactionary?', *One Man's Chorus*, pp. 236–237.

282 Burgess, 'Why Were the Revolutionaries Reactionary?', p. 237.
283 Anthony Burgess, Lecture at Tufts University, 4 March 1975.
284 Burgess, Lecture at Tufts University, 4 March 1975.
285 Bakhtin, *Problems of Dostoyevsky's Poetics*, p. 79; Burgess, *The Clockwork Testament*, p. 60.
286 Burgess, *The Clockwork Testament*, p. 60.
287 Burgess, *The Clockwork Testament*, p. 61.
288 Burgess, *The Clockwork Testament*, p. 60.
289 Henry Louis Gate Jr, *Thirteen Ways of Looking at a Black Man* (New York: Vintage Books, 1997), p. xvi; Burgess, *The Clockwork Testament*, p. 48.
290 Bakhtin, *Problems of Dostoyevsky's Poetics*, p. 83.
291 Burgess, *The Clockwork Testament*, p. 63.
292 Saunders, *Self Impression*, p. 5.
293 George Shea, 'To the Editor: Anthony Burgess at Fordham', *Times Literary Supplement*.
294 Shea, 'To the Editor'.
295 Anthony Burgess, 'Viewpoint', *Times Literary Supplement*, 22 June 1973, p. 718.
296 Leo Hamalian, 'Anthony Burgess at Fordham: To the Editor', *Times Literary Supplement*, n.d., Burgess, 'Viewpoint', p. 718.
297 Burgess, *The Clockwork Testament*, p. 99.
298 Burgess, *The Clockwork Testament*, p. 125.

5

Earthly Powers (1980)

> Writing is excruciatingly hard, and the more you write the harder it gets. Yeats' words – 'The fascination of what's difficult'– are pertinent to my kind of novelist. Masochism comes into it too. Also, and this is hard to articulate, there is a profound personal need to say something – not directly, like a Mafioso or politician (I see now those examples are ill-chosen) but deviously, laterally, wrapping the message in so many layers of paper art that, with luck, the reader may fail to get the message and take in only the art. (Anthony Burgess, 'Why I Wrote *Earthly Powers*: The Genesis of *Earthly Powers*')[1]

Introduction

Although both *Earthly Powers* (1980) and *The End of the World News* (1982) are littered with references to the United States, the discussions to tackle these references are generally only echoes of previously discussed ideas and biographical material that Burgess infused into his fiction. These two novels are far less blatantly autobiographical, or autobiograficational, and exhibit a more dialogized and heteroglottal fiction and authorial act. In the case of *Earthly Powers*, Burgess's longest novel and considered by many to be his masterpiece, there exists a wide-ranging narrative provided by the novel's protagonist, Kenneth Toomey, a gay author – a term Burgess bemoans as being 'appropriated' by 'sodomites' – which takes place over half a century and throughout more than ten countries, and although the novel does have its flaws, it is a much more *achieved* work in the sense that Burgess presents characters who more closely meet Bakhtin's standards of a polygottal, heteroglossic, and dialogized artistic achievement which is evidenced in the characters being more self-contained and therefore more autonomous, thus creating a larger distance between them and the author.[2] *The End of the World News* does something similar in resurrecting historical figures, as was a common practice for Burgess in the last two decades of his life, with only his science fiction *Puma* narrative as an aberration, though as a piece of pure fiction this story is more dialogized from the works discussed previously. Although particularly *American* in theme and setting, the narrative is not riddled with examples of biographical authorial intervention which are meant to act as the concealed voice of the author.

Be that as it may, the two shorter chapters dedicated to these novels will explore the more limited American influences on the texts and how those influences can be recognized as examples of Burgess's American authorial heteroglossia, this time only with glimmers of autobiografictional elements and slight monoglossia. Because these two works present repeated American-themed biographical content, much of what will be discussed is understanding the novels through a historical and authorial context that has been firmly established throughout the previous chapters, and which will be more drawn out in Chapter 7 on *Enderby's Dark Lady, or No End to Enderby* (1984). In the Bakhtinian sense, what this chapter does is carry forth the argument that Burgess has particularly American texts within his canon that exhibit 'language already permeated with many voices' from his past novels and public expostulations in the form of collateral language, themes, context, and ideas.[3] It may even be that *Earthly Powers* is the supremely heteroglossic novel of Burgess's career, a kind of culmination or crucible of Burgess's artistic life up until 1980, all baked into a novel where every line tells, alludes, and reflects, so that the details of the story all carry with them added inter-, intra-, and extratextual meaning/s, singularly and literarily for Toomey to the non-Burgess scholar, and historically and biographically for a reader critically aware of Burgess's life and canon.

Earthly Powers is a prime example of how Burgess's literature is essentially also a rumination on his real life, despite how many times Burgess claimed it was all fiction or how many times Burgess scholars have tiptoed around finding parallels between Kenneth Toomey and Burgess. Andrew Biswell, Anthony Burgess's biographer and head of the International Anthony Burgess Foundation, explained this irony by drawing a comparison between Burgess and Kenneth Toomey, the novel's protagonist, stating that in *Earthly Powers*, 'Kenneth Toomey's fictional autobiography, Burgess, much like Toomey ... casts himself as the unreliable narrator of his own life's story' as he soliloquys about 'confabulations' and how 'all memories are disordered. The truth, if not mathematical, is what we think we remember'.[4] Biswell additionally points out the fact that 'at the beginning of *Little Wilson and Big God* [Burgess explains] that it is a book about memory, and that he has not checked any facts apart from the spelling of Malay words'.[5] Unfortunately, or fortunately depending on one's view of the veracity of this type of approach, this Old Historicist lens can be aptly applied to Burgess's life and works despite such protestations that 'no serious critic of *Earthly Powers* would wish to appear naïve enough to equate the two', and will therefore be utilized when applicable, because unlike some other authors, Burgess's life lends a lot of context to his fiction, and even protestations concede in the end that the author and narrator of *Earthly Powers*, as well as Enderby in New York, all stand for the '"cultural conservatism" reminiscent in its spirit of the crusade' that supported the type of 'cultural elitism' evident in Burgess and Toomey alike, ultimately resulting in a 'libertarian economic philosophy' of both author and character.[6] There is no illogic in this approach because Burgess was a highly autobiographical author, and since there is no avoiding this, it is important to understand the connections between his life and his fiction. In novels like *The Doctor Is Sick*, where Burgess presents a character, Edwin Spindrift, 'who is mad about words and language', Burgess's readers and biographers can see that this character is likely in fact 'a kind of self-caricature, and that Burgess was well aware of the dangers of putting language and literature before life' a problem the character must grapple with.[7] After publishing *The Worm and the Ring* (1961), Burgess was sued for libel due to the representation of real people in a novel where the characters taught at a school closely resembling the Banbury Grammar School Burgess taught at in the 1950s. *The Malayan Trilogy* (1956–59) abounds in real-life inspirations for the fictional plots and characters. *The Right to An Answer* (1960), *Honey for the Bears* (1963), *A Vision of Battlements* (1965), *Beard's Roman Women* (1976), and *The Pianoplayers* (1986) all have tremendous amounts of biographical information spliced into the texts as literary material moulded to a fictional construction.[8] During his American years, who Burgess *was* is important for understanding his literature because he even more frequently used his real-life experiences to help fuel his literary output; to ignore this aspect would not only be disingenuous to Burgess research but would also deprive his writings of contextuality and depth.

Scope, background, and *Earthly Powers* as autobiography

Burgess's longest and most achieved authorial vision rests within the over 600 pages of *Earthly Powers*, a novel so dense and packed with allusions that it begs for a book-length investigation of its own. But since the other novels addressed in this monograph better display the sustained formation of Burgess's *American* turn in literature, *Earthly Powers* will be assessed briefly and concisely through a selective reading which foregrounds the figure of Ralph in order to assess questions of race in an American context, which, though still significant, includes less autobiograficational elements among the lingering authorial monoglossia that is infused with Burgess's American heteroglot.[9]

Having begun writing the novel in 1970, and with the climax hinging upon an American cult leader, *Earthly Powers* has several pronounced American influences.[10] Again, too, with the focus on the homosexual character, Kenneth Toomey, a world-renowned author who at one point has an African American lover, and who also travels to the United States, such circumstances allow the text to navigate literary and biographical terrain, as William Empson details in *7 Types of Ambiguity* (1966), where 'the word means one relation or one process … an intention to mean several things, a probability that one or other or both of two things has been meant, and the fact that a statement has several meanings', a tactic, as has been one of the main purposes of this monograph, which Burgess deployed in basically every novel of his, though most glaringly concerning the topic of the United States in the novels discussed in this analysis.[11] Adding to this American side of the text is also the fact that the novel makes dozens of references to American authors, American works of literature, American cities and citizens, and takes place in the United States for a significant amount of time. What these aspects of the novel reveal is still a heavily American-inspired text, though cursorily, and not one whose infrastructure is solely supported by some American theme. The exception to this statement, though, is with the White integrationist Godfrey Manning, the American cult leader who is perhaps evil incarnate, modelled after Jim Jones of the People's Temple – 'There is a massacre on the lines of the recent James Jones affair. The girl dies with hundreds of others' – who is born and raised in the fictional town of Pring, Indiana, and who perhaps exists as a symbol of the dangers of Americanism and the United States, 'the home of the cult of personality', a criticism that is indeed brought to the text through authorial double-voicing, despite being on the whole a more dialogic and cosmopolitan literary display, largely inhabited by far more fully formed and independent characters compared to the final two Enderby novels.[12]

Unlike *The Clockwork Testament, or Enderby's End* (1974) and *Enderby's Dark Lady, or No End to Enderby* (1984), Toomey, and most of the cast of characters in the novel, reach, or are close to reaching, what Bakhtin called a 'plurality of consciousness', resulting in these characters not being the 'voiceless slaves' that appear in the last two Enderby novels but '*free* people, capable of standing *alongside* their creator, capable of not agreeing with him and even rebelling against him'.[13] Since 'with every role we assume, whether voluntary or compulsory, our fictive personality is defined in the vocabulary of society', *Earthly Powers* cannot help but be steeped in the American cultural milieu that Burgess experienced throughout the 1960s and 1970s.[14] Similarly to the multi-voiced Burgessian cultural epitextual stratagem that assists in Burgess producing his own authorial myth through a cacophony of publicly voiced truths and semi-truths, Toomey relates to his audience that the tale which is about to be relayed, although autobiographical, cannot be trusted, since specifics from his life cannot 'be taken as a verbatim account of what happened' because he 'cannot remember' specific details and therefore must embellish – still, he maintains, 'the gist is true'.[15] In fact, it could be argued that Burgess's entire canon could fit under this indefinite truism, that 'the gist is true' of his fiction, non-fiction, journalism, lectures, interviews, and correspondence – all of his work has an air of truth and fiction, the hyperbolized and the honest, the accurate and the inaccurate. Readers should therefore embark upon *Earthly Powers* in the same way that they should embark on Burgess's autobiographies, with a suspension of disbelief, always remembering that regardless of 'if the author gives the hero traits that mirror nearly exactly traits that exist in the author, the hero is "consummated" in the language of the text, and once the author finishes writing the life of the hero, the author's life continues'.[16] This may not be entirely accurate, since the life of John Wilson has ended, but the life of his characters, Anthony Burgess as much as Kenneth Toomey, lives on in the texts which are evocative of, as Philippe LeJeune notes in *On Autobiography* (1989), 'that sign of reality which is the previous production *of other texts*' which must be recognized as existing within the 'indispensable ... autobiographical space' where the 'author is, then, the same name of a person, identical, taking upon himself a series of different published texts' who therefore 'draws his reality from the list of his other works'.[17] Under these terms, *Earthly Powers* is thus an autobiography, that of Toomey's creation, a loosely autobiographical novel, in the resemblances to Burgess's life, *and* an achieved heteroglottal and dialogic novel with characters who have complete personalities and yet very much live within the self-allusive universe of Burgess's writing, therefore making a Bakhtinian analysis of the text beneficial in the sense that such an approach, which works '"from the inside out"', helps to assess the 'difficulties of "active understanding"' in order to make room for the explicit 'conditions of possibility of that understanding and of past understandings of the text'.[18] Such a disposition opens the text up to a myriad of different interpretations, while also aligning those interpretations according to a particular stratum of ontological textual identification. As such, the second stratum, that of the loosely autobiographical novel, is the most revealing for this monograph, since investigating this exposes cracks in the narrative which reveal glimmers of Burgess's self-allusive and monologic qualities.

Toomey, Burgess, and the United States

Examples of Burgess's life seeping into *Earthly Powers* exist throughout the novel at varying levels of relation between Toomey and Burgess, setting and

Burgess, characters and Burgess, and plot and Burgess, though each instance where this arises also has more or less accuracy. The instances to be discussed here will be the most profound points at which Burgess, the author of the book, creeps into the narrative, displaying at times, though much less than in the past, monoglossia, hidden polemics, and double-voiced discourse. Like Toomey, whose 'diaries and notebooks [include] considerable lacunae', archives of Burgess's ephemera also exist and can inform scholarship of the epitextual contextual evidence that surrounds his life and work in a similar way that Toomey attempts to reconstruct his past, though in a much less speculative manner.[19]

It is well known that Burgess fashioned Toomey out of the author William Somerset Maugham, who was, according to Burgess, no stranger to producing autobiografiction, as he discussed in *On the Novel*, saying that 'Fiction need not be fictitious. The presentation of factual material as art is the purpose of such thinly disguised biographies as Somerset Maugham's *The Moon and Sixpence*.'[20] Other inspirations include Noël Coward, and of course Burgess himself, with Toomey often inhabiting 'the physical world of Burgess' despite vastly deviating from the author in many ways.[21] The record of Burgess's own life is therefore source material which can be used to assess the significance of Toomey's travels, and one of the most significant trajectories in the novel includes the United States. Noteworthy is a *Los Angeles Times* review of *Earthly Powers* that takes note of Burgess's autobiografictional elements by distinguishing between Burgess the public intellectual and Burgess the author:

> Burgess the essayist and Burgess the novelist too often seem at cross purposes with one another. Just as Burgess begins to develop the subsidiary characters – Toomey's sister Hortense, his brother Tom and the various lovers and friends – Burgess II pulls him away to less relevant pursuits. ... Though Burgess never has kept his essays and his fiction entirely separate, the books since *The Clockwork Orange* [sic] have shown an increasing tendency toward collaboration with himself ... often dazzling as fiction, sometimes equally impressive as lecture, but always verging on disintegration into isolated segments.[22]

This mix of public figure and comedic writer appears to have been a perfect fit for American audiences, and it seems it was inevitable that Burgess's satirical, provocative, and bawdy style would be appreciated in the United States and therefore signify the place his future success lay, something he could not help but recognize in the 1960s. Although there was certainly not unanimous praise for Burgess in the United States, it still appears that even in 1977 Burgess was more distraught by the criticism he received from England than from American reviewers, as he responded to a series of bad reviews about *Beard's Roman Women* in *Harper's Magazine* that he was exhausted about claims of autobiographical elements being in his fiction, arguing that readers should

> never automatically assume that a novel is autobiography. I am tired of being identified with my main character, as so often in the reviews of this new book, and I am often forced to rush into the correspondence columns and deny the identification, since silence might imply acceptance and conceivably have dangerous legal consequences, especially in England, where the laws of libel are very strict. Do please at least think it possible that the novelist may be capable of contriving his own characters and situations, however much they may appear to be God's.[23]

Perhaps these reviewers got this idea not directly from the highly autobiographical novel itself, but actually from Burgess, who had said just three months previously in the *Times Literary Supplement* that the 'novel [*Beard's Roman Women*] was written on commission. … I must have been lacking in inventiveness at the time, so I fell back more than ever I would normally on the facts of my own life'.[24] The novel too, he reveals, found its genesis due to a 'young Bostonian' requesting Burgess provide some writing to accompany the individual's 'very good photographs of Rome' – the relationship with David Robinson, the photographer, soured after the first publication, with Liana writing in 1977 that she had closed association with Bertha Klausner and David Robinson 'as far as her representation abroad of BEARD'S ROMAN WOMEN' since the contract apparently stated that 'when the novel is published without photographs David Robinson gets 40% of the novel written by Anthony Burgess? Are you serious, or is it some sort of joke?'.[25] This is further evidence that during the writing of and publication in 1980 of *Earthly Powers*, Burgess's authorial content and business negotiations were tightly wrapped up with the United States, as well as a persisting and growing attention to autobiografictional ingredients in his work.

As the novel opens, on Toomey's eighty-first birthday in 1971, there begins a request to Toomey by the Archbishop of Malta to dig into his past so as to recall his relationship with the now-deceased Carlo Campanati, known as Pope Gregory XVII, who is under consideration for canonization. By chapter 11, the reflection of Toomey's life begins in London, 1916, at the age of twenty-six, though the crux of the story being investigated for Campanati occurred in 'Chicago in the twenties'.[26] Campanati, it is learned, is also half-American, with his Italian father meeting their American mother during a business trip – Americans, of course, always having something to do with money-making ventures in Burgess's fiction.[27] Although seemingly connected through fate, the diametrically opposed *earthly power* on which the novel's plot hinges is the American Godfrey Manning, the former faith healer and tolerance priest and now cult leader who, it is revealed, is the same child that Campanati miraculously cured in a Chicago hospital at about six years old and who goes on to organize a mass suicide.[28] Such an ethically nuanced dilemma of a plot point, similar to Toomey saving the Nazi leader Heinrich Himmler from a gunshot, upends common binary definitions of *good* and *evil*, and appears to suggest that both the solution and the cause of some of the world's most pressing problems emanate from the United States.[29]

In many ways, *Earthly Powers*, albeit Burgess's greatest literary achievement, is a reservoir of previously used and discussed themes, ideas, and places by Burgess, though this time, as opposed to the Enderby novels, Burgess makes a much more concerted effort to produce more independent and dialogic characters than the monologic and stereotypical caricatures of *The Clockwork Testament* and *Enderby's Dark Lady*. Still, though, Burgess cannot help but trickle in, with slight interjections along the way that nod towards his personal opinions, or at least allude to topics he had discussed elsewhere in his public and professional life. There are many examples of this, but several significant ones include Toomey criticizing Hermann Hesse as being a 'much overrated German novelist of my acquaintance', where Burgess himself had described Hesse as a writer focused on ideas and morals rather than form and style, which is why he believed young readers were attracted to him: 'The studies of struggling youth presented by Hermann Hesse became, after his death in 1962, part of an American campus cult indicating the desire of the serious young to find literary symbols for their own growing problems.'[30] And the rest of *Earthly Powers* is filled with allusions to literary talents Burgess had written articles and monographs on, as well as mentioned publicly, including all, to only name a few, of the following prominent American figures in some capacity: Walt Whitman, Ernest Hemingway, Ezra Pound, Ralph Ellison, James Baldwin, and J.D. Salinger. Again, too, people from Burgess's own life appear, and in the American context perhaps the most important is the allusion to Ben Forkner, an acquaintance of Burgess since his time at the University of North Carolina at Chapel Hill in 1969, founder of the Anthony Burgess Centre at the University of Angers, and editor of *One Man's Chorus* (1998), who gets a cameo in *Earthly Powers* through 'Sindy was Cynthia, nee Forkner, a starlet from North Carolina and Domenico's third wife' – though why the male, Ben Forkner, is represented as a woman remains unclear to scholars and to Forkner himself.[31]

One of the most telling instances of Burgess sewing himself into *Earthly Powers* is when Burgess uses Toomey to voice almost verbatim opinions of Burgess's he had expressed publicly in lectures, articles, and interviews. Stating in 1966 that the 'novel derives its material from the human community, since it makes its plot of patterns out of human actions, and since every action carries the aura of an implied moral judgement, then the novelist trembles on the edge of a kind of commitment – though, in the best writers, it is of the most general kind', this turns into Toomey's contemplative remark that he cannot 'accept that a work of fiction should be either immoral or moral', since it 'should merely show the world as it is and have no moral bias', which means presenting in a novel 'the nature of the motives of human actions and perhaps learn something, too, of the motives behind the social forces which judge those actions and which, I take it, we call a system of morality'.[32] Two years after *Earthly Powers* was published, Burgess presented a lecture at the University of Pennsylvania where he argued that the 'job of the novelist, I think, is to impose a pattern on this flux of human experience – make it seem significant and interesting and perhaps teach the reader, if teach is the right word, that various aspects of life, which didn't seem to him to be connected before are now in fact connected'.[33] Finally, this 'isolated rhetorical polemic' that Burgess and Toomey both expressed manifests in a previously unpublished article in 1991, entitled 'Can Art Be Immoral?', where Burgess yet again echoed himself and his character by remarking that

> static pleasure ... moves down the continuum in the direction of either the didactic or the pornographic. ... Art is in the deepest sense ethical in the sense that it accepts the holiness of the human imagination. ... Art cannot be immoral. If it seems to be immoral, it is not art.[34]

It is not only people and topics which Burgess referred to in *Earthly Powers* as a form of double-voiced discourse but also the places Toomey visits and the language he encounters along the way, which refer, sometimes strictly, to experiences Burgess himself had. Toomey, like Burgess, comes either directly or indirectly into contact with a litany of institutions, states, and countries that the author himself engaged with, including quite early in the novel when Sarah Lawrence College is mentioned as the school where Mr Sciberras, the Maltese poet, says that he met Hortense in Bronxville while 'reading poems, some of them mine. ... She was at the little party afterwards', being a school that Burgess visited in order to present the lecture 'The Writer's Daily Damnation' on 19 January 1972.[35] Although *Earthly Powers* abounds in international travelling similarities between Toomey and Burgess, with Kuala Kangsar, Malaysia, Adelaide, Australia, Malta, Monte Carlo, and so on, several other instances in the United States where author and character coincide include trips to Colorado, New York City, Oklahoma, and California. Although all authors are called on to give lectures, talks, and attend events, in Burgess's case, the similarities between fictional author-character and author-author are too close to ignore being incorporated into the novel. At Colorado College on 17 March 1969, a lecture given by Burgess entitled 'The Novel in Our Culture' ended up focusing on pornography and didacticism in literature, with Toomey presenting a similar lecture in *Earthly Powers* entitled 'What Now in the Novel?' which is also an article Burgess republished in *Urgent Copy* (1968) and is also very similar in name to Burgess's non-fiction books, *The Novel To-Day* (1963), *The Novel Now* (1967), and *On the Novel* (1975).[36] Again, Toomey follows a very similar, if not identical, lecture trip to Burgess when he lectures at the University of Oklahoma 'on Monday' and then spends 'tomorrow night in New York'.[37] In 1969, while holding a writer-in-residence position at the University of North Carolina at Chapel Hill, Burgess also held a lecture series at the University of Oklahoma between 1 and 3 December 1969, before returning to campus for several days and then leaving the following weekend for New York City in order to speak at 92nd Street Y and Columbia University.[38] Other instances exist too, like chapter 71's reference to tour dates that include schools and cities Burgess visited, such as the 'town in Pennsylvania confusingly named California' which coincides with Burgess's scheduled lecture at California State College in California, Pennsylvania on 8 November 1972, or the mention of Toomey visiting San Francisco, a place where Burgess presented the lecture 'Wild World of the Modern Novel' at the City College of San Francisco on 20 March 1969, and finally Toomey's redolent encounter at the Marlborough Street Court, where instead of defending *Last Exit to Brooklyn* like Burgess, Toomey defends Radclyffe Hall's *The Well of Loneliness* (1928) against attacks of being categorized as pornography.[39] In the interests of avoiding enumerative prose about Burgess's movements, it's more important now to turn to why this novel utilizes these places, these characters, and these themes, which Burgess used elsewhere to present fiery condemnations of the United States, but here he presents in more relaxed terms.

The significance of the United States in *Earthly Powers*

Once the United States is introduced in the novel, the image of the country exists in the background but slowly and steadily rises like a celestial body to prominence, reaching the apex of American exceptionalism in the final pages with Manning's atrocity, only to quickly drop off and settle back down into the background where it, in Toomey's world, belongs. The United States of *Earthly Powers* is yet again a debased place, intellectually torpid, and lacking in morals and secular understanding, too prone to mythologize itself – again in cartoons: 'Her mythology's the Saturday morning TV show of kids' cartoons' – and to exhibit traits of anti-intellectualism.[40] While talking to Ann, Toomey's niece, he reflects on the generational and cultural divide between him and Ann's child, Eve, by voicing opinions expressed by Burgess, so that it could be conceived that readers are hearing Burgess through Toomey:

> What do they teach them these days? ... She started to read *The Catcher in the Rye* but couldn't get on with it, found it kind of hard going. It's difficult for someone of my generation, to converse about Superman and Donald Duck and Debbie Reynolds. God, you were brought up on French and Italian, but she knows no languages. They read twenty lines of Virgil at school in bad English prose. She saw a movie about Helen of Troy. The past is dead and the world outside the United States doesn't exist.[41]

This sounds like a line right out of *M/F*, or an article like 'The Purpose of Education' in which Burgess reprimand's younger generations and the democratization of education as producing a 'teenage God, finger-clicking to a pop-mass, worshipped in pop-lyrics; the travesty-art of The Beatles is elevated to the Beethovian; drug sessions will give you instant beatification'.[42] Toomey and Burgess lash out at the vacuous minds and stomachs of the American youth who cannot even handle the simplest and most moral literature there is to offer in *The Catcher in the Rye*, a novel, although included in his *99 Novels* (1984) for 1951, Burgess said, not necessarily complimentarily, was a 'book of great moral probity', and with digestion that cannot handle real food, like the Coca-Cola and hamburger college students of *M/F* and *The Clockwork Testament*:[43]

> 'Haven't you even taken her to Europe?'
>
> 'We went to France but the food made her sick.'
>
> 'I fear,' I said, prophetically, 'the great vacuum. You can fill it for a time with Walt Disney but some big wind is going to blow that fluff away. Stronger anodynes. She tells me that one of her instructors was on to drugs. He'd read a book by some guy, she said, I might know him, it turned out to be my old friend Aldous Huxley. All about visions and reality and you got the truth the easy way, like switching on the TV.'[44]

Eve, as her name suggests, is the new American woman of the second half of the twentieth century, and Toomey's experiences are evocative of a theme explored by Burgess and other writers of the period of 'the cultured Englishman in barbarous America', a situation Burgess could empathize with easily.[45] Borrowed from William Blake's *The Marriage of Heaven and Hell* (1793), Huxley's monograph on drug experimentation, *The Doors of Perception* (1954), would go on to supply Jim Morrison, an icon of drug culture and lead singer of The Doors, with his band's name in 1965, and Timothy Leary's counter-cultural motto of the era and of drug experimentation, 'Turn on. Tune in. Drop out'; Burgess refers to a cultural phenomenon in the United States which he disparaged on several occasions.[46] Only a year after the publication of *Earthly Powers*, Burgess presented a lecture in Washington, DC on the subject of 'Excellence' for the LTV Corporation, where he best contextualized and articulated how he saw the American counter-culture movement of the 1960s and 1970s, as well as the continued hangover from such cultural change. Burgess argued, as a kind of support or justification for Toomey here, that Americans held 'a philosophy which stands midway between Oriental essentialism and French existentialism', which demanded that *action* was 'not a necessary mode of proving ourselves that we take up hopelessly. Action does not necessarily lead to fascism, consumerism, pollution and the rest of the shibboleths of the so-called alternative society. Action is not drugs: only drugs', but to Americans, action, in and of itself, stood as a form of 'positive definition' that was 'dedicated to the maintenance and furtherance of civilization'.[47] The 'vacuum', or immoral and ignorant suck that both Burgess and Toomey see as the Americanization of the world, which resulted in a denigration of standards, was stronger than other counter-cultural currents, and this was why the United States after World War Two had somehow usurped the role of im/moral world leader, making the European sensibility only, as Toomey puts it, a 'matter of waiting for the Americans to move'.[48] The story of Toomey in *Earthly Powers* is also the tale of a European who is slowly aged out of the new world, a world subsumed and controlled by the United States but who finds in the Mediterranean – similarly to Miles at the end of *M/F* – a place to avoid the chaos of the rapidly changing world.

The destructive, impulsive, and uninformed actions of American youth, as has been previously explained, greatly bothered Burgess, especially since he felt that the country tended to too easily fall in step behind youth movements and ideas, instead of ignoring them and forcing them to appeal to higher standards. In *You've Had Your Time*, Burgess calls these students the 'American young, children of the new anarchy', whose actions he claims to have witnessed on campuses with a 'burnt-out college library', committed by, as stated previously, a 'candidate for a PhD in English literature' who was not allowed to study Hermann Hesse – in an earlier utterance of this same story in 'Believing in or Abominating the Past' for *The Minneapolis Star* in November 1972, Burgess says the student smashed windows.[49] An act of arson also arises in *Enderby's Dark Lady, or No End to Enderby* with 'a disaffected busboy or bellhop, mandatorily stoned [who] had filled a familysize Coca-Cola bottle with gasoline siphoned from the hotel manager's car, glugged this inflammable out in the empty thirdfloor bedroom two doors away from Enderby's own and then enflamed it' only to escape the incident with 'a cashbox containing something under a hundred dollars'.[50] This type of destructive futility is what Burgess abhorred about Americans, more specifically American youth. Speaking to students in the 1950s,

Toomey carries with him the same Burgessian dissuasion for the 1960s and 1970s American college students, as he reflects that in his memory of the 'five hundred students and faculty' in the audience, he tended 'to see the students in memory as jeaned and afroed, but this was the fifties and they were dressed as young ladies and gentlemen'.[51] The use of the aforementioned Coca-Cola bottle in *Enderby's Dark Lady*, family-sized meaning large, is likely used to signify the image of excess in American culture, a common trope of Burgess's – though he enjoyed the soft drink: 'against which let no man say a word' – to symbolize Americanization through a large corporate entity and as a foodstuff that is essentially void of nutrition, providing only sugar to American youth, and possibly one of the culprits for Eve's inability to eat actual cuisine.[52]

Sugar soda is also used as a more general metonym for American culture in Burgess's fiction, featuring American characters of his, like the African American Ralph Pembroke in *Earthly Powers* who, after being jumped by black-skinned Arabs in Tangier, desires to return home 'where the white liberals are real nice to n-----s so long as they don't claim their rights. Cokes and burgers and Jello'.[53] Meant to shock Ralph out of what Toomey calls Ralph's 'black militancy' that included the belief that African Americans had it worse than anyone else, Toomey reminds his partner that outside of the United States all anyone sees him as is an *American*, not a race, and therefore he lived in wealth and luxury.[54] Again, what Burgess's non-fiction and fiction focuses on is his perception of the ridiculousness and illogic of racism, not the racism that actually exists in American culture, especially not endemic, systemic, and historical racism.

Race and *Earthly Powers*

Ralph's entrance into the novel brings up the final and most significant American theme of the novel: race, a topic to be explored here and at more length in Chapter 7 on *Enderby's Dark Lady*. This subject must be analysed in two chapters because of the redundancies in Burgess's authorial acts, and to expose the authorial monoglossia that occurs when the topic of race, prejudice, and racism arises in his fiction, often out of important epitextual non-fiction and public appearances.

In an essay republished in *Urgent Copy* in 1968, Burgess commented that it was the American Jew and African American, namely J.D. Salinger and James Baldwin, who elicited a moral response from their readers, due to presenting scenarios where the 'success or failure of the innocent, the misfit, the minority to adjust to a complex, vital but ruthless urban society ... is simplified to sheer morality: there is a demand that sympathy be given to the desperate teenager or Negro or sexual invert'.[55] Burgess decisively, perhaps for this reason, made it a point to altogether avoid this supposed sentimentalism with African Americans in his fiction in order to instead call out what he believed were hypocritical and ahistorical protestations about their treatment and lineage. He did so not in the vein of White supremacists, intent on distorting facts or producing counter-narratives that assert white hegemony, but in order to express that he felt Black Americans needed to relax and understand that they themselves did not possess a 'monopoly of abuse', and therefore had to understand their situation in a more worldly context and forget about 'hating tyrants who don't exist any more', arguing that 'it would be unfair to direct one's enmity at either liberal Germans or (in the case of blacks) breast-beating Americans'.[56] This is problematic in many ways, especially how he presented Black characters and, Paul Gilroy's term in *The Black Atlantic* (1993), the 'Eurocentric rationalism' used to dismiss past transgressions against peoples of colour, but this also provides proof of Burgess's lack of 'astonishing humanity' in his literature, a term that Richard Wright claimed Carson McCullers had when writing characters of colour, characters with disabilities, and non-binary characters.[57] Rather, Burgess was an ideologue who conformed his world and the worlds of his characters into the shapes he discerned, patterning these worlds into his view of reality that was largely influenced and maintained by a former middle-class, ex-Mancunian lapsed-Catholic identity, all fuelled by a self-imposed outsider status. Although *Earthly Powers* breaks with some of Burgess's rote and contrived dialogue and plots that are aimed at proving his points, the demise of Ralph Pembroke in the novel is undoubtedly the most monologic pattern in the novel, with Ralph yearning for Africa, only to be beaten up by Africans and pushed back into the, it is suggested, 'civilized' Western society he owes his life to, in order to inevitably and ironically take up a prestigious 'Black Studies' professorship position at an Ivy League institution. The irony is of course satirical.

Despite this, Ralph, former lover of Kenneth Toomey, is one of Burgess's most versatile and complete Black characters – with Miles Faber, the protagonist of *M/F*, being the most completely individualized, though he is seemingly only Black to play out a contrived sub-narrative about race consciousness and myth – but the characterization still lends itself to the stock Anglo representation of Blackness in that Ralph exists in *Earthly Powers*, as Toni Morrison explains in *Playing in the Dark* (1992), in no capacity or 'no sense that matters' except to introduce matters of ethnic division existing throughout the twentieth century and for Burgess to voice more of his opinions about the Black Power Movements of the 1960s and 1970s through Toomey upon Ralph as a sounding board.[58] Ralph exists in the text as a gay lover of Toomey's in order to utilize Burgess's motif of interracial relationships and as an example of what he argued on multiple occasions was a misdirected Black identity movement in the United States. Burgess showcases what he saw as the futility of such a movement by placing Ralph in Tangier, northern Africa, where he is robbed by a group of Black people, and Toomey comforts him only with this: 'A rich American, Ralph, that's all you are to them', to dampen his dreams of Pan-Africanism.[59] Economics and nationality appear to be the international reigning signifiers of importance according to Toomey, and, indeed, Burgess. The plot point seems to be an attempt to expose the hypocrisy behind the Pan-African Movement that ignores the immense diversity of Africa and separation of time between the peoples enslaved and those who remained in Africa. Indeed, these are actual truthful realities, in which an idea like Pan-Africanism ignores the 'divisions in the imagined community of the race and the means to comprehend or overcome them', but recognizing this does not change the fact that Ralph's presence in *Earthly Powers* is not that of a human per se but as a simulacrum, a symbol, an allusion that works as a 'decorative display' signalling 'the facile writer's technical expertise' that is about nothing other 'than the "normal," unracialized, illusory, white world that provides the backdrop for the work'.[60] Ralph, Lloyd Utterage in *The Clockwork Testament, or Enderby's End*, and April in *Enderby's Dark Lady, or No End to Enderby* – who is quite literally a character that is demarcated as being owned by another character, Enderby, in the title of the book and as being Shakespeare's Dark Lady – all stand in as stock stereotypes and motifs with prescribed qualities that fit the image of the stereotypical Black character – though the stereotypes are not all the same – fulfilling what Morrison equates to 'blackface' qualities 'meant to render permissible topics that would otherwise have been taboo' in order 'to employ an imagined Africanistic persona to articulate and imaginatively act out the forbidden in American culture'.[61] Ralph and Lloyd especially are characters who do not move the novels' plots forward, while April, though more essential, just acts more or less as yet another sounding board for Burgess's other characters, largely Enderby, and is an actress, both literally and figuratively, who is only capable of reciting lines; if anything significant, these characters only provide empty conflict which is meant as a catalyst that allows Toomey or Enderby to act upon them or respond to them in ways that reveal more about the protagonists' own personal character – or the motives of the author – than anything concerning their Black counterparts.

In one instance, Ralph argues that 'Educated black speech is probably the finest sound of all North America', to which Toomey replies, Enderbianly, 'No, dearest Ralph, no and again no. If you want to write a pamphlet, of a severely polemical nature, do so. Tell the world of the sufferings of the American Negro, but don't try to turn it into art. Because you can't do it, you know.'[62] In this scene, the reader learns more about Toomey's aesthetic aims – and for anyone aware of Burgess's public opinions, that Toomey is simultaneously amplifying his own author's points – more than anything about Ralph. Ralph's argument, a subjective bait for the overly opinionated Toomey, is simply meant to lure out Toomey's convictions and allow Burgess to again develop a riposte to such claims as they relate to African American literature, language, and culture. Again, Ralph's rants act as ridiculous, emotion-filled expostulations only to be rejected and derisively sneered at by Toomey, a man of the world, of higher proclivities than politics and race issues, the achieved White author: '"Ralph," I said tiredly, "I refuse to take the blame for the wrongs perpetrated by a few Anglosaxon slaveowners. The men you should blame are resting at peace in expensive graves"'.[63] Ralph responds to the patronizing comment with the same vigour and anger as Lloyd Utterage in *The Clockwork Testament* as an act of again fulfilling the role of the angry Black man hell-bent on achieving revenge from the White man: 'You bastard white fucker. The sight of your white skin makes me want to fucking throw up. ... Fucking English. You even robbed us of our own fucking language. I'll answer the letter when I feel like doing it, you ofay pig ... you effete decadent etiolated moribund sonofabitching white bastard' – *ofay* being an African American pejorative slang word used to signify a White person.[64] Despite Ralph's erudite and esoteric lexicon, there is still little depth or diversity to Burgess's Black characters as they are set against a backdrop of a hierarchical White lattice assembled out of White perceptions, White aesthetic boundaries, and Anglo and Anglo-Saxon Eurocentric White historiographies. Ralph is in way over his head by design and made into a caricature of the radical and angry 1960s and 1970s Black American, the type Burgess no doubt witnessed in his time in the United States or perceived in a gay, Black author-intellectual like James Baldwin, but was by no means a majority, although in Burgess's fiction this is all that is ever presented, aside from maybe Dorothy Alethea Pembroke (Dotty), Hortense's lover and Toomey's friend: '"A black lady. She used to be a nightclub singer. A very handsome black lady"' who '"went to City College. She had a fancy for French, God knows why. Now she reads Flaubert and Anatole France. A very skeptical black lady"'.[65] Further on, and upon running into the quondam Archbishop of York, who looks like the composer Frederick Delius and who is blind, not even knowing he speaks to a Black man, he responds to some of Ralph's generational anger with an assimilatory dismissal that sounds Burgessian, asking the Black character to relent and give up any attempts to define his own culture because it is gone, subsumed and melted into the fabric of White American and European fabrics: 'You can't do it, you know', the old man says about Ralph's desire to get away from White people:

> You've absorbed too much from them. You might become Moslem, of course, but that would, in your view, only be exchanging one exotic abomination for another. Whatever you do, my boy, don't yearn after some longburied juju. And never feel bitter about slavery. All races have at one time or another been enslaved by another race. Slavery is a mode of cultural transmission.[66]

As with so many depictions of Black people in literature by the authorial hand of White authors, this dialogue and interaction are not for the eyes of the Black reader; rather, this is, as Toni Morrison notes in her seminal study of Blackness as presented through White literary imaginations, an example of the 'subject of the dream' being 'the dreamer'.[67] These interlocutors, discussing the matters of Black assimilation into White culture, are through an act of monoglossic hidden polemic Burgess's pleas, the author's arguments squeaking through into his characters, since Burgess himself believed that Blackness, especially African American Blackness, had been absorbed into American culture and could not, should not, attempt to identify itself outside of the larger national milieu, believing that the rise in 'Black studies' meant, as Allan Bloom did in his popular *The Closing of the American Mind* (1987), of which Burgess owned a copy, that this was just a type of 'new segregationism that would allow the white impresarios to escape from the corner they had painted themselves into'.[68] To be *American*, Burgess assumed, meant that any connection to previous lives, countries, cultures, and so on had to be let go of, and the United States, that all-encompassing and expansive monolithic cultural, national identity, had to take over as the leading point of social identification.[69]

Committing the cardinal authorial sin of commodifying characterization and conforming characters to the biased wills of the author – as opposed to simply letting the character exist as an autonomous personality – Toomey, the text, and the author attempt to rid Ralph of his beliefs, not because of any aesthetic aim or to accurately present the verisimilitude of real-life discourse about race relations, but they all appear to do so in an attempt to again endorse Burgess's vision of the 'big miscegenation', or the ultimate mixing of all ethnicities and cultures which he believed was inevitable.[70] The mixing of ethnicities did not bother Burgess in the least, but as evidenced in *Earthly Powers* and his public discussions, he could not let go of what he argued were the inaccuracies adopted by the Black empowerment movements of the 1970s: 'All I'm suggesting is that one ought to look a little more seriously at what is meant by negritude' – a French movement started in the 1930s in which displaced African French authors protested France's colonial rule, a movement which was adopted by Harlem Renaissance African American authors – 'and to consider that the particular kind of negritude that black Americans represent may not be representative of the whole of Africa but only a very small, rather unusual segment of Africa.'[71]

He elaborates on this further in his article 'Pioneer', about Ronald Firbank, in which he calls Firbank's American title to his novel *Sorrow in Sunlight*, *The Prancing Nigger*, 'gross', arguing further that the novel made 'black things chic' and that it was 'no exaggeration to state that the Paris adoration of all things negro – with Josephine Baker as a black goddess – that flourished in the 1920s owed a good deal to Firbank' and that the 'cult of *negritude* had nothing to do with the explosion of "black power"' because:

> Blackness was a kind of *décor*, jazz was a new and piquant form of elegance in which, as in the paintings of the Douanier Rousseau, the jungle was tamed and considered rather charming. To see Josephine Baker's lithe body gyrating was not to savour the rank meat of tribalism: the Parisians received their Africa through the alembic of Dior and the *Shocking* of Schiaparelli. Behind the exotic thrills lay the over-civilised *frissons* of Firbank.[72]

In the previous article, before stating that Englishmen 'have had a lot to do with Africa, far more than America has', Burgess goes on to argue that 'this black-oppression business gets in the way of other modes of oppression' and therefore distorts and drives 'out of our sights the long history of oppression against the Jews, and also the oppression of various forms of white man'.[73] He states this before, as he did on multiple occasions, equating his ancestry with the oppression of Jews and Africans, explaining that

> I feel that I myself, as a northern English Catholic, have been oppressed for many centuries. My ancestors were threatened with actual state execution for refusing to become Protestant, and after that, they were unable to become members of the total national culture because of education and job discrimination that still goes on.[74]

While reviewing *Uncle Tom's Cabin* by Harriet Beecher Stowe, Burgess made a similar claim, apparently disturbed by the attention the mistreatment of African Americans had received in popular media and that an emphasis in the United States on Black slavery had made 'Negro servitude in the South seem not only the type of all slavery but the only one we ought to feel guilty about. We can forget what happened to the Jews, or what is still going on under Islam'.[75]

In the first and second decades of the twenty-first century, many of these comments would force an author into the realm of a social pariah and, likely, a voice for what could be considered the *alt-right*, but it is crucial here to remember *when* Burgess was making these comments. In the 1970s, a tumultuous and tense time for race relations coming off the heels of the Civil Rights Movement, Americans were, as they continue to be, struggling to grapple with their country's history of chattel slavery, Jim Crow laws, failed reconstruction, and the Great Migration, all social phenomena which were countered with institutionalized and systemic racism that came in the form of unethical race-centric incarceration, housing practices, voting intimidation, policing practices, and unofficial segregation in communities and schools, among many other examples, resulting in large-scale disenfranchisement that continues in varying capacities into the 2020s.[76] White people largely continued to attempt to rationalize and make sense of such attacks on human rights through historical precedence and juxtaposition, using the Holocaust or African complicity in slavery – with Burgess saying in his 1974 *Playboy* interview that the 'white was responsible for slavery, but between the white man and the slave was the black slave trader, the tribal chief who was black and who has as many bad qualities in him as the white man' – as facile arguments to apparently quell guilt and, though intellectually dishonest, assert power over the supposedly historically contextualized narrative.[77]

Historians have largely discredited many of these assertions, though, in one popular instance with Howard Zinn explaining that the slavery which occurred in Africa before the implementation of the Middle Passage 'is hardly to be praised' as the greater evil since it was 'far different from plantation or mining slavery in the Americas, which was lifelong, morally crippling, destructive of family ties, without hope of any future'.[78] The slavery that had occurred in African countries before Western White people got involved 'lacked two elements that made American slavery the cruelest form of slavery in history: the frenzy for limitless profit that comes from capitalistic agriculture; the reduction of the slave to less than human status by the use of racial hatred', which became manifest in the 'relentless clarity based on color, where white was master, black was slave'.[79] More recently, Roxanne Dunbar-Ortiz's *Loaded: A Disarming History of the Second Amendment* (2018) states that although the brutality of the United States's North American colonization was not necessarily 'exceptional' when compared to other countries' violence that was 'imposed to achieve sovereignty', what was different, and which extended to chattel slavery, was 'rather the historical narratives attached to that violence and their political uses, even today' – narratives that, it must be noted, were nearly impossible to penetrate in the latter half of the twentieth century.[80]

It is surprising that Burgess was not aware of these realities, or did not *intersect* with these facts, having read so widely, but it appears that the period's own struggles with ascertaining truth, and Burgess's own history, his own personal myth, somewhat influenced by Burgess's Irish–British lineage – a group of people in the nineteenth century who were often blamed for the 'painful problems of the new urban industrial age' and summarily 'othered' as 'the foil against which the English and later the British had defined themselves' – trumped emerging historical and social narratives and shifting paradigms of thought.[81] Often fond of writers like Ralph Ellison and James Baldwin, Burgess still could not reconcile his own ancestral struggles with the struggles of African Americans. However, in 1969, he voiced his opinion that progress had to be made between different races because 'social progress depends on our understanding the past; because new ideas don't sprout *in vacuo* but spring from the study, and sometimes rejection, of old ones; because there is such a thing as aesthetic pleasure obtainable from even very ancient books'.[82] Still, though, Burgess then used this point to selectively and subjectively decide what texts, ideas, and histories were worthy of such retrospective study, and those that were not – namely African American histories – both here and in his general summaries of literature such as in *They Wrote in English* (1989), which will be discussed at more length in the next chapter.[83]

In a 2016 interview, Ben Forkner described some of these conflicts Burgess had with race through several instances he remembers sharing with Burgess. In France, where Forkner has lived for decades, and where Burgess visited him several times for lectures at the University of Angers and Nantes, Forkner remembers one occasion on which a Black scholar was talking with Burgess, and Burgess proposed a question to the scholar, asking, as Forkner remembers it, 'You know, I've had some trouble with: don't you think I should be able to call a black man a bastard? Because there are a lot of bastards among the blacks, just as there are a lot of bastards among the whites', to which the Black scholar replied, 'Certainly.'[84] This is a point Burgess expressed somewhat privately, but also in his 1967 'London Letter' in *The Hudson Review* that 'verbal releases are a fine thing' and that he called his 'Border collie a black bastard, which I do frequently', but give him 'a white dog, and I'll gladly call him a white bastard' and his 'grey cat ... a loud-mouthed grey sod', so therefore he believed that 'our coloured immigrants have reached a phase of confidence which would not be offended by insulting references to their ethnic differentiators'; though meant humorously, this is a somewhat shocking display of callousness and false equivalency.[85] As usual with Burgess, it was the restriction of language that bothered him more than the nuances of the historical content of the discussion, and he predominantly refused to regulate his diction around issues of race – taking only two dozen pages of *Earthly Powers* to use both 'black bastard' and 'black bitch', familiar territory in the Burgess canon, all the way back to *Time for a Tiger*, where Rivers says that '"They're all the same .... N-----s. Black bastards'".[86] Although these instances may not necessarily be acts of double-voiced discourse, they do reveal a pattern of epitextual social heteroglossia that finds its way into the text from the lived life of Anthony Burgess, a life where such ideas, terms, concepts, and thinking were displayed, used, and applied routinely, and where the authorial Burgess, not unlike practically every White writer to some extent of the period, developed these topics into dialogic banter to be used between fictional characters, which ultimately connects and overlaps with the overall historical authorial utterance, therefore urging such an analysis.

And perhaps most disturbingly of all, because of all this, it could be argued that the Ralph, Rukwa, John, and Laura track of *Earthly Powers* is a rather aggressive monoglot plot device used to establish what Burgess saw as the difference between African Americans and Africans, as well as the potential dangers of Black movements making a motto of 'slay the white bastard', with Dawson Wignall proclaiming that 'Ralph Pembroke should have shut up' with his radical opinions which caused Wignall to warn Toomey to 'get your delightful and talented sister out of an America full of very aggressive blacks'.[87] The deaths of Laura and John at the hands of the (as Toomey says, while also condemning ' "filthy Ralph" ') ' "filthy fucking Africans, cut the white man's balls off", who have taken the Eucharist too seriously – describing in his proposal for the novel, initially entitled *Eagles in My Life*, *The Creators*, or *The Prince of the Powers of the Air*, that

> John died as a result of the 'Africanisation' of the Christian rite, together with the use of a dialectical liturgy, which had the effect of convincing the African parishioners, easily persuaded to the belief by the Mau Mau, that it was a good thing to crucify the pastor of the Christian flock, since this was what happened to Christ. The blessing in the sacrifice of the bread and wine is converted, in the local dialect, to an injunction to eat physical flesh and blood. John's horrible death is directly caused by the vernacularization decreed in the Second Vatican Council.[88]

This not only beckons back to the cannibalistic *The Wanting Seed*, and indeed colonial literature describing indigenous populations as *savages* and *brutes*, but is ultimately a point of failure in the *Earthly Powers* narrative that reveals Burgess's inability to let well enough alone, and to grant the characters and plots the freedom to take on a life outside of his own convictions, which is, as Bakhtin has noted, the supreme power of Dostoevsky and the sign of achieved fiction. Although Burgess's exploration of these matters here may reflect some sort of reality, and though these characters and their dialogue is 'entangled, shot through with shared thoughts, points of view', what it all lacks are 'alien value judgements and accents' that point in different directions away from the monologism of the author and his 'specific conceptual horizon'.[89] Instead, a faceless, valueless, indeterminate mob of Africans descend on the more actualized White people; there is no dialogue, no equal play – this plot point is decidedly one-sided in its display of authorial monologic.

Conclusion

Despite all of these often problematic remarks, it still should be remembered that Burgess was quite progressive and tolerant in his views for the time – his positive representations of non-heterosexual characters in novels like *Honey for the Bears* (1963), *Nothing Like the Sun* (1964), *Earthly Powers* (1980), *The Pianoplayers* (1986), and *Dead Man in Deptford* (1993) during periods when discriminatory laws were bountiful and his attempted dialogic representation of Malays (even going so far as to learn their language) during the end of British colonial rule must be acknowledged, and his wide reading and general interest in at least attempting to understand the lives of other peoples should force any honest scholar to take these aspects into consideration and see that Burgess saw his writing as a way of learning, so that 'Possibly by writing a lot you can learn to understand [things] better.'[90]

Since he was an inescapably definite product of the early twentieth century, though, this still doesn't negate the fact that *Earthly Powers*, as achieved as the novel is, still has remnants of Burgess's particularly nasty monoglossia when it comes to race and chastising the United States. And the story itself, as discussed in the introduction to this chapter, also exists as a kind of fabricated homage to Burgess's own life that is wrapped up in an authorial heteroglossic display of dialogic strewn out over decades of a fictional twentieth-century literary author. In this sense, there is no denying the America*ness* of the text and its inspirations, whether in addressing the counter culture, race, and/or the modernization/Americanization of the world, since *Earthly Powers* runs off the fuel of American intervention, a novelistic vision which would have lacked, were it not for Burgess's years in the United States, a complete and complex view of Toomey's twentieth century without it.

Notes

1 Anthony Burgess, 'Why I Wrote *Earthly Powers*: The Genesis of *Earthly Powers*', *Washington Post Book World*, 23 November 1980, p. 1.

2 Anthony Burgess, 'Artist's Life', *One Man's Chorus: The Uncollected Writings of Anthony Burgess*, ed. by Ben Forkner (New York: Carroll & Graf, 1998), p. 209; Graham Foster, 'Earthly Powers at 40', International Anthony Burgess Foundation, 20 April 2020, www.anthonyburgess.org/earthly-powers-40/earthly-powers-at-40; Andrew Biswell, 'The Earthly Powers Bookshelf: St Nicholas', International Anthony Burgess Foundation, 11 December 2020, www.anthonyburgess.org/blog-posts/the-earthly-powers-bookshelf-st-nicholas

3 Wayne C. Booth, 'Introduction' to Mikhail Bakhtin, *Problems of Dostoyevsky's Poetics*, ed. by Caryl Emerson, Theory and History of Literature, volume 8 (Minneapolis, MN: University of Minnesota, 1984), p. xxi.
4 Andrew Biswell, 'Anthony Burgess Webchat – Biographer Andrew Biswell on His Sexuality, Best First Lines and More', *The Guardian*, 31 March 2017; Anthony Burgess, *Earthly Powers* (New York: Europa Editions, 1980; 2012), p. 645.
5 Biswell, 'Anthony Burgess Webchat', para. 11.
6 Ákos Farkas, *Will's Son and Jake's Peer: Anthony Burgess's Joycean Negotiations* (Budapest: Akadémiai Kiadó, 2002), pp. 125, 127.
7 Farkas, *Will's Son and Jake's Peer*, pp. 125, 127.
8 Biswell, 'Anthony Burgess Webchat'.
9 Saul Bellow, *The Adventures of Augie March* (New York: Penguin Books, 1953; 1984).
10 Vanessa Thorpe, 'Burgess Papers Reveal Alternatives to Notorious Earthly Powers "Catamite" Opening', *The Observer*, 17 May 2020.
11 William Empson, *7 Types of Ambiguity* (New York: New Directions, 1966), pp. 6–7.
12 Burgess, *Earthly Powers*, p. 551; Anthony Burgess, 'The Prince of the Powers of the Air: A Novel of Circa 250,000 Words', 1979, University of Texas at Austin: Harry Ransom Center, box 12, pp. 1–10.
13 'Race and the Peoples Temple', *PBS*, n.d., www.pbs.org/wgbh/americanexperience/features/jonestown-race; Bakhtin, *Problems of Dostoyevsky's Poetics*, p. 6.
14 Jochem Riesthuis, 'This, That and the Other: Anthony Burgess Inscribes His Modernist Differences in *Little Wilson and Big God*', *Anthony Burgess and Modernity* (Manchester: Manchester University Press, 2008), p. 181.
15 Burgess, *Earthly Powers*, p. 62.
16 Michael F. Bernard-Donals, *Mikhail Bakhtin: Between Phenomenology and Marxism* (Cambridge: Cambridge University Press, 1994), p. 29.
17 Philippe LeJeune, *On Autobiography*, ed. by Paul John Eakin, trans. by Katherine Leary (Minneapolis, MN: University of Minnesota Press, 1989), p. 12.
18 David Shepherd, 'Bakhtin and the Reader', *Bakhtin and Cultural Theory*, ed. by Ken Hirschkop and David Shepherd (Manchester: University of Manchester Press, 2001), p. 151.
19 Burgess, *Earthly Powers*, p. 156.
20 Graham Foster, 'The Earthly Powers Podcast: Part 1 – Who Is Kenneth Toomey?', The International Anthony Burgess Foundation; Anthony Burgess, *On the Novel* (Manchester: International Anthony Burgess Foundation, 1975; 2019), p. 34.
21 Foster, 'The Earthly Powers Podcast'.
22 Elaine Kendall, '"Earthly Powers" Is Ambitious but Long-Winded', *The Akron Beacon Journal*, 21 December 1980, p. 107.
23 Anthony Burgess, 'A Shrivel of Critics: Modest Proposals for Reviewers', *Harper's Magazine*, February 1977, p. 90.
24 Quoted in Paul Boytinck, *Anthony Burgess: An Annotated Bibliography and Reference Guide* (New York: Garland Publishing, 1985), p. 8.

25 Quoted in Boytinck, *Anthony Burgess*, p. 8; Liana Burgess, Letter to Gladys Carr, 31 January 1977, Series III. Contracts and Royalty Statements, 1956–97: HRC Anthony Burgess Papers, 85.1; Liana Burgess, Letter to Bertha Klausner, 30 January 1977, Series III. Contracts and Royalty Statements, 1956–97: HRC Anthony Burgess Papers, 85.1.
26 Burgess, *Earthly Powers*, p. 43.
27 Burgess, *Earthly Powers*, p. 108.
28 Burgess, *Earthly Powers*, pp. 293, 610.
29 Burgess, *Earthly Powers*, p. 386.
30 Burgess, *Earthly Powers*, p. 34; Burgess, *On the Novel*, p. 62.
31 Burgess, *Earthly Powers*, p. 490; Benjamin Forkner, email to Christopher Thurley, 9 May 2021: Forkner explains that the two men did discuss the similarity between Forkner and Faulkner, and Burgess even used 'Forkner' again in *Any Old Iron* (1989) as Pfc. Forkner from South Carolina (p. 183).
32 Anthony Burgess, 'Speaking of Books: The Writer's Purpose', *The New York Times*, 1 May 1966, para. 11; Burgess, *Earthly Powers*, p. 181.
33 Anthony Burgess, 'Contemporary Authors: The Works of Anthony Burgess', Pennsylvania State University, 1982.
34 Anthony Burgess, 'Can Art Be Immoral?', *The Ink Trade: Selected Journalism 1961–1993*, ed. by Will Carr (Manchester: Carcanet Press, 2018), p. 245.
35 Burgess, *Earthly Powers*, p. 29; Anthony Burgess, 'Anthony Burgess Lecture: "The Writer's Daily Damnation"', Sarah Lawrence College: Sarah Lawrence College Archives, 19 January 1971.
36 Burgess, *Earthly Powers*, p. 558; Anthony Burgess, 'What Now in the Novel?', *Urgent Copy* (New York: W.W. Norton, 1968), pp. 153–156.
37 Burgess, *Earthly Powers*, p. 560.
38 Robert Finley, 'English Critic, Novelist Talk at Symposium', *The Oklahoma Daily*, 2 December 1969; 'Anthony Burgess Reading from New Work', The Poetry Center; Frank MacShane, Letter to Anthony Burgess, Columbia University, 22 December 1969, University of Texas at Austin: Harry Ransom Center Archives.
39 Burgess, *Earthly Powers*, pp. 568, 518.
40 Burgess, *Earthly Powers*, p. 569.
41 Burgess, *Earthly Powers*, p. 569.
42 Anthony Burgess, 'The Purpose of Education', *The Spectator*, 3 March 1967, p. 11.
43 Anthony Burgess, *99 Novels: The Best in English since 1939* (New York: Summit Books, 1984); Anthony Burgess, 'Thoughts on Excellence', n.d., Harry Ransom Center, p. 79.
44 Burgess, *Earthly Powers*, p. 570.
45 John J. Stinson, *Anthony Burgess: Revisited* (Boston, MA: Twayne, 1991), p. 96.
46 Stephen Davis, *Jim Morrison: Life, Death, Legend* (New York: Penguin Books, 2005), p. 47.
47 Anthony Burgess, 'Thoughts on Excellence', *Excellence: The Pursuit, the Commitment, the Achievement* (Washington, DC: LTV Corporation, 1981), p. 26.

48 Burgess, *Earthly Powers*, p. 326.

49 Anthony Burgess, *You've Had Your Time: Being the Second Part of the Confessions of Anthony Burgess* (London: Penguin Books, 1990), p. 196; Anthony Burgess, 'Believing in or Abominating the Past', *The Minneapolis Star*, 28 November 1972, p. 6.

50 Anthony Burgess, *Enderby's Dark Lady; or No End to Enderby* (New York: McGraw-Hill, 1984), p. 78.

51 Burgess, *Earthly Powers*, p. 497.

52 Anthony Burgess, n.d., n.p., The University of Texas at Austin: Harry Ransom Center Archives.

53 Burgess, *You've Had Your Time*, p. ix; William Manley, phone interview with Christopher Thurley, 6 December 2017; Burgess, *Earthly Powers*, p. 516.

54 Burgess, *Earthly Powers*, p. 484.

55 Anthony Burgess, 'The Jew as American', *Urgent Copy*, p. 132.

56 Anthony Burgess, *The Clockwork Testament; or, Enderby's End* (London: Hart-Davis, MacGibbon, 1974), p. 60; Anthony Burgess, 'Prime Time for Hitler', *Saturday Review*, 23 June 1979.

57 Sarah Schulman, 'White Writer', *The New Yorker*, 21 October 2016; Paul Gilroy, *The Black Atlantic* (Cambridge, MA: Harvard University Press, 1993), p. 54.

58 Toni Morrison, 'From *Playing in the Dark: Whiteness and the Literary Imagination*', *The Critical Tradition: Classic Texts and Contemporary Trends*, ed. by David Richter (Boston, MA: Bedford/St. Martin's, 2007), p. 1793.

59 Burgess, *Earthly Powers*, p. 516.

60 Gilroy, *The Black Atlantic*, p. 24; Morrison, 'From *Playing in the Dark*', p. 1793.

61 Morrison, 'From *Playing in the Dark*', p. 1800.

62 Burgess, *Earthly Powers*, p. 484.

63 Burgess, *Earthly Powers*, p. 496.

64 Burgess, *Earthly Powers*, p. 496. This appears to confirm, even in 1980, the famous W.E.B. DuBois adage that "'White Americans are willing to read about Negroes but they prefer to read about Negroes who are fools, clowns, prostitutes, or at any rate in despair and contemplating suicide. Other sorts of Negroes do not interest them'" (quoted in Robert Fikes Jr, 'Adventures in Exotocism: The "Black Life" Novels of White Writers', *The Western Journal of Black Studies*, 26.1 (2002), 8); 'ofay', *Oxford English Dictionary*, www-oed-com.mmu.idm.oclc.org/view/Entry/130555?redirectedFrom=ofay&

65 Burgess, *Earthly Powers*, p. 465.

66 Burgess, *Earthly Powers*, p. 511. The reverberations extend throughout other works of Burgess's such as in *Beard's Roman Women* (1976) where Beard says, 'You must get over this colour business' (p. 65).

67 Morrison, 'From *Playing in the Dark*', p. 1793.

68 Allan Bloom, *The Closing of the American Mind* (New York: Simon and Schuster, 1987), p. 95.

69 Anthony Burgess, *The Great Cities – New York* (Amsterdam: Time-Life Books, 1976).

70 Geoffrey Aggeler, *Anthony Burgess: The Artist as Novelist* (Tuscaloosa, AL: University of Alabama Press, 1979), p. 204.
71 Anthony Burgess, 'Playboy Interview: Anthony Burgess; A Candid Conversation', *Playboy*, September 1974, p. 82; The Editors of Encyclopedia Britannica, 'Negritude', *Encyclopedia Britannica.*
72 Anthony Burgess, 'Quiet Pioneer', *One Man's Chorus*, p. 306.
73 Burgess, 'Playboy Interview', p. 82.
74 Burgess, 'Playboy Interview', pp. 82–84.
75 Anthony Burgess, 'Making de White Boss Frown', *Urgent Copy*, p. 121.
76 Michelle Alexander, *The New Jim Crow* (New York: The New Press, 2010); Roxanne Dunbar-Ortiz, *Loaded: A Disarming History of the Second Amendment* (San Francisco, CA: City Lights Books, 2018).
77 Burgess, 'Playboy Interview', pp. 82, 84.
78 Howard Zinn, *A People's History of the United States* (New York: Harper Perennial – Modern Classics, 1980; 2003), p. 58.
79 Zinn, *A People's History of the United States*, p. 28.
80 Dunbar-Ortiz, *Loaded*, chapter 2.
81 Mervyn Busteed, *The Irish in Manchester, c. 1750–1921* (Manchester: Manchester University Press, 2016), p. 34.
82 Anthony Burgess, 'Letter from Europe', *American Scholar*, 38.4 (Autumn 1969), 684–685.
83 Anthony Burgess, *They Wrote in English* (proof copy, International Anthony Burgess Foundation Archive, 1989).
84 Benjamin Forkner, phone interview with Christopher Thurley, 28 July 2016.
85 Anthony Burgess, 'London Letter', *The Hudson Review*, 20.1 (Spring 1967), pp. 102–103.
86 Burgess, *Earthly Powers*, p. 25; Anthony Burgess, *The Malayan Trilogy* (London: Vintage Books, 2000), p. 66.
87 Burgess, *Earthly Powers*, p. 628.
88 Anthony Burgess, 'The Prince of the Powers of the Air: A Novel of Circa 250,000 Words', n.p., 1979, University of Texas at Austin: Harry Ransom Center, box 12, pp. 1–10; Burgess, *Earthly Powers*, pp. 581–582; Roger Lewis, *Anthony Burgess: A Biography* (New York: St. Martin's Press, 2002).
89 Mikhail Bakhtin, *The Dialogic Imagination: Four Essays*, ed. by Michael Holquist, trans. by Caryl Emerson and Michael Holquist (Austin, TX: University of Texas Press, 1981), pp. 276, 282.
90 Anthony Burgess, 'Going on Writing till Ninety or One Hundred', *Conversations with Anthony Burgess*, ed. by Earl Ingersoll and Mary Ingersoll (Jackson, MS: University Press of Mississippi, 2008), pp. 14–15; Dana Gioia, 'Talking with Anthony Burgess', *Inquiry*, 2 February 1981, p. 25.

6

The End of the World News (1982)

> The three greatest events of all time? My dear child, that's too much. Event, anyway, is too instantaneous, too much of the big bang. Let's say the moment when an animal brain stood for the first time revealed as a human brain, the completion of the invention of writing, the (don't laugh, I mean it) abolition of slavery in the West ... greatest events of the past century – discovery of the unconscious by Sigmund Freud, the Trotskian doctrine of world socialism, and the invention of the space rocket ... put that in your college magazine if you like. To you my love. XXXXXXXXXXX, old as I am. (Anthony Burgess, *The End of the World News*)[1]

Introduction

Evidence suggests that on multiple occasions, and displayed throughout this monograph, Burgess perceived the United States in the 1960s and 1970s as being the location of literary innovation which started with authors willing to push the boundaries of the novel. The perceived malaise of Europe after World War Two, as Burgess saw it, was a kind of hangover from the violence and destruction seen across Europe throughout the first half of the twentieth century. The United States, hardly disrupted at home from the war, was a place free from the emotional exertion placed on the body politic, leaving it with energy left to spare: energy to argue, energy to polemicize, energy to fight, and energy for change – perhaps memorialized in the American Trotsky-infused dictum, 'We'll fight all right if we must. / In God, meaning us, meaning US us, / We kind of trust'.[2] In *They Wrote in English* (1989), Burgess stated that 'without doubt the best fiction to come out of World War II, big and ambitious', was coming from the United States in novels like Norman Mailer's *The Naked and the Dead* (1948), even though he claims this particular novel borrowed the innovative device of flashbacks from another American's work, John Dos Passos's *U.S.A.* trilogy.[3] In 1979, Burgess explained that despite the British having got 'over our World War

II enmities' and the United States getting over 'the revolutionary notions of 1776', it was now time for Britain to attain a 'will to work' whereas Americans needed 'a little Old World modernism' since the 'long flirtation with Europe has become arid' and thus the British were 'waiting to be turned into an honest GI bride'.[4] The sarcasm is thick here, though he essentially witnessed this supposed titillation playing out when he was considered the first choice sought out to write an apocalypse story distinctly in the American vein.[5] Such an admission was also simultaneously a confirmation that Burgess too was a kind of American in the sense that he was innovative and diverse in his writing genres and forms, therefore he fit in to some extent, and even though *The End of the World News* may be a disingenuous and unintentional creation, it stands as an example of such inventiveness.[6]

In *Earthly Powers*, Kenneth Toomey remarks that he was just thinking 'that those two kids prefer to go and see the end of the world through the southward drift of toxic atomic dust than to hear the new word of the Lord in Madison Square Garden', which may be an allusion to the *Puma* narrative of Burgess's *The End of the World News* (1982), one of two stories out of the three total, the other two being the 'Freud escaping Nazi Germany' or 'That Man Freud'[7] and 'Trotsky's in New York!' (first conceptualized as a 'Broadway-style musical') narratives, the latter of which takes place in the United States and therefore exhibits much of Burgess's previously explained motifs and allusions.[8] In this chapter, it's important to briefly discuss the second of the two less significant, the first being *Earthly Powers*, though still ardently, *American* novels by Burgess because although having been largely written in and taking place in the United States, the significance in understanding Burgess's American influence here dwindles. This diminishment occurs due to several reasons: first, the narratives in this book were commissioned and created for the stage or film and therefore have a different tone than that of Burgess's literature; second, these genres change the purposes of the texts from cultural commentary to something closer to mere spectacle or amusement, or as the subtitle deems it, 'An Entertainment'; and third, much of what Burgess presents here is recycled material that often repeats points made throughout his earlier career, with little unique glimmers of his authorial heteroglossia. Still, delving into the *Puma* and 'Trotsky in New York' narratives makes the overall goal of this monograph complete by covering all points of Burgess's American-inspired novels, and the authorial heteroglossia that emerges from such texts in the shape of thinly veiled monological commentary and criticism of the United States.

Chock-full of Burgess references, organized around a peculiar narrative introduction, and supposedly meant to be a reflection of certain 'poetic values' that stand as a 'recognition of the ineluctably growing authority of the visual media, particularly television' – though the final product resembles the pre-Information Age experimental writing of E.T.A. Hoffman's *The Life and Opinions of Tomcat Murr* (1820–22) – makes *The End of the World News* a distinctly unique text in Burgess's canon, though the content to be analysed here is somewhat repetitive, since the topics addressed have been discussed at more length in previous chapters concerning more elaborate displays of these themes in other novels.[9] Because of the strange 'Foreword' of this novel in three parts, there must first be an assessment of what this means and how this distorts our understanding of both this text and where/how this fits into Burgess's *American* canon. By presenting a 'Foreword', written by 'John B. Wilson, BA', which is of course Burgess's birth name, that introduces a collection of 'posthumous work' from the author, Anthony Burgess, readers enter into territory much like that of the narrative techniques used by authors, in the American context, such as Washington Irving with Diedrich Knickerbocker, Nathaniel Hawthorne in 'Rappaccini's Daughter' (1844) with M. de l'Aubépine, Vladimir Nabokov in *Lolita* (1955) with John Ray, Jr, PhD and *Pale Fire* (1962) with John Shade and Charles Kinbote, and Philip Roth in *My Life as a Man* (1974) with Nathan Zuckerman and Peter Tarnopol, where a fictional character comments on their work or the work of another author, occasionally by even stumbling upon these works, as is the case with Wilson, M. de l'Aubépine, and Knickerbocker – not to mention into the Burgess realm as well, as is evidenced by Burgess's initial draft of *Enderby Outside* that prefaces the novel with a note from its *new* author, thus killing off his previous *nom de guerre*, Joseph Kell: 'Before he died, Joseph Kell bequeathed to Anthony Burgess not merely his copyrights and royalties but also his identity. His dying wish was that Mr Burgess should conclude the story about Enderby, the poet, already half-told in *Inside Mr Enderby*' – though Liana does write that *The Pianoplayers* was, initially at least, attributed as the 'first novel by Josephine Kell'.[10] In prefacing *The End of the World News* in this manner, even by perhaps alluding to *Pale Fire* with the Wilson character stating that he hoped not to 'displease' his friend's 'shade', Burgess not only separates himself from the work by arguing that the real individual, John Wilson, has found a now-deceased Burgess's papers, but also attempts to cast doubt on the authorial act (for who has actually created these works and for what reason?) and gives him a chance to yet again self-explicate his own work, as he does too in *1985* (1978).[11]

With knowledge of the work's production, it could be gleaned that instead what Burgess is doing is shallowly reconstituting old work into the shape of some experimental *new* work by *ex post facto* authorial artifice. When expedient, as has been an argument throughout this monograph, Burgess shields himself from the words of his works by erecting barriers of public, personal, and authorial identities (e.g. John Wilson, Anthony Burgess, Joseph Kell,

F.X. Enderby, and Kenneth Toomey), what Roger Lewis called a 'suite of aliases' that gave him the 'freedom of an actor who swaps costumes and parts'.[12] What the facts of the publication reveal, and all its exterior heteroglot influences and paratextual play, is, despite Alan Roughley's astute analysis which argues that the novel gave way to 'a playful writing that challenges the limits of thematic criticism and opens up serious yet simultaneously playful questions about the forms of literature, the power of writing and the playful exuberance of writing that is willing to throw its own being – or at least the being of its author – into question', that *The End of the World News* appears to be more of a rudimentary and fiscally provoked literary response, playful in its literary ambitions only as an afterthought, which is meant to allow the author-figure, Anthony Burgess, who has created the nominal, fictional, and reportedly deceased 'John B. Wilson', to save face while affording him room to contradict himself, present a shoddy conglomeration, and ultimately protect the brand of the author with purported complexity.[13] In what might be called an act of multi-voiced corroboration, the author of Anthony Burgess's autobiography, *You've Had Your Time*, presumably Burgess or Wilson, sticks with this story and explains that although the three narratives which make up *The End of the World News* were separately commissioned 'projects to fulfil in the sphere of show business', through an act of serendipity, empirical author *Anthony Burgess* had the epiphany that, while the texts sat unused and all written in the mid-1970s, each narrative was one aspect of a larger story, that of 'the twentieth century, in which the major discoveries have been of the human unconscious', in order to will this unlikely formation into justified authorial and inspirational being.[14] The support for this possibly being an attempt to justify recycling work is that Burgess allowed for the *Puma* narrative, initially intended as a standalone project and minus any references to the other narratives of *The End of the World News*, to be published separately in *Omni* magazine in 1983, which is even further supported when Burgess explicitly provided directions for *Puma* to be published as a separate novel from *The End of the World News* when outlining his intentions for the Irwell critical editions of his work, proving, as Paul Wake, editor of the recently published critical Irwell edition of *Puma*, notes, just how 'loose the stitches holding the three strands of that book together are'.[15]

More importantly for this monograph's purposes, Wake notes that *Puma* 'had its genesis in the United States, primarily in Iowa City and New York' – Burgess spent four weeks at the University of Iowa from 5 October to 31 October 1975 – and that three 'particular contexts might be said to be key to *Puma*'s composition: Burgess's life in New York in the 1970s; his sense of his identity as an author, in particular to his sense of himself as an author of science fiction; and his "vestigial Catholicism" '.[16] Aside from what archival research has turned up about *The End of the World News*, and by association, *Puma*, it's clear just through the peritextual 'Foreword', which should really be considered part of the fictional work as a whole, that this is a text inspired by American culture, with an innately American theme, where the thinly veiled *authors* beg the reader to connect the 'evident clue as to this intention' with a letter to Jenny, 'clearly a student in an American university' and a comment in the fictional, and assumed, author's notebook.[17] However contrived, Burgess's hand feeds the point through a fictionalized self, who says that after seeing a 'photograph of late President Carter and wife in White House late at night eating hamburgers and watching television' with three screens playing 'simultaneously' – which is either misremembered or fictionalized since this famous image is of former president Lyndon Johnson – the fictional Burgess, Wilson, wonders if this is a glimmer of the future 'viewing pattern': 'True visual counterpoint. Is this also possible future of the novel?'[18] Double-voiced discourse and Burgess's peculiar heteroglossic authorial utterance occurs, yet again, as Burgess repeats the line of his *fictional* executor, Wilson, in Burgess's autobiography, where it is explained that *The End of the World News* acts as a 'tripartite novel in a form appropriate to the television age', where the 'television zapper has trained us to take in quasi-simultaneously a number of diverse programmes', and so these stories are his attempt to 'apply this zapping technique to prose fiction'.[19] Even more metafictionally layered, there also exists an 'author's note on the dust-jacket of the original Hutchinson edition' which reads 'It is the new way of reading, derived from the new way of watching television. To view one channel at a time is no longer enough: we need three distinct yet simultaneous imaginative stimuli: the family of the middle and late 1980s will have to be a three-screen family', thus continuing to throw into question the engineering and history of the text, its supposedly financial emphasis with the blurb's 'puffy gobbet of sales talk', Burgess's elaborate crafting of old texts into a supposed parody of the modern novel, and his ever-present and ubiquitous presence in and surrounding his fictions.[20]

And this 'television age' is undoubtedly an age closely associated with the United States, since the idea for the story, in the form of a screenplay for a disaster movie *à la manière de When Worlds Collide* (1933) and *After Worlds Collide* (1934), came directly from Richard D. Zanuck and David Brown at Universal Pictures in California, who Burgess described as naturally thinking 'in terms of the end of America and an American spaceship saving the élite of America, who would build a new America somewhere in the outer blackness'.[21] Additionally, the Trotsky narrative that takes place in New York City, which was at first planned to have a musical score written by American composer Stanley Silverman, though this went unfulfilled, was also at one point meant to be an off-Broadway stage-play, therefore making these two strands of the overall *The End of the World News* narrative a refashioning of unused American show-business content.[22] Paid generously once already for *Puma* ($65,000 in 1975), having written the disaster story 'for the money, for the money' – though Burgess was adamant that, quoting from Samuel Johnson, 'a man was a "blockhead" if he did not write for money' – none of the three narratives actually came to fruition for their original intentions (Hollywood film, Canadian television, and Broadway theatre), leaving Burgess with almost 400 pages of unused material as an artist who 'hated waste', so it's no surprise that something had to be made of these works, and so, with the American literary market, there exists *The End of the World News*.[23]

Epitexts and context

The *Puma* narrative was started in summer 1975 and finished in late January 1976 and the prose Trotsky narrative/libretto was completed in 1977 (musical score in 1979), meaning that Burgess was writing *Puma* between and during American lecture tours and the Trotsky narrative at a time when his most peripatetic American years were now behind him, having largely disappeared from the American lecture circuit after late 1976.[24] In addition to all this activity, Burgess had, in the 1970s, also held teaching positions at the City College of New York, Columbia University, the University of Iowa, and the State University of New York at Buffalo, all while also publishing *Joysprick* (1973), *Napoleon Symphony* (1974), *The Clockwork Testament* (1974), *New York* (1976), *Moses* (1976), *A Long Trip to Teatime* (1976), and *Beard's Roman Women* (1976), in addition to writing a stage-play on Houdini and scripts and treatments on Roald Amundsen, Attila the Hun, Edward the Black Prince, Cyrus the Great, Marco Polo, Samson, Aristotle Onassis, Beethoven, the shah of Iran, and Merlin, with multiple other projects commissioned about the life of Christ, Sigmund Freud, and William Shakespeare.[25] Needless to emphasize, Burgess's life at this point was wrapped up very closely with the United States, so it's no wonder that he was 'approached by two big men in Paramount, or rather Universal' who had 'made a lot of money out of these disaster films, you know, *Earthquake* and *Jaws*', to make the 'ultimate disaster film'.[26] Believing that Americans loved disaster films because 'there hasn't been a great deal of disaster here of the kind that we've had in the West ... I beg your pardon, in Europe', Burgess's slip here may even reveal that he felt the United States was outside of the *Western* world, and something different entirely, that was in need of fictive relief in the form of imaginary disaster. In fact, Burgess believed that tapping into the soul of the country was impossible until it had dealt with tragedy on the European scale: 'I think possibly New York has this soul but has not had a chance to demonstrate it and show it exists; no disaster has been big enough yet to explore its soul'.[27] And perhaps Burgess was right at the time – though he may have changed his stance after the events of 11 September 2001 – so, he saw his task when writing the *Puma* narrative as attempting to capture the essence, the soul, and the myth of the United States in his writing, something this monograph has argued he was trying to do since he first started work on *M/F* (1971).

The End of the World News, though an 'entertainment', is no different from all of Burgess's other work in the sense that the text(s) are bursting with Burgessian self-allusions and authorial heteroglossia which are infused, in the Trotsky and *Puma* narratives, with a socio-ideological language, that of American culture. From the fictional Freud family viewing Sophocles' play, *Oedipus Rex*, which is of 'course Burgess's own translation that they are hearing' and which was produced and presented at the Guthrie theatre in Minneapolis, Minnesota, to the secret code in the *Puma* narrative being the same as Tristram Foxe's and Burgess's military numbers, the text is littered with references to Burgess's life and to his most repeated topics of concern, such as pornography, race in the United States, incest, religion, and American culture and language.[28]

Although reviewers at the time of the book's publication recognized Burgess's ingenuity with the form and shape of the novel, they were not so congratulatory about the actual content, with one reviewer in *Christian Science Monitor* remarking that the 'novel retains Burgess's franchise on technical ingenuity but perhaps not a place for itself on that spaceship', and another in *Time* saying that Burgess had, despite being innovative, 'abused his poetic license; he is often perverse for perversity's sake, and he can be more outrageous than illuminating'.[29] Although the *Encounter* called it 'insolently unpolished', Michael Wood at the *New York Times* argued that *The End of the World News* was derivative but revivifying by ultimately parodying 'the forms of writing that might survive the death of literature: the libretto, the novel ripe for a television series and science fiction'; Lorna Sage in *The Observer* called it 'a sardonic anti-book' where 'each of its narratives gets lots of space, but none of them is done with real gusto or venom', and J.G. Ballard wrote in *The Guardian* that the book was a 'brilliant extravaganza'.[30] As has been a theme throughout all critical responses to Burgess's work, though, little has been said about how the United States is conceptualized in Burgess's fiction, and how such an analysis resounds with the rest of his oeuvre.

In 2018, though, Wake's 'Introduction' and annotations to *Puma* have finally spotlighted this reality and started to pull this significant point of inspiration from the text and out into the critical arena. Wake notes that if

'Burgess's life as a lecturer in New York in 1972 provided inspiration for some of the early adventures of *Puma*'s protagonists, then his research for *New York*, Time-Life's glossy picture book, plays a more direct role in the detail of the city that dominates the story'.[31] With *M/F*, *The Clockwork Testament*, *New York*, *Trotsky's in New York!*, and *Puma* all being published in the 1970s – Burgess's New York quintet – there exists ample evidence that information gathered for each book began to spill over into his other work, with *Puma* being a prime example. Wake points out that the 'novel's frequent reference to the history of the city' is derived from his work on the Time-Life book and that some of the non-fiction stories that 'make up the narrative' of *New York* appear in *Puma* as well – Burgess's notebooks around this period, which also include a draft of dialogue between the characters of the story (meant for the screenplay), also contain detailed maps and pictures of New York City as well as mileage maps with the distances between American cities.[32] Another instance of Burgess's authorial heteroglossia, *The End of the World News* still does not necessarily meet Bakhtin's standards of a literary heteroglot exhibiting autonomous, free-thinking characters, but what remains is Burgess's peculiar brand of the heteroglot where 'in the novel heteroglossia is by and large always personified, incarnated in individual human figures, with disagreements and oppositions individualized', which is always a clearly ordained stratagem that, though it rests shallowly below the surface of the text, emanates from Burgess's life and works which are infused with the language that Burgess had acquired, in this case, while living in the United States.[33] As has been the goal of this entire monograph, *The End of the World News*, though not a shining example of the American inspirations in his fiction like *M/F*, *The Clockwork Testament*, or *Enderby's Dark Lady*, still stands as a significant example of how Burgess's centralized 'verbal-ideological thought' is influenced 'within a heteroglot national language' that is then transmuted into 'language as a world view, even as a concrete opinion', which then exposes a stratum of 'mutual understanding in all spheres of ideological life' as can be deduced between text and epitext.[34] Burgess's public life in the United States was no different, and his prose here, just like all the other pieces discussed, drips with socio/verbal-ideological discourse of the Burgess variety that is 'utilized to refract the author's intentions' in an act of incorporating an 'impersonal form "from the author," alternating (while ignoring precise formal boundaries) with direct authorial discourse'.[35] Burgess does this not only in the preface but once again intrinsically by splicing in biographical elements into the text, though not nearly as authorially directed as the last two Enderby novels. Doing so in *The End of the World News* creates a 'dialectics of the object' that is swollen and 'interwoven with the social dialogue surrounding it'.[36] The object of course is the United States, and in *Puma* the 'earth, meaning America', down to New York City, and then to specific characters, locales, and so on, since New York City acts as the point of historical catalyst, centre of history, all focused around an Americano-centric reality – something, Burgess suggests, Americans are quite used to.[37] As Bakhtin notes, a kind of literature with evidence of such voice and utterance carries with it significance that the 'object is a focal point for heteroglot voices among which his [the author's] own voice must also sound', with the characters and dialogue essentially creating the background voices 'necessary for his own voice' to elevate 'the social heteroglossia surrounding'.[38] By framing the novel around an invented deceased author of the same name, whose executor of his fiction is also a persona of the actual author of the book *The End of the World News*, with characters who inhabit the same spaces as the author known as Anthony Burgess – with Valentine (Val) Brodie, the novel's author/academic-protagonist, being published by an Iowa City press from a university, also where the first monograph on Burgess's work came from in 1971 with Rexford Brown's work, to the language of the characters spilling over in references to places Burgess visited himself as is the case with Harvard, Columbia, Princeton, Choate, and others – it's clear to any informed reader of Burgess, aware of the author's travels, non-fiction, interviews, and the secondary academic commentary on his work, that the space this text occupies is indefinitely mired within an authorial heteroglot.[39]

The United States in *The End of the World News*

As another distinctly *American* text, Burgess does resort back to familiar themes in *The End of the World News*, with rather stock characterizations and dialogue, especially with his slights and backhanded compliments against the United States, but also with references to pornography and reproductive anatomies.[40] In creating characters who see the United States, much like in earlier novels, as 'but a word, a noise, an abstraction' in *The End of the World News*, a kind of surreal entropy surrounds the spirit of the two American narratives, with both narratives dealing with different topics Burgess himself was concerned with as a public commentator. One such topic was the duelling dichotomy behind capitalism and the social contract, which Trotsky, in 1917 – the year of Burgess's birth, the Russian October Revolution, and the United States's entrance into World War One: 'My birth thus coincided with that of the modern age – American hegemony, the dissolution of Christendom' – speaks out against, arguing for Americans to forget the abstraction since there 'are two nations only, the nation of labour and the nation of capital. Prepare for the first and the last battle between them'.[41] Desiring to write a similar historical piece to

Tom Stoppard's *Travesties* (1974), Burgess focused on Trotsky's brief visit to New York City in 1917, saying that Trotsky called the city a place of 'prose and fantasy' where the narrative says the city is a place where the 'world's here', 'all the nations, all the races', and that when Burgess had finished all three projects that ended up becoming *The End of the World News*, he claims to have seen now 'that they were aspects of the same story. They were the story of the twentieth century', with very little context or explanation surrounding the failure of each to be accepted on their own, therefore supposedly coming to the realization that he had actually written this purportedly ingenious 'tripartite novel', and not just refashioned loose works without contracts – which is all wrapped up neatly in his autobiography acting as a self-fashioned justification for and commentary on his own previous work.[42] Burgess the autobiographer encapsulates these terms inside a story in *You've Had Your Time* when he remarks on the flawed system of capitalism at the core of the United States's industry of mythological and fictional distractions with institutions like Hollywood with its 'mad spending' – that ironically funded *The End of the World News* – as a 'phenomenon to which I found it difficult to adjust, and it was figured in the London lifestyle of these Americans who took over our capital without diffidence, dragging me with them to restaurants with an indigestible cuisine and night clubs where expensive whores clung to them'.[43] Burgess's Trotsky is much more dialogized than other characters of Burgess's, since Trotsky is a historical figure who Burgess fictionalizes – although the story takes place in New York City, this text is not an especially important text for understanding Burgess's American commentary outside of the fact that he simply chose to write about a Russian political figure visiting the United States – but fissures still expose some of Burgess's monoglottism becomes exposed. One such instance is when Trotsky is verbally accosted by an American, something Burgess himself was no stranger to, whether on television, lecturing, or through print. Indeed, his public comments about American life sometimes provoked threats, like in this letter he received in October 1971:

> Communist bastard, stay out of the U.S.A. Who wants you bastard and your theories about communal life? Communist bastard and the aditors [sic] of the N.Y.Times, scum of the earth, be damned for your theories of communal life, go to Russia bastard and be hapy [sic] thery [sic] with your communistic way of lify [sic]. … P.S. Only the communist aditors [sic] of the N.Y.Times can give you space for the trush [sic] you writing, bastard Burges [sic]. Be damned communist bastard.[44]

In *The End of the World News*, Trotsky hears something similar: '"Go back to Moscow," cries a heckler', but Trotsky remarks humorously, having far less attachment to the country than Burgess, 'I would if I could and I will yet. I am an unwilling exile from my native land'.[45]

Burgess's relationship with the United States, as has been displayed repeatedly, was contentious and was described by Burgess as being in a sense sadomasochistic since he loved to hate the country that afflicted him.[46] This is not entirely dissimilar to the Russians who visit with Trotsky and attempt to make sense of the Americans, something Burgess had been trying to do since 1966. When the fictionalized Nikolai Bokharin [sic] in the narrative says that the Americans are a 'frivolous people' who cannot 'stand anything that goes on too long', whether that be, in the case Bokharin refers to, apocopes which could be a metaphor for a lack of attention span, there exists a glimmer of monologism that beckons towards Burgess's condemnation on the youth he encountered across the nation's universities and colleges who dismissed literature before the twentieth century as lacking relevance; this was a topic tackled by Burgess in his 1970 *New York Times* article, 'Is Shakespeare Relevant?', as well as publicly on multiple other occasions, stressing, as he might be here to his American audience, that society and culture must be respectful of and 'teach the great lesson of historical perspective' and not just be focused on the here and now.[47] Although Trotsky's crew makes this loaded monoglot generalization, here in just a brief observation, it is in the *Puma* narrative that this criticism is further developed.

The presence of Burgess in *The End of the World News* is yet again evident through a kind of a monoglottal double-voiced discourse, constructed out of Val, a science fiction author and perhaps another autobiographical facet of Burgess in his fiction, who laments metatextually that 'science fiction, is let's be honest, ultimately triviality .... It's brain-tickling, no more. The American mediocrity, which rejects Shakespeare, Milton, Harrison and Abramovitz, has led us to this nonsense – a university course in, let's face it, trash. Christ, we should be studying Blake and Gerard Manley Hopkins'.[48] A point redolent of Burgess's, or perhaps Toomey's, or Enderby's, own convictions, Val and the text are reduced to one of the most pronounced instances of the authorial monoglot, when Val contemplates that there 'is only the past, and the glory of the past is not order, for order is an abstraction imposed by that non-existent thing called the present', so therefore as an enlightened culture, people had to 'glory in having added more and more to the past, increased the roar of its music and the chaotic profusion of its flowers'.[49] Geoffrey Aggeler describes Burgess's echoing and authorial heteroglot sentiment thus: 'Burgess has also been disturbed that American students have "cut themselves off completely from the past, from the whole of the past" '.[50] Here Val, as a creation of Burgess's, is particularly autobiograficational in that both authors are science fiction writers in this instance and each are echoing the other's points through a double-voiced discourse, making this instance simultaneously also an example of hidden polemic, which is easily evidenced and supported when accessing Burgess's authorial heteroglossia. In an article entitled 'Believing in or Abominating the Past' in *The Minneapolis Star* in 1972, Burgess stated outright a very similar opinion to that of Val: that he 'believed the past had something to teach me [and] that it was important to me to know the language of Virgil and Horace', whereas the young people he was encountering across the United States tended to 'abominate the past as the source of all hypocrisy, humbug and evil'.[51] More like Val with every sentence, Burgess then says that such a stance, to desire to 'study Vonnegut and Kesey and, God help us, even my own work', was disturbing, though like Val, who ultimately saves the human race, Burgess may actually take himself more seriously, envisioning himself steering his own *American* spaceship away from the country as a saviour of culture, since the 'only way we can learn about the general progress, the general movement of man in society is to see what has happened in the past' – a point he had been arguing to the American public and the American collegiate youth since at least 1966, and mentioned throughout every chapter of this monograph, and indeed how Burgess ends *Puma* in the 'Epilogue', similar to the teacher/narrators of *Nothing Like the Sun* and time-travelling voyeurs of the Enderby tetralogy:

> Val sighed. A ship. It was impossible to convince them. The business of *getting somewhere* was left to computers. Had been, indeed, for the last millennium. A sceptical, tough, hard-brained generation. They would believe nothing. Science fiction, indeed. The end-of-session bell rang. 'All right,' he said. 'Class dismissed.' They went running off for their protein and synthevedge. They had forgotten the story already.[52]

The dichotomy between economics and social institutions, as well as the monoglottal Val, is not the only evidently American-themed point Burgess expressed in *The End of the World News*, as the text repeatedly utilizes the juxtaposition, as has been discussed previously, between the United States and Russia. In *Honey for the Bears* (1963), the two countries are conflated when discussing 'Georgia', 'Russian Georgia, not the one where they hang all the n-----s' and when it's argued that 'Americans and Russians are all the same. You promise things and you don't keep your promises. You just can't be trusted, that's what it is'.[53] In this sense, *The End of the World News*'s Trotsky narrative could be perceived as Burgess finally getting to explore two international powers that had intrigued him for decades and worried him into the 1980s, as he remarked on a television show that he was a little 'scared' about nuclear weapons and that the European continent could become a 'battlefield between America and Russia', all because the earth's most powerful governments had not 'learned how to conduct a peace economy'.[54] Mentioned previously, this goes right along with Burgess's discontent about the United States's form of capitalism – though he benefitted from it – and, in a display of his authorial heteroglot, a mutual concern he had voiced two decades earlier in *Honey for the Bears*, that 'Americanism and America's Russianism [would] make plastic of the world'.[55]

Getting to the core of the concerns Burgess had with the United States and Russia in an interview in 1973, Burgess qualifies that what he was always suspicious of was 'the use of power to change others', evoking his decades-long interest in and rejection of the American psychologist B.F. Skinner's behaviourist conditioning techniques, stating that it, as mentioned previously, 'seems strange to me that this is the way both the USA and Russia seem to think things ought to be done. In that respect they are coeval.[56] Into 1982, while reviewing American television, Burgess even condemned the two-dimensionality of the fictional characters who appeared in television shows as being indicative of Americans thinking of 'intellectual excitement or human complexity as dangerous', which Burgess surmised was in line with Soviet Russian concepts of human individuality, 'but hardly for the greatest democracy the world has ever seen'.[57] The existence of Russian influences on Burgess's life, thinking, and work should be explored in more depth elsewhere, but what Russia and the United States helped codify in Burgess's mind was a kind of cultural foil that revealed mythic and structuralist aspects of the human experience.

The same kind of idealism in Americans that resulted in them saving the world in the *Puma* narrative with spaceships called *America I*, *America II*, *III*, *IV*, and so on, 'literally to the crack of doom', was the typical display of narcissism that Burgess had come to expect from the country and why the narrator explains that to call these spacecrafts 'anything other than plain *America* was somehow to diminish the achievement, to make it appear primitive and experimental and, in a sense, already a dead thing'.[58] This actually acts as a perfect metaphor for a point discussed in Chapter 5 regarding the founding of the United States, where Burgess claimed that the 'United States had emerged boldly and idealistically, influenced by a treatise on law, *De l'esprit des lois*, written by the French philosopher Montesquieu', a point repeated multiple times, perhaps most importantly in what may be his most explicit and detailed commentary on American politics, the article 'Thoughts on Irangate' written in 1987, which states that, after having read the Tower Commission Report, the United States government had exposed 'a flaw in the United States Constitution which has persisted ever since Montesquieu formulated *la séparation des pouvoirs*', which permits 'the American system ... any amount of presidential machiavellianism behind the collective back of Congress'.[59] It was this kind of overstylized approach to governance which Burgess uses as a metaphor here in

The End of the World News. Further still, the characters appear to be sarcastic and mocking as they criticize the lack of foresight of the 'inalienable right of all Americans' that was guaranteed by the Constitution, but which dissolved under a need for pragmatism: 'the pursuit of happiness, also of enemies and harmless uneatable animals. Come on, we need protection'.[60]

Significance and conclusion

The End of the World News, like so many of Burgess's texts, can, with knowledge of his other works and his life, turn into a kind of scavenger hunt for heteroglottal Burgessian allusions, so much so that the lexicon becomes distinctly idiomatic. In fact, if *M/F* was Burgess's American sex novel, *The Clockwork Testament* his American violence novel, and *Enderby's Dark Lady* his literary *au revoir*, then *The End of the World News*, particularly *Puma*, is his American destruction novel, the culmination of the corrosive, hubristic, and selfish ahistorical conservancy of American culture as it embarks into otherworldly future territories – again, emanating from the United States's heart, New York City, but retreating – in 'anabasis' – into its geographical midwestern heart.[61] The benefit of such an approach is not integral to enjoying Burgess's fiction, since all of his novels could easily be read and potentially enjoyed without such epitextual and biographical knowledge, but for any authoritative, academic, and scholarly investigation into Burgess's works, this is an essential and intellectually productive way towards understanding the larger and more encompassing authorial vision which stretches out across and over every piece of Burgess's entire canon, both published and unpublished, fiction and non-fiction. This is perhaps not applicable to, or even possible for, every author, but for Burgess the key to understanding him is through his texts, and his texts through understanding him.

A reference to Hopkins alone brings with it connections to at least half a dozen other pieces of Burgess's that exist in various mediums, from music to non-fiction, journalism to fiction, interview to correspondence, and so on, so that when various terms, ideas, names, and topics arise, there exists a kind of coded expression in need of unpacking. Scholars such as Wake are aware of this, as he unpacked in the footnotes that a singular reference to a Thomas Wolfe novella also nods towards the author's upbringing in Chapel Hill, North Carolina where Burgess taught in 1969, therefore revealing the layered nature of Burgess's biographical references.[62] When dialogue such as this appears in *The End of the World News*, 'Doidy? A doidy book?', someone versed in Burgess's discourse must then work to reveal the context, the layers of meaning packed into such an expression in order to get a more complete view of Burgess's artistic vision.[63] In this case, this supposedly phonetically spelled New York accent is also used in *M/F*, and should then elicit a query into Burgess's long and storied interaction and commentary on 'dirty books', incest, and pornography, as well as his commentary on New York vernacular and phonetics.[64] Even easier is when Burgess blatantly reuses material, as when the Livedog from *The Wanting Seed* returns in *The End of the World News* in order to allude not just to 'god and devil backwards' (and evil), but once again also to the authorial heteroglot, this time concerning Burgess's decades of commentary on population, the Eucharist, and anthropophagy.[65]

Recognizing these instances isn't imperative to the text, but in pulling these aspects out of the fiction, which has been the purpose of this entire monograph, with respect to the presence of the United States within Burgess's canon, what is revealed is an immense inner-authorial dialogue; in other words, a kind of canonic double-voiced discourse in which pieces from Burgess's entire canon, throughout all mediums, all authorial voices, and all personages, are communicating with and about one another. To begin to pinpoint these examples, in this case, reveals the profound significance Anthony Burgess's experiences with the United States had on his life and work, and therefore exposes the complexities of such a relationship, all while beginning to frame a more unifying vision of Burgess's canon and life in the American context.

Notes

1 Anthony Burgess, *The End of the World News* (London: Penguin Books, 1982; 1984), pp. ix–x.
2 Burgess, *The End of the World News*, p. 69.
3 Anthony Burgess, *They Wrote in English* (proof copy, International Anthony Burgess Foundation Archive, 1989), p. 19.
4 Anthony Burgess, 'Isn't It Time for Britain to Become a GI Bride?', *The Los Angeles Times*, 16 May 1979, p. 63.
5 Paul Wake, 'Introduction', *Puma* (Manchester: Manchester University Press, 2018), p. 2.
6 Anthony Burgess, *You've Had Your Time: Being the Second Part of the Confessions of Anthony Burgess* (London: Penguin Books, 1990), p. 326.
7 'John McGreevy Productions has engaged your services as writer for a proposed film and television series on the life of Sigmund Freud, provisionally entitled THAT MAN FREUD. The manuscript for the said motion picture and television series (of approximately 80,000–100,000 word) to be completed April 30th, 1978, with a copy made available to John McGreevy Productions ... the sum of $7,000 (Canadian dollars) upon receipt of sign contract, $3,000 upon receipt

of manuscript, $30,000 when the major financing comes into place, for adaptation' (John McGreevy Productions, Letter to Anthony Burgess, 26 January 1978, University of Texas at Austin: Harry Ransom Center, box 77, fols. 1–5).

8 Anthony Burgess, *Earthly Powers* (New York: Europa Editions, 1980; 2012), p. 569; Paul Phillips, *A Clockwork Counterpoint: The Music and Literature of Anthony Burgess* (Manchester: Manchester University Press, 2010), pp. 238, 393.

9 Burgess, *The End of the World News*, p. viii; E.T.A. Hoffmann, *The Life and Opinions of Tomcat Murr* (London: Penguin, 1820; 1999).

10 Burgess, *The End of the World News*, p. vii; Anthony Burgess, *Enderby Outside* typed draft, n.d., n.p., University of Texas at Austin: Harry Ransom Center, box 19, fol. 1; Liana Burgess, Letter to Gladys Carr, 8 Giugno 1977, Series III. Contracts and Royalty Statements, 1956–97: HRC Anthony Burgess Papers, 85.1.

11 Burgess, *The End of the World News*, p. x.

12 Roger Lewis, *Anthony Burgess* (London: Faber, 2002), p. 46.

13 Alan Roughley, '*The End of the World News*: "The End of the Book and the Beginning of Writing"', *Anthony Burgess and Modernity*, ed. by Alan Roughley (Manchester: Manchester University Press, 2008), pp. 73–74.

14 Burgess, *You've Had Your Time*, pp. 326–327.

15 Wake, 'Introduction', p. 8.

16 Wake, 'Introduction', pp. 5, 9.

17 Burgess, *The End of the World News*, p. ix.

18 Burgess, *The End of the World News*, p. ix.

19 Burgess, *You've Had Your Time*, p. 327.

20 Andrew Biswell, *The Real Life of Anthony Burgess* (London: Picador, 2005), p. 384; Roughley, '*The End of the World News*', p. 73.

21 Burgess, *You've Had Your Time*, p. 327.

22 Burgess, *The End of the World News*, p. 154; Anthony Burgess, 'Cucarachas and Exiles, Potential Death and Life Enhancement', *New York Times*, 29 October 1972, pp. 28, 37; Burgess, *You've Had Your Time*, p. 327.

23 Burgess, *You've Had Your Time*, p. 326; Paul Wake, 'Introduction', pp. 2, 7; Biswell, *The Real Life of Anthony Burgess*, p. 384; Alayne Merenstein, 'A Clockwork Success', *The Panther*, 28 February 1973, p. 2.

24 John J. Stinson, *Anthony Burgess: Revisited* (Boston, MA: Twayne Publishers, 1991), p. 136; Paul Phillips, *A Clockwork Counterpoint: The Music and Literature of Anthony Burgess* (Manchester: Manchester University Press, 2010), p. 393; Paul Wake, 'Introduction', *Puma*, p. 8.

25 Stinson, *Anthony Burgess*, p. 136; Wake, 'Introduction', p. 8; Jim Clarke, *The Aesthetics of Anthony Burgess: Fire of Words* (Cham: Palgrave Macmillan, 2017), p. 145.

26 William M. Murray, 'Working on Apocalypse', interview with Anthony Burgess, *Conversations with Anthony Burgess*, ed. by Earl Ingersoll and Mary Ingersoll (Jackson, MS: University of Mississippi, 1977; 2008), p. 105.

27 Murray, 'Working on Apocalypse', p. 106.

28 Biswell, *The Real Life of Anthony Burgess*, p. 345; Lewis, *Anthony Burgess*, p. 117.
29 Roderick Nordell, 'Burgess Novel: Ultimate Questions, No Answers', *Christian Science Monitor*, 11 May 1983, p. 9; J.D. Reed, 'Dividing Gall into Three Parts', *Time*, 121.12, 21 March 1983, p. 76.
30 A.N. Wilson, 'Faith and Uncertainty: Recent Novels', *Encounter*, 60.2 (February 1983); Michael Wood, 'A Love Song to What Would Be Lost', *New York Times Book Review*, 6 March 1983; Lorna Sage, 'Jape of Things to Come', *Observer*, 24 October 1982, p. 33; Wake, 'Introduction', p. 17.
31 Wake, 'Introduction', p. 11.
32 Wake, 'Introduction', p. 11; Anthony Burgess Notebook on End of the World News, University of Texas at Austin: Harry Ransom Center, box 15.
33 Mikhail Bakhtin, *The Dialogic Imagination: Four Essays*, ed. by Michael Holquist, trans. by Caryl Emerson and Michael Holquist (Austin, TX: University of Texas Press, 1981), p. 326.
34 Bakhtin, *The Dialogic Imagination*, p. 271.
35 Bakhtin, *The Dialogic Imagination*, p. 311.
36 Bakhtin, *The Dialogic Imagination*, p. 278.
37 Burgess, *You've Had Your Time*, p. 326.
38 Bakhtin, *The Dialogic Imagination*, p. 278.
39 Burgess, *The End of the World News*, pp. 130, 159.
40 Burgess, *The End of the World News*, p. 195.
41 Anthony Burgess, *Little Wilson and Big God: Being the First Part of the Autobiography* (New York: Weidenfeld & Nicolson, 1986), p. 17; Burgess, *The End of the World News*, p. 155.
42 Burgess, *You've Had Your Time*, pp. 120, 327; Burgess, *The End of the World News*, p. 72.
43 Burgess, *You've Had Your Time*, p. 159.
44 Ex-American G.I., Letter to Anthony Burgess, 7 October 1971, University of Texas at Austin, Harry Ransom Center Archives.
45 Burgess, *The End of the World News*, p. 154.
46 Anthony Burgess, 'Anthony Burgess Lecture: "The Writer's Daily Damnation" ', Sarah Lawrence College: Sarah Lawrence College Archives, 19 January 1971, p. 23.
47 Burgess, *The End of the World News*, p. 74; Anthony Burgess, 'Is Shakespeare Relevant?', *New York Times*, 11 December 1970; Mary Ann Grossman, 'Banned Books Testify to Fear of Ideas', *St. Paul Pioneer Press*, 28 September 1985, the University of Texas at Austin: Harry Ransom Center Archives, 'Anthony Burgess Papers'.
48 Burgess, *The End of the World News*, p. 30.
49 Burgess, *The End of the World News*, p. 216.
50 Geoffrey Aggeler, *Anthony Burgess: The Artist as Novelist* (Tuscaloosa, AL: University of Alabama Press, 1979), p. 99.
51 Anthony Burgess, 'Believing in or Abominating the Past', *The Minneapolis Star*, 28 November 1972, p. 6.

52 Burgess, 'Believing in or Abominating the Past', p. 6; Anthony Burgess, 'A Candid Interview with the Author of *A Clockwork Orange*', interview with Katherine Pritchard, *Seventeen*, 32.8 (August 1973), p. 249; Anthony Burgess, *Puma* (Manchester: Manchester University Press, 2018), p. 224.
53 Anthony Burgess, *Honey for the Bears* (New York: W.W. Norton, 1963; 1996), pp. 99, 162.
54 'The English Author Anthony Burgess', *NRK TV*, 16 October 1981, https://tv.nrk.no/program/FOLA02008681
55 Burgess, *Honey for the Bears*, p. 255.
56 'An Interview with Anthony Burgess: "The Challenge of Our Time"', *Jim Nelson Black* (The University of Texas at Arlington, 15 May 1973; 2016), p. 8.
57 Anthony Burgess, 'Cardboard Character', *TV Guide*, 1982 (unpublished; International Anthony Burgess Foundation Archive), p. 3.
58 Burgess, *The End of the World News*, pp. 113, 224.
59 Anthony Burgess, *The Great Cities – New York* (Amsterdam: Time-Life Books, 1976), p. 161; Anthony Burgess, 'Thoughts on Irangate', 1987, University of Texas at Austin: Harry Ransom Center Archives, Gabriele Pantucci Collection, container 7, p. 1.
60 Burgess, *The End of the World News*, p. 290.
61 Burgess, *Puma*, p. 221.
62 Paul Wake, 'Notes', *Puma*, p. 309.
63 Burgess, *The End of the World News*, p. 288.
64 Anthony Burgess, *M/F* (London: Jonathan Cape, 1971), p. 35.
65 Burgess, *The End of the World News*, p. 161.

7

Enderby's Dark Lady, or No End to Enderby (1984)

> But all the plots of Shakespeare are, as the kids discover, pregnant with present relevance. Black is beautiful (Othello and Cleopatra), also powerful, but Mister Charlie does for them. Women outtalk men (Beatrice), succeed in the professions (Portia, La Pucelle), plot murder (Lady Macbeth). Useless wars kill men and destroy civilizations (the history plays); dictators come to sticky ends (the Roman plays). Wealth is a snare (Timon of Athens), virginity a joke (Measure for Measure), colonialism intolerable (Caliban – Shakespeare's one American character – in The Tempest). (Anthony Burgess, 'Is Shakespeare Relevant?')[1]

Introduction and background

Taking place just three years after the events of *The Clockwork Testament, or Enderby's End* (1974), in 1976, but along a different timeline, Enderby, in *Enderby's Dark Lady, or No End to Enderby* (1984), returns to the United States by visiting two states Burgess had spent some time in: Indiana and North Carolina.[2] Published the same year as William Boyd's *Stars and Bars* (1984), in which another Englishman – who carries around sabres for fencing, not unlike Enderby's swordstick in *The Clockwork Testament* – visits New York City and the American South only to encounter humorous disasters and disappointments, where valuable art is burned, guns and business dealings are plentiful, and the native Brit struggles with Ameringlish, *Enderby's Dark Lady* exists only as a partially farcical tale, being surrounded by Shakespeare short stories, that is far more callous and focused on Enderby, a character who, dissimilar to Boyd's, Henderson Dores, 'wants change – he wants to be different from what he is. And that, really, is why he is here', but is still, exhaustingly and frustratingly, the same angry and bitter Enderby of *The Clockwork Testament*, who appears again conjured to take on Burgess's own quibbles.[3] In having Enderby return to the United States, 'condemned to visit ... there to suffer', the text and character dialogues take on, in the Bakhtinian sense, the roles of existing as refracted authorial 'discourse in the language of a character and finally the discourse of a whole incorporated genre', that of parody, which, through close biographical analysis, expose the 'oppositions between individuals [who] are only surface upheavals of the untamed elements in social heteroglossia'.[4] At the beginning of the short novel, deemed a novella by Burgess, Enderby explains that he 'should have gone to New York to become a professor for a time. A consequence of *The Wreck of the Deutschland*, you know. It was a question of one or the other. So I chose this. More creative than Creative Writing, if you see what I mean', which is representative and evocative of an important bifurcation involving Burgess's own fractured view of his time in the United States where he, more successfully than Enderby, though not without his frustrations, made a living as a literary author, public intellectual, visiting professor, and freelance writer.[5] Since in all areas of 'life and ideological activity, our speech is filled to overflowing with other people's words, which are transmitted with highly varying degrees of accuracy and impartiality', it is no wonder that the peripatetic life of Burgess is strikingly exhibited in *Enderby's Dark Lady* as an example of an 'intensive, differentiated and highly developed ... social life of a speaking collective' with a greater importance placed 'among other possible subjects of talk, to another's word, another's utterance'.[6] This approach to novelistic fiction is not new in Burgess's canon or this monograph's analysis, but more so than in other novels, in *Enderby's Dark Lady*, Burgess appears to attempt to bring his arguments concerning American culture to a close through a fictional text, by dealing specifically through a theme of American cultural criticism that looks at show business and the commoditization of art, race, and language. In many ways Enderby's death at the conclusion of *The Clockwork Testament* acts as a condemnation of the United States's obsession with fame, its treatment of literature in society, and its mission in higher education, while *Enderby's Dark Lady* allows Burgess/Enderby to revisit the United States with less animosity, although Enderby's, and by association Burgess's, disgust is still potent, in order to use the United States as a backdrop for creative release in the shape of science fiction, myth, and cultural criticism, as the author and the fictional character bid farewell to the country that afforded Burgess consternation coupled with opportunity, going on to visit the United States fewer than a half-dozen times in the last decade of this life, a striking contrast to the two decades previous. *The Clockwork Testament* is a harsh castigation of all that Burgess saw as wrong with the United States, while *Enderby's Dark Lady* acts as a parodic *carmen cygni*, or literary *au revoir*, from Burgess to the American public, which is made clear in the mere fact that after 1984, when *Enderby's Dark Lady* was published, Burgess did not write another novel that prominently showcased the

United States, effectively ending his two-decades-long artistic relationship with the country, only to return a handful of times and under strict circumstances of payment and accommodations before his death in 1993 – though near the end of his life, he did at least have writing ideas that still involved the United States, and Canada, chief among them being the proposed *Our Lady of the Snows* novel and *The Hunters Are Up in America*, surviving as two short outlines, neither of which was fully realized before his death.[7]

Again, the novels chosen for this monograph are texts in which the United States is prominently displayed in and through Burgess's characters and plots, which also present dialogized echoes between the fiction and the author's own life, and therefore must be critically positioned in and recognized as existing within a historical and biographical context in order to make complete sense of the text, since these representations tend to be under the pressure of an authorial monologism. This is not necessarily an aesthetic objection *per se*, since, by Bakhtinian standards, 'objectivity is not a supreme goal' due to objectivity being intrinsically 'unattainable, in itself, because the author's voice is always present, regardless of how thoroughly it is disguised', and *Enderby's Dark Lady* is no different, though, as with *The Clockwork Testament*, these novels tend to be much more autobiographical than some of Burgess's other work, with Enderby, as Rob Spence has noted, existing in these novels not so much as a fully autonomous and idealized character but as what Henry James would have called 'a vessel of consciousness, albeit a shaky and porous one'.[8]

The character/author similarities are again pronounced in Enderby's final journey, wherein Burgess literarily returns, fifteen years later, to the first American university where he held an extended position as a writer-in-residence, at the University of North Carolina at Chapel Hill in November and December 1969. Echoing Burgess in *You've Had Your Time* (1990), where he incorrectly remarks that he was 'a visiting professor' at the 'oldest state university in the Union' – he was a writer-in-residence and the University of North Carolina is the first to begin instruction to students, but is not the oldest since the University of Georgia was chartered in 1785, four years before the University of North Carolina's charter – the third-person omniscient narrator of *Enderby's Dark Lady* informs readers that Enderby was approaching the 'first of the United States state universities', effectively ensuring that the lives of Burgess and Enderby have yet again entwined.[9] The University of North Carolina at Chapel Hill was Burgess's grand entrance into the United States, and it revealed both the positive aspects and frustrations of this new relationship he was to build with England's cantankerous neighbour across the Atlantic – what with his proposed doctoral ambitions being denied while he spent his first full month in a single American city and university campus, while being a kind of campus-wide intellectual celebrity, something that would be routine over the next several years, but which really *started* in Chapel Hill – so it's unsurprising that Enderby ends his four-book lifespan where Burgess began becoming an American personality by acting out, yet again, an autobiograficational double-voiced discourse which reeks of American heteroglossia, all wrapped up (though less than *The Clockwork Testament*) in a monologic authorial *au revoir* and hidden polemic directed at the country which, arguably perhaps most significantly impacted his life financially, artistically, and professionally.[10]

Background of *Enderby's Dark Lady*

At its core, this is a book, partially a novella, which is a hybrid construction of authorially indeterminate stories surrounding a narrative of a recurring partially autobiographical character from a known novelist. It is experimental, it is diverse, and though every piece provides context for explaining Burgess and his artistic processes, it is in essence all about Shakespeare, with the Enderby narrative thrown in as a disappointing farewell to the character and to Burgess writing the United States into his fiction. Such a criticism is not unlike other reviews of the novella that came out after the book's publication, wherein much of the feedback was similar to a *Kirkus Review* which called the story 'limp' and missing 'the two strengths of the previous novels', while another critic argued the satire of the book was 'misplaced' and, finally and most accurately, that the book produced 'collapses of tone' resulting in a 'simply bewildering, neither amusing nor to any discernible point' of a novel that exhibited 'mild flings at parody' which 'seem to cancel each other out', with Burgess appearing 'to have lost real enthusiasm for the cultural battle as he has waged it before'.[11] This is telling, since although still bombastic, caustic, insulting, gross, and disturbing, in *Enderby's Dark Lady*, Enderby does seem to have lost some of his viciousness which is tampered by his existence in the American mid-West, either due to the environment or to Burgess's disinterestedness with the United States and/or Enderby – 'Enderby's demand to be resurrected has come inconveniently' – at the time of producing this strange and clunky excuse of a novella.[12] In *Enderby's Dark Lady*, the Enderby of *The Clockwork Testament* who flashes swordstick and cuts marauders on the subway is exchanged for an Enderby whose libido is in need of satiating (remember that the Enderby of *Inside Mr Enderby* believes in the 'act of creation. Sex. That was the trouble with art. Urgent sexual desire aroused with the excitement of a new image or rhythm'), where he, much like Alexander Portnoy and Peter Tarnopol of Philip Roth's novels *Portnoy's Complaint* (1969) and *My Life as a Man* (1974), can't seem to contain his sexual desires, which results in him having to find 'a small and overdainty lavatory' so that he could pound 'his load out furiously' and having to 'cart' his 'engorged shlong three times into the bathroom and, on a face towel monogrammed with a fanciful S, fiercely discharge his heat', both times while thinking of Shakespeare in some capacity.[13] It may even be that *The Clockwork Testament* was the American *violence* novel and *Enderby's Dark Lady* is the American *sex* novel, this time with Enderby resembling Roth's Portnoy who, as a child, ejaculates 'three drops of something barely viscous into the tiny piece of cloth where my flat-chested eighteen-year-old sister has laid her nipples, such as they are', during his 'fourth orgasm of the day', and Roth's Tarnopol who masturbates in public and 'smears' and leaves his semen 'places', or 'Tarnopol's silver bullet'.[14] Still, with Portnoy questioning his incestuous urges towards his mother and sister, with Enderby running off to a bathroom to wipe his penis, in a state of detumescence, 'on a handy face towel' in a public bathroom after a séance where he believes Shakespeare sent him a message by pounding '46' on the table, it seems all these characters are struggling to figure out, like Tarnopol after too smearing his semen on public items, 'What does it mean!' about their peculiar predicaments – something to do with sexual frustration, lust, and the production of art, just like Bloom's masturbation in the 'Nausicaa' episode of *Ulysses* (1922) with his post-ejaculation 'little limping devil' – but Burgess here seems far more derivative than novel, more crude than humorous, more lazy than inventive than his contemporary or his predecessor.[15]

As *Enderby's Dark Lady* begins to take shape, Enderby is put into a situation that Burgess was familiar with, being requested to visit an American city to do literary work of some capacity, this time being enlisted to collaboratively work on a 'ridiculous musical ... play on the career of William Shakespeare to celebrate, for the commission was inevitably American, the second American centennial conjoined with the three hundred and sixtieth anniversary of Shakespeare's death', a strange proposition to Enderby since it 'was not immediately clear what connection there could be between the death of a poet and the birth of a sort of nation'.[16] Even stranger, Enderby learns upon landing in the United States that the idea for the play supposedly came from Shakespeare's posthumous communication with the clairvoyant Mrs. Allegramente, who has, the Americans claim, spoken to the Elizabethan poet from the 'Happy House' or 'mansion of the blessed' in the afterlife and has said that he 'was delighted that America had achieved two hundred years of free nationhood' and that he, Shakespeare, 'wished to be associated in song and dance with our celebrations'.[17] A strange, surreal, mythic, and illogical place, Enderby is yet again equipped with another coffee mug emblazoned with an American city, 'CHICAGO – MY KIND OF TOWN' – in *The Clockwork Testament* it's 'five bags in a pint mug with ALABAMA gilded onto it' and a 'GEORGIA tea mug' – a vessel given to Enderby 'by a Jewish visitor to Tangiers, citizen of that city full of wind, who claimed acquaintanceship with a Jewish novelist called [Saul] Bellow'.[18] Enderby, in this parallel universe, opens the novella again questioning what he has gotten himself into in visiting the United States, this time being 'forced into "prostituting" [his] art to cheap popular entertainment', which in Enderby's case is compounded by the reality that the actress, April Elgar, who plays 'Lucy Negro, the dark-skinned woman', a name coming from an Elizabethan prostitute whom Burgess speculated was Shakespeare's 'Dark Lady' – a topic investigated by such Shakespearean scholars who Burgess reviewed such as Alfred Leslie (A.L.) Rowse who claimed to have figured out the identity of the 'dark lady' in his 1973 monograph *Shakespeare the Man* and who went on *The Dick Cavett Show* in October 1978 and said that Burgess was a 'low-brow writer' whose comments on Shakespeare weren't 'of any real value' and that he, Rowse, was 'not interested in [Burgess]', since Rowse was 'only really interested in first-rate writers' – has also been sold, 'ironically, into white slavery' in the shape of the American acting and stage performance scene.[19] Since all of Burgess's literature is at its core 'a process of self-identification and self-discovery', there exists no difference here from the other works discussed in this monograph except that *Enderby's Dark Lady* may tie with *The Clockwork Testament* as being the most prominent and quintessential examples of Burgess's authorial catharsis acting itself out autobiographically through vaguely fictional texts.[20] Within this paradigm of self-discovery through literary production, *Enderby's Dark Lady* acts as a step backward into Burgess's past and a step forward into Burgess's future, in the sense that this text reverts back to common themes approached in Burgess's previous Enderby novels, as well as fictionally in *Nothing Like the Sun* (1963) and as non-fiction in *Shakespeare* (1970), but *Enderby's Dark Lady* – all three texts of which were simultaneously in print in 1984 – breaks that mould by turning the novella into a metafictional Künstlerroman about the parallel experiences of Enderby and Burgess – Burgess having written the screenplay *Will!, or the Bawdy Bard*, which turned into the ballet *Mr WS* – as well as a science fiction genesis story about the interstellar artistic inspirations of an interdimensional William Shakespeare (in *Inside Mr Enderby* (1963), this Enderby too is inspired by travellers from the future when a kiss from a time-travelling student 'has prodded a sleeping inspiration. Listen. *My bedmate deep / In the heavy labour of unrequited sleep*').[21] Additionally, and comparatively, *Enderby's Dark Lady* may be building upon Burgess's friend Jorge Luis Borges's proclamation in 'Tlön, Uqbar, Orbis Tertius' that 'All men, in the vertiginous moment of coitus, are the same man. All men who repeat a line from Shakespeare are William Shakespeare', and/or it is a response to Borges's story, 'Shakespeare's Memory' (1983), which came out the year before *Enderby's Dark Lady* and describes a man given the option to live in Shakespeare's mind but who loses his own identity – the similarities to these fictional representations of Shakespeare thus have the effect of contributing to a broader literary epitextual dialogue occurring during a specific chronotope, just outside the text.[22]

The science fiction portion of the novel, chapter 12, 'The Muse' – the title of the short story being left out initially but where Burgess pencilled into the proof copy for it to be added – was also in the works for years before *Enderby's Dark Lady*, with the idea being commissioned by Kingsley Amis to write a story for a science fiction anthology in 1964; the book was never produced but Burgess ended up publishing the story, entitled 'The Muse: A Sort of SF Story', in the spring 1968 edition of the *Hudson Review*, going on to have it reprinted, without its original subtitle, in the seventh edition of *Penguin Modern Stories* (1971) and finally in the University of Buffalo professor and friend/colleague of Burgess Leslie Fiedler's edited collection, *In Dreams Awake* (1975).[23] Thinking of combining Shakespeare and science fiction for years, Burgess, jocularly or apocryphally, even suggested at one point that this part of *Enderby's Dark Lady* was included as a 'response to a suggestion by a PhD candidate moonlighting as a cab driver that he write a science fiction story about the Bard', and so 'The Muse' in *Enderby's Dark Lady* appears with several slight revisions from the original but is essentially the exact same story, and is placed as an epilogue that seems to converse with the historical fiction short story, 'Will and Testament', that opens the book – a 're-working of Rudyard Kipling's short-story of 1934, "Proofs of Holy Writ" ', which Burgess presented 'as part of the International Shakespeare Association Congress in Washington D.C. in April 1976' and which was published by Plain Wrapper Press in a limited edition printing in 1977 – leaving the novella in the middle bookended by Elizabethan short stories that are not seemingly unrelated to the Enderby text except through the theme of Shakespeare and Enderby the poet, who, although he 'did not read novels' and, as stated in *Inside Mr Enderby*, 'Prose was not his *métier*', is the implied author of the short stories which surround the text of Enderby's journey.[24] Andrew Biswell, Burgess's biographer, argues that these pieces have an 'overall effect within *Enderby's Dark Lady*' of enriching 'the short story by adding new layers of meaning which were not present in its previous incarnations. Deftly redeploying his story in a self-mocking comic novel, Burgess provides a metafictional commentary on his own practice as a historical novelist', and though this may be true to some extent, background information is needed to come to this conclusion, since without knowing this textual history, instead, *Enderby's Dark Lady* comes off as an unfocused and confusing bricolage of a work, not entirely dissimilar to

The Clockwork Testament, but to a fuller degree less cohesive.[25] Significant for the purposes of this monograph, though, to stress this again, is that the sheer extent of epitextual elements, authorial multi-voicedness, and simultaneous authorial narratives makes conducting a Bakhtinian analysis of Burgess's 'dialogic imagination', where 'context prevails over text', as Marilyn Middendorf explains about Bakhtin's concepts, not only beneficial to better understand Burgess's works but also to better understand the historical, cultural, and biographical pressures that weigh on the text, as a way to assess the pulsating sphere of the 'life-world' of the novel and its author, while also acknowledging the 'tentative and multivoiced humanity' at the core of human experience.[26]

Similar to the alien Shakespeare in the final chapter, the Enderby in *Enderby's Dark Lady* is from another timeline in a similarly satirized and caricatured United States to the Enderby of *The Clockwork Testament*, with this new iteration of Enderby being exposed yet again to, as Farkas astutely explains, 'American philistinism but, unlike in the first ending of the sequel where he confronts the aggressive ignorance of the New World ... here Enderby is suspended, Hamlet-like as it were, on the horns of the artistic dilemma whether to please or not to please'.[27] Reflective of Enderby, both Burgess and his character are subjected to being, as Burgess explains in the 'Prefatory Note' which opens the book, 'condemned to visit the United States, there to suffer', either by 'going to Manhattan to teach creative Writing' or in 'being employed to write the libretto for a ridiculous musical about Shakespeare in a fictitious theatre in Indianapolis', where Enderby only *experiences* one or the other, but where Burgess experienced both realities.[28] *The Clockwork Testament* was Burgess's cathartic release and *Enderby's Dark Lady* acts similarly, but more so as a goodbye, a kind of exorcism meant to expunge any remaining frustrations he had towards the country. He does so through the ever-static Enderby who learns and grows little, but is less vituperative now in *Enderby's Dark Lady*, in an Enderbian farewell to the United States and to the character of Enderby. As is apparent by tracking Burgess's authorial and public discourse, juxtaposed with the language of the text, *Enderby's Dark Lady* is yet again another autobiograficational monoglottal production which rarely allows characters to be, as Bakhtin explains in *Problems of Dostoyevsky's Poetics*, '*subjects of their own directly signifying discourse*', since the text as a whole does not allow for the 'consciousness of a character' to be given 'as *someone else's* consciousness, another consciousness', because Enderby, and indeed the other characters, tend to turn into objects which are 'closed' from autonomy due to them being by-products 'of the author's consciousness'.[29] Once again, as Bakhtin notes, this time in *Dialogic Imagination*, 'our speech is filled to overflowing with other people's words, which are transmitted with highly varying degrees of accuracy and impartiality', and what is evident in *Enderby's Dark Lady* is that Burgess has made less of an attempt to create autonomous characters than in his other works in order to present a satire and parody of his own life in fictional form, as a kind of commentary on his life and his opinions.[30] Although biographically significant, and literarily complex enough to attract interpretation, this does not necessarily make for an achieved novelistic vision, since when contextualizing *Enderby's Dark Lady*, what emerges is a 'monologic artistic world' where 'the idea, once placed in the mouth of a hero who is portrayed as a fixed and finalized image of reality, inevitably loses its direct power to mean, becoming a mere aspect of reality, one more of reality's predetermined features, indistinguishable from any other manifestation of the hero', which results in the ideas being expressed by these characters as ceasing to contain meaning inside the text alone, becoming only 'simple characterizing feature[s]' with potent allusiveness to the author's life and public language.[31] Enderby is of course versatile for Burgess, really being a different character almost entirely from novel to novel, working various jobs and taking on different moods, but it is this imprecision that results in Enderby being more of an affixed appendage to Burgess, a 'fixed and finalized' image of the distorted reality Burgess chooses and focuses *through* this protean self-projection, as needed, and especially in the final two Enderbian iterations.

Autobiography in *Enderby's Dark Lady*

Enderby's Dark Lady is a novella that works into what Jim Clarke calls Burgess's 'autobiographical turn in the 1980s, which transpired to be more confabulated than factual', existing as a 'counterfactual or speculative biography' that once again breaks with the Enderby that readers had been introduced to earlier in *Inside Mr Enderby* (1963) and *Enderby Outside* (1968), to an Enderby whose story acts as an 'editorial comment upon Burgess's own interactions with Shakespeare and the world of theatre'.[32] This does not go far enough, though, because Enderby's presence in *Enderby's Dark Lady* is yet another act too of self-mythologization for Burgess, since, by placing his most autobiographical character into a 'Goddess paradigm … conflated with the reality of a black woman, just as it is in *Nothing Like the Sun*', in order for Burgess to extend the American and 'the Enderby mythos' – 'Godgeorge. America, by Gorge', as the text alludes to Burgess's own unfinished American 'George Trilogy' – he allows for both character and author to extend their mythos, all while also revisiting the author's own past both in Chapel Hill, North Carolina and in Indiana in order to present a final castigation of the United States in the guise of reconciliation.[33]

Arriving in Indiana, much as Burgess did in Minneapolis, Minnesota in 1972 as the 'literary consultant and writer' for the Tyrone Guthrie Theater – a relationship which would result in two stage-plays and adaptations for Burgess in *Oedipus the King* (1972) and *Cyrano* (1971/85) – Enderby has been 'commissioned to write not only verse but mock Tudor dialogue' for an American stage-play.[34] Enderby describes Indiana, the fictional Terrebasse, as being 'generally known as the Hoosier State [with] 91 per cent of total area farmland. Iron, glass, carriages, railroad cars, woolens, etc. Climate remarkably equable. Leading cities Indianapolis, Fort Wayne, South Bend, Evansville, Gary. Terrebasse not mentioned'.[35] In French, Terrebasse means 'low land', which stands in contrast to the real town of Terre Haute, Indiana, which means 'high land', in order to, again redolent of Dante's *Divine Comedy* that was an inspiration for *The Clockwork Testament*, signify a descent into ludicrousness and depravity, which all takes place during the production of an Americanized Shakespeare play that is disrupted due to a 'Union regulation' issue – similar to *Inside Mr Enderby* with Walpole's concerns about Enderby not being in a union – and Enderby scaring the audience into evacuating by uttering, '*Fire*. … "There's no fire, I just said fire, that's all." *Fire* came again', the mere thought of a conflagration, or inferno, scattering the 'no discipline' American audience.[36] Beyond the apparent wordplay, Burgess's decision to choose Indiana, 'why Indiana, a part of the United States I do not know very well?', may be partially explained by looking elsewhere in his canon.[37] Burgess did visit Indiana on several occasions for lectures: visiting Purdue University in 1973 and Earlham and Wabash Colleges in 1975, spending only a collective three days there, but more importantly readers of *Earthly Powers* (1980) will remember that it is Indiana where the cult leader, Godfrey Manning, grew up, a place the novel describes as being filled with racism, violence, and hypocritical Christian authority.[38] Although Manning appears as a religiously devout White American who was opposed to the rampant racial prejudice and bigotry in the fictional Pring, Indiana, when given some backstory, he goes on to commit a Peoples Temple, Jim Jones-like religious massacre in California before trying to escape the United States. Converting the name of the Indiana city Enderby visits to mean lowland, and being the home-state of Manning, urges readers of Burgess's canon to then see Indiana as, especially as *Enderby's Dark Lady* continues, a depraved, debased, and delusional space which lacks any sound morals. But there may be more to this. Burgess describes Manning's backstory thus:

> Manning's parents had died in a road accident near Dectur, Illinois, and he had gone to live with an uncle and aunt. The town of Pring was a Ku Klux Klan centre where custom defied law and said that no n----- had better have the sun setting on his head if he didn't want gunshot in his ass. … Sick of

> the racism of Pring, he dropped out of its high school whose principal was a loud voice of intolerance and enrolled in a school in the bigger town of Richmond [before entering] Indiana University in Bloomington. … He was jeered at during church services; dead cats were stuffed into the church toilets. N-----LOVER was chalked on the church wall. He became a parttime student at Butler University, took ten years to get a bachelor's degree and was finally ordained as a minister of the Disciples of the Lord Jesus. … He continued to suffer the enmity of racists. Talking to a black brother at a bus stop he was hit by a hurled beer bottle. His wife was spat upon in a supermarket. He saw his church as a garrison besieged by a mad and dangerous world.[39]

Pring, Indiana does not exist, but *pring* is an Andalusian dish made of slow cooked meat. Andalusia being an autonomous nation-state in southern Spain, a connection can be found via the Spanish-founded town of Valparaiso, Indiana that rests just south of Chicago and north of Terre Haute – high land and low land – the town's name in Spanish meaning 'Paradise Valley', a misnomer and oxymoron that ironically contrasts with Manning's rough rise in Indiana to be accepted into the 'Disciples of the Lord Jesus', leading him to eventually create a cult. Finally, to wrap this labyrinthine speculation up, Godfrey Manning's name provides even more clues to support these connective claims and to pull Chapel Hill into the mix. Godfrey, being pronounced *God-free*, evokes the idea of godlessness or *God-freed* where spirituality is held captive or rejected entirely, as Enderby feels both types of oppression in *Enderby's Dark Lady*. Stranger still, while at Chapel Hill in 1969, as previously mentioned, due to the Civil Rights and Black Power Movements on the University of North Carolina at Chapel Hill's campus when Burgess was there, the Lenoir Hall cafeteria was closed due to a demonstration and protest headed by the Black Student Movement president at the time, Preston Dobbins, a name that would have more than likely been mentioned to Burgess by Thomas Stumpf or some other such individual. Dobbins, born in St Louis but raised in Chicago, walked through the cafeteria sweeping food off people's tables and forced the school to relocate the dining hall to 'a sort of ersatz cafeteria out of Manning Hall' that drew in the attention of the North Carolina armed state police who subsequently surrounded Manning Hall and 'disturbed the Burgesses quite a bit'.[40]

This is possibly why it is unsurprising that Enderby is immediately met with an unwelcoming, stereotypical, and hostile environment upon arriving that vaguely resembles some sort of entrance into the underworld: 'The immigration officials seemed to let everyone in, even Americans, very grudgingly and only after looking up every name in a big book like a variorum edition of something', while the Americans behind Enderby growl, 'looking at their watches and muttering for Chrissake, as in an American novel'.[41] Enderby's descent appears to be into an *enfer*-like habitat where the 'dark lady who was to play the Dark Lady was completing a nightclub engagement', and the sacrosanct artist, William Shakespeare, is caricatured and commoditized into an *Übermensch* comical character screen-printed on Mrs. Schoenbaum's – her surname also alluding to the American Shakespeare scholar Samuel Schoenbaum, who mentioned Burgess's work on Shakespeare in *Shakespeare's Lives* (1970) and *Shakespeare: A Documentary Life* (1974) – the daughter, a college 'dropout', therefore embodying American hubris and anti-intellectualism, was 'greasy as though basted', and wears a T-shirt that 'had Shakespeare as bigfisted flying Superman on it with the legend WILL POWER' to yet again signal Americans' inability to be both learned and refined – the T-shirt perhaps even being a nod to the 'Shakespeare teeshirt I bought for him [his son, Paolo Andrea] at the conference' in Washington, DC in April 1976.[42] All this occurs as Enderby is led down a metaphorical River Styx to sell his soul to Mephistopheles – no apparent coin under his tongue for Charon, though – for money and fame, the Faustian bargain succumbed to by Mann's composer Adrian Leverkühn, as Enderby relinquishes his high artistic sense for the almighty dollar, subjecting himself to a kind of servitude or bondage that takes shape in the American system of show business.[43] His guide, the widow Mrs. Schoenbaum, to the low land is an archetype for the American obsession with financial wellbeing, whose husband 'was dead from making money', and who appears to Enderby to be 'clearly enjoying her widowhood. ... Her silver hair was frozen into a photographed stormtossed effect, clicked into sempiternal tempestuousness on a Wuthering Heights of the American imagination', is accompanied by 'one overweight man ... from the University of Indianapolis'.[44] The eternal woman with her gluttonous companion then take off into the low lands to embark on a dramaturgical nightmare, in a collapsed-Tower-of-Babel culture where Enderby cannot even understand the language, with him thinking 'dropout' means 'combining knockout and coughdrop' and where he ascertains that 'junkfood' is 'presumably food for junkies'.[45]

While in Terrebasse, Indiana, Enderby encounters a similar environment to the lawless land where 'custom defied law' that Manning encountered growing up, an environment evocative of 'a mad and dangerous' American tableau.[46] While naked in his corporatized Holiday Inn hotel room, awakened by a 'lavish ejaculation' at four in the morning brought on by the 'power of a woman he had not even seen and knew to be' in the mental image of April Elgar, Enderby squints at himself in the mirror, this time a 'long bathroom mirror' so he could see his entire naked being, something he could not do, he claims, in overly conservative Tangier, while coming to the realization that anything 'went down all right in this mad America' – clothes symbolizing the right level of permissiveness, with the United States starkly bare and Tangier fully covered and overly conservative.[47]

Perhaps most blatantly autobiographical, and unabashedly compared by Burgess himself, was the overlap between Burgess and Enderby when discussing the American author and Nobel Prize winner John Steinbeck. To begin chronologically, Burgess claims in *They Wrote in English* (1979) that after he had won the 1962 Nobel Prize, when asked by Burgess 'what he proposed to do with the money', John Steinbeck replied, 'Mind your own goddamn business'.[48] In *Enderby's Dark Lady*, Enderby tells a very similar story, to Mrs. Schoenbaum and Allegramente, after hearing that the latter has apparently communicated with Steinbeck and Shakespeare in the afterlife, telling the two American women that

> 'I met Steinbeck,' Enderby said, 'when he was given, unjustly I thought and still think, the Nobel, oh I don't know though when you consider some of these dago scribblers who get it, think it was an unjust bestowal. There was a party for him given by Heinemann in London. I asked him what he was going to do with the prize money and he said: *Fuck off*'.[49]

Reviewing Jackson Benson's biography of Steinbeck, *The True Adventures of Steinbeck, Writer: A Biography* (1984), Burgess eliminates any question of authorial double-voicedness in *Enderby's Dark Lady* when he admits that 'I have just published a novella in which, by happy chance, Steinbeck is mentioned' and after quoting the same above passage, he explains further by saying that Benson's book doesn't mention the party, but to clarify, what 'Steinbeck said to Enderby he really said to me. The rudeness was not typical but Steinbeck was very tired'.[50] Although Burgess occasionally equivocated when describing the similarities between him and his creation, here the barrier between fiction and non-fiction, author and character is stripped and collapsed, proving that Enderby, especially since *The Clockwork Testament*, had increased in his similarities to his creator and here is explained to be living out the same experiences almost exactly, thus dismantling any attempts to disregard the significance of the similarities between the two, and to therefore take up the challenge of analysing and deconstructing the meanings and influences behind Burgess crafting such autobiografictional Enderby novels – or as Saunders explains, the 'almost autobiographical' which is in 'the realm of autobiografiction' where the 'indeterminacy of the "almost" recognizes the difficulty of demarcating what is autobiography from what is invention' – as well as his fictional *American* narratives that address issues very close to the author-figure himself and conditional to his American experiences.[51]

The repetitive themes of American permissiveness, the rampant consumerism ('rather exciting, really, all this consumerism'), the out-of-place European in barbaric America and unabashed onanism in an American setting, the wordplay, the focus on race, the overlapping between Burgess and Enderby, and the locations all point to yet another autobiograficational Enderbian, and *American*, experience taking place, infused as it is with the heteroglossia of Burgess's own literary work and public life so as to assemble Enderby's final journey to the United States, and simultaneously to wrap up several loose ends that Burgess had left undone in *M/F* (1971), *The Clockwork Testament* (1974), *New York* (1976), *Earthly Powers* (1980), and *The End of the World News* (1982).

American sex, show, and business in *Enderby's Dark Lady*

Enraptured and enticed by both the United States and April, Enderby is enveloped in the country's culture slowly, silently, and morbidly. The alluring April entrances Enderby as he loses sight of his inclinations and attachments to the past that he had held in such high esteem, remarking that although she 'was black America, which was better than Cedar Rapids', she was 'not Elizabethan London. Nor, God help him, were his own rhythms', all while Enderby ponders Shakespeare's own possible attraction to a woman of dark complexion: 'what right had he, Enderby, to assume that Shakespeare had fallen for a genuine negress (inadmissible term nowadays, he had been told)?' – though also a poetic term, this would be inadmissible at the time Enderby is using the word, since, aside from being categorized as 'offensive' by the *Oxford English Dictionary*, the word was also very outdated by the 1980s, considering its popularity dropped precipitously after the early twentieth century.[52] Resonant with Burgess – as evidenced in his class on Shakespeare at the City College of New York during the spring semester of 1973 – the author wondered, just as Enderby does, if Shakespeare had fallen in love with a Black woman, though a 'dark lady was not necessarily a black lady'.[53] Explaining to his City College class that it was regular for visitors, even in New York City, to send word to a brothel to have a 'negress' ready for them, Burgess argues that Shakespeare was, in Sonnet 127, the first to say 'black is beautiful', reciting, 'In the old age black was not counted fair, / Or if it were, it bore not beauty's name; / But now is black beauty's successive heir, / And beauty slandered with a bastard shame'.[54] Enderby, as he slowly believes himself to be turned into Shakespeare – 'Enderby enWilled himself' to become a mixture of the two with 'Will Enderby', 'Enderspeare', 'Shakeserby', 'Willerby', 'Shakesby', 'Enderwill', 'Shenderspeare', and/or 'Spearsby', and the completion of the metamorphosis, 'I am William Shakespeare' – believes he has caught the same lust and passion for a 'dark lady' by being 'corrupted in advance, he had *wanted* a black lady, and nobody had questioned his assumption'.[55] Enderby's translation into Shakespeare is provoked and urged on by the

United States, but it's a transformation Enderby is unworthy of, since, as the novella concludes, 'Shakespeare looked at Enderby from the mirror and coldly nodded' when asked to remove his costume; to make such an attempt appears to have come at a Mephistophelian, or Faustian, price, since Enderby did not heed his own warnings to leave Shakespeare alone and not tamper with him, and so Enderby's pride and identity are stripped as the story progresses.[56] Although not the first time for Enderby to see figures in mirrors – remember that he 'was shocked to see the image of his stepmother in the big Gilbey's Port mirror' in the 'saloon-bar of the Neptune' pub, who then nods at Enderby, 'as out of some animated painting in a TV commercial, raised its glass in New Year salutation, then seemed to hobble out of the picture, into the wings, thus disappearing' in the opening chapters of *Inside Mr Enderby* (1963) on New Year's Day – this suggests that Enderby has a history of seeing beyond reality in mirrors, whether they be apparitions or delusions.[57] Another legitimate interpretation that could very well lead to this same outcome would be that Enderby is not seeing himself as Shakespeare but an actual apparition of Shakespeare exists in the mirror, both valid likelihoods since Enderby believes, without any substantive proof – and not to mention that the narrative isn't entirely trustworthy as an Enderby and Burgess third-person conglomeration – that Shakespeare is haunting the entire production, especially after Enderby believes the playwright to have signalled a warning to him during a séance: ' "But it was him all right. And you don't know why, do you, eh?" He wagged a finger at her [Mrs. Allegramente]. "Leave him alone is my advice. Don't meddle. Good friend for Jesus' sake forbear, remember that" ... "I'm getting out of here" '.[58] Enderby repeats the warning on Shakespeare's grave – 'Good friend for Jesus sake forbeare, / To dig the dust enclosed here. / Blessed be the man that spares these stones, / And cursed be he that moves my bones' – after the table was knocked on four and six times to signal Shakespeare's addition of his name into Psalm 46 of the King James Bible.[59] Strangely, as will be discussed, the eery encounter provokes Enderby to masturbate shortly afterwards, thus signalling that sex, and death (this could include violence), are the urges most human, most discomforting, perhaps most American, and paradoxically the most literary and non-literary: ' "It's the death urge, I suppose, death and sex come very close together – oh, we're damned, we're damned, we're damned".'[60]

Writing in 'Pornography: "The Moral Question Is Nonsense"; For Permissiveness, With Misgivings' in the *New York Times* in July 1973, Burgess argued that the age of sexual permissiveness, especially in the United States, resulted in an age that permitted 'any kind of subject matter in fictional art or sub-art', which inevitably led to the 'bad artist, or the merely money-grubbing sub-artist, exploit[ing] the whole range of sex and violence, since these are what interest people most'.[61] Enderby, conditioned by the Americanization of the world even before entering the United States, encounters this swiftly with April and the poor art of the fictional Peter Brook Theater. Castrated and consumed whole by the United States – 'Pete Oldfellow said in heat: "She's got him by the balls, she's made him pussy-drunk, she eats him for dinner"' – Enderby is acclimatized predominantly against his will.[62] Enderby's ironic allure to the United States is matched by Burgess's own, as Enderby reflects that he 'had been drawn into the celebration of America, not Shakespeare. What voice from the dead had condoned the travesty to come? ... He should have read the small print before signing. Sold into slavery, by God. Suable if he reneged. Best embrace one's enforced corruption', a submissive and sexual sentiment similarly shared by Burgess in the mid-1980s in the unpublished article, 'Ah, Liberty', in which Burgess bemoans American Fourth of July celebrations where the Statue of Liberty is praised and reproduced, even with 'six-foot plastic replicas of the statue' and an 'inflatable version which the sex-starved may take to bed', which is 'quite an achievement, since, in this country so adept at the exploitation of female beauty, Miss Liberty is the one woman who totally lacks sexual allure. She has too many clothes on'.[63] Continuing, Burgess casts aspersions on American exceptionalism through faint praise which is worth producing here from this unpublished piece of writing:

> For my part, I remain touched by that curious combination of sagacity and innocence which characterizes America in search of that very American commodity which reconciles entertainment and uplift. Disneyland is a monstrous work of mechanical and electronic genius, and so are the Liberty celebrations. It is entirely appropriate that the switch which lights up the effigy should be in the control of a president who began his career as a film actor [Ronald Reagan].[64] In America the art of entertainment is big business, and big business is politics – or vice versa. Television, with all its uncountable channels, has been scouring the archives for entertaining fodder that should be appropriate to this special July 4, but it has not come up with a film about the struggle to get Miss Liberty erected in the first place. It has come as close as it can get with a cinematic biography of the [John Philip] Sousa who composed the 'Stars and Stripes For Ever'. Those brassy sounds are the very noise of American hope and innocence.[65]

Taking the concept of ridiculous sexual urges, a theme in American media from the novels of Philip Roth, Gore Vidal, and Terry Southern, to popular 1970s blaxploitation and porn films with voyeuristic sex scenes like in *Sweet Sweetback's Baadasssss Song* (1971) and the Golden Age pornography movies of *Behind the Green Door* (1972) and *Deep Throat* (1972), in *Enderby's Dark Lady*, Enderby, acting as Shakespeare, nearly forgets his histrionic role when he notices the 'sturdy filling of his codpiece' onstage with April during a sex scene.[66] Never fulfilled, though, Enderby feels 'inter-crucial wetness' inside his pants from pre-ejaculate, the potentially public sexual display ceases to appease the American audience and is disrupted by union protest, and thus Enderby's attraction to April ceases to be consummated and he ceases to become Shakespeare.[67]

Since the last two Enderby novels show a strong resemblance between author and literary character, as readers we then become 'obliged to introduce a fourth symmetrical term on the side of utterance, an extratextual referent that could be called the prototype, or better yet, the *model*', in this case being the storied public life of John Anthony Burgess Wilson which is evidence of Burgess's inability, or disregard, 'to get out of the self; that is to say, to represent, equally with our own, a point of view different from our own'.[68] Although Philippe LeJeune, here quoted, would likely disagree with equating auto/biographical and fictional texts as referential texts, Bakhtinian notions of heteroglossia, as David Shepherd argues in 'Bakhtin and the Reader', which seep into an authorial monologism, beg that they be, especially in texts like *Enderby's Dark Lady* which appear to nod and suggest the need to provide a 'restoration of an often excluded history' outside and around the text, in the epitextual boundaries.[69] On numerous occasions in *Enderby's Dark Lady*, Enderby again gives voice to some of Burgess's own grievances and denunciations so that an unrestrained honesty is transmuted from the author and vocalized through Enderby's polemics. A prime example of this is when Enderby goes into a diatribe in a local bar, waxing poetical about the licentiousness and contradictory nature of Americans after a hard-hatted group of 'workmen' yell out to Enderby, calling the 'Queen of England a whore'.[70] Enderby responds to the men by quoting the Gettysburg Address by President Abraham Lincoln as a cantrip, or mischievous trick, in order to disguise himself as red-blooded, albeit temporarily visiting, American capable of quoting quintessential American speeches that have been elevated to the mythical, to the religious, therefore quelling the xenophobia with much appreciated jingoism: 'The workmen looked solemn, as in church. ... They bought Enderby the same again. He was told that it was only kidding about the Queen of England being a whore.'[71] Enderby clarifies the quip by stating that the queen's 'circumstances hardly allow it', before going on the offensive, so as to denigrate the position of president and uphold the role of monarch: 'Of course, your President Kennedy was a whoremaster or lecher, but that sort of thing is expected in a male leader. A double standard, you know.'[72] Enderby is aware of the provincial patriotism which enshrouds some political and entertainment figures in American culture, as he ruminates that Kennedy's sexual life had established him and his mistress, Marilyn Monroe, as mythic gods who, he was told, were 'screwing away in heaven. No such place as heaven. It's got to be heaven if you're screwing Marilyn Monroe' and in 1987 that 'If Marilyn Monroe was America's Brunnhilde, [Arthur] Miller, a bespectacled New York Jew, was an unlikely Siegfried.'[73] Reviewing Marilyn Monroe's life in 1992, thirty years after her death, Burgess described Marilyn as one of only two, with Jean Harlow, 'blonde goddesses of the silver screen', who had 'an American face that exuded American optimism – alas, terribly misplaced. But since America dominates our age, it is proper that its chief sexual icon should come from that land of promise. Promise unfulfilled, like Marilyn herself'.[74] The allusion to Monroe in *Enderby's Dark Lady* seems to evoke similar feelings, that of pure sexual charge, and, as the story continues, consummation and artistic achievement left unfulfilled and ultimately irretrievably shattered.

The Americans in the text don't just lash out at foreign ways of governance, but they are also protective of the capitalist mindset and their brand of English, as they exhibit their unmitigated and colloquial nastiness. Particularly, this comes through when, earlier in the story, an American lawyer attacks Enderby's foreignness based on nothing else except his accent, Americans having 'no discipline, too prone to panic'.[75] The lawyer 'discloses his madness' by slipping into a cautionary dictum to Enderby after he mentions the 'Late Late Show', which showed movies 'interspersed with commercials for cutprice ah discs', which the lawyer then takes as being an attack on capitalism from the more socialized British: 'Don't knock free enterprise. Free enterprise made this country what it is.' 'I'm not ah er knocking anything –' 'We don't need smartass, pardon me, Laura, Europeans coming over here to knock American institootions. This next year we have our bicentennial.' ... 'We don't need smartass sarcasm, pardon me Laura and Mrs Allegramente, from smartass knockers of American traditions. We celebrate two centuries of American knowhow. Also liberty of conscience and expression.'[76] Replying certainly British-*ly*, and perhaps sardonically, Enderby says, '"As I am certainly well aware. My heartiest felicitations." ... "I most heartfeltly congratulate you"', which is perceived as being, for lack of a more accurate word, a smarmy, as well as evasive and insincere, British reply.[77] Sensing this, the lawyer retorts to Enderby, 'Don't give us that. There's a tone of voice that grates on me', to which Enderby replies, inevitably and inescapably the foreigner in this pugnacious land, 'I can't help being a bloody Englishman.'[78]

Speaking on *The Dick Cavett Show* on 12 October 1972, Burgess firmly positioned himself as the 'bloody Englishman', forever a 'foreigner' and an 'outsider' in the United States, before claiming that he did indeed like 'the great American public' but they concerned him for allowing themselves to be 'bulldozed by three elements: the mafia, the government, and by the tycoons', the last of which had 'determined that if you get a good talk show with a lot of wit, a lot of interest, a lot of talk, which is what a talk show is for, you've got to get rid of it. Or cut it down to the minimum', a comment which received loud audience applause.[79] The Enderby of *Enderby's Dark Lady* also comments on his outsider status, as well as the status of business in American culture through yet another act of double-voiced discourse, where Burgess's own points and topics of conversation, influenced by the cultural heteroglossia of the United States, leak into the mouths of his characters, especially Enderby. Remarking in his winter 1972–73 'Letter from Europe', in which he frequently gave an outsider's perspective of the United States, Burgess says similarly that he had been 'dubbed' a fascist for not having subscribed to the 'left-wing of "progressive" interpretation of my work' since there was 'no open-mindedness, no willingness to accept new parameters or even that traditional view of art as art and not a device of persuasion' because the 'great domestic theme is a kind of chimera of corruption whose head is the church, whose body is the state and whose many limbs such assorted agents as the mafia and Italo-American big business', all while Americans still maintain and bear a supposed 'immigrant twang' that does well 'in the dining saloon'.[80] Focusing on the disingenuousness of American media and show business, instead of seeing how corporate greed and an emphasis on consumerism could deteriorate American media, as Burgess expressed on *Cavett*, Enderby instead encounters Americans unabashedly and uncritically protecting capitalism, exactly what Burgess claimed on *Cavett* had worried him 'greatly' and caused something to happen 'to the American psyche', a *something* that is displayed prominently in the last two Enderby novels.[81] And curiously, since Enderby was used by Burgess for so many years, with critics and scholars noticing the connections between author and character, between epitext and text, it almost appears as if, as Bakhtin explains, 'while these two voices are dialogically interrelated, they – as it were – know about each other (just as two exchanges in a dialogue know of each other and are structured in this mutual knowledge of each other); it is as if they actually hold a conversation with each other'.[82] In fact, the texts which Burgess created are not only presenting dialogue which is soaked in the external authorial heteroglossia in which Burgess existed, making it particularly monoglottal, but *Enderby's Dark Lady* furthers or continues both Enderby and Burgess's discourses and also communicates directly with *The Clockwork Testament* when Enderby says that he should have gone to New York City as a 'consequence of *The Wreck of the Deutschland**', in which the peritextual asterisk denotes a footnote at the bottom of the page which reads, '*See *The Clockwork Testament*' with no other explanation.[83] In addressing the epitextual 'life-world' of such a text which is monoglottal and reaches back, allusively, to other texts by the same author; it must be recognized, whether intended or not, that not only does this tactic produce a dual-textual dialogue but it also must be seen as a marketing tool.[84] Here too, Enderby, although in a conversation with a fellow traveller on a flight, appears to be in more conversation with Burgess and the reader than any actual character, by using this 'small-talk' as a way to inform and explain the groundwork for the novella when Enderby says he 'should have', 'you know', 'I chose', and 'if you see', as a way to suggest he has autonomy, though at first it almost appears as if this is exposition by Burgess, again stating, as he did at the start of the book, an answer to 'people's notions of plausibility [which] demands that I try to explain why Enderby, having died of a heart attack in New York about ten years ago, should be alive three years later in the state of Indiana'.[85] Although Burgess claims that Enderby demanded 'to be resurrected', and that either narrative is correct, though both cannot be, this argument would then contradict the (para)peritextual asterisk which appears to be an authorial move (since Burgess handwrote this into the undated typescript of the novel), or else a publisher's decision to try to sell more books.[86] Either way, what continues to occur in *Enderby's Dark Lady* on from *The Clockwork Testament* is again a demonstrably monoglottal authorial voice which is inspired by the author's American experiences, but one that doesn't *listen* to the actual voices of his surroundings, or as Bakhtin explains, the author of a monoglottal vision is 'deaf to organic double-voicedness and to the internal dialogization of living and evolving discourse', and therefore may not 'comprehend, or even realize, the actual possibilities and tasks of the novel as a genre'; Bakhtin continues by even defining such a supposedly novelistic conception as being ignorant of the purposes of the novel:

> He may, of course, create an artistic work that compositionally and thematically will be similar to a novel, will be 'made' exactly as a novel is made, but he will not thereby have created a novel. The style will always give him away. We will recognize the naively self-confident or obtusely stubborn unity of a smooth, pure single-voiced language (perhaps accompanied by a primitive, artificial, worked-up double-voicedness) … he simply does not listen to the fundamental heteroglossia inherent in actual language; he mistakes social overtones, which create the timbres of words, for irritating noises that it is his task to eliminate. … In such a novel, divested of its language diversity, authorial language inevitably ends up in the awkward and absurd position of the language of stage directions in plays.[87]

Parodied into two-dimensionality, many of the Americans portrayed in *Enderby's Dark Lady* and *The Clockwork Testament* are, though 'internally dialogized mutual illumination[s] of [language as] *stylization*', so stripped down that Burgess's attempts to produce 'authentic stylization' through 'artistic representation of another's linguistic style, an artistic image of another's language', however accurate the diction may be, the nuance and tone become overrun with Burgess's monologism as the one who '*represents* (that is, the linguistic consciousness of the stylizer)' and thus takes over 'the one that is *represented*, which is stylized', effectively producing shallow American characters as Burgess saw this demographic.[88] A population he believed were so fearful of other ways of life and so overly or justifiably, depending on the bias, arrogant about their successes and ways of life, the American citizens of Burgess's novels are often defensive of any foreign influence, which, although generalized and parodied, is not altogether an entirely inaccurate stereotype of a lay American. Double-voiced by the authorial presence, wherein, as Bakhtin states in *Problems of Dostoyevsky's Poetics*, 'someone else's words' are introduced into the author's 'own speech' and 'inevitably assume[s] a new ([their] own) interpretation and become subject to [their] evaluation of them; that is, they become double-voiced', such an act of transmission 'leads to a clash of two intentions within a single discourse', and this is increasingly obvious in *Enderby's Dark Lady*.[89] As occurs many times in Burgess's fiction, there exists more overlap between fictional content and the author's own arguments, in this case when the reference to 'two centuries of American know-how' is actually redolent of a previously mentioned lecture Burgess gave at Clark University in 1975, close to the time when Enderby is experiencing the events of *Enderby's Dark Lady*, where he sarcastically warned Americans not to 'gloat over your Bicentennial' because they needed to remember 'that your country was founded by men who could not make it at home' – sounding like his reasoning that Americans, whether they admit it or not, are 'all foreign immigrants'.[90] In the unpublished article 'tercenart' Burgess goes so far as to even prognosticate an American tricentennial where the 'triunited states of america, canada and mexico' in 2076 are looking forward to the 'forthcoming restoration of the monarchy and the reestablishment of the democratic actuality after decades of presidential abuse', a common theme of Burgess's American political commentary mentioned previously, once again making its way into one of his novels, effectively marrying the American bicentennial with Shakespeare's legacy, perhaps because, as he said in 1976 during an interview for the *Christian Science Monitor*, 'I'm very worried about America. America is all we have, the only bastion of art, free speech, culture.'[91]

Despite his many proclamations of being an 'outsider' in the United States, though he said 'I'm an American' in that very same *Christian Science Monitor* interview, Burgess's time in the country and the pages spent commenting on it actually made him into a peculiarly American construction, and a staple authorial voice in American commentaries between the mid-1960s and early 1990s as a temporarily visiting public émigré intellectual, whose career blossomed due to the very American institutions he chided, and whose literary canon from 1966 onward was greatly influenced and reflective of his years in the United States.[92]

Problems of race in *Enderby's Dark Lady*

Readers aware of Burgess's life and works, as well as Enderby's previous stories, find much of the same in *Enderby's Dark Lady*. Similar to *The Clockwork Testament*, attacks on the refusal of Americans to understand and focus on the past sprout up throughout the text, but importantly, what occurs in *Enderby's Dark Lady*, as the title suggests, is much more focused on attitudes of race, which exposes Burgess's most profound contradiction: how can Burgess condemn African Americans for focusing on America's past wrongs while simultaneously growing disgruntled on their fixation with the present? In this way, *Enderby's Dark Lady* is very much about Burgess's struggles to understand African Americans, American history, and how American English exists as a backdrop to these topics.

Speaking to April Elgar about what he perceives as Americans' refusal to acknowledge the past, pushing blindly, as Enderby and Burgess alike see it, into the future, Enderby is dispirited with what he sees, remarking that, ' "It's as if there's no sense of the past here in America" ', only to have April respond that, ' "Well, who wants the past? Like the cigarette commercial says, we've come a loooong way, baby. This past you talking about is a bad bad time. You ask my mother" '.[93] Alluding to aggression towards African Americans in the South, much like V.S. Naipaul, the Trinidadian United Kingdom citizen, finds in *A Turn in the South* (1989), quoting an American travelling companion as saying, " 'We've had too much of the past" ', Burgess begins laying out an Enderby narrative that attempts, though callously and uncritically, to understand and comment on the plight of African Americans in the United States and the Black experience as he saw it in the 1970s.[94] At least vaguely, although how critically is unclear, aware of the poor treatment of African Americans in the United States, Burgess still tended to be cavalier about racism in the country especially, but also racism as it existed in other places he had visited and lived in – Burgess rarely discussed racism and appears to have thought that racism was not that big of a problem in the world, as evidenced while once lecturing at the City College of New York, and repeated in his 'London Letter' (1967), arguing that the British were not racist towards immigrants, but rather they exhibited xenophobia due to a fear of losing jobs and that was it.[95] Aside from being ridiculous, since racism exists everywhere, not least in a former international colonial power, this claim is also somewhat ahistorical, as Andrew Biswell notes in the 'Introduction' to *1985* (1978) as he assesses the illogic of the novel's plot being due to Burgess experiencing a rather profound 'detachment from the reality of British life in the mid-1970s' from having been away for so long, something Burgess partially actually admits himself in his article, 'Cut Off': 'A few years ago I produced a brief novel called *1985* that is hopeless prophecy because it is so ignorant about what was going on in 1976 – the year of writing it.'[96] Taking these fantastical and inaccurate claims into account, Burgess's dismissive comment waving off British racism – 'Manchester was not really a xenophobic, but in the Cheetham Hill area there could be sporadic anti-semitism' – may then simply allude to earlier issues like the dock-workers' union strike in 1968 in support of Tory MP Enoch Powell who had 'warned the nation against opening the "floodgates" to black immigrants' in his 'Rivers of Blood' speech, which supporters of his claimed was not racist, similarly to Burgess through what may now be called veiled or covert racism, because these comments were only concerned with immigration and economics.[97]

Such opinions, though, were not uncommon during the 1970s and 1980s, especially in conservative ideological camps, during the years of 'the so-called "history wars"', when political conservatives insisted 'that historical narratives should cultivate pride in America's past and highlight the nation's exceptionalism and continual progress toward greatness', while the left, or liberal-leaning, and indeed a large portion of those working or participating in higher education, with the introduction of New Historicism and growing emphases on cultural studies, believed that 'celebratory, patriotic versions of United States history [ignored] the reality of racism and oppression in America's past and [failed] to encourage critical thinking and active citizenship'.[98] It was likely this left-leaning tendency, which often the young sided with, that dissuaded Burgess from actively engaging with these ideas, leaving him to largely refuse or be unwilling to admit to the pernicious and ubiquitous nature of racism. By 1982, in 'Grunts from a Sexist Pig', as mentioned previously, Burgess was still belittling civil rights battles conducted by marginalized communities, stating that their arguments for equality were simply 'militant organizations pleading the rights of the supposedly oppressed – blacks, homosexuals, women', which inevitably began 'with reason' and good intentions, but soon abandoned those principles.[99] By ignoring the historical and sociological importance of the movements, and the fact that, as Ashraf H.A. Rushdy noted in their 2004 essay, 'The Neo-Slave Narrative', 'the Civil Rights Movement in many ways forced historians undertaking studies of the American slave past to revise their views', Burgess essentially, but selectively, blinded himself towards a better understanding of the systemic and endemic racism that existed in American society, despite having clearly been introduced to such concepts through reading Black American authors like Ralph Ellison and James Baldwin, and while conducting research for *New York* (1976).[100] It is Burgess's wide reading too that must be taken into consideration when assessing his views on race, since although he may at first appear outright and willingly ignorant, and has been 'described as a die-hard conservative, a male chauvinist, a heterosexist and even a racist', the reality of his beliefs is more complex, and contradictory than that, since on the other hand, Burgess's canon – which includes far more dialogized characters and narrators who are female, gay, and Black – is an attestation to the fact that, however clumsily, he, through many of his works, 'went out of his way to challenge every form of bigotry, whether racial, religious or gender-based in the name of his own brand of British egalitarianism and Christian humanism', as Farkas reminds us.[101] It is important to understand, as Bernard Bergonzi did in his *The Situation of the Novel* (1972), that the conservative mentality Burgess harboured did 'not stem from any pattern of systematic political convictions', but was instead designed and crafted around a background in 'metaphysical and religious' sensibilities coupled with a British–Irish Catholic family history.[102] Such a background provoked him to, on several occasions, exaggeratingly equate the treatment of the Irish in England pre-1900s with African slavery, while often detailing Irish/Catholic victimization at the hands of the British as a counter to African American claims of victimization. This is most prominently outlined when describing his family history in the first chapter of *Little Wilson and Big God* (1986) where he briefly explains the persecution of Catholics under Protestant rule.[103] And although the history of racism and persecution against the Irish and Scottish is well reported as being particularly detrimental to those populations – as Mervyn Busteed describes specifically in *The Irish in Manchester, c. 1750–1921* (2016), with people like James Phillips Kay arguing that the 'Irish were "a less civilized race than the natives"' – to make this comparison with 300 years of the African slave trade and then another 100 more years of Jim Crow laws in the United States ignores a plethora of other factors, including institutionalized racism in the form of voting rights and economic security, as well as the realities of chattel slavery, physical treatment, skin colour alone, and legacy, to only name a few, which made racism against those of colour particularly more egregious, persistent, and elongated.[104]

It was not that he was entirely naïve to the realities of racism in the United States either, since he acknowledged on multiple occasions the lingering and virulent racism that the country was capable of harbouring, stating that he was aware of the fact that the 'slave-owning mentality is not confined to the Southern States of America' in his 'Making de White Boss Frown' article reviewing *Uncle Tom's Cabin* (1852) by Harriet Beecher Stowe, which also compares James Baldwin to the 'brilliantly articulate escaped slave George' and argues that Stowe's work is far more resistant to the 'technique of morality ... than is evinced in much present-day protest literature – Baldwin's *Blues for Mister Charlie*, for instance'.[105] Although he commended writers like James Baldwin and Ralph Ellison, including works from them (*Another Country* and *Invisible Man*) in his *99 Novels: The Best in English since 1939* (1984), it was that some of Baldwin's approaches to the subject of racism, as well as his contemporaries, Burgess found too aggressive, admitting in 1968 that 'England has her racial problems, but no novelist with Baldwin's fire – which I, in my tepid English way, sometimes think too hot for its subject – has yet come forward here'.[106] Indeed, Burgess did apply positive assessments of many writers of colour throughout his career, most prominently perhaps in *On the Novel* (1975), where he takes time to enumerate and briefly compliment dozens of writers around the world, but when it came to discussing African American authors, he claimed that they presented a 'segmented spirit' and therefore grouped them with other authors who could only capture 'the spirit of an age-group, social group or racial group, and not the spirit of an entire society', such as the 'beat-generation books of Jack Kerouac, the American Jewish novels of Bellow, Malamud and Philip Roth, and the Negro novels of Ralph Ellison and James Baldwin'.[107]

Although he admired all of these authors to varying degrees, and recognized their writing skill and ability, the political moralizing of African American authors bothered Burgess and went against his own aesthetic philosophies and pursuits, putting him directly at odds with the African American literary tradition which for generations largely adhered to an aesthetic standard similar to W.E.B. DuBois's dictum that he 'did not care a damn for any art that is not used for propaganda', and become an American tradition that would go on to challenge 'the primacy of the written text and the relation of art to politics and propaganda'.[108] The paradigm shift that African American art presented caused Burgess, in his 1979 non-fiction history of English literature, *They Wrote in English*, to refuse to even discuss African American writers of the twentieth century in the 'Now and America' chapter because too 'many surveys of literature stress duty as opposed to pleasure', remarking that Black poets such as James Weldon Johnson, Paul Laurence Dunbar, Langston Hughes, and Countee Cullen were not worthy enough to be discussed because, as Burgess argues, he did not 'think that black poetry is, as yet, very important poetry', since too much of it 'proclaims that black experience aggressively and thus approaches propaganda rather than art. Only when a poet can generalize racial wrongs into universal wrongs, speaking for mankind and not just a part of it, can he or she produce genuine literature'.[109] Burgess's argument, though weak since a gestalt term like 'mankind' would signal that 'racial wrongs' *are* 'universal wrongs', is that the literature to come from the United States, despite the fact that the late 1970s were by his estimations, 'especially in America ... sad, turbulent, full of rage, self-pity, [and] despair', had to reach beyond the pale of contemporary frustrations in order to produce literature and art that was aesthetically worthwhile and therefore withstand the test of time and remain relevant.[110] Despite the argument's seeming logical legitimacy and sanguine aspirations, the other aforementioned white authors and contemporary books mentioned throughout this monograph clearly contradict this line of thought; additionally, it could be argued that all literature encompasses the contemporary frustrations of the work's author, a point that is clearly evident in many of the White authors Burgess listed elsewhere in *They Wrote in English* – largely when discussing the impact of World War Two on European authors – and by Enderby himself saying that all art, even 'bad art ... is made out of elemental cries for help'.[111] It appears that *Black* frustrations were of a separate paradigm in which Burgess applied different rules, as is incredibly evident in *Enderby's Dark Lady* and elsewhere in his fiction and non-fiction.

Indeed, most arguments about racial identity and grappling with the United States's institutional slavery in the 1980s appeared as confusing and arbitrary to Burgess as they do to Enderby puzzling 'fuzzily' at the American production of a play on Shakespeare 'to celebrate the second American centennial conjoined with the three hundred and sixtieth anniversary of Shakespeare's death' to be associated with the arithmetical justification of 'Thomas Jefferson, Augustan voice of liberty, [who] had possessed 360 slaves. With 360 degrees a wheel came full circle. With two centuries you came full circle twice. It was all a lot of nonsense'.[112] Aside from being incorrect – the official Monticello estate itself admits that 'Jefferson enslaved over 600 human beings throughout the course of his life' – Burgess utilizes this invented history in order to evoke the dizzying illogic of Americans attempting to legitimize their place in history and associate the country with a great writer – a 'sort of nation' indeed.[113] The attempt for the United States to also embed itself in myth seems to be part of the text's grand scheme to paint the American world Enderby enters into as a kind of upside-down world, full of illusion and anti-reality, the likes of which Burgess embodies not just in the environment but also within the Black body of April Elgar, who is described as a kind of 'goddess', and therefore a symbol which is 'mediated by women, the nature of the relationship with the Muse [which] is conflated with the reality of a black woman, just as it is in *Nothing Like the Sun*'.[114] Although WS's muse in *Nothing Like the Sun* (1964) may be syphilis and not necessarily Shakespeare's Dark Lady, it is the Dark Lady who gives WS syphilis and therefore is the conjurer of inspiration, or else the Eros who delivers the passion and inspiration.[115]

Blackness and language in *Enderby's Dark Lady*

April, the titular 'Dark Lady' of Enderby's world, is the second most important character of the novella, only to Enderby – though Shakespeare is the common element through all three stories – but only as a symbolically stereotyped monoglottal and metonymic device meant to signify a source of inspiration, an American Black person, a naïve American, a sexualized American, and as a symbol of African American vernacular English, whose very existence in the text voices Burgess's heteroglottal understanding of the American vernacular and conceptualization of American life, but which is a voice that does 'not sound' as character alone, without understanding Burgess's commentary on matters of American culture which accrued over decades of travelling the United States.[116] Recognizing April as such, 'in essence, as a *thing*, [which] does not lie on the *same* plane with the real language of the work' since her voice is only a 'depicted gesture of one of the characters and does not appear as an aspect of the world doing the depicting', makes it easier to see how she embodies and reflects Burgess's perspective of Americans rejecting introspection and ignoring the past.[117] Therefore, April also acts as a symbol of Burgess's own misunderstanding of the United States and its struggles to deal with the treatment of African American populations in the country since it was, and remains, predominantly White Americans who have distorted or turned away from an understanding of the Black American experience through various avenues of propaganda, revisionist histories, selective narratives, and overt disregard.[118] April is only separated from the 'bad bad' past by two generations, but she assumes the position of a stock stereotyped character who resembles the variety Burgess used when admonishing college students whom he had encountered on American campuses and attacked in both *M/F* and *The Clockwork Testament*.[119] Additionally, April's speech is reflective not only of a 1970s African American vernacular but one particularly similar to the caricatured and hyperbolized language used in blaxploitation films of the era such as *Sweet Sweetback's Baadasssss Song* (1971), *Shaft* (1971), *Coffy* (1973), *Foxy Brown* (1974), and *Dolemite* (1975), with the Black characters of the novella appearing as parodies who more often than not speak in sing-song, slangy, and oversimplified diction and utterances – of their own volition and/or intentional or not is a different argument entirely. Much like the students in Enderby's classes in *The Clockwork Testament*, who utilized 'maaan' to evoke hippiedom, April speaks frequently with the idiomatic and partially sexualized epithets 'honey', 'baby', and 'kid', as well as slipping into antebellum African American Southern dialect with sentences like 'ah doan want none of dem lil old virginals, whatever de shit dey are. Dey doan fit mah personality no way no how', like something straight out of a Charles

Chesnutt, Joel Chandler Harris, Mark Twain, or, worse, Thomas Nelson Page story.[120] The first of Chesnutt's 'Uncle Julius', 'local color' stories, and the only Black American author mentioned here, was 'The Goophered Grapevine' (1887) which depicts a Black character who speaks in colloquial Black Southern dialect – used by Chesnutt somewhat ironically, this style would go on to be mocked and mimicked not only in plantation myth stories like those from Page but also in minstrel shows with White actors performing in blackface between the 1830s and 1960s – opening up his tale of a bewitched farm by telling the White land prospector that '"I would n' spec' fer you ter b'lieve me 'less you know all 'bout de fac's. But of you en young miss dere doan' min' lis'n'in' ter a ole n----- run on a minute or two w'ile you er restin', I kin 'splain to yer how it all happen"'.[121] Harris, friends with Twain, in his famed 'Uncle Remus' stories, has a character in 'The Wonderful Tar-Baby Story' (1881) who uses a similar vernacular dialect not just to Chesnutt, but to Burgess here too, which coming from the mouths, or pens, of White men takes on a tone of mocking or caricature: '"How you come on, den? Is you deaf?" sez Brer Rabbit, sezee. "Kaze if you is, I kin holler louder," sezee'.[122] Finally, and most problematical, is the 'Marse Chan' chapter of *A Tale of Old Virginia* (1887), wherein the 'Old South' sympathizer and romanticizer, Thomas Nelson Page, paints the image of slaves content in their lackadaisical plantation lives, reminiscing about the good times before the end of the Civil War:

> 'Dem wuz good ole times, marster – de bes' Sam ever see! Dey wuz, in fac'! N-----s didn' hed nothin' 't all to do – jes' hed to 'ten' to de feedin' an' cleanin' de hosses, an' doin' what de marster tell 'em to do; an' when dey wuz sick, dey had things sont 'em out de house, an' de same doctor come to see 'em whar 'ten' to de white folks when dey wuz po'ly. Dyar warn' no trouble nor nothin'.[123]

For Burgess to try this out in the 1980s as a White European is not only offensive and insulting but generally just in poor taste and it comes off as being very outdated. Even more out of touch, Burgess uses this antiquated stereotype as a stand-in for the epitome of Blackness, 'She was black America', which not only proves that April is nothing but a caricature or symbol but also that the inspiration for this caricature can be traced to the monoglottal authorial vision, influenced by the external heteroglossia of his travels, resulting in April existing as the figurehead, and her community as mindless cardboard characters meant as a sounding board for Enderby's vitriol, which is more often than not particularly double-voiced with the author.[124] In profound naiveté and myopia, key to the hyperbole of Enderby, Burgess's character enumerates the grievances he has with the American Black population by giving a tone-deaf and insensitive sermon to a room full of African American parishioners:

> 'Martyrs, I said, and I say again martyrs. Your people have been martyrs, witnesses to the devilry and Godlessness of racial oppression. You think of the white man as the enemy, but I ask you to remember that white men have suffered, if you can accept the Jews as white, women too. My own people suffered in England in the times of the Godless Tudors, a sort of gingerhaired people from the principality of Wales' ... They all looked at him in wonder, no cries of dat right and I hearin ya. 'My family stuck to God's truth as taught by the Church of Rome, and, by Christ, we suffered for it. Later, of course,' he added speedily, 'we became Baptist, another true faith battered by the forces of oppression. Oppression,' he then cried, 'intolerance, hatred – ah, by God, do we know them? By God we do, and will go on knowing them. Today, as some of you will know, we celebrate the birth of Jesus Christ in a filthy stable. He was on the side of intolerance, saying I come to bring not peace but a sword, and on the side of hatred, as of the Pharisees and of even your own father and mother if they got in the way of the truth and the light. Christians have been oppressors throughout the history of the faith, as you know, for it was at least nominal Christians who oppressed your people during the dark days of slavery. Christians oppressing Jews as well as blacks as well as Muslims, for the most part teetotal pederastic people, and of course the other way round, although neither Jews nor blacks have had much opportunity to be oppressive, except in Israel and Africa. Still, everything comes to those that wait.'[125]

As if Enderby could not entrench himself further in this insensitive diatribe, which it is important to recognize is also part of the supposed humour of the scene, since this is meant to be farcical and not seriously homiletic, he goes on to justify slavery as being a mode of – a term he used in *This Man and Music* when discussing structuralist Oedipal myth and in *Earthly Powers* between the Archbishop of York and Ralph – '*cultural transmission*, meaning that if you had not been enslaved and oppressed you would still be worshipping sticks and stones and sucking jujus in the heart of darkness, well, not quite, most of you coming from West Africa, an explanation of your natural artistry'.[126] Spouting still-used White supremacist talking points, Enderby then articulates Burgess's own opinions by asking the audience not to 'bother to try to learn Swahili, that is an East Coast *lingua franca*', a point which Burgess had expressed in his 1969 'Letter from Europe' and 1974 *Playboy* interview, saying that there was 'little point in black Americans learning Swahili unless they propose, which none of them does, emigrating to Mombasa or Zanzibar', in the first article, and, almost identically to Enderby, this in the second article:

> I've often wondered why American blacks want to learn Swahili. That's not their language at all. Swahili is a language from the east coast of Africa, with a strong Islamic-Arabic element in it; but the American black is a west-coast black almost entirely. His language is a language of the west coast – Ibo, which nobody is willing to learn. The American black is a very special kind of black who is extremely artistic.[127]

This is problematic in the sense that Burgess is evidenced here voicing the almost verbatim pseudoscientific nonsense of a character of his creation who is meant to be giving a parodic speech. This begs the question, then: who is being serious, if anyone? If we are to accept that Burgess's article and interview are accurate verbal displays of the author's opinions, which this monograph asserts, then is Burgess using Enderby for a hidden polemic or are both Burgess and Enderby, Burgeby or Endergess, both fictional creations disseminated from John Wilson, all in play? This is unlikely, though, since this would then force readers and scholars of Burgess to disregard all of his journalism, non-fiction, interviews, and correspondence as mere histrionics, a public display of art to be analysed like literature and not historically or biographically, all in all an unrealistic proposition and an improbable feat to achieve for any person, let alone a prominent author and public intellectual and teacher.

Bakhtin acknowledges that when looking at the 'artistic speech phenomena' in a novel, the discourse that exists in them must have a 'twofold direction' which points 'both toward the referential object of speech, as in ordinary discourse, and toward *another's discourse,* toward *someone else's speech*', and to ignore such a reality would be to misperceive 'stylization or parody' as 'ordinary speech' and therefore misunderstand satire and caricatures.[128] What Burgess is doing here, though, defies the boundaries of parody which Bakhtin outlines, that 'parody introduces into that discourse a semantic intention that is directly opposed to the original one', because there is no dialogue at the moment Enderby expresses this supposedly parodic homily – it is simply Enderby sermonizing his own creator's opinions to an imagined and captive two-dimensional audience.[129] What Bakhtin does grasp about what is happening here is that parody of any type 'is an intentional dialogized hybrid', which, inside it, includes 'languages and styles [that] mutually illuminate one another', in this sense the undeniable autobiograficational element of the novel, by utilizing the author's heteroglossia as proof of hidden polemics and monoglottal double-voiced discourse between author and text, character and author.[130] Since 'it can be safely said that parody is indeed the readiest means of transgression for Bakhtin and Enderby-Burgess alike', *Enderby's Dark Lady* becomes even more problematic for the pseudoscientific and ignorant, perhaps even racist, content outlined in Enderby's speech.[131] Again, this is a truth and reality of the text and author that must be recognized and dealt with intellectually and contextually, since this text, this artefact, carries with it authorial, historical, and literary significance, but it is also very much a product of a worldview carried by an author of an earlier generation and from a different continent and culture – as any critical intellectual historicism purports to do, the text *must* be met on *its* terms, not the sagacity gained at the point at which scholarly criticism is applied, since, as New Historicism demands, the purpose of such historical analyses is not to 'demote art' or to 'discredit aesthetic pleasure', but rather to find and evaluate the 'creative power that shapes literary works *outside* the narrow boundaries in which it had hitherto been located, as well as *within* those boundaries' as a way to 'locate inventive energies more deeply interfused within it'.[132]

Not unlike Burgess's idol, James Joyce, who parodies himself in Stephen Daedalus and Leopold Bloom, Burgess's parodying is far more antagonistic and prejudiced, despite the fact that the Enderby of *Enderby's Dark Lady*, as Stinson notes, 'has a bit more balance and dimension', though he is clearly not 'less prejudice[d]' or 'less prone to sermonize', since he literally provides a sermon.[133] When Enderby wraps up his obloquy by asking his audience of Black parishioners to 'move forward to an age in which one of these things will happen, except in the Godless media, of which the damnable stage is one, and try to get on with the job, whatever it happens to be, insurance or singing or bongo drumming, and let us try to make a little money for our children and our children's children and, if the hideous future which has not yet come about but, by heaven, will come about will permit it, even our children's children's children, yea, unto seventy times seven', the question of whether this text is indeed genuinely monoglottal and homiletic, and therefore a 'poor work of art' as Bakhtin defines, must be asked, since if it is, then it also needs to be recognized that such monologism, especially when focused on marginalized peoples, has an air of implicit and subconscious (since neither Burgess nor Enderby seem to be aware of how their views could be classified as *racist* considering they believe they're just talking about aesthetics and culture) racism in it.[134] Tony Crowley explains in 'Bakhtin and the History of the Language' that such monoglot literary representations carry with them, in the Bakhtinian sense of contextualized language used, 'the force and violence of colonial oppression' that strips the audience of agency and, while not producing 'absolute silence', it does present 'the colonial subject with a problem to which there appears to be no answer: how to engage in discourse without, in using the oppressor's language, reinforcing one's own dispossession'.[135] The answer to whether this parodic sermon, and other elements of Enderby's story, is racist or not is a resounding 'yes', especially under current twenty-first-century understandings of the many different ways in which racism manifests itself, but not necessarily by early 1980s standards, and therefore *Enderby's Dark Lady* should be categorized as a novella which has distinctly racist elements in it with decidedly little literary merit in the Enderby narrative, though the bookend stories have more significance and the book as a whole is still essential for understanding Burgess's aesthetic and cultural discourses.

Contra the critics, and to this analysis, John Stinson saw the novella as providing 'some of his American antagonists both a bit of wit and hints of a third dimension' so that the 'cultural clash is still starkly presented, but it is presented more realistically' through what Stinson argued was the 'presence of humour that is slightly subtler' as a kind of correction for the 'revelation of some antiblack prejudice in *The Clockwork Testament*', with Burgess here presenting 'his black Americans as both morally worthy and well balanced'.[136] In fact, this adulatory assessment may also be a symptom of the same ethnocentric blindness expressed by both Burgess and Enderby, and therefore is intellectually bereft since this 'well balanced' presentation, aside from possibly April, is expressed not to fully characterized and idealized Black characters but to a stock and silent human background meant for the play of both author and character. No other voices are heard in the crowd of African American parishioners, except for crude stereotypes of hypothetical Black catechistic expulsions with 'no cries of dat right and I hearin ya'.[137] If Enderby is the worst of Burgess, or at least a distortion in some cases, this is quite an alarming sermon that utilizes White supremacist ideologies to rationalize historical oppression and slavery, with portions that align almost completely with the author's public responses on the same matters.

More importantly, though, concerning Burgess's representation of a Black, female character, he once again cannot help but to reduce April to a collection of stereotypes that lacks any defining realistic characterization – or at least the ersatz realism that Burgess fashions around any and all of the *background* or *peripheral* characters in the Enderby novels – and this therefore says more about how Burgess, as a White man, perceived American female Blackness than about the American Black female. Having done so follows a long historical pattern of White writers misrepresenting and deconstructing Black people, but especially women, as mere objects to be acted upon that goes back to the founding of the United States, even to Thomas Jefferson with his mistress Sally Hemings, only to confirm Malcolm X's oft-quoted aphorism from his 'Who Taught You to Hate Yourself' 1962 speech that African American women, the 'black woman', have, has, and perhaps continues to be the 'most disrespected', 'neglected', and 'unprotected' demographic in the United States.[138] For this reason, for Burgess to present a two-dimensional and stereotypical character as April only compounds his overall obliviousness of the struggles of Black Americans throughout history, and why the renowned African American scholar Henry Louis Gates Jr made it a point to state that much of his 'scholarly and critical work has been an attempt to learn how to speak in the strong, compelling cadences of my mother's voice. ... And for us as scholar-critics, learning to speak in the voice of the black female is perhaps the ultimate challenge of producing a discourse of the critical Other'.[139] Of course, Burgess is only one of many White authorial voices to commit such an insensitive solecism, as African American author and scholar Toni Morrison notes that there exists a storied history of 'misreadings that characterize these peoples in Eurocentric eyes', which epitomizes the 'lack of restraint attached to the uses of this trope. As a disabling virus within literary discourse'.[140] What is the ultimate frustration of Burgess's work is that he appears to have changed or grown negligibly over three decades of writing, but at the very least the inspirations behind some of these views can be followed back to language above any other variable.

It was not only African American literature and the tendency for Black people to seek equity and political identity through literature and protest during the 1960s, 1970s, and early 1980s that bothered Burgess – 'I don't know what we mean by identity; I don't think it matters ultimately. One is defined by what one does. If one ceases to act, one ceases to have any identity. The whole business about names and so forth is all rather amusing but fundamentally irrelevant to the whole business. Call me X. Call me K. It doesn't really matter' – but it was also what Burgess dubbed 'Black English', different from the condescending antebellum dialect mentioned previously, that annoyed him, and is yet another theme he explored vicariously through Enderby in *Enderby's Dark Lady*.[141] On multiple occasions, Burgess argued that the speaking patterns of African Americans signified, as he does here in 1986, a 'tongue of deprivation' and agreed wholeheartedly with anyone who would berate 'teachers who sentimentally drool over its alleged expressive virtues'.[142] Furthermore, Burgess believed what was once called Ebonics, but is now classified as African American vernacular English in the twenty-first century, was a 'ghetto dialect known as "black English" ', which signalled a person's attempt, or desire, to 'opt out of English' and by relation then to 'opt out of New York and America'.[143] But in holding such opinions, it is really Burgess who is singularly detached from American culture in thinking that African American vernacular English is un-American because it deforms English, which is to ignore the fact that African American vernacular English is intrinsically *American* and not a tongue of deprivation, but a living historical remnant of oppression, as well as resilience.

While criticizing the youth of the United States in 1972 on William F. Buckley's *The Firing Line*, Burgess explained his issues with this form of English in more detail by explaining that such language expresses a 'desire to simplify, to make highly complex situations easily manageable. I see this, for instance, with the attempt on the part of some pundits to regard what they call "black English" as a valuable language in itself. Well, of course, it is a language of deprivation. It is a slave language. It has the reek of slavery and the clank of the trains [sic] [chains][144] in it'.[145] Having at least a modicum of sense, as a public individual on a nationally syndicated television show, he refrained from quoting or caricaturing 'black English now, but you know precisely what I mean, the way in which words become mere counters for resentment and not devices for analysis'.[146] As a polyglot author known for utilizing, literally, heteroglottal elements in his novels, whether invented slang languages or the use of Russian, Malay, Chinese, French, Italian, and Arabic (as well as pidgin languages which form between these languages and English), among other languages and registers, as well as different dialects and polyphones in his novels – begging for a more linguistic Bakhtinian analysis in Burgess studies – Burgess's outright dismissal and condemnation of 'Black English' is telling and supportive of accusations of bias against African Americans.

In this instance it becomes clearer that what Burgess had a larger problem with was when the exactitude and specificity of language was tampered with, which he felt 'Black English' did. There of course exists a parallelism with Enderby here, who similarly despises slang and colloquial language and finds it to be unintelligible, as shown when he comments on April's use of rhyme: ' "Sharp as a pistol, brought up in Bristol. The white man's knavery sold me in slavery." ... "At least," Enderby said, "You've stopped saying *shit* all the time. That's a word I've heard Americans use even at table. They don't take in the referent of the word. It's become just a neutral expletive" ' – a word Burgess harped on publicly frequently, explaining in *A Mouthful of Air* (1992) in the section about swear words that 'fuck', 'cunt', 'shit', and 'piss' are not slang but are rather 'ancient words long buried by a social decorum not so mindlessly repressive as our permissive age seems to think' – before going on to paraphrase April's speech as being full of 'Baby honey-bunch and then an unintelligible duet in what Enderby took to be Black English', which makes Enderby's penis, or 'shlong', settle 'to neutrality. Black bitch and so on'.[147] Enderby mocks the use of the word *schlong* (the accepted spelling), an American-Yiddish slang neologism first popularly published by Philip Roth in 1967 from the Yiddish word for 'serpent', for his phallus in order to signify that April's diction had made her unsexed and unappealing in the eyes of Enderby, but only temporarily because of Enderby's sapiosexuality, which April appeases at certain points.[148] In falling in love with April, this therefore places Enderby in the same seat as Shakespeare being inspired by a 'dark lady' which manifests in the story with Enderby literally playing Shakespeare in the play that Enderby is working on, effectively mythologizing himself and allowing Burgess to write Enderby into history and turn him into a character within a character who enacts longevity and immortality, making Enderby, as the title alludes to, have no *End* and therefore to perpetually *Be*, as an answer to Hamlet's eternal question. Again, April is just a set-piece, her significance dependent, and her voice essentially a monologized caricature of the heteroglossia Burgess encountered but could never internalize and understand.

As with Burgess's entire canon, but specifically with novels like the *Malayan Trilogy* (1956–59), *The Doctor Is Sick* (1960), *A Clockwork Orange* (1962), *Nothing Like the Sun* (1964), and the Enderby tetralogy (1963–84), language is the supreme indicator of reality and worth in the narration and in the mouths of the characters in each text, or so Burgess would have likely wished or argued, simply because he felt that language persisted while issues of race, classicism, economics, and so on fell into states of obsolescence and futility. Still, it's undeniable that even though Burgess purported to not be concerned with race – stating in his 1969 'Letter from Europe' that it was arbitrary to stratify humans based on their ethnicity, opting instead for classification based on 'anthropology and art' – he could not stand the fact that societal pressures on different ethnicities resulted in different ways of utilizing language.[149] To even describe someone as *Black* to Burgess was a misnomer and absurd: 'I had better say now that I use the term "black" under duress', especially in the United States, because the Blackest people Burgess encountered were 'the Tamils of Madras and Jaffna, and they call themselves not blacks but Indians. "Black", as used in America, has a very parochial ring and the expression assumes a cultural, racial and political unity hardly subscribed to by all the blacks outside America', which is why he preferred the more accurate term, by his estimation and more contemporaneously, '"Afro-American"', despite 'black insistence on its use. Of this I say no more'.[150] Contradicting himself, as he did frequently, Burgess did say more about the use of the word *Black*, but this time he took to *Enderby's Dark Lady*, where Enderby, while professing his love to April, also reflects on *Whiteness* compared to the beauty Enderby sees in April and her *Brownness*: 'If you think I like being white you're wrong. I see myself white writhing over your divine brownness. An abomination. ... I can start writing poems again. Love poems. From a distance. Me white in Africa, you black here. Not really black, of course. A damnable politicoracial abstraction', a connective term which turns up in *Earthly Powers* too when describing Dotty, Hortense's lover.[151] Enderby, having lived in Tangier – a place Burgess spent time in with William S. Burroughs in 1963 and 1965 – before his visit to Indiana, also comments on the fact that when he first saw April he was shocked because before that moment he had never recognized beauty in a Black body, or a 'black American beauty', as Enderby calls her.[152] He explains that the 'women of darker hue' whom he had encountered had always 'showed only ankles under robes and kohled eyes over yashmaks' – not enough skin to entice Enderby who is only able to recognize literal shades and hues of colours.[153]

To see beauty in an African American woman stuns Enderby aesthetically, describing her as glowing in 'deep content with her Blue Mountain glow and exact sculpted line of feature. Quadroon? Octoroon? Blasphemous terms, obsolete musical instruments squeaking in accompaniment to a celestial choir'.[154] Once again reaching back into antiquated terms, which Enderby acknowledges as being 'apt only for damnable race laws. Doubloon was more like it: hot gold, also cool', and dismisses their use, Enderby still utters them and Burgess puts them to the page, despite being 'obsolete' and discordant (squeaking) with humanly pursuits, thus confirming these words as parts of their idiosyncratic lexicons, as language steeped in a kind of mathematical and scientific racism to designate a human who was 'three quarters white and one-quarter black' and a person who was 'by descent seven-eighths white and one-eighth black'.[155] However facetiously or not, Enderby does admit that certain words had become archaic, which also confirms his wherewithal to associate politics, history, and race with certain words, thus proving that he, and indeed Burgess, recognize that certain words carry more cultural weight than others, but that both character and author would act as the supreme judges for approving what words were acceptable or not.[156] Still, in admitting that there are antiquated and offensive words, Enderby deviates slightly from Burgess's views since he consciously recognizes how outdated diction with emotional connections present political and societal anachronisms that become 'blasphemous' and 'obsolete' in the 'celestial choir' of modern society. Specific words, to Enderby, therefore, do not exist in the neutral space and vacuum that Burgess hypothesizes but upends in his fiction. It may be that Enderby's love for April is what partially emotionalizes him and pulls him away from the world of words and into the world of feelings, which is detached from the unfeeling of linguistics and philosophy.

Still, the mere presence of the epithets in the text can be perceived as a sarcastic interjection by Burgess to the ongoing American discussions on these matters by a protagonist even more naïve than his creator regarding manners and modes of linguistical oppression. It appears that Burgess's philosophy on the aesthetics and ontology of language met resistance in the United States because he realized that there was indeed cultural and historical weight in language, that words were never detached from emotions, regardless of how much he wished they were, and that language is intrinsically attached to historical matter that cannot always be intellectually disentangled – in the Bakhtinian sense, all language is borrowed.[157]

In one of his more scholarly, or academic, books that has sections which 'are particularly taxing', as D.J. Enright noted in the *Times Literary Supplement*, *A Mouthful of Air* (1992), which was still somewhat favourably reviewed in Enright's article and in the *New York Times*, Burgess summarizes what he believes is the ridiculousness of racially tinged language as just being a by-product of the human condition.[158] Burgess addresses the relationship between race and language when he says that 'race is one of the most sensitive themes of our age, with racism subject to state laws', to the point that it 'might be expected that terms like "n-----," "wop," "kike," "limey," and so on would disappear, with either new euphemisms or neutral "dictionary" terms replacing what we must call cacophemisms (Greek *kako*, as in "cacophony")' because, he continues, 'no race has ever really liked other races. There is always the prospect of war between them, and this explains the large number of euphemisms that has appeared in the period following the Second World War, accepting the principle of national aggression but hypocritically trying to disguise it'.[159] Language, therefore, to Burgess, is both meaningless and simultaneously the most important facet of human life and the human experience. Not meaning to be ironic, Burgess presents the paradox of language in a way that makes sense from a strictly linguistic perspective, where language acts as humans' seminal mode of communication and expression, but more philosophically, it is ultimately fragile, ineffective, and absurd by the mere fact that symbols are presented in order to approximate meaning and consciousness.

The problem is, though, as Burgess ran into in his 1976 *New York Times* Guest Observer article 'Dirty Words', discussed in Chapter 4, is that he plays off of the two premises – that language is reality creating and therefore rife with meaning, and yet in essence arbitrarily created and thus meaning*less* – in a mutually exclusive fashion, ignoring the first premise when expedient and vice versa.[160] In one of Burgess's particularly ignorant moments that stems from his disinterest in contemporary racial issues, he decided to take on the taboo of racially charged slurs and epithets, used in the United States and beyond, without an ounce of sympathy and a failure to take socio-linguistic factors into account. It is quite a startling argument that takes shape, which Burgess alleges on several different occasions, where he looks at language as essentially meaningless in the Saussurean lens and demands that words like 'n-----', 'kike', 'wap', 'dago', 'chink', and the massive false equivalency of 'honky', when juxtaposed to the other derogatory terms, be considered essentially neutral and should be socially acceptable to use so as to strip them of their power, being just a series of signs.[161] In fact, linguistically, Burgess appears to align with a more structuralist linguistic model, one created by Ferdinand de Saussure, which, although it acknowledges the *parole*, speech from a person, Saussure's ideas fail, in Bakhtinian terms, to, according to Michael Holquist writing about Bakhtin in *Dialogism: Bakhtin and His World* (1990), 'discover a dialogic relation between the self/other aspects of language as they are present in individual speakers', which is also where Bakhtin and Saussure are crucially different, since Bakhtin placed more emphasis on 'the simultaneous presence of features that are idiosyncratic to the speaker *and* features that he or she shares with others'.[162] This distinction is important because like the main argument of this monograph,

Burgess's language is assessed through a specific historical, cultural, and lexical contextual-chronotope, so that his utterances are evaluated in relation to his existence or the 'particular combinations of time and space as they have resulted in historically manifested narrative forms', so that social influences on his texts may be diagnosed, defined, and established as significant and consequential vestigial epitextual appendages of his texts, but what Burgess often argued about language – the word, the utterance – was that it did not hold such weight and power or connection with the larger social setting outside of it.[163] In this specific case, it's clear that this hermetic and ahistorical stance, as well as his own personal racial sensibilities, could clearly not break through his supposed, though selective, allegiance to structuralist linguistics, and his opinions regarding this matter do not seem to have been fuelled by any sense of empathy as Burgess pounds through the atonal and tone-deaf claim that 'human history does not depict the progressive throwing off of chains' by banning words, since this would be merely exchanging 'one set of chains for another, or two others'.[164]

In the same article, Burgess agreed that the controversial comedian 'Lenny Bruce was right in crying "n-----, n-----" at his audience, along with "kike" and "bohunk" and, I hope, "limey"'.[165] In a spectacular display of Enderbiac obliviousness to audience and naiveté, Burgess argued that Bruce

> wanted to demonstrate that harm cannot properly reside in a word, only in the attitude that animates it. You can't outlaw attitudes by outlawing words. You drive the word into an area of private darkness where it becomes more obscene. You can only cleanse words of obscenity by driving obscenity from your own mind.[166]

Bruce, a Jew, and Burgess are right, of course, but only in an academic setting: language is, through a Saussurean lens, ostensibly arbitrary and subjective *in vacuo*, as well as entropic and nonsensical, but this is to ignore completely the human element indelibly and intrinsically wound into language that mirrors humanity's love as much as its hate. Operating in the post-modern period, still reeling from the horrors of World War Two and its continued effects, the fear of any sort of censorship is understandable especially after having witnessed the McCarthy trials (1954), but it's also a rather benighted view considering the effectiveness of World War Two propaganda and outright racism that helped incite and provoke the Axis powers. Burgess believed language and literature, at their most aesthetically charged points, had to be hermetically sealed and removed from the vicissitudes of societal life, despite such a claim being preposterous and antithetical to the aesthetic evolutions of the last 100 years which have been shaped by war and politics, which only seems to support Bakhtin's dictum that, as Holquist summarizes, existence is 'the event of co-being; it is a vast web of interconnections each and all of which are linked as participants in an event whose totality is so immense that no single one of us can ever know it', and therefore the 'mutuality of differences' is where language, and aesthetics, must be met to find meaning as it sprouts up 'between words in language, people in society, organisms in ecosystems, and even between processes in the natural world'.[167]

As an onlooker on American life, and as a writer, Burgess believed that 'harm', however this could be defined, could not logically 'reside in a word', but it appears that the United States had proved him wrong in this assumption, allowing only Enderby, almost singularly, to comment on these matters after the mid 1970s.[168] To be fair to Burgess, as a cosmopolitan and a widely read individual, and to position him too in the correct historical and biographical context, it was quite common during the 1970s for White Americans to 'not see why they should individually be made to pay for the collective sins of their ancestors', and being British made this even more indecipherable.[169] This was not a singularly American problem, but the United States's problems with bigotry were, and continue to be, often far more severe than experienced in the European social spectrum.

Attempting to move the discussion back to linguistics, in 1974, for his *Playboy* interview, Burgess equated British English with African American speech, as a kind of digraphia, perhaps as a way to understand or play with his notions of English language use:

> There's a curious sympathy between American blacks and Englishmen that lies in the fact that they speak in the same way. The typical black voice is not an American voice. It's not a mid-western voice or a Brooklyn voice or a Bronx voice; it's very much more like an English voice. The Englishmen say fatha, motha; and blacks, of course, speak in precisely the same way. Of course, it's not a black lingo at all, it's Southern lingo. The 'rrr,' as in father or mother which you get in the North derives straight from 1620's mode of speech; whereas the Southern states, for the most part, developed in the late 17th and early 18th centuries. And some of the features of the later development of English are retained in Southern speech.[170]

On *The Dick Cavett Show* in 1985, a year after having written *Enderby's Dark Lady*, Burgess argued for understanding the historical context of certain words, making the claim that if humans were to bash any literature based solely on racial divides, racism, sexism, and so on collected within its pages, then a whole lot of literature would have to be thrown out. Instead, Burgess emphasized the necessity of reading as widely as possible in order to understand the progression of humanity, where everything must be understood within its context of the time of its creation, echoing the large push in literary explication during this period of the post-structuralist view of New Historicism, when it arrived around 1982 through Stephen Greenblatt.[171]

One such example of Burgess combatting anachronistic applications to words, ideas, and literary texts argued for the democratic use of language to Cavett, stating that people, readers in particular, should not be offended by offensive language because historical awareness was needed:

> N----- which is a terrible word ... but you've got to accept these in the historical context. We don't say n----- today; it's a desperate word, but in Mark Twain's time they used it. ... You've got to get to a kind of frame. And, you know, we've not only had this trouble with *Huckleberry Finn*, we've had with Shakespeare's *A Merchant of Venice*. ... We have to develop a historical perspective. ... We're too squeamish.[172]

Burgess, the word-man, also saw this use of words as simply being a product of human nature and historical consequence. Finding it essential to mention concerns with language usage, because language is made by and for humans, Burgess was not naïve to the fact that humans are filled with hate, racism, and fear, as much as they are with love, acceptance, and benignity, and so language had to reflect this – a point made in Alex's lexicon in *A Clockwork Orange*. This is what led him to believe that racist terms used by people had to stay or, at the very least, had to be understood before they slipped into obscurity because they acted as types of relics and artefacts of human lexical ingenuity and ability to inflict pain.

Aside from Burgess's apparent distaste for African Americans mulling over their past in the United States, while simultaneously denouncing their American desire to push into the future and disregard the past, at the core of Burgess's distaste is yet again language. The creator of one of the most popular literary slangs, in Nadsat, Burgess found American slang to be both (1) a sign of a healthy language since it was 'able to take in slang, colonial solecisms, the terminology of linguistics and, of course, the rich snarls of Yidglish, as well as the chattery', something not all regional languages were capable of, and (2) a sign of laxness and loss of meaning.[173] Enderby even remarks that 'the British have no real slang on the American pattern, I mean not one diffused throughout the entire social system, if you see what I mean'.[174] To the Enderby of *Enderby's Dark Lady*, this is frustrating since the Americans of the novel use *shit* without being disgusted with the referent bodily excretion, which results in a loss of meaning and vitality, or an attachment to the tangibility of the signified. Enderby sees the United States, especially in *Enderby's Dark Lady* but also in *The Clockwork Testament*, as a place that is losing its grip on reality in part due to colloquialisms invading the lexicon and detaching meaning from the signified world – despite Burgess having begun, though never completing, a dictionary of slang, commissioned by Penguin Books in 1965 and at least partially inspired by his relationship with the lexicographer Eric Partridge, Burgess's interest in slang appears to have been more an interest in lexical inventiveness, not so much in how language changes in a lay-public's mouth, as evidenced in the remaining pages of this work where Burgess left 'personal assessments' of words: '"Arse is a noble word; ass is a vulgarism"'.[175] Not unsurprisingly, this was a fear shared by Burgess's early contemporary, George Orwell, in his seminal article 'Politics and the English Language' (1946), in which Orwell remarks that sloganizing and utilizing clichéd language could 'construct your sentences for you – even think your thoughts for you, to a certain extent – and at need they will perform the important service of partially concealing your meaning even from yourself'.[176] American English's ability to be fluid, inclusive, and diverse in being spoken 'variously and vigorously' led Burgess to remark that the use of American English was 'the final repository of spoken English', but there was also the problem that, despite this, there did not exist a 'mode of American speech that is not self-conscious, giggly, without using slang. There's also a folksiness that I can't stand'.[177] Because of this, the inclusion of so much new diction, without a strict understanding of the referents attached, meant that American English needed 'an Oscar Wilde. It needs to accommodate itself to greater wit, greater tonal variety. ... Americans tend to use the front and back parts of their mouths, not enough in the middle'.[178]

In *Enderby's Dark Lady*, Enderby grows similarly frustrated by this supposed deprivation of tongue by lashing out at April and her race's use of English, remarking that he could not stand her 'Topsy act, the slangy front to the world, the virtues of deprivation and so on. What I mean is. Well, it was you who mentioned the noumenon and the phenomenon aspect of things. I take your image to bed with me and devour it growling'.[179] This allusion refers to the character in Harriet Beecher Stowe's 1852 novel, *Uncle Tom's Cabin*, mentioned previously, in which Topsy refers to a Black child raised in poverty who is essentially reduced to the level of a house pet and entertainer by her slave owners.[180] This is what Burgess and Enderby feared about the American tongue, a language that produces elements with no corresponding reality, or rather a noumenonic set of phrases, diction created in a vacuum of *ding an sich*, Immanuel Kant's philosophical approximation, as the *Oxford English Dictionary* defines, of things 'not mediated through perception by the senses or conceptualization, and therefore unknowable', which pulled language away from human phenomena into a realm of unreality.[181] April is wise enough to know these philosophical terms, but as with many of Burgess's American characterizations, she cannot apply that knowledge to the real world and instead uses what intellect she has in order to procure dollars:

> 'Like that thing in Kant, I guess. Noumenon and phenomenon. May Johnson is the dingus an sich.' Enderby gaped. But, of course, everybody in this country

> got educated at the State U, a kind of superior high school. Then they forgot their bit of education in order to make money. Very sound, really. And then they could paralyse their interlocutors with Kant when they didn't expect it.[182]

Americans were dangerous in this sense, both Burgess and Enderby gathered, for they were inventive, progressive, and learned, but these qualities were only operated and extended superficially. American slang was just another example of this quickly rotating and gyrating American machine that muscled through language as much as it did through anything else, like politics, technology, and so on. Believing that the United States owed much of its 'vigorous charm' to 'slang which, by its nature, must quickly die to make way for fresh slang', he tied, in *Language Made Plain* (1964), this reality to a preoccupation with the youth which had the unfortunate side effect of reducing British English to a state of lexical subservience to its former colonies: ' "That's the way the cookie crumbles" has gone into British currency, it is already old hat in America. Beatnik terms (*nik* is Jewish-Slavonic) and beatnik syntax ("Like he's crazy, man") already have a lavender smell about them', examples which, to Burgess, substantiated the 'American claim that its brand of language has a right to be regarded as distinct and different from British English'.[183] Enderby hopelessly tries to linguistically assimilate in *Enderby's Dark Lady*, subsequently cementing the divide between him and April, which is quintessentially displayed during a debate about the pronunciation of *Indiana*: ' "It's not Indiaaaaahna, it's Indianna, like in banana." "Banahna," Enderby corrected' – inescapably British.[184]

In fact, part of his arguments about the difference between British and American English have a history in North Carolina, Enderby's final place of travel in the Enderby series. During his last visit to North Carolina on 17 April 1973 at Duke University, Burgess presented a lecture entitled 'British and Ameringlish' at The Blackburn Literary Festival. Burgess's lecture at Duke was most likely a concoction of several other articles he wrote; an unpublished typescript entitled 'Neologism', which was adapted into 'Ameringlish and Britglish', both archived at the International Anthony Burgess Foundation, is what is believed to be what Burgess used when he spoke at the festival and subsequently what turned into his 9 September 1973 *New York Times* article, 'A Gift of Tongues: Ameringlish Isn't Britglish'.[185] In the articles, there exists an identical line of the phonetic spelling of 'ham and grits': 'Short vowels in many varieties of American speech tend to be lengthened. This happens especially in the South, where "grits" become something like "gree-ets" and "man" has the triphthong "ay-en".'[186] This spelling is also reproduced in *Enderby's Dark Lady* but is lacking one single 'e' as Enderby mimics Mrs. Johnson while in Chapel Hill, a place Enderby 'could see himself for ever here', when being asked to eat the 'white porridge (get dem greeerts down, dey'll do you gud)'.[187] In quintessential display of his own fictional, authorial, public, and private heteroglossia, Burgess even used this same approximate phonetical spelling in a personal letter to Max Steele on 3 February 1970, remarking that Burgess and Liana 'both miss Chapel Hill very much, despite the ham any [sic] greerts and hayem [sic] and guns and so on, and do hope we're going to make this visit in the spring', while also repeating the line from *Enderby's Dark Lady* in his autobiography, *You've Had Your Time*, but this time without the phonetic spelling: 'Normally grits were not merely in good supply but compulsory, Get 'em down, son, they'll do you good.'[188] As just another prime example of his public heteroglossia and authorial monologism, 'hominy grits' even appears in *Tremor of Intent* and *Earthly Powers* as yet another word, term, concept, item, idea, and utterance that appears multiple times throughout Burgess's oeuvre, and with it, the weight of his cultural and personal context.

Conclusion

Business, entertainment, and language are the predominant gifts that Enderby sees the United States bestowing on the rest of the world, and he even throws in a sexually transmitted disease, syphilis, as being 'America's gift to Europe', presumably linking the disease to the country's intrinsic sexual permissiveness, tied all the way back to Shakespeare and to Burgess's own *Nothing Like the Sun*.[189] To Enderby, all of the United States's gifts to the world corrupt, corrode, or else degrade the societies in which their gifts are received through either ideological and linguistical conflagration, acidic poisonous cuisine, contaminative greed, war, or impudent cultural assertiveness.

Burgess, although he chastised the United States for its obsession with earning money, partook of and benefitted from this frequently, so of course Enderby had to succumb to the same desires. Indeed, Burgess's first encounter with show business reflects what Enderby encountered in *Enderby's Dark Lady*, when Burgess described his first visit to Hollywood, with its, again, 'mad spending' and 'whores'.[190] So, it appears that these many distasteful qualities were aspects of American culture he thought about for some time, and he allowed his most cantankerous character, Enderby, to expose and experience the same elements he adored and despised through a piece of particularly inventive and yet lacklustre autobiografictional parody. It is in *Enderby's Dark Lady* that Burgess brings Enderby's fictional existence to an end, in the second most biographical and monoglot of the novels assessed in this monograph. In this text, Burgess and Enderby engage in a ventriloquist-like dialogue with one another, where the diction each of them uses emanates from a single mind but which is refracted through different mediums, for different purposes, and at different times. Like all the novels chosen for this monograph, this text is a reflection of the heteroglossia Burgess accumulated while interacting with American culture, be that acquired from faculty and students at universities, newspapers, films, literature, and/or the stage and film industry, though here there exists, again, little attempt to conceal the link between Enderby and Burgess, Burgess and Enderby.

Notes

1 *New York Times*, 11 December 1970, para. 7.
2 Anthony Burgess, 'A Prefatory Note', *Enderby's Dark Lady; or No End to Enderby* (New York: McGraw-Hill, 1984), p. 7.
3 William Boyd, *Stars and Bars* (New York: Viking Penguin, 1984), p. 15.
4 Burgess, 'A Prefatory Note', p. 8; Mikhail Bakhtin, *The Dialogic Imagination: Four Essays*, ed. by Michael Holquist, trans. by Caryl Emerson and Michael Holquist (Austin, TX: University of Texas Press, 1981), p. 324–326.
5 Anthony Burgess, 'Living for Writing', *But Do Blondes Prefer Gentlemen? Homage to Qwert Yuiop and Other Writings* (New York: McGraw-Hill Book Company, 1986), p. 377; Anthony Burgess, *Enderby's Dark Lady; or No End to Enderby* (New York: McGraw-Hill, 1984), p. 39.
6 Bakhtin, *The Dialogic Imagination*, p. 337.
7 Andrew Biswell, International Anthony Burgess Foundation, email sent to Christopher Thurley, 21 May 2021; Anthony Burgess, 'Letter to Robby Lantz' in International Anthony Burgess Foundation Archive, 6 November 1976; Anthony Burgess, *Beard's Roman Women* (New York: McGraw-Hill Book Company, 1976), p. 17.
8 Wayne C. Booth, 'Introduction', *Problems of Dostoyevsky's Poetics* (Minneapolis, MN: University of Minnesota Press, 1984; 1999), p. xix; Robert Spence, 'The Reputation of Anthony Burgess' (Manchester: University of Manchester dissertation, unpublished, 2002), p. 112.
9 Anthony Burgess, *You've Had Your Time: Being the Second Part of the Confessions of Anthony Burgess* (London: Penguin Books, 1990), p. 204–205; 'Anthony Burgess Is Visiting Writer', *The Daily Tar Heel*, Chapel Hill, NC, 13 November 1969, p. 3; 'First Public University in the United States', https://museum.unc.edu/exhibits/show/davie/silhouette1820; Burgess, *Enderby's Dark Lady*, p. 108.
10 Christopher W. Thurley, 'Grits, Pornography, Epiphanies and Ph.D.'s: Anthony Burgess and the University of North Carolina at Chapel Hill', n.p., 2022.
11 'Kirkus Review of *Enderby's Dark Lady*', 15 March 1984; Anatole Broyard, 'Books of the Times', *The New York Times*, 14 April 1984; Walter Kerr, 'The Poet and the Pop Star', *Late City Final Edition Section*, 22 April 1984.
12 Burgess, 'A Prefatory Note', p. 7.
13 Anthony Burgess, *Enderby* (New York: Ballantine Books, 1963; 1968; 1969; 1973), p. 23; Burgess, *Enderby's Dark Lady*, pp. 66, 82.

14 Philip Roth, *Portnoy's Complaint* (New York: Vintage International, 1969; 1994), p. 22; Philip Roth, *My Life as a Man* (New York: Rinehart, and Winston, 1974), pp. 212–213.
15 Burgess, *Enderby's Dark Lady*, p. 66; Roth, *My Life as a Man*, p. 213; James Joyce, *Ulysses* (New York: Dover Publications, 1922; 2009), p. 353.
16 Burgess, 'A Prefatory Note', p. 8; Burgess, *Enderby's Dark Lady*, p. 36.
17 Burgess, *Enderby's Dark Lady*, p. 61.
18 Anthony Burgess, *The Clockwork Testament; or, Enderby's End* (London: Hart-Davis, MacGibbon, 1974), pp. 19, 38; Burgess, *Enderby's Dark Lady*, p. 36.
19 Ákos Farkas, *Will's Son and Jake's Peer: Anthony Burgess's Joycean Negotiations* (Budapest: Akadémiai Kiadó, 2002), p. 101; Anthony Burgess, Lecture at the City College of New York, International Anthony Burgess Archives, 27 February 1973; A.L. Rowse, *Shakespeare the Man* (New York: St Martin's Press, 1973); 'A.L. Rowse Interview with Dick Cavett, Pt. 2', *The Dick Cavett Show*, WNET Television Network – PBS, Daphne Productions and Rollins & Joffe Productions, 31 October 1978.
20 Jim Clarke, *The Aesthetics of Anthony Burgess: Fire of Words* (Cham: Palgrave Macmillan, 2017), p. 161.
21 Anna Edwards, 'Fictional Shakespeares', International Anthony Burgess Foundation, n.d., www.anthonyburgess.org/anthony-burgess-and-shakespeare/fictional-shakespeares; Clare Preston-Pollitt, 'Mr WS: Burgess's Shakespeare Ballet', The International Anthony Burgess Foundation, n.d., www.anthonyburgess.org/anthony-burgess-and-shakespeare/mr-ws-burgesss-shakespeare-ballet; Anthony Burgess, *Shakespeare* (New York: Carroll & Graf, 1970; 2002); Anthony Burgess, *Nothing Like the Sun* (New York: W.W. Norton, 1964; 2013); Jorge Luis Borges, *The Book of Sand and Shakespeare's Memory* (New York: Penguin Books, 1983; 2007); Burgess, *Enderby*, p. 8.
22 Jorge Luis Borges, 'Tlön, Uqbar, Orbis Tertius', *Sur*, May 1940; 1961; Borges, *The Book of Sand and Shakespeare's Memory*.
23 Andrew Biswell, 'Anthony Burgess as Time Traveller', *No End to Enderby* (LUX, December 2020); Anthony Burgess, *Enderby's Dark Lady or No End to Enderby*, undated, typescript, University of Texas at Austin: Harry Ransom Center, 19.3; Anthony Burgess, 'The Muse', *The Hudson Review*, 21.1 (Spring 1968), pp. 109–126; Anthony Burgess, 'The Muse', *Penguin Modern Stories 7* (Harmondsworth: Penguin, 1971); Leslie Fiedler, editor of *In Dreams Awake: A Historical-Critical Anthology of Science Fiction* (New York: Dell Publishing, 1975).
24 Paul Phillips, *A Clockwork Counterpoint: The Music and Literature of Anthony Burgess* (Manchester: Manchester University Press, 2010), p. 251; 'The Fictional Shakespeares of Anthony Burgess', International Anthony Burgess Foundation, www.anthonyburgess.org/shakespeare/fictional-shakespeares; Burgess, *Enderby's Dark Lady*, p. 35; Burgess, *Enderby*, p. 31.
25 Biswell, 'Anthony Burgess as Time Traveller'.
26 Marilyn Middendorf, *Journal of Basic Writing*, 11.1 (1992), 35–36; Christine Gallagher and Stephen Greenblatt, *Practicing New Historicism* (Chicago, IL: The University of Chicago Press, 2000), pp. 12–13.

27 Farkas, *Will's Son and Jake's Peer*, p. 100.
28 Burgess, 'A Prefatory Note', pp. 7–8.
29 Mikhail Bakhtin, *Problems of Dostoyevsky's Poetics*, ed. by Caryl Emerson, Theory and History of Literature, volume 8 (Minneapolis, MN: University of Minnesota, 1984), p. 7.
30 Bakhtin, *The Dialogic Imagination*, p. 337.
31 Bakhtin, *Problems of Dostoyevsky's Poetics*, p. 79.
32 Clarke, *The Aesthetics of Anthony Burgess*, pp. 114–115; Burgess, *Enderby's Dark Lady*, p. 37.
33 Clarke, *The Aesthetics of Anthony Burgess*, pp. 114–115; Robert McCrum, 'The "Lost" Novels That Anthony Burgess Hoped Would Make Him Rich', *The Guardian*, 18 March 2017; Burgess, *Enderby's Dark Lady*, p. 37.
34 'Novelist Anthony Burgess Will Join the Staff of the Guthrie Theater', *Pittsburgh Post-Gazette*, 9 March 1972; Sophocles, *Oedipus the King*, trans. and adapt. by Anthony Burgess (Minneapolis, MN: University of Minnesota Press, 1972); Edmund Rostand, *Cyrano de Bergerac*, trans. and adapt. by Anthony Burgess (New York: Applause Theatre & Cinema Books, 1985; 1998); Burgess, *Enderby*, p. 101; Burgess, *Enderby's Dark Lady*, p. 36.
35 Burgess, *Enderby's Dark Lady*, p. 37.
36 Burgess, *Enderby's Dark Lady*, p. 139; Burgess, *Enderby*, p. 101.
37 Burgess, *Enderby's Dark Lady*, pp. 7–8.
38 Burgess, 'A Prefatory Note', pp. 7–8; Anthony Burgess, *Earthly Powers* (New York: Penguin, 1980), pp. 610–611.
39 Burgess, *Earthly Powers*, pp. 610–611.
40 Thomas Stumpf, in-person interview with Christopher Thurley, 1 July 2015. Another possible influence for choosing 'Manning' as a surname resides in the fact that Burgess was close with Olivia Manning, the British writer, in the early 1960s and apocryphally may have even proposed to marry her after the death of Lynne in 1968, despite the fact that she was married and Burgess was friends with her husband ('Object of the Week: Burgess's Library of Inscribed Books'). He said of the writer in 1980 that she 'was never, like so many women novelists, limited to the experiences of her own sex. She recognized, unlike so many of the fictional proponents of feminism, the need for a creative point of view which transcended what her personal life could give her, and this is an aspect of her important as a novelist and short-story writer' (Anthony Burgess, 'A Talent to Remember', *Observer*, 27 July 1980, p. 28).
41 Burgess, *Enderby's Dark Lady*, pp. 40–41.
42 Burgess, *Enderby's Dark Lady*, pp. 43, 60–61; Samuel Schoenbaum, *Shakespeare's Lives* (Ann Arbor, MI: University of Michigan Press, 1970; 1991); Samuel Schoenbaum, *Shakespeare: A Documentary Life* (Oxford: Oxford University Press, 1977); Anthony Burgess, Letter to Ann Jennalie Cook, 9 August 1984, University of Texas at Austin: Harry Ransom Center, box. 73.
43 Burgess, *Enderby's Dark Lady*, p. 83; Thomas Mann, *Doctor Faustus: The Life of the German Composer Adrian Leverkühn as Told by a Friend*, trans. by John E. Woods (New York: Vintage Books, 1947; 1999).

44 Burgess, *Enderby's Dark Lady*, p. 57. This was a fictional university at the time of writing the novel; although the Methodist Indiana Central College is now known as the University of Indianapolis, they did not take on this name until 1986.
45 Burgess, *Enderby's Dark Lady*, p. 60.
46 Burgess, *Earthly Powers*, pp. 614–615.
47 Burgess, *Enderby's Dark Lady*, pp. 67–68.
48 Anthony Burgess, *They Wrote in English* (proof copy, International Anthony Burgess Foundation Archive, 1979; 1989), p. 16.
49 Burgess, *Enderby's Dark Lady*, pp. 61–62.
50 Burgess, 'Living for Writing', p. 377.
51 Max Saunders, *Self Impression: Life-Writing, Autobiografiction, and the Forms of Modern Literature* (Oxford: Oxford University Press, 2010), p. 302.
52 Burgess, *Enderby's Dark Lady*, p. 97; 'Negress', *Oxford English Dictionary*, www-oed-com.mmu.idm.oclc.org/view/Entry/125887?redirectedFrom=negress#eid
53 Burgess, *Enderby's Dark Lady*, p. 97; Burgess, *Enderby's Dark Lady*, p. 97; Anthony Burgess, Lecture at the City College of New York, International Anthony Burgess Archives, 22 March 1973.
54 Burgess, Lecture at the City College of New York, 22 March 1973.
55 Burgess, *Enderby's Dark Lady*, pp. 75, 76, 136, and 97.
56 Burgess, *Enderby's Dark Lady*, p. 66.
57 Burgess, *Enderby*, pp. 15, 18–19.
58 Burgess, *Enderby's Dark Lady*, p. 66.
59 Burgess, *Enderby's Dark Lady*, p. 65.
60 Lynn Darling, 'The Haunted Exile of Novelist Anthony Burgess.', *Washington Post*, 26 December 1980.
61 Anthony Burgess, 'Pornography: "The Moral Question Is Nonsense"; For Permissiveness, with Misgivings', *New York Times*, 1 July 1973, pp. 18–19.
62 Burgess, *Enderby's Dark Lady*, p. 95.
63 Burgess, *Enderby's Dark Lady*, p. 83; Anthony Burgess, 'Ah, Liberty', International Anthony Burgess Foundation Archive, unpublished, 1986, pp. 3–5.
64 'The odium attached to Reagan is not that of villainy but of incompetence. He came closest to malpractice in permitting a network of private assistance to the Contras to be run out of the Security Council offices in apparent contravention of a Congressional ban. But his real crime was failure to fulfill his executive function, ignorance of the actions of his creatures, self-contradiction in his efforts at justification of those actions. This, in the art of the possible, may be more reprehensible than open-eyed machiavellianism. The morality of politics is one of failure or success' (Anthony Burgess, 'Thoughts on Irangate', 1987, University of Texas at Austin: Harry Ransom Center Archives, Gabriele Pantucci Collection, container 7).
65 Burgess, 'Ah, Liberty', pp. 3–5.
66 *Behind the Green Door*, dirs. Artie and Jim Mitchell (Jartech, 1972); *Deep Throat*, dir. Gerard Damiano (Gerard Damiano Film Productions, 1972); Burgess, *Enderby's Dark Lady*, p. 138.

67 Burgess, *Enderby's Dark Lady*, p. 138.
68 Philippe LeJeune, *On Autobiography*, ed. by Paul John Eakin, trans. by Katherine Leary (Minneapolis, MN: University of Minnesota Press, 1989), pp. 22, 45.
69 David Shepherd, 'Bakhtin and the Reader', *Bakhtin and Cultural Theory*, ed. by Ken Hirschkop and David Shepherd (Manchester: University of Manchester Press, 2001), p. 149.
70 Burgess, *Enderby's Dark Lady*, p. 85.
71 Burgess, *Enderby's Dark Lady*, p. 85.
72 Burgess, *Enderby's Dark Lady*, p. 85.
73 Burgess, *Enderby's Dark Lady*, p. 85; Anthony Burgess, 'Miller and Marilyn', 1987, University of Texas at Austin: Harry Ransom Center Archives, Gabriele Pantucci Collection, container 7.
74 Anthony Burgess, 'Marilyn', *One Man's Chorus: The Uncollected Writings of Anthony Burgess*, ed. by Ben Forkner (New York: Carroll & Graf, 1998), pp. 377, 380.
75 Burgess, *Enderby's Dark Lady*, p. 139.
76 Burgess, *Enderby's Dark Lady*, pp. 62–63.
77 Burgess, *Enderby's Dark Lady*, p. 63.
78 Burgess, *Enderby's Dark Lady*, pp. 62–63.
79 'Interview with Anthony Burgess', *The Dick Cavett Show*, ABC Television Network: Daphne Productions and Rollins & Joffe Productions, 12 October 1972.
80 Anthony Burgess, 'Letter from Europe', *American Scholar*, 32.1 (Winter 1972–3), 136.
81 'Interview with Anthony Burgess', *The Dick Cavett Show*, 12 October 1972.
82 Mikhail Bakhtin, 'Discourse in the Novel', *The Dialogic Imagination: Four Essays*, p. 324.
83 Burgess, *Enderby's Dark Lady*, p. 39.
84 Middendorf, *Journal of Basic Writing*, pp. 35–36; Gallagher and Greenblatt, *Practicing New Historicism*, pp. 12–13.
85 Burgess, *Enderby's Dark Lady*, pp. 39, 7.
86 Burgess, *Enderby's Dark Lady*, pp. 39, 7; Anthony Burgess, *Enderby's Dark Lady or No End to Enderby*, undated, typescript, University of Texas at Austin: Harry Ransom Center, 19.3, p. 31.
87 Bakhtin, 'Discourse in the Novel', p. 327.
88 Bakhtin, 'Discourse in the Novel', p. 362.
89 Bakhtin, *Problems of Dostoyevsky's Poetics*, p. 195.
90 Burgess, *Enderby's Dark Lady*, p. 39; John White, 'Thus Spoke the Novelist', *The Scarlet*, Clark University, 18 April 1975; Burgess, 'Marilyn', p. 378.
91 Anthony Burgess, 'Tercenart', n.p., n.d., International Anthony Burges Foundation Archive; Louise Sweeney, 'What Would Shakespeare Write Today? Interview with Anthony Burgess', *Christian Science Monitor*, 12 May 1976, p. 14.
92 Sweeney, 'What Would Shakespeare Write Today?', p. 14.
93 Burgess, *Enderby's Dark Lady*, p. 99.

94 V.S. Naipaul, *A Turn in the South* (New York: Vintage International, 1989), p. 8.
95 Anthony Burgess, Lecture at the City College of New York, International Anthony Burgess Archives, 13 March 1973; Anthony Burgess, 'London Letter', *The Hudson Review*, 20.1 (Spring 1967), 102–103.
96 Andrew Biswell, 'Introduction', *1985* (London: Serpent's Tail, 1978; 2013), p. xi; Anthony Burgess, 'Cut Off', *One Man's Chorus*, p. 97.
97 Robert Miles Robert, 'Class Relations and Racism in Britain in the 1980's', *Revue européenne des migrations internationales*, 1987, pp. 223–238; Sarfraz Manzoor, 'Black Britain's Darkest Hour', *The Guardian*, 24 February 2008, www.theguardian.com/politics/2008/feb/24/race; Anthony Burgess, 'Manchester as Was', *One Man's Chorus*, p. 89.
98 Renee Romano, 'Hamilton after *Hamilton*', *Utne Reader* (Spring 2019).
99 Anthony Burgess, 'Grunts from a Sexist Pig', *But Do Blondes Prefer Gentlemen?*, p. 1.
100 Ashraf H.A. Rushdy, 'The Neo-Slave Narrative', *The African American Novel*, ed. by Maryemma Graham (Cambridge: Cambridge University Press, 2004), p. 88; Anthony Burgess, *The Great Cities – New York* (Amsterdam: Time-Life Books, 1976).
101 Ákos Farkas, Personal Lecture Notes, n.p., n.d.
102 Bernard Bergonzi, *The Situation of the Novel* (London: Pelican Books, 1972), p. 211.
103 Anthony Burgess, *Little Wilson and Big God: Being the First Part of the Autobiography* (New York: Weidenfeld & Nicolson, 1986).
104 Mervyn Busteed, *The Irish in Manchester, c. 1750–1921* (Manchester: Manchester University Press, 2016), p. 27.
105 Anthony Burgess, 'Making de White Boss Frown', *Urgent Copy: Literary Studies* (New York: W.W. Norton, 1968), pp. 114, 117–118.
106 Anthony Burgess, *99 Novels: The Best in English since 1939* (New York: Summit Books, 1984); Anthony Burgess, 'The Postwar American Novel: A View from the Periphery', *Urgent Copy*, p. 129.
107 Anthony Burgess, *On the Novel* (Manchester: International Anthony Burgess Foundation, 1975; 2019), pp. 37, 87.
108 Simon Lee-Price, 'African American Literary History and Criticism', *The Cambridge History of Literary Criticism: Twentieth-Century Historical, Philosophical and Psychological Perspectives*, volume 9 (Cambridge: Cambridge University Press, 2008), p. 249.
109 Burgess, *They Wrote in English*, p. 33.
110 Burgess, *They Wrote in English*, p. 33.
111 Burgess, *They Wrote in English*; Burgess, *Enderby's Dark Lady*, p. 111.
112 Burgess, *Enderby's Dark Lady*, p. 36.
113 'Slavery FAQs – Property', *The Jefferson Monticello*, www.monticello.org/slavery/slavery-faqs/property; Burgess, *Enderby's Dark Lady*, p. 36.
114 Clarke, *The Aesthetics of Anthony Burgess*, pp. 114–115.
115 Burgess, *Nothing Like the Sun*, p. 227.
116 Bakhtin, *The Dialogic Imagination*, p. 278.
117 Bakhtin, *The Dialogic Imagination*, p. 287.

118 'On Views of Race and Inequality, Blacks and Whites are Worlds Apart', Pew Research Center, 27 June 2016, www.pewsocialtrends.org/2016/06/27/on-views-of-race-and-inequality-blacks-and-whites-are-worlds-apart; Ira Berlin, 'Slavery as Memory and History', Library of Congress, November 1998, www.loc.gov/loc/lcib/9811/slavery.html. This is a well-studied area of research in African American studies, and these two cited sources are only summaries of the much larger discourse that proves this point through exhaustive research that reveals many deeper nuances. For the sake of this monograph, though, it would be digressive to go further into this. Suggested reading includes studies and discourses by James B. Stewart, Thomas Edge, and, of course, Henry Louis Gates Jr and W.E.B. DuBois, to name only a few.

119 Burgess, *Enderby's Dark Lady*, p. 99.

120 Burgess, *Enderby's Dark Lady*, p. 76.

121 Vicky Gan, 'The Story behind the Failed Minstrel Show at the 1964 World's Fair', *Smithsonian Magazine*, 28 April 2014, www.smithsonianmag.com/history/minstrel-show-1964–worlds-fair-180951239; Charles W. Chesnutt, 'The Goophered Grapevine', *The Literature of the American South*, ed. by William L. Andrews (New York: W.W. Norton, 1998), p. 340.

122 Joel Chandler Harris, 'The Wonderful Tar-Baby Story', *The Literature of the American South*, p. 289.

123 Thomas Nelson Page, 'Marse Chan', *The Literature of the American South*, p. 314.

124 Burgess, *Enderby's Dark Lady*, p. 97.

125 Burgess, *Enderby's Dark Lady*, p. 114.

126 Burgess, *Enderby's Dark Lady*, p. 114 (my emphasis).

127 Burgess, *Enderby's Dark Lady*, p. 114; Anthony Burgess, 'Letter from Europe', *American Scholar*, 38.4 (Autumn 1969), 684; Anthony Burgess, 'Playboy Interview: Anthony Burgess; a Candid Conversation', *Playboy*, September 1974, p. 82.

128 Bakhtin, *Problems of Dostoyevsky's Poetics*, p. 185.

129 Bakhtin, *Problems of Dostoyevsky's Poetics*, p. 193.

130 Bakhtin, *The Dialogic Imagination*, p. 76.

131 Ákos Farkas, 'Honey from the Bears: Burgess, Bakhtin and That Other in the East' (unpublished conference paper, Second International Anthony Burgess Symposium, International Anthony Burgess Foundation: Liverpool Hope University, 27 July 2007), p. 10.

132 Gallagher and Greenblatt, *Practicing New Historicism*, p. 12.

133 John J. Stinson, *Anthony Burgess: Revisited* (Boston, MA: Twayne, 1991), p. 100.

134 Burgess, *Enderby's Dark Lady*, p. 114; Bakhtin, *Problems of Dostoyevsky's Poetics*, p. 185.

135 Tony Crowley, 'Bakhtin and the History of the Language', *Bakhtin and Cultural Theory*, ed. by Ken Hirschkop and David Shepherd (Manchester: University of Manchester Press, 2001), p. 196.

136 Stinson, *Anthony Burgess*, p. 100.

137 Burgess, *Enderby's Dark Lady*, p. 114.

138 'Thomas Jefferson and Sally Hemings: A Brief Account', *Monticello*, www.monticello.org/thomas-jefferson/jefferson-slavery/thomas-jefferson-and-sally-hemings-a-brief-account; Matthew Rodriguez, 'Here's the Malcolm X Speech about Black Women Beyoncé Sampled in "Lemonade"', *Mic*, 23 April 2016, www.mic.com/articles/141642/here-s-the-malcolm-x-speech-about-black-women-beyonce-sampled-in-lemonade
139 Henry Louis Gates Jr, 'The Master's Pieces: On Canon Formation and the African-American Tradition', *Loose Canons: Notes on the Culture Wars* (New York: Oxford University Press, 1992), p. 42.
140 Toni Morrison, 'From Playing in the Dark: Whiteness and the Literary Imagination', *The Critical Tradition: Classic Texts and Contemporary Trends*, ed. by David Richter (Boston, MA: Bedford/St. Martin's, 2007), p. 1792.
141 Anthony Lewis and Anthony Burgess, '"I Love England, but I Will No Longer Live There"', *New York Times*, 3 November 1968, pp. 285–310; Burgess, *Enderby's Dark Lady*, p. 81.
142 Burgess, 'Ameringlish', *But Do Blondes Prefer Gentlemen?*, p. 212.
143 Anthony Burgess, *The Great Cities – New York*, pp. 140–141.
144 This is transcribed as 'trains', but Burgess says 'chains' in the actual interview.
145 Anthony Burgess, 'The Young', *The Firing Line*, Southern Educational Communications Association, 21 December 1972; 31 December 1972. University of Buffalo Archives.
146 Burgess, 'The Young'.
147 Anthony Burgess, *A Mouthful of Air: Language, Languages ... Especially English* (New York: William Morrow and Company, 1992), p. 319; Burgess, *Enderby's Dark Lady*, p. 81.
148 'schlong', *Oxford English Dictionary*, www-oed-com.mmu.idm.oclc.org/view/Entry/241992?redirectedFrom=schlong&
149 Anthony Burgess, 'Letter from Europe', *American Scholar*, 38.4 (Autumn 1969), 684.
150 Burgess, *The Great Cities – New York*, p. 35; Ben L. Martin, 'From Negro to Black to African American: The Power of Names and Naming', *Political Science Quarterly*, 106.1 (Spring 1991), 83–107.
151 Burgess, *Enderby's Dark Lady*, p. 116; Burgess, *Earthly Powers*, p. 474.
152 Graham Foster, 'Burgess and American Literature: Part Two', The International Anthony Burgess Foundation, www.anthonyburgess.org/blog-posts/burgess-and-american-literature-part-two; Burgess, *Enderby's Dark Lady*, p. 71.
153 Burgess, *Enderby's Dark Lady*, p. 71.
154 Burgess, *Enderby's Dark Lady*, p. 71; Reg in *Any Old Iron*, published in 1989, uses these terms to describe the 'halfbreed from Tiger Bay', Terry MacMahon, after he first speaks as the 'quadroon or octoroon' (Anthony Burgess, *Any Old Iron* (New York: Washington Square Press – Pocket Books, 1989), p. 320).
155 Burgess, *Enderby's Dark Lady*, p. 71; 'octoroon', *Oxford English Dictionary*, www-oed-com.mmu.idm.oclc.org/view/Entry/130358?redirectedFrom=octoroon#eid; 'quadroon', *Oxford English Dictionary*, www-oed-com.mmu.idm.oclc.org/view/Entry/155757?redirectedFrom=quadroon#eid

156 Burgess, *Enderby's Dark Lady*, p. 116.
157 Bakhtin, *The Dialogic Imagination*, p. 339.
158 D.J. Enright, 'Feasting on Tongues', *Times Literary Supplement*, 13 November 1992, p. 25; Herbert Mitgang, 'Two English Languages, a Vast and Fertile Field', *New York Times*, 27 July 1993, C16; Burgess, *A Mouthful of Air*.
159 Burgess, *A Mouthful of Air*, pp. 329–330.
160 Anthony Burgess, 'Guest Observer: Dirty Words', *New York Times*, 8 August 1976.
161 Burgess, 'Guest Observer: Dirty Words'. This sentiment resurfaces in *You've Had Your Time* when Burgess describes the changing of the times by explaining that the 'old taboos were vanishing, but new taboos were coming in: one was not allowed to say kike or "n-----"' (Burgess, *You've Had Your Time*, p. 194).
162 Michael Holquist, *Dialogism: Bakhtin and His World* (London: Routledge, 1990), pp. 46, 44.
163 Holquist, *Dialogism: Bakhtin and His World*, p. 109.
164 Burgess, 'Guest Observer: Dirty Words', p. 5.
165 Burgess, 'Guest Observer: Dirty Words', p. 5.
166 Burgess, 'Guest Observer: Dirty Words', p. 5.
167 Holquist, *Dialogism: Bakhtin and His World*, p. 41.
168 Burgess, 'Guest Observer: Dirty Words'.
169 Hugh Brogan, *The Penguin History of the USA*, 2nd edition (London: Penguin Group, 1999), p. 676.
170 Burgess, 'Playboy Interview', pp. 82, 84.
171 'Interview with Anthony Burgess', *The Dick Cavett Show*, ABC Television Network: Daphne Productions and Rollins & Joffe Productions, 14 September 1985.
172 'Interview with Anthony Burgess', *The Dick Cavett Show*, ABC Television Network: Daphne Productions and Rollins & Joffe Productions, 14 September 1985.
173 Anthony Burgess, 'One of the Minor Joys ...', 1972, n.p., International Anthony Burgess Foundation Archive.
174 Burgess, *Enderby's Dark Lady*, p. 80.
175 Dalya Alberge, 'Anthony Burgess's Lost Dictionary of Slang Discovered', 3 June 2017, www.theguardian.com/books/2017/jun/03/anthony-burgesss-lost-slang-dictionary-discovered#:~:text=The%20writer%20Anthony%20Burgess%20invented,three%20letters%2C%20has%20been%20discovered
176 George Orwell, 'Politics and the English Language', *A Collection of Essays* (New York: Doubleday Anchor Books, 1954), pp. 171–172.
177 Anthony Burgess, 'What the Famous Are Saying', *The Philadelphia Inquirer*, 12 February 1975.
178 Burgess, 'What the Famous Are Saying'.
179 Burgess, *Enderby's Dark Lady*, p. 106.
180 Burgess alludes to *Uncle Tom's Cabin* one more time in *Enderby's Dark Lady* when Enderby daydreams about April's grandparents: 'Enderby said, catching with no pleasure an image of elephanthided men called Cudge whining

under Simon Legree whips in the cottonfields, what time old massa in the parlour read with mild interest a great record of the conversation of the English Enlightenment' (Burgess, *Enderby's Dark Lady*, p. 103).

181 'noumenon', *Oxford English Dictionary*, www-oed-com.mmu.idm.oclc.org/view/Entry/128690?redirectedFrom=noumenon#eid

182 Burgess, *Enderby's Dark Lady*, p. 88.

183 Anthony Burgess, *Language Made Plain* (New York: Thomas Y. Crowell Company, 1964; 1965), pp. 178–179.

184 Burgess, *Enderby's Dark Lady*, p. 115.

185 Anthony Burgess, 'A Gift of Tongues: Ameringlish Isn't Britglish', *New York Times*, 9 September 1973; Anthony Burgess, 'Ameringlish and Britglish', International Anthony Burgess Foundation Archive, 1973; Anthony Burgess, 'Ameringlish Usage', *New York Times*, 20 July 1980; Anthony Burgess, 'Ameringlish', *But Do Blondes Prefer Gentlemen?*, pp. 211–214.

186 Burgess, 'A Gift of Tongues', p. 93.

187 Burgess, *Enderby's Dark Lady*, p. 111.

188 Anthony Burgess, Letter to Max Steele, 3 February 1970. TS; Lija, Malta (Letters to Anthony Burgess. Max Steele Papers. The Louis Round Wilson Special Collections Library. Southern Historical Collection. University of North Carolina at Chapel Hill); Burgess, *You've Had Your Time*, p. 204.

189 Burgess, *Enderby's Dark Lady*, p. 50.

190 Burgess, *You've Had Your Time*, p. 159.

8

After America

> You fell for Glamour as much as I did. You fell for the Big American Glamour like you all do and pretend not to. Yap yap yapping about Deadly Transatlantic Influence and hardly able to lap lap lap it up fast enough. Oh you do so much want to be Absorbed. The only way you can go on existing, I guess, is to become an Idea in somebody's mind. A ready-made memory, that's what it is, ready to be bought up by a mind that thinks it's oh so classy to have a long memory and not much trouble in acquiring it. That means you won't have to trouble about the practical side of surviving when you just become the Big American Museum. (Anthony Burgess, *Honey for the Bears*)[1]

In a letter to Leslie Fiedler at the University of Buffalo in 1978 after having received his final request for a visit from the school, Burgess responded with, 'It looks rather as if my lecturing days are over.'[2] After the late 1970s, Burgess's trips to and around the United States dropped off precipitously, though not entirely, nor did this stop him from discussing matters of American import and practice or mean that everything he had said up until this point did not still reveal inspirations and influence on his fiction both before and after his American journeys. Inevitably, with a country with such a short attention span, the signs of Burgess's consternation began in the 1970s and reached a fever pitch in the mid 1980s, and by the early 1990s Burgess appears to have felt that his writing popularity in the United States had ended, and the publishing world had changed, saying to Geoffrey Aggeler in a letter that he had noticed that 'American publishers don't seem to want British authors any more. Nor, perhaps, American ones either'.[3]

Burgess had very little patience for students, or the American public, who argued about *relevance* in studies of history and literature. Enderby, more naïve than Burgess, imagines a world intrinsically connected to the past and to the world of fine arts, thinking that people, Americans specifically, would view a movie based on a poem and seek out the poem to further educate themselves, thinking that his film script could be seen 'as the tribute of one poet to another' provoking people who saw the film to 'then go and read the poem. They would see the poem as superior art to the film'.[4] This, of course, may be how scholars, artists, and the appreciators of art wish the world operated, but any individual with knowledge of popular culture and humans who exist outside the realm of 'superior art' knows that this never has been or will be the case. *The Deutschland* movie in *The Clockwork Testament*, based on Enderby's film script derived from Gerard Manley Hopkins's poem, *The Wreck of the Deutschland*, is consumed without any such contextual knowledge, and even the actors in the film are devoid of understanding the material they have just worked with. Asked to be on the Sperr Lansing Show by Midge Tauchnitz, as mentioned previously, Enderby encounters the insipid ignorance of an individual working in the television industry when he attempts a joke with Midge about Hopkins being deceased and therefore not available for comment:

> 'In the eschatological sense, I should think it's pretty certain that –' 'Pardon me?' 'But in the other it's no wonder. 1844 to 89,' he twinkled. 'Oh, I'll write that down. But it doesn't sound like a New York number –' 'No no no no no. A little joke. He's dead, you see'.[5]

An encounter like this is what drove Burgess mad: Americans having absolutely no higher cultural awareness and erudition. Personal accounts of Burgess during the late 1980s describe a man dispirited and annoyed with America and Americans, as William Manley recalls in his article, 'The Manley Arts: Anthony Burgess', about an encounter with the author in June 1986, though his narrative was not published until 2000. Manley claims that Burgess had lashed out at the journalist for mentioning *A Clockwork Orange*, saying, 'I hate that fucking movie, I hate the fucking American edition of the book and you two gentlemen are a couple of fucking arseholes.'[6] The next day Manley ran into Burgess again, and this time he had an explanation for his behaviour:

> 'I want to apologize,' he says 'I had a wretched day, and I hate it when Americans bring up *Clockwork*. It bothers me that in this fucking country the only thing anyone seems to have read by me is *Clockwork*. I've written over 50 books, you know. Once, a few years ago, some arsehole even mistook me for a former baseball player!'[7] … 'You haven't read any of my other books have you?'[8]

If Manley's account can be trusted as being verbatim, at least in sentiment, then what appears here is Burgess at a point in his life where he's beginning to realize that his large body of work may be swallowed up entirely by one book, a devastating realization to him, especially after so many years of such multivariate work. Talking with William Manley in 2017, the journalist explained that even his father, after having told him about meeting Anthony Burgess, asked if he meant Smoky Burgess, the baseball player, as either yet another example of the point made in his essay or a conflation of his experience and Burgess's supposed commentary, prompting Manley, in our discussion, to think that it was just that type of limited knowledge that enraged Burgess regarding Americans.[9]

During a 1981 colloquium entitled 'Thoughts on Excellence' in Washington, DC, where Burgess was introduced to speak by the writer Tom Wolfe, Burgess recalled in a post-event article that despite being at the conference with genius scientists, writers, philosophers, and musicians, none of these individuals

> achieved a standing ovation except one man, whose name may conceivably be unfamiliar to my readers. This man was Fran Tarkenton, a professional football player. He spoke vehemently and obscenely about his progress in the art of being a quarterback, his success in the discipline, and his apotheosis as a shrewd man of business when his limbs and reflexes became too slow for the football field. When he had finished his harangue to us all to build a great country and work like hell, every tycoon present rose to his feet and cheered. For Rostropovich, Tom Wolfe and myself, to say nothing of the distinguished architect, philosopher and historian who also participated in the conference, there was no such gesture of love and admiration. Fran Tarkenton got it all.[10]

Although Burgess benefitted from the American obsession with celebrity, it was exactly this peculiar brand of philistinism and idolatry that bothered him deeply, and instead of producing polemics against such blatant acts of ignorance – though he mocks this in the unpublished article 'Signing', saying, 'Americans have contrived a new secondary occupation for novelists. It is called signing', an appropriate outcome from 'the land that invented mass-production' – Burgess allowed Enderby to mock such shortsighted appeals in American popular culture. He knew that, just as Enderby realized, regardless of what took place in a society, be it sycophantic idolatry of minor celebrities, or a lack of appreciation for the works of great humanistic value, it was art that would always be blamed for society's problems by the charlatans, the demagogues, and the vapid: 'Art was neutral, neither teaching nor provoking, a static shimmer, he would tell the bastards.'[11]

Although the United States provided him with his most significant public platform, which resulted in him selling the number of books he did, writing music to be performed, having lecturing gigs, teaching, and appearing on television and radio, he had apparently realized that for posterity only one piece of that far more immense corpus would be generally remembered. It was not only the United States's obsession with *A Clockwork Orange* that irked him, but also the cult of personality, as he saw it, around the director of the film, Stanley Kubrick. Remarking in 'The Maestro Heresy', reprinted in *But Do Blondes Prefer Gentlemen? Homage to Qwert Yuiop and Other Writings* (1986), Burgess argued that it is

> inevitable that I should want to diminish the glory of the mere interpreter, since I have for the last thirty-odd years practised an art which doesn't depend on interpretation at all. With the novel nothing – save the printer's errors – stands between the giver and the taker. The critics are, of course, ready to interpret for the reader and tell him what he is really reading and what the author, without knowing it, really meant, but there's no obligation to read the critics. As soon as I have brought such narrative gifts as I have to a medium – such as film, stage or television – which depends on interpreters, then I have gone through hell.[12]

Americans' infatuation with the concept, elucidated in Somerset Maugham's *Cakes and Ale* (1930) by the character Alroy Kear, an oft-quoted sentiment by Burgess, that ' "The Americans prefer a live dog to a dead lion. That's one of the things I like about Americans" ', was what Burgess most certainly did not like, explaining that it 'is probably America, so much concerned with the present and palpable, that has done most to deify the interpreter: it may have something to do with the Hollywood star system, in which actors became gods and writers were merely schmucks with Remingtons'.[13] Regarding his own experience with this kind of laudation for the 'interpreters', Burgess explains that 'it is bad enough to have to cope with the ill-informed egos of actors, but there is that new, very twentieth century, phenomenon the director to deal with, who has produced the "director's theatre" and the *cinéma d'auteur*', and that at one point, years earlier, he was even

> asked to write a definitive essay on Stanley Kubrick, who had made a film of one of my novels. It was assumed that I would be honoured to follow around my own interpreter with a tape recorder, conceding that he was more important than the primary creator: no insult was intended, but umbrage was taken. If Shakespeare were alive today, he would be asked to take time off from *The Tempest* to write an epic poem on the first interpreter of Hamlet – Richard Burbage – or even on the clown Will Kemp.[14]

What he likely didn't know or realize upon his death was that his wife and a handful of scholars would go on to ensure that his legacy was carried on and that his vast body of work would be included in the enduring conversations regarding British, and now American, twentieth-century literature. In fact, the goal of this monograph is to again reveal another layer to the Burgess story. What has been achieved here is a grand display of the sheer immensity of his other forms of *work*, and how this work was continually influenced by his American experiences, and how the end of that influence left him as a person. In this sense, the title of this chapter is a misnomer because there never was an 'After America' for Burgess, but rather just a pre-American-influenced life and career, and then his authorial history of post-American influence. Although Burgess may have been or appeared to have been, as Manley puts it, 'a lonely man, who felt unappreciated' and undervalued and/or misunderstood in his art, the fact remains that the United States essentially benefitted Burgess in all the ways he hoped it would and this monograph is finally the testament to those experiences, those influences, and that larger perspective of his life and works – it just came thirty years too late for him to witness.[15]

Possibly one of the last examples, or at least the most unsettlingly oblique, of Burgess's lassitude towards the United States closer to the end of his life came in an unpublished article, 'Ah, Liberty', which describes a visit to New York City in July 1986.[16] Towards the end of the article, Burgess expresses that he had grown tired of the 'manifestation of American energy, skill, harmless chauvinism and sheer joy of life' and in effect this place had 'overwhelmed me and doused my centers of thought'.[17] Exuding ennui, Burgess's tone is one of exhaustion, sick of the United States's hollow slogans during a time when New York City celebrated the Statue of Liberty while underneath the surface these simple citizens, with 'manifestations of liberty claimed and liberty denied ... filling the air', he remarks, were comforted through blind adherence to a creed, without question or critical thought, the 'easy way of hailing Liberty, massive and newly washed, as a safe abstraction', since, as Burgess states in a private notebook in 1940 under 'Notes on Cultural Reconstruction', 'What is "liberty" but a negative thing we occasionally bolster up by positive talk of national heritage?'.[18] Most assuredly, Burgess's entanglements with America never led him to blind adulation or patriotism towards the country, but he remained mystified at the peculiarity that is the United States, a suspicion and interest that assisted in guiding so many of his American commentaries. In 'Ah, Liberty' Burgess ruminates on the fact that he had witnessed an American culture shocked and stunned the Vietnam War experience, which he argues had destroyed the United States's sense of being morally 'clean', and yet the country, and perhaps Americans, maintained its/their 'curious combination of sagacity and innocence' which, in effect, produced 'that very American commodity which reconciles entertainment and uplift'.[19] And it may have been that sentiment, that resilience, however blind, that helped him recognize how he needed to spend his final days, weeks, months, and years: time in Europe to digest, shed, reflect, and write. And write Burgess had to do, for he felt he had exhausted his options in the American lecture and personality circuit, and by the 1980s he was quite obtuse about what he wanted to do for the rest of his life, when he remarked in a letter responding to a professorial request from Louisiana State University in 1985 that he was 'afraid that I am probably now too old to consider assuming an academic appointment in the United States. Moreover I have a great deal of writing to do before the grim reaper mows me down'.[20] Which of course he did. Having largely had enough of and from the United States, he resorted back to his craft and his raison d'être, to be *un homme de mots et des lettres humaines* indelibly and crucially influenced by the United States of America and American culture.

Still, his legacy in American literary and academic circles remained steadfast in the years up until his death, with descriptions of him existing as being 'one of the last remaining men of letters, Burgess can be matched by few if any writers today in breadth of topics, much less in terms of wit and insight'.[21] Burgess's editor at McGraw-Hill, Gladys Justin Carr, even described him as being 'the literary Merlin of our time' who was 'far too prolific for any single publisher to "own"', where she then relays a time when the publisher had 'asked him to do [a] book ... suggesting that the time was right for such a collection', but then

> Arbor House requested that we not publish in the same season as *The Kingdom of the Wicked*. We agreed. It seemed in everyone's best interest – including the author's – to spread Burgess around, thereby avoiding an embarrassment of riches for booksellers. After all ... Burgess is not only an author for many publishers, he is an author for all seasons.[22]

At last, the final resemblance of the United States in the dispositions of Burgess may not have anything at all to do with art but rather his insistence on capital, on economics, and on earning a living through hard work. The capitalist mentality of Burgess is one more hospitable to the American psyche and why he had the effect on some Americans, such as James Klein Fleming at the University of Iowa, of adulation for his work ethic, as expressed in a letter to the author where he tells Burgess that

> if nothing else your visit, Anthony, taught me something about the author as producer, as Walter Benjamin would have it. Jeez, man, how Oregon pulp forests must fear you. ... And let me throw whatever weight my hamburger and Coca-Cola diet has visited upon me behind a choice for your return.[23]

This fact, of Burgess's always incessant concern with money and *producing* – a topic he was for years somewhat bashful about to his editors, agents, and publishers – is what turned him into the kind of writer-for-hire that the United States desired and why certain entities respected Burgess. Closer to the end of his life, this bashfulness was almost entirely eliminated to the point where Burgess would explicitly request funds *before* producing work: 'Do you pay me? That sounds a very capitalistic question, but authors in the West are very much on their own and must earn what they can.'[24] The stereotype of the money-obsessed American, an image Burgess utilized in his own fiction, was also characteristic of his own proclivities. He was far more American than he probably ever liked to admit, which is why, possibly, he felt the need to abandon the American landscape; to shield himself away from what the United States might have made of him had he stayed. The

United States was always the temptress to Burgess; indeed, perhaps his most potent professional and artistic muse.

Notes

1 New York: W.W. Norton, 1963; 1996, p. 201.
2 Anthony Burgess, Letter to Leslie Fiedler, 22 March 1978, University of Texas at Austin: Harry Ransom Center Archive, 80.3.
3 Anthony Burgess, Letter to Geoffrey Aggeler, 5 January 1991, International Anthony Burgess Foundation.
4 Anthony Burgess, *The Clockwork Testament; or, Enderby's End* (London: Hart-Davis, MacGibbon, 1974), p. 16.
5 Burgess, *The Clockwork Testament*, p. 25.
6 William Manley, 'The Manley Arts: Anthony Burgess', *Booklist*, The American Library Association: Chicago, IL (1 March 2000), p. 1176.
7 Forrest Harrill 'Smoky' Burgess was the player Burgess refers to here. Ironically, when Manley told his father later in the day that he had been talking to Burgess, his father responded that he should have invited him to meet the baseball player, which was 'precisely what drove Burgess crazy about Americans. ... That's still the case with Americans. If you make literary allusions, people generally don't know what you're talking about' (William Manley, phone interview with Christopher Thurley, 6 December 2017).
8 Manley, 'The Manley Arts: Anthony Burgess', p. 1176.
9 William Manley, phone interview with Christopher Thurley, 6 December 2017.
10 Anthony Burgess, 'A Trip to Washington', n.pub., February 1981, Harry Ransom Center Archive, p. 3.
11 Anthony Burgess, 'Signing', n.p., 1985, University of Texas at Austin: Harry Ransom Center, box 60, p. 1; Burgess, *The Clockwork Testament*, pp. 26–27.
12 Anthony Burgess, 'The Maestro Heresy', *But Do Blondes Prefer Gentlemen? Homage to Qwert Yuiop and Other Writings* (New York: McGraw-Hill, 1986), p. 580.
13 Burgess, 'The Maestro Heresy', p. 584.
14 Burgess, 'The Maestro Heresy', p. 580.
15 William Manley, phone interview with Christopher Thurley, 6 December 2017.
16 William Manley, phone interview with Christopher Thurley, 6 December 2017.
17 Anthony Burgess, 'Ah, Liberty', International Anthony Burgess Foundation Archive, unpublished, 1986.
18 Burgess, 'Ah, Liberty'; Andrew Biswell, 'Introduction', *A Vision of Battlements* (Manchester: Manchester University Press – Irwell Edition, 2017), p. 12.
19 Burgess, 'Ah, Liberty', p. 3.
20 Anthony Burgess, Letter to James Olney, Louisiana State University, 29 January 1985, University of Texas at Austin: Harry Ransom Center Archives, box 81, fol. 2.

21 A.R. Nourie, *Choice*, September 1986, American Library Association, Series III. Contracts and Royalty Statements, 1956–97: University of Texas at Austin: Harry Ransom Center, Anthony Burgess Papers, 85.1.

22 'New Burgess Collection Due from McGraw-Hill', *Publishers Weekly*, 25 October 1985, Series III. Contracts and Royalty Statements, 1956–97: University of Texas at Austin: Harry Ransom Center, Anthony Burgess Papers, 85.1.

23 James Klein Fleming, Letter to Anthony Burgess, 13 November 1976, Correspondence: University of Texas at Austin: Harry Ransom Center, Anthony Burgess Papers, Box 82.

24 Anthony Burgess, Letter to Vladimir Abarinov, 20 June 1987, University of Texas at Austin: Harry Ransom Center Archives, Gabriele Pantucci Collection, container 7.

Conclusion: The beginning of the end

> Novels, which I have to write in order to live, are supposed to be brief or not so brief chronicles of the novelist's own time, society, culture, manners, and, above all, speech. Cut off from these, how can I practice my craft? (Anthony Burgess, 'Cut Off')[1]

The last known time Anthony Burgess was in the United States was between December 1992 and January 1993, when he was receiving cancer treatment at Memorial Sloan Kettering Cancer Center in New York City. Less than a year later he would be dead of lung cancer in London, England. Leaving behind more than fifty books, hundreds of musical scores, and hundreds of thousands of documents and archived materials, the task of fully biographically and historically contextualizing his work remains monumental for the scholars, archivists, and enthusiasts who have been digging through this material for the last three decades. This monograph, *Anthony Burgess and America*, took on this very same challenging task by exploring a large and significant part of Burgess's life left practically uncharted, uncategorized, and unexplored. In uncovering so many historical and biographical materials, this analysis then attempted to make critical sense of Burgess's authorial multi-voicedness when considered alongside his fiction.

Burgess's life in and commentary on the United States, though erratic, constitutes a period filled with some of the most busy, well-paid, and public days, weeks, months, and years of his life. What he absorbed from his time in the United States is stamped upon his fiction of the era, the fiction analysed here, though these influences are often veiled and therefore overlooked. The methods, theory, and research conducted here provide in-depth explanations to the hidden, and visible, American influences stretched out over decades of fiction, non-fiction, journalism, letters, lectures, and interviews, revealing a complex web of interconnections that have been forged into the socio-ideological language he inherited from the American cultural milieu he encountered and which was transmuted and subsumed into the heteroglossic language of his fiction, which was often distorted through a monologic authorial approach. This is easily evident through the research conducted here across diverse mediums of authorial utterance, which have all been buttressed upon Mikhail Bakhtin's theories of the dialogic, which states that language, especially the language of an author, reflected in a text via narrative and dialogue is the 'authentic sphere where language *lives*', having been charged with the 'entire life of language, in any area of its use (in everyday life, in business, scholarship, art, and so forth)', therefore making such language 'permeated with dialogic relationships'.[2] Literary characters then 'clothe themselves in discourse, become utterances, become the positions of various subjects expressed in discourse, in order that dialogic relationships might arise among them', and Burgess's *American* fiction is a quintessential example of such a phenomenon intratextually, but more importantly when considering the extratextual influences, or epitexts.[3] Bakhtin's theories of language and philosophical anthropology are particularly well suited for the various displays of writing and communication which Burgess produced throughout his professional career. Doing so has produced a worthwhile and beneficial approach that is needed for the advancement of Burgess scholarship, so as to better understand the author's life, while also opening up new avenues of textual hermeneutics. In contextualizing Burgess's position in and response to American culture, by taking his biographical materials – and other epi/paratextual evidence – into consideration and by assessing the auto/biografictional aspects of his life and work as a cosmopolitan writer and author, such an approach affords Burgess scholarship to look upon Burgess's authorial canon wholly, completely, and through a more complex lens than it has before. Complex in the sense that, in order to do so, close reading and secondary sources are not enough to make such a case, but rather historical, biographical, theoretical, literary, and sociological research and analyses must take place in order to reach a more complete and kaleidoscopic view of Burgess's life and works. Never before has Burgess scholarship attempted to intertwine the many modes of communication Burgess utilized during his time as an author, as a way to make better sense of his authorial inventions. Although some scholars and biographers have attempted to do so, the closest contextualization of Burgess's work in this realm of comparative and historico-biographical insights may simply be the new Manchester University Press scholarly Irwell editions of his works, which include detailed scholarly prefaces and extensive endnotes. The difference is of course that one is an editing and research task, while what this monograph has done is argue for new ways of seeing Burgess's texts *through* such a biographically and historically aligned and orientated lens, and more specifically in an American context. Because of the biographical and historical nature of such an approach, it's essential that such an exegesis attempt to achieve objectivity and avoid speculation, which is why the philosophers and theorists chosen for this were used in order to ensure that such an approach is not chaotic, futile, editorial, and/or uncritical; this is why certain literary theory rules and models have been applied to this examination so as to make more scholarly sense of all the elements used to analyse Burgess's texts so as to be qualifiers that refine the overall analysis presented in the previous pages.

Of course, it is true that, as David Lodge noted in *After Bakhtin* (1990), 'it is not that the real author's comments are without interest but that they do not have absolute authority', so when investigating Burgess's own discourse on the subject of the United States, and indeed his commentary on his own work and inspirations, it was necessary to engage with the cultural, biographical, critical, and historical milieu that surrounded his autobiograficational authorial monologue/s.[4] Even though a large majority of this monograph utilized Burgess's authorial utterances, in various capacities, as proof of the interconnected nature of his authorial heteroglot – since his body of work acts as a singular autobiografictional act – it is important to recognize and remember that autobiography, through John Sturrock's analysis in *The Language of Autobiography* (1993), 'does not report only on the inner life of its author, but on the commerce with the outside world by which that inner life has been conditioned ... cultural and historical context ... self-presentation ... self-portraiture in art'.[5] Therefore, juxtaposing Burgess's work with the literature of the era, with American social events, and with historical background was all essential to understanding the cultural heteroglossia Burgess was immersed in and influenced by. Although insight gained from this approach may be 'more likely to be historical than theoretical', it is in the historical paradigm, especially concerning Burgess's time in the United States, that the influence of Burgess's life on his fiction has been most egregiously ignored.[6] In his analysis of Bakhtin's work, Lodge notes that since a 'literary text is an intentional act – it does not come into existence by accident', it is then vital, and indeed 'logical' (in this case with Burgess's fiction, having been produced by the public figure and sundry author that he was), to be analysed alongside and within a historical and biographical frame of reference which presumes 'that every component of a literary text has or ought to have some kind of point or function or purpose'.[7] To miss out on the influences from his surroundings and what he absorbed from the cultures he was enmeshed within, despite being particularly monoglottal in his approach to fiction, is to miss out on the 'life-world' of Burgess within his texts; indeed, to miss an entire dimension of the works and leave them incomplete in the mind of the reader and lacking full critical realization.[8] That job, too, is not complete with this monograph or even with the Irwell editions, but instead this is just the beginning of new and more nuanced, broad, and critical approaches – or a critical apparatus – to analysing and assessing how Burgess's life intertwined with this work, and vice versa.

Recognizing this, at least when critically engaging with an author like Burgess, is an attempt to achieve what Bakhtin calls 're-accentuation', or the socio-linguistic, historical positioning of a novel and its author, so as to 'rigorously coordinate the style under consideration with the background of heteroglossia, appropriate to the era, that dialogizes it'.[9] In addition to this, recognizing this re-accentuation through an analysis of, to use Genette's paratextual term, the 'realm of influence', which has been assessed, measured, and scrutinized, such an intricate application has opened up productive avenues of understanding Burgess's texts as intricately intra-, inter-, and-extra-literarily dialogized historical *and* auto/biographical documents.[10] The final product of such an exploration is a kind of catalogue of historical, authorial, and literary evidence with varying degrees of overlap and which exist across a non-linear spectrum of gradations that makes it 'impossible to lay out the languages of the novel on a single plane, to stretch them out along a single line', since all of these strands of utterance instead create a 'system of intersecting planes' which cohabitate with the space of the authorial voice intra-, inter-, and extra-literarily.[11] By acknowledging Burgess's epitextual orchestras of utterances, what is achieved is a recognition of the 'temporal orientation ... with this zone of contact' where the 'novel's special relationship with extraliterary genres, with the genres of everyday life and with ideological genres' reveals itself as existing within its present reality, its point of composition, which is 'incomplete' and where every 'specific situation is historical'.[12] This is then why it is so important to take into account the authorial utterance of a novel alongside the epitexts of private correspondence, interviews, non-fiction, lectures, and the author's canon, since all of these acts of expression are just constituent elements of a larger authorial narrative or orchestra, and without acknowledging all of these facets, the critical understanding of any literary text is forever incomplete. Thus, and as this monograph has argued at length, Burgess's characters, diegesis, settings, narrators, themes, and dialogues should be recognized as being 'located in a zone of potential conversation with the author, in a zone of *dialogical contact*' where the 'author can express some of his most basic ideas and observations only with the help of this "language"'.[13] The 'language' mentioned here is the Bakhtinian sense of language, not just 'bluntly distinct national languages ... that exist as the normative material of dictionaries and grammars, but also the scores of different "languages" that exist simultaneously within a single culture and a single speaking community', though such a linguistic examination of Burgess's multilingual-languagedness would also be critically insightful.[14] Since Burgess argued, in different ways and on multiple occasions, that he was 'an American – I'm an Englishman, therefore I'm an American. I'm not playing jokes. It's the language that does it, the language and the culture', his pleas for cultural identity, whether genuine or not, should at least be taken into consideration and examined, since, as has hopefully been proven throughout this monograph, Burgess clearly absorbed from and was immersed within an American culture whose heteroglossic elements seeped into his authorial, private, and public lexicon.[15]

Ever the outsider, Burgess was nevertheless, to repeat, greatly impacted by his time in the United States artistically, financially, and linguistically, as he ruminated in 1973:

> My four-year exile from England, my tendency to visit America rather than England in order to refresh my spoken English – these are subtly turning me into a person who is more at home with 'elevator', 'sidewalk', 'attorney', than with 'lift', 'pavement', 'lawyer'. I automatically turn 'zed' into 'zee' and avoid talking of 'fortnight' instead of 'two weeks'. But I am unlikely to be changed into an American writer. I join rather that group which uses a kind of English but seeks a subject-matter remote from both British and American experience.[16]

The 'subject-matter' Burgess mentions here is unclear, but he appears to be referring to his expatriate status and the cosmopolitan nature of his fiction and life, as well as the heavily allusive intertextual challenges to his readers in his novels, and possibly to his repetitive use of eschatological themes which are overlaid across his characters and plots, which he perhaps suggests, especially in the *M/F* structuralist sense, were not meant to codify a specific nationality but rather humanity as a whole. Whatever it is that he is alluding to, going on to say that he is essentially 'nothing', a man without a country who has experienced 'deracination', not only is this remark a great testimonial from the author to bring this discussion to close but it is also a nearly perfect summary of the United States's lasting influence on Burgess, despite the incongruence between author and country.[17] Significant, too, is that this claim also acts as proof of the socio-ideological language influence that penetrated Burgess's thinking and was then laid out in his fiction, albeit in more complex terms. What came from this was an infused American heteroglossia which birthed his monologic narratives, with the side effect of producing suggestive trails of resonances, allusions, interdependent utterances, and a complex web of authorial linguistical play.

Upon close examination, these *languages*, authorial, biographical, and social, can be accessed, assessed, catalogued, and tied back to Burgess and his literary work, and thankfully, and necessary for this approach, there is a lot to begin from. Not all authors fulfil the function of providing paratexts, and even fewer do so with 'great conscientiousness', but with Burgess there exist webs of epitexts waiting and ready for examination, seemingly put there as yet more and more strands of symphonic utterance to be heard with and read alongside his published oeuvre.[18]

The end of Burgess and the United States

As has been proven, the United States had a profound and significant impact on the life and work of Burgess, and his texts alone provide credence for such a claim. It is entirely reasonable to state that were it not for Burgess's American audiences, American popular media, and his career in the United States, the legacy of Burgess that exists today would not have been possible. This is true both financially and popularly, since Americans were Burgess's largest audience while living, and the institutions of the United States were what helped him accrue millions of dollars throughout the last three decades of his life – even admitting in a letter in 1978 that the 'fact is, however, that I rely on the US for my livelihood, there being none available in the publication of books in Britain' – a point that is also in line with Bakhtinian analysis, and therefore should be at least briefly addressed.[19] In his Marxist literary criticism, Bakhtin argued, along with Pavel Medvedev, that a literary structure,

> like every ideological structure, refracts the generating socioeconomic reality, and does so in its own way. But, at the same time, in its 'content,' literature reflects and refracts the reflections and refractions of other ideological spheres (ethics, epistemology, political doctrines, religion, etc.). That is, in its 'content' literature reflects the whole of the ideological horizon of which it is itself a part.[20]

Therefore the more tangible and materialist aspects of this argument should not be wholly removed from this discussion or forgotten, since, for added emphasis, Burgess, as will be discussed in the next paragraph, recognized that American authors had time and the finances to experiment with literature as authors in other countries did not. Similarly, and comparatively, in many ways too it could be argued that Burgess oscillated more congenially within the literary orbital echelons of Norman Mailer, Vladimir Nabokov, William Burroughs, Henry Miller, John Barth, Gore Vidal, Philip Roth, Saul Bellow, Terry Southern, Joseph Heller, and so on than he did with his British and European contemporaries. Believing that the 'American city is the arena where contemporary Western man must find himself', it's no stretch, after looking at these five novels, that the influence the United States had on Burgess was consequential, influential, and inspiring, in both positive and negative ways, aesthetic and financial.[21] In some ways too, though Burgess had not seen himself as an *American* author – though in a 1983 interview he described himself as writing in a 'dialect of American, not in a dialect of British, English' – the American literary scene in some respects certainly did, with the Directory of American Poets and Fiction Writer reaching out to him in 1984 to be included in their repository of the *Who's Who in America*, 43rd edition, which Burgess gladly responded to with information about himself.[22]

Although Burgess found the United States to be 'full of understanding', he noted that the 'rivers are polluted, the air is polluted, but man knows this in America, and although he doesn't do a great deal about it, at least he's aware, and awareness of the process is the beginning of wisdom'.[23] That same 'awareness' and so-called 'wisdom' was often disconcerting elsewhere, as he remarked in the late 1970s that he had a 'curious irrational fear of even going to America' at that time due to his feelings of 'distrust about the Carter administration which one has to live in CIA-ridden Europe really to appreciate'.[24] Even though the United States consistently occupied space in his consciousness, he still found the place unfavourable for the writing of literature, though it was helpful for ideas: 'it's impossible to write anything of length in the US because of distractions'.[25] Ironically, the inspiration to write which came from the United States did not afford the conducive atmosphere needed to put those ideas into fiction, since 'America allows one to indulge the lesser talent of talking, performing, making a possible fool of oneself'.[26] And even though for years he took advantage of the American systems of support for authors and intellectuals, he was never able to fully assimilate to the country or its institutions in the ways that other, usually born-and-raised American, authors could, like John Barth who received a 'sinecure on a campus' and could therefore 'take his time … to write very long novels, full of the most intricate symbolism, because he happens to be on the campus at Buffalo'.[27] Indeed, Burgess lamented, in what is a quintessential example of his evolution of utterance and struggle to fit as a writer and intellectual in either the United States or England, that 'British universities were wrong in not welcoming writers for a brief time – not a year, not even a term – to talk to students', while also arguing that Barth could not have produced 'his fictional monsters without a professional subsidy', in what appears to be a pseudo-complimentary remark that is right in line with Burgess's 1967 review of Barth's *Giles Goat-Boy* (1966), included in Burgess's *99 Novels* (1984), where he stated that the novel makes 'much contemporary British fiction look very lightweight. Interpret that in what sense you like'.[28] In sum, Britain could not do, literarily or academically, what Burgess wanted and needed for his career, and although the United States did provide ground for the lecturing he wanted to do and the literary experimentation he wanted to test out, this country was also not a perfect fit, assuredly fixing Burgess into some borderland, straddling the two, atavistically connected to his old homeland and yearning to fit in with the new world.

As Burgess saw it on at least the occasion of writing the article 'Endtime', with humans being birthed with 'the end of the world with us ever since the world began, or nearly', and in that vein, therefore, all humans had to be 'solipsists', meaning that when we die 'the world dies with us', the United States of Burgess's experiences, in his mind, is indeed dead and gone with him, but what the texts chosen for this monograph attest to is that a fraction of the reality experienced from his life still lives on, as vestigial elements, in the pages of his writings and the recordings of his voice.[29] It is quite fitting actually that David Foster Wallace, arguably one of the pioneers of American post-modernist, or post-post-modernist, literature, used the very same above quote as an epigraph for his story, 'Westward the Course of Empire Takes Its Way' – a title originally from George Berkeley's poetry and used for German-American painter Emanuel Leutze's famous 1860 painting as well as being mentioned in Pynchon's *Gravity's Rainbow* (1973) – about the next wave of American creative writing – by in fact leaving John Barth (Dr Ambrose) behind – since Burgess too pushed the boundaries of what it meant to be a late modernist all the way up to what could be classified as the post-modernist period of literature, largely due in part to his emphasis and interest in the culture and literary experimentation of the United States.[30]

In closing, despite all of the archival work, the hundreds of books read, the connections pored over, listed, contextualized, and discussed, and though there is indefinitely, as Hayden White declares, an increased *knowledge* of the American influences on Burgess's life and work, there is still, inevitably, not necessarily an increase in *understanding*, as is unfortunately the case with any historical work.[31] But perhaps, as the maestro of his own one-man chorus, Burgess was aware of the Gordian knot he had tied, and knew of its convoluted nature, so that, in his penultimate final novel he published while still alive and which he spent his last tour in the United States promoting in December 1991, for a *Mozart and the Wolf Gang*, there exists his final veiled communiqué regarding a literary career of profound authorial multi-voicedness; as usual, displayed on the tongues of his characters: 'Idiot tongues fracture syntax. Unreason appeals to reason, and reason is revealed as unreason. But treason rhymes with it. My reading is jumbled. My mastery of the syllogism of no account. The one truth: we will believe what we wish to believe.'[32] In an American context, we may say that Burgess is even Whitmanesque in the sense that his famous quote from 'Song of Myself' in *Leaves of Grass* (1855) helps explain his convoluted multi-voicedness: 'Do I contradict myself? / Very well then I contradict myself, / I am large, I contain multitudes'.[33]

Ultimately, still more archival work is needed to fully understand Burgess's time in the United States, with thousands of pieces of evidence likely still to be uncovered and strewn across the country, in both private and public hands. Finally, bridging Burgess's non-literary and literary work is perhaps the most important achievement here, *and* the factor least developed. Burgess's literature *should* be understood, in order to achieve as complete an understanding of his work as possible, as it existed alongside his life, his autobiographies, his journalism, his poetry, his music, his interviews, and his lectures and teaching, because that is what his books were assembled from: the life he led. Burgess's novels, though in varying degrees of being detached from their author, as has been evidenced in the previous chapters, were largely not polyphonic in the Bakhtinian sense that polyphonic characters 'possess extraordinary independence', though they most certainly do exist '*alongside* the author's word, and in a special way combine[d] with it'.[34] The key difference between Bakhtin's Dostoevskian polyphonic character and Burgess's heteroglossic authorial monological character is that although the author's and characters' words may align, Burgess's most monologic characters actually were, in part, Burgess and are therefore incapable of being presented as 'full and equally valid voices' as Bakhtin argued Dostoevsky's characters did – though, perhaps with further research into the life of Dostoevsky, Bakhtin would have had to adjust his argument.[35] This is all to say that the many utterances of Burgess are, and should be recognized as such, essential epitexts to his published novels, and the novels are all epitexts to the utterances, so that the novels could be recognized as extended digressions which branched out from the author's lived and uttered dialogue, while always remaining on the same trajectory. Although many beneficial approaches to Burgess's life and work exist, the scholarly activity bridging these facets is only just beginning, though it is crucial for the next evolution in Burgessian scholarship. With scholarly editions, interview and journalism collections, lost works, and letter collections already being formally curated for publication in the years and decades to follow, there is no doubt that this is only the beginning of understanding the auto/biografictional authorial multi-voicedness of the writer, speaker, poet, musician, journalist, reviewer, and personality named Anthony Burgess.

Notes

1 From *One Man's Chorus: The Uncollected Writings of Anthony Burgess*, ed. by Ben Forkner (New York: Carroll & Graf, 1998), p. 95.

2 Mikhail Bakhtin, *Problems of Dostoyevsky's Poetics*, ed. by Caryl Emerson, Theory and History of Literature, volume 8 (Minneapolis, MN: University of Minnesota, 1984), p. 183.

3 Bakhtin, *Problems of Dostoyevsky's Poetics*, p. 183.

4 David Lodge, *After Bakhtin: Essays on Fiction and Criticism* (London: Routledge, 1990), p. 145.

5 John Sturrock, *The Language of Autobiography: Studies in the First Person Singular* (Cambridge: Cambridge University Press, 1993), p. 10.
6 Sturrock, *The Language of Autobiography*, p. 10.
7 Lodge, *After Bakhtin*, p. 144.
8 Christine Gallagher and Stephen Greenblatt, *Practicing New Historicism* (Chicago, IL: The University of Chicago Press, 2000), pp. 13 and 51.
9 Mikhail Bakhtin, *The Dialogic Imagination: Four Essays*, ed. by Michael Holquist, trans. by Caryl Emerson and Michael Holquist (Austin, TX: University of Texas Press, 1981), p. 422.
10 Gérard Genette, *Paratexts: Thresholds of Interpretation*, trans. by Jane E. Lewin (Cambridge: Cambridge University Press, 1987; 1997), p. 409; Bakhtin, *The Dialogic Imagination*, p. 420.
11 Bakhtin, *The Dialogic Imagination*, p. 48.
12 Bakhtin, *The Dialogic Imagination*, p. 33.
13 Bakhtin, *The Dialogic Imagination: Four Essays*, p. 45.
14 Caryl Emerson, 'Editor's Preface', *Problems of Dostoyevsky's Poetics* (Minneapolis, MN: University of Minnesota Press, 1984; 1999), p. xxxi.
15 Louise Sweeney, 'What Would Shakespeare Write Today? Interview with Anthony Burgess', *Christian Science Monitor*, 12 May 1976, p. 14.
16 Anthony Burgess, 'Viewpoint', *Times Literary Supplement*, 23 March 1973, p. 322.
17 Burgess, 'Viewpoint', p. 322.
18 Genette, *Paratexts*, p. 409.
19 Anthony Burgess, Letter to Henry Hardy, 27 December 1978, University of Texas at Austin: Harry Ransom Center, box 77, fols. 1–5.
20 Mikhail Bakhtin and P.N. Medvedev, *The Formal Method in Literary Scholarship* (Cambridge, MA: Harvard University Press, 1978; 1985), pp. 16–17.
21 Anthony Burgess, 'The Jew as American', *Urgent Copy: Literary Studies* (New York: Norton, 1968), p. 136.
22 'Ten O'Clock News; Anthony Burgess'. 1983-04-12. WGBH, American Archive of Public Broadcasting (GBH and the Library of Congress), Boston, MA and Washington, DC, http://americanarchive.org/catalog/cpb-aacip-15-mg7fq9qg1t; 'Poets and Writers', Letter to Anthony Burgess, 15 October 1984, University of Texas at Austin: Harry Ransom Center, box 77, fols. 1–5; Brad Treiman, Letter to Marquis Biographee, n.d., Series II, Correspondence, 1956–97: University of Texas at Austin: Harry Ransom Center, Anthony Burgess Papers, 78.1–5; Anthony Burgess, Biographical Questionnaire, 30 July 1985, Series II, Correspondence, 1956–97: HRC Anthony Burgess Papers, 78.1–5.
23 Anthony Burgess, 'Playboy Interview: Anthony Burgess; a Candid Conversation', *Playboy*, September 1974, p. 84.
24 Anthony Burgess, Letter to Geoffrey Aggeler, 22 April 1977, International Anthony Burgess Foundation Archive.
25 Anthony Burgess, 'A Conversation with Anthony Burgess', *CBS News*, December 1980.
26 Burgess, 'Viewpoint', p. 322.

27 Anthony Burgess, ed. by George Malko, 'Penthouse Interview: Anthony Burgess', *Penthouse*, June 1972, p. 118.

28 Anthony Burgess, 'Writer among Professors', *But Do Blondes Prefer Gentlemen? Homage to Qwert Yuiop and Other Writings* (New York: McGraw-Hill Book Company, 1986), p. 11; Anthony Burgess, *99 Novels: The Best in English since 1939* (New York: Summit Books, 1984); Anthony Burgess, 'Caprine Messiah', *Spectator*, 21 March 1967, p. 369.

29 Anthony Burgess, 'Endtime', *But Do Blondes Prefer Gentlemen?*, pp. 12–13.

30 David Foster Wallace, 'Westward the Course of Empire Takes Its Way', *Girl with Curious Hair* (New York: W.W. Norton, 1989), p. 232; Thomas Pynchon, *Gravity's Rainbow* (New York: Penguin, 1973), p. 214.

31 Hayden White, 'The Historical Text as Literary Artifact', *The Critical Tradition: Classic Texts and Contemporary Trends*, ed. by David Richter (Boston, MA: Bedford/St. Martin's, 2007), p. 1390.

32 Anthony Burgess, *Mozart and the Wolf Gang* (London: Vintage, 1992), p. 90.

33 Walt Whitman, 'Song of Myself', *Leaves of Grass* (New York: Penguin, 1855; 1961), lines 1314–1316.

34 Bakhtin, *Problems of Dostoyevsky's Poetics*, p. 7.

35 Bakhtin, *Problems of Dostoyevsky's Poetics*, p. 7.

Index

EU authorised representative for GPSR:
Easy Access System Europe, Mustamäe tee 50,
10621 Tallinn, Estonia
gpsr.requests@easproject.com

www.ingramcontent.com/pod-product-compliance
Lightning Source LLC
LaVergne TN
LVHW052015230825
819359LV00004B/119

* 9 7 8 1 5 2 6 1 7 4 1 4 7 *